Pearson
BTEC National
Sport

CW00919157

Student Book 1

PEARSON

Published by Pearson Education Limited, 80 Strand, London,
WC2R 0RL.

www.pearsonschoolsandfecolleges.co.uk

Copies of official specifications for all Edexcel qualifications may be
found on the website: www.edexcel.com

Text © Pearson Education Limited 2016
Edited by Rob Crane
Page design by Andy Magee
Typeset by Tech-Set Ltd
Original illustrations © Pearson Education Ltd
Illustrated by Tech-Set Ltd
Cover design by Vince Haig
Picture research by Susie Prescott
Cover photo/illustration © Rocksweeper / Shutterstock.com

The rights of Mark Adams, Matthew Fleet, Adam Gledhill, Chris Lydon,
Chris Manley, Alex Sergison, Louise Sutton and Richard Taylor to
be identified as authors of this work have been asserted by them in
accordance with the Copyright, Designs and Patents Act 1988.

First published 2016

19 18
10 9 8 7 6 5 4 3

British Library Cataloguing in Publication Data
A catalogue record for this book is available from the British Library

ISBN 978 1 292 13400 0

Printed in Great Britain by Bell and Bain Ltd, Glasgow

Acknowledgements

We would like to thank Nicky Bourne, James Fleming, Katherine
Howard, Wade Nottingham, Gretel Redwood and David Spencer-Smith
for their invaluable help in reviewing this book.

The authors and publisher would like to thank the following individuals
and organisations for permission to reproduce photographs:

(Key: b-bottom; c-centre; l-left; r-right; t-top)

123RF.com: 56tr, Daniel Ernst 175tr, Inspirestock International 243cr;
Alamy Images: Chatchai Somwat 332b, Colin Hawkins / Cultura
Creative (RF) 185cr, Dave Johnson 457tl, dpa picture alliance archive
137tl, 274tl, Hero Images Inc 122tr, Imageplotter 18tc, Juice Images
219tr, 228t, Kidstock / Blend Images 168c, Neil Tingle 322c, pa european
pressphoto agency b.v. 438br, Radius Images 365tr, Ulrich Doering 66cl,
Zoonar GmbH 1, 373cl; **Corbis:** Christophe Dupont Elise / Icon SMI
48cr, Image 100 / Glow Images 154b, Lu Bo'an / Xinhua Press 213, Phil
McElhinney / Demotix 35br, Thomas Peter / Reuters 257; **Courtesy
of Bodystat Ltd:** 236t; **Courtesy of SKLZ:** 115tr; **Courtesy of Sports
Coach UK:** 149tl; **Food Standards Agency:** © Crown copyright 2016
62b; **Fotolia.com:** antiksu 211tr, bst2012 341tr, ffongbeer69 110c,
Intellistudies 470tl, leungchopan 425tr, mimagephotos 255tr, Monkey
Business Images 357cl; **Functional Movement Systems:** 488b; **Getty
Images:** Adam Pretty 351bl, Adrian Peacock 145tl, Andrew yates /
AFP 185br, Andy Lyons 305, annebaek 232bl, ANTONIN THUILLIER
/ AFP 385, Bryn Lennon 348cl, China Photos 156t, Clive Brunskill
130br, Clive Rose 184l, Fuse 127, Gary Dineen / NBAE 287tl, Glyn Kirk
/ AFP 289tc, Ian Hoten / SPL 479c, Ian Walton 24br, Jana Chytilova /
Freestyle Photography 177, Joosep Martinson 471, Kali Nine LLC 204b,
londoneye 383tr, Mariano Sayno / husayno.com 59, Minas Panagiotakis
270bl, olga Akmen / Anadolu Agency 314br, PhotoAlto / Sandro Di
Carlo Darsa 343, quavondo 113br, Quinn Rooney 427, Stu Forster 14bl,
Westend61 186br; **Pearson Education Ltd:** Gareth Boden 176tl, 256tl,
426tl; **Physiotherapist: Jessie Wong:** Model: Elisa Wong 487tl; **Press
Association Images:** Gareth Copely / PA Archive 337tr, Steve Parsons
431bl; **Rex Shutterstock:** Derek Catten 461cr, Vaughan Pickhaver 447tr;
Science Photo Library Ltd: Arthur Glauberman 70c; **Shutterstock.
com:** A and N photography 303tr, Andrey Khrolenok 132tl, Dziurek
353bl, Featureflash 47tr, IAKOBCHUK VIACHESLAV 98c, Istvan Csak 26bl,
Kaliva 366tr, MaraZe 64br, Mitch Gunn 139cr, Monkey Business Images
212tl, Pal2iyawit 393tc, PT Images 515tr, Rido 105br, 304tl, 516tl, Roger
Jegg - Fotodesign-Jegg.de 342tl, Sergey Nivens 166t, wavebreakmedia
384tl; **Squawka Ltd:** 492b; **Stuart Smith:** 469tr; **Takei Scientific
Instruments Co.,Ltd:** 225tr; **UK Anti-Doping :** 2016 437tr
Cover images: *Front:* **Shutterstock.com:** Rocksweeper
All other images © Pearson Education**Websites**

The publisher would like to thank the following organisations for their
kind permission to reproduce their materials:

Case Study (**p 35**), Menu (**p 65**), Table 2.4 (**p 68**) all taken from the NHS.
Used with permission of NHS Choices. Research (**p 63**) Health survey
data **© 2015,** re-used with the permission of the Health and Social Care
Information Centre. All rights reserved. Table 2.4 (**p 69**), Extracts from
legislation (**pp 144-7**) taken from UK GOV. Table 2.10 (**p 86**) Calculating
BMR adapted from Schofield, W.N. (1985) Predicting basal metabolic
rate, new standards and review of previous work, *Human Nutrition.
Clinical Nutrition* 39 Suppl 1: 5–41. US National Library of Medicine.
USA Gov. Table 2.14 (**p 92**) by Bush, Gledhill, Mackay. Reproduced
with permission of Pearson Education Ltd. Theory into practice (**p 94**)
Taken from Nutritionists at the English Institute of Sport. Used with
permission. Multidimensional model of sport leadership (**p 282**) used
with permission of Dr. Chelladurai. Case study (**p 451**) with information
taken from XPRO. Used with permission of EXPRO.org. Table 28.7 (**p 485**)
taken from Davis, B. *et al* (2000) *Physical Education and the study of sport,*
4th edition, Spain: Harcourt. Used with permission.

A note from the publisher

In order to ensure that this resource offers high-quality support for
the associated Pearson qualification, it has been through a review
process by the awarding body. This process confirms that this resource
fully covers the teaching and learning content of the specification
or part of a specification at which it is aimed. It also confirms that it
demonstrates an appropriate balance between the development of
subject skills, knowledge and understanding, in addition to preparation
for assessment.

Endorsement does not cover any guidance on assessment activities
or processes (e.g. practice questions or advice on how to answer
assessment questions), included in the resource nor does it prescribe
any particular approach to the teaching or delivery of a related course.

While the publishers have made every attempt to ensure that advice on
the qualification and its assessment is accurate, the official specification
and associated assessment guidance materials are the only authoritative
source of information and should always be referred to for definitive
guidance.

Pearson examiners have not contributed to any sections in this
resource relevant to examination papers for which they have
responsibility.

Examiners will not use endorsed resources as a source of material for
any assessment set by Pearson.

Endorsement of a resource does not mean that the resource is required
to achieve this Pearson qualification, nor does it mean that it is the
only suitable material available to support the qualification, and any
resource lists produced by the awarding body shall include this and
other appropriate resources.

Contents

How to use this book

Welcome to your BTEC National Sport course!

A BTEC National in Sport is one of the most popular BTEC courses. It is a vocational qualification that will help prepare you for a huge range of careers. You may be thinking of pursuing a career as an elite sports performer or as a coach. At present, there are around 1.2 million coaches in Britain. You may be considering joining the health and fitness industry as an exercise professional. This job requires you to supervise and instruct people who are taking part in exercise classes or training sessions.

Research shows a clear link between an active lifestyle and good health. As a result, the health and fitness industry has grown significantly over the last 10 years, and will probably continue to grow. There is a demand for exercise professionals and there are good employment opportunities, some of which you will find out more about in this book.

How your BTEC is structured

Your BTEC National is divided into **mandatory units** (the ones you must do) and **optional units** (the ones you can choose to do).

The number of mandatory and optional units will vary depending on the type of BTEC National you are doing. This book supports all the mandatory units and the most popular optional units to allow you to complete the:

▶ Certificate

▶ Extended Certificate

▶ Foundation Diploma.

This book also contains a number of mandatory and optional units for the Diploma and the Extended Diploma. Pearson's BTEC National Sport Student Book 2 covers the remaining mandatory and optional units for these qualifications, as well as the remaining optional units for the Foundation Diploma.

Your learning experience

You may not realise it but you are always learning. Your educational and life experiences are constantly shaping your ideas and thinking, and how you view and engage with the world around you.

You are the person most responsible for your own learning experience so you must understand what you are learning, why you are learning it and why it is important both to your course and to your personal development. Your learning can be seen as a journey with four phases.

Phase 1	Phase 2	Phase 3	Phase 4
You are introduced to a topic or concept and you start to develop an awareness of what learning is required.	You explore the topic or concept through different methods (e.g. research, questioning, analysis, deep thinking, critical evaluation) and form your own understanding.	You apply your knowledge and skills to a task designed to test your understanding.	You reflect on your learning, evaluate your efforts, identify gaps in your knowledge and look for ways to improve.

During each phase, you will use different learning strategies to secure the core knowledge and skills you need. This student book has been written using similar learning principles, strategies and tools. It has been designed to support your learning journey, to give you control over your own learning, and to equip you with the knowledge, understanding and tools you need to be successful in your future studies or career.

Features of this book

In this student book there are lots of different features. They are there to help you learn about the topics in your course in different ways and understand it from multiple perspectives. Together these features:

▶ explain what your learning is about
▶ help you to build your knowledge
▶ help you understand how to succeed in your assessment
▶ help you to reflect on and evaluate your learning
▶ help you to link your learning to the workplace

In addition, each individual feature has a specific purpose, designed to support important learning strategies. For example, some features will:

▶ get you to question assumptions around what you are learning
▶ make you think beyond what you are reading about
▶ help you make connections across your learning and across units
▶ draw comparisons between your own learning and real-world workplace environments
▶ help you to develop some of the important skills you will need for the workplace, including team work, effective communication and problem solving.

Features that explain what your learning is about

Getting to know your unit

This section introduces the unit and explains how you will be assessed. It gives an overview of what will be covered and will help you to understand why you are doing the things you are asked to do in this unit.

Getting started

This is designed to get you thinking about the unit and what it involves. This feature will also help you to identify what you may already know about some of the topics in the unit and act as a starting point for understanding the skills and knowledge you will need to develop to complete the unit.

Features that help you to build your knowledge

Research

This asks you to research a topic in greater depth. These features will help to expand your understanding of a topic and develop your research and investigation skills. All of this will be invaluable for your future progression, both professionally and academically.

Worked example

Worked examples show the process you need to follow to solve a problem, such as a maths or science equation, or the process for writing a letter or memo. They will help you to develop your understanding and your numeracy and literacy skills.

Safety tip

These tips give advice about health and safety when working on the unit. They will help to build your knowledge about best practice in the workplace, as well as making sure that you stay safe.

Theory into practice

In this feature, you will be asked to consider the workplace or industry implications of a topic or concept from the unit. This will help you to understand the relevance of your current learning and the ways in which it may affect a future career in your chosen sector.

Discussion

Discussion features encourage you to talk to other students about a topic, working together to increase your understanding of the topic and to understand other people's perspectives on an issue. These features will also help to build your teamworking skills, which will be invaluable in your future professional and academic career.

Key terms

Concise and simple definitions are provided for key words, phrases and concepts, giving you, at a glance, a clear understanding of the key ideas in each unit.

Link

Link features show any links between content in different units or within the same unit helping you to identify knowledge you have learned elsewhere that will help you to achieve the requirements of the unit. Remember, although your BTEC National is made up of several units, there are common themes that are explored from different perspectives across the whole of your course.

Further reading and resources

This feature lists other resources – such as books, journals, articles or websites – you can use to expand your knowledge of the unit content. This is a good opportunity for you to take responsibility for your own learning and prepare for research tasks you may need to complete academically or professionally.

Features connected to your assessment

Your course is made up of mandatory and optional units. There are two different types of mandatory unit:

▶ externally assessed
▶ internally assessed.

The features that support you in preparing for assessment are below. But first, what is the difference between these two different types of unit?

Externally assessed units

These units will give you the opportunity to demonstrate your knowledge and understanding, or your skills, in a direct way. For these units you will complete a task, set directly by Pearson, in controlled conditions. This could take the form of an exam or it could be another type of task. You may have the opportunity to prepare in advance, to research and make notes about a topic which can be used when completing the assessment.

Internally assessed units

Most of your units will be internally assessed and will involve you completing a series of assignments, set and marked by your tutor. The assignments you complete will allow you to demonstrate your learning in a number of different ways, from a written report to a presentation to a video recording and observation statements of you completing a practical task. Whatever the method, you will need to make sure you have clear evidence of what you have achieved and how you did it.

Assessment practice

These features give you the opportunity to practise some of the skills you will need during the unit assessment. They do not fully reflect the actual assessment tasks but will help you to prepare for them.

Plan - Do - Review

You will also find handy advice on how to plan, complete and evaluate your work. This is designed to get you thinking about the best way to complete your work and to build your skills and experience before doing the actual assessment. These questions will prompt you to think about the way you work and why particular tasks are relevant.

Getting ready for assessment

For internally assessed units, this is a case study of a BTEC National student, talking about how they planned and carried out their assignment work and what they would do differently if they were to do it again. It will give you advice on preparing for your internal assessments, including Think about it points for you to consider for your own development.

Getting ready for assessment

This section will help you to prepare for external assessment. It gives practical advice on preparing for and sitting exams or a set task. It provides a series of sample answers for the types of question you will need to answer in your external assessment, including guidance on the good points of these answers and ways in which they could be improved.

Features to help you reflect on and evaluate your learning

Ⅱ PAUSE POINT

Pause Points appear regularly throughout the book and provide opportunities to review and reflect on your learning. The ability to reflect on your own performance is a key skill you will need to develop and use throughout your life, and will be essential whatever your future plans are.

Hint
Extend

These sections give you suggestions to help cement your knowledge and indicate other areas you can look at to expand it.

Features which link your learning with the workplace

Case study

Case studies throughout the book will allow you to apply the learning and knowledge from the unit to a scenario from the workplace or industry. Case studies include questions to help you consider the wider context of a topic. They show how the course content is reflected in the real world and help you to build familiarity with issues you may find in a real-world workplace.

THINK ▶FUTURE

This is a special case study where someone working in the industry talks about the job role they do and the skills they need. This comes with a *Focusing your skills* section, which gives suggestions for how you can begin to develop the employability skills and experiences that are needed to be successful in a career in your chosen sector. This is an excellent opportunity to help you identify what you could do, inside and outside of your BTEC National studies, to build up your employability skills.

National BTEC awards

Every year Pearson hosts an award ceremony celebrating excellence in BTEC Nationals. Teachers and tutors nominate their outstanding BTEC students (in 2015, there were over 800 nominations) and a judging panel gives prizes to the student judged to be the most outstanding for each subject. We talked to Joe Holland, the Outstanding BTEC Sport Student of the Year in 2014, who shared his experience of studying for a BTEC – and what he went on to do in the future.

Why did you do the BTEC National in Sport?

I'm a very sporty person so I took BTEC First Sport in Year 10, came out with maximum marks, so thought I'd carry on with my BTEC in Year 12/13. I thought about what I wanted to do after school and I wanted to go to university and become a teacher. The BTEC was even better than I thought it would be. It taught me lots of different things, like life skills. It's a very independent course and teaches you a lot about yourself.

In Year 12 I set up a sports leadership programme, to help train other leaders to help younger students. I do a lot of volunteering in Sport and when I approached my teachers with this idea they really liked it. The first year of doing it went better than I thought – to be honest it was amazing. BTEC gave me this opportunity, and I wouldn't have had it on other subjects.

How did you set up the sports leadership programme?

I came up with a plan, tweaked it with my teachers and then went round each PE class and asked people if they were interested. I started with 50 and trained them up. This went really well so I was able to bring in a couple of Year 12s to help. I trained them to run their own sessions: so training them to train others. This also meant when I left school I was able to pass the programme on so it kept going and going. I made sure when I left that they had my notes, but said they also need to do something new with it: otherwise year after year the sports leaders are going to be doing the same stuff and that is not going to get them to develop. It was hard at first but now it has built a legacy that will keep going – I'm quite proud of it!

Setting up the programme really helped me understand what I want to do. I enjoy teaching, I enjoy watching people develop. It really helped me develop and to understand more about myself. Because I set the course up I became a role model for the younger students. When I go back to the school to teach, they still know me and tell me about what they're doing. It's amazing.

What are you doing now?

I'm in my second year at university, studying Physical Education and Sport Science. Choosing this course allows me to go into either of these areas. I also work for School Games which is a big organisation to help put sports competition into young people's lives. I run events and also volunteer in schools. I'm a recreational assistant at ActiveLife and I work for the Youth Sports Trust, which is a big sports organisation. The BTEC Award helped me to get these opportunities. I also won the Youth Sports Trust award, giving me the opportunity to volunteer at the national event. From there I was approached for a job as one of 40 Team Leaders. This opportunity all came first from BTEC.

What are your plans for the future?

I want to be a PE teacher but I'm also looking to go to Camp America for a year or two in the Summer and look into Sport Development. I love the vibe at the Youth Trust, and enjoy working with the children and the other coaches. I'm a bit torn at the moment, but teaching is my main aim. It will be a hard road getting there, but that's the plan.

What would you say to people starting BTECs?

It will teach you a lot of things but don't take a subject you don't want to do in the future. BTEC offers a lot of opportunities for the future. It's structured but very free: you get the information and then go to work, developing a university style of working.

About the authors

Mark Adams

Mark is a senior standards verifier for the QCF and NQF BTEC Sport qualifications and has worked for Pearson for over 10 years. He has taught BTEC qualifications in schools and colleges and most recently in an elite sports environment. Mark is currently Head of Education at a Premier League football club. He has contributed as a writer and series editor for a number of BTEC Sport text books at Level 2 and Level 3.

Matthew Fleet

Matthew is a senior lecturer in PE and Coaching at Southampton Solent University. During the last decade, he has worked in over 150 schools and colleges, leading to extensive expertise in physical education. Matthew has also worked as an external verifier, moderator and lead examiner and as a teacher trainer for physical education, helping to support and develop both new and experienced teachers.

Adam Gledhill

Adam has 15 years' experience working within further and higher education. He works within qualification development for Pearson and is a co-author of previous editions of this book. Adam has experience of providing interdisciplinary sport science support to different athlete populations; from youth and senior international football players, to youth athletes in a range of sports. Among his consultancy roles, he has worked as Head of Sport Science for an FA Women's Super League team and as Head of Psychosocial Development for a Football Association Licensed Girls' Football Centre of Excellence.

Chris Lydon

Chris has worked in further and higher education for twenty years as a senior sports science lecturer specialising in anatomy and physiology and fitness training. He has also worked as an external standards verifier for Pearson and an external examiner for a number of universities. He is currently employed as an Assistant Principal at a large FE college where he is responsible for the recruitment and support of staff and students. Chris has previously written a number of books relating to BTEC sports qualifications.

Chris Manley

Chris splits his time between roles as a Postgraduate Education Tutor at Canterbury Christ Church University and as a Senior Practitioner at an FE college. Chris has been a National League basketball coach, tutor and referee and was a successful slalom canoeist. He has a Master's degree in Education and postgraduate qualifications in the sociology of sport, and works in a variety of roles related to BTEC for Pearson. Chris has published for BTEC and for teaching professionals studying teaching qualifications.

Alex Sergison

Alex has worked in the sports industry for 15 years and specialises in outdoor education. He has acted as a consultant for a number of small businesses as well as running his own. He manages Weymouth College's outdoor education department based on Portland. Alex has been involved with Pearson as a course writer and study guide writer for the last 6 years.

Louise Sutton

Louise is a principal lecturer in sport and exercise nutrition at Leeds Beckett University. She has a particular interest in the practical application of sport dietetics in elite environments over the past 20 years, having advised elite athletes from a range of professional sports. She has extensive experience in delivering nutrition education programmes to support junior athlete development and was recently awarded the British Dietetic Association's Roll of Honour for her contribution to the development of the Sport and Exercise Nutrition Register.

Richard Taylor

Richard is a former rower and personal trainer with several years of experience in teaching Further and Higher Education sports programmes and PE in schools. Currently a tutor for Gillingham FC's academy, Richard has worked with a number of professional football clubs, written several higher education sports programmes and contributed to previous editions of this book.

Anatomy and Physiology 1

Getting to know your unit

To understand what happens during sport and exercise, you must know about body systems. This unit explains how the body is made up of a number of different systems, how these systems interact and work together, and why they are important to sports performance. You will:

▶ be introduced to the structures and functions of the five key systems and the effects that sport and exercise has on them

▶ investigate the structure and function of the skeletal and muscular systems and their role in causing movement in sport and exercise

▶ examine the structure and functions of the cardiovascular and respiratory systems

▶ understand why the heart works as it does and how it works with the lungs to allow sportspeople to cope with the demands of sport

▶ look at the three different energy systems and the sports in which they are predominantly used.

This is a mandatory unit and introduces knowledge that will link with all other units in the course.

How you will be assessed

This unit will be assessed by an examination set by Pearson. The examination will contain a number of short answer and long answer questions. You will be assessed for your understanding of the following topics in relations to sports performance:

▶ the skeletal system

▶ the muscular system

▶ the respiratory system

▶ the cardiovascular system

▶ the energy system.

During this examination you will need to show your knowledge and understanding of the interrelationships between these different body systems for sports performance.

Throughout this unit you will find assessment practice activities to help you prepare for the exam. Completing each of these activities will give you an insight into the types of question that will be asked and, importantly, how to answer them.

Unit 1 has five assessment outcomes (AO) which will be included in the external examination. Certain 'command words' are associated with each assessment outcome. Table 1.1 explains what these command words are asking you to do.

As the guidelines for assessment can change, you should refer to the official assessment guidance on the Pearson Qualifications website for the latest definitive guidance.

The assessment outcomes for the unit are:

▶ **AO1** Demonstrate knowledge of body systems, structures, functions, characteristics, definitions and other additional factors affecting each body system
   • Command words: identify, describe, give, state, name
   • Marks: ranges from 1 to 5 marks

▶ **AO2** Demonstrate understanding of each body system, the short- and long-term effects of sport and exercise on each system, and additional factors that can affect body systems in relation to exercise and sporting performance
   • Command words: describe, explain, give, state, name
   • Marks: ranges from 1 to 5 marks

▶ **AO3** Analyse exercise and sports movements, how the body responds to short-term and long-term exercise, and other additional factors affecting each body system
   • Command words: analyse, assess
   • Marks: 6 marks

▶ **AO4** Evaluate how body systems are used and how they interrelate in order to carry out exercise and sporting movements
   • Command words: evaluate, assess
   • Marks: 6 marks

▶ **AO5** Make connections between body systems in response to short-term and long-term exercise and sport participation. Make connections between muscular and all other systems, cardiovascular and respiratory systems, energy and cardiovascular systems
   • Command words: analyse, evaluate, assess, discuss, to what extent
   • Marks: 8 marks

▶ **Table 1.1:** Command words used in the assessment outcomes

Command word	Definition – what it is asking you to do
Analyse	Identify several relevant facts of a topic, demonstrate how they are linked and then explain the importance of each, often in relation to the other facts.
Assess	Evaluate or estimate the nature, ability, or quality of something.
Describe	Give a full account of all the information about a topic, including all the relevant details of any features.
Discuss	Write about the topic in detail, taking into account different ideas and opinions.
Evaluate	Bring all the relevant information you have on a topic together and make a judgement (for example, on its success or importance). Your judgement should be clearly supported by the information you have gathered.
Explain	Make an idea, situation or problem clear to your reader by describing it in detail, including any relevant data or facts.
Give	Provide examples, justifications and/or reasons.
Identify	State the key fact(s) about a topic or subject. The word *Outline* is similar.
State/name	Give a definition or example.
To what extent	Review information and then bring it together to form a judgement or conclusion, after giving a balanced and reasoned argument.

Getting started

Anatomy and **physiology** are essential ingredients in all sport and exercise performance. List the changes that your body experiences when you take part in sport or exercise. When you have done this, consider each change and try to identify which body system is being affected.

 A # The effects of exercise and sports performance on the skeletal system

Key terms

Anatomy – study of the structure of the body such as the skeletal, muscular or cardiovascular systems.

Physiology – study of the way that the body responds to exercise and training.

Structure of the skeletal system

Before we look at the functions of the skeletal system, it is important to understand which bones make up the skeleton and how they are used to perform the vast range of techniques and actions required in sport. Without bones, you would be a shapeless mass of muscle and tissue, unable to move. The skeletal system is made up of bones, cartilage and joints.

Your skeleton is made up of 206 bones which provide a framework that supports your muscles and skin and protects your internal organs.

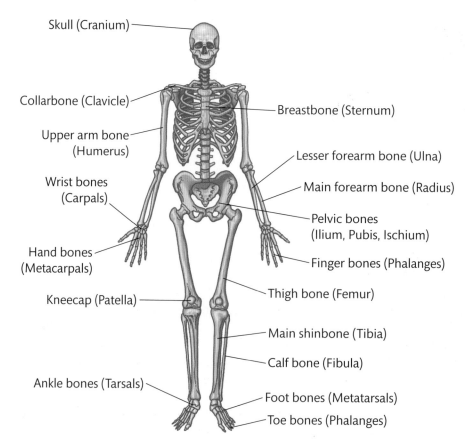

▶ **Figure 1.1:** Bones of the human skeleton; Latin names are shown in brackets

Many terms are used to describe the location (or anatomical position) of bones. These are described in Table 1.2. You might find it useful to make a note of them.

▶ **Table 1.2:** Terms used to describe the location of bones

Term	Meaning
Anterior	To the front or in front
Posterior	To the rear or behind
Medial	Towards the midline or axis, an imaginary line down the centre of the body
Lateral	Away from the midline or axis
Proximal	Near to the root or origin (the proximal of the arm is towards the shoulder)
Distal	Away from the root or origin (the distal of the arm is towards the hand)
Superior	Above
Inferior	Below

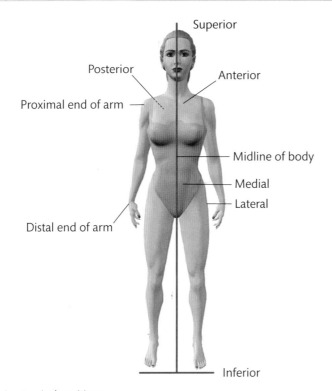

▶ **Figure 1.2:** Anatomical positions

Types of bone

The skeleton has five main types of bone according to their shape and size. These can be classified as:

▶ **long bones** – the bones found in the limbs. They have a shaft known as the **diaphysis** and two expanded ends known as the **epiphysis**. – *Tibia*

▶ **short bones** – small, light, strong, cube-shaped bones consisting of **cancellous bone** surrounded by a thin layer of compact bone. The carpals and tarsals of the wrists and ankles (introduced later in this section) are examples of short bones.

▶ **flat bones** – thin, flattened and slightly curved, with a large surface area. Examples include the scapulae, sternum and cranium.

▶ **irregular bones** – have complex shapes that fit none of the categories above. The bones of the spinal column are a good example.

▶ **sesamoid bones** – have a specialised function and are usually found within a tendon. These bones provide a smooth surface for the tendon to slide over. The largest sesamoid bone is the patella in the knee joint.

> **Key term**
>
> **Cancellous bone** – light and porous bone material that has a honeycomb or spongy appearance.

→ *Tarsals*

Areas of the skeleton

The skeleton can be divided into two parts: 80 bones form your **axial skeleton** – the long **axis** of your body; the other 126 bones form your **appendicular skeleton** – the bones that are attached to this axis.

Axial skeleton

The axial skeleton is the main core or axis of your skeleton and consists of:

▶ the skull (including cranium and facial bones)

▶ the thoracic cage (sternum and ribs)

▶ the vertebral column.

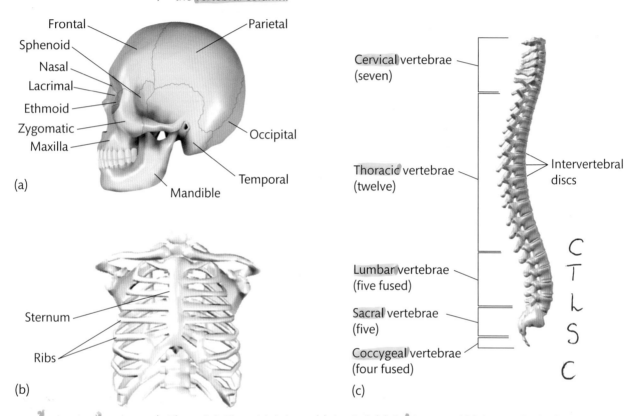

▶ **Figure 1.3:** The axial skeleton: (a) the skull, (b) the thorax and (c) the vertebral column

Appendicular skeleton

The appendicular skeleton consists of the bones that are attached to the axial skeleton. These bones will be introduced in more detail later in this section, but the appendicular skeleton consists of the following parts.

▶ The upper limbs consist of 60 bones (30 in each arm) including the humerus, radius, ulna, carpals, metacarpals and phalanges.

▶ The lower limbs consist of 60 bones (30 in each leg) including the femur, tibia, fibula, patella, tarsals, metatarsals and phalanges.

▶ The shoulder girdle consists of four bones – two clavicles and two scapulae – which connect the limbs of the upper body to the thorax.

▶ The pelvic girdle is made of three bones: the ilium, pubis and ischium. These fuse together with age and are collectively known as the innominate bone. The main function of the pelvic girdle is to provide a solid base through which to transmit the weight of the upper body. It also provides attachment for the powerful muscles of the lower back and legs, and protects the digestive and reproductive organs.

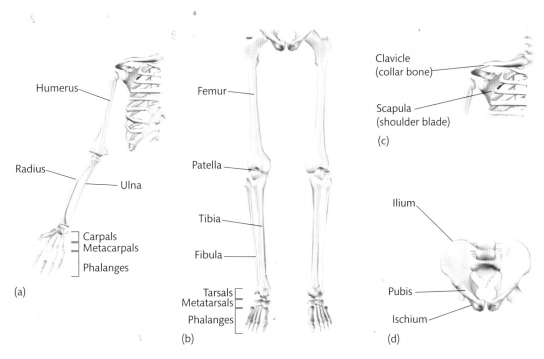

▶ **Figure 1.4:** The appendicular skeleton: (a) the upper limbs, (b) the lower limbs, (c) the shoulder girdle and (d) the pelvic girdle

The spine or vertebral column

The vertebral column is commonly known as the spine or backbone and extends from the base of the cranium to the pelvis, providing a central axis for the body. It is made up of 33 irregular bones called **vertebrae**.

The vertebral column accounts for around 40 per cent of a person's overall height. The vertebrae are held together by powerful **ligaments**. These allow little movement between adjacent vertebrae but a considerable degree of flexibility along the spine as a whole.

The vertebral column can be classified into five sections or regions (see Figure 1.3(c)):

▶ **cervical vertebrae** – the seven vertebrae of the neck. The first two are known as the atlas (C1) and the axis (C2). They form a pivot joint that allows the head and neck to move freely. They are the smallest and most vulnerable vertebrae of the vertebral column.

▶ **thoracic vertebrae** – the 12 vertebrae of the mid-spine, which articulate with the ribs. They lie in the thorax, a dome-shaped structure that protects the heart and lungs.

▶ **lumbar vertebrae** – the five largest of the movable vertebrae, situated in the lower back. They support more weight than other vertebrae and provide attachment for many of the muscles of the back. The discs between these vertebrae produce a **concave** curve in the back.

▶ **sacral vertebrae** – the five sacral vertebrae are fused together to form the **sacrum**, a triangular bone located below the lumbar vertebrae. It forms the back wall of the pelvic girdle, sitting between the two hip bones. The upper part connects with the last lumbar vertebra and the bottom part with the coccyx.

▶ **coccygeal vertebrae** – at the bottom of the vertebral column there are four coccygeal vertebrae, which are fused together to form the **coccyx** or tail bone.

Key terms

Ligaments – short bands of tough and fibrous flexible tissue that hold bones together.

Concave – having an outline or surface that curves inwards.

The vertebral column has many functions. It protects the spinal cord and supports the ribcage. The larger vertebrae of the lumbar region support a large amount of body weight. The flatter thoracic vertebrae offer attachment for the large muscles of the back. These, along with the **intervertebral discs**, receive and distribute impact associated with sporting performance, reducing shock.

Postural deviations

The 33 vertebrae of the spine have a distinctive shape when stacked on top of one another. The normal shape consists of a curve in the cervical (neck), thoracic (mid back) and lumbar (low back) regions when viewed from the side. A **neutral spine** refers to a good posture with the correct position of the three natural curves. When viewing the spine from the front (anterior), it should be completely vertical. Occasionally the spine may suffer from disorders which can cause the natural curves to change.

▶ **Kyphosis** – the excessive outward curve of the thoracic region of the spine resulting in a 'hunchback' appearance. This is often caused by poor posture but can be caused by deformities of the vertebrae.

▶ **Scoliosis** – the abnormal curvature of the spine either to the left or to the right (lateral curvature). Most likely to occur in the thoracic region. Often found in children but can be found in adults. This condition is not thought to be linked to bad posture and the exact reasons for it are unknown, although it seems to be inheritable.

Major bones of the skeletal system

The skeletal system includes the following bones.

▶ **Cranium** – this box-like cavity (space) consists of interlinking segments of bone that are fused together. The cranium contains and protects the brain.

▶ **Clavicles** – these are commonly known as the collar bones and are the long, slim bones that form the anterior part of the shoulder girdle. This provides a strong attachment for the arms.

▶ **Ribs** – there are 12 pairs of ribs and they form part of the **thoracic cage**. The first seven pairs are attached to the sternum (see below) and are known as true ribs; the remaining five pairs are known as false ribs as they do not attach to the sternum. The ribs are long, flat bones.

▶ **Sternum (breast bone)** – this is the elongated, flat bone that runs down the centre of the chest and forms the front of the thoracic cage. Seven pairs of ribs are attached to the sternum, which provides protection and muscular attachment.

▶ **Scapula** (plural: scapulae) – commonly known as the **shoulder blades**, these large, triangular, flat bones form the posterior part of the shoulder girdle.

▶ **Humerus** – this is the long bone of the upper arm and is the largest bone of the upper limbs. The head of the humerus articulates (joins) with the scapula to form the shoulder joint. The distal end articulates with the radius and ulna to form the elbow joint.

▶ **Radius and ulna** – the ulna is the longer of the two bones of the forearm. The ulna and radius articulate distally (see Table 1.2) with the wrist.

▶ **Carpals** – these are the eight small bones that make up the wrist. They are irregular, small bones arranged in two rows of four. They fit closely together and are kept in place by ligaments.

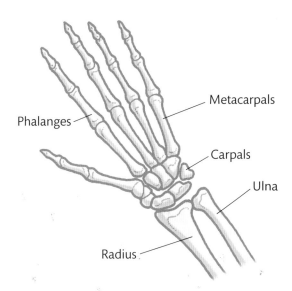

▶ **Figure 1.5:** The bones of the wrist and hand

▶ **Metacarpals** – five long bones in the palm of the hand, one corresponding to each digit (finger or thumb). These run from the carpal bones of the wrist to the base of each digit in the hand.

▶ **Phalanges** – the bones that make up the thumbs, fingers and toes. Most fingers and toes have three phalanges, but the thumbs and big toes have two.

▶ **Pelvis** – the pelvis is made up of two hip bones which in turn consist of three sections (**ilium**, **ischium** and **pubis**) which fuse together during puberty to form one bone. The ilium structure provides the socket for the ball and socket joint (see Figure 1.8) of the femur, allowing the legs to be attached to the main skeleton.

▶ **Femur** – the longest and strongest bone in the body, sometimes referred to as the **thigh bone**. The head fits into the socket of the pelvis to form the hip joint; the lower end joins the tibia to form the knee joint.

▶ **Patella (kneecap)** – the large, triangular sesamoid bone found in the quadriceps femoris **tendon**. It protects the knee joint.

▶ **Tibia and fibula** – the long bones that form the lower leg. The tibia is the inner and thicker bone, also known as the **shin bone**. The upper end of the tibia joins the femur to form the knee joint, while the lower end forms part of the ankle joint. The fibula is the outer, thinner bone of the lower leg; it does not reach the knee, but its lower end does form part of the ankle joint.

▶ **Tarsals** – along with the tibia and fibula, seven bones known collectively as the tarsals form the ankle joint including the heel. The calcaneus, or heel bone, is the largest tarsal bone. It helps to support the weight of the body and provides attachment for the calf muscles via the Achilles tendon. The tarsals are short and irregular bones.

▶ **Metatarsals** – there are five metatarsals in each foot; they are located between the tarsals and the phalanges (toes). Each metatarsal has a similar structure, with a distal and proximal head joined by a thin shaft (body). The metatarsals are responsible for bearing a great deal of weight, and they balance pressure through the balls of the feet. The metatarsals are a common site of fracture in sport.

Key term

Tendon – strong fibrous tissue that attaches muscle to bone.

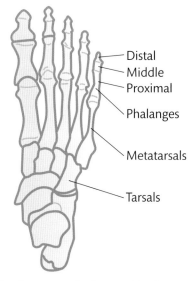

▶ **Figure 1.6:** The bones of the foot

Hint

Consider a sport of your choice and identify the bones that are used in the main actions involved in that sport.

Extend

How could understanding how these bones work affect your performance in sport? For each action you identified, explain the functions of the listed bones.

Key term

Calcium – a mineral essential for bone growth and found in a wide range of foods including milk, cheese, yoghurt, nuts, broccoli and beans.

Process of bone growth

Bone is a living organ that is continuously being reshaped through a process called remodelling. **Ossification** is the process in which bones are formed. Throughout this process parts of the bone are reabsorbed so that unnecessary **calcium** is removed (via cells called **osteoclasts**) while new layers of bone tissue are created.

The cells that bring the calcium to your bones are known as **osteoblasts** and are responsible for creating bone matter. Osteoblast activity increases when you exercise, so your bones will become stronger the more exercise you do. This means your bone calcium stores increase to cope with the demand for calcium, so exercising also reduces the risk of osteoporosis. Activities that can build stronger bones include tennis, netball, basketball, aerobics, walking and running.

The ends of each long bone contain growing areas – or plates – which allow the bone to grow longer. This continues throughout childhood until they reach full maturity. These areas are called the **epiphyseal plates** and allow the long bones to extend. Once a long bone is fully formed, the head – or end of each bone – fuses with the main shaft (diaphysis) to create the **epiphyseal line**.

Function of the skeletal system

Your skeleton has a number of important functions both in sport and in everyday life. When performing sport or exercise there are eight main functions.

▸ **Support** – collectively, your bones give your body shape and provide the supporting framework for the soft tissues of your body.

▸ **Protection** – the bones of your skeleton surround and protect vital tissues and organs in your body. Your skull protects your brain, your heart and lungs are protected by your thorax, your vertebral column protects your delicate spinal cord, and your pelvis protects your abdominal and reproductive organs.

▸ **Attachment for skeletal muscle** – parts of your skeleton provide a surface for your skeletal muscles to attach to, allowing you to move. Tendons attach muscles to bone, providing leverage. Muscles pulling on bones act as levers, and movement occurs at the joints so that you can walk, run, jump, kick, throw etc. Type of joint (see page 12) determines the type of movement possible.

▸ **Source of blood cell production** – your bones are not completely solid, as this would make your skeleton heavy and difficult to move. Blood vessels feed the centre of your bones, and stored within the bones is **bone marrow**. The marrow of your long bones is continually producing red and white blood cells. This is an essential function as large numbers of blood cells, particularly red cells, die every minute.

▸ **Store of minerals** – bone is a reservoir for minerals such as calcium and phosphorus, which are essential for bone growth and the maintenance of bone health. These minerals are stored and released into the bloodstream as required, balancing the minerals in your body.

▶ **Leverage** – the bones provide a lever system against which muscles can pull to create movement.

▶ **Weight bearing** – your bones are very strong and will support the weight of your tissue including muscles. During sport large forces are applied to your body, and your skeleton provides the structural strength to prevent injury.

▶ **Reducing friction across joints** – the skeleton has many joints of different types. Synovial joints secrete fluid that prevents bones from rubbing together, reducing friction between the bones.

Main function of different bone types

The bones in your body have many different functions, depending on their shape and location. Consider the bones of the arms and legs and how they are used in sport. In conjunction with your muscles, these long bones can produce large movements such as kicking or throwing as the long bones act like levers. The flat bones of the body are also important in sport as they can provide protection from impact, ensuring your vital organs remain functioning. Look at Table 1.3 for examples of the different bones and their main functions.

▶ **Table 1.3:** Function of different bones types

Type of bone	Function	Examples
Long	Movement, support, red blood cell production	Femur, humerus, tibia, radius, ulna
Short	Fine or small movements; shock absorption, stability, weight bearing	Carpals, tarsals
Flat	Attachment for muscles; protection	Sternum, scapula, pelvis, cranium
Sesamoid	Protection; reduction of friction across a joint	Patella, pisiform (wrist)
Irregular	Protection (spinal cord); movement	Vertebrae

⏸ PAUSE POINT   What are the main functions of the skeleton? Why are these important in sport and exercise?

   Write down the main functions of the axial skeleton and the appendicular skeleton.

    Consider a sporting action. What are the roles of the axial and appendicular skeleton in this action?

Joints

You have seen that your skeleton is made up of bones that support and protect your body. For movement to occur, the bones must be linked. A joint is formed where two or more bones meet. This is known as an **articulation**. The adult human body contains around 350 joints, which can be classified in different ways depending on their structure.

Key term

Articulation – where two or more bones meet.

The bones of the shoulder are shown in Figure 1.4(c) on page 7 and the bones of the hip, knee and ankle are shown in Figure 1.4(b). The structure and movement of the vertebrae are described on pages 7–8 under the heading 'The spine or vertebral column'.

Classification of joints

There are three types of joint, classified according to the degree of movement they allow:

▶ fixed – *bone plates in cranium*
▶ slightly movable – *vertibrae*
▶ synovial. – *ankle, shoulder, knee*

Fixed joints

Fixed joints, or **fibrous** or **immovable joints**, do not move. Fixed joints form when the bones interlock and overlap during early childhood. These joints are held together by bands of tough, fibrous tissue and are strong with no movement between the bones. An example is between the bone plates in your cranium, which are fixed together to provide protection for your brain.

Slightly movable joints

Slightly movable or **cartilaginous joints** allow slight movement. The ends of the bone are covered in a smooth, shiny covering, known as articular or hyaline cartilage, which reduces friction between the bones. The bones are separated by pads of white fibrocartilage (a tough cartilage that is capable of absorbing considerable loads). Slight movement at these joining surfaces is made possible because the pads of cartilage compress, for example between most vertebrae.

Synovial joints

Synovial joints or **freely movable joints** offer the highest level of mobility at a joint and are vital to all sporting movements. Most of the joints in your limbs are synovial.

A synovial joint (see Figure 1.7) consists of two or more bones, the ends of which are covered with articular cartilage, which allows the bones to move over each other with minimum friction. Synovial joints always have a synovial cavity or space between the bones. This cavity is completely surrounded by a fibrous capsule, lined with a synovial membrane, whose purpose is to release or secrete fluid known as synovial fluid into the joint cavity. This lubricates and nourishes the joint. The joint capsule is held together by tough bands of connective tissue known as ligaments. These ligaments provide the strength to avoid dislocation, while being flexible enough to allow a wide range of movement.

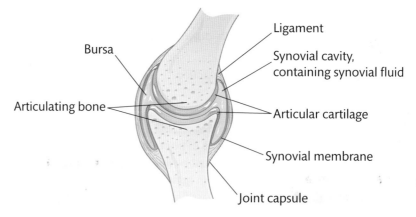

Bursa

Articulating bone

Ligament

Synovial cavity, containing synovial fluid

Articular cartilage

Synovial membrane

Joint capsule

▶ **Figure 1.7:** A synovial joint

All synovial joints contain the following features.

▶ A **joint capsule** or fibrous capsule - an outer sleeve to help to hold the bones in place and protect the joint. This capsule will also contain the main structure of the synovial joint.

▶ A **bursa** – a small fluid-filled sac which provides a cushion between the tendons and the bones, preventing friction. Bursae are filled with synovial fluid.
▶ **Articular cartilage** on the ends of the bones – provides a smooth and slippery covering to stop the bones rubbing or grinding together.
▶ A **synovial membrane** – the capsule lining that releases synovial fluid.
▶ **Synovial fluid** – a viscous (thick) liquid that lubricates the joint and reduces the friction between the bones, preventing them from rubbing together. Synovial fluid also provides nutrients to the articular cartilage.
▶ **Ligaments** – hold the bones together and keep them in place.

Reduce Friction

Types of synovial joint

There are six types of synovial joint, categorised according to their structure and the movements they allow. These joints will permit specific movements and, combined, will allow you to perform complex techniques such as a somersault or a tennis serve.

▶ **Hinge** – These allow movement in one direction only (similar to the hinge of a door). Elbow and knee joints are typical examples and only allow movements forwards and backwards. Exercise examples include running with the knee bending or a bicep curl.

Flexion + Extention

▶ **Ball and socket** – The round end of one bone fits into a cup-shaped socket in the other bone, allowing movement in all directions. Examples include hip and shoulder joints, used in running and in throwing an object such as a javelin.

Rotation, abduction, adduction

▶ **Condyloid** – Also known as ellipsoidal joints. These are similar to ball and socket joints, in which a bump (condyle) on one bone sits in the hollow formed by another. Movement is backwards and forwards and from side to side. Ligaments often prevent rotation. An example of a condyloid joint in action is during a basketball game when a player is dribbling or bouncing the ball, with the wrist being used to create this action.

▶ **Gliding** – These joints allow movement over a flat surface in all directions, but this movement is restricted by ligaments or a bony prominence, for example in the carpals and tarsals of wrists and ankles. This can be seen in a netball jump with the foot pointing downwards.

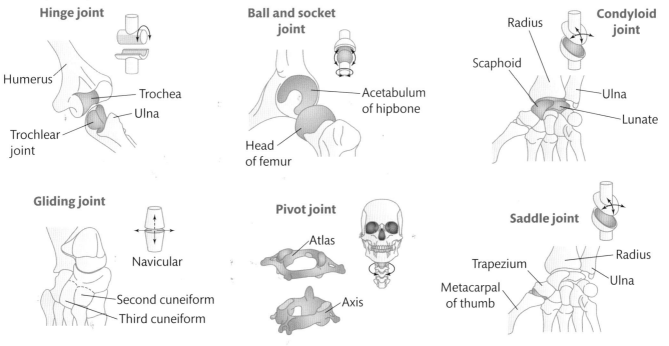

▶ **Figure 1.8:** Types of synovial joint

Key terms

Concave – where the bone curves or is hollowed inwards.

Convex – where the bone curves outwards.

▶ **Pivot** – A circular bone fits over a peg of another bone, allowing controlled rotational movement, such as the joint of the atlas and axis in the neck. This joint allows you to turn your head from side to side. When you turn your head in sport you will be using a pivot joint.

▶ **Saddle** – These are similar to condyloid joints but the surfaces are **concave** and **convex**. The joint is shaped like a saddle with the other bone resting on it like a rider on a horse. Movement occurs backwards and forwards and from side to side, such as at the base of the thumb. You would use a saddle joint when gripping a racket in tennis or squash.

Ⅱ PAUSE POINT   What are the different types of joint? Can you identify the location of each of these types of joint?

           Hint   Describe the location of each of the synovial joints in the body.

          Extend   Draw a synovial joint, labelling the main structural features.

Key terms

Flexibility – the range of movement around a joint or group of joints.

Soft tissue – the tissue that connects, supports and surrounds structures such as joints or organs. It includes tendons, ligaments, skin, fat and muscles.

The range of movements at synovial joints

The type of movement that each synovial joint allows is determined by its structure and shape. Sporting techniques usually use a combination of different joints to allow a wide range of movement or techniques. For example, a cricketer bowling a ball will use joints in the fingers (phalanges), wrist, elbow and shoulder. They will also use the joints of the foot, ankle, knee and hip when running.

It is important when studying sports performers in action that you are able to break down these techniques and identify the specific movements at each joint. A coach will often analyse the movements produced by an athlete in order to improve technique, and it is common to see movements filmed and analysed in detail using computer software.

The range of motion is the amount of movement at a joint and is often referred to as joint **flexibility**. Flexibility will also depend on a number of factors including age, the tension of the supporting connective tissues (tendons) and muscles that surround the joint, and the amount of **soft tissue** surrounding the joint.

The following movements are common across a wide range of sports and are important when performing sport and exercise techniques.

▶ **Flexion** – reducing the angle between the bones of a limb at a joint: muscles contract, moving the joint into a bent position. Examples include bending your arm in a bicep curl action or bending the knee when preparing to kick a football.

▶ **Extension** – straightening a limb to increase the angle at the joint, such as straightening your arm to return to your starting position in a bicep curl action or the kicking action when taking a penalty in football with the knee straightening.

▶ **Dorsiflexion** – an upward movement, as in moving the foot to pull the toes towards the knee in walking. *– decrease in angle*

▶ **Plantar flexion** – a movement that points the toes downwards by straightening the ankle. This occurs when jumping to shoot in netball.

▶ **Lateral flexion** – the movement of bending sideways, for example at the waist.

▶ **Horizontal flexion** and **horizontal extension** – bending the elbow (flexion) while the arm is in front of your body; straightening the arm at the elbow is **extension**.

▶ Cricketers use a large number of joints and movements when bowling

▶ **Hyper-extension** – involves movement beyond the normal anatomical position in a direction opposite to flexion. This occurs at the spine when a cricketer arches his or her back when approaching the crease to bowl.

▶ **Abduction** – movement away from the body's vertical midline, such as at the hip in a side-step in gymnastics. *– Cartwheel*

▶ **Adduction** – movement towards the body's vertical midline, such as pulling on the oars while rowing. *– star jump*

▶ **Horizontal abduction and adduction** – this is the movement of bringing your arm across your body (flexion) and then back again (extension).

▶ **Circumduction** – this is a circular movement that results in a conical action.

▶ **Rotation** – circular movement of a limb. Rotation occurs at the shoulder joint during a tennis serve.

Reflect

Think about a common sporting movement such as a javelin throw. Consider the movement at each joint and identify the type of action that is occurring.

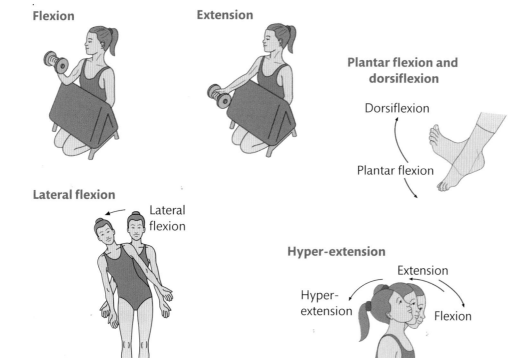

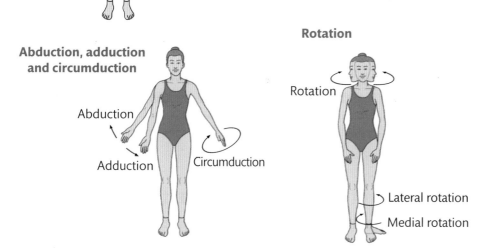

▶ **Figure 1.9:** Anatomical and biomechanical terms relating to muscle action

Many sporting movements look complex but in reality they can be viewed and analysed as separate, smaller movements. It is commonplace for modern coaches to use video equipment to film specific techniques so that the series of movements can be analysed and discussed with the athlete.

Consider the action of throwing a ball. You will use a number of different joints including the ball and socket joint of the shoulder, the hinge joint of the elbow and the gliding joints of the wrist (carpals). In combination with the skeletal muscles, you will be able to use the long bones as levers to produce a large powerful movement in order to throw the ball.

Now consider a tennis serve and the joint actions used. How are these similar to the action of throwing a ball? Many different sporting techniques will use similar joint actions and muscles that are refined to meet the needs of the specific sporting technique.

Check your knowledge

1 Can you think of any other sporting techniques that are similar?

2 What sports share the same movements?

3 How would a PE teacher or coach benefit from being able to identify different and identical sporting movements?

Responses of the skeletal system to a single sport or exercise session

You are probably aware that during exercise your heart rate and breathing rate increase, but did you know that your skeletal system will also respond to exercise? This is sometimes overlooked as the changes are small and out of sight. When you exercise or take part in sport your body's systems will adapt almost instantaneously so that your body is prepared for the additional stresses that will be put on it. This is one of the reasons why you should always complete a well-planned and performed warm-up before starting any physical activity.

Your skeletal system will respond to exercise in the short term by producing more synovial fluid in the synovial joints. This is so that the joints are lubricated and can protect the bones during the increased demands that exercise puts on the skeleton and joints. The fluid will also become less **viscous** and the range of movement at the joint will increase. The release of synovial fluid from the synovial membrane will also provide increased nutrients to the articular cartilage.

Another **acute response** to exercise is the increased uptake of minerals within the bones. Just as muscles become stronger the more you use them, a bone becomes stronger and denser when you regularly place exercise demands upon it. The body will absorb minerals such as calcium which will increase your bone mineral density. This is especially important for weight bearing exercises such as bench pressing. When more stress and force is applied to the bones they must be strong enough to cope with these increased demands.

Adaptations of the skeletal system to exercise

Your body responds to the stress of exercise or physical activity in a variety of ways. Some of these are immediate and are often referred to as acute responses to exercise. Others are long-term, and are often referred to as **chronic responses** or adaptations that contribute to improved fitness for sports participation and reduced health risk.

Like other systems of the body, the skeletal system will adapt to exercise. Exercise will increase your bone mineral density and over time this will result in stronger bones which will be more resistant to the forces found in sport such as kicking, jumping or running.

Long-term physical activity will also increase the strength of the ligaments which attach your bones together at synovial joints. When you exercise as part of a training programme, your ligaments will stretch a little further than normal and as a result will become more pliable over time, resulting in increased flexibility.

⏸ **PAUSE POINT**   When you exercise, what are the immediate responses your body makes?

> Hint   Think about your warm-up before exercise. What happens to your body and why?
>
> Extend   Research and draw up a list of the changes that occur in the skeletal system and explain why they happen during exercise.

Additional factors affecting the skeletal system

The benefits of taking part in regular exercise or physical activity are huge. People who take part in regular exercise are more likely to live longer and are less likely to develop serious diseases. Exercise should be part of a healthy lifestyle and it is common to hear about the benefits of physical activity in preventing heart disease and controlling weight. Regular exercise can also help common skeletal diseases such as arthritis and osteoporosis.

Arthritis

Arthritis is a condition where there is an inflammation within a synovial joint, causing pain and stiffness in the joint. The most common type of arthritis is osteoarthritis. This is caused by general wear and tear over a long period of time. This reduces the normal amount of cartilage tissue, which may result in the ends of the bones rubbing together. This natural breakdown of cartilage tissue can be made worse by injury to the joint.

However, regular exercise can prevent arthritis. During physical activity your joints will produce more synovial fluid which will not only improve the joint lubrication, reducing friction between the bones, but will also provide important minerals to the cartilage. Exercises such as stretching will also improve the joint range of motion, lengthen the ligaments holding the bones in place and improve flexibility.

Osteoporosis

Osteoporosis is the weakening of bones caused by a loss in calcium or a lack of **vitamin D**. As you get older your bones slowly lose their mineral density and naturally become brittle, fragile and more likely to break under stress. However, physical activity and exercise can help prevent osteoporosis by promoting increased uptake of minerals within the bones, resulting in an increase in bone mineral density. Resistance training is a good method of preventing osteoporosis, as overloading the skeleton will increase bone density.

Age

The skeletal system is a living tissue that is constantly growing and repairing itself so that it can provide support and protection. Generally, exercise and sports will benefit you. The exception to this is resistance training (weight training) in children, as this can cause more harm than good. The reason for this is that a child's bones are still growing and putting too much force on them can damage the epiphyseal plates which are found at each end of the long bones. Damage to these plates during childhood and puberty can result in stunted bone growth.

> **Key term**
>
> **Vitamin D** – is used to regulate the amount of calcium in the body and is produced from sunlight on our skin; it is created under the skin. Small amounts of vitamin D can also be found in oily fish and eggs.

1 Explain how the bones of the skeleton are used in movement for sport. **(2 marks)**

2 Jack has the first stages of osteoporosis. He has been advised to take part in exercise to help prevent this condition from worsening. Identify one type of exercise that Jack could take part in to prevent the osteoporosis from getting worse. **(1 mark)**

3 Explain why weight bearing exercises will prevent osteoporosis from getting worse. **(3 marks)**

4 Analyse how movement at the synovial joints in the upper skeleton allows a tennis player to serve the ball as shown in the picture. **(6 marks)**

Plan
- What is the question asking me to do? Do I need to give sporting examples?
- What are the key words that I will need to include relating to the skeletal system?

Do
- I will write down the key terms that need to be included in each answer.
- I will ensure that I have given sufficient examples relating to the number of marks available.

Review
- I will check my answer. Is it clear? Do I give suitable examples?

B The effects of exercise and sports performance on the muscular system

There are over 640 named muscles in the human body and these make up approximately 40 per cent of your body mass. The muscles that move your bones during activity are called **skeletal muscles**. In this section you will learn about the principal skeletal muscles, their associated actions, and muscle fibre types. This section also looks at the different types of muscles and their specific functions, as well as the responses and adaptations of the muscular system to sport or exercise.

Characteristics and functions of different types of muscle

There are three main types of muscle tissue in the human body.

Connect to bone
Voluntary
Fatiguing

- **Skeletal muscle** – also known as striated or striped muscle because of its striped appearance when viewed under a microscope, this type of muscle is voluntary, which means it is under conscious control. Skeletal muscles are critical to sport and exercise as they are connected to the skeletal system via tendons and are primarily responsible for movement. Skeletal muscles contract and, as a result, pull on your bones to create movement. They can become fatigued during exercise. Skeletal muscles are explored in more depth from page 19.

Continuously
Involuntary
Non fatiguing
Heart

- **Cardiac muscle** – this type of muscle tissue is only found in the wall of your heart. It works continuously. It is involuntary, which means it is not under conscious control. It is composed of a specialised type of striated tissue that has its own blood supply. Its contractions help to force blood through your blood vessels to all parts of your body. Each contraction and relaxation of your heart muscle as a whole represents one heartbeat. The cardiac muscle does not fatigue, which means that it does not get tired during exercise.

▶ **Smooth muscle** – an involuntary muscle that works without conscious thought, functioning under the control of your nervous system. It is located in the walls of your digestive system and blood vessels and helps to regulate digestion and blood pressure.

Involuntary
Digestive system
Regulate digestion

Discussion

In small groups, compare the different types of muscle tissue and their function. Discuss the importance of each of function in relation to the characteristics of the muscle.

Major skeletal muscles of the muscular system

Skeletal muscles are voluntary muscles which means that they are under your control. For example, you must send a conscious signal from your brain to your muscles to perform any sporting action. Skeletal muscles are attached to your skeleton by tendons which pull on specific bones when a muscle contracts. Skeletal muscles not only provide you with movement, strength and power but are also responsible for maintaining posture and generating heat which maintains your normal body temperature.

It can be difficult to remember the names, location and function of all the major skeletal muscles in the body. Figure 1.10 and Table 1.4 will help you to locate the main ones which are important to sport and exercise. You should be able to identify the main muscles used when performing common movements such as a kick in rugby, a tennis serve or a simple exercise such as a press-up.

▶ **Table 1.4:** Major skeletal muscles and their function

Muscle	Function	Location	Origin	Insertion	Exercise/activity
Triceps	Extends lower arm	Outside upper arm	Humerus and scapula	Olecranon process	Dips, press-ups, overhead pressing
Deltoids	Abducts, flexes and extends upper arm	Forms cap of shoulder	Clavicle, scapula and acromion	Humerus	Forward, lateral and back-arm raises, overhead lifting
Pectorals	Flexes and adducts upper arm	Large chest muscle	Sternum, clavicle and rib cartilage	Humerus	All pressing movements
Biceps	Flexes lower arm at elbow	Front of upper arm	Scapula	Radius	Bicep curl, pull-ups
Wrist flexors	Flexes hand at wrist	Front of forearm	Humerus	Metacarpal	Bouncing a basketball when dribbling
Wrist extensors	Extends or straightens hand at wrist	Back of forearm	Humerus	Metacarpal	Straightening of wrist
Supinators	Supinate forearm	Top and rear of forearm	Humerus	Ulna	Back spin in racket sports, spin bowl in cricket
Pronators	Pronate forearm	Top and front of forearm	Humerus	Ulna	Top spin in racket sports, spin bowl in cricket

: Major skeletal muscles and their function – *continued*

	Function	Location	Origin	Insertion	Exercise/activity
Abdominals	Flex and rotate lumbar region of vertebral column	'Six-pack' muscle running down abdomen	Pubic crest and symphysis	Xiphoid process	Sit-ups
Hip flexors	Flex hip joint (lifting thigh at hip)	Lumbar region of spine to top of thigh (femur)	Lumbar vertebrae	Femur	Knee raises, lunges, squat activation
Quadriceps • rectus femoris • vastus lateralis • vastus medialis • vastus intermedius	Extends lower leg and flexes thigh	Front of thigh	Ilium and femur	Tibia and fibula	Squats, knee bends
Hamstrings • semimembranosus • semitendinosus • biceps femoris	Flexes lower leg and extends thigh	Back of thigh	Ischium and femur	Tibia and fibula	Leg curls, straight leg deadlift
Gastrocnemius	Plantar flexion, flexes knee	Large calf muscle	Femur	Calcaneus	Running, jumping and standing on tip-toe
Soleus	Plantar flexion	Back of lower leg	Fibula and tibia	Calcaneus	Running and jumping
Tibialis anterior	Dorsiflexion of foot	Front of tibia on lower leg	Lateral condyle	By tendon to surface of medial cuneiform	All running and jumping exercises
Erector spinae	Extension of spine	Long muscle running either side of spine	Cervical, thoracic and lumbar vertebrae	Cervical, thoracic and lumbar vertebrae	Prime mover of back extension
Teres major	Rotates and abducts humerus	Between scapula and humerus	Posterior surface of scapula	Intertubercular sulcus of humerus	All rowing and pulling movements, face pulls, bent over rows
Trapezius	Elevates and depresses scapula	Large triangular muscle at top of back	Continuous insertion along acromion	Occipital bone and all thoracic vertebrae	Shrugging and overhead lifting
Latissimus dorsi	Extends and adducts lower arm	Large muscle covering back of lower ribs	Vertebrae and iliac crest	Humerus	Pull-ups, rowing movements
Obliques	Lateral flexion of trunk	Waist	Pubic crest and iliac crest	Fleshy strips to lower eight ribs	Oblique curls
Gluteals	Extends thigh	Large muscle on buttocks	Ilium, sacrum and coccyx	Femur	Knee-bending movements, cycling, squatting

---

‖ PAUSE POINT   What are the different muscle types?

 List the characteristics and functions of each muscle type.

Extend   Explain the importance of the different types of muscle to sport and exercise.

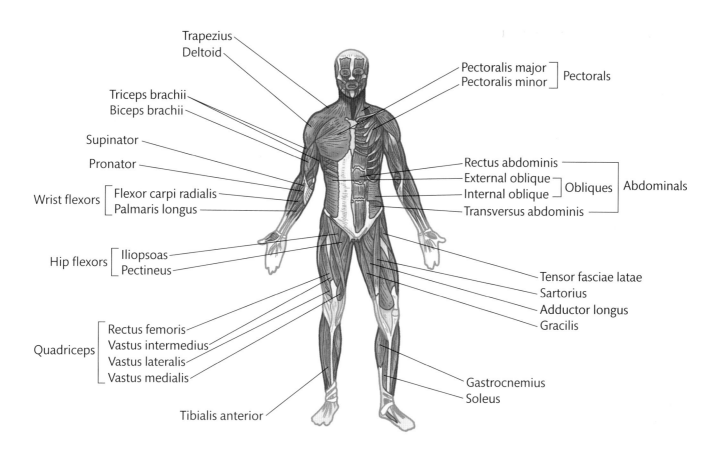

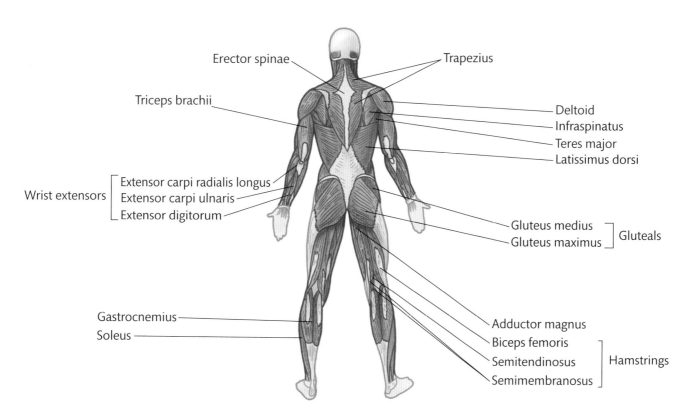

▶ **Figure 1.10:** Major skeletal muscles and their location

Antagonistic muscle pairs

When a muscle contracts, it exerts a pulling force on the bones to which it is attached, causing them to move together around the joint. Muscles must cross the joints that they move. If a muscle did not cross a joint, no movement could occur.

Under normal circumstances, muscles are in a state of partial contraction, ready to react to a stimulus from your nervous system. When a stimulus from the nerve supply occurs, muscle fibres work on an 'all or nothing' basis – either contracting completely or not at all. At the point of contraction your muscles shorten and pull on the bones to which they are attached. When a muscle contracts, one end normally remains stationary while the other end is drawn towards it. The end that remains stationary is known as the **origin**, and the end that moves is called the **insertion**.

Muscles do not work in isolation. They are assembled in groups and work together to bring about movement. They act only by contracting and pulling. They do not push, although they are able to contract without shortening, and so hold a joint firm and fixed in a certain position. When the contraction ends, the muscles become soft but do not lengthen until stretched by the contraction of the opposing muscles. Many muscles work in antagonistic pairs; for example, Figure 1.11 shows how the bicep and tricep work together to perform a bicep curl.

Key terms

Origin – the fixed end of the muscle that remains stationary.

Insertion – the end of the muscle that moves. The insertion normally crosses over a joint to allow movement when the muscle shortens.

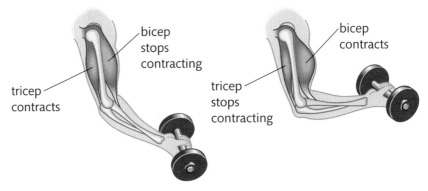

bicep stops contracting

tricep contracts

bicep contracts

tricep stops contracting

▶ **Figure 1.11:** Bicep and tricep muscles work together during a bicep curl

Reflect

Consider the main muscle contracting and the opposite muscle relaxing during a movement. What happens when the opposite movement occurs?

The muscle that shortens to move a joint is called the **agonist** or prime mover. This is the muscle principally responsible for the movement taking place – the contracting muscle.

The muscle that relaxes in opposition to the agonist is called the **antagonist**. This is the muscle responsible for the opposite movement, and the one that relaxes as the agonist works. If it did not relax, movement could not take place. Antagonists exert a 'braking' control over the movement.

Synergists are muscles that work together to enable the agonists to operate more effectively. They work with the agonists to control and direct movement by modifying or altering the direction of pull on the agonists to the most advantageous position.

Fixator muscles stop any unwanted movement throughout the whole body by fixing or stabilising the joint or joints involved. Fixator muscles stabilise the origin so that the agonist can achieve maximum and effective contraction.

❚❚ PAUSE POINT Can you name the main skeletal muscles and where they are located?

> Hint   Consider a sport and describe the role of the specific muscles in this sport.
>
> Extend   Think of a sporting movement and list the pairs of muscles being used for each phase of the movement.

Theory into practice

When your body is in action during sport and exercise, your muscles shorten, remain the same length or lengthen.

1 Using a dumbbell or other suitable resistance weight, bend your forearm upwards so that your elbow bends in a bicep curl action. Consider your bicep muscle. What is happening?

2 Now return your arm to the starting position by slowly lowering the forearm. What is happening to the bicep muscle now? Consider the action of the tricep muscle on the other side of the elbow joint.

3 Consider how these muscles work as a pair. How do these muscles control the movement?

Types of skeletal muscle contraction

There are three different types of muscle contraction which will be used depending on the sporting technique or exercise action.

Isometric

During an isometric contraction the length of a muscle does not change and the joint angle does not alter. However, the muscle is actively engaged in holding a static position. An example is the abdominal plank position. This type of muscle work is easy to undertake but rapidly leads to fatigue. It can cause sharp increases in blood pressure as blood flow is reduced.

- length does not change
- static
- fast fatigue

Concentric

When you make any movement such as a bicep curl, your muscle will shorten as the muscle fibres contract. In the bicep curl, the brachialis and bicep shorten, bringing your forearm towards your upper arm. Concentric contractions are sometimes known as the **positive phase** of muscle contraction.

- muscle shortens

Eccentric

An eccentric muscular contraction is when a muscle returns to its normal length after shortening against resistance. Again using the bicep curl as an example, this is the controlled lowering of your arm to its starting position. At this point your muscles are working against gravity and act like a braking mechanism. This contraction can be easier to perform, but it does produce muscle soreness.

- muscle lengthens

Eccentric contractions occur in many sporting and daily activities. Walking downstairs and running downhill involve eccentric contraction of your quadriceps muscles which are used to control the movement. Eccentric contraction can be a significant factor in the stimulus that promotes gains in muscle strength and size. Eccentric contractions are sometimes known as the **negative phase** of muscle contraction.

Discussion

Muscles can only pull on a bone, they can never push. In small groups, discuss a rugby scrum where a pushing force is required. Explain how a pushing force is created when muscles can only pull. What muscles are being used to create this movement?

❚❚ PAUSE POINT   Can you explain the importance of different muscle contractions in sport?

Hint   Think of a press-up. Which muscles are working as antagonistic pairs in the shoulder?

Extend   What types of contraction are taking place for each phase of a press-up at the shoulder joint?

Fibre types

All skeletal muscles are made up from muscle fibres. These fibres fall into two main categories depending on their speed of contraction: Type I ('slow-twitch') and Type II ('fast-twitch'). The mix of fibres varies from individual to individual, and within the individual from muscle group to muscle group. To a large extent this fibre mix is inherited. However, training can influence the efficiency of the different fibre types.

Type I

Type I (slow-twitch) fibres contract slowly and with less force. They are slow to fatigue and suited to longer-duration **aerobic** activities. Aerobic activity describes exercise where energy is produced using oxygen. The opposite of this is **anaerobic** activitiy, where movements are produced using energy that has been created without oxygen. Slow-twitch fibres have a rich blood supply and contain many **mitochondria** to sustain aerobic metabolism. Type I fibres have a high capacity for **aerobic respiration**. They are recruited for lower-intensity, longer-duration activities such as long-distance running and swimming.

Type IIa

Type IIa fibres (also called fast-twitch or fast-oxidative fibres) are fast-contracting, able to produce a great force, and are also resistant to fatigue. These fibres are less reliant on oxygen for energy supplied by the blood and therefore fatigue faster than slow-twitch fibres. Type IIa fibres are suited to speed, power and strength activities such as weight training with repeated repetitions (10–12 reps) and fast running events such as the 400 metres.

Type IIx

Type IIx fibres (also called fast-twitch or fast-glycolytic fibres) contract rapidly and have the capacity to produce large amounts of force, but they fatigue more readily, making them better suited to **anaerobic activity**. They depend almost entirely on **anaerobic respiration** and are recruited for higher-intensity, shorter-duration activities. They are important in sports that include many stop–go or change-of-pace activities such as rugby or football.

▶ Sprinters use type IIx fast-twitch fibres

Key terms

Mitochondria – the organelles (parts of cells) in the body where aerobic respiration takes place.

Aerobic respiration – the process of producing energy using oxygen, where energy is released from glucose.

Anaerobic activity – activity where your body uses energy *without* oxygen; that is, activity that results in muscle cells using anaerobic respiration.

Anaerobic respiration – the process of breaking down glucose without oxygen to produce energy.

All or none law

For a muscle to contract it must receive a nerve impulse, and this stimulus must be sufficient to activate at least one motor unit which contains the motor neuron (nerve cell) and the attached muscle fibres. Once activated, **all** the muscles fibres within the motor unit will contract and produce a muscle twitch. This is known as the 'all or none' law, as muscle fibres either respond completely (all) or not at all (none).

❚❚ PAUSE POINT   Can you explain how different muscle fibre types affect sport?

> Hint   List three sports and the types of muscle fibre required for each.

> Extend   Explain why your chosen sports require these types of fibre and how an athlete can improve their performance by understanding this.

Responses of the muscular system to a single sport or exercise session

When you exercise or take part in sport your muscles will respond in a variety of ways. Some of these responses are immediate and are known as acute responses. Responses that take place over a longer period of time are known as chronic responses.

Discussion

In small groups, list the changes in your body immediately after starting a high-intensity exercise. What is happening to your body? Why? Now think about different sports that require different intensities. How do sportspeople train to meet the demands of these physical activities?

Increased blood supply

The short-term effects of exercise on your muscles include an increase in metabolic activity (the rate at which the muscles produce and release energy so that movement can take place). As a result of this increase in metabolic activity, there is a greater demand for oxygen and glucose in the muscles, which is met by an increase in blood supply. Blood vessels expand or get wider to allow more blood to enter your muscles. This is called **vasodilation**. Blood flow increases significantly to ensure that the working muscles are supplied with the oxygen they need as well as to remove waste products such as carbon dioxide.

Increased muscle temperature

When you exercise you get warmer. This is because your muscles need energy from fuels such as fats and carbohydrates, which are broken down using chemical reactions that produce heat as a waste product. The more you exercise or the harder you train, the more energy your muscles need. This results in more heat being produced. The amount of heat your muscles produce is in direct relation to the amount of work they perform – the harder you work out, the more heat your muscles will produce. This principle is used in a warm-up which prepares your muscles for exercise by slowly increasing their temperature.

Increase muscle pliability

The warming of your muscles during activity makes them more pliable and flexible. Pliable muscles are less likely to suffer from injuries such as muscle strains. An increase in pliability will improve joint flexibility, as warm and pliable muscles are able to stretch further.

Lactate (high intensity exercise)

You may have experienced an uncomfortable burning sensation in your muscles during high-intensity exercise. This is most likely caused by the build-up of **lactic acid** which is a waste product produced during anaerobic exercise. This build-up of acid in the muscle tissue will result in rapid fatigue and will impede muscular contractions if it is not removed quickly.

Micro tears (resistance exercise)

During resistance training such as weight training, your muscles are put under stress to the point that tiny tears occur in the muscle fibres. These micro tears cause swelling in the muscle tissue which causes pressure on the nerve endings and pain. Training improvements will only be made if the body has rest and time to repair these micro tears, making the muscle a little bit stronger than it was before. Proteins are used to repair muscle tissue.

Delayed onset of muscle soreness

Delayed onset of muscle soreness (or DOMS) is the pain felt in muscles 24–48 hours (typically) after taking part in strenuous exercise. The soreness usually occurs at least a day after exercise and can last up to 3 days. DOMS is caused by the microtears that occur when you exercise, particularly if you are unaccustomed to the intensity of exercise. DOMS is often associated with exercises where **eccentric muscle contraction** has occurred.

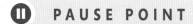

> **Key term**
>
> **Eccentric muscle contraction** – where a muscle lengthens as it contracts. Such contractions occur when controlling a force or movement.

PAUSE POINT   What are the immediate responses your muscles make when exercising?

 Hint   Why do these changes happen during exercise?

 Extend   What aspects of the warm-up are used to prevent muscle injury? Why is a warm-up before exercise important to your muscles?

Adaptations of the muscular system to exercise

Training or exercising regularly over a long period of time will allow your body's muscular system to change and adapt. For example, you will notice that your muscles change in size if you undertake a strength or resistance training programme. Such changes are known as chronic adaptations to exercise.

Hypertrophy

Regular resistance training where the muscles are overloaded will increase muscle size and strength. The increase in muscle size is a result of the muscles fibres becoming larger due to increases in protein in the muscle cells; this is known as hypertrophy. The muscle fibres increase in size over time so that they can contract with greater force.

Increased tendon strength

Tendons are tough bands of fibrous connective tissue designed to withstand tension. Like muscles, tendons adapt to the overloading of regular exercise. Ligaments and tendons, the connective tissue structures around joints, will increase in flexibility and strength with regular exercise. Cartilage also becomes thicker.

Increase in number and size of mitochondria

When muscles are overloaded as part of resistance training, the muscle fibres will become bigger (hypertrophy). Within these muscle fibres are tiny structures called mitochondria which are responsible for energy production. Because of the increase in

▶ Hypertrophy occurs when muscles are regularly overloaded

fibre size, there is room for more and larger mitochondria, which results in the muscles being able to produce more aerobic energy which will improve aerobic performance.

Increase in myoglobin stores

Myoglobin is a type of haemoglobin (the red protein found in blood used for transporting oxygen) that is found exclusively in muscles. It is responsible for binding and storing oxygen in the blood within skeletal muscles. By following a planned exercise programme, you can increase the amount of myoglobin stored in your muscles. This is important as myoglobin will transport oxygen to the mitochondria which in turn will release energy. The more myoglobin you have, the more energy will be available for the muscle.

Increase in storage of glycogen

Your body needs a constant and steady supply of **glycogen** in order to produce energy. As your body adapts to long-term exercise, your muscles are able to store more glycogen. This means that you will be able to train at higher intensities for longer, as muscle glycogen does not require oxygen to produce energy.

Increase in storage of fat

You are able to use your fat stores to produce energy through a process called **aerobic glycolysis**. Well-trained athletes are able to use these fats more efficiently, breaking them down into fatty acids and into energy using oxygen. This enables them to use fats as an energy source when **carbohydrate** becomes scarce.

Increased tolerance to lactate

Anaerobic training stimulates the muscles to become better able to tolerate lactic acid, and clear it away more efficiently. With endurance training the capillary network (see page 39) extends, allowing greater volumes of blood to supply the muscles with oxygen and nutrients. The muscles are able to use more fat as a fuel source, and become more efficient at using oxygen, increasing the body's ability to work harder for longer without fatiguing. The net result is an increase in the body's maximal oxygen consumption.

> **Key terms**
>
> **Glycogen** – the stored form of glucose.
>
> **Carbohydrate** – the sugars and starches found in foods such as potatoes, wheat and rice. Carbohydrates are broken down by the body into sugars which are used for energy production.

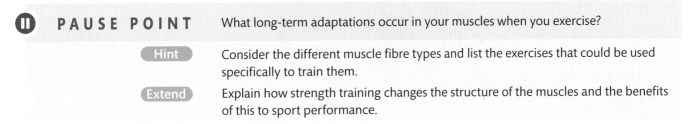

❚❚ PAUSE POINT What long-term adaptations occur in your muscles when you exercise?

Hint Consider the different muscle fibre types and list the exercises that could be used specifically to train them.

Extend Explain how strength training changes the structure of the muscles and the benefits of this to sport performance.

Additional factors affecting the muscular system

There are two primary additional factors that will affect your muscular system and in turn affect exercise and sports performance.

Age

As you get older your muscle mass will decrease. The onset of this muscle mass loss begins around the age of 50 and is referred to as **sarcopenia**. Muscles become smaller, resulting in a decrease in muscle strength and power.

Cramp

Cramp is the sudden involuntary contraction of your muscle. The sensation of muscle spasm where you have no control of the tightening of the muscle fibres can be painful and can be prompted by exercise. The muscles of the lower leg are particularly susceptible to cramp during exercise. Cramp can last from a few seconds up to 10 minutes.

There are a number of factors that can contribute to cramp. The most common one in sport is dehydration which can result in the inadequate supply of blood to the muscles, reducing the supply of oxygen and essential minerals. To prevent cramp you should ensure that you drink plenty of fluid during exercise and sport, especially if the weather is hot. Stretching can also help to prevent cramp as this will lengthen the muscle fibres and improve muscle flexibility.

Assessment practice 1.2

Nancy is a netball player. She uses weighted lunges as part of her training as shown.

1 Explain how the use of weighted lunges will improve Nancy's performance in netball. **(3 marks)**

2 Two days after Nancy's training session she experiences delayed onset of muscle soreness (DOMS). Describe why Nancy's training may cause DOMS. **(1 mark)**

3 Explain how muscle adaptation occurs as a result of Nancy's resistance training. **(2 marks)**

4 The second picture shows Nancy training on a resistance machine. Explain how Nancy's muscles work as antagonistic pairs for each phase of the movement. **(4 marks)**

Plan
- What are the key terms and words being used?
- Do I need to include specific examples such as different types of movement?

Do
- I will write down the key words and explain each of them.
- I will make sure I contextualise my answers by giving relevant examples.

Review
- Have I given sufficient examples linked to the marks available?
- Have I broken down any movements into key phases and explained all the key terms used?

The effects of exercise and sports performance on the respiratory system

The respiratory system provides oxygen to all living tissue in your body, as well as removing waste products such as carbon dioxide, heat and water vapour. Oxygen is required for every cell in your body to function. Central to the respiratory system are your lungs, which enable oxygen to enter the body and carbon dioxide waste to be removed through the mechanism of breathing. Your body's ability to inhale and transport oxygen while removing waste products is critical to sports performance: the better your body is at this process, the better you will be able to train or perform in sport.

Structure and functions of the respiratory system

Air is drawn into your body via the nose and sometimes via the mouth, and passes through a series of airways to reach the lungs. This series of airways is referred to as the **respiratory tract** and can be divided into two main parts. The upper respiratory tract includes the nose, nasal cavity, mouth, pharynx and larynx. The lower respiratory tract consists of the trachea, bronchi and lungs.

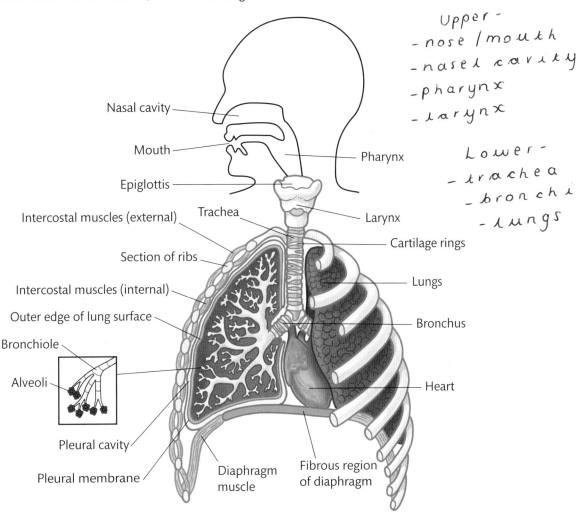

Upper-
- nose / mouth
- nasal cavity
- pharynx
- larynx

Lower-
- trachea
- bronchi
- lungs

▶ **Figure 1.12:** Bronchi, bronchial tree and lungs

Nasal cavity

When you breathe in, air enters the nasal cavity by passing through the nostrils. Hairs within the cavity filter out dust, pollen and other foreign particles before the air passes into the two passages of the internal nasal cavity. Here the air is warmed and moistened before it passes into the nasopharynx. A sticky mucous layer traps smaller foreign particles, which tiny hairs called cilia transport to the pharynx to be swallowed.

Pharynx

Commonly called the throat, the pharynx is a small tube that measures approximately 10–13 cm from the base of the skull to the level of the sixth cervical vertebra. The muscular pharynx wall is composed of skeletal muscle throughout its length. The funnel-shaped pharynx connects the nasal cavity and mouth to the larynx (air) and oesophagus (food). It is a passageway for food as well as air, so special adaptations are required to prevent choking when food or liquid is swallowed.

Larynx

The larynx, or voice box, has rigid walls of muscle and cartilage, contains the vocal cords and connects the pharynx to the trachea. It extends for about 5 cm from the level of the third to sixth vertebra.

Trachea

The trachea or windpipe denotes the start of the lower respiratory tract. It is about 12 cm long and 2 cm in diameter. It contains rings of cartilage to prevent it from collapsing, and it is flexible. It travels down the neck in front of the oesophagus and branches into the right and left bronchi.

Epiglottis

The epiglottis is the small flap of cartilage at the back of the tongue which closes the top of the trachea when you swallow to ensure food and drink pass into your stomach and not your lungs.

Lungs

Your lungs are the organ that allows oxygen to be drawn into the body. The paired right and left lungs occupy most of the thoracic cavity and extend down to the diaphragm. They hang suspended in the right and left pleural cavities straddling the heart. The left lung is smaller than the right.

Bronchi

The bronchi branch off the trachea and carry air to the lungs. By the time inhaled air reaches the bronchi, it is warm, clear of most impurities and saturated with water vapour.

Once inside the lungs, each bronchus subdivides into lobar bronchi: three on the right and two on the left. The lobar bronchi branch into segmental bronchi, which divide again into smaller and smaller bronchi. Overall, there are approximately 23 orders (sizes) of branching bronchial airways in the lungs. Because of this branching pattern, the bronchial network within the lungs is often called the **bronchial tree**.

Bronchioles

Bronchioles are small airways that extend from the bronchi and connect the bronchi to small clusters of thin-walled air sacs, known as alveoli. Bronchioles are about 1 mm in diameter and are the first airway branches of the respiratory system that do not contain cartilage.

Alveoli

At the end of each bronchiole is a mass of air sacs called alveoli. In each lung there are approximately 300 million gas-filled alveoli. These are responsible for the transfer of oxygen into the blood and the removal of waste such as carbon dioxide out of the blood. This process of transfer is known as **gaseous exchange**. Combined, the alveoli have a huge surface area for maximal gaseous exchange to take place – roughly the size of a tennis court. Surrounding each alveolus is a dense network of **capillaries** to facilitate the process of gaseous exchange. For more on gaseous exchange, see page 32.

 PAUSE POINT   Explain how air enters the body and how it is used.

   List the journey of air from the mouth to the alveoli.

Draw a diagram of the journey of air from the nose to the alveoli. Label each part of the respiratory system on your diagram.

Diaphragm

The diaphragm is a flat muscle that is located beneath the lungs within the thoracic cavity and separates the chest from the abdomen. The diaphragm is one of several components involved in breathing, which is the mechanism of drawing air – including oxygen – into the body (inhalation) and removing gases including carbon dioxide (exhalation). Contraction of the diaphragm increases the volume of the chest cavity, drawing air into the lungs, while relaxation of the diaphragm decreases the volume of the chest cavity, pushing air out.

Thoracic cavity

This is the chamber of the chest that is protected by the thoracic wall (rib cage). It is separated from the abdominal cavity by the diaphragm.

Internal and external intercostal muscles

The intercostal muscles lie between the ribs. To help with inhalation and exhalation, they extend and contract.

▶ The **internal intercostal** muscles lie inside the ribcage. They draw the ribs downwards and inwards, decreasing the volume of the chest cavity and forcing air out of the lungs when breathing out.

▶ The **external intercostal** muscles lie outside the ribcage. They pull the ribs upwards and outwards, increasing the volume of the chest cavity and drawing air into the lungs when breathing in.

Mechanisms of breathing

Breathing or **pulmonary ventilation** is the process by which air is transported into and out of the lungs, and it can be considered to have two phases. It requires the thorax to increase in size to allow air to be taken in, followed by a decrease to allow air to be forced out.

Inspiration

Inspiration is the process of breathing air into the lungs. The intercostal muscles between the ribs contract to lift the ribs upwards and outwards, while the diaphragm is forced downwards. This expansion of the thorax in all directions causes a drop in pressure within the lungs to below atmospheric pressure (the pressure of the air outside the body), which encourages air to be drawn into the lungs.

> - intercostals contract
> - ribs move up + out
> - diaphragm moves ↓

Expiration

The opposite of inspiration is expiration, and this occurs when the intercostal muscles relax. The diaphragm relaxes, moving upwards, and the ribs move downwards and inwards. Pressure within the lungs is increased and air is expelled or pushed out of the body.

> - intercostals relax
> - diaphragm relaxes
> - ribs move down + in

During sport or exercise, greater amounts of oxygen are required, so the intercostal muscles and diaphragm must work harder. This results in an increase in your breathing rate and an increase in the force of your breath.

Control of breathing

Neural control

Breathing is a complex process that is largely under involuntary control by the respiratory centres of your brain. Inspiration is an active process, as the diaphragm muscle is **actively** contracting which causes air to enter the lungs. Expiration is a passive process, as the diaphragm muscle **relaxes** to allow air to exit the lungs. This process is controlled by neurones (cells that conduct nerve impulses) in the brain stem. Neurones in two areas of the **medulla oblongata** are critical in respiration.

> **Key term**
>
> **Medulla oblongata** – located in the middle of your brain, this is responsible for involuntary functions such as breathing, heart beat and sneezing.

These are the dorsal respiratory group (DRG) and the ventral respiratory group (VRG). The VRG is thought to be responsible for the rhythm generation that allows rhythmic and continuous breathing.

Chemical control

Other factors that control breathing are the continually changing levels of oxygen and carbon dioxide in the blood. Sensors responding to such chemical fluctuations are called **chemoreceptors**. These are found in the medulla and in the **aortic arch** and **carotid arteries**. These chemoreceptors detect changes in blood carbon dioxide levels as well as changes in blood acidity, and send signals to the medulla that will make changes to breathing rates.

Gaseous exchange

Gaseous exchange is the process by which one type of gas is exchanged for another. In the lungs, gaseous exchange occurs by **diffusion** between air in the alveoli and blood in the capillaries surrounding their walls. It delivers oxygen from the lungs to the bloodstream and removes carbon dioxide from the bloodstream to the lungs.

The alveolar and capillary walls form a **respiratory membrane** that has gas on one side and blood flowing past on the other. Gaseous exchange occurs readily by simple diffusion across the respiratory membrane. Blood entering the capillaries from the pulmonary arteries has a lower oxygen concentration and a higher carbon dioxide concentration than the air in the alveoli. Oxygen diffuses into the blood via the surface of the alveoli, through the thin walls of the capillaries, through the red blood cell membrane and finally latches on to haemoglobin. Carbon dioxide diffuses in the opposite direction, from the blood plasma into the alveoli.

- Oxygen is diffused into the blood stream
- CO² is diffused out of the blood stream and into the lungs to be exhaled

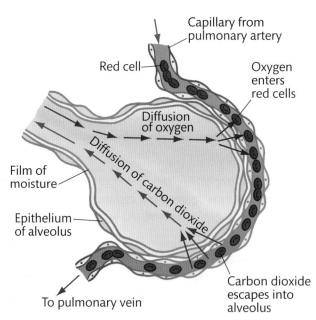

▶ **Figure 1.13:** Gaseous exchange in action in an alveolus

Lung volumes

What happens to your breathing when you are exercising or training? Your lungs are designed to take in more air during exercise so that more oxygen can reach the alveoli and more carbon dioxide can be removed. Your breathing will become deeper and more frequent to cope with the demands that exercise puts on your body.

Your **respiratory rate** is the amount of air you breathe in one minute. For a typical 18-year-old, this represents about 12 breaths per minute at rest, during which time about 6 litres of air passes through the lungs. It can increase significantly during exercise, by as much as 30–40 breaths per minute.

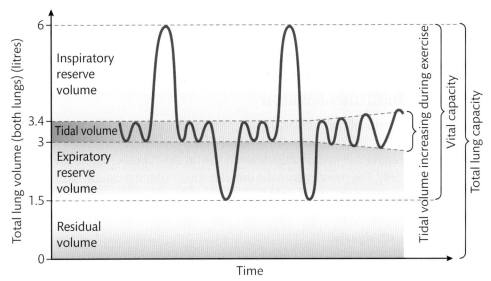

▶ **Figure 1.14:** Lung volume and capacities of a healthy adult

Tidal volume

Tidal volume is the term used to describe the volume of air breathed in and out with each breath. Under normal conditions this represents about 500 cm³ of air breathed, both inhaled and exhaled. Of this, approximately two-thirds (350 cm³) reaches the alveoli in the lungs where gaseous exchange takes place. The remaining 150 cm³ fills the pharynx, larynx, trachea, bronchi and bronchioles and is known as dead or stationary air.

Normal volume of air

During exercise, tidal volume increases to allow more air to pass through the lungs. The volume of air passing through the lungs each minute is known as the **minute volume** – it is determined by the breathing rate and the amount of air taken in with each breath.

Increases during exercise – more O₂ needed

▶ The lungs normally contain about 350 cm³ of fresh air, 150 cm³ of dead air and 2500 cm³ of air that has already undergone gaseous exchange with the blood.
▶ The lungs are never fully emptied of air, otherwise they would collapse. The air that remains in the lungs after maximal expiration, when you breathe out as hard as you can, is referred to as **residual volume**. The volume is around 1200 cm³ for an average male.

air left in the lungs after max exhalation – stays the same

▶ **Vital capacity** is the amount of air that can be forced out of the lungs after maximal inspiration. The volume is around 4800 cm³.
▶ By breathing in deeply, it is possible to take in more air than usual so that more oxygen can reach the alveoli. This is especially important during exercise. You can breathe in up to an additional 3000 cm³ of fresh air in addition to the normal tidal volume – this is known as the **inspiratory reserve volume.**

amount of air that can be forced out after maximal inhalation

▶ The **expiratory reserve volume** is the amount of additional air that can be breathed out after normal expiration. This can be up to 1500 cm³. At the end of a normal breath, the lungs contain the residual volume plus the expiratory reserve volume. If you then exhale as much as possible, only the residual volume remains.
▶ **Total lung volume** is your total lung capacity after you have inhaled as deeply and as much as you can, after maximal inspiration. It is normally around 6000 cm³ for an average-sized male.

after maximal inspiration

PAUSE POINT   Can you remember the different lung volumes?

> Hint
>
> Write a list of the different lung volumes and briefly describe each one.
>
> Extend
>
> Think about how your breathing changes during exercise. Explain what is happening to each specific lung volume.

Responses of the respiratory system to a single sport or exercise session

Your body is surprisingly insensitive to falling levels of oxygen, yet it is sensitive to increased levels of carbon dioxide. The levels of oxygen in arterial blood vary little, even during exercise, but carbon dioxide levels vary in direct proportion to the level of physical activity. The more intense the exercise, the greater the carbon dioxide concentration in the blood. To combat this, your breathing rate increases to ensure the carbon dioxide can be expelled through expiration.

Increased breathing rate

Exercise results in an increase in the rate and depth of breathing. During exercise your muscles demand more oxygen, and the corresponding increase in carbon dioxide production stimulates faster and deeper breathing. The capillary network surrounding the alveoli expands, increasing blood flow to the lungs and pulmonary diffusion.

A minor rise in breathing rate prior to exercise is known as an anticipatory rise. When exercise begins there is an immediate and significant increase in breathing rate, believed to be a result of receptors working in both the muscles and joints.

After several minutes of aerobic exercise, breathing continues to rise, though at a slower rate, and it levels off if the exercise intensity remains constant. If the exercise is maximal, the breathing rate will continue to rise until exhaustion. After exercise the breathing rate returns to normal, rapidly to begin with and then slowly.

Increased tidal volume

During exercise, tidal volume increases to allow more air to pass through the lungs. Tidal volume is elevated by both aerobic and anaerobic exercise. During exercise, oxygen is depleted from your body, triggering a deeper tidal volume to compensate.

During strenuous exercise, oxygen diffusion may increase by as much as three times above the resting level. Likewise, minute ventilation depends on breathing rate and total volume. During exercise adults can generally achieve minute ventilation approximately 15 times greater than the resting values.

Adaptations of the respiratory system to exercise

Like the cardiovascular system, the respiratory system undergoes specific adaptations in response to an organised and regular training programme. These adaptations help to maximise the efficiency of the respiratory system; oxygen can be delivered to the working muscles to meet the demands of the exercise while waste products can be removed quickly.

Increased vital capacity

Your vital capacity increases in response to long-term physical training to provide an increased and more efficient supply of oxygen to working muscles.

Increased strength of respiratory muscles

The diaphragm and intercostal muscles increase in strength, allowing for greater expansion of the chest cavity. This will mean that it is easier to take deeper breaths as the stronger and more pliable muscles will allow the chest cavity to expand further.

Increase in oxygen and carbon dioxide diffusion rate

Your respiratory system adapts to regular training, allowing oxygen and carbon dioxide to diffuse more rapidly. An increase in diffusion rates in tissues means that you can train longer and harder, as your muscles will be supplied with more oxygen and the increased carbon dioxide will be removed more quickly.

❚❚ PAUSE POINT   Why is the respiratory system so important to sports performance?

> **Hint**   Describe how the respiratory system adapts to long-term exercise.
>
> **Extend**   Explain why each adaptation can improve sport and exercise performance.

Additional factors affecting the respiratory system

Although regular training will improve the efficiency of your respiratory system, there are a number of additional considerations that can affect this system.

Asthma

Asthma is a common condition where the airways of the respiratory system can become restricted, making it harder for air to enter the body, resulting in coughing, wheezing or shortness of breath.

During normal breathing, the bands of muscle that surround the airways are relaxed and air moves freely. However, asthma makes the bands of muscle surrounding the airways contract and tighten so that air cannot move freely in or out of the body. Asthma can have a negative effect on sports performance as people with the condition will not be able to get enough oxygen into their lungs to supply their muscles, especially with the increased amounts required during exercise.

However, regular exercise will strengthen your respiratory system and help prevent asthma. Regular aerobic training can help to improve breathing and muscular strength, and endurance training will also improve oxygen uptake.

> **Safety tip**
>
> If you suffer from asthma always carry your inhaler. If you begin to experience the symptoms of asthma then stop the exercise immediately.

> **Research**
>
> For more information about asthma, see NHS Choices – www.nhs.uk/Livewell/asthma.

Case study

Paula Radcliffe

World record marathon runner Paula Radcliffe has had exercise-induced asthma all of her life. However, through determination and the correct medication, she has been able to compete successfully at the highest level and is currently the world record holder for the women's marathon with her time of 2 hours, 15 minutes and 25 seconds.

To ensure that she is able to train and compete, Paula always warms up gently and gradually so that her asthma does not interfere. When training she will use her preventer inhaler first thing in the morning and then her reliever inhaler before she starts exercising.

Paula's message is clear: 'control your asthma, don't let it control you'.

Check your knowledge

1   How does asthma affect sporting performance?

2   What is the difference between a preventer inhaler and a reliever inhaler?

▶ Paula Radcliffe is one of many elite athletes who compete successfully despite suffering from asthma

Effects of altitude/partial pressure on the respiratory system

Many elite athletes like to train at high altitude as the air pressure is lower and the oxygen particles are farther apart. This means that the density of oxygen in the air is lower and it is harder to breathe (inspire) this oxygen into your body due to lower partial pressure. Over time the athletes' respiratory system will adapt to this lower pressure and become more efficient.

In the short term, the effects of altitude on the body are that your lungs have to work harder. Symptoms can include shortness of breath, dizziness, headaches and difficulties in concentrating. The decreased availability of oxygen at higher altitudes can quickly lead to hypoxia, which occurs when the body has insufficient access to oxygen. To cope with the decrease in available oxygen, you must breathe faster and deeper.

Like other systems of the body, the respiratory system will adapt over a long period of time so that it can cope with the decrease in available oxygen at higher altitudes. Your lungs will acclimatise by becoming larger which enables them to take in more oxygen. The body will also produce more red blood cells and capillaries, enabling the lungs to oxygenate the blood more efficiently.

Athletes who train at altitude feel the benefits of a more efficient respiratory system when they return to compete at lower altitudes. Athletes who were born at high altitude benefit even more, having grown up and developed in that environment.

Assessment practice 1.3

Freddie is a football player.

1 Explain the short-term effect of taking part in football on Freddie's tidal volume. **(3 marks)**

2 Explain the role of carbon dioxide in the chemical control of breathing during exercise. **(3 marks)**

3 Explain how increasing the strength of the respiratory muscles aids performance in long distance running. **(4 marks)**

Plan
- I will plan longer answers by noting the key words and likely examples.
- I will look at the marks available and allow time to write a full answer.

Do
- I will write a structured answer, especially for questions that offer more marks.
- I will give relevant examples linked to the key theories.

Review
- Have I reread my answers? Have I included a response to the key terms?
- Have I fully answered the question, making the relevant number of points linked to the marks available?

 The effects of exercise and sports performance on the cardiovascular system

The cardiovascular system is sometimes referred to as the **circulatory system** and consists of the heart, blood vessels and blood. The cardiovascular system is the major transport system in your body, carrying food, oxygen and all other essential products to cells, and taking away waste products of respiration and other cellular processes, such as carbon dioxide. Oxygen is transported from the lungs to the body tissues, while carbon dioxide is carried from the body tissues to the lungs for excretion.

Structure of the cardiovascular system

The heart

The heart is a unique hollow muscle and is the pump of the cardiovascular system. It is located under the sternum (which provides protection) and is about the size of a closed fist. The function of the heart is to drive blood into and through the arteries in order to deliver it to the tissues and working muscles.

The heart is surrounded by a twin-layered sac known as the pericardium. The cavity between the layers is filled with pericardial fluid, whose purpose is to prevent friction as the heart beats. The heart wall itself is made up of three layers: the epicardium (the outer layer), the myocardium (the strong middle layer that forms most of the heart wall), and the endocardium (the inner layer).

The right side of the heart is separated from the left by a solid wall known as the **septum**. This prevents the blood on the right side coming into contact with the blood on the left side.

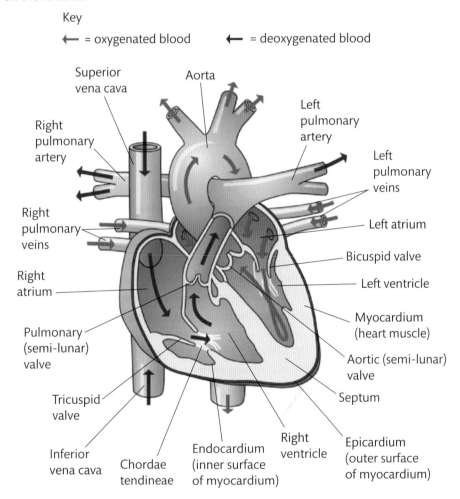

▶ **Figure 1.15:** Diagram of the heart

The heart can be thought of as two pumps: the two chambers on the right (the right atrium and the right ventricle) and the two chambers on the left (the left atrium and the left ventricle; see Figure 1.15). The chambers on the right supply blood at a low pressure to the lungs via the pulmonary arteries, arterioles and capillaries, where gaseous exchange takes place. This blood is then returned to the left side of the heart via the capillaries, venules and veins.

When the chambers of the left side of the heart are full, it contracts simultaneously with the right side, acting as a high-pressure pump. It supplies oxygenated blood via the arteries, arterioles, and capillaries to the tissues of the body such as muscle cells. Oxygen passes from the blood to the cells and carbon dioxide (a waste product of aerobic respiration) is taken on board. The blood then returns to the right atrium of the heart via the capillaries, venules and veins.

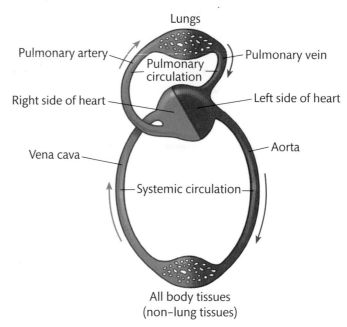

▶ **Figure 1.16:** Double circulation through the heart

The main parts of the heart are as follows.

Key terms

Oxygenated blood – blood containing oxygen.

Deoxygenated blood – blood without oxygen (containing carbon dioxide).

▶ **Coronary arteries** – these are the blood vessels that supply oxygenated blood to the heart muscle. There are two coronary arteries, the left and right.
▶ **Atria** – these are the upper chambers of the heart. They receive blood returning to your heart from either the body or the lungs. The right atrium receives **deoxygenated blood** from the superior and inferior vena cava. The left atrium receives **oxygenated blood** from the left and right pulmonary veins.
▶ **Ventricles** – the pumping chambers of the heart. They have thicker walls than the atria. The right ventricle pumps blood to the pulmonary circulation for the lungs, and the left ventricle pumps blood to the systemic circulation for the body including the muscles.
▶ **Bicuspid (mitral) valve** – one of the four valves in the heart, situated between the left atrium and the left ventricle. It allows the blood to flow in one direction only, from the left atrium to the left ventricle.
▶ **Tricuspid valve** – situated between the right atrium and the right ventricle, it allows blood to flow from the right atrium to the right ventricle and prevents blood from flowing backwards.
▶ **Semi-lunar valves (aortic valve and pulmonary valve)** – the aortic valve is situated between the left ventricle and the aorta and prevents flow from the aorta back into the left ventricle. The pulmonary valve is situated between the right ventricle and the pulmonary artery.

The major blood vessels connected to the heart are as follows.
▶ **Aorta** – this is the body's main artery. It originates in the left ventricle and carries oxygenated blood to all parts of the body except the lungs.
▶ **Superior vena cava** – a vein that receives deoxygenated blood from the upper body to empty into the right atrium of the heart.

- **Inferior vena cava** – a vein that receives deoxygenated blood from the lower body to empty into the right atrium of the heart.
- **Pulmonary vein** – carries oxygenated blood from the lungs to the left atrium of the heart.
- **Pulmonary artery** – carries deoxygenated blood from the heart back to the lungs. It is the only artery that carries deoxygenated blood.

PAUSE POINT Explain the function of the heart in the cardiovascular system.

Hint Close the book and draw a diagram of the heart. Try to label each part of your diagram.

Extend Label the blood flow through the heart, showing where the blood is flowing to and from.

Structure of blood vessels

As the heart contracts, blood flows around the body in a complex network of vessels. Around 96,000 km of arteries, arterioles, capillaries, venules and veins allow the blood's circulation throughout the body. The structure of these different vessels is determined by their different functions and the pressure of blood within them.

Blood flowing through the arteries appears bright red due to its oxygenation. As it moves through the capillaries it drops off oxygen and picks up carbon dioxide. By the time it reaches the veins it is a darker shade of red than oxygenated blood.

Arteries

Arteries carry blood **away** from the heart, and with the exception of the pulmonary artery they carry oxygenated blood. They have thick muscular walls to carry blood at high speeds under high pressure. When the heart ejects blood into the large arteries, the arteries expand to accommodate this blood. They do not require valves as the pressure within them remains high at all times, except at the point where the pulmonary artery leaves the heart. Arteries have two major properties: **elasticity** and **contractility**.

NO VALVES
- blood away from the heart
- thick muscular walls
- carry blood at high pressures

The smooth muscle surrounding the arteries enables their diameter to be decreased and increased as required. This contractility of the arteries helps to maintain blood pressure in relation to changes in blood flow. The arteries are mostly located deep within the body, except where they can be felt at a pulse point. These vessels branch into smaller arterioles that ultimately deliver blood to the capillaries.

- found deep within the body

Arterioles

Arterioles have thinner walls than arteries. They control blood distribution by changing their diameter. This mechanism adjusts blood flow to the capillaries in response to differing demands for oxygen. During exercise, muscles require an increased blood flow in order to get extra oxygen, so the diameter of arterioles leading to the muscles dilates, or gets wider. To compensate for this increase in demand for blood by the muscles, other areas, like the gut, have their blood flow temporarily reduced, and the diameter of their arterioles is decreased. Arterioles are essentially responsible for controlling blood flow to the capillaries.

- increase and decrease in diameter depending on the need for blood

Capillaries

Capillaries connect arteries and veins by uniting arterioles and venules. They are the smallest of all the blood vessels, narrow and thin. The number of capillaries in muscle

- pressure is higher than veins but lower than arteries

- allow gaseous exchange

- carry deoxygenated blood back to the heart

- thin with large diameter

- flow slow and at a low pressure

- have valves

- found close to surface of skin

may be increased through frequent and appropriate exercise. They form an essential part of the cardiovascular system as they allow the diffusion of oxygen and nutrients required by the body's cells. Capillaries that surround muscles ensure they get the oxygen and nutrients they require to produce energy. The walls of capillaries are only one cell thick, allowing nutrients, oxygen and waste products to pass through. The pressure of blood within the capillaries is higher than that in veins, but lower than in the arteries.

Veins

Veins facilitate **venous return** – the return of deoxygenated blood to the heart. They have thinner walls than arteries and a relatively large diameter. By the time blood reaches the veins, it is flowing slowly and under low pressure. Contracting muscles push the thin walls of the veins inwards to help squeeze the blood back towards the heart. As these muscle contractions are intermittent, there are a number of pocket valves in the veins that help to prevent any backflow when the muscles relax. Veins are mainly close to the surface and can be seen under the skin. They branch into smaller vessels called **venules**, which extend to the capillary network.

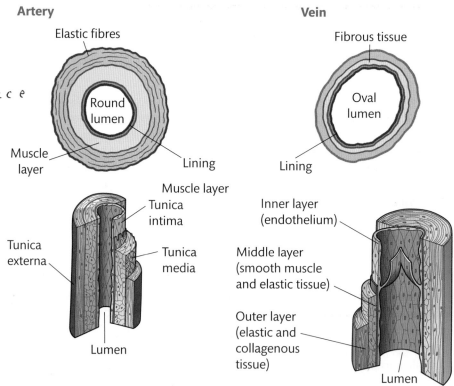

▸ **Figure 1.17:** Structure of arteries and veins

▸ **Table 1.5:** Comparison between veins and arteries

Veins	Arteries
Carry blood from the tissues of the body to the heart	Carry blood away from the heart to the tissues of the body
Usually found just beneath the skin	Found deeper within the body
Have less muscular walls than arteries	Are more muscular than veins, with much more elastic fibres
Have valves to prevent the backflow of blood	Do not contain valves
Contain blood under low pressure	Contain blood under high pressure

Venules

Venules are the small vessels that connect the capillaries to the veins. The venules will take the blood from the capillaries and transport this deoxygenated blood under low pressure to the veins which, in turn, will lead back to the heart.

 PAUSE POINT   Explain the functions of veins, venules, arteries, arterioles and capillaries.

> Hint   Close the book and list the differences between arteries and veins.
>
> Extend   Explain why there are structural differences between arteries and veins.

Composition of blood

The average adult has approximately 4–5 litres of blood. This blood is composed of:

▶ **red blood cells** (erythrocytes) – the main function of red blood cells is to carry oxygen to all living tissue. All red blood cells contain a protein called haemoglobin which gives blood its red colour and when combined with oxygen forms oxyhaemoglobin. Red blood cells are round, flattened discs with an indented shape which gives them a large surface area and allows them to flow easily within plasma. A drop of blood contains millions of red blood cells.

▶ **plasma** – the straw-coloured liquid in which all blood cells are suspended. It is made up of approximately 90 per cent water as well as electrolytes such as sodium, potassium and proteins. The plasma also carries carbon dioxide, dissolved as carbonic acid.

▶ **white blood cells** (leucocytes) – the components of blood that protect the body from infections. White blood cells identify, destroy and remove pathogens such as bacteria or viruses from the body. White blood cells originate in the bone marrow and are stored in your blood.

▶ **platelets** (thrombocytes) – disc-shaped cell fragments produced in the bone marrow. The primary function of platelets is clotting to prevent blood loss.

Function of the cardiovascular system

There are a number of important functions that the cardiovascular system plays during exercise and sports performance.

Delivering oxygen and nutrients

The key function of the cardiovascular system is to supply oxygen and nutrients to the tissues of the body via the bloodstream. During exercise your body will need more of these so the cardiovascular system responds to ensure that there is a suitable supply to meet the increased demands. When the cardiovascular system can no longer meet these demands, fatigue will occur in the muscles and performance will deteriorate.

Removing waste products – carbon dioxide and lactate

As well as providing oxygen and nutrients to all the tissues in the body, the circulatory system carries waste products from the tissues to the kidneys and the liver, and returns carbon dioxide from the tissues to the lungs. During exercise your muscles will produce more carbon dioxide and lactate and it is essential that these are removed, otherwise muscle fatigue will occur.

Thermoregulation

The cardiovascular system is responsible for the distribution and redistribution of heat within your body to maintain thermal balance during exercise. This ensures that you do not overheat during exercise.

- diameter increases

- increases blood flow

- decreases body temperature

- diameter decrease

- limits blood flow

- increases body temperature

Your cardiovascular system uses the following ways of controlling and distributing heat around your body.

▶ **Vasodilation of blood vessels near the skin** – during exercise, vasodilation of blood vessels occurs in the parts of the active muscles where gaseous exchange takes place. Vasodilation is caused by the relaxation of the involuntary muscle fibres in the walls of the blood vessels and causes an increase in the diameter of blood vessels. This decreases resistance to the flow of blood to the area supplied by the vessels. This will result in a decrease in body temperature as heat within the blood can be carried to the skin surface.

▶ **Vasoconstriction of blood vessels near the skin** – blood vessels can also temporarily shut down or limit blood flow to tissues. This process is known as vasoconstriction and causes a decrease in the diameter of blood vessels. This will result in an increase in body temperature, as heat loss is reduced as blood is moved away from the surface.

Fighting infection

Leucocytes (white blood cells) are constantly produced inside the bone marrow. They are stored in, and transported around the body by, the blood. They can consume and ingest pathogens (substances that cause illness) and destroy them, produce antibodies that will also destroy pathogens, and produce antitoxins which will neutralise the toxins that may be released by pathogens.

Clotting blood

Clotting is a complex process during which white blood cells form solid clots. A damaged blood vessel wall is covered by a fibrin clot to help repair the damaged vessel. Platelets form a plug at the site of the damage. Plasma components known as coagulation factors respond to form fibrin strands which strengthen the platelet plug. This is made possible by the constant supply of blood through the cardiovascular system.

Platelet   Red blood cell   Broken blood vessel wall   Activated platelet   Clot   Fibrin

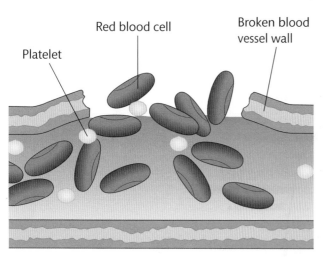 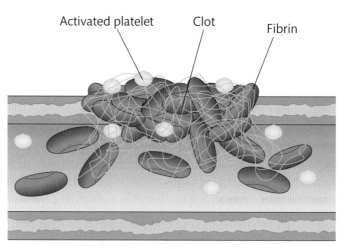

▶ **Figure 1.18:** Clotting prevents excessive bleeding when a blood vessel is damaged

Ⅱ PAUSE POINT   Identify the functions of the cardiovascular system and explain why they are important to sports performance.

Hint   Describe the main functions of the cardiovascular system.

Extend   Explain each of the main functions of the cardiovascular system and why they are so important to sport and exercise performance.

Nervous control of the cardiac cycle

Your heart pumps (or beats) when the atria and ventricles work together. Both the atria and the ventricles contract independently, pushing blood out of the heart's chambers. The process of the heart filling with blood followed by a contraction where the blood is pumped out is known as the **cardiac cycle**. The electrical system of your heart is the power source that makes this possible.

Your heart's electrical system is made up of three main parts: the sinoatrial node, the atrioventricular node, and the Bundle of His and Purkinje fibres (Figure 1.19).

Sinoatrial node (SAN)

The sinoatrial node (SAN) is commonly referred to as the heart's pacemaker and is located within the wall of the right atrium. The SAN sends an impulse or signal from the right atrium through the walls of the atria, causing the muscular walls to contract. This contraction forces the blood within the atria down into the ventricles.

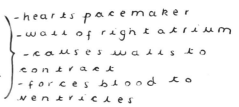

- hearts pacemaker
- wall of right atrium
- causes walls to contract
- forces blood to ventricles

Atrioventricular node (AVN)

The atrioventricular node (AVN) is located in the centre of the heart between the atria and the ventricles, and acts as a buffer or gate that slows down the signal from the SAN. Slowing down the signal allows the atria to contract **before** the ventricles, which means that the ventricles are relaxed (or open) and ready to receive the blood from the atria at the top of the heart.

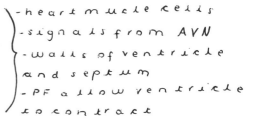

- centre of heart
- atria and ventricle
- slows down signal
- allows ventricles to relax

Bundle of His and Purkinje fibres

Bundle of His are specialist heart muscle cells that are responsible for transporting the electrical impulses from the AVN. They are found in the walls of the ventricles and septum. At the end of the Bundle of His are thin filaments known as Purkinje fibres which allow the ventricle to contract at a paced interval. This contraction causes the blood within the ventricle to be pushed up and out of the heart, either to the lungs or to the working muscles.

- heart mucle cells
- signals from AVN
- walls of ventricle and septum
- PF allow ventricle to contract

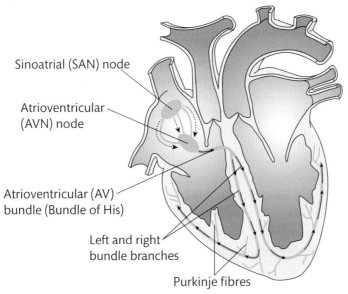

Sinoatrial (SAN) node

Atrioventricular (AVN) node

Atrioventricular (AV) bundle (Bundle of His)

Left and right bundle branches

Purkinje fibres

▶ **Figure 1.19:** The heart's electrical system

Effects of the sympathetic and parasympathetic nervous system

The autonomic nervous system is the part of the nervous system that regulates body functions such as breathing and your heart beating, and it is involuntary.

This system can be further divided into the following nervous systems.

▸ **Sympathetic nervous system** – prepares the body for intense physical activity and is often referred to as the 'fight or flight' response.

▸ **Parasympathetic nervous system** – relaxes the body and inhibits or slows many high energy functions. This is often referred to as the 'rest and digest' response.

During exercise and sport the **sympathetic nervous system** will cause the heart to beat faster and your lungs to work harder, allowing you to produce more energy and meet the demands of the exercise.

After exercise your heart rate will need to slow down to its normal resting levels. It is the job of the **parasympathetic nervous system** to do this; if the parasympathetic nervous system did not function then your heart rate would continue to be elevated.

Responses of the cardiovascular system to a single sport or exercise session

During exercise your contracting muscles require a continual supply of nutrients and oxygen to support energy production. These requirements are over and above those required to support normal activities at work or rest. Your heart has to beat harder and faster to meet these increased demands. If these demands are repeated frequently as a result of a systematic training programme, over time your heart will become stronger and your cardiovascular system will become more efficient at supplying oxygen and removing waste products.

Anticipatory increase in heart rate prior to exercise

You may have experienced the feeling that your heart is beating faster than usual immediately before a sports match. This is known as an **anticipatory response**. Your heart rate will increase just before exercise in order to prepare for the increased demands that are about to be put on your body. Nerves that directly supply your heart and chemicals in your blood can rapidly alter your heart rate. The greatest anticipatory heart-rate response is observed in short sprint events.

Increased heart rate

In order for your muscles to receive more oxygenated blood, your heart rate will increase during exercise. Nerve centres in your brain detect cardiovascular activity and this results in adjustments that increase the rate and pumping strength of your heart. At the same time, regional blood flow is altered in proportion to the intensity of the activity undertaken.

Increased cardiac output

Cardiac output is the amount of blood pumped out of the left side of the heart to the body in one minute. It is the product of heart rate (beats per minute) and stroke volume (the amount of blood per heart beat):

▸ cardiac output = heart rate × stroke volume

During participation in sport and exercise, cardiac output will be greater as a result of increases in heart rate and/or stroke volume. Stroke volume does not increase significantly beyond the light work rates of low-intensity exercise, so the increases in cardiac output required for moderate to high-intensity work rates are mostly achieved by increases in heart rate. Your maximum attainable cardiac output decreases with increasing age, largely as a result of a decrease in maximum heart rate.

Increased blood pressure

Blood pressure is the pressure of the blood against the walls of your arteries and results from two forces:

▸ **systolic pressure** – the pressure exerted on your artery walls when your heart contracts and forces blood out of the heart and into the body

▸ **diastolic pressure** – the pressure on the blood vessel walls when the heart is relaxed between beats and is filling with blood.

During exercise your systolic blood pressure increases as your heart is working harder to supply more oxygenated blood to the working muscles. Your diastolic blood pressure stays the same or decreases slightly.

When blood pressure is measured, it is written with both the systolic and the diastolic pressure noted.

The top number is the **systolic pressure** and the bottom number is the **diastolic pressure**, e.g. $\frac{120}{80}$ mm Hg

[handwritten margin note: Systolic / Diastolic. Systolic increases during exercise. Diastolic does not increase]

Redirection of blood flow

To ensure that blood reaches the areas of the body that need it the most during exercise (i.e. the working muscles), your body will redirect and redistribute the flow of blood. This ensures that the maximum amount of oxygenated blood can reach the muscles, but other areas of the body that need less oxygen during exercise will receive less blood. The body does this using vasodilation and vasoconstriction – refer back to the section on thermoregulation starting on page 41 for more information.

Theory into practice

In pairs, choose a sport that you both enjoy. Take 8–10 minutes to perform a thorough warm-up and then take part in your chosen activity for at least 20 minutes at moderate intensity levels. At the end of the session take approximately five minutes to cool down.

During each part of the activity, pay close attention to the changes that are taking place in your body. Get your partner to record these for you.

1 During the warm-up, what changes occurred to your heart rate and breathing?

2 During the main exercise what changes occurred? Think about how you felt: did you get hot? How did your body adapt to control your temperature? What do you think would have happened if you had exercised at higher intensities?

Adaptations of the cardiovascular system due to exercise

If you undertake a purposeful and well-planned exercise programme, your cardiovascular system will adapt over time and you will become fitter and more able to cope with the demands of exercise. The extent of these changes will depend on the type, intensity and frequency of exercise undertaken, and the overload achieved.

Cardiac hypertrophy

Cardiac hypertrophy is the enlargement of your heart over a long period of time. Training will cause the walls of your heart to get thicker. In particular the wall of the left ventricle will thicken, increasing the strength potential of its contractions.

Increase in resting and exercising stroke volume

Stroke volume is the amount of blood that can be ejected from the heart in one beat. In simple terms, the more blood that can be pushed out of the heart, the more oxygen can get to the muscles. Stroke volume at rest has been shown to be significantly higher after a prolonged endurance-training programme. The heart can therefore pump more blood per minute, increasing cardiac output during maximal levels of exercise. Blood flow increases as a consequence of an increase in the size and number of blood vessels. This allows for more efficient delivery of oxygen and nutrients.

Decrease in resting heart rate

The result of cardiac hypertrophy and an increase in stroke volume through long-term exercise is that your resting heart rate falls, reducing the workload on your heart.

Reduction in resting blood pressure

Exercise causes your blood pressure to rise for a short time. However, when you stop, your blood pressure should return to normal. The quicker it does this, the fitter you are likely to be. Research indicates that regular exercise can contribute to lowering blood pressure. For people suffering from high blood pressure (hypertension), steady aerobic exercise is often recommended to reduce this.

Decreased heart rate recovery time

Heart rate recovery is a measure of how much your heart rate falls during the first minute after exercise. The fitter your heart, the quicker it returns to normal after exercise. Fitter individuals generally recover more rapidly because their cardiovascular system can adapt more quickly to the imposed demands of exercise.

Capillarisation of skeletal muscle and alveoli

Long-term exercise, particularly aerobic exercise, can lead to an increase in the number of capillaries in the cardiac and skeletal muscle. Blood flow increases as a consequence of this increase in the size and number of blood vessels. This allows for more efficient delivery of oxygen and nutrients.

Increase in blood volume

Your blood volume represents the amount of blood circulating in your body. It varies from person to person, and increases as a result of training. Blood volume increases as a result of capillarisation. An increase in blood volume means your body can deliver more oxygen to your working muscles and your body will also be able to regulate your body temperature more effectively during exercise.

 **PAUSE POINT**   What is meant by 'cardiac output'?

 Hint   Describe what happens to your cardiac output during exercise.

Extend   Consider the two components of cardiac output. What are the long-term adaptations affecting your cardiac output due to an exercise programme?

Additional factors affecting the cardiovascular system

Regular training has many long-term benefits for the cardiovascular system. However, when considering any training programme there are a number of additional factors that can affect the cardiovascular system which will impact on exercise and sport performance. Therefore when starting any new training programme, and especially if you have not exercised for a long period of time, you should see a doctor to get checked over.

Sudden arrhythmic death syndrome (SADS)

Sudden arrhythmic death syndrome (SADS) is a genetic heart condition that can cause sudden death in young, apparently healthy people even though the person has no disease affecting the structure of the heart. If the heart's normal, natural rhythm becomes disrupted then the heart can stop beating, which can cause death. There have been a number of high-profile cases where elite sportspeople have suffered from SADS, such as Bolton Wanderers footballer Fabrice Muamba.

Case study

Fabrice Muamba

Fabrice Muamba was a professional footballer playing for Bolton Wanderers in the English Premier League. During an FA Cup match between Tottenham Hotspur and Bolton on 17 March 2012 he suffered a cardiac arrest (heart attack) and collapsed on the pitch.

Muamba received lengthy treatment on the pitch to revive him and he was transferred to a specialist heart hospital, where it was later revealed that his heart had stopped beating for 78 minutes. Muamba made a full recovery, although due to the seriousness of the incident he has retired from football.

This incident highlights that even elite athletes who are seemingly fit and healthy can suffer from serious illness, and many clubs now have regular specialist heart testing for all of their athletes.

In pairs, find out more about Sudden Arrhythmic Death Syndrome (SADS). Visit the Cardiac Risk in the Young (CRY) website, www.c-r-y.org.uk.

Check your knowledge

1 Find examples of SADS in sport.

2 What is being done to help protect sportspeople from SADS?

3 Report back your findings to the rest of the group.

▶ In 2012 footballer Fabrice Muamba, aged 23, collapsed on the pitch during Bolton Wanderers' game against Tottenham Hotspur

High and low blood pressure

The long-term benefits of exercising are enormous. However, exercise can affect your blood pressure, especially during exercise. When you start to exercise, your blood pressure will increase as your heart works harder and pushes more blood out of the heart with greater force. If you already suffer from high blood pressure (**hypertension**), this sudden increase in demand on the heart can be dangerous as too much force may be exerted on the heart and arteries. Anybody suffering from hypertension should seek medical advice before starting an exercise programme.

- Too much force on the heart and arteries can cause damage to the walls

Low blood pressure (**hypotension**) means that your blood is moving slowly around your body, which can restrict the amount of blood reaching vital organs and muscles. Symptoms of low blood pressure include dizziness, fainting and tiredness. If you suffer from low blood pressure then it will be harder for your cardiovascular system to respond during exercise; if your muscles are not receiving enough oxygenated blood, this will affect performance. If insufficient blood is supplied to the brain then fainting may occur. As with hypertension, anybody suffering from hypotension should seek medical advice before starting an exercise programme.

- Too little O₂ going to the brain and muscles
- dizzyness

Vasodilation - cools the body

Hyperthermia/hypothermia

All athletes should be aware of hyperthermia and hypothermia, and their causes and symptoms.

▸ **Hyperthermia** is the prolonged increase in body temperature that occurs when the body produces or absorbs too much heat. When you exercise your body produces heat as a waste product. Your cardiovascular system will regulate your body temperature by dilating the blood vessels closer to the body's surface and making you sweat so that the heat can dissipate. However, if you are exercising in a hot environment it is difficult for the heat to be removed. Likewise, if you are wearing incorrect clothing that traps the heat then you may suffer from hyperthermia.

▸ Exercising in hot conditions can contribute to hyperthermia

Vasoconstriction - warms the body

▸ **Hypothermia** is where your body becomes too cold, with your core temperature dropping below 35°C. (The ideal internal body temperature for humans is 37°C.) Symptoms will include shivering, confusion and, in severe cases, an increased risk of your heart stopping. Hypothermia may occur if you are training in a cold environment without adequate clothing.

Assessment practice 1.4

1 Describe the pathway of blood flow from the heart through the major blood vessels to the body and lungs. **(4 marks)**

2 State the function of the bicuspid valve. **(1 mark)**

3 Describe the nervous control of the cardiac cycle. **(4 marks)**

4 Grace is a basketball player. The table shows Grace's heart rate at rest and then one minute before taking part in basketball. Grace has been taking part in regular basketball for over 8 months. In this time Grace's resting heart rate has decreased from 77 to 70 bpm (beats per minute). Explain why Grace's resting heart rate has decreased. **(3 marks)**

Resting heart rate (bpm)	Heart rate one minute before taking part in basketball (bpm)
70	80

5 Explain the change in Grace's heart rate shown in the two columns of the table. **(4 marks)**

Plan
- I will plan my answer and have a clear idea of the point I am making. I will make sure this point comes across in everything I write.
- When reading through a question, I will write down notes on a blank page.

Do
- I will try to answer all the simpler questions first and then come back to the harder questions.
- I will allow time to answer all the questions and to check my answers.

Review
- I will reread my answers and make any corrections.

The effects of exercise and sports performance on the energy systems

All movement requires energy. The method by which your body generates energy is determined by the intensity and duration of the activity being undertaken. Activities that require short bursts of effort, such as sprinting or jumping, require the body to produce large amounts of energy over a short period. In contrast, marathon running or cycling require continued energy production over a longer period and at a slower rate.

The body's energy systems facilitate these processes. The energy systems of the body can function aerobically (with oxygen) or anaerobically (without oxygen). Movements that require sudden bursts of effort are powered by energy systems that do not require oxygen – anaerobic systems – whereas prolonged activities are aerobic and require oxygen.

All energy systems work together, but the type of activity and its intensity will determine which system is predominant.

The role of ATP in exercise

Energy is required in order to make the muscle fibres contract. This energy is obtained from the breakdown of foods in the diet, particularly carbohydrate and fat. The body maintains a continuous supply of energy through the use of **adenosine triphosphate (ATP)**, which is often referred to as the energy currency of the body.

ATP is a molecule that stores and releases chemical energy for use in body cells. When ATP is broken down, it gives energy for immediate muscle contractions. It is the only molecule that can supply the energy used in the contraction of muscle fibres (see Figure 1.20).

ATP consists of a base (adenine) and three phosphate groups. It is formed by a reaction between an **adenosine diphosphate (ADP)** molecule and a phosphate. Energy is stored in the chemical bonds in the molecules; when a bond is broken, energy is released.

(a) ATP is formed when adenosine diphosphate (ADP) binds with a phosphate

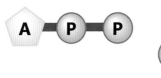

(b) When a cell needs energy, it breaks the bond between the phosphate groups to form ADP and a free phosphate molecule

▶ **Figure 1.20:** ATP and energy released from the breakdown of ATP

ATP works like a rechargeable battery. Energy is released by converting ATP to ADP, which is the 'uncharged' form. By binding a phosphate back with the ADP to resynthesise ATP, the 'battery' is charged again and ready to be used for immediate and powerful muscular contractions.

However, your muscles have only very small amounts of ATP stored in them, so to replenish ATP quickly, the body has to use a number of other systems as well.

[Handwritten margin notes:]
Carbs + fats broken down
↓
ATP formed
↓
stores and releases energy
↓
causes immidiate muscle contractions

Base - adenine
+
Three phosphate groups
↓
when the cell needs energy it breaks a bond and forms ADP

The ATP–PC (alactic) system in exercise and sports performance

The ATP–PC (alactic) system is **anaerobic**, which means that it does not require oxygen to produce energy. This is important in sports where sudden and powerful movements are required, such as shot put or sprinting, as the muscles can use ATP to produce energy and movement without having to 'wait' for oxygen to be delivered.

A muscle cell has a small amount of ATP in it that it can use immediately, but there is only enough to last for about three seconds. To replenish the ATP levels quickly, muscle cells also contain a high-energy phosphate compound called creatine phosphate (or phosphocreatine, or PCr). When the high-energy bond in PCr is broken, the energy it releases is transferred to ADP to resynthesise ATP.

The ATP–PC system only supports high-intensity exercise for short periods of time (approximately 10 seconds) as the PC store runs down quickly. If exercise continues at a high intensity these stores will only partially replenish, as there will not be enough energy available for creatine and phosphate to reform phosphocreatine. A ratio called the 'work-to-rest ratio' can be used to determine how quickly a system will replenish. For the ATP–PC system this ratio is 1:10–12. This means that for every second of work you need to allow 10–12 seconds for recovery.

The lactate system in exercise and sports performance

The lactate system is a short-term energy system and is used to meet energy requirements of higher intensity over a longer period, such as during a 400-metre race. It is an **anaerobic** process that does not require oxygen and therefore is not sustainable over a long duration.

The body breaks down most carbohydrates from the foods we eat and converts them to a type of sugar known as glucose. When the body does not need to use the glucose for energy, it stores some of it in the liver and muscles where it is easily accessible for energy production and is known as **glycogen.**

In the lactate energy system, ATP is made by the partial breakdown of glucose and glycogen through the process of **anaerobic glycolysis**. Around 60–90 seconds of maximal work are possible using this system.

Anaerobic glycolysis

When the ATP–PC system begins to fade at around 10 seconds, the process of anaerobic glycolysis begins. This system breaks down liver and muscle glycogen stores without needing the presence of oxygen. The breakdown of glucose and glycogen releases energy which can be used to resynthesise ATP; the breakdown of glucose produces two molecules of ATP, whereas the breakdown of glycogen can produce three molecules of ATP.

Lactic acid production

Unfortunately, anaerobic glycolysis produces lactic acid as a by-product. Lactic acid is the limiting factor of the anaerobic system. It accumulates and diffuses into the tissue fluid and blood. If this substance is not removed quickly enough by the circulatory system, it builds up to impede muscle contraction and cause fatigue. You may have experienced this as an uncomfortable burning sensation and soreness in your muscles during intense exercise.

A recovery time of approximately eight minutes will aid the removal of lactic acid from the muscles as well as the storage of glycogen in your muscles.

The aerobic system in exercise and sports performance

The **aerobic** energy system is the long-term energy system. If plenty of oxygen is available, as it is during everyday movements and light exercise, glycogen and fatty acids break down to yield the largest amounts of ATP. This produces carbon dioxide and water, which do not affect the ability of muscles to contract, unlike the lactic acid produced by the lactate system.

Aerobic energy production occurs in the mitochondria of the muscle cells. The aerobic system relies on the breakdown of carbohydrates and stored fats to produce energy, and improved aerobic fitness makes it easier for the body to convert these food sources.

The production of energy within the aerobic system is slow to engage because it takes a few minutes for the heart to deliver oxygenated blood to working muscles. Long, continuous and moderate exercise, such as long-distance running, produces energy using this system.

The aerobic energy system can be broken down into three processes.

1 **Aerobic glycolysis** – this is the first stage of **aerobic metabolism** (the breakdown of foods into energy). It converts carbohydrates (in the form of either glucose or glycogen) into pyruvic acid using oxygen. This breakdown requires 10 chemical reactions: another reason why the aerobic system is slower to deliver energy and is suited to steady sports performance. The process of aerobic glycolysis produces two molecules of ATP.

2 **Krebs cycle** – sometimes known as the **citric acid cycle**, this is the second phase in the process of anaerobic metabolism. It takes place in the mitochondria. The pyruvic acid that was produced during aerobic glycolysis enters the mitochondria and is converted to citric acid. This results in two molecules of ATP being produced, with carbon dioxide and hydrogen being produced as waste products. The carbon dioxide will be exhaled by the lungs and the hydrogen will be used in the next phase of energy production, the electron transport chain.

3 **Electron transport chain** – the hydrogen that was released as part of the Krebs cycle is vital in the production of energy. The electron transport chain is the most important step in energy production and is where the majority of ATP is created. This process will create 34 molecules of ATP from glucose. The hydrogen created as part of the Krebs cycle is accepted by the hydrogen acceptor found in the mitochondria where, in the presence of oxygen, ATP can be produced.

In total the aerobic energy system will produce 38 molecules of ATP from one molecule of glucose. Depending on the duration and intensity of the exercise, as well as your level of fitness, recovery of the aerobic energy systems can range from a few hours to 2–3 days.

The energy systems in combination

During exercise the body does not switch from one system to another – energy at any time is derived from all three systems. However, the emphasis changes depending on the intensity of the activity relative to the efficiency of your aerobic fitness, i.e. your ability to deliver and utilise oxygen. Table 1.6 shows different types of sport and the relative contributions made by the different energy systems. Figure 1.21 illustrates the contribution of different energy systems during exercise.

Handwritten margin notes:
- Long term energy system
- Glycogen and fatty acids are broken down
- Occurs in the mitochondria
- For long duration and moderate intensity exercise (long distance running)
- breakdown of foods into energy
- forms pyruvic acid
- pyruvic acid enters mitochondria
- converted to citric acid
- 2 ATP forms
- uses the hydrogen released from the Krebs cycle
- forms 34 molecules of ATP

When you start running, the following process takes place.

▸ The muscle cells burn off the ATP they already contain in about three seconds.

▸ The creatine phosphate system kicks in and supplies energy for 8–10 seconds. This would be the major energy system used by the muscles of a 100-metre sprinter or a weightlifter, where rapid acceleration, short-duration exercise occurs.

▸ If exercise continues, the lactic acid energy system kicks in. This occurs in short-distance exercises such as a 200- or 400-metre run or a 100-metre swim.

▸ If exercise continues, the aerobic energy system takes over. This occurs in endurance events such as an 800-metre run, a marathon run, rowing, cross-country skiing and distance skating.

▸ **Table 1.6:** The different lengths of time for each energy system, with sport examples

Duration	Classification	Energy supplied by	Sport example
1–3 seconds	Anaerobic	ATP (in muscles)	A punch in boxing
3–10 seconds	Anaerobic	ATP + PC	100-metre sprint
10–45 seconds	Anaerobic	ATP + PC + muscle glycogen	200-metre run
45 seconds–2 minutes	Anaerobic, Lactic	Muscle glycogen	400-metre run
2 minutes–4 minutes	Aerobic + Anaerobic	Muscle glycogen + lactic acid	1500-metre run
Over 4 minutes	Aerobic	Muscle glycogen + fatty acids	Marathon running

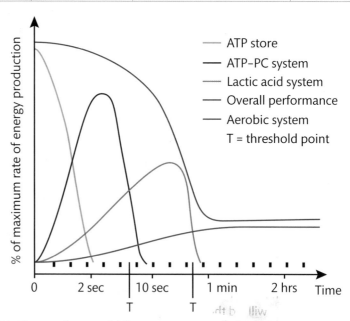

▸ **Figure 1.21:** The contribution of different energy systems during exercise

 PAUSE POINT

Why do different sports use different energy systems?

Hint   Choose a sport. What is the main energy system that is used?

Extend   Now consider a team sport and a specific position. Are different energy systems used during a performance? If so, why?

Mo Farah versus Usain Bolt

As part of his charity, the Mo Farah Foundation, Mo Farah has challenged the world 100-metre champion, Usain Bolt, to race over a distance that would not suit either runner. Mo Farah is the current Olympic champion over 5000 metres and 10,000 metres, while Usain Bolt is the Olympic champion over 100 metres and 200 metres. Farah has suggested that they race between 600–800 metres.

1 Suggest an optimum distance that would be fair for both athletes.

2 Why do you think that one athlete is better suited to one distance than another distance?

Adaptations of the energy systems to exercise

Long-term exercise will allow the body's energy systems to adapt to the physical demands of exercise. This means that by following an exercise programme it is possible to train each energy system so that you can perform for longer and at increasingly harder intensities.

Increased creatine stores

Short-duration, interval training sessions using high-intensity exercises will improve your ability to produce anaerobic energy. Your body will adapt and be able to store more creatine in the muscles which will improve the ATP–PC system. This will result in you being able to exercise anaerobically for longer using fast and powerful movements.

Increased tolerance to lactic acid

Anaerobic training stimulates the muscles to become better able to tolerate lactic acid and to clear it away more efficiently. With endurance training the capillary network extends, allowing greater volumes of blood to supply the muscles with oxygen and nutrients. The muscles are able to use more fat as a fuel source and become more efficient at using oxygen, increasing the body's ability to work harder for longer without fatiguing. The net result is an increase in the body's maximal oxygen consumption.

Aerobic energy system

Long-term exercise will improve the ability of the aerobic energy system to produce energy, as improvements in the cardiovascular system will allow for increased oxygen to be delivered which is needed to produce ATP aerobically. Likewise, adaptations of the cardiovascular system will aid the removal of lactic acid through oxidisation.

Increased use of fats as an energy source

Fat is the primary energy source during low-intensity exercise. Fat combustion powers almost all exercise at approximately 25 per cent of **aerobic capacity** (which is approximately 60–70 per cent of your maximum heart rate). Fat oxidation increases if exercise extends to long periods, as glycogen levels deplete. When considering the effects of long-term exercise, the trained athlete has a greater opportunity to burn fat as a fuel than the non-trained athlete because they have a more efficient system of delivering oxygen to the working muscle, as well as a greater number of mitochondria.

Key term

Aerobic capacity – the maximum amount of oxygen that can be consumed during maximal exercise.

Increased storage of glycogen and increased numbers of mitochondria

Muscles increase their oxidative capacity with regular training. This is achieved by an increase in the number of mitochondria within the muscle cells, an increase in the supply of ATP and an increase in the quantity of enzymes involved in respiration. The ability of the muscles to store more glycogen is also increased, meaning that anaerobic glycolysis can last for longer.

> **Link**
>
> You can find more information on this topic in *Unit 5: Application of Fitness Testing*.

Additional factors affecting the energy systems

There are two main additional factors that must be considered when examining the energy systems and their impact on sport and exercise performance.

Diabetes and hypoglycaemic attack

Diabetes is a condition where the amount of glucose in your blood is too high. This is known as type I diabetes. It develops when glucose cannot enter the body's cells to be used as fuel. **Insulin** is the hormone produced by the pancreas that allows glucose to enter the body's cells, where it is used as fuel for energy. If you have diabetes, your body cannot make proper use of this glucose so it builds up in the blood and cannot be used.

Hypoglycaemia is an abnormally low level of glucose in your blood. When your glucose (sugar) level is too low, your body does not have enough energy to carry out its activities. Hypoglycaemia mainly occurs if someone with diabetes takes too much insulin, misses a meal or exercises too hard. Typical early warning signs are feeling hungry, trembling or shakiness, and sweating. Additional symptoms include confusion, and you may have difficulty concentrating. In severe cases, a person experiencing hypoglycaemia can lose consciousness.

Children's lack of lactate system

Although we all possess the same body systems, a child's body systems are still growing and developing, with significant changes occuring during puberty. One such area is the lactate energy system, which is not fully developed in children. During high-intensity exercise, lactic acid will build up in the muscles and, due to their developing cardiovascular system, it is more difficult for children to remove this waste product. Therefore it is generally recommended that children exercise aerobically.

Assessment practice 1.5

1 Explain why it is an advantage for marathon runners to have high numbers of mitochondria. **(2 marks)**

2 Describe the process of ATP production from carbohydrates through the aerobic energy system. **(5 marks)**

3 The graph (Figure 1.22) shows the ATP–PC stores in a performer's muscles while competing in a rugby match. Explain why playing in a rugby match will have this effect on muscle ATP–PC stores. **(3 marks)**

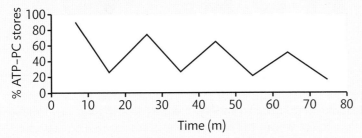

▶ **Figure 1.22:** ATP is the only immediately usable source of energy in the human body

4 Compare and contrast the importance of the aerobic and anaerobic energy systems for an elite 100-metre sprinter in competition and in training. **(8 marks)**

5 Denise is training for a marathon. Analyse how adaptations to Denise's cardiorespiratory system could improve her marathon-running performance. **(8 marks)**

6 Identify four key long-term adaptations that are linked to aerobic training and explain the benefit of each adaptation. **(8 marks)**

Plan
- I will listen to, and read carefully, any instructions that I am given.
- I will look for the command words in the question and plan a response to them.

Do
- I will make sure I write a detailed response for the questions with more marks.
- I will include key words and information and use them to structure my answer.

Review
- I will check that I have answered all the questions.
- I will check that I have given examples and that they are clear.

Further reading and resources

Books

Bartlett, R. (2014) *Introduction to Sports Biomechanics*, London: Routledge.

Marieb, E. (2015) *Human Anatomy and Physiology*, Oxford: Pearson.

Palastanga, N. (2012) *Anatomy and Human Movement: Structure and Function*, London: Churchill Livingstone.

Sharkey, B.J. and Gaskill, S.E. (2006) *Fitness and Health*, Champaign, IL: Human Kinetics.

Tortora, G.J. and Derrickson, B.H (2008) *Principles of Anatomy and Physiology*, London: John Wiley and Sons.

Websites

www.humankinetics.com – Human Kinetics: educational resources relating to all areas of sport and physical activity.

www.sportsci.org – Sport Science: research into sport, including articles considering the functions of different bodily systems in sport.

www.topendsports.com – Top End Sports: information on many aspects of anatomy and physiology.

THINK ▶FUTURE

Helen Reardon

Sports Therapist

I have been working as a sports therapist for seven years, and over this time I have worked with a wide range of people in a variety of places. In any given day I will work with different people, each of whom will have specific fitness goals. For example, I may provide one-to-one support for somebody training to run a marathon or work with an athlete who is returning from a long-term injury.

Having a detailed knowledge of anatomy and physiology is essential to my job, as I have to understand how each body system works and how the body will be affected by exercise. In particular I have to understand anatomy and physiology so that I can manage and prevent sporting injuries. It is essential that I understand the adaptations the body makes so that I can set each of my clients personal and challenging goals and develop specific training programmes. Often I will be working with clients who are returning from injury, so it is essential that the programmes I set are at the correct level so that the injury does not reoccur. I have to ensure that each of my clients can train safely and use the correct techniques so that they do not injure themselves.

As part of my job I am responsible for providing sports massage and giving advice on preventive and rehabilitative exercises to help prevent and manage injuries. My work also involves testing joints for ease and range of movement, strapping and taping, and advising on stretching and warm-up and cool-down exercises.

One of the most important skills for a successful sports therapist is the ability to motivate people. Being able to get a client to reach their goal when they are tired or returning from injury is challenging but also one of the most rewarding parts of my job. Seeing individuals and teams achieve their long-term goals and knowing that you were key to their success is hugely satisfying.

Focusing your skills

Think about the role of a personal trainer. Consider the following questions.

- What types of people will you work with and how will you support them?
- What role will you play in helping them achieve their goals?
- What different types of exercise will you recommend and how will these affect each of the body's systems?

- What types of training goals will you need to help people with? Will you work with elite athletes or people who are trying to lose weight?
- What skills do you currently have? What skills do you think may need further development?

Getting ready for assessment

This section has been written to help you to do your best when you take the assessment test. Read through it carefully and ask your tutor if there is anything you are still not sure about.

About the test

The assessment test will ask a range of short answer questions as well as some longer answer questions.

Remember that all the questions are compulsory and you should attempt to answer each one. Consider the question fully and remember to use the key words to describe, explain and analyse. For longer questions you will be required to include a number of explanations to your response; plan your answer and write in detail.

As the guidelines for assessment can change, you should refer to the official assessment guidance on the Pearson Qualifications website for the latest definitive guidance.

Preparing for the test

To improve your chances on the test you will need to make sure you have revised all the key **assessment outcomes** that are likely to appear. The assessment outcomes were introduced to you at the start of this unit.

Do not start revising too late! Cramming information is stressful and does not work.

Useful tips

- **Plan a revision timetable** – identify all the topics you need to revise and try to spend several short revision sessions on each of them. Coming back to each topic several times will help you to reinforce the key facts in your memory.

- **Take regular breaks** – short bursts of 30–40 minutes are more effective than long hours of revision. Remember, most people's concentration lapses after an hour and they need a break.

- **Allow yourself rest** – do not fill all your time with revision. You could schedule one evening off a week, or book in a 'revision holiday' of a few days.

- **Take care of yourself** – stay healthy and rested, and eat properly – this will help you to perform at your best. The less stressed you are, the easier you will find it to learn.

Revise all the key areas likely to be covered – draw up a checklist to make sure you do not forget anything!

Read each question carefully before you answer it to make sure you understand what you have to do.

Sitting the test

- Listen to, and read carefully, any instructions you are given. Lots of marks are lost because people do not read questions properly and then fail to complete their answers correctly.

- Most questions contain command words (see Table 1.1). Understanding what these words mean will help you understand what the question is asking you to do.

- The number of marks can relate to the number of answers you are expected to give – if a question asks for two examples, do not only give one! Similarly, do not offer more information than the question needs: if there are two marks for two examples, do not give four examples.

- Plan your time carefully. Work out what you need to answer and then organise your time. You should spend more time on longer questions. Set yourself a timetable for working through the test and then stick to it – do not spend ages on a short 1–2 mark question and then find you only have a few minutes for a longer 7–8 mark question.

- It is useful when reading through a question to write down notes on a blank page. This way you can write down all the key words and information required and use this to structure your answer.

- If you are writing an answer to a longer question, try to plan your answer before you start writing. Have a clear idea of the point you want to make, and then make sure this point comes across in everything you write.

- If you finish early, use the time to re-read your answers and make any corrections – this could really help to make your answers even better and could make a big difference to your final mark.

Sample answers

For some questions you will be given some background information on which the questions are based. Look at the sample questions which follow and our tips on how to answer them well.

Answering short answer questions

☐ Read the question carefully and highlight or underline key words.

☐ Note the number of marks available.

☐ Make additional notes that you can include in your answer.

☐ Make the same number of statements as there are marks available. For example, a two-mark question needs two statements.

Worked example

Explain the effects of taking part in exercise on tidal volume. [3]

Answer: Tidal volume increases during exercise because during exercise a person has to take in (inhale) more air. More air is required as it contains oxygen which is needed to provide energy for the working muscles.

> This answer gives a brief description of what happens to tidal volume during exercise (1 mark) plus an explanation of how (1 mark) and why this increases (1 mark).

Answering extended answer questions

Example:

Craig is a 17-year-old swimmer who has asthma. Discuss the effects of participating in swimming on the respiratory system for an individual suffering with asthma. [6]

Answer: Craig may experience both positive and negative effects of swimming. The positive aspects of swimming for an asthma sufferer are that the air breathed in will be moist and warm, which reduces the chances of an exercise-induced asthma attack. Exercise will also increase Craig's vital capacity and strengthen the respiratory muscles. This will allow more air to be breathed, which will help reduce the effects of asthma.

The negative or disadvantage of exercise for Craig is that he may suffer from an exercise-induced asthma attack. This may result in wheezing while breathing or coughing. Craig may experience tightness in his chest. If asthma occurs then the bronchi may become inflamed or the airways might narrow, which will reduce the amount of air getting into the lungs.

> For a question using the word 'discuss', you must do more than just explain. You might need to talk about the issues or the advantages (positive) and disadvantages (negative) of an approach or theme.

> This answer describes the causes and symptoms of asthma in general as well as in relation to exercise. Further discussion includes the advantages and disadvantages of exercise with specific reference made to swimming.

> When answering an extended answer question, you may write several paragraphs. Remember to make notes before you start to answer the question and ensure that you plan all aspects of your longer answer to gain all the available marks.

Fitness Training and Programming for Health, Sport and Well-being

2

In this unit, you will explore the ways of screening clients and assessing their lifestyle and nutritional habits. The ability to screen clients and assess fitness training programmes is essential for anyone working in the health and fitness industry, and for sports coaches looking to improve individuals' or teams' performance.

This unit has been selected as an externally assessed unit, as it introduces many of the skills and processes required in the industry. This unit links with *Unit 5: Application of Fitness Testing* and *Unit 7: Practical Sports Performance*.

How you will be assessed

This unit will be assessed externally using an examination set by Pearson. The examination will contain two parts.

▶ **Part A** is supplied a set period of time before your examination so that you can carry out independent research about a scenario based on an individual who requires guidance on training, lifestyle and nutrition.

▶ **Part B** is a written examination under controlled conditions in which you can use your research notes to complete a task that builds on Part A.

As the guidelines for assessment can change, you should refer to the official assessment guidance on the Pearson Qualifications website for the latest definitive guidance.

You will be assessed for your understanding of the following topics:

▶ lifestyle factors and their effect on health and well-being
▶ recommendations to promote health and well-being
▶ screening processes for training programming
▶ programme-related nutritional needs
▶ training methods for different components of fitness
▶ appropriate training activities to meet the needs of a specific client
▶ principles of fitness training programming.

Throughout this unit you will find activities that will help you to work towards your assessment. Completing these activities will not mean that you have achieved a particular grade, but you will have carried out useful research or preparation that will help you later when you do your external assessment.

Unit 2 has five assessment outcomes (AO) which will be included in the external examination. Certain 'command words' are associated with each assessment outcome. Table 2.1 explains what these command words are asking you to do.

The assessment outcomes for the unit are:

▶ **AO1** Demonstrate knowledge and understanding of the effects of lifestyle choices on an individual's health and well-being

▶ **AO2** Apply knowledge and understanding of fitness principles and theory, lifestyle modification techniques, nutritional requirements and training methods to an individual's needs and goals

▶ **AO3** Analyse and interpret screening information relating to an individual's lifestyle questionnaire and health monitoring tests

▶ **AO4** Evaluate qualitative and quantitative evidence to make informed judgements about how an individual's health and well-being could be improved

▶ **AO5** Be able to develop a fitness training programme with appropriate justification

▶ **Table 2.1:** Command words used in this unit

Command word	Definition
Justification	Give reasons or evidence to: • support an opinion or decision • prove something right or reasonable
Qualitative evidence	Descriptive information from interviews or questionnaires
Quantitative evidence	Numerical or statistical information
Interpretation	Drawing the meaning, purpose or qualities of something from source material
Relevance	Importance to the matter at hand

Getting started

Consider how athletes train to meet the physical demands of their sport at an elite level. Now consider the rising levels of obesity and heart disease in the world. How can knowledge of fitness training and programming help in both these different scenarios?

A Examine lifestyle factors and their effect on health and well-being

Positive lifestyle factors and their effect on health and well-being

Evidence suggests that leading a healthy lifestyle by following a sensible diet, participating in regular physical activity, maintaining a healthy body weight and avoiding smoking, excessive alcohol consumption and stress, is important to health and well-being.

> **Reflect**
>
> Think about your own lifestyle and what pressures may affect your ability to train or compete. Consider five factors that may limit the amount of time you have for sporting activities. How could you begin to overcome these pressures?

Exercise and physical activity

There is overwhelming scientific evidence to prove that people leading active lives are less likely to die early or suffer from chronic disease such as **cancer**, **coronary heart disease (CHD)** or **type 2 diabetes**. They are also better able to cope with stress and anxiety. Figure 2.1 shows just some of the benefits of physical exercise.

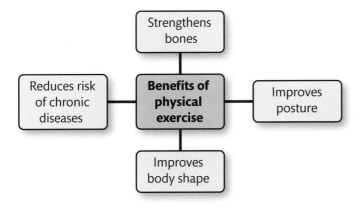

▶ **Figure 2.1:** Benefits of exercise and physical activity on health and well-being

The Department of Health recommends people do at least 30 minutes of moderate exercise at least five days a week. 'Moderate' means you must get a little warmer and slightly out of breath – the more vigorous the activity, the greater the gain in cardiovascular health. The exercise can be anything that raises energy expenditure above resting level, which is enough to expend approximately 200 calories. This may include brisk walking, swimming, cycling, jogging or even gardening.

> **Key terms**
>
> **Cancer** – a group of diseases characterised by uncontrolled growth of abnormal cells that can spread throughout the body.
>
> **Coronary heart disease (CHD)** – when your coronary arteries (which supply your heart muscle with oxygen-rich blood) become narrowed by a gradual build-up of fatty material within their walls.
>
> **Type 2 diabetes** – a disorder characterised by an increase in blood glucose levels that usually develops in adulthood.

Physical exercise can also have social, economic and psychological benefits. Some of these are shown in Table 2.2.

▶ **Table 2.2:** Wider benefits of physical activity and exercise

Social	Economic	Psychological
• Encourages social interaction	• Reduces NHS costs	• Relieves stress
• Improves social skills	• Creates employment	• Reduces depression
• Reduces isolation	• Supports local businesses	• Improves mood
• Enhances self-esteem and confidence	• Reduces absenteeism from work	• Improves concentration

Balanced diet

'Diet' refers to your typical food consumption, while a 'balanced diet' is one that provides the correct amount of nutrients required by your body.

Eatwell Guide

The Eatwell Guide is a way in which the UK government promotes a balanced diet. It is made up of the following food groups:

▶ bread, rice, potatoes, pasta and other starchy carbohydrate foods
▶ fruit and vegetables
▶ dairy and alternatives
▶ meat, fish, eggs, beans, pulses and other protein
▶ oil and spreads.

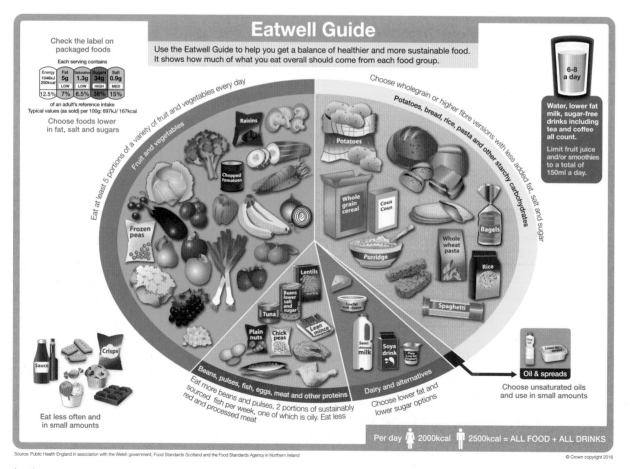

▶ **Figure 2.2:** The Eatwell Guide

The model identifies the types and proportions of food from each group required to achieve a healthy, balanced diet. It is illustrated by a plate with divisions of varying sizes representing each of the five main food groups (see Figure 2.2). The larger the slice of the plate, the more that food group should feature in your diet, while those with smaller slices should be consumed in smaller portions or only occasionally.

Benefits of a healthy diet

Improved immune function

A poor diet can force the immune system – the body's natural defence that fights off disease – to work without enough nutritional support, reducing its ability to protect the body. A weakened immune system leads to a higher risk of illness, which can cause a loss of appetite. This then weakens the immune system further, creating a cycle that has to be broken to allow recovery. In contrast, a healthy diet helps boost the immune system and prevents this cycle of poor nutrition leading to ill-health.

Maintaining a healthy body weight

A healthy diet and regular exercise can help you avoid excess weight gain and maintain a healthy weight. Eating a low-fat and low-sugar diet can also help to control weight. Starting the day with a healthy breakfast may help to reduce snacking later in the day. The government recommends incorporating 'five a day' – five portions of fruits and vegetables which are low in calories and high in nutrients – into your diet to help with weight control.

> **Research**
>
> Data available from the Health Survey for England (HSE) suggests that in 2012 around 28 per cent of children aged 2–15 years of age were classed as either overweight or obese. Similar figures available in 2007 suggest the figure was around 24 per cent.
>
> Research the possible causes of this increase in childhood obesity. Consider the types of food and drink available, and the opportunities children have to exercise, both at home and in school.

Reduced risk of chronic disease

A healthy diet can reduce the risk of chronic diseases such as coronary heart disease, stroke, and **hypertension** by increasing the levels in our body of high-density lipoprotein (HDL) or 'good' cholesterol and decreasing the levels of low-density lipoprotein (LDL) or 'bad' cholesterol. This keeps your blood flowing smoothly, reducing the risk of heart disease and hypertension. A healthy diet can also help prevent or manage a range of other chronic health problems, including diabetes, depression, cancer, and osteoporosis.

Fluid intake requirements

The water of the body fluids makes up 55–60 per cent of an adult's body. All of the body's chemical reactions occur there, and water is the main transport mechanism in your body, carrying nutrients, waste products and internal secretions. Water also plays a vital role in regulating your temperature, particularly during exercise, and aids the passage of food through your digestive system. Therefore, it is vital to remain hydrated at all times.

Around 10 per cent of your daily fluid requirements come from the **metabolic processes** that release water within your body. The other 90 per cent come from your diet. Approximately 60 per cent of this comes from fluids and the rest from food, particularly food with a high water content.

> **Key terms**
>
> **Hypertension** – also known as high blood pressure, it is a chronic medical condition in which the blood pressure in the arteries is continually raised. It is considered a potential threat to health and well-being.
>
> **Metabolic processes** – chemical reactions that take place in the body to sustain life.

Caffeine – a mildly addictive central nervous system stimulant found in coffee, tea and some energy drinks.

Metabolic rate – the energy expended by an individual over a period of time, usually expressed in units of energy per unit of body mass, per unit of time.

Stimulant – a substance that raises levels of physiological or nervous activity in the body.

Moderation of caffeine intake

Caffeine provides no nutritional value. However, because it is an addictive, mild **stimulant**, it can affect your mood and cause physical side effects. Caffeine is found in coffee, tea, energy drinks and some fizzy drinks (particularly colas). Moderate caffeine consumption, of around 400 mg caffeine or the equivalent of up to 4–5 cups of coffee per day (depending on the blend strength), can be considered part of a healthy balanced diet.

Research shows that caffeine can improve physical performances requiring speed and strength. However, a larger caffeine consumption can lead to negative physiological side effects such as hypertension and digestive problems.

Discussion

In 2004, caffeine was taken off the World Anti-Doping Agency (WADA) list of banned substances. However, research has shown that caffeine can raise heart rate and enhance sports performance. Why did the WADA take caffeine off the list of banned substances? Do you think it was the right choice? Discuss this as a small group.

Strategies for improving dietary intake

Sportspeople should eat foods that can enhance their preparation for, and recovery from, training and competition. Most sportspeople will obtain all the energy and nutrients they need by eating when they are hungry and choosing a balanced and varied diet. To improve their dietary intake, sportspeople should consider the following factors:

▶ **Timing of meals** – What you eat has an impact on your health and well-being. However, when and how you eat can also have an impact. You should aim to eat every 3–4 hours. Timing your meals in this way will improve fat burning, help to control your appetite and balance your stress hormones. You should also try to eat your meals at the same time every day.

It is important to start your day with a good breakfast. Research has shown that people who regularly skip breakfast are more susceptible to weight gain (perhaps because they are more likely to snack during the day) and type 2 diabetes.

Eating too close to bedtime raises your body temperature and increases blood sugar levels. These factors interfere with the quality of your sleep and the natural fat-burning benefits of a good night's rest.

▶ Eating a healthy breakfast kick-starts your metabolism for the day

▶ **Eating less/more of certain food groups** – as we have seen, the Eatwell Guide illustrates that, in order to have a healthy and balanced diet, you should try to eat a good balance of different foods, with approximately two thirds of your diet consisting of:

- fruit and vegetables
- starchy foods, such as bread, rice, potatoes and pasta.

Some sportspeople change the balance of their diet depending on their requirements at the time, such as eating more protein (to aid muscle recovery) or carbohydrates (to provide slow-release energy before an event).

Case study

Menu for an Olympic rower

A heavyweight rower in training for the Olympics will undergo a rigorous and often punishing training regime involving three training sessions per day for 6 days a week. To maintain the intensity of this regime, the rower will need to consume around 6000 calories a day. The daily meal plan shown in Table 2.3 gives an indication of what type of diet an elite-level athlete needs in order to train and compete.

▶ **Table 2.3:** Example daily meal plan for an Olympic rower

Time	Meal
7 a.m.: breakfast	<ul><li>large bowl of cereal or porridge and 500 ml skimmed milk</li><li>2 slices of wholemeal bread with honey</li><li>glass of fruit juice</li><li>1 litre fruit squash</li></ul>
8 a.m.: training	<ul><li>1 litre isotonic sports drink during training</li></ul>
9:30 a.m.: post-training	<ul><li>4 scrambled eggs</li><li>2 rashers grilled bacon</li><li>portion grilled tomatoes</li><li>2 slices of wholemeal bread with honey</li><li>1 litre of fruit squash</li></ul>
11 a.m.: training	<ul><li>1 litre isotonic sports drink during training</li><li>500 ml protein shake immediately after training</li></ul>
12:30 p.m.: lunch	<ul><li>pasta with grilled chicken breast</li><li>green side salad</li><li>piece of fruit</li><li>1 litre fruit squash</li></ul>
4 p.m.: training	<ul><li>1 litre isotonic sports drink during training</li></ul>
5:30 p.m.: post-training	<ul><li>large bowl of cereal or porridge and 500 ml skimmed milk</li><li>piece of fruit</li><li>500 ml of water</li></ul>
7:30 p.m.: dinner	<ul><li>grilled lean meat or fish</li><li>6–8 new potatoes or 1 cup of boiled rice</li><li>large portion of steamed vegetables</li><li>1 low-fat yoghurt</li><li>piece of fruit</li><li>750 ml of fruit squash</li></ul>
9:30 p.m.: bedtime snack	<ul><li>1 cereal bar</li></ul>
10:30 p.m.: bed	

Key term

Fibre – an indigestible dietary component with no calorie content that helps to decrease the time food takes to pass through the digestive system.

In the UK, many people eat and drink too many calories, too much fat, sugar and salt, and not enough fruit, vegetables, oily fish and **fibre**. It is important to have some fat in your diet, but as part of a healthy diet try to avoid foods that are high in fat and/or sugar.

▶ **Five a day** – 'Five a day' highlights the health benefits of including five 80 g portions of fruit and vegetables as part of a healthy diet. It is based on advice from the World Health Organization (WHO), which recommends eating a minimum of 400 g of fruit and vegetables to lower the risk of chronic health problems.

Including fruit and vegetables in your diet is an excellent way of improving your dietary intake because fruit and vegetables:

- are good sources of vitamins and minerals
- are an excellent source of dietary fibre, which helps to maintain a healthy digestive system
- can help to reduce the risk of heart disease, stroke and cancer
- are generally low in fat and calories, so they can help maintain a healthy weight.

Case study

Sports Scientist: Jack Donnelly and the nutrition dilemma

Jack is a qualified sports scientist at a professional football club. He works with the club's academy, where boys and girls from 9 to 16 years old are developed into football players. Jack is responsible for a range of duties, including monitoring all the players' height and weight throughout the training season, and working with coaches to set training programmes, improve fitness and give nutritional advice.

A balanced diet is vital for the players' health, well-being and sports performance, so Jack must make sure the

advice he gives is up-to-date and correct so the players, regardless of their age or ability, get the best out of their sessions with him. He gets to work with all ages as part of his job and having the opportunity to improve their dietary habits is rewarding.

Recently, Jack was approached by the parents of an under-9 player who were worried that their son would not eat much in the way of fruit or vegetables. They were concerned it might be affecting his performance as he was tired after training and matches.

Check your knowledge

1 Discuss as a group what advice you would give the parents if you were in Jack's position.

2 Come up with a five-point plan that deals with the gaps in the player's diet and explains to the parents what they need to consider when addressing their son's eating habits.

3 Present this plan as a verbal discussion, in an email to the parents or by producing a leaflet that could be used as guidelines for similar occasions.

▶ **Reducing salt intake** – Too much salt can raise your blood pressure, putting you at increased risk of heart disease and strokes. A diet high in salt can raise your blood pressure (hypertension) – this condition currently affects more than one third of adults in the UK. Adding salt to your diet is often unnecessary: 75 per cent of the salt we eat is already in our diet in the form of bread and breakfast cereals. Reducing added salt is only a small part of the solution. You need to become aware of the salt that is already in the foods you buy, and choose lower-salt options. Adults should eat no more than 6 g of salt per day.

▶ **Healthy alternatives** – Opting for a healthier diet may simply involve small changes to what you eat. Try to eat fewer foods high in fat, salt or sugars and substitute them with fruit or vegetables. For example, choose skimmed or semi-skimmed milk instead of full-fat milk, or wholegrain instead of white bread. A simple way to monitor your diet and what you eat is to look at the front-of-pack red, amber and green nutrition labels. These have been in effect since 2013 and show you if the food has high, medium or low amounts of fat, saturated fat, sugars and salt.

Healthy eating can also involve adding new foods to your diet. Soya foods can simulate meat and dairy products such as milk, cheese and yogurt. Soya offers health benefits as it is high in protein, vitamins, minerals and fibre. Vegetarians tend to enjoy diets high in carbohydrates, fibre and vitamins. Research shows vegetarians are less likely to suffer from obesity, type 2 diabetes and hypertension.

❚❚ PAUSE POINT   Do you understand the elements of a balanced diet and their contribution to general health and well-being?

> Hint   A balanced diet consists of the correct amounts of nutrients required by the body.

> Extend   What additional sources of information are available to you that support and promote a positive lifestyle in terms of a balanced diet?

Positive risk-taking activities

Not all risk-taking is bad. In fact, some risks are good and promote healthy development. Risk-taking is linked to developmental changes in the brain that help you to become a healthy adult. An element of positive risk-taking is necessary for children and young adults so they can test their boundaries and develop as individuals.

Discussion

Research shows that many children in the UK prefer to watch television, play computer games or go online rather than play outdoors, and parents – for a variety of reasons – simply agree to their children's less active preferences. Do you think a childhood that lacks outdoor play will have a detrimental effect on later adult life? Discuss this complex issue as a class debate.

Outdoor and adventurous activities

Outdoor and adventurous activities are increasingly popular with adults as team-building exercises or as part of their continued professional development (CPD). What makes these activities risky is that they involve the potential for failure. Learning how to win and lose, succeed and fail, take risks to help others and meet challenges in unfamiliar surroundings are important factors for people's development.

Safety tip

Although risks should always be minimised to prevent harm or injury, these risks can be managed to be within acceptable boundaries to promote healthy development. To achieve this, you should consider what might cause harm and decide if you are taking reasonable steps to prevent this from happening.

Key terms

Endorphins – hormones that reduce the sensation of pain and affect emotions, generally in a positive way, during and after exercise.

Neurotransmitter – a chemical released across a synapse of a neurone (the space between two neurones where signals are passed) which affects the activity of muscle fibres or organs.

Endorphin release

Have you heard of thrill-seekers feeling ecstatic after a bungee jump or a tandem parachute jump? This 'high' is because **endorphins** are released into the brain when you exercise. Endorphins are **neurotransmitters**, chemicals that can be linked with an energetic and positive outlook on life. They possess other potential benefits too, by:

▶ reducing stress
▶ helping to fight anxiety and depression
▶ boosting self-esteem
▶ promoting restful sleep.

Improved confidence

Exercise can impact your health and well-being by improving your confidence in a number of ways.

▶ You feel better physically and mentally, helping to develop a positive attitude.
▶ Exercise can help build your self-esteem by improving the physical condition of your body and how you think about it.
▶ When you witness what your body is physically capable of, your self-confidence may increase.
▶ You feel a sense of accomplishment from achieving your exercise goals.

Government recommendation/guidelines

UK government recommendations

To promote a healthy population, the UK government issues guidelines. The hope is that people will follow these suggestions and enjoy a healthy lifestyle, reducing the amount of money the NHS has to spend to combat obesity and smoking-related disease.

In terms of **physical activity**, the government advises adults aged 19–64 years old to do two types of exercise each week: aerobic and strength exercises. The reccomendations for children are slightly different (see Table 2.4).

▶ **Table 2.4:** Government advice on physical activity

Age of participants	Types of exercise
Children aged 5–18 years old	At least 60 minutes of physical activity every day such as cycling and playground activities, and vigorous activity, such as running or tennis. On three days a week, these activities should involve exercises for strong muscles, such as push-ups, and exercises for strong bones, such as running and jumping.
Adults 19–64 years old	Should be active daily and should do at least 150 minutes of moderate aerobic activity such as cycling or fast walking every week, and strength exercises on two or more days a week that work all the major muscle groups.

Alcohol is a drug that affects every organ in your body. It is a central nervous system depressant that is quickly absorbed by your stomach and small intestine into the bloodstream. 'Binge drinking' (excessive alcohol consumption in a single day or night) is a major public health concern. Current government guidelines for **alcohol consumption** are 14 units per week for men and women (equivalent to about half a pint of lager, beer or cider or one 175 ml glass of wine per day). Any alcohol intake should be spread across a week to avoid binges and should include two or three alcohol-free days each week. One unit is equivalent to 8 grams of alcohol, typically a small glass of wine, half a pint of beer, lager or cider, or a single pub measure of spirits.

The government takes **healthy eating** seriously and has introduced a number of initiatives designed to encourage improved dietary practices – see Table 2.5 for more details.

▶ **Table 2.5:** Government healthy eating initiatives

Initiative	Details
Love your labels	The best way of checking what you are eating is to look at food labels, as they can tell you what is inside the food. Once you know how to use them, you will soon be able to make healthier choices when shopping.
Eatwell Guide	The Eatwell Guide helps you eat a balanced diet by showing you how much of each type of food to eat at each meal.
Eat a little slower	It takes time for the brain to register you are full, so try to pace yourself and eat more slowly.
Aim to feel satisfied, not stuffed	Try eating just one plate of food and do not go back for seconds.

Negative lifestyle factors and their effects on health and well-being

Smoking

Tobacco smoke contains **nicotine** and tar which are both damaging to health. When you smoke, more than 7000 chemicals spread throughout your body and all of your organs. Nicotine is one of these chemicals, a powerful drug that causes addiction. It stimulates the central nervous system and increases heart rate and blood pressure. Tar is a complex mixture of chemicals, many of which cause cancer. Tar largely collects in the respiratory tract and is then gradually absorbed.

Health risks associated with smoking

The risk of disease increases not only with the volume of smoking and number of years smoked, but also how deeply the smoke is inhaled.

▶ **Coronary heart disease (CHD)** – a generic term to describe conditions caused by an interrupted or reduced flow of blood through the coronary arteries to the heart. Smokers have a higher risk of developing **atherosclerosis** (a build-up of fatty deposits in the arteries) which is a primary contributor to CHD. Smoking alone leads to an increased risk, but when it is combined with other risk factors – such as high blood pressure, high cholesterol and physical inactivity – it increases the likelihood of the blood clotting, leading to a heart attack.

▶ **Cancer** – lung cancer is the most common form of cancer worldwide and the type most commonly associated with smoking. The earlier in life you begin to smoke, the higher your risk of developing lung cancer. A study of ex-smokers showed those who started smoking before the age of 15 had twice as many cell mutations (a key factor in the development of cancer) as those who started after the age of 20. Smoking not only leads to an increased risk of cancer in the lungs – studies have shown it is also linked to cancers of the mouth, oesophagus, bladder, breast, cervix, colon, liver and kidneys.

▶ **Lung disease** – smokers are likely to suffer more respiratory tract infections than non-smokers. They are more likely to suffer from colds and flu, and take longer to recover. Pneumonia is a serious lung infection and is more likely to be fatal among smokers due to the effects of smoking on their lungs. Smoking is by far the biggest cause of **emphysema**, a chronic disease of the lungs that causes breathing

Key term

Nicotine – an addictive chemical found in tobacco that stimulates the central nervous system. Research suggests nicotine has a negative impact on physical performance because of its effects on the cardiorespiratory system.

difficulties. Emphysema leads to damage to the tissues supporting the shape and function of the lungs. Sufferers' lungs are gradually unable to hold their shape properly when they exhale, making the lungs inefficient when transferring oxygen into, and removing carbon dioxide from, the blood. This leads to about 25,000 deaths in the UK each year.

▶ **Bronchitis** – a condition that inflames the lining of the bronchial tubes; it can be an **acute** or **chronic** condition. The most common symptom of bronchitis is coughing. Acute bronchitis is often caused by a viral or bacterial infection, while chronic bronchitis is most often seen in smokers. Smoking causes damage to the **cilia** lining the airways; over time they become less efficient at clearing debris and irritants, making the lungs more susceptible to infection.

▶ **Infertility** – smokers are likely to have more fertility problems than non-smokers. Female smokers have an increased chance of developing ovulation problems. Male smokers can suffer a lower sperm count and erectile dysfunction. Second-hand or passive smoking is also linked to fertility problems, as well as a range of other health-related issues.

Key terms

Acute – a condition which develops rapidly and occurs for a short duration.

Chronic – a condition which develops slowly and occurs over a long duration.

Cilia – tiny hairs that protect the respiratory tract by filtering particles and mucus away from the lungs.

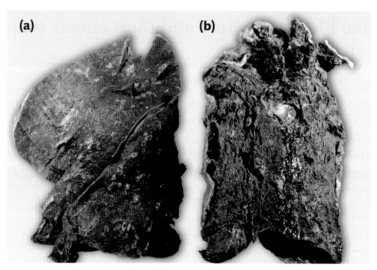

(a)   (b)

▶ The internal effects of smoking: (a) a healthy lung and (b) a smokers lung

Alcohol

Moderate alcohol consumption is thought to help reduce the risks of heart disease. However, too much alcohol can cause health problems such as malnutrition, cirrhosis of the liver, certain types of cancer and psychological health problems.

Health risks associated with excessive alcohol consumption

▶ **Stroke** – this occurs when brain tissue dies as a result of sudden and severe disruption of blood flow to the brain. Heavy alcohol use is associated with increased risk of stroke.

▶ **Cirrhosis** – chronic abuse of alcohol over a prolonged period can lead to cirrhosis, the progressive replacement of healthy liver tissue with **scar tissue**, which may result in liver failure and death.

▶ **Hypertension** – the relationship between alcohol use and blood pressure is important as hypertension is a key factor in the risk of coronary heart disease and stroke. Hypertension is defined as a **systolic blood pressure** above 140 mm Hg and a **diastolic blood pressure** above 90 mm Hg.

▶ **Depression** – excessive alcohol consumption can cause depression. Alcohol dependence and depression can occur together, and depression is commonly reported in people being treated for alcohol dependence.

Key terms

Scar tissue – connective tissue replacing damaged tissue that failed to heal itself.

Systolic blood pressure – pressure exerted in the arteries when the heart contracts.

Diastolic blood pressure – pressure exerted in the arteries when the heart relaxes and fills with blood.

⏸ PAUSE POINT Do you understand the likely risks of excessive alcohol consumption to health and well-being?

> **Hint** Think about the four main health conditions associated with excessive alcohol consumption.

> **Extend** Find out, from government statistics, how many people were affected by each of these four health conditions in the last calendar year.

Stress

Stress is a physiological and mental response to your environment. Factors that lead to stress are known as 'stressors' and they take on different forms. Potential stressors include major life events, such as divorce and moving house; injury or trauma; and environmental situations such as a demanding work environment or even sporting competition. Whatever the stressor, the responses usually include feelings of **anxiety** and tension.

Health risks associated with excessive stress

Many health problems are caused by, or exacerbated by, stress.

▸ **Hypertension** – the body produces a surge of hormones (**adrenaline** and **cortisol**) when faced with a stressful situation. These hormones – adrenaline in particular – cause a temporary sharp increase in blood pressure. These short-term spikes in blood pressure added together over time may put you at risk of developing long-term hypertension.

▸ **Angina** – associated with chest pain and usually a symptom of coronary heart disease (CHD) when the narrowing and hardening of the coronary arteries limits blood flow to the heart. Stress increases heart rate and blood pressure, and if the coronary arteries are narrowed, the blood will be unable to reach the heart efficiently, often causing chest pain.

▸ **Stroke** – stress causes a temporary rise in blood pressure. The main cause of stroke is high blood pressure which, in turn, can weaken the arteries in the brain and make them split or rupture, causing a bleed on or around the brain.

▸ **Heart attack** – although it is difficult to link stress directly with heart attacks, symptoms of stress (such as hypertension and the exposure to persistently high levels of stress hormones) may contribute to heart attacks.

▸ **Stomach ulcers** – it was believed that lifestyle factors such as stress and alcohol caused stomach ulcers. However, recent research suggests there is little evidence to confirm this, though such lifestyle factors may make the symptoms of a stomach ulcer worse.

▸ **Depression** – short-term stress can be good for you – it keeps you alert and ready for action. However, chronic stress can lead to depression. If stress responses fail to shut off once a difficult situation passes, elevated levels of cortisol and reduced levels of serotonin, a 'feel good' hormone, can lead to depression.

> **Key terms**
>
> **Anxiety** – a feeling of apprehension and heightened physiological tension.
>
> **Adrenaline** – a hormone responsible for preparing the body for the 'fight or flight' mechanism by increasing heart rate, breathing rate and metabolic rate. It can also improve the force of muscle action and delay the onset of fatigue.
>
> **Cortisol** – a hormone associated with stress that increases blood sugar levels, suppresses the immune system and aids the metabolism of macronutrients.

Lack of sleep

Health risks associated with lack of sleep

Sleep allows your body to rest and restore itself and plays a vital role in healthy living. Getting the right amount of sleep can help protect your mental and physical health, and improve your quality of life. A lack of sleep is linked with an increased risk of heart disease.

Research by the National Sleep Foundation suggests that a healthy adult requires between seven and nine hours of sleep per night. Athletes often require more sleep due to the added recovery and repair requirements as a consequence of training.

▶ **Depression** – one of the symptoms of depression is insomnia or an inability to sleep properly. This in turn can have a negative effect on general health and well-being, leading to a cycle of chronic mental and physical symptoms if not treated.

▶ **Overeating** – how much we sleep plays an important role in regulating how much we eat, the number of calories we burn and when we eat. Eating when we should be sleeping may increase weight gain.

Sedentary lifestyle

Physical inactivity in general terms counts as doing less than 30 minutes physical activity per week. **Sedentary** behaviour refers to activities that use little energy (for example, watching television or sitting down). Physical inactivity and sedentary behaviour have both been shown to be significant risk factors in the increase in chronic diseases such as CHD, stroke, type 2 diabetes, certain types of cancer and hypertension. Physical inactivity can also add to feelings of depression.

Key term

Sedentary – applied to an individual who is relatively inactive and has a lifestyle characterised by sitting.

Lifestyle modification techniques

Common barriers to change

Poor health is a drain on national resources and increases the amount spent on healthcare by the government. However, many people encounter difficulties in living a healthy lifestyle. Age, ethnicity and social and economic status may all present challenges to achieving wellness.

▶ **Time** – modern lifestyles are busy and time seems to be at a premium. Working hours constantly change and working from 9 a.m. to 5 p.m. is not the norm for everyone. Finding the time to exercise or simply undertake some form of physical activity may prove difficult. To overcome this, some people put more physical activity into how they get to work (such as cycling), what they do at work, or what they do during their leisure time. It is important to make an effort to exercise during the day and try to enjoy it.

▶ **Cost** – if people have the time and money, they can join a gym. If not, some forms of physical activity are basically free. Walking to work or increasing the physical activity you do at home (for example, housework or gardening) does not cost anything. Buying a pair of running shoes and a tracksuit and going walking or jogging is another cheaper alternative to a gym.

▶ **Transport** – many gyms, health clubs and even open spaces are only a short car journey away. Not everyone has access to a car though, so many people rely on public transport to get there. This may add an additional expense. How reliant on a car are you for journeys of less than 5 miles? Could you walk or cycle any of these journeys? It would save you money and help to increase your fitness levels.

▶ **Location** – where you live often influences your lifestyle choices. The availability of leisure activities, their cost and the ease in getting there often decide the type and level of physical activity we do. However, we often forget what we can do in our immediate surroundings. If, for example, you live in a flat, you could walk up and down the stairs instead of taking the lift. Always consider how your location and environment can be used for maximum exercise benefit.

Strategies to increase physical activity levels

Despite the strong case for keeping active, many people find it difficult to take up exercise. For some people exercise conjures up unpleasant thoughts, such as boring exercise classes, or rough competitive sports with a risk of injury.

People who have never exercised before, or who are in poor shape, should not expect immediate results. Achieving physical fitness requires time and consistency, but there are strategies that can be used in their everyday lives to help produce improvements.

At home

Increasing physical activity at home is probably easier than you think. Its main advantage is that you can manage your own time, and it will help to encourage others (such as children) to be active. Activities can be added to daily routines and household chores can be enhanced to increase general fitness, for example:

▶ going for a short walk – from 10–30 minutes – before breakfast

▶ doing housework instead of hiring someone to do it or, if you already do your own housework, doing it more vigorously

▶ standing up while talking on the telephone

▶ gardening – just 30 minutes per day will help improve fitness levels

▶ taking a dog for a walk.

At work

Evidence suggests that moderate-intensity lifestyle activities, such as taking the stairs instead of the lift, can be more successfully promoted than vigorous exercise programmes. Stair climbing can occur throughout the day and, with an energy cost of approximately 8–10 kcals per minute, can help with weight control, as well as leg power, bone strength and cardiovascular fitness. People can also be encouraged to go for a run or gentle jog during their lunch hour for 20 minutes – leaving time for a shower and something to eat.

During leisure time

There are lots of opportunities for physical activity during leisure time. If time permits, people can play a new sport, join a club that promotes physical activity (walks, tours, dancing, etc.) or plan family outings that include physical activity (such as hiking, walking, swimming, etc.). People can also listen to music – which can increase motivation – while exercising. Whatever they choose, as it is their leisure time, they should enjoy it.

Method of transport

Scientific evidence supports the benefits of regular walking for health and well-being. It is an easy and economical way to become and stay active. All ages can participate and it can be a social activity.

To achieve health benefits, you will aim for 10,000 steps a day (about 5 miles). The average sedentary individual achieves around 2000–3000 steps a day. If they can walk to a destination rather than taking the car or bus, they may be surprised how many additional steps – and calories – they will use. A **pedometer** can be used as a motivational tool to measure progress towards achieving a target. A sensible approach to reaching the 10,000 a day target is to increase daily steps by 500 each week until the 10,000 target is reached. If a person commutes to work, they could increase their steps by getting off a stop earlier and walking the remaining distance.

> **Key term**
>
> **Pedometer** – an instrument for estimating the distance travelled on foot by recording the number of steps taken. Many smartphones now include a pedometer app.

With around 70 per cent of all car trips being less than 5 miles, cycling can be an excellent form of transport, not least because you can cover much greater distances than when walking. Cycling is also an effective and enjoyable form of exercise. Daily cycling has been shown to lead to significant health benefits. People of most fitness levels can participate in cycling, although anyone with heart disease or other pre-existing conditions should consult their doctor beforehand.

Ⅱ   PAUSE POINT   Can you recognise and explain the barriers to changing a sedentary lifestyle?

> Hint   Using paper, a whiteboard or a tablet, list the barriers to change.
>
> Extend   How best do you think these barriers can be overcome? How would you go about changing or advising people with a sedentary lifestyle?

Quitting smoking strategies

Smoking increases the risk of lung cancer and heart disease. As with most behaviour-changing goals, to give up smoking the smoker must want to stop. After this there are several methods that can help.

▶ **Acupuncture** – a traditional Chinese therapy which may help someone to stop smoking by increasing the body's production of mood-enhancing endorphins that reduce or alleviate withdrawal symptoms.

▶ **NHS smoking helpline** – this was launched in 2000 as part of an initiative to encourage 1.5 million people in the UK to stop smoking by 2010. The helpline offers information, advice and support.

▶ **NHS smoking services** – the range of services promoted include group and one-to-one counselling and information on nicotine replacement therapy. Studies show you are more likely to quit smoking if you do it through the NHS.

▶ **Nicotine replacement therapy** – this refers to a range of products (gums, patches, lozenges and sprays) available to help smokers give up. They are available on prescription and are suitable for most smokers, although pregnant women or anyone taking regular medication should consult their doctor first. Unlike cigarettes, they do not contain the harmful cancer-causing toxic chemicals.

▶ **Quit Kit support packs** – funded by the NHS, these kits offer free support. Smokers can obtain a Quit Kit, download an app, and receive an email programme or text messages that will help keep them focused on giving up smoking.

Strategies to reduce alcohol consumption

Key term

Alcoholism – a chronic disorder characterised by a dependence on alcohol.

When alcohol consumption becomes both excessive and frequent, it has a severe and negative impact on health. This is called **alcoholism**. Alcoholics have an intense craving for alcohol and become physically dependent on it. Alcoholism is serious, but recovery is possible if the alcoholic is strongly motivated to stop. Some possible treatments are covered below.

▶ **Self-help groups** – successful treatment depends on sufferers recognising they have a problem. Self-help groups such as Alcoholics Anonymous (AA) help many sufferers through a step-by-step recovery programme.

▶ **Counselling** – individual or group counselling is provided by specially trained therapists; this might involve other family members as well. Counselling and therapy often focus on exploring and developing awareness of the triggers for alcohol consumption and on changing behaviour. Relapse, or slipping back into previous habits, is often high for alcoholics, so preventing this is a key feature of the process.

Treatment for alcohol abuse often begins with detoxification and withdrawal from alcohol. This is necessary when alcohol consumption has continued for long periods of time. It can be an uncomfortable process with unpleasant withdrawal symptoms. In extreme cases it can be fatal (which is why detoxification is usually undertaken under supervision within an alcohol treatment facility).

▶ **Alternative treatments** – some alcohol users may seek alternative treatments and therapies such as acupuncture and hypnosis which are thought to lessen the symptoms of withdrawal. However, there are mixed views about their value within the medical profession.

Ⅱ PAUSE POINT   Do you understand the effects of alcohol on the body?

         Hint   Consider three of the negative implications (physical and/or mental) of excessive alcohol consumption on health and well-being.

         Extend   Research the impact of excessive alcohol consumption on the lives of former footballers George Best, Tony Adams or Paul Merson. Has the modern footballer's approach to alcohol consumption changed and, if so, how?

Stress management techniques

There are two general approaches to controlling stress.
▶ Try to reduce the amount of overall stress.
▶ Develop coping or stress management techniques.

To reduce overall stress, the factors promoting stress should be identified and, if possible, eliminated or reduced. Careful time management and prioritisation of workloads and commitments may help an individual to manage their stress better.

It is not possible to eliminate all the stresses in daily life. Therefore, having techniques or participating in activities to reduce stress levels will have a positive impact on health and well-being. Exercise can be viewed as a positive stress for the body. Other ways to manage stress are described below.

▶ **Assertiveness training** – the ability to express your feelings and rights while respecting those of others. Assertiveness may come naturally to some, but it is a skill that can be learned. It can help people deal with conflict situations that may be a cause of stress in their daily life.

▶ **Goal setting** – properly set goals can be motivating and rewarding. Achieving these goals can build self-confidence and reduce stress.

▶ **Time management** – this is a critical element of effective stress management. Time management is about achieving your tasks in good time by using techniques such as goal setting, task planning and minimising time spent on unproductive activities.

▶ **Physical activity** – this can have a positive effect on anxiety, depression, self-esteem and mood. It can be a stress reliever by producing an outlet for frustration, releasing endorphins (the 'feel good' hormones that lift mood) and providing a distraction from stressors.

▶ **Positive self-talk** – this is the inner dialogue you have with yourself. It influences most of your emotional life and reflects how you respond to your thoughts, feelings and actions. Self-talk can be negative or positive. Positive self-talk involves taking an optimistic view of life and your situation. In daily life you will face many challenges, difficulties and deadlines – taking a positive view of these and having constructive ways of dealing with them helps to reduce and manage stress.

▶ **Relaxation** – relaxation is not lying on a sofa or going to sleep but a mentally active process that ensures the body is relaxed and calm. When you relax, a series of responses are activated that decrease your heart rate, lower your breathing rate, decrease your blood pressure and help your muscles to relax. There is no single relaxation technique that works for everyone, but techniques such as meditation or breathing techniques generally work for most people.

- **Breathing techniques** – exercises that focus on breathing are a simple way of trying to control or reduce stress. They involve controlled inhalation and exhalation, and are best undertaken when the participant is quiet and comfortable.
- **Meditation** – meditation produces a deep state of relaxation and a calm mind. During meditation, an individual will focus their attention on eliminating any thoughts causing stress. This can promote a sense of calm and balance that benefits both physical and mental well-being.

▶ **Alternative therapies** – these can work best when used alongside traditional treatment such as counselling or medication. Alternative therapies can include herbal remedies. Research continues to investigate the effects of herbal remedies to treat stress and anxiety, so it is a good idea to speak with your doctor before beginning any alternative treatment since some herbal remedies can cause complications if combined with certain prescription medicines.

▶ **Changes to work–life balance** – the pressure of an increasingly demanding work culture is a significant factor on stress levels. People can think more about their approach to work and consider:
- taking proper breaks at work
- ensuring a line is drawn between work and leisure by trying not to take work home
- informing employers if you feel stressed
- using relaxation techniques after work
- engaging in leisure activities and spending time with family and friends.

Assessment practice 2.1

You have secured a position as an assistant community coach at a local tennis club as part of your course's work experience requirement. In addition to assisting the full-time coach with fitness coaching and fitness programming for boys and girls aged from 9 to 16, you have been asked to design a presentation on general health and well-being as part of an induction evening at the tennis club.

The club is expecting about 30–40 sets of parents and their children, the players. You are on first and you have a 30-minute slot (20 minutes for the presentation and 10 minutes for questions and answers). The general manager of the club has asked you to prepare a presentation in a format of your choice (PowerPoint, posters, slideshow, etc.) but it must address the following key points:
- positive lifestyle factors
- negative lifestyle factors
- lifestyle modification techniques.

You will need to carry out some research on these three points and demonstrate you understand what each of the three points mean and how they may be applicable to your audience (players and parents). Make sure your presentation is relevant and informative. You will need to outline the importance of the positive lifestyle factors and how they might benefit performance, how the negative factors can contribute to an unhealthy lifestyle and a likely decrease in performance, and how lifestyle modification techniques may help reduce unhealthy practices.

Plan
- What is the task? What is my presentation being asked to address?
- How confident do I feel in my own abilities to complete this task? Are there any areas I think I may struggle with?

Do
- I know how to examine lifestyle factors and their effect on health and well-being.
- I can identify when my presentation may have gone wrong and adjust my thinking/approach to get myself back on course.

Review
- I can explain what the task was and how I approached the construction of my presentation.
- I can explain how I would approach the more difficult elements differently next time (i.e. what I would do differently).

Understand the screening processes for training programming

Screening processes

Poor training programmes or the wrong type of training lead to a lack of motivation and few training gains. Collecting appropriate information about your client through an efficient screening process that may include goals, lifestyle information, medical history and physical activity history, means you will produce a more effective programme for your client.

Screening questionnaires

Lifestyle questionnaires

When designing a training programme, you need to know about the client's lifestyle factors such as alcohol intake, diet, time availability, occupation, family and financial situation – all of these will influence how you design their training programme. The training programme should be built into a routine rather than becoming an extra stress, as this will help your client to stick with the programme and will produce the best results. You can gather this information using a lifestyle questionnaire similar to the one shown in Figure 2.3.

Physical Activity Readiness Questionnaires (PAR-Q)

For most people, physical activity is safe and will pose no problems or hazards. However, some people will need to check with their doctor before they start regular physical exercise. Completion of a PAR-Q is a recommended first step if a client is planning to start or increase the amount of regular exercise they undertake. The PAR-Q is designed to identify those people for whom physical activity might be inappropriate, or who should consider medical advice regarding which type of activity will be most suitable for them.

If your client is aged between 15 and 69 years old, the PAR-Q will tell you if they should check with their doctor before they start. If your client is over 69 years old, and not used to being physically active, it is vital they check with their doctor before starting a physical exercise programme. Before you design an exercise programme for a client, ensure your client answers a PAR-Q of a similar format to the example in Figure 2.4.

If a client answers 'Yes' to one or more questions on the PAR-Q, they need to talk to their doctor before taking any fitness tests or starting a training programme. If a female client is, or may be, pregnant they should also consult a doctor before starting.

Legal considerations

Collecting information about your client is important, not only to make your programme effective, but also for health and safety reasons. If you are a self-employed fitness instructor or personal trainer, it is also important for your own insurance. Remember that the information you possess about clients is privileged and is subject to the **Data Protection Act**. This means you have to keep their personal information secure and inaccessible to other people. Client confidentiality should be maintained at all times.

Before you being any training programme, or administer any health or fitness test, you must make sure your client has completed an informed consent form. This shows that you have given your client all the information they need about what the programme or test will involve and any possible consequences. You can find out more about informed consent forms in *Unit 5: Application of Fitness Testing*.

> **Key term**
>
> **Data Protection Act** – a law that controls how personal information is used by organisations, businesses or the government.

Lifestyle questionnaire

Work
1. What is your occupation?
2. How physically demanding is your job?   ☐ Not at all ☐ Moderately ☐ Extremely
3. On an average day, how much time do you spend sitting down?   ☐ 0–2 hours ☐ 2–5 hours ☐ 5–10 hours ☐ 10+ hours
Sleep
4. How many hours of sleep do you usually get each night?
5. When you wake up, do you feel refreshed?   ☐ Always ☐ Usually ☐ Occasionally ☐ Never
6. Do you have trouble falling asleep or often wake up at night?   ☐ Always ☐ Usually ☐ Occasionally ☐ Never
Lifestyle
7. Do you smoke? ☐ Yes ☐ No
8. If yes, roughly how many cigarettes do you smoke each day?
9. If you have smoked in the past, how long ago did you stop?
10. Do you drink alcohol? ☐ Yes ☐ No
11. If yes, roughly how many units of alcohol do you drink per week?
Exercise
12. On a scale of 1–10 (1 = not active, 10 = very active), how active are you on a daily basis?   1 2 3 4 5 6 7 8 9 10
13. What exercise do you do in an average week? (*e.g. Do you participate in a regular sporting activity, or go to the gym on a regular basis?*)

▶ **Figure 2.3:** An example lifestyle questionnaire

PHYSICAL ACTIVITY READINESS QUESTIONNAIRE (PAR-Q)

1.	Has your doctor ever told you that you have a heart condition and should only do physical activity recommended by a doctor?	☐ Yes ☐ No
2.	Have you ever felt pain in your chest when you do physical exercise?	☐ Yes ☐ No
3.	Have you ever felt pain in your chest when NOT exercising?	☐ Yes ☐ No
4.	Have you ever suffered from unusual shortness of breath while resting or during mild exercise?	☐ Yes ☐ No
5.	Do you often feel faint, have dizzy spells, or lose consciousness?	☐ Yes ☐ No
6.	Has your doctor ever told you that you have a bone or joint problem that could be made worse by exercise?	☐ Yes ☐ No
7.	Do you have high blood pressure?	☐ Yes ☐ No
8.	Do you have low blood pressure?	☐ Yes ☐ No
9.	Do you have insulin-dependent diabetes or any other metabolic disease?	☐ Yes ☐ No
10.	Has your doctor ever told you that you have high cholesterol levels?	☐ Yes ☐ No
11.	Are you currently taking any prescribed medication?	☐ Yes ☐ No
12.	Is there any history of coronary heart disease in your family?	☐ Yes ☐ No
13.	Are you, or is there any possibility you might be, pregnant?	☐ Yes ☐ No

If you answered Yes to any of these questions, please provide details below.

....

▶ **Figure 2.4:** An example PAR-Q

⏸ PAUSE POINT   At which point during a screening process would you refer a client to see a GP?

Hint   Think about the questions on the PAR-Q and answers that might raise concerns.

Extend   How would you tell a client that they might be unable to continue with their health tests, training programme and exercise? What skills should you ideally possess to explain your decision?

Health monitoring tests and their results

Before planning a training programme for a client, you should also do some health monitoring tests. These include calculating their blood pressure, heart rate, body mass index (BMI) and waist-to-hip ratio. These tests can be done again during and after the fitness programme to help measure progress.

It is important to follow the correct protocol when undertaking health monitoring tests. If you do a test one way and then re-do it in a slightly different way, the results will be invalid and you will not be able to compare against normative data (see below). Always bear in mind that the client may be nervous during a test – health-related tests can have far-reaching outcomes, so always treat your client with courtesy and respect and try to help them relax.

Interpreting results against normative data

You can use published data interpretation tables to compare your clients' results against data for sports performers and elite athletes. Your choice when selecting data tables for interpretation of fitness test results will depend on your selected individual, their needs and their personal goals. However, most individuals will be interested to know how they compare against normative data.

PAUSE POINT How might negative lifestyle factors discussed in this unit influence the results of a resting heart rate test?

Hint Consider how each of the negative lifestyle factors might affect resting heart rate. Use websites such as **www.nhs.uk/Livewell** to find more information.

Extend What are the signs that a client may be under the influence of negative lifestyle factors? Make a list of what to look out for.

Population norms

Making judgements about the results of health monitoring tests can be subjective. You should bear in mind that you are dealing with an individual, and individuals are all different. When judging tests against population norms, remember that these norms are benchmarks that exist to guide your next action with your client. They are not a method of diagnosing a client with an illness or disorder.

Norms for sports performance

It is difficult to interpret norms for sports performance. The best advice that can be given is that they should be between the population average and elite athletes.

Norms for elite athletes

It is reasonable to expect the results of health monitoring tests for elite athletes to be at the top end of what can be expected. There are no definitive data sets for elite athletes, but it is fair to say that it is unlikely someone would be able to compete at an elite level if their test results were average compared to population norms.

Blood pressure test

Blood pressure can be measured using a digital blood pressure monitor, which provides a reading of blood pressure as: systolic blood pressure/diastolic blood pressure (expressed in units of mm Hg).

Accepted health ranges

Table 2.6 shows the accepted health ranges of blood pressure results for men and women.

▶ **Table 2.6:** Accepted blood pressure ranges for men and women

Rating	Blood pressure reading (mm Hg)
Average (desirable)	120/80 mm Hg
Above average (borderline hypertension)	140/90 mm Hg
High blood pressure (hypertension)	160/100 mm Hg*

* An individual should seek advice from their GP if blood pressure is >160/100 mm Hg on at least two separate occasions.

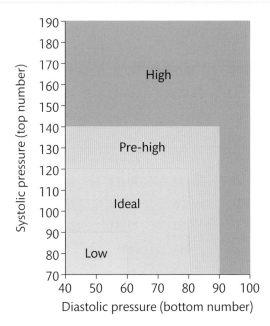

▶ **Figure 2.5:** Blood pressure chart

Ⅱ PAUSE POINT   What might you need to keep in mind when conducting a blood pressure test? What anomalies might occur during the test and why?

Hint   Think about how you might feel if you were having your blood pressure tested.

Extend   How might you prepare a client for fitness tests? What strategies might you use to ensure your tests are accurate and your client is relaxed?

Resting heart rate test

This can be measured manually via the radial artery in the wrist or using a digital blood pressure monitor. Resting heart rate is measured in beats per minute (bpm). The average resting heart rate for a male is 68 bpm and for a female is 72 bpm. This difference is because males generally have larger hearts than females, which can pump a greater volume of oxygenated blood around the body per beat. A high resting heart rate (**tachycardia**) is above 100 bpm.

Key term

Tachycardia – a fast heart rate characterised by a resting heart rate of over 100 bpm or 20–30 beats above normal heart rate.

Accepted health ranges

Tables 2.7 and 2.8 show the accepted health ranges for men and women.

▶ **Table 2.7:** Resting heart rate data for men (bpm)

Age	18–25	26–35	36–45	46–55	56–65	65+
Athlete	49–55	49–54	50–56	50–57	51–56	50–55
Excellent	56–61	55–61	57–62	58–63	57–61	56–61
Good	62–65	62–65	63–66	64–67	62–67	62–65
Above average	66–69	66–70	67–70	68–71	68–71	66–69
Average	70–73	71–74	71–75	72–76	72–75	70–73
Below average	74–81	75–81	76–82	77–83	76–81	74–79
Poor	82+	82+	83+	84+	82+	80+

▶ **Table 2.8:** Resting heart rate data for women (bpm)

Age	18–25	26–35	36–45	46–55	56–65	65+
Athlete	54–60	54–59	54–59	54–60	54–59	54–59
Excellent	61–65	60–64	60–64	61–65	60–64	60–64
Good	66–69	65–68	65–69	66–69	65–68	65–68
Above average	70–73	69–72	70–73	70–73	69–73	69–72
Average	74–78	73–76	74–78	74–77	74–77	73–76
Below average	79–84	77–82	79–84	78–83	78–83	77–84
Poor	85+	83+	85+	84+	84+	84+

Body mass index (BMI) test

BMI is a measure of **body composition** (expressed in kg/m^2) and is used to determine whether a person is a healthy weight. It is only an estimate, as the test does not take into account the individual's frame size or muscle mass.

To calculate someone's BMI:

1 Measure the individual's body weight in kilograms and height in metres.
2 Divide their weight by their height.
3 Divide the answer by their height again to find a value for their BMI (expressed in kg/m^2).

Research shows a significant relationship between high BMI and incidence of cardiovascular disease, and high BMI and diabetes. The risk of cardiovascular disease increases sharply at a BMI of 27.8 kg/m^2 for men and 27.3 kg/m^2 for women.

Worked example

A man is 1.8m tall and weighs 78 kg. Calculate his BMI.

1 $78 \div 1.8 = 43.33$

2 $43.33 \div 1.8 = 24.07$

The man's BMI is 24.07 kg/m^2.

Accepted health ranges

Table 2.9 shows the accepted health ranges for the BMI of both men and women.

▶ **Table 2.9:** BMI data for men and women

BMI	Comments
<18.5	You are underweight; consult your GP to discuss a plan to achieve a more healthy weight
18.5–24.9	Healthy range
25–30	Above the healthy range – you may be overweight and likely to be heavier than is healthy for someone of your height
>30	Classed as obese; being obese puts you at an increased risk of health problems (e.g. CHD, stroke and type 2 diabetes)

⏸ **PAUSE POINT** Is BMI an accurate measure of whether or not an individual is potentially overweight?

> Hint   Consider athletes such as rugby players, weightlifters and boxers. They may have BMIs over 25 but are considered elite athletes.

> Extend   What might explain these high BMIs? Think in terms of the specific types of body composition that are important in these sports.

Waist-to-hip ratio test

The waist-to-hip ratio can determine levels of obesity and help identify those at risk of heart disease. Use a tape measure placed firmly against the individual's skin to measure their waist circumference in centimetres at the narrowest level of the torso. Next, measure the individual's hips by placing the tape measure at the maximum circumference of the buttocks. Make sure the tape measure is level when taking measurements. Divide the waist measurement (cm) by the hip measurement (cm) to obtain the waist-to-hip ratio.

Accepted health ranges

A ratio of 1.0 or more in men or 0.85 or more in women indicates an individual is carrying too much weight.

Theory into practice

The results of health monitoring tests can be the first step in identifying an underlying chronic health problem or disorder that has gone unnoticed for years. Although a GP will treat any problem or disorder, they are busy professionals and may not have the time to conduct such tests on a regular basis.

What do you think are the wider social or economic benefits of trained sport scientists or sports health practitioners conducting health monitoring tests on patients for GPs as part of a referral scheme?

Your role at a local tennis club is going well and you are in the final week of your work experience requirement. Following your presentation on health and well-being, the tennis club is now offering general health checks for all members. The general manager has asked you to design a new health monitoring booklet to be used by the full-time fitness coach and given to club members. The booklet will have three sections:

1 A description of each test and why it is carried out.

2 A blank template for each test into which the results can be inserted.

3 An exemplar test with mock results filled in and analysed.

The design of the booklet is up to you, but it must be in these three parts and should include the following key features:

- PAR-Q
- written confirmation of a commitment to client confidentiality
- blood pressure test and interpretation of results
- resting heart rate test and interpretation of results
- body mass index (BMI) test and interpretation of results
- waist-to-hip ratio test and interpretation of results.

You will need to carry out research to complete this task. You should be able to show you understand each of the three sections and how the key features fit into the format of the booklet. Make sure your booklet is relevant and informative. You will need to highlight healthy results and flag up potential areas for concern (maybe using a traffic light system).

Plan
- What is the task? What is my booklet being asked to address?
- Are there any areas of the test analysis that I think I may struggle with?

Do
- I know how to design my own booklet, put a PAR-Q into practice, carry out the health monitoring tests and interpret the results of these tests correctly.
- I can identify where my booklet may have gone wrong and adjust my thinking to get back on course.

Review
- I can explain what the task was and how I approached the construction of my booklet.
- I can explain how I would approach the more difficult parts differently next time.

C Understand programme-related nutritional needs

Common terminology

The health and fitness industry uses some fairly standard terms when talking about nutrition. It is important you understand what these terms mean so that you can properly engage with other professionals working in the industry and explain the terms to your clients.

Dietary Reference Values (DRVs)

Dietary standards have been used in the UK since the 1940s. The first set of standards focused on a Recommended Daily Allowance (RDA) for each nutrient, which aimed to prevent nutritional deficiency. In the late 1980s, the government set up a panel of experts to review the RDAs and new **Dietary Reference Values** (DRVs) were established. The panel imagined a group of people and worked out the nutritional requirements of the people in that group to see what 'usual' requirements were. DRVs are now the responsibility of the European Food Safety Authority and, following a European regulation of 2011, RDAs are no longer used. The term 'dietary reference value' covers all of the following measures of nutrient intake:

▶ **Reference Nutrient Intake (RNI)** – the best estimate of the amount of nutrient considered to be sufficient for 97 per cent of people in the group.

▶ **Estimated Average Requirements (EAR)** – the nutrient intake needed to meet the average (median) requirements of the group. About half these people will usually need more than the EAR and half will usually need less.

▶ **Lower Reference Nutrient Intake (LRNI)** – the amount of a nutrient that is sufficient for only a few members of the group who have exceptionally low requirements. Intakes below the LRNI by most individuals within the group will almost certainly be inadequate.

▶ **Safe Intake (SI)** – the range of intakes of a nutrient for which there is not enough information to establish RNI, EAR or LRNI. It is an amount sufficient for the majority of the group but not so large that it causes negative side-effects.

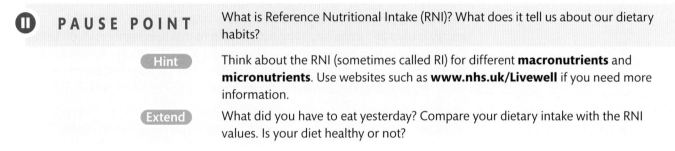

Ⅱ PAUSE POINT   What is Reference Nutritional Intake (RNI)? What does it tell us about our dietary habits?

> **Hint**   Think about the RNI (sometimes called RI) for different **macronutrients** and **micronutrients**. Use websites such as **www.nhs.uk/Livewell** if you need more information.

> **Extend**   What did you have to eat yesterday? Compare your dietary intake with the RNI values. Is your diet healthy or not?

Energy

Energy comes from the foods we eat. It is used to support your **basal metabolic rate** and all additional activity carried out at work and leisure. Energy is measured in **calories** or **joules**. As both these units are small, they are multiplied by 1000 and referred to as **kilocalories** (the UK system) or **kilojoules** (the metric or international system).

> **Key terms**
>
> **Macronutrients** – nutrients required in large amounts (carbohydrates, fats and proteins) to maintain health and well-being.
>
> **Micronutrients** – nutrients required in small amounts (vitamins and minerals) to maintain health and well-being
>
> **Basal metabolic rate (BMR)** – minimum rate of metabolism in an individual who is not digesting or absorbing food. BMR represents the lowest rate of energy usage that can sustain life.
>
> **Calories** – one calorie is the energy needed to raise the temperature of 1 gram of water by 1°C.
>
> **Joules** – 1 joule of energy moves a mass of 1 gram at a velocity of 1 metre per second. Approximately 4.2 joules = 1 calorie.
>
> **Kilocalories (kcal)** – one kilocalorie is the energy required to raise the temperature of 1 litre of water by 1°C. It is equal to 1000 calories and used to state the energy value of food. Kilocalories are often simply referred to as calories.
>
> **Kilojoules (kJ)** – a unit of energy, equivalent to 1000 joules.

Energy balance

You are in 'energy balance' when the amount of energy you take in as food and drink (your energy input) is the same as the amount of energy you expend (your energy output). You will be neither losing nor gaining weight.

There are four major components of energy output: resting metabolic rate, dietary thermogenesis, physical activity and adaptive thermogenesis.

▶ **Resting metabolic rate** (RMR) – this is the metabolic rate of a person at rest and accounts for 60–75 per cent of total energy output. It represents the largest component of the total daily energy expenditure. RMR is closely related to lean body mass and is influenced by the composition of your body: muscle tissue is much more metabolically active than fat tissue (muscle burns energy more quickly than the same weight of fat). Gains in muscle mass will result in increases in RMR. RMR is also influenced by your age, gender, and genetic background.

▶ **Dietary thermogenesis** (DT) – refers to any energy expended over RMR for digestion, absorption, transport and storage of food. It is influenced by the calorie content and composition of your diet and your own nutritional needs. High energy intakes and a regular eating pattern help to maintain higher rates of dietary thermogenesis. In a healthy individual this means that DT accounts for about 10 per cent of the total energy expenditure per day, while skipping meals and other restrictive dietary practices reduces this number.

▶ **Physical activity** (PA) – represents the most variable component of your total energy expenditure. This is the additional energy expended above RMR and DT, and in active individuals it can be the highest total daily energy use. Exactly how much it is depends on how active your general lifestyle is – how often, how energetically and for how long you participate in sport and exercise, and what type of activity you do.

▶ **Adaptive thermogenesis** (AT) – this is energy expenditure that comes from environmental or physiological stresses that may require you to respond by shivering, or stress that causes anxiety or fidgeting.

Basal metabolism

To estimate energy requirements, you first need to calculate basal metabolic rate (BMR) in kilocalories per day. The way of doing this for men and women of different ages is shown in Table 2.10.

▶ **Table 2.10:** Calculating BMR

	Age (years)	Basal metabolic rates in kcal per day (W = weight in kg)
Males	10–17	BMR = 17.7W + 657
	18–29	BMR = 15.1W + 692
	30–59	BMR = 11.5W + 873
	60–74	BMR = 11.9W + 700
Females	10–17	BMR = 13.4W + 691
	18–29	BMR = 14.8W + 487
	30–59	BMR = 8.3W + 846
	60–74	BMR = 9.2W + 687

BMR is affected by a number of different factors.

▶ **Age** – basal metabolism decreases with age. After the age of 30, it falls by approximately 2 per cent per decade.

▶ **Gender** – males generally have greater muscle mass than females, so generally have a higher basal metabolic rate.

▶ **Climate** – exposure to hot or cold climates causes an increase in basal metabolism to maintain the body's internal temperature.

▶ **Physical activity** – to estimate total energy requirements you also need to consider your level of physical activity and training. This involves taking account of the calories used in different physical activities and the intensity and length of time over which you did the activity. Your intensity levels can be estimated by wearing a heart rate monitor and calculating your resting heart rate to work out your health range (see Tables 2.7 and 2.8).

Components of a balanced diet

All activity affects your body's need for fuel and fluid. Knowing the nutrients your body requires, along with their different functions, is the basis for understanding nutrition.

Macronutrients

Nutrients in food are categorised according to the relative amounts required by your body. Carbohydrate, protein and fat are termed **macronutrients**, as they are required in relatively large amounts on a daily basis. These nutrients are also the energy-providing nutrients of your diet.

Carbohydrate

Carbohydrates are your body's most readily available source of energy and can be accessed rapidly. One gram of carbohydrate provides approximately 4 kcal of energy. Carbohydrate foods are divided into two basic types: simple and complex.

Simple carbohydrates are sugars. They are easily digested and absorbed to provide a quick energy source. The simplest carbohydrate unit is monosaccharide (**saccharide** means 'sugar', **mono** means 'one'). Simple carbohydrates are found in most sweet-tasting foods such as fruit, fruit juices and honey.

Longer chains of simple sugars are called polysaccharides or **complex carbohydrates**. Complex carbohydrates are found in bread, rice, pasta, potatoes, beans and lentils.

Complex carbohydrates are an important source of energy since they are broken down slowly in your body to release energy over longer periods. They should form the largest percentage of your total carbohydrate intake. Unrefined sources such as wholemeal bread, wholegrain rice and wholemeal pasta are best as they also contain a higher nutritional value from macronutrients and provide a source of fibre.

After you eat foods containing carbohydrates your body sugar level rises. This causes the pancreas to release the hormone insulin. Insulin normalises blood sugar levels and helps the transport of **glucose** from the blood to the cells. Glucose is then used directly by the cells for energy or stored as **glycogen** in your liver and muscles. Glycogen is a crucial source of glucose for fuelling activity.

Around 80 per cent of glycogen is stored in your muscles while the rest is stored in your liver, with a small amount of glucose circulating in your bloodstream as blood glucose. Excess carbohydrate not required for glycogen stores is converted to fat and stored in your body's adipose tissue.

Key term

Saccharide – a compound containing sugar or sugars.

Key terms

Glucose – a monosaccharide that is converted to glycogen in the body.

Glycogen – type of blood sugar and major fuel source that the body converts from dietary carbohydrates.

Carbohydrate can only be stored as glycogen in limited amounts – approximately 375–475 grams – in an average adult, equivalent to approximately 1500–2000 kcal. Day-to-day stores of glycogen are influenced by dietary carbohydrate intake and levels of physical activity or training. Regular exercise can encourage muscles to adapt to store more glycogen. This is an important training adaptation for elite athletes, particularly in endurance-type sports.

A general recommendation is that carbohydrates should comprise 45–70 per cent of your total calories consumed. If your activity level is high, for example in endurance sports, you will need nearer 70 per cent to replace your depleted glycogen stores. A lower activity level, for example distance walking, will need nearer 45 per cent.

▶ **Table 2.11:** Sources of carbohydrate

Simple carbohydrates 'Quick release' energy	**Complex carbohydrates** 'Slow release' energy
Sugar, syrup, jam, honey, marmalade, sugary fizzy drinks, boiled sweets, fudge, fruit juice, sports drinks, energy gels.	Bread, bagels, crispbread, crackers, rice, pasta, noodles, couscous, potatoes, breakfast cereals, pulses, root vegetables.

Fats

Fat is an essential basic nutrient and the body's most concentrated source of energy. Each gram of fat gives approximately 9 kcal of energy. Fats also provide the body with heat insulation, mechanical cushioning and buoyancy.

Triglycerides are the basic component of fats. Each triglyceride is made from a glycerol molecule with three fatty acids attached. When triglycerides are digested and absorbed by your body they break down into these two substances. Fats come from animal and vegetable sources and there are two main types:

▶ **Saturated fats** – fatty acids, mainly from animal sources; along with cholesterol, they are linked to the build-up of fatty substances on artery walls. Saturated fats are usually solid at room temperature.

▶ **Unsaturated fat** – fatty acids usually liquid at room temperature and considered less likely to build up fatty acids on artery walls.

Most dietary experts recommend cutting back on fat intake. Many people in the UK eat too much saturated fat. The government recommends an average man should have no more than 30 g a day, and an average woman no more than 20 g.

Cutting back on fat intake is particularly good advice for athletes as it allows them to gain a greater proportion of their energy intake from carbohydrates (maintaining glycogen stores), to support training and competition. The primary function of fats is to provide a concentrated source of energy, forming your body's largest potential energy source. Even the leanest people have large amounts of energy stored as fat. Fat is more than twice as energy-dense as other macronutrients, yielding 9 calories per gram.

Fats protect and cushion your vital organs, provide structural material for cells and act as an insulator. Animal fats are a source of the fat-soluble vitamins A, D, E and K. Fats add flavour and texture to foods, which can be the reason for over-consumption.

All fats in your diet are a mixture of three fatty acid types (see Table 2.12). Fats that contain mostly saturated fatty acids (such as butter and ordinary margarine) are generally solid at room temperature and are usually found in meat, eggs and dairy foods. The two exceptions are palm and coconut oil, which are plant sources. Fats composed mainly of unsaturated fatty acids are usually liquid at room temperature, for instance, olive or sunflower oils.

▶ **Table 2.12:** Sources of fat

Saturated	Monounsaturated	Polyunsaturated
Full-fat dairy products, butter, hard margarine, lard, dripping, suet, fatty meat, meat pies, pâté, cream, cakes, biscuits, chocolate, coconut, coconut oil	Olive oil, olive oil spreads, rapeseed oil, corn oil, peanuts, peanut butter, peanut oil	Soft margarine, low-fat spreads labelled as high in polyunsaturated fats, sunflower oil, safflower oil, soya oil, oily fish, nuts

Protein

Proteins are essential for maintaining health and physical performance. They play a vital role in the structure and function of cells, enzymes, hormones and antibodies.

The smallest units of protein are **amino acids**. You do not need to know the names and functions of the 20 individual amino acids, but the body needs all of them to be present simultaneously in order to grow and function properly. Different proteins contain different numbers and combinations of amino acids. The eight your body is unable to make are called **essential amino acids** (EAAs) – they are a necessary part of your diet. The remaining amino acids are called non-essential – your body is able to synthesise them if all the essential ones are present.

The chief role of protein in your body is to build and repair tissue. Proteins may also be used as a secondary source of energy when carbohydrate and fats are limited, such as towards the end of prolonged endurance events or during severe energy restriction that may accompany dieting.

Proteins, like carbohydrates, have an energy value of approximately 4 calories per gram. Unlike carbohydrate and fat, excess protein cannot be stored in your body. All proteins carry out functional roles, so daily protein ingestion is required. If your protein intake exceeds your requirements for growth and repair, excess intake is used to provide energy immediately or converted to fat or carbohydrate and stored.

Protein foods are classified into two groups (see Table 2.13). The value of foods for meeting your body's protein needs is determined by their amino acids. Foods that contain all of the EAAs are known as first-class or **complete proteins**. These are mainly from animals (for instance, eggs, meat, fish, milk and other dairy products) and soya. Foods lacking in one or more of the EAAs are called second-class or **incomplete proteins**. These come from plant sources such as cereals, bread, rice, pasta, pulses, nuts and seeds.

Vegetarians and vegans must make sure they eat a variety of incomplete proteins in careful combinations to ensure an adequate intake of all EAAs. For example, beans and wheat complement each other well.

> **Key term**
>
> **Amino acids –** the chemicals which form the building blocks of protein.

▶ **Table 2.13:** Sources of protein

Complete proteins	Incomplete proteins
Meat, poultry, offal, fish, eggs, milk, cheese, yoghurt, soya	Cereals, bread, rice, pasta, noodles, pulses, peas, beans, lentils, nuts, seeds

On average, men should eat 55 g and women should eat 45 g of protein per day. This is roughly two palm-sized portions of protein.

Micronutrients

Vitamins and minerals are referred to as micronutrients as they are required in much smaller amounts than macronutrients. Despite the relatively small requirements for these nutrients, many play a critical role in regulating the chemical reactions in your body.

Vitamins A, B, C and D

Vitamins are vital, non-calorific nutrients required in very small amounts. They perform specific metabolic functions and prevent particular deficiencies and diseases. For example:

▸ **Vitamin A** – helps with the normal functioning of the eyes and respiratory tract. Vitamin A is found in green vegetables and carrots.

▸ **Vitamin B** – this group of vitamins plays an essential role in releasing energy from foods. The B vitamins are found in lean meats, eggs, cereals, wholegrains and milk.

▸ **Vitamin C** – essential for the formation and healthy functioning of collagen (major component of skin, bone and connective tissue) and a stimulant for the body's defence mechanisms. Vitamin C is found in vegetables and citrus fruits.

▸ **Vitamin D** – helps with the absorption of calcium and phosphorus to aid bone health. Vitamin D is found in oily fish, eggs and margarine, or it is produced in the skin by the action of ultraviolet light.

Most vitamins required to maintain health cannot be produced by your body and must be supplied by your diet. The exceptions are vitamin D, which your body is able to synthesise by the action of sunlight on the skin, and vitamin K, which can be produced by the bacteria in the large intestine. Vitamins play an essential role in regulating the many metabolic processes in your body, particularly those that release energy. They also support growth and the immune and nervous system, and some are involved in producing hormones.

Specific vitamins have specific functions and are required in differing amounts, suggested by the Dietary Reference Values (DRVs) – refer back to page 84 for more information. A balanced and varied diet with adequate energy content should supply sufficient intake of all vitamins.

It is important to note that large amounts of some vitamins can harm your health. This is particularly true for fat-soluble vitamins, as they can be stored in your body. The only situation in which large doses of any vitamin may be good for you is when the body has a severe lack of a particular vitamin or is unable to absorb or metabolise vitamins efficiently.

Vitamins are obtained from a variety of plant and animal sources and are broadly grouped depending on whether they are fat- or water-soluble. Vitamins A and D are in the fat-soluble group, with B and C being water-soluble.

▸ All fat-soluble vitamins such as A and D have common features. They are found in fatty or oily parts of foods. Once digested they are absorbed and transported in the lymphatic system to the blood. Because they are insoluble in water, they are not removed from the body in urine and can build up in the liver and **adipose tissue**.

▸ Vitamins B and C are water-soluble. Many B vitamins serve similar functions, helping the use of energy within your body. Excess vitamins of this type are excreted in urine, so your body has only limited stores, meaning you need to have a regular intake of them. Many of these vitamins are destroyed by food processing and preparation.

Minerals

Minerals are non-calorific nutrients that are essential to life. Like vitamins they are required in small or trace amounts. Minerals are classified in two categories depending on the relative amounts required by your body:

▸ **Macrominerals** such as calcium are required in relatively large amounts, sometimes as much as several hundred milligrams per day.

▸ **Trace elements** such as copper (found in seafood, nuts, seeds and wholegrains) and selenium (found in seafood, fish, lean meat and wholegrains) are required in much smaller quantities (micrograms per day).

Calcium

This mineral is essential for the development of healthy bones and teeth, and general health and well-being. Calcium is the most abundant mineral found in the body – over 1 kg is found in the average adult – and is required for blood clotting, muscle and nerve activity, and cell permeability.

Sources of calcium include meat, poultry, fish, vegetables, dairy products and nuts. In the UK, the calcium Reference Nutrient Intake (RNI) for adult males and females is 700 mg.

Iron

This mineral is a component of haemoglobin, and is essential for general health and well-being. A lack of iron leads to a condition known as anaemia which decreases oxygen transport in the blood, leading to apathy and fatigue.

Sources of iron include red meat, liver, dried fruit, vegetables and nuts. In the UK, the iron Reference Nutrient Intake (RNI) for adults aged 19–50 is 8.7 mg for men and 14.8 mg for women.

Key terms

Adipose tissue – tissue containing a high proportion of fat-storing cells that generally forms under the skin where it can act as an insulator or shock absorber.

Trace elements – minerals required by the body in relatively small amounts (less than 100 mg per day).

Discussion

How closely should governments be involved in what we eat? Do you think multivitamins or 'five a day' should be available to all, without charge, on the NHS? Would this help lower the risk of chronic diseases or reduce the impact of poor diet? Or is diet a personal choice and any health issues something the NHS should deal with, rather than preventing the causes?

In small groups discuss this dilemma and consider whether or not the government should focus on prevention or cure.

Fitness, Training and Programming for Health, Sport and Well-being

Do you understand why micronutrients are an important part of dietary intake?

Hint

Micronutrients (vitamins and minerals) have different specific roles in the body.

Extend

Find out the Reference Nutrient Intake (RNI) values for all vitamins and essential minerals for a healthy adult male and female.

Hydration

Water is the main transport mechanism in your body, carrying nutrients, waste products and internal secretions. It also plays a vital role in temperature regulation, particularly during exercise, and helps the passage of food through your digestive system.

Water makes up around 50–60 per cent of your total body weight – actual amounts vary depending on age, gender and body composition. Muscle has higher water content than fat tissue, so leaner individuals have higher water content than fatter individuals of the same body mass.

Water can be lost from your body in a number of ways, including urine, faeces, evaporation from the skin and breathing out. If water loss is high, your body becomes dehydrated. Normally your body maintains a balance between fluid input and output. Table 2.14 shows the balance between water intake and water loss.

▶ **Table 2.14:** Daily water balance for a sedentary 70 kg adult male (Source: Bush *et al.* (2012) *Foundations in Sports Science*, London: Pearson Education Ltd)

Daily water input		Daily water output	
Source	**Millilitres**	**Source**	**Millilitres**
Fluids	1200	Urine	1250
Food	1000	Skin	850
Metabolism	350	Lungs	350
		Faeces	100
Total	**2550**	**Total**	**2550**

Different types of fluid intake

Around 10 per cent of your daily fluid requirements come from metabolic processes that release water within your body. The other 90 per cent is taken from your diet. Approximately 60 per cent come directly from fluids and the rest comes from food. Factors that affect the amount of fluid you need are listed below:

▶ **Climate** – where you live or train, and its climate, will affect the level of fluid intake you need. A hot climate requires an increase in fluid intake and a **humid** climate even more so, due to the body's reduced ability to keep cool due to the high water content in the surrounding atmosphere. Athletes who train or compete in hot or humid conditions need to monitor **electrolyte** levels due to the amount of minerals and salts lost due to sweating.

▶ **Levels of exercise** – athletes should begin training fully hydrated and drink plenty of water both during and after activity. Training is an opportunity to practise fluid-replacement strategies for competitive situations. Many factors influence the effectiveness of fluid-replacement strategies during exercise. Make sure your hydration strategy is correct, especially for long-duration aerobic events. Fluid replacement can be accelerated by drinking reasonable volumes of still, cool water drinks. They should not be too concentrated, and must be ready to drink.

Key terms

Humid – air containing a high amount of water or water vapour.

Electrolytes – substances such as potassium, magnesium, calcium and sodium which are dissolved in bodily fluids and lost through sweat. Without electrolytes, your cells and organs will not be able to function correctly.

The more intense the activity, the more the absorption of fluid is slowed. Unpleasant symptoms experienced when drinking during exercise usually means you started drinking too late and your body is already dehydrated. Try to drink regularly during exercise, especially if you are exercising for more than an hour.

▶ **Time of year** – athletes should be encouraged to take more care when hydrating in the summer months due to higher outdoor temperatures. Although outdoor temperatures are often lower during winter months, it is still essential to make sure correct hydration takes place.

Dehydration and hyperhydration

Dehydration can reduce strength, power and aerobic capacity. Severe dehydration can cause heatstroke and may be fatal. A water loss as small as 2 per cent of body mass can be enough to affect your ability to perform muscular work. For a 75 kg male this would mean a fluid loss of only 1.5 litres. Remember, thirst is a poor indicator of your body's hydration status. Warning signs include:

▶ lack of energy and early fatigue during exercise

▶ feeling hot and/or clammy or flushed skin

▶ not needing to go to the toilet

▶ nausea, headache or disorientation

▶ shortness of breath.

Hyperhydration is when you have more water than the normal body water content. Starting exercise in a hyperhydrated state can improve thermoregulation, improving heat dissipation and exercise performance. However, a hyperhydrated state can also be dangerous, causing symptoms similar to dehydration.

Hyperhydration can also cause **hyponatremia**, a potentially fatal condition resulting from a low level of sodium in the body fluids, made worse by excessive water consumption. Endurance athletes, who often lose large volumes of water and sodium through sweating, are particularly at risk from hyponatremia if they replace water volumes but not sodium (further diluting their already reduced sodium levels). The drinking of electrolyte replacement sports drinks is recommended to prevent this.

> **Key terms**
>
> **Dehydration** – a reduction in the normal water content of your body, when you lose more fluid than you take in. Dehydration can lead to decreased blood pressure, increased heart rate and increased core body temperature.
>
> **Hyperhydration** – an increase in the normal water content of your body, when you take in more fluid than you lose.
>
> **Hyponatremia** – a state of low sodium levels in the body fluids.

 PAUSE POINT   Complete a daily nutrition audit on yourself or a friend.

   Hint   List what you or a friend ate yesterday and break down this daily intake into macronutrients, micronutrients and hydration categories.

   Extend   Can you identify gaps in the daily nutritional intake? Make recommendations about what foods could be eaten to cover these gaps.

Nutritional strategies for individuals taking part in training programmes

Adapting diet to gain or lose weight

Weight can be gained by increasing the amount of fat or the amount of lean body mass. Both will register as increases in weight on a set of scales, but your body composition results will be very different. Gains in fat weight are relatively easy to achieve. However, gains in lean body mass can only be achieved from the body's responses to a progressive strength training programme, supported by an adequate diet, high in protein (to aid muscle growth) and low in fat. These diets generally involve adding additional lean meat, fish or poultry to your diet, or low-fat protein drinks.

Key terms

Optimal body weight – an ideal weight for a body composition that enables an athlete to perform successfully in a specific sport or activity.

Ergogenic aids – any aid that enhances physical performance.

Most athletes are concerned with achieving and/or maintaining an **optimal body weight**. Sports that group participants by weight category include body-building, boxing, horse racing, martial arts and rowing. Participants in these sports must compete within a certain weight range.

For some sports, low body weight may be crucial. In some cases this may be below a person's natural weight. These sports can be called weight-controlled sports, and include distance running, gymnastics, figure skating and diving. Inappropriate weight-loss practices affecting athletes include fasting or skipping meals, laxative abuse, bingeing and purging, and deliberate dehydration via sweatsuits or saunas.

When most athletes talk about achieving weight loss, they usually mean fat loss. Losses in muscle mass may result in unfavourable changes in their power-to-weight ratio.

Theory into practice

Chris Hoy and Nairo Quintana are both professional cyclists, but their sizes are very different. Hoy is a track cyclist who specialised in sprint events; he is 1.85 m tall and weighs 92 kg. Nairo Quintana is a road cyclist who specialises in long-distance events such as the Tour de France; he is 1.66 m tall and weighs 58 kg.

Hoy's event requires muscular power to achieve high speeds over short distances on the indoor track. This power is provided by large muscles that add to Hoy's overall bodyweight. Quintana's event requires considerable endurance, allowing him to cycle up to 200 km per day, sometimes up steep mountains. This requires excellent muscular endurance, cardiorespiratory fitness and much lighter overall bodyweight.

Quintana's smaller bodyweight is ideal for long-distance cycling. Any additional weight will affect his performance over long distances, as more energy will be required to move just one additional kilogram of bodyweight over 200 km. Hoy does not have to worry too much about this; his event is over in minutes.

Do you think Chris Hoy would be able to compete effectively on a 200 km mountain stage of the Tour de France?

Using ergogenic aids in training programmes

Athletes and coaches are always looking for ways to gain a competitive advantage and improve athletic performance. In response to this, a range of **ergogenic aids** are marketed and sold to athletes at all levels. Some are commercially available and legal, others available on prescription only, while some are illegal and their use and possession may result in criminal investigation or sporting penalties.

Energy gels and bars

Energy gels are designed to replenish depleted carbohydrate stores after exercising. Remember, the body relies on carbohydrate – glycogen – as its primary fuel source when exercising. Generally, the greater the exercise intensity, the greater the percentage of fuel that comes from carbohydrates. However, we can only store a limited amount of carbohydrate in our skeletal muscles and liver.

Energy gels do not provide a simple one-to-one replacement because the glycogen you ingest from gels does not always get to the working muscles. For glycogen to get to the muscles, it must be digested, and then absorbed by the muscles. This takes time and is inefficient, especially during exercise when blood is diverted from the digestive system. Energy gels consumed at least 30 minutes before exercise can give maximum benefit.

Protein drinks

Protein is used for the production of muscle, to manufacture hormones, enzymes and immune system components. If you do not consume enough protein, your body cannot put together the structures that make up cells, tissues and organs, nor will muscles heal as quickly, which could lead to injury.

Solid food takes longer to digest, and breaking down protein to send it to the muscles can take hours. A protein drink taken after a workout will only take about 30 minutes to reach the muscle area after ingestion.

Carbohydrate loading

Carbohydrate loading (also known as 'glycogen loading') is used by endurance athletes before an event to maximise storage of glycogen in skeletal muscles. Carbohydrate loading involves increasing your intake of carbohydrate and decreasing your training for approximately three days before competition. Carbohydrate loading is based on a regular, controlled diet and is legal.

Your body can store enough glycogen to sustain approximately 90 minutes of exercise. After this, without extra fuelling, you are in danger of running out of energy. Carbohydrate stores can be maximised two to three days before an event by increasing your carbohydrate intake at mealtimes, with an approximate guide being 10 g of carbohydrate per kilogram of bodyweight. Increase the carbohydrate content of your diet by adding larger portions of wholemeal bread, pasta, rice, potatoes and plenty of fruit juice at mealtimes. Two hours before the event, try to eat a high carbohydrate snack such as citrus fruits or muffins.

Case study

Sports Scientist: Jack Donnelly and the new menu

Jack is progressing well as the football club's new sports scientist. Now the academy manager has asked him to help the club's chef ensure the academy players get the correct nutrition during their daily meals with the club. He has been asked to make sure all components of a balanced diet are present in the correct amounts. Failure to do so may result in impaired performance and the players leading a less-than-healthy lifestyle.

Jack is due to sit down with the chef and compose a dietary plan for a five-day week, including breakfast, lunch, dinner and all hydration.

Check your knowledge
Draw up a five-day (Monday to Friday) dietary plan for the players.

- Research the recommend amounts for an athlete of each macronutrient (carbohydrates, fats, proteins).
- Ensure all macronutrients are included and in the correct amounts.
- Use ergogenic aids (energy gels and bars, protein or carbohydrate drinks) if you deem them appropriate.
- Make sure you include hydration times and amounts.
- Think about the most appropriate times for each meal.

Theory into practice

Nutritionists at the English Institute of Sport (EIS) (www.eis2win.co.uk/) use the term 'unleash the power of food'. Their belief is that through the science of nutrition, athletes have been able to reduce injuries, increase capacity to train, and improve competitive performance. They have done this by being involved in all aspects of nutrition from getting the food right at hotels to ergogenic aids.

Consider how these principles might be adapted to a more local coaching role, say at a school, college or local sports club. Do you think you could get a local team or athlete to embrace the same methods?

Using sports drinks

Most sports drinks provide three nutrients: carbohydrates to replace energy, water to replace fluid and electrolytes to replace minerals lost in sweat. The carbohydrate is usually glucose, fructose, sucrose or maltodextrins, which are all saccharides that are quickly absorbed. Sports drinks often contain a range of minerals and vitamins, but most often include the electrolytes sodium and potassium – both these macrominerals are lost in sweat. Sodium promotes the absorption of glucose and water. Magnesium is another mineral lost in sweat, and is present in water and most sports drinks.

Isotonic

Isotonic drinks contain the same concentration of glucose to water as blood (4–8 per cent or up to 8 g per 100 ml of water). Because of this, although they are hydrating, they have no effect on the volume of tissues or cells. They usually also contain sodium, making them quicker to absorb into the bloodstream. They are useful for prolonged exercise or during warmer weather. They can also be used before exercise.

Hypertonic

Hypertonic drinks are high-energy, concentrated sports drinks containing over 8 per cent of carbohydrate; they are absorbed more slowly than isotonic drinks. Although they provide carbohydrates, they are not ideal for optimal rehydration and may need to be consumed with other fluids. They have a higher total salt concentration than body fluids and are best used in the recovery phase after exercise.

Hypotonic

Hypotonic drinks have a lower concentration of carbohydrates and are more diluted than isotonic or hypertonic drinks. They contain less than 4 per cent carbohydrates (4 g per 100 ml of water) and are generally easily absorbed and well tolerated. Although water is adequate for non-endurance athletes or when sweat losses are small, these drinks encourage fluid replacement. Their salt concentration is lower than body fluids.

Discussion

Energy drinks are big business: they promote the benefits of hydration and electrolyte balance and may improve your sports performance, but they can be expensive. Are they any more beneficial than tap water or less-expensive orange squash? In small groups, discuss this and consider whether or not energy drinks are worth the expense. Feed back your findings to the group in the form of a sales pitch for both alternatives.

Assessment practice 2.3

Your health monitoring booklet has proved a success and is currently being used by the full-time fitness coach on a daily basis. Because of your efforts and commitment over your work experience placement, the general manager of the tennis club has asked you to stay on in a part-time capacity to perform fitness training and programming, and to assist the fitness coach in giving clients the correct health advice.

The first job the fitness coach has asked you to do is prepare an information leaflet for all members explaining their nutritional needs while they are training for and competing in tennis tournaments. Your leaflet should contain the following information:

- an explanation of common nutritional terminology (e.g. RNI and energy balance)
- components of a balanced diet (e.g. macronutrients, micronutrients and hydration)
- different strategies used by tennis players taking part in training programmes.

The design of the leaflet is up to you, but the coach has asked you to state the key nutritional requirements and explain why they are important to the members if they are undertaking his training programmes. Once the coach is happy with the leaflet, he will give copies to all members, telling them to contact you if they have any further questions.

Plan

- What is the task? What is my leaflet being asked to address?
- How confident do I feel in my own abilities to complete this task? Are there any areas of the nutritional requirements and their impact that I think I may struggle with?

Do

- I know how to design my own leaflet, include all the necessary nutritional information and explain why this information is important.
- I can identify where my leaflet may have gone wrong and adjust my thinking/ approach to get myself back on course.

Review

- I can explain what the task was and how I approached making my leaflet.
- I can explain how I would approach the more difficult parts differently next time.

D Examine training methods for different components of fitness

Components of fitness to be trained

Fitness is the ability to meet the demands of your environment. It includes social, spiritual, psychological, emotional and physical well-being. Though it is often defined as one of the following, it is not only concerned with muscle size, body tone or the ability to run far or fast.

- ▶ **Physical fitness** – focusing on the health-related aspects of fitness – good scores in components in this area mean you have only a small chance of developing health problems.
- ▶ **Skill-related fitness** – fitness that allows the individual to perform an activity, task or sport (also known as motor fitness).

Physical fitness

Physical fitness involves six main components:

- ▶ **Aerobic endurance** – also known as stamina or cardiorespiratory endurance, it is the ability of the cardiovascular and respiratory systems to work efficiently and supply the muscles with nutrients and oxygen to maintain exercise over time. It is important not only for daily tasks such as walking to work, but also for a range of sport, leisure and recreational activities. A number of events rely on aerobic endurance, and poor aerobic endurance can lead to poor performance in some sports.

- **Strength** – the ability of a specific muscle or muscle group to exert a force in a single maximal contraction. When you think about strength, you might think about weightlifters or boxers, but strength is required in most sports. For instance, a Formula 1 driver needs strong neck muscles to withstand the pressure put on their head when going round corners fast.

- **Muscular endurance** – this is needed where a specific muscle or muscle group makes repeated contractions over a significant period of time (possibly over a number of minutes) against a light to moderate fixed resistance load. Sporting examples include:
  - a boxer making a repeated jab
  - continuous press-ups or sit-ups
  - the 400 metres in athletics.

▶ Boxers need muscular endurance to make repeated jab punches

- **Flexibility** – this is important for all sports and for health. It relates to having an adequate range of motion in all joints of the body and the ability to move a joint fluidly through its complete range of movement.

- **Speed** – a component of physical fitness, speed is required to maximise performance in order to move the whole body quickly or limbs rapidly. It is the ability to move over a distance in the quickest possible time. Athletic sports such as the 100-metre sprint and long jump require high levels of speed.

- **Body composition** – the amount of body fat and fat-free lean body tissue an athlete has. It is important from a health and sports performance perspective. Lean body mass includes the combined weight of the vital organs, bones, muscles and connective tissues.

Skill-related fitness

Skill-related fitness involves five main components.

- **Agility** – the ability of an athlete to quickly and precisely move or change direction while maintaining control of the movement.

- **Balance** – being able to maintain stability or equilibrium while performing. There are two forms of balance: **static balance**, where the athlete is stationary, for example in a handstand in gymnastics, and **dynamic balance**, where the athlete is moving, for example a footballer sprinting with the ball.

- **Coordination** – the ability to control movement of two or more body parts, smoothly and efficiently, to perform a task. Most sporting movements require different joints and muscles to be used in a specific order.

▶ **Reaction time** – the time taken for a sports performer to respond to a stimulus and initiate their response. An obvious example is a starting pistol (the stimulus) and the sprint start (the movement) in sprint events.

▶ **Power** – the ability to produce a maximal force in the shortest possible period of time, or to generate and use muscular strength quickly. Stronger athletes tend to produce a greater amount of power during an action. Power is generally needed more by athletes in specific sports and is developed using advanced training methods. For example, sprinters need power when pushing away from the blocks, golfers need it to strike a long-range drive and boxers for delivering a punch.

Training methods for physical fitness-related components

To develop different components of fitness to meet the needs of different sports, athletes, coaches and personal trainers often need to use a variety of training methods. These methods might be in indoor or outdoor environments or using a range of equipment.

Aerobic endurance training methods

The three most common methods used to improve aerobic endurance (also known as **VO$_2$ max**) are:

▶ continuous training

▶ fartlek training

▶ interval training.

Circuit training is also used. There is insufficient evidence to suggest which aerobic training method is best, but all will lead to improvements in aerobic endurance.

Aerobic endurance training is often used by people who want to lose or manage their weight by reducing their body fat content; as such, aerobic training is often used during pre-season by football and rugby teams. Body fat is reduced because training results in increased levels of the hormones **epinephrine** and **norepinephrine** which then help break down fat to be used as an energy source.

As well as the health benefits of aerobic endurance training methods, they have different benefits for sport-specific performance: they can help to improve blood volume, improve mitochondrial size and density, develop neuromuscular patterns and improve muscle tone.

Training thresholds

Different intensities of aerobic exercise can be classed as different training thresholds or zones of training. In order to use training thresholds in your training, you need to understand the principles behind **maximum heart rate**. When the body is in action, **cardiac output** can increase by five to seven times in order to accelerate the delivery of blood to exercising muscles, and meet their aerobic demands. This is a result of increases in either heart rate, **stroke volume** or both. Since stroke volume does not increase significantly beyond the light work rates of low intensity exercise, the increases in cardiac output required for moderate- to high-intensity work rates can only be achieved by increases in heart rate.

> ### Key terms
>
> **VO$_2$ max** – the maximum amount of oxygen that can be taken in by and used by the body. Also a measure of the endurance capacity of the cardiovascular and respiratory systems and exercising skeletal muscles.
>
> **Epinephrine** – a chemical in the body used for communication between cells in the nervous system and other cells in the body. It works with norepinephrine to prepare the body for the 'fight or flight' response.
>
> **Norepinephrine** – a chemical in the body used for communication between cells in the nervous system and other cells in the body. It works with epinephrine to prepare the body for the 'fight or flight' response.
>
> **Cardiac output** – the volume of blood pumped out (in litres) by the left ventricle in one minute.
>
> **Stroke volume** – the volume of blood pumped out (in millilitres) by the left ventricle during one heartbeat.

Maximum heart rate can be estimated using the following formula:

Maximum heart rate = 220 – age (in years)

The formula includes the person's age because heart rates vary with age: children have relatively higher rates than adults, and maximal cardiac output decreases with age (as a result of a decrease in maximum heart rate).

Once you know someone's maximum heart rate (MHR), you can get them to target specific heart rate zones during their training which will have different effects on how their body develops (see Table 2.15).

▶ **Table 2.15:** Training zones

Training zone	% MHR	Purpose
Warm-up or cool-down zone	50%	Mainly for the sedentary or unfit person who wants to start training.
Active recovery zone	60%	Useful for aiding recovery and removing waste products, and provides a good next step for those new to aerobic training.
Fat burning (or weight management) zone	60–70%	A progression for people once they have increased their fitness levels, but also used by athletes training for long-distance events such as a marathon. You may use continuous training when training in this zone.
'Target heart rate' zone	60–75%	Some coaches have been known to expand this zone as high as 85 per cent. This zone has the greatest benefits for cardiovascular health and for improving the body's ability to use fats as an energy source.
Aerobic fitness zone	70–80%	The zone where you develop your aerobic endurance. This zone is suitable for more active or trained athletes.
Peak performance zone	80–90%	The highest zone of aerobic training is geared towards competitive sport and helps develop the anaerobic threshold. You will often use up-tempo methods such as fartlek and interval training when training through the aerobic fitness and peak performance zones.
Anaerobic threshold	80–100%	Exercising with legs that are starting to get hot, tight and achy, with much more laboured breathing is a sign you are close to your anaerobic threshold. This is the point where you can no longer meet the energy requirements of exercise using your aerobic energy system, so your body compensates by producing energy using your anaerobic systems. This is the point that your **blood lactate** levels increase significantly. (Refer to Unit 1 for more information.) Training at high percentages of your maximum heart rate helps to increase this threshold, allowing you to train at higher intensities and longer durations while still using your aerobic energy system. Training close to your anaerobic threshold significantly stresses your cardiovascular system, so it is not suitable for inexperienced trainers. Training at 100% of maximum heart rate is only recommended for highly experienced and elite athletes.

Key term

Blood lactate – lactate dissolved in blood as a result of a build-up in blood carbon dioxide levels. Lactate is not the same thing as lactic acid.

Ⅱ PAUSE POINT

How would you differentiate the aerobic training zone of an 18-year-old athlete and a 40-year-old trying to get fit and healthy?

Hint What is your maximum heart rate and what heart rate would you see in your aerobic training zone?

Extend What training methods might you use to progress an experienced athlete into the peak performance zone?

Types of aerobic endurance training methods

Continuous training

Also known as steady-state or long, slow distance training: the athlete trains at a steady pace over a long distance. The intensity of continuous training should be moderate (approximately equal to or less than 70 per cent of VO_2 max) over a long distance and time.

This method is suited to long-distance runners and swimmers. Due to the lower level of intensity, an athlete can train for longer. It can also be useful for:

▶ beginners who are starting structured exercise
▶ athletes recovering from injury
▶ 'specific population' individuals such as children or elderly people.

Its disadvantages include a higher risk of injury when running long distances on harder surfaces. It can also be boring and it is not always **sport specific**: the sport specific benefits are small.

Continuous training can be performed in a gym using a range of cardiovascular equipment (for example, treadmill, cross-trainer or exercise cycle) or outdoors at a suitable park or track area.

Fartlek training

Fartlek training is designed to improve an athlete's aerobic endurance. It is based on running outdoors, and varies the intensity of work according to the athlete's requirements. The intensity of training is changed by varying terrain, such as sand, hills, soft grassland or woodland, or by running at a more sustained pace to a landmark such as a lamp post or tree.

Some of the benefits of this training method include improving aerobic endurance, improving muscular endurance and improving balance and **proprioception** in the ankle, knee and hip, all of which have a variety of benefits ranging from improved sport performance during a game to helping with injury rehabilitation.

Fartlek training can be more useful than continuous training because it can be individual- and sport-specific. This method also uses both aerobic and anaerobic energy systems to improve aerobic endurance and can involve changes in direction, so it is useful for team sports players as it can mimic the sport.

In fartlek training there is no rest period, but the athlete has more control and is able to decrease intensity at any time to rest. The benefits of fartlek training are that:

▶ it is less technical than other methods (such as interval training), making it easier to use
▶ athletes control their own pacing
▶ the boredom of conventional training is reduced.

Fartlek training can be done in a gym using a range of cardiovascular equipment (for example, treadmill, cross-trainer or exercise cycle) so long as the speed, resistance or gradient can be changed regularly. Fartlek training can be undertaken outdoors at a suitable park area where the intensity can be changed by varying terrain.

> **Key terms**
>
> **Sport specific** – a training activity that reproduces an element of the sport that is being trained for. For instance, although footballers do lots of running during their sport, they do not do it for long, continuous periods of time but in short bursts.
>
> **Proprioception** – the awareness of the body's position in space.

> **Research**
>
> Fartlek training can use both aerobic and anaerobic energy systems, involving changes in gradient, pace, resistance and direction, closely mimicking the requirements of a specific sport. Some common examples of fartlek sessions include Astrand, Gerschler, Saltin and Watson methods. Research these examples and examine their different approaches.

Interval training

Interval training improves both anaerobic endurance components and aerobic endurance by varying the intensity and length of the work periods. In interval training, athletes perform a work period, followed by a rest period, before completing another work period. They can repeat this pattern many times, depending on their fitness levels. When designing an interval training programme, you should consider:

▶ the number of intervals (rest and work periods)
▶ the intensity of the work and rest intervals
▶ the duration of the work and rest intervals.

'Sets' and 'reps' are common terms that provide structure and organisation when referring to the number of exercises in the training programme.

▶ **Reps** is short for repetitions and describes how many times you perform an exercise.
▶ A **set** tells you how many times you repeat that exercise for the set number of reps.

An example of an interval training programme for aerobic endurance could be one set of three repetitions of five-minute runs interspersed with two minutes of rest. This would be written in a training diary as *1×3×5:00 Work: Rest 2:00*. This method of training allows clear progression and **overload** to be built into the programme by increasing the intensity of work periods, increasing the number of intervals, decreasing the duration of the rest period or increasing the intensity of the rest period (for example, using a slow jog rather than a walk).

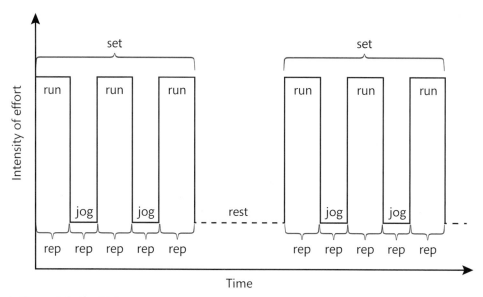

▶ **Figure 2.6:** Combining reps into a set

▶ Interval training can be performed in a gym using a range of cardiovascular equipment (for example, treadmill, cross-trainer or exercise cycle) so long as the speed, resistance or gradient can be changed at the required intervals, or outdoors at a suitable park or track area where running or cycling can be undertaken safely.

Circuit training

In a circuit training session, a number of different exercises (or 'stations') are organised around a room. Each station contains a different activity. Individuals are set a time limit to do these exercises, e.g. one minute per station. Between the stations there should be a rest period dependent on the individual or groups completing the circuit.

A circuit can be designed to improve aerobic endurance, muscular endurance or strength, or a combination of all three. To avoid fatigue, the stations should allow consecutive exercises to use different muscle groups: for example, repeated sprints (legs) may be followed by press-ups (upper body). To increase progression and overload, the individual may wish to:

▶ decrease the rest periods
▶ increase the number of stations
▶ increase the number of circuits
▶ increase the time spent at each station
▶ increase the number of circuit sessions per week.

Circuit training can be performed in a gym using a range of equipment, though space for all the stations can be an issue. Circuit training can use cardiovascular equipment, free weights, resistance machines or simple body weight exercises at the stations. Circuit training can also be performed outdoors at a suitable park or track area so long as you have equipment mobile enough to take with you for use at any of the stations.

Muscular strength training methods

If you visit a gym or fitness suite, you will often see people lifting different weights at different speeds. This is because a number of the training methods used to improve muscular strength can also be used to improve muscular endurance simply by doing the training differently, for example by altering the weight, the number of repetitions and the number of sets. Common training methods used to improve muscular strength and muscular endurance include:

▶ resistance machines
▶ free weights (such as dumbbells)
▶ medicine ball training
▶ circuit training
▶ core stability training.

If you think about how a person's appearance changes after using muscular strength training in a gym, you may say they look 'built' or 'pumped'. These changes are due to increased muscle tone and muscle **hypertrophy**. Muscle tone is where muscles have a more defined appearance, whereas muscle hypertrophy is the growth of the muscle and happens when the **muscle fibres** increase in size.

Principles when training for strength

Strength is the ability of a specific muscle or muscle group to exert a force in a single maximal contraction. Strength training can provide benefits and improvement to health and well-being by increasing muscle, bone and connective tissue strength, improving cardiovascular function and increasing bone density and metabolic rate. Sports where strength training is important include weightlifting, track and field, rugby, wrestling, rowing, boxing and, increasingly, football and basketball.

The basic principles for strength training are to use a high weight, low repetitions and a high set count. This is because strength training targets predominantly the Type IIa and Type IIx fast-twitch muscle fibres (as described in Unit 1). Type IIx fibres use anaerobic metabolism to transfer energy and are the classic 'fast' twitch muscle fibres that produce quick, powerful bursts of speed. This muscle fibre has the highest rate of contraction of all fibre types but also has a much faster rate of fatigue. Type IIa fibres (also known as intermediate fast-twitch fibres) can use both aerobic and anaerobic metabolism to transfer energy, and can exhibit similar properties to Type IIx fibres.

Key terms

Hypertrophy – an increase in the size of muscle tissue (or organs) due to growth of individual cells without an increase in the overall number of cells.

Muscle fibres – the contractile element of muscle tissue which appears banded or striped under a microscope. A single muscle contains between 10,000 and 450,000 fibres.

Link

This content links to *Unit 1: Anatomy and Physiology.*

It is important to establish a one-repetition maximum (or 1RM) before undertaking strength training. This is the most force the participant can apply in a single attempt at an exercise movement. For example, their 1RM for the bench press may be 80 kg.

▶ **Repetitions and sets** – the potential for fatigue when using a heavy load is high. Therefore, the numbers of repetitions tend to be lower (6–10 repetitions) so the participant is doing **low reps and high loads**. Strength training generally relies on a high number of sets to work the fast-twitch muscle fibres for longer. The number of sets depends on your level of fitness, training experience and the muscle area being worked. Large muscle groups (for example, chest or legs) can tolerate a higher number of sets (5–8 sets), whereas smaller muscle groups (for example, arms) can tolerate fewer sets (4–6 sets). An experienced gym user training their chest muscles for strength might perform the workout shown in Table 2.16.

▶ **Table 2.16:** A workout for an experienced gym-user training their chest muscles

Exercise	Reps	Sets	Weight (% of 1RM)
Bench press	8	6	75% = 60 kg

▶ **Rest periods between sets** – fast-twitch muscle fibres take longer to recover from exercise than slow-twitch muscle fibres. Because fast-twitch muscle fibres are fundamental for achieving increased strength, a rest period of 2–4 minutes between sets is ideal. The higher your training intensity and the more demanding it is on your body, the longer you should rest between sets. If your training intensity is lower and less demanding on your body, your rest period should be towards the shorter end of the range. The chest muscle workout shown in Table 2.16 can be adapted to specify a rest period (see Table 2.17).

▶ **Table 2.17:** Updated workout targeting chest muscles

Exercise	Reps	Sets	Weight (% of 1RM)	Rest period
Bench press	8	6	75% = 60 kg	3 minutes

▶ **Order of exercise to prevent or maximise muscle fatigue** – a general order of exercise to prevent muscle fatigue is to work the largest muscle groups first, then proceed to the smaller groups. Include all major muscle groups to avoid strength imbalances in the body. It is recommended you train your abdominal muscles at the end of a workout to make sure they are fresh to help stabilise your body while exercising other muscle groups in your next workout. An example of a workout designed to prevent muscle fatigue is shown in Table 2.18.

▶ **Table 2.18:** Order of exercise (muscle groups) to prevent muscle fatigue

Order	Muscle groups – muscles
1	chest – pectorals
2	back – latissimus dorsi, trapezius
3	legs – quadriceps, hamstrings, glutes, calves
4	shoulders – deltoids
5	arms – biceps, triceps
6	core – abdominals, erectus spinae

> **Key term**
>
> **Repetitions until failure** – an exercise (usually with free weights or bodyweight) during which the set is performed until the muscles worked can no longer achieve a further full contraction due to fatigue.

Maximisation of muscle fatigue is used in a specific exercise method. To truly fatigue a muscle, it should be exercised with **repetitions until failure**, an advanced training method that requires a 'spotter' – someone to support the participant. The order in which you should approach this type of training is similar to Table 2.18, allowing all muscle groups to be trained to their fullest extent.

Methods

Pyramid sets are a highly effective training technique that use an upward, then downward sequence in weight, reps and sets to maximise muscular strength and endurance goals. Pyramid sets have a number of benefits. Starting with a light weight allows joints and muscle tissue to warm up so your body is better prepared for later, heavier lifts. It also creates an intense routine as muscles become overloaded. The chest muscle workout shown in Tables 2.16 and 2.17 could be adapted to become a pyramid set (shown in Table 2.19).

▶ **Table 2.19:** A pyramid set

Set number	Reps	Weight	Rest
1	12–15	50% 1RM = 40 kg	2 minutes
2	10–12	70% 1RM = 56 kg	2 minutes
3	8–10	80% 1RM = 64 kg	2 minutes
4	4–6	90% 1RM = 72 kg	2 minutes
5	8–10	80% 1RM = 64 kg	2 minutes
6	10–12	70% 1RM = 56 kg	2 minutes
7	12–15	50% 1RM = 40 kg	2 minutes

When you go back down in weight (sets 5–7 in Table 2.19), your muscles will be increasingly fatigued, your strength will decrease and you may not be able to complete as many reps as you did at the start (sets 1–4).

Pyramid sets can be used at an advanced training level. This usually involves adaptations such as a small weight increase for sets 5–7, and/or repetitions until failure at set 7.

Equipment

▶ **Free weights** – barbells or dumb-bells, allowing an individual to have a constant resistance during dynamic action. Free weights increase strength in the short term, increase the range of movements and allow focus on certain movements or muscle groups, and some movements aid the training of balance and coordination. However, the use of free weights can increase the risk of injury. For safety reasons when using larger weights, helpers (or 'spotters') are required to oversee (or 'spot') for an individual.

▶ **Fixed-resistance machines** – your local fitness centre will have a number of fixed-resistance machines, allowing individuals to change the load based on their training programme. Variable resistance ranges from 0–100 kg on most machines, allowing the programme to include overload and progression, pyramid training, etc. These machines are expensive, making them impractical for home use. Due to their design they are limited to specialist exercises such as chest or leg press. On the positive side, they have an increased safety element compared to free weights, and can be used by novice trainers still learning different movement patterns. The range of movement can be changed at a specific joint by adjusting the machine's setting. Fixed-resistance machines are ideal for novice trainers undertaking strength training for the first time, regardless of whether they train with a helper or not – the risk of injury from repetition failure or over-extending joints is far less with resistance machines than with free weights.

▶ People using larger free weights should have a 'spotter' to maintain safety

⏸ PAUSE POINT   If you start a free weight strength routine with chest exercises, is there any danger of exhausting other muscle groups first?

Hint   What muscle groups facilitate the chest press action and help to move the barbell?

Extend   Research other chest exercises that isolate the chest muscle and place less stress on smaller assisting muscle groups.

Muscular endurance training methods

Principles when training for endurance

Muscular endurance is the ability of a specific muscle or muscle group to make repeated contractions over a significant period of time (possibly over a number of minutes). To develop muscular endurance you must train the muscle to overcome fatigue. Unlike muscular strength training methods, muscular endurance is not developed by increasing the weight lifted, but by increasing the amount of time a muscle spends contracting against a given resistance. Muscular endurance training should be a progression after several months of training and should come after strength training (low reps and high load) because the greater a muscle's strength, the more force it can exert during endurance training.

Muscular endurance training has similar benefits to muscular strength training. Muscle tone can increase and muscles will experience hypertrophy (although to a lesser extent). The additional benefits happen within the muscle cell. Muscular endurance places stress on the slow-twitch muscle fibres and as a result they can increase in size. This means there is more space for mitochondrial activity. The increase in size and number of **mitochondria** is important because they are the part of the muscle that synthesises aerobic energy. By increasing their size and number, you can increase aerobic performance and the efficiency of **type I muscle fibres** (and some type IIa muscle fibres).

Another important change within muscle fibres is that there is a large increase in **myoglobin** content. This is important for aerobic performance, as myoglobin carries oxygen to the mitochondria. If you have more myoglobin, you can produce more aerobic energy in the mitochondria. These changes can increase VO_2 max by up to 20 per cent. Sports where strength training is key include athletics, football, hockey, boxing, rowing and tennis.

Muscular endurance training helps the body deal with fatigue and increases tolerance to blood lactate. The training uses relatively light to medium loads of 40–60 per cent of 1RM, lifted for a set time or number of repetitions.

Key terms

Mitochondria – organelles (parts of cells) containing enzymes responsible for energy production. Mitochondria are the part of a muscle cell responsible for aerobic energy production.

Type I muscle fibres – slow twitch or slow oxidative fibres containing large amounts of myoglobin and mitochondria. They have a slow contraction velocity and are resistant to fatigue.

Myoglobin – a form of haemoglobin found in muscles that binds and stores oxygen in the mitochondria.

Muscular endurance training can be either long-term or short-term in its approach. Long-term muscular endurance training is suitable for continuous, steady-state sports such as long-distance running, triathlon, rowing and distance swimming. Light resistance or loads are used so that the training can be sustained for a prolonged period. Rest periods are kept to a minimum to reflect the continuous nature of the event. Short-term muscular endurance is suitable for shorter duration events or ones which are continuously stop–start in nature. Light to medium resistance or loads are used and rest periods are short (10–30 seconds) in duration. Free weights, fixed resistance machines and circuits are all suitable methods for training muscular endurance.

▶ **Repetitions and sets** – muscular endurance training works on the principle of performing many repetitions against a given resistance for a prolonged period of time, or **high reps and low loads**. Depending on the resistance, muscular endurance training reps can range from 15 to 30, and the number of sets from 4 to 6. Muscular endurance is highly (though not entirely) dependent on Type I slow-twitch fibres. Given their resistance to fatigue, exercise should involve a higher number of repetitions than strength training; therefore, lower loads (40–60 per cent of 1RM) are appropriate. An experienced gym user training their shoulders (1RM for dumbbell shoulder press is 25 kg) towards the end of a muscular endurance session might perform the exercise shown in Table 2.20.

▶ **Table 2.20:** A workout for an experienced gym-user training their shoulders

Exercise	Reps	Sets	Weight (% of 1RM)
Shoulder press	15	4	50% = 12.5 kg

▶ **Rest periods between sets** – one aim of muscular endurance training is to increase resistance to fatigue and improve tolerance to blood lactate, so rest periods between sets are fewer and shorter than in strength training. Typical rest periods range from 30 to 60 seconds, depending on exercise intensity and the experience of the individual. The shoulder workout shown in Table 2.20 can now be updated (as shown in Table 2.21).

▶ **Table 2.21:** Updated workout targeting shoulders

Exercise	Reps	Sets	Weight (% of 1RM)	Rest period
Shoulder press	15	4	50% = 12.5 kg	30 seconds

▶ **Order of exercises to prevent muscle fatigue** – as with strength training methods, a general order of exercise to prevent muscle fatigue is to work the largest muscle groups first and then proceed to the smaller groups (see Table 2.18). Make sure you include all major muscle groups to avoid strength imbalances.

Methods

▶ **Circuit training** – most sports, whether they are team or individual, largely feature moments of intense exercise lasting 30–120 seconds, followed by periods of less intense aerobic exercise. Examples include football and tennis. Circuits are a suitable muscular endurance training method that aids the training for both intense and less intense periods and replicates the needs of the athlete. The principle of high reps and low loads remains the same, but the rest periods are generally replaced by active recovery periods when the athlete transfers from one station to another. A footballer may undertake a muscular endurance circuit over a period of 6 weeks similar to the one shown in Table 2.22.

	Week 1	Week 2	Week 3	Week 4	Week 5	Week 6
Intensity	Low	Medium	High	Low	Medium	High
Squats with medicine ball	30 seconds	40 seconds	50 seconds	30 seconds	40 seconds	50 seconds
Crunches	15	20	25	15	20	25
Dumbbell lunges	30 seconds	40 seconds	50 seconds	30 seconds	40 seconds	50 seconds
Press-ups	15	20	25	15	20	25
Plank	30 seconds	40 seconds	50 seconds	30 seconds	40 seconds	50 seconds
Back extensions	15	20	25	15	20	25
Calf raises	30 seconds	40 seconds	50 seconds	30 seconds	40 seconds	50 seconds
Changeover time	20 seconds	15 seconds	10 seconds	20 seconds	15 seconds	10 seconds

▶ **Fixed-resistance machines** – useful during muscular endurance training (either with or without a helper). The risk of injury from repetition failure or over-extending joints is far less with resistance machines than free weights.

▶ **Free weights** – allow an individual to have constant resistance during exercise, which adds to the 'endurance' element. The use of free weights can increase the risk of injury. For safety reasons, even when using smaller weights compared with strength training, helpers (or 'spotters') should oversee an individual as there is a risk of muscular failure towards the end of the set.

▶ **Resistance bands/tubing** – these can be used for single muscle exercises, as part of a muscular endurance circuit when the resistance required is light, or for working a specific muscle group (for example rotator cuff) not suited to free weight, body weight exercise or resistance machines.

Ⅱ PAUSE POINT Is it difficult to further overload specific muscle groups as part of a muscular endurance programme?

> **Hint** In sets you can use different exercises, one after another, within the same set, so long as they target the same muscle group.

> **Extend** Research the training methods known as 'super sets' and 'super giant sets'. What level of athlete uses these methods?

Core stability training methods

Core stability training exercises the deep muscles of the torso all at the same time. It is vital to most sports because the core muscles stabilise the spine and provide a solid foundation for movement in the arms and legs. The core is the centre point for all sporting actions – it reduces postural imbalance and plays an important role in injury prevention.

Methods

▶ **Yoga** – an ancient form of exercise focusing on strength and flexibility combined with breathing techniques to enhance physical and mental wellbeing. It is one of the best ways to build core stability, strength and flexibility in your muscles, as it focuses on the abdominal and back regions. Yoga can be performed using light free weights which create additional forces on the muscles and joints, increasing the overall strength and core stability requirements of each exercise or pose. Resistance bands can also target areas requiring precision movement while applying an additional resistance. Yoga exercises are varied but can target every area required for core stability. Exercise examples are shown in Figure 2.7 and are described below.

- **Side plank** strengthens the obliques, while abdominal muscles stabilise the body.
- **Floating triangle** lengthens and strengthens the obliques, abdominals and back muscles.
- **Boat** engages all the abdominal muscles.
- **Dolphin** works the abdominals while flexing the spine.
- **Locust** strengthens the muscles around the spine and is ideal to counter all previous exercises and maintain an exercise balance.

▶ **Figure 2.7:** Yoga positions

▶ **Pilates** – developed by Joseph Pilates, who believed mental and physical health were interlinked. His method was influenced by other forms of exercise, including gymnastics, boxing and wrestling. Pilates is similar to yoga and aims to strengthen the body with particular focus on the body's core to improve strength, general fitness and well-being. Resistance bands can also target areas requiring precision movement while applying additional resistance. Pilates develops whole-body strength, flexibility, coordination, balance, and good posture, with a decreased risk of injury compared with other forms of exercise.

▶ **Gym-based exercises** – because core stability training methods tend to use body weight exercises (for example, yoga and Pilates), they can also be performed on a gym mat. Exercises such as plank, bridge and V-sit can also be done on a mat and there are various resistance machines (for example, back extension machines and abdominal crunch machines) that work aspects of core stability. Gym-based core stability exercises can incorporate a variety of equipment to aid training, such as resistance bands. A stability ball will further engage the core muscles by introducing the need for additional coordination and balance due to the 'wobble' effect. Kettle bells engage your core muscles with almost every lift, and free weights can add additional resistance to an exercise. All can be combined for a core stability circuit training programme.

Flexibility training methods

Both **static flexibility** and **dynamic flexibility** can be developed using a range of training methods. The main methods of flexibility training are:

▶ static stretching

▶ dynamic stretching

▶ proprioceptive neuromuscular facilitation (PNF) stretching.

The general principle of flexibility training is to overload a specific muscle group by stretching the muscles beyond what they are used to. The aim is to increase the range of movement, and work must be targeted towards the joints and muscle groups requiring improvement. The movement should not exceed the tolerance level of the tissue. For improvements in flexibility, an individual should increase the time (duration) of stretching and the number of repetitions to allow overload to take place.

As flexibility is significantly affected by the temperature of muscles and connective tissues, flexibility training is best completed at the end of a training session or after some form of aerobic training. If using stretching activities as part of a warm-up, you should make sure the stretching is low-intensity and does not stretch the muscle or joint too far, too soon.

▶ Stretching is a key way to improve flexibility

The three main types of stretch are:

▶ **Maintenance stretches** – used to return a worked muscle to its normal length. They are performed after an exercise session. They should be held for 10–15 seconds. Stretching after an exercise session is one of the most neglected areas of fitness training. Research shows individuals who regularly stretch after training reduce the risk of injury, reduce muscle tension and improve muscle coordination.

▶ **Developmental stretches** – used to increase muscle length or muscle flexibility. They are performed at the end of an exercise session. They should be held for an initial 6–10 seconds, then developed slightly further for another 20–30 seconds. They are a key method of increasing muscle flexibility and an individual's range of movement. However it is not solely about achieving more flexibility, but should be considered a specialised area of stretching designed to aid and improve posture and general well-being.

▶ **Pre-activity stretches** – used to get the muscle ready for exercise. They should be performed standing and held for 8–10 seconds and be performed after the warm-up phase of your exercise programme. Pre-activity stretches should focus on the muscles or muscle groups that the exercise programme will target.

Static stretching

To improve flexibility, you can use static stretches, which are controlled and slow. There are two types:

▶ **Active** – can be done individually. Active stretching involves voluntary contraction of specific muscles. Research shows that this can lead to gains in range of motion and increased functional mobility.

▶ **Passive** – also known as assisted stretching, it requires the help of another person or an object such as a wall. The other person applies an external force (push or pull) to force the muscle to stretch. Passive stretching is one of the safest methods of stretching and also most helpful for relaxation.

Dynamic stretching

Think about when you have watched football players, rugby players or basketball players going through their warm-up. You will see them performing a range of movements that are like the sports movements they need during the game. These are dynamic flexibility exercises. Dynamic flexibility is important for sports that have high-speed movements and movements that take a muscle or joint past its normal range of static flexibility.

Proprioceptive neuromuscular facilitation (PNF) technique

Proprioceptive neuromuscular facilitation (PNF) stretching is an advanced form of stretching and one of the most effective ways of increasing flexibility. The types of movement vary between different muscles and muscle groups, but the general process is the same:

▶ Stretch the target muscle group to the upper limit of its range.

▶ **Isometrically** contract the muscle or muscle group against a partner for 6–10 seconds.

▶ Relax the muscle or muscle group as your partner stretches it to a new upper limit or range of movement (you should be able to stretch it further this time).

When using this type of stretching remember that pain is the body's signal that you are working out too hard in some way, so when this activity hurts too much you have taken it too far.

> **Key term**
>
> **Isometric** – an exercise in which an engaged muscle group produces no movement of the joint at which the muscles are attached.

Equipment

▶ **Towel** – wrapping a towel around, for example, your feet or a stable fixing in a gym, and holding on to both ends of it can help you to stretch a muscle a few centimetres further while keeping the rest of the body stable.

▶ **Belt** – can be used to maintain correct limb alignment during stretches to increase flexibility and mobility.

▶ **Band** – resistance bands come in many forms and strengths, and are ideal for adding a resistance or supportive element to a stretch while stabilising the movement.

▶ **Mat** – an essential piece of kit while stretching. Most stretches are done on the floor so, to aid concentration and support, it is important you remain comfortable throughout, without pressing your bodyweight against a hard floor which may lead to injury.

▶ **Partner** – important when performing PNF stretching. Partner up with someone who knows your physical abilities or experience so they know your upper-limit range of movement when assisting in a stretch.

Speed training methods

Principles of speed training

Speed is an essential component of fitness in most sports, and good acceleration is vital. Acceleration from a standing position is critical for success in sports such as sprinting and in team-based sports such as rugby league, where a player has to accelerate with the ball past opponents, changing pace rapidly.

Although there are general guidelines for speed-based interval training, the more specific requirements are geared towards the requirements of specific sports and specific positions within those sports. Speed training should take place after a rest period of low-intensity training to reduce the risk of injury or overtraining. Speed training should take place after the warm-up, and any other training within the session should be low-intensity.

▶ **Training thresholds** – maximum speed training works largely in the anaerobic training zones, while the recovery phases – jogging or walking – work in the aerobic training zones. A general guideline for speed training is that there should be a work-rest ratio of 1:5. If you were to have a 10 second maximal sprint, this would be followed by a 50 second rest period. Interval training is used in aerobic endurance training and speed training, so you can use Table 2.23 to plan a training session targeting different energy systems.

▶ **Table 2.23:** Guidelines for speed-based interval training

Energy system	Time (min:sec)	Sets	Reps per set	Work : relief ratio	Relief interval type
ATP–PC	0:10	5	10	1:3	Walking
	0:20	4	10	1:3	
ATP–PC–LA	0:30	5	5	1:3	Jogging
	0:40	4	5	1:3	
	0:50	4	5	1:3	
	1:00	3	5	1:3	
	1:10	3	5	1:3	
	1:20	2	5	1:2	
LA–O_2	1:30–2:00	2	4	1:2	Jogging
	2:00–3:00	1	6	1:1	
O_2	3:00–4:00	1	4	1:1	Walking
	4:00–5:00	1	3	1:0.5	

▶ **Percentage of maximum heart rate** – as speed training should achieve maximal sprint speeds, it is working in the anaerobic zone. At peak speed an athlete should be working towards 90–100 per cent of maximum heart rate. However, peak speed is only a small percentage of the total training time – the remainder will be recovery time when an athlete is working towards a heart rate of 60 per cent of maximum.

▶ **Recovery periods between sets** – depending on the intensity, repetitions and sets used as part of your training programmes, you may require rest periods of 1–3 minutes in between sets. These will be essential for you to replenish energy stores, maintain correct technique and reduce the risk of injury.

Methods

▶ **Hollow sprints** – team sports such as football or rugby and individual sports such as tennis require participants to vary their speed while competing. This change of pace requires practice, and hollow sprints are designed to do this. Hollow sprints involve sprinting for a set distance, slowing down, and then accelerating again for another set distance. This process helps train the Type IIx and Type IIa fast-twitch muscle fibres and conditions them to accelerate quickly over short distances. The distances should be variable throughout the activity. An example of a hollow sprint programme is shown in Table 2.24.

▶ **Table 2.24:** A typical hollow sprint training programme

Start	15 m	5 m	10 m	5 m	5 m	5 m	2 minute rest
	Sprint	Jog	Sprint	Jog	Sprint	Jog	

▶ **Acceleration sprints** – this is an aerobic training method where running speed is gradually increased from an initial jog to **striding** then sprinting at maximum speed. Each section should be approximately 50 metres long (150 metres in total). The speed increase is incremental – this reduces the risk of muscle injury.

▶ **Interval training** – can improve anaerobic endurance. The work intervals for aerobic endurance training tend to be long in duration and low in intensity in order to train the aerobic system. By contrast, for anaerobic endurance, work intervals will be shorter but more intense (near to maximum). Interval training can help athletes improve speed and anaerobic endurance (speed endurance). Athletes should work at a high intensity. Overload and progression can be brought in by making changes, e.g. decreasing the rest period.

▶ **Resistance drills** – one of the best methods to increase speed, resistance band exercises place an additional resistance against an accelerating athlete over short distances. This additional resistance makes the muscle work harder during the acceleration phase. When the resistance bands are removed, the athlete will be ready to move and accelerate faster in their role or sport. A similar principle is applied if the athlete trains with a parachute instead of a resistance band, or uses a sled or bungee ropes. An alternative is to simply add resistance by getting the participant to run up a hill.

Equipment

The following types of equipment will provide an additional load to speed training. This load works against the athlete over short distances, making the muscles work harder during the acceleration and speed phases of movement.

▶ **Resistance bands/tubes** – inexpensive equipment used during resistance drills. The resistance can be varied according to the ability of the athlete. Resistance bands are limited to a short distance unless a partner is holding either end and follows the athlete. The tension within the band/tube provides the additional load.

▶ **Parachutes** – similar to resistance bands but with the advantage that they are not limited to a set distance. Air resistance within the parachute provides the additional load.

▶ **Bungee rope** – similar to resistance bands but, due to their greater length, bungee ropes allow the athlete to run a greater distance. The tension within the rope provides the additional load.

▶ **Resistance tyres** – a tyre is attached by a rope to a harness or belt worn by the athlete. This equipment works on a similar principle to parachutes, but friction between the tyre and the ground provides the resistance rather than the air resistance of the parachute.

Key term

Striding – long, continuous steps that are quicker than walking but slower than sprinting.

▶ Speed training can use parachutes to increase the challenge of resistance drills

Training methods for skill-related fitness components

Agility training methods

Agility is the ability to change direction quickly without losing speed or balance. Exercises involve changing the body position quickly and with control and include **SAQ (Speed, Agility, Quickness)**. These combine speed, the maximum velocity an athlete can achieve and maintain, and quickness (rapid and energetic movements). SAQ works over short distances, usually over 5 metres. Each drill is performed as quickly as possible without compromising technique and might involve running between cones in a zig-zag pattern, forcing rapid changes of direction. SAQ is designed to replicate specific movements in sports such as rugby and football.

Balance training methods

Static balance exercises focus on retaining the body's centre of mass above the base of support **when stationary** – if you can stand on one leg without holding onto anything for at least 20 seconds, your static balance is good. Balance training is useful on two fronts. First, a controlled wobble engages your core muscles and second, it can prepare you for a rapid change of direction. An example of static balance training is the one-legged balance. You start with your feet together, raise one foot – knee facing forward or to the side – and hold the position with eyes open, then closed. Switch feet and repeat for four to six reps with each foot.

In contrast, **dynamic balance** exercises focus on retaining the body's centre of mass above the base of support **when moving**. Ideally, balance training requires that both right and left sides of the body allow for an equal range of motion of your body's joints. A wobble cushion or balance board trainer can help if one side of your body is weaker than the other. An example of dynamic balance training is the Plank Progression, which improves your balance of one shoulder at a time. You start in a standard plank position with your elbows on top of the dome and hold for 30 seconds. Then, progress to one elbow at a time and add a rotation if possible.

An effective balance routine progresses from static to dynamic balance moves: for instance, you could move from a basic squat to a squat on one leg, keeping support near in case you lose balance. This type of progression helps improve your functional balance.

Coordination training methods

Coordination training methods are exercises that use two or more body parts at the same time. Coordination training often leads to improved execution of sport-specific skills because continued practice and repetition aid coordination. For example, continued forehand practice in tennis will increase coordination of the forehand shot.

An example of coordination training is the tennis ball toss. Mark a distance from the wall at which you stand facing the wall. Throw a tennis ball from one hand in an underarm action against the wall, and try to catch it with the opposite hand. Throw the ball back against the wall and catch it with the initial hand. By adding a set time limit to complete a number of throws, you can also add the factor of working under pressure.

Reaction time training methods

Reaction time is vital in many sports, especially timed and short-duration sports. Consider how important the start is in the 100-metre sprint. Reaction time to the gun is often where the race is won and lost. But other sports such as table tennis also call for quick reaction times. The following pieces of equipment may be used:

▶ **Stopwatch** – used to time the participant's reactions.

▶ **Whistle** – an excellent stimulus to get athletes to react. Most athletes are used to hearing a whistle.

▶ **Visual stimuli** – coloured or traffic lights, flags or hand signals are examples of visual stimuli to indicate when athletes should react and carry out a sport-specific skill or move.

▶ **Auditory stimulus** – shouting or a range of electronically-created sounds can be used to get athletes to react. A good training practice is to have a range of sounds, with each sound followed by a different reaction or movement.

▶ **Reaction Ball** – a six-sided ball used to enhance reaction time and hand–eye coordination. The random movement of the Reaction Ball requires the athlete to react quickly and seize – or catch – the ball before it bounces and changes direction. Reaction Balls can be used in sports-specific training drills such as those used by cricket fielders.

▶ A Reaction Ball

Power training methods

Plyometric training is designed to improve explosive power. It is a useful training method because it engages and stretches the target muscle or muscle groups during the same exercise movement. Plyometric training is ideal for sports and activities involving explosive actions, such as a slam dunk in basketball or a 100-metre sprint start.

If you stretch a contracted muscle it becomes stronger, and muscles produce more force if they have previously been stretched. Plyometric activities help this process of force production by taking the muscle through an eccentric muscle action followed by a powerful concentric muscle action. This process causes the muscle spindles to cause a stretch reflex, preventing any muscle damage and producing a maximum force at a rapid rate.

Different activities are used in plyometric training sessions. Lower body activities include hurdle jumps, single leg bounds, alternate leg bounds, box drills, and depth jumps. Upper body activities include plyometric press-ups and medicine ball throws.

Equipment that may be used includes the following:

▶ **Ladders** – these are portable pieces of equipment, 2–10 m in length, ideal for developing speed and agility but also useful for plyometric training. Hops are a basic plyometric exercise that can be adapted using ladders. You lay the ladder out and stand at one end with feet together; get yourself into a squat position and hop down the length of the ladder on both feet from ladder segment to segment. A progression of this exercise is to switch to single foot hops.

▶ **Cones** – cone routines are simple but effective. Cones are laid out on the ground and a routine or pattern is explained which generally involves a series of one-legged jumps from one cone to another, usually side-to-side. These jump routines can be performed as low-level plyometric exercises but they also develop coordination and balance.

▶ **Jump ropes** – jump rope routines are flexible and are ideal for developing speed, agility and balance and improving your hand–eye–foot coordination. Jump rope routines can be performed as low-level plyometric exercises: keep both feet together and jump quickly while turning the rope, coming no higher than 5–10 cm off the ground with a slight skip between each jump. Repeat the exercise for 50–100 repetitions depending on fitness and experience.

- ▶ **Medicine ball** – the chest push using a medicine ball is a plyometric exercise.
  - From a kneeling position, hold a medicine ball with both hands against the chest.
  - Carry out the pass by pushing the medicine ball in an explosive, rapid movement outwards from the chest, pushing as far forward as possible.
  - Allow the body to fall forward with the momentum and catch yourself on the floor with the palms of your hands.
- ▶ **Hurdles** – can be used to perform a variety of exercises that are simple to set up and adapt. A simple yet effective leg exercise is hurdle jumps with a bounce. With feet together, you jump over one hurdle. After landing, bounce once then jump the next hurdle. Continue this sequence until you reach the final hurdle.
- ▶ **Benches** – bench jumps are a highly effective exercise designed to increase leg power and strength. Difficulty can be increased by using a taller bench, but care must be taken to ensure the bench is stable, otherwise injury may occur.

Ⅱ PAUSE POINT Can you think of any potential safety concerns when doing plyometric exercise?

> Hint   The intense movements used in repetition increase the stress on joints and the potential for injury.

> Extend   How might you go about implementing low-intensity variations to make plyometrics safe and effective for more people?

Assessment practice 2.4

The fitness coach calls you into his office. He tells you that in 3 months' time he is going to Spain to work with the National Tennis Academy. He has agreed with the general manager that you should undertake a Level 2 gym instructor award, just in case you have to take over his duties while he is away. The tennis club has kindly agreed to pay for this course on condition that you prove you have existing knowledge of different training methods and different components of fitness, and how these can be used at the tennis club.

The fitness coach suggests that you produce an article for the next issue of the tennis club's magazine that covers all the components of fitness to be trained. Where possible you should apply each component using tennis as the sporting example. If this is not possible, he suggests you choose any other sport of your choice, but remember to give each component a sporting context.

If this article is of a good standard, the general manager has promised to publish it in the next issue of the magazine, so all members will have the opportunity to read it.

Plan

- What is the task? What am I being asked to address in the article?
- Are there any fitness training components I am not comfortable with?
- The article may be published in a magazine, so the design and its impact are important. Is this something I may struggle with?

Do

- I know all the components of fitness, and will include all the necessary information, with sporting examples, and explain why this information is important. I will make sure details are brief and to the point, without too much detail to overload the readers.
- I can identify where my article may have gone wrong and adjust my thinking/approach to get myself back on course.

Review

- I can explain what the task was and how I approached the construction of my article.
- I can explain how I would approach the more difficult parts differently next time.

Understand training programme design

Reflect

Consider your own training or coaching experiences. How might you have adapted that coaching and training if you were planning the programme now? How would you analyse the training requirements for your sport? What training methods might you now employ and what nutritional requirements would you consider?

Link

This section will provide useful knowledge that you can apply if you are studying *Unit 4: Sports Leadership* and are asked to develop a session.

Principles of fitness training programmes

When designing training programmes, there are two key questions:

▶ What am I trying to improve?

▶ How am I going to improve it?

You need detailed knowledge of different components of fitness, and the different training methods used to improve them, to answer these questions.

Before you can design a training programme, you will need to set individual goals. Without these, you will not know what to direct your training towards. The programme must be flexible but capable of meeting these goals and personal needs. Each individual has different ambitions and aspirations, and your programme should reflect these.

The athlete's aims and objectives should be broken down into short-term (up to one month), medium-term (one to three months) and long-term goals (three months to one year). Goals should be SMARTER targets:

▶ **Specific** – they say exactly what you mean (e.g. to improve flexibility in the hamstring muscle group)

▶ **Measurable** – you can prove you have reached them (e.g. increase flexibility by 5 cm using the sit and reach test)

▶ **Achievable** – they are actions you can achieve (e.g. practise and improve flexibility through training)

▶ **Realistic** – you will be able to achieve them but they will still challenge you (e.g. the increase in flexibility must be manageable – a 20 cm increase in two weeks is not achievable)

▶ **Timed** – they have deadlines (e.g. to reach the target within six weeks)

▶ **Exciting** – ensure you look forward to and never get bored with your training programme

▶ **Recordable** – keep accurate records of everything you do in a training diary. This will be an excellent resource and source of inspiration to keep you fit and healthy.

You must also consider the resources you will need for the training programme. The range you could choose from is huge, including free weights, resistance machines, cardiovascular machines, mats, resistance bands, kettle bells, suitable clothing and footwear, etc. The training location should also be considered and might have a considerable impact on the equipment available.

Principles of training

One of the most important principles when planning individual sessions and full training programmes is the **FITT principle**. FITT stands for Frequency, Intensity, Time, Type.

▶ **Frequency** of a training session or programme refers to the number of training sessions per week. While the frequency of sessions is important, intensity and duration of training are more important. Novice trainers should not train more than three times per week until their levels of fitness can cope with the increased training load. Once your levels of fitness have increased, you could progress to five times per week.

▶ **Intensity** of a programme is closely linked with the training principle of overload – it is how hard you are working during your training. Intensity is one of the most important factors when designing a training programme and relates to factors such as weight, distance, heart rate percentages and speed.

▶ **Time** relates to the length of each training session, how long the session(s) will last for.

▶ **Type** of exercise you complete will be related to your individual needs. It is the mode of training you will complete, for example free weight training.

Additional principles of training

There are also other principles to consider in planning a training programme.

▶ **Specificity** – the principle of specificity means that you should plan your training programme around the needs of the sport or activity (such as specific muscle groups, components of fitness or sporting actions) and your individual needs (such as targets that are specific to you rather than just general targets).

▶ **Progression** – this is important because your body will only adapt to training if you keep making the training progressively harder (increasing the levels of overload). Without correct levels of overload and progression, your training gains will start to level off or 'plateau'. Be careful when planning progression, because poor performances may result from too little progression or a training programme that overloads the system. As well as poor performance, excessive overloading may lead to injury or illness through over-training.

▶ **Overload** – overload is stretching the body systems beyond their normal functional level and is an essential aspect of gaining training effects. The following areas can be adapted (increased or decreased) to control the level of overload:

  • frequency: the number of sessions a week, for example, increasing from two to four

  • intensity: the amount of energy needed to perform a particular exercise or activity

  • duration: the total time an exercise session or activity takes, for example, one 20-minute session could be increased to a 30-minute session.

▶ **Reversibility** – the loss of training benefits and adaptations when you stop training.

▶ **Rest and recovery** – the need for adequate time to recover from training or competition. Your ability to recover from training is just as important as the workout itself.

▶ **Adaptation** – the way the body 'programmes' the muscles to remember movements or skills. The process of repeating these movement or skills encourages the body to adapt so they become easier to perform.

▶ **Variation** – regular changes in training intensity, duration or volume often yield increased gains in performance.

▶ **Individual needs** – the personal fitness needs based on age, motivation, fitness level and gender, and/or the aims or requirements of a specific sport, all form part of a successful training programme.

During your training, you will normally be trying to progress the overload to make sure that you keep seeing training effects, but there are times when you will want or need to reduce the overload. These include:

▶ signs of over-training or burnout, such as injury, illness or severe decrease in motivation

▶ different times of the season (for example, off season or close to a major competition).

Ⅱ PAUSE POINT   What risks are involved with overload?

> **Hint**   Consider the difference between constructively overloading a client and pushing them beyond their capabilities.

> **Extend**   How can you control the level of overload so that your client makes progress rather than suffering injury or burnout?

Periodisation

Most people in sport use a training programme based on a structured cycle. This is known as 'periodisation'. Periodisation can benefit you because it ensures continued physiological and psychological changes, it prevents over-training injuries and boredom, and it helps to achieve peak performance for key events.

The training cycle is split into **macrocycles**, **mesocycles** and **microcycles**.

Macrocycles

The first layer of a training programme may be based on a 1-year to 4-year cycle, which is known as a macrocycle. For example, a football player will train based on a 1-year cycle, from June to May, aiming to peak for a weekly or bi-weekly match, whereas an Olympic athlete will have a 4-year macrocycle, aiming for peak performance to coincide with the Olympic Games.

Mesocycles

The macrocycle is divided into a number of mesocycles, usually lasting 4–24 weeks. The mesocycle is the main method of controlling the work-to-rest ratios. For example, if you have a work-to-rest ratio of 3:1, you will have a four-week mesocycle with three working weeks followed by one active rest week. If you are an inexperienced trainer, you may have a ratio of 2:1, but if you are an advanced trainer, you could have a ratio of up to 6:1.

Mesocycles can be **step loaded**. This technique uses a repetitive work-to-rest ratio; for example, with a 4-week mesocycle, you could have a ratio of 3:1 and repeat this cycle three times but increase the intensity of the work weeks at the start of each cycle.

Microcycles

Each mesocycle is divided into a number of microcycles. The microcycle is planned with a specific adaptation in mind and should follow the principles of FITT training. Microcycles typically last for one week, but can range from 5–10 days. A typical periodised training programme is shown in Table 2.25.

▶ **Table 2.25:** A typical periodised training programme.

Macrocycle											
Mesocycle 1				Mesocycle 2				Mesocycle 3			
Microcycle 1	Microcycle 2	Microcycle 3	Microcycle 4	Microcycle 5	Microcycle 6	Microcycle 7	Microcycle 8	Microcycle 9	Microcycle 10	Microcycle 11	Microcycle 12
Work	Work	Work	Rest	Work	Work	Work	Rest	Work	Work	Work	Rest

Ⅱ **PAUSE POINT**   What factors or events might disrupt the periodisation of a training programme?

> **Hint**   Injuries, illness and unforeseen circumstances happen all the time. We cannot plan for them, only adapt to them.

> **Extend**   How would you get a client back on track after a 6-week injury? Would you re-write or adapt their training programme?

Case study

Sports Scientist: Jack Donnelly and the fitness training challenge

Jack is now well established as the football club's new sports scientist. Having performed a number of tasks throughout the club over the year, Jack has now been asked to work on the more specific training and fitness requirements of the under-16 boys' squad.

Jack found this a step-up in terms of the required sports-specific knowledge. Therefore, Jack has taken it upon himself to gain a Personal Trainer qualification to aid his role at the football club and help the under-16s in their aim to be fitter and stronger. Jack has identified the following steps to achieve his aim:

- **Step 1** – Be realistic: are you in good shape and able to demonstrate or perform exercises in front of trained athletes? Before you start, make sure you are reasonably fit, have an interest in fitness training and programming and are comfortable in a gym setting.

- **Step 2** – Undertake a Level 2 Gym Instructor qualification. This is the first step into fitness training and the fitness industry, and it is the foundation for further progression to becoming a Personal Trainer or Athletic Trainer.

- **Step 3** – Once qualified as a Level 2 Gym Instructor, consider progressing to a Level 3 Diploma and Advanced Diploma in Personal Training. These courses will provide you with advanced knowledge and the development of your gym skills. You may even want to run your own business from this point.

- **Step 4** – The knowledge gained from your academic qualifications combined with a start at Level 2 Gym Instructing will help you carry out and supervise fitness programmes.

Take a look at the websites of some local health and fitness clubs and see if they are advertising for gym instructors. See what their work might be like and compare it to the other health and fitness clubs. There are also opportunities for fitness trainers, personal trainers and strength and conditioning coaches at professional sports clubs. What differences are there between these jobs and those in health and fitness clubs?

Assessment practice 2.5

The fitness coach has a six-month contract to work at a tennis academy in Spain. The general manager has asked if you will fill in until his return. Naturally, you said yes!

However, you have taken over the fitness training duties at a busy time and the general manager has asked you to put together a general training programme for a typicala competitive adult tennis player. This 'off the shelf' training package will help you free up more time to devote to training the rising stars of the under-16s group.

This programme can be written in whichever format you wish, but it must include the following information to ensure the club continues to offer the best training advice possible:

- fitness training programme design: aims and objectives; SMARTER goals; resources required
- principles of training: FITT; specificity; overload; progression; rest and recovery
- periodisation (6 months): macrocycles; mesocycles; microcycles.

The programme should be geared towards the annual tennis club tournament which is in 6 months' time, when the fitness coach will be returning.

Plan

- What is the task? What does the training programme need to address?
- How confident do I feel in my own abilities to complete this task? Are there any areas of fitness training programme design and its impact that I think I may struggle with?

Do

- I know how to design a fitness training programme, and will include all the necessary information and explain why this information is important. It is a six-month programme, so I will keep the detail fairly brief – too many details may overload the clients.

Review

- I can explain what the task was and how I approached the design of my fitness training programme.
- I can explain how I would approach the more difficult parts differently next time.

Further reading and resources

Books

Bean, A. (2013) *The Complete guide to Sports Nutrition*, London: Bloomsbury.

Bean, A. (2015) *Which Sports Supplements Really Work*, London: Bloomsbury.

Brooks, D. (2004) *The Complete Book of Personal Training*, Champaign, IL: Human Kinetics.

Coulson, M. (2013) *Complete Guide to Personal Training*, London: Bloomsbury.

Delavier, F. (2013) *Strength Training Anatomy*, London: Bloomsbury.

Websites

www.eis2win.co.uk – English Institute of Sport: information about the nutritional principles used by the EIS to improve athlete performance.

www.uksca.org.uk – UK Strength and Conditioning Association: information and advice about how to become an accredited strength and conditioning coach.

www.bases.org.uk – British Association of Sport and Exercise Sciences: news and other information about sport and exercise sciences.

www.nhs.uk/livewell – NHS Live Well: tips for leading a healthy lifestyle.

THINK ▶FUTURE

Siobhan Barber

Personal Trainer

I studied a BTEC National Sports course and soon took an interest in fitness training and programming. Early in the course, I knew I wanted to be a Personal Trainer. Soon after starting the course, I took my Level 2 gym instructor's award. The BTEC course helped me pass the exam. Soon after passing, I was able to get a part-time job at a local health club while I continued my studies at college. After my BTEC course I had saved up enough money to do a 12-month Level 3 Personal Trainer course. It was hard work, but I am now a fully qualified Advanced Personal Trainer with a list of clients at a health club.

The role is varied and I see many of my clients either early in the morning or later in the evening, as most work regular hours during the day. The free hours during the day are great as they allow me to relax and give me time to plan my weekly schedule, send out invoices, manage my cash flow and ensure all my insurance and administration is up-to-date. When relaxing, I catch up on the latest research and articles for the fitness industry, just to stay one step ahead for the benefit of my clients. The job is very rewarding but it is vital to have a good rapport with clients, to help them feel comfortable and good about themselves. Their health, well-being and achievements are a reflection of my efforts, so I am also very proud of my clients and all they have accomplished in the gym.

Personal training is my dream job. Throughout my BTEC course I knew it was what I wanted to do, and this focus helped me finish that course and all the subsequent courses. I make a good living and I am just about to put down a deposit on a flat as a first-time buyer. Would I change anything about my work? Not a single thing.

Focusing your skills

Conducting health monitoring tests

It is important to follow 'correct protocol' in health monitoring tests. Clients may feel nervous so you need to put them at ease.

- An ability to communicate with clients is important, so treat them with courtesy and respect, and help them to relax.
- Ensure all equipment is clean, hygienic and ready to use, e.g. all monitors have batteries and all cuffs and callipers have been wiped with anti-bacterial wipes.
- Carry out your tests in a suitable environment and in a professional manner. Explain what you are doing and maintain an air of calm authority throughout.
- Emphasise that results are confidential and will not be passed on without the client's consent.

- Explain results in a considered manner and say how they will be used to develop any training programme.
- Ensure the testing area is left exactly as you found it and all testing equipment is safely stowed away.

Fitness knowledge

- A personal trainer requires sophisticated knowledge about how the body moves and functions. This is based on human anatomy, physiology, psychology, nutrition and exercise programming.
- You are both coach and tutor to your clients, and need to combine long-term goals and motivational techniques in a training programme.
- You are tasked with developing individual training programmes, all of which are different and require careful planning, coordination and organisation.

Getting ready for assessment

This section has been written to help you do your best when you take the assessment test. Read through it carefully and ask your tutor if there is anything you are still not sure about.

About the test

The assessment test is in two parts. Part A will contain a scenario based on an individual who needs guidance on training, lifestyle, and nutrition upon which secondary research is to be conducted. This scenario will be released to you a set period of time before Part B. Part B will include supplementary stimulus information building on the scenario information in Part A. As the guidelines for assessment can change, you should refer to the official assessment guidance on the Pearson Qualifications website for the latest definitive guidance.

Preparing for the test

To improve your chances during the assessment you will need to revise all the key assessment outcomes that are likely to appear. The assessment outcomes were introduced to you at the start of this unit. To help plan your revision, it is useful to know what type of learner you are. Look at the following table and decide which descritpion sounds most like you.

Type of learner	Visual learner	Auditory learner	Kinaesthetic learner
What it means	• Need to see something or picture it to learn it	• Need to hear something to learn it	• Learn better when physical activity is involved – learn by doing
Helpful ways to prepare for the test	• Colour-code information on your notes • Make short flash cards (so you can picture the notes) • Use diagrams, mind-maps and flowcharts • Use post-it notes to leave visible reminders for yourself	• Read information aloud, then repeat it in your own words • Use word games or mnemonics to help • Use different ways of saying things – different stresses or voices for different things • Record short revision notes to listen to on your phone or computer	• Revise your notes while walking – use different locations for different subjects • Try and connect actions with particular parts of a sequence you need to learn • Record your notes and listen to them while doing chores, exercising etc. – associate the tasks with the learning

- Once you receive the scenario for Part A, you should independently conducte research and make notes over the time period before the supervised assessment. Plan a timetable to address each topic contained in the scenario and prepare a set of notes to take into the supervised assessment. Make sure you are familiar with the content by the time you undertake Part B.
- Read carefully any instructions and all the content you are given on the day for Part B. Make sure you refer to your prepared notes and consider how the new supplementary stimulus information builds on the scenario in Part A – write down notes on a blank page.

> Do not start revision too late! Cramming information is stressful and does not work.

- Most questions contain command words. Understanding what these words mean will help you understand what the question is asking you to do. The command words were introduced at the start of this unit.
- Planning your time is an important part of succeeding on a test. Work out what you need to answer and then organise your time. If you are writing an answer to a longer question, try to plan your answer before you start writing. Have a clear idea of the point you want to make, and then make sure this point comes across in everything you write, so it is all focused on answering the question you have been set.

Worked example

David Smith is 30 years old and works a 40-hour week in an office administration role. He has not undertaken any exercise for at least five years. He takes the train to work each day, a journey that last approximately 15 minutes. While on holiday recently, he noticed he had gained weight (10 kg in the last two years). His best friend has suggested that he starts playing football with him and his friends again, but David is worried he will not be able to play like he once could and will suffer on account of his increased weight and obvious lack of fitness.

Look carefully at how the question is set out to see how many points you need to include in your answer.

David has decided to join a local gym and undergo a full fitness assessment, so that in the weeks ahead, he may be able to start playing five-a-side football again. He has completed a PAR-Q form and indicated that he has no medical conditions and is fit to take part in physical activity. Consequently, David has been given a 6-week training programme to follow.

Lifestyle questionnaire

Section 1: Personal details			
Name	Mr D Smith	Date of birth	01/07/1986
Address	10 The Drive, Milltown		
Phone (home)	01234 566786	Phone (mobile)	07785879657
Occupation	Office worker		
Hours worked	9 a.m. to 6 p.m. with a 1-hour lunch break		
How far do you live from your workplace?	Approx. 5 miles		
How do you travel to work?	Train		
Section 2: Current activity levels			
How many times per week do you currently take part in physical activity?	None		
Section 3: Your lifestyle			
How many units of alcohol do you usually consume per week?		16	
Do you smoke?		No	
Do you experience stress on a daily basis?		Yes	
If yes, what causes your stress?		Work deadlines	
On average, how many hours of sleep do you get per night?		6	
Section 4: Health monitoring tests			
Blood pressure	140/90 mm Hg		
Resting heart rate	88 bpm		
BMI	31		
Waist-to-hip ratio	1.3		
Section 5: Physical goals			
What are your physical/sporting goals?	Start playing competitive 5-a-side football again and lose at least 10 kg in weight		
Signed (client): D. Smith			

With reference to the lifestyle questionnaire shown, interpret the lifestyle factors and screening information for the client. [12]

Answer: *Client is 30 years old and his BMI suggests he is overweight and needs to lose between 8 and 10 kg. His blood pressure is too high and he should drink less alcohol. He has an office job and does not get any exercise during the day or at home. Says he wants to play football again but afraid he will make a fool of himself because he is too fat and not fit enough. Wants to change his lifestyle.*

This answer is generally relevant to the client's lifestyle factors but it does not cover some of the information provided by the client (i.e. travel method used, resting heart rate, stress factors, etc.). 5 marks awarded.

Suggest relevant training methods for the client. [8]

Answer: *Client's aims are to lose weight and get fit for football. Suggest Week 1 training of 3 days per week concentrating on cardiovascular fitness to underpin later muscular endurance, agility, flexibility and further cardiovascular fitness. To review blood pressure after three and six week intervals. Try to make training football-specific if possible. Initial cardiovascular training to concentrate on low to moderate treadmill exercises to get client's base fitness levels up. Begin Week 1 with low intensity resistance machines with focus on the legs to aid football.*

This answer suggests the use of training methods that have specific relevance to the client's requirements. It takes into account his current level of fitness and suggests adaptations to the training programme specific to the client's requirements (football). 7 marks awarded.

Design weeks 1 and 6 of a 6-week training programme for the client. [6]

Answer:

Week 1	
	Physical activity
Monday	Gym: • 5 min CV warm-up on treadmill – low intensity • Static stretch – all major muscle groups • Chest press and leg press on resistance machines (2 × 15 reps – low resistance) • 20 min run on treadmill at 8 km/h • 2 × 10 arm curls – low resistance • 2 × 10 crunches • 5 min CV cool down on exercise cycle • Cool down stretching
Tuesday	Walk to work
Wednesday	Gym: • 5 min CV warm-up on exercise bike – low intensity • Static stretch – all major muscle groups • Seated rows and leg extensions on resistance machines (2 × 15 reps – low resistance) • 20 min row at low intensity • 2 × 10 tricep extensions – low resistance • 2 × 10 leg raises • 5 min CV cool down on treadmill • Cool down stretching
Thursday	Rest

Friday	Gym:
	• 5 min CV warm-up on treadmill – low intensity
	• Static stretch – all major muscle groups
	• Shoulder press and leg extensions on resistance machines (2 × 15 reps – low resistance)
	• 20 min run on treadmill at 8 km/h
	• 1 × 5 press-ups
	• 2 × 10 crunches
	• 5 min CV cool down on exercise cycle
	• Cool down stretching
Saturday	30 min walk around local park
Sunday	• Rest

Week 6: Progression

	Physical activity
Monday	Gym:
	• 10 min CV warm-up on treadmill – low intensity
	• Static stretch – all major muscle groups
	• Chest press and leg press on resistance machines (3 × 15 reps – low resistance)
	• 30 min run on treadmill at 8 km/h
	• 3 × 10 arm curls – low resistance
	• 2 × 10 crunches
	• 10 min CV cool down on exercise cycle
	• Cool down stretching
Tuesday	Gym:
	• 10 min CV warm-up on exercise bike – low intensity
	• Static stretch – all major muscle groups
	• Seated rows and leg extensions on resistance machines (3 × 15 reps – low resistance)
	• 25 min row at low intensity
	• 3 × 10 tricep extensions – low resistance
	• 2 × 10 leg raises
	• 10 min CV cool down on treadmill
	• Cool down stretching
Wednesday	Walk to work
Thursday	Gym:
	• 10 min CV warm-up on treadmill – low intensity
	• Static stretch – all major muscle groups
	• Shoulder press and leg extensions on resistance machines (3 × 15 reps – low resistance)
	• 30 min run on treadmill at 8 km/h
	• 2 × 10 press-ups
	• 2 × 10 crunches
	• 10 min CV cool down on exercise cycle
	• Cool down stretching
Friday	Gym:
	• 10 min CV warm-up on exercise bike – low intensity
	• Static stretch – all major muscle groups
	• Seated rows and leg extensions on resistance machines (3 × 15 reps – low resistance)
	• 25 min row at low intensity
	• 3 × 10 tricep extensions – low resistance
	• 2 × 10 leg raises
	• 10 min CV cool down on treadmill
	• Cool down stretching
Saturday	Rest
Sunday	Rest

This answer demonstrates specific relevance to the individual's training requirements with a clear progression from Week 1 to Week 6. It includes appropriate rest periods and exercise periods away from the gym to keep the client interested and motivated. 6 marks awarded.

Professional Development in the Sports Industry

3

Getting to know your unit

The sports industry in the UK is larger than ever. People now have more leisure time and this has seen an increase in participation in leisure and sports activities. To have a successful career you will need to understand all the different opportunities available in the sports market and the different career development steps you will need to follow to reach your chosen goal. Learning how to build a career plan will be a major part of your work in this unit. When you have finished this unit you will have a much better understanding of what the sports industry is and the job opportunities that exist within it.

How you will be assessed

This unit will be assessed internally by a series of tasks set by your tutor. These tasks might take the form of presentations or written documents. There is also likely to be a strong emphasis on practical demonstrations during which you will be observed.

The assignments set by your tutor may result in you producing:
▶ detailed written reports demonstrating analytical skills
▶ evidence of extensive research
▶ completed action plans and reviews
▶ evidence of participation in interviews.

You will discover that the range and type of employment in the sports industry goes beyond jobs such as PE teacher or lifeguard, and the assessment of this unit reflects both that range of possible positions and the skills and expectations of potential employers.

The overall aim of this unit is to help you focus your attention on a specific employment role in the sports industry, to help you narrow your focus and decide on a career path, and to compare and contrast roles within the industry.

For Learning Aim A, you are likely to be asked for a report that examines two career pathways that are linked to your own career aspirations.

Learning Aims B, C and D will be more practically focused and may involve a role play scenario in which you take on the roles of both interviewer and interviewee. In this role play, you will demonstrate your competence and ability to be self-critical, while using recognised analytical tools.

The exercises in this unit are designed to help you practise and gain skills that will help you to complete your assignments. The theories in the unit will give you background information to help you to complete the assignments but will not guarantee you a particular grade.

To pass this unit you must ensure that you have covered all of the Pass grading criteria. If you are seeking a Merit or Distinction grade then you must be able to show that you are capable of analysis of the key areas of focus, specifically employment opportunities and requirements, personal and developmental requirements and needs. For Distinction grades, you are required to justify your focus on specific careers, demonstrate a high level of self-management in producing plans and display the ability to evaluate concisely and offer recommendations.

Assessment criteria

This table shows what you must do in order to achieve a **Pass**, **Merit** or **Distinction** grade, and where you can find activities to help you.

Pass	Merit	Distinction
Learning aim Understand the career and job opportunities in the sports industry		**AB.D1** Justify how own skills audit outcomes, and development action plan, align to chosen career pathway based on a comprehensive knowledge and understanding of the career. **Assessment practice 3.1** **Assessment practice 3.2**
A.P1 Explain the different career pathways, the associated job opportunities and their requirements in the sports industry. **Assessment practice 3.1**	**A.M1** Analyse the professional development requirements and opportunities for specialism or promotion in different career pathways and the associated job opportunities in the sports industry. **Assessment practice 3.1**	
A.P2 Explain the development pathway into a selected career in the sports industry. **Assessment practice 3.1**		
Learning aim Explore own skills using a skills audit to inform a career development action plan		
B.P3 Explain how selected sports industry career matches outcomes of own personal skills audit. **Assessment practice 3.2**	**B.M2** Analyse own personal skills audit outcomes against a selected career in the sports industry. **Assessment practice 3.2**	
B.P4 Develop a career development action plan to meet the requirements of intended sports career, using skills audit outcomes. **Assessment practice 3.2**	**B.M3** Develop a career development action plan that has specific relevance to the requirements of intended sports career and skills audit outcomes. **Assessment practice 3.2**	
Learning aim Undertake a recruitment activity to demonstrate the processes that can lead to a successful job offer in a selected career pathway		
C.P5 Prepare appropriate documentation for use in selection and recruitment activities. **Assessment practice 3.3**	**C.M4** In interviews and activities demonstrate analytical responses and questioning and activities to allow assessment of skills and knowledge. **Assessment practice 3.3**	**CD.D2** Demonstrate individual responsibility and effective self-management during the recruitment activity. **Assessment practice 3.3**
C.P6 Participate in the selection interviews and activities, as an interviewee. **Assessment practice 3.3**		**CD.D3** Evaluate how well the documents prepared, and own performance in the interview activities, supported the process for accessing the selected career pathway. **Assessment practice 3.3** **Assessment practice 3.4**
Learning aim Reflect on the recruitment and selection process and your individual performance		
D.P7 Review own performance in role in the interviewing activities, supported by an updated SWOT analysis. **Assessment practice 3.4**	**D.M5** Analyse the results of the process and how your skills development will contribute to your future success. **Assessment practice 3.4**	

Getting started

There are many different careers available in the sports industry. Draw a circle in the middle of a sheet of paper and write 'Jobs in the sports industry' inside it. Then draw lines off the circle and, at the end of each line, write the name of a sports industry job, e.g. lifeguard. See how many jobs you can name in the sports industry.

A Understand the career and job opportunities in the sports industry

Scope and provision of the sports industry

The sports industry is large and diverse, and includes employment opportunities as different in nature as a personal trainer, a sports journalist or even a bingo caller!

Since the UK hosted global sports events such as the 2012 London Olympic and Paralympic Games and the 2015 Rugby World Cup, there has been significant growth in employment in areas such as coaching, fitness and event management. This is despite many people feeling they have less spare income and fewer leisure hours. The industry supports over 450,000 jobs in the UK, and the 2012 Olympics alone will continue to contribute £16.5 billion to the overall gross domestic product (the overall value of the UK economy) up to 2017.

Sport is now considered one of the top 15 mainstream employers in the UK economy, above legal services, accounting, telecommunications, advertising and publishing. According to Sport England, sport now accounts for 2.3 per cent of the UK workforce.

Sports provision

The types of **sports provision** available to you depend to a certain extent on where in the UK you live. Outdoor activities – such as climbing, kayaking, rambling and sailing – are more suited to rural or coastal areas. Large international sporting events are usually hosted in or near large cities, often as a practical convenience for those competing from overseas who have to fly into the country and stay in hotel accommodation.

Sports such as running, cycling and swimming are being promoted as local and national governments encourage people to take more exercise. Success in competitive sport by professional sportspeople also helps boost interest: cycling has grown more popular with the success of such figures as Tour de France winners Sir Bradley Wiggins and Chris Froome, and multiple Olympic and World medallist Victoria Pendleton. Their success, coupled with the minimal environmental impact of cycling, has been used to promote the sport at all levels, targeting all ages and classes of society.

> **Key term**
>
> **Sports provision** – the total range of sport and leisure activities offered to the public.

▶ Athletes such as Victoria Pendleton have increased the popularity of cycling

In October 2014, British Cycling achieved a membership of over 100,000 people for the first time, and the overall number of people taking part in local competitions in road, BMX and mountain biking has increased. Since 2011, it is thought that more than 700,000 people have begun riding bikes at least once a month, and the cycling industry is said to contribute £3 billion to the UK economy and employ more than 23,000 people.

Research what has caused this huge increase in the popularity of cycling. Take a look at the kinds of employment opportunities that now exist in cycling. Be prepared to present your findings as a small group to the rest of your class.

Geographical factors

While some traditional sports, such as football, continue to grow in popularity in the UK, others are suffering as newly-emerging sports – such as *parkour* (free running), paddle boarding and Cyclocross – attract participants at their expense. The national governing bodies for both netball and cricket report a downturn in participants.

The type of sport or physical activity that you participate in is largely influenced by where you live. Those living in inner-city areas generally have better access to traditional and non-traditional sports. However, participation in other sports is more likely in rural areas, for example show jumping, other equine sports and those requiring large amounts of space.

Inner city sports provision is not only limited to space-friendly activities. Even the largest, most densely populated cities now often make very clever use of space. Golf courses often surround parkland in built-up areas, and lakes and waterways – originally designed for industrial use – often host a range of powered and non-powered water sports such as jet-skiing, water jet-packing, canoeing and angling.

Discussion

What causes a sport or activity to go in or out of fashion? Why do you think that traditional sports such as netball and rounders are declining in popularity? Similarly, what is it about new 'emergent' sports such as free running and paddle boarding that make them popular? Think carefully about how people are influenced, why they might choose a particular sport and what makes it so appealing to them.

The environment

Everything we do has an environmental impact. Since sport and leisure participation levels are higher than ever, it follows that the impact on the environment is also greater than ever. This is not restricted to the use of fuel to travel to and from sports and sporting events. The sector most aware of its own impact is the outdoor sector, which includes sports such as canoeing, climbing and mountain biking. Legislation has sought to limit the erosion of paths and tracks caused by thousands of walkers and ramblers (one of the fastest-growing activities in the UK).

However, it is not only outdoor activities that are aware of their impact. In England there are 92 football clubs in the top four professional leagues, and hundreds more non-league clubs, many with their own stadia. These clubs use a vast amount of water to treat their pitches – one report suggested in excess of 20,000 litres a day at some grounds (the same volume as a small swimming pool). The many thousands of travelling fans also leave an environmental footprint.

Outdoor activities – friend or foe?

Countryside motor sports such as moto-cross and quad biking have become more popular in recent years.

These activities can have a devastating effect on the landscape and have a significant **carbon footprint** due to their use of fossil fuels.

Other outdoor activities can have a similar effect on the environment. For example, a large BMX event at a track can attract hundreds of competitors and spectators. Due to the remote location of many BMX facilities there are two main considerations: travel and parking.

Check your knowledge

1 As a group, discuss the potential environmental impact of a large number of competitors and spectators all travelling to the same location. What different environmental impacts might this have?

2 Discuss the impact of vehicles and large numbers of competitors and spectators on the area put aside for parking. Develop a three-point plan to deal with that impact. This action plan could be used as a guideline for future events.

Sports infrastructure

Sports **infrastructure** is largely determined by the popularity of a particular sport in an area and the historical development of that sport. Large popular sports generally have their national governing bodies based in big cities such as London. However, regional popularity means that Rugby League is based in the north west (Leeds), surfing in the south west (Newquay) and curling in Scotland (Newbridge). Other sports are popular in all parts of the country, such as cycling, triathlon and military-style fitness classes.

The accessibility of sports and activities is also influenced by the local population. For example, a squash player who wants to join a local league has a far greater chance in a big city than in a remote rural area. The more potential users or participants, the greater the demand.

Research

Look at the different participation rates of similar organised events that are staged throughout the UK. Parkrun, which offers hundreds of 5 km runs in all areas of the UK, could make for an interesting comparison – see www.parkrun.org.uk.

The presence or absence of appropriate facilities, space, transport or equipment will also affect participation – leisure provision is dependent upon available resources and particularly space. Consider the facilities and space required for football, which in a rural area might be played on a village green, compared to an enclosed fenced space in a built-up city.

Discussion

Consider the impact of available space on your sport. Find out how your sport is provided for in built-up towns compared to semi-rural and rural areas.

Socio-economic factors

There are approximately 125,000 sports clubs in the UK with over 6 million members. However, participation can be limited to those who can afford to join or who have sufficient free time to participate. For example, joining a golf club involves not only the cost of membership and green fees, but also the cost of equipment and a fee to play each round. This means the cost of playing golf on a regular basis can run into thousands of pounds. For many low wage earners, it can be too expensive to participate – a **socio-economic** block to participation.

In contrast, running by yourself in the evening is a cheap activity. But if you have to work long hours, will you be too tired to go running after work?

If a whole geographical area is economically disadvantaged, then the facilities on offer in that area might also be affected – they might be run down or neglected, whereas an affluent area might be able to afford maintenance and improvement costs.

> **Key term**
>
> **Socio-economic factors**
> – the social and economic experiences and realities that help shape your personality, attitudes and lifestyle. The factors can also define whole regions and neighbourhoods – Public Service agencies throughout the UK, for example, often cite the socio-economic factor of poverty as being related to areas with high crime rates.

> **Discussion**
>
> Think about the opportunities for participation that female football players have compared with males. Discuss this as a group.

The way that many sports have developed in the UK reflects both their socio-economic origins and current participation. Sports such as rugby, cricket, rowing and hockey developed in public schools and as a result some of the more successful clubs and players are located in fairly affluent areas. Other sports such as basketball, football and skateboarding have their roots in more working-class areas.

> **Research**
>
> What is the social history of your sport? Choose a sport that you enjoy or that interests you, and research the history and development of that sport in the UK. Try to find reasons for the way that the sport developed: for example, did it begin in public schools, is it played in rural or urban areas or is it derived from another sport (e.g. beach volleyball from traditional volleyball)? Present your findings in a short presentation to your peers.

Seasonal factors

Some sports and activities are affected by seasonal factors, many of them weather related.

▶ Open air swimming pools in the UK usually operate between April and September (the number of people wanting to swim outside in the autumn and winter is far smaller than in the spring and summer).

▶ Summer camps for a number of sports tend to be aimed at younger people and take place in the long school summer break when participants are available.

▶ Most sports have a clearly defined season, many running from September to April/May. Others such as Rugby League operate in the summer to take advantage of available resources and weather conditions.

▶ Training camps are often held at specific times of the year, avoiding the competitive season for that sport. Often pre-season training camps are held in warm weather or at high altitude in preparation for the upcoming season or event.

Do you understand the size and diversity of the sports industry and how it affects the kind and amount of sport in your area?

Hint

Think about what sports you and your friends play.

Extend

What does your local authority do to support sport? Find out what they are doing and what their plan is for the next few years.

Careers and jobs in the sports industry

Employment opportunities in the sports industry are varied. It can be helpful to break down the industry into a few categories (see Table 3.1). Many of these categories cross over and their skills are useful in different areas too. For example, if you wanted to be a successful personal trainer you would certainly want to have the skills of both a fitness instructor and a nutritionist in order to be effective in your work.

▶ **Table 3.1:** Categories of job in the sports industry

Category	Possible job roles
Sport and leisure	• Duty management, e.g. leisure centres, holiday parks, adventure and outdoor, coach management • Promotions, sales and marketing • Theme park and cinema management • Sports journalism, web-based media work • Sports development, National Governing Body officers and administrators • Outdoor instructor, sports coach and GP exercise referral • Groundskeeper and lifeguard
Sports science	• Nutritionist • Sports psychologist • Sports injury management
Exercise and therapies	• Massage therapist • Exercise or gym instructor, personal trainer, strength and conditioning coach • Sports physiotherapist, Sports therapist • Lifestyle consultancy and wellness
Teaching and education	• PE teacher, further education tutor • Sports technician
Playwork	• Play worker • Early Years Development and Children's Partnership officers • School assistants who provide and facilitate sport
Gaming	• Casino managers, dealers, cashiers, inspectors, betting shop managers and cashiers, bingo and lottery callers • Online gaming, gaming software

Depending on your employer, you may also be required to perform a range of duties that change on a regular basis in response to changing leisure trends. For example, in a sports centre a recreation assistant's role is primarily that of a lifeguard and to set up and break down sports equipment. However, industry guidelines for this role are only advisory, which means employers are free to shape the nature of the role to suit the facility. Similar job titles for the same job include 'leisure attendant' and 'customer care attendant' – the different names reflect the priorities of the different employers.

Sectors in the sports industry

Sport and leisure in the UK can be categorised into three sectors: the public, private and voluntary sectors. Within these sectors, employment in the sport and leisure industry is usually available at either local or national level.

▶ **Local level** jobs are those that focus on sport or leisure within a local area, for example a local leisure centre. These jobs exist within all sectors.

▶ **National level** employers focus on the whole country. Examples include national governing bodies (NGBs) like the Rugby Football Union (RFU) and Basketball England (BE). Not everyone who works at a national level will be in contact with elite sportspeople – most work to set policy within their sport. NGBs generally:

- organise and run national teams
- train and develop coaches and officials
- offer services such as insurance to their members
- manage the interpretation of the rules of their sport
- where possible, invest any surplus profit back into the national game.

The public sector

The public sector is one of the largest providers of sport in this country. Public sector facilities are usually owned by the local council or local authority and include swimming pools, leisure centres, tennis courts and even some golf courses.

They are open to the general public and provide a service to the community, aiming to make sport accessible to all, particularly those who have not traditionally taken part in sport. Sometimes public sector facilities are run by an organisation that the council has selected. If a private company is appointed to run a facility in this way, it is responsible to the council and must meet targets for local participation and prove its value to the community.

The public sector does not only exist at a local level. The government includes the Department for Culture, Media and Sport (DCMS), which is a public sector employer that provides public funding (money raised through taxes) to promote sport participation and excellence.

The private sector

The private sector has enjoyed large growth over the last few years. Private sector facilities are usually for the use of members only and aim to provide an excellent service to people who pay an initial joining fee followed by monthly membership fees.

Much of the private sector leisure that can be accessed by the general public is fitness focused. Most local private sector employers are fitness centres such as Nuffield Health, David Lloyd and Virgin Active. Members are normally tied to a minimum 1-year contract.

Some private sector centres are specialist, such as tennis, snooker or squash centres, but many provide a wider service. They aim to make a profit for the owners, and most of the management team will have a **performance-related pay** agreement. At a higher level, the company will aim to reward its investors by paying them 'dividends' that share some of the company's profits.

Private sector organisations are usually owned either by individuals or by a wider group of shareholders. Some centres are owned and run on a **franchise** basis; this allows them to benefit from corporate marketing and branding while providing a personal service.

Some professional sports clubs such as Chelsea FC are large multi-national private sector organisations with financial turnovers of millions of pounds a year.

The voluntary sector

The voluntary sector is by far the largest sector in terms of numbers of people involved. It provides most of the sport in this country through volunteers who enjoy sport and want to develop their club or team. Examples include local clubs that meet in the evenings or at weekends, such as football teams, swimming clubs and basketball teams.

Voluntary sector clubs and teams usually cover their costs by collecting subscriptions ('subs') each week or having an annual membership fee. They do not normally own their facilities but rent them from local councils or private organisations.

Volunteers have played a huge role in helping to provide sport in this country for many years, and are often described as the backbone of UK sport. This was especially true at the London 2012 Olympic Games.

The third sector

The third sector is a range of organisations that are neither public nor private. It is essentially another name for the voluntary sector and includes providers such as community organisations, charities, religious associations and other community groups. These organisations are typically 'value driven', choosing to reinvest any profits to improve the performance of the organisation or to address targets such as improving people's health by encouraging sports participation.

Public/private partnerships

Dual use, community use and partnership centres are also growing sectors.

Public/private partnerships are when both public and private organisations are involved in the funding, operation or use of a facility. This can be beneficial, as it may release funding to build a new facility that a public organisation could not afford alone.

For example, a local council might give a private property developer permission to build a large shopping centre but insist that they also make a contribution to the community by building a new facility, such as a leisure centre. This is called a 'planning gain'. It can lead to a partnership between the public and private sectors.

London 2012 Games Makers

One of the main challenges when hosting a major national or international sports tournament such as the Olympic and Paralympic Games is its size. When London was awarded the 2012 Games, one of the key factors in its success was an ambitious proposal that, alongside paid professionals, there would be a team of 70,000 volunteers, carefully recruited for a number of specialist and non-specialist roles. Over 240,000 people applied for these roles.

One of the most enduring images of the games was the army of purple-dressed volunteers who were in the middle of the games and important to their success. Many of these 'Games Makers' had roles that dealt with members of the public, showing them where to go, providing them with sun screen, dealing with problems and generally working as ambassadors to improve the overall quality of the event.

Many of the Games Makers committed to multiple shifts, all of them as volunteers, many taking time out of their normal everyday jobs. The success of this Games Maker programme has prompted the hosts of other international events to recruit in the same way.

Check your knowledge

1 What is the benefit of using volunteers, aside from saving money?

2 Do you have to sacrifice quality if you are not paying?

3 Why were so many people competing for voluntary roles?

4 What are the potential drawbacks of using volunteers?

Football in the community (FITC) schemes are also growing in popularity. The majority of Premier and Football League clubs in England see the benefit of offering football coaching in their area. For the club the advantages can be huge: it can win new fans who will visit the club and buy merchandise, and at the same time club scouts can spot any emerging talent for their youth programmes.

There is nothing to stop a club (in the private sector) from running a FITC scheme on its own – many do so successfully – but a relationship often exists between a club and the local council. The club takes advantage of the council's facilities, education contacts and marketing resources, and in return the council (in the public sector) promotes healthy activity within the local population without having to recruit its own staff to deliver the activity.

Discussion

Consider the role of a community football coach in a FITC scheme. They are far more than just a coach. Discuss how they will need to work closely with the council to ensure that a quality service is offered. Draw up a list of what the local authority would want to ensure and discuss the relative importance of these considerations.

⏸ **PAUSE POINT**   What are the categories of employment in the sports industry and what are the main job roles in each category?

Hint   Using paper, a whiteboard or a tablet, see how many sports or leisure jobs you can name.

Extend   Could the UK sports industry survive without volunteers? How would you go about recruiting volunteers for a sports project?

Sources of information about careers in sport

There are a number of ways to find out about careers in the sports and leisure industry. Each of the sectors has a number of **websites** that give advice about and promote employment in that sector. Most NGBs also have a list of national and local vacancies for a specific sport – a few examples are shown in Table 3.2.

▶ **Table 3.2:** Sources of career guidance

Health and fitness	Sports coaching and sciences
Leisure Opportunities – www.leisureopportunities.co.uk	BASES – www.bases.org.uk The Youth Sport Trust – www.youthsporttrust.org
Leisure and the outdoors	**Education and PE**
Skills Active – www.skillsactive.com The Football Association – www.thefa.com The Independent Schools Football Association – www.isfa.org.uk	Association for Physical Education – www.afpe.org.uk Times Education Supplement – www.tes.com/jobs
General careers advice	
Get Smaart Magazine – www.getsmaart.com Careers in Sport – www.careers-in-sport.co.uk/jobs Human Kinetics – www.humankinetics.me/jobs-careers Sporting Coaching Abroad – www.sportingopportunities.com UK Sport – www.uksport.gov.uk/jobs-in-sport	

County and regional sports partnerships also have recognised and clearly defined careers links with employment providers, primarily for those seeking employment in the public sector. Many sports and sports organisations have **magazines** that include job adverts and sector news, and increasingly job opportunities can also be found on **social media sites** such as Facebook and Twitter.

Specialist **trade organisations** such as the Institute of Groundskeepers and the Society of Sports Therapists use their own websites and social media accounts to promote job vacancies suitable for their membership.

Types of employment

Full-time

Full-time employees usually have one job, at which they work for between 35 and 45 hours a week. In the sports industry this is hardly ever a 9 a.m. to 5 p.m. job and full-time sports professionals should generally expect to work some evenings and weekends.

Full-time employees usually have the advantage of good conditions and benefits such as Statutory Sick Pay (SSP), which means that they will still be paid if they are too ill to work. They are also entitled to paternity/maternity pay, receive regular salary payments (usually once a month), and often have pension contributions paid by their employer.

Theory into practice

A personal trainer will have clients who work in 9–5 jobs and are unlikely to want training sessions during those times. This means that personal trainers will need to compromise their own working hours in order to be available at convenient times. This may mean working unsocial hours.

Research the typical day for a personal trainer, either online or by asking someone in the industry. Try to plan out a typical week. Consider how you might continue to have a social life and what compromises you may be prepared to make, thinking about the advantages and disadvantages of this lifestyle.

Part-time

Part-time employees do not work as many hours as full-time employees. The advantage of working part-time is that it can offer more flexibility, such as working in school hours to offset additional childcare costs. Some people combine two part-time jobs instead of one full-time job because they prefer the variety and flexibility this offers.

There are many reasons why people may choose to work part-time rather than full-time.

▶ They may be studying full-time, which is expensive, and choose to work part-time to help themselves financially.
▶ They may be close to retirement and choose to work fewer hours so they have more time to themselves while remaining in touch with the industry.

Some key sports roles are part-time. Top-level cricket umpires work part-time but remain at the highest level of the game. Similarly, while many top flight football officials are full-time, the vast majority of referees work on a part-time basis, often officiating at several games per week. This part of the sports industry could not afford to pay for full-time officials so part-time workers are vital. Swimming coaches, weekend lifeguards, football in the community officers, sports administrators and reporters are also often part-time employees.

Recent changes to employment law mean part-time employees are entitled to many of the same benefits as full-time employees.

▶ Top-level cricket umpires like Aleem Dar are part-time

Fixed-term contracts

A fixed-term contract has a clearly defined start and end date. This is useful when an employer has limited financial resources or is not able to commit for a long period, or when the appointment will not exist after a short-term period. For example, a tournament director will work before and during an event but will not be required after the tournament ends. Other examples of people who work in the sports industry on fixed-term contracts include:

▶ PE and sport educational consultants, who deliver small-group workshops to help PE teachers learn about changes to courses or new ways of teaching
▶ pop-up sports merchandisers, who sell sports clothing and merchandise at events like world championships, invitational competitions and super leagues but are only required for the duration of the event.

Self-employment

A self-employed person generates their own income, customers and partners, and is responsible to themselves and any employees. Self-employed sports professionals, such as some sports therapists, personal trainers and sports psychologists, can work **independently** and are free to trade with whoever they want.

Other self-employed people prefer to offer their product or services on a **sub-contract** basis. This is where a larger organisation will engage a self-employed person on a sub-contract. For example, a Rugby League team may not wish to employ a full-time sports psychologist but may want to have one available for its players on a case-by-case basis. This means their players can still be treated by a reputable psychologist, but the club does not need to pay for their services when they are not being used.

> **Theory into practice**
>
> Many sports therapists are self-employed and treat their clients in only one or two locations, such as a hotel. The hotel might agree to promote their services and offer them a reduction on the hire cost of facilities such as treatment rooms. What are the benefits of this arrangement to the therapist and the hotel?

Zero-hours contracts

Zero-hours contracts have attracted attention in recent years as they are often seen as contentious and unpopular, with several high-profile controversies. Someone who has signed a zero-hours contract agrees that they may be required to work at any reasonable time but understands that when business is slow they may not be given any hours to work.

Zero-hours contracts have advantages and disadvantages:

▶ **Advantages:** workers have greater flexibility as they have no obligation to accept work when it might impact on their studies or training. For the professional sportsperson this might also mean that they are free to travel and take extra time off when they are competing and training overseas.

▶ **Disadvantages:** zero-hours work often has unpredictable shift patterns that suit the business rather than the worker. A worker is likely to be required at short notice and may feel under pressure to take on work rather than refuse and risk being offered less or no work in the future. With this type of contract there is also no guarantee of any income.

Large sports retailers often offer zero-hours contracts, as do companies that provide security at sporting events and some fitness providers for positions such as personal trainer.

Apprenticeships

An apprenticeship is a training programme that is carried out mostly in the workplace while 'on the job', with additional training delivered by an education partner such as a further education college.

Apprentices spend most of their working week with their employer, working at a rate of pay specific to their age or level of training, until they are fully qualified. Apprenticeships vary in length: even within the sports industry some are as short as 1 year, while others are as long as 6 years depending on the level of the training.

Apprenticeships are most common in the manufacturing, engineering and construction industries but there are several examples in sport. The PE and School Sports Apprenticeship recruits new PE staff, such as PE teaching assistants. As part of their training, the apprentices are involved in day-to-day PE teaching support, activity leadership and sports coaching, as well as gaining relevant qualifications in the industry.

Professional training routes, legislation and skills in the sports industry

Different career pathways in sport

There are a range of different ways to seek employment in the sports industry and many people follow quite different routes to arrive at the same job. The following profiles offer ideas as to how you can pursue a career in sport.

Becoming a sports coach

Sports coaches are the key to successful performance. Whether they are working with a top performer who needs small adjustments to succeed, or a complete novice who needs help and support to achieve, the role of the coach is critical. As with all professions it is necessary to train, practise and qualify. This is a typical pathway for a cycling coach.

- Start by gaining some work experience, perhaps working as an assistant to a coach who has recognised qualifications and experience, and at the same time apply for Cycling Coach qualifications at Level 1 and upwards, and look for volunteering opportunities at local cycling events.

- While you are doing this, take an active interest, and train where opportunities exist, in areas such as safeguarding and child protection. Develop your knowledge of all disciplines – BMX, Cyclocross, mountain biking (MTB) and road cycling.

- Continue gaining experience across all disciplines, including working with children and coaching disability cycling. Where possible, develop your reputation by working with high-level athletes.

- Gain additional qualifications that will add to the required set of skills, such as becoming a *commissaire* (a race official) or training in first aid and cycle mechanics.

Becoming a sports scientist

The key jobs in the UK for sports scientists are nutritionist, sports psychologist, sports therapist and injury specialist. Other jobs are connected with performance enhancement and exercise and fitness, such as strength and conditioning coaches. Employment opportunities in sports science are increasing, but it is a competitive field with more than 10,000 sports science places offered every year at universities in the UK alone.

- A good starting point for a sports scientist is to take a sports science or similar degree at university. Most universities offer more than one course of this type; some specialise in health and fitness and others in nutrition or psychology.

- Since the market is competitive, many graduates of sports science go on to further studies and Master's degrees in specialist areas such as Biomechanics or Strength and Conditioning. Many take on post-graduate teaching programmes with a view to teaching or lecturing in sports sciences.

- Becoming recognised in sports sciences usually involves affiliation with, or membership of, one or more professional organisations such as the British Association of Sport and Exercise Sciences (BASES), the British Psychological Society, or the Society of Sports Therapists.

Becoming a sports development officer

Sports development officers (SDOs) generally work in the public sector. This means working for either national or local government. Sports-specific development officers are generally recruited from their sports and will have considerable experience, perhaps as a coach, performer or administrator.

- A major part of every SDO's role is understanding and interpreting national and local strategies. This means that you will need to have a good standard of general education, particularly in maths and English.
- University courses in Sports Development do exist, but most SDOs are well-educated and have significant experience or expertise in particular areas, such as managing budgets, leading teams of sporting volunteers or experience in a specific sport.
- SDOs generally manage budgets and are expected to produce evidence of the effectiveness of their work against targets.
- Management and marketing courses are also useful and will help the SDO with the day-to-day demands of their work.

Becoming a leisure manager

The leisure industry continues to grow in the UK, and its demand for excellence has never been higher. Leisure managers are responsible for large numbers of employees with very different roles, from administrators and receptionists to catering and grounds staff, as well as the more traditional roles of lifeguard and recreation assistant.

- Experience in the leisure industry is important. You could gain this by working as a lifeguard or as a receptionist.
- This kind of experience can lead to a role as a duty manager (the person who manages or supervises a team of staff on a day-to-day basis and whose role is operational). This involves dealing with customer issues and complaints, staffing issues, rotas, and communication with staff.
- The next level of management is more strategic, with involvement in planning and making sure that the leisure facility meets the targets it has set for participation in the most profitable way. Managers at this level will have a lot of experience in the leisure industry and may have studied leisure management, either at university or with a professional body such as the Chartered Institute for the Management of Sport and Physical Activity (CIMSPA).

Becoming a sports tutor or PE teacher

Every secondary school and most further education colleges have a sport or PE department. They teach and assess vocational sports programmes such as BTEC Sport. These classes are taught by teachers and tutors.

- Tutors work full or part-time and are recruited for their experience and qualifications. A sports tutor is usually educated to degree standard and has a teaching certificate, as does a PE teacher. This usually means they have studied a sports science degree and then completed a teaching qualification.
- Many PE teachers have progressed to university, via GCSEs and A levels. Others have studied in other areas such as BTEC Level 2 Sports courses, progressing to Level 3 and then on to university.
- Another route is to have built a good reputation in a recognised field, for example as a high-level sports coach, a sports nutritionist or a sports therapist. When an industry specialist is employed they nearly always study for a teaching qualification while they are teaching. Many young people value the experience that someone from industry can bring, especially if they need guidance on working in a particular field.

Job descriptions

Every job role should have a job description. This is a statement that identifies what the person doing the job will be required to do. A **person specification** is more focused on the skills and qualities of the individual, and will usually be derived from the job description. Some example job descriptions are shown in Figure 3.1.

Sports psychologist

Job description

Day-to-day roles will vary according to the setting that you are working in and the level of performance. Typically this will involve some or all of the following:

- dealing with stress, arousal and anxiety
- improving self-confidence
- mental toughness for training and competing
- improving concentration and focus
- developing coping strategies for those with sports injuries
- controlling aggression
- goal setting

Person specification

- a British Psychological Society (BPS) accredited degree in psychology leading to the Graduate Basis for Chartered Membership (GBC)
- relevant work experience
- a BPS accredited Master's degree in sport and exercise psychology
- an interest in sport
- an interest and ability in science and maths
- excellent communication and listening skills
- the ability to motivate people
- good problem-solving and decision-making skills

PE teacher

Job description

Typically, this role will involve some or all of the following:

- lesson preparation
- teaching and making sure that everyone learns
- managing behaviour
- administering and arranging fixtures in and out of school
- implementing health and safety and safeguarding protocols
- setting and marking homework and assignments
- preparing for examinations and coursework
- attending meetings and training
- speaking with parents and carers about each student's progress
- attending general school events such as open days and social activities

Person specification

- personal fitness to carry out your duties
- University education degree
- Qualified Teacher Status (QTS) number
- knowledge of physical education and its impact on young people's development
- knowledge of the National Curriculum applying to the subjects you teach
- the ability to develop good working relationships with a wide range of people
- the ability to work in a team as well as use your own initiative
- enthusiasm for your subject to inspire all students
- the ability to prepare students for exams
- good organisation and time-management skills
- the ability to manage classes and deal with challenging behaviour
- excellent communication skills
- patience and a good sense of humour

Sports therapist

Job description

Typically, this role will involve some or all of the following:

- examining and diagnosing injuries
- planning treatment programmes
- using methods such as manipulation, massage, heat treatment, electrotherapy and hydrotherapy
- keeping records of patients' treatment and progress

Person specification

- an interest and ability in health science and sport
- experience in the treatment and management of sports injuries
- concern for the health and wellbeing of patients
- the ability to educate, advise and motivate people
- the ability to work well as part of a multi-disciplinary team
- good communication skills
- good organisational and administrative skills

▶ **Figure 3.1:** Example job descriptions

Sector-specific legislation that impacts on job roles

Safeguarding

In recent years the sports industry has become aware of the important role it has in protecting young and vulnerable people.

> **Research**
>
> Child protection in sport is vital to get right. Different sports have different ways in which they ensure child protection training is delivered. One of these ways is through normal coach education. Research how Level 2 coaches in rugby, netball or basketball are trained in safeguarding issues.

Safeguarding refers to the process of protecting children and vulnerable groups in order to provide safe and effective care. Child protection is part of the safeguarding process, protecting individual children from harm. An organisation's child protection procedures will detail how to respond to any concerns about a child's welfare.

From an employment perspective, safeguarding is essential. Not only are employees who have direct contact with children or vulnerable adults required to complete a Disclosure and Barring Service (DBS) check, employers are also required – by law – to ensure that this process is robust and effective. Failure to ensure that this kind of safeguarding has taken place will have serious consequences for that employer, which could result in legal action.

One of the characteristics of safeguarding is that it is always changing interpretations, reporting procedures and even legislation. As a result of this there is a need to train on a regular basis and be prepared to update your training. Training is usually delivered face-to-face, though it is increasingly available via online and interactive sessions as well.

The Disclosure and Barring Service (DBS)

Many jobs in the sports industry require the job holder to pass a DBS check. This helps employers and sporting organisations such as NGBs and clubs prevent unsuitable people from working with vulnerable groups such as children. People working as coaches, officials, teachers, lifeguards or other positions that involve access to children and vulnerable adults are required to complete detailed forms that are then sent to the police and other government agencies for checking. This check will highlight any reasons there might be for that individual to be prevented from working with children or vulnerable adults.

Many sports careers require **enhanced disclosures** which not only search criminal databases but also ask police if they have any additional concerns. An enhanced disclosure contains all of the information in a normal DBS disclosure plus other relevant information held in police records. It indicates whether the job applicant is not allowed to work with children or vulnerable adults.

Health and Safety at Work Act (1974)

The main health and safety legislation is the Health and Safety at Work Act (1974). This sets out the general duties that employers, the self-employed and those in control of premises have towards their employees and others who could be affected by their work activities (such as customers and clients). It gives employees the duty to ensure the health and safety of themselves and each other.

Case study

Joanna is a lifeguard at a busy swimming pool. She has been a lifeguard for a number of years. Lots of people think that the job is easy because they think you simply stand and watch the swimming pool, but there are actually a lot of other duties. Joanna recommends the following steps to become a lifeguard, based on her experience.

- **Step 1** – Be realistic: are you in good physical health and can you swim? Before you start, make sure you can follow the Royal Lifesaving Society (RLSS) guidelines for lifesaving fitness, including being able to swim at least 50m, tow a casualty, dive, retrieve a weighted object from the deepest part of the pool and tread water.
- **Step 2** – Get an RLSS approved Pool Lifeguard qualification. Many local pools offer these courses, mostly for staff but also to attract new people. Some pools may pay for you, if you agree to work for them afterwards. The course takes just over a week and you will learn how to deal with a variety of incidents

and emergencies, resuscitation methods, how to move those with spinal injuries and how to supervise swimmers safely.
- **Step 3** – Once qualified you can find a job. Nearly all swimming pools – whether in hotels, leisure centres or private clubs – need lifeguards, so finding a job should not be too hard.
- **Step 4** – The job normally has a range of duties as well as lifesaving. You will probably be involved in routine cleaning and chemical testing, and you will be required to train on a regular basis and keep a record of your training in a training folder.

1 Look at three of the swimming pools closest to you. Look at their websites and see if they are advertising for lifeguards. Consider and imagine what working at each pool might be like and compare it with the other pools/facilities.

2 There are also opportunities for other lifeguarding jobs, like those at outdoor pools in the summer. Lifeguards are also employed by holiday providers and caravan parks. See if you can spot any jobs like these. What differences are there between these jobs and those in indoor pools?

3 Having researched these opportunities, draw up a seven-point action plan that shows how you could progress from having no or limited experience to gaining employment. This does not have to be for a lifeguard role but it should be for a position in the sports industry.

The principles of the Health and Safety at Work Act are to:

▸ secure the health, safety and welfare of people at work

▸ protect people other than those at work against risks to health and safety arising from the activities of people at work

▸ control the handling and storage of dangerous substances

▸ control the emission into the atmosphere of noxious or offensive substances from premises.

It is the duty of the employer, as far as is reasonably practicable, to safeguard the health, safety and welfare of the people who work for them as well as that of non-employees (for example, customers, visitors and members of the general public) while they are on the premises. The term 'reasonable and practicable' means that in any situation you must use your own judgement to decide on the best course of action. You should carefully consider all the options, thinking about the consequences (i.e. what could happen as a result of this decision?), how quickly you can decide to do something and the available resources. At that time, you need to decide what you consider to be reasonable and practicable.

Under the Health and Safety at Work Act the employee also has responsibilities. Employees are responsible for:

▸ taking care of their own health and safety

▸ taking care of the health and safety of others who may be affected by their actions

▸ cooperating with the employer and other relevant organisations to ensure that the requirements of the act are met (including notifying supervisors of unsafe equipment or practices)

▸ not misusing equipment provided to maintain health and safety.

Reporting of Injuries, Diseases and Dangerous Occurrences Regulations (RIDDOR), 1995

The reporting of accidents and incidents is covered by the Reporting of Injuries, Diseases and Dangerous Occurrences Regulations (1995). These regulations are also known as RIDDOR. RIDDOR places a legal duty on employers, the self-employed and those in control of premises to report:

▸ work-related deaths

▸ major injuries or over-3-day injuries

▸ work-related diseases

▸ dangerous occurrences (near-miss accidents).

RIDDOR is in place to allow the **Health and Safety Executive (HSE)** to:

▸ follow up, report and check safety practices and operational procedures

▸ ensure a standardised report form is used

▸ send officers to advise organisations on prevention of further accident and illness

▸ allow an investigation to prosecute, prohibit and make improvements where necessary.

Personal Protective Equipment (PPE), 2002

The Personal Protective Equipment (2002) regulations cover the use of **personal protective equipment (PPE)**. The regulations require PPE (such as safety helmets, gloves, eye protection and high-visibility clothing) to be supplied and used at work wherever there are risks to workers' health and safety that cannot adequately be controlled in other ways. The regulations require that PPE is:

▸ properly assessed before use to ensure its suitability for the work being done

▸ maintained and stored correctly

▸ supplied with adequate instructions so that users know how to use it safely

▸ worn correctly by the user.

Control of Substances Hazardous to Health (COSHH), 2002

Hazardous substances include all substances or mixtures of substances classified as dangerous to health under the Chemicals (Hazard Information and Packaging for Supply) Regulations 2002 (CHIP), such as:

▸ substances used directly in work activities (for example, adhesives, paints and cleaning agents such as markings used for sports pitches)

▸ substances generated during work activities (for example, fumes from chemicals used in swimming pools)

▸ naturally-occurring substances (for example, grain dust)

▸ biological agents (for example, bacteria and other microorganisms such as those in swimming pools or spas).

The COSHH regulations can be complied with by following an eight-step process. The steps and example activities associated with each step can be seen in Table 3.3.

Key terms

Health and Safety Executive (HSE) – the organisation responsible for proposing and enforcing safety regulations throughout the UK.

Personal Protective Equipment (PPE) – all equipment (including clothing affording protection against the weather) which is intended to be worn or held by a person at work and which protects them from one or more risks to their health or safety, for example, safety helmets, gloves, eye protection, high-visibility clothing and safety footwear.

▶ **Table 3.3:** The eight steps of the COSHH regulations

Step	Example activities
1. Undertake a risk assessment (to be carried out by an appropriately trained individual)	• Identify hazardous substances • Consider the risks these substances might present
2. Decide what precautions are needed	• Decide on all actions, such as measures to prevent hazardous substances being absorbed through the skin
3. Prevent or adequately control exposure (do what is reasonably practicable)	• Change the process or activity so that hazardous substances are not needed or generated • Replace hazardous substances with a safer alternative • Use in a safer form, for example, cones instead of markings
4. Ensure that control measures are used and maintained	• Provide staff training • Display notices • Ensure managers or supervisors carry out necessary checks
5. Monitor exposure	• Measure the concentration of hazardous substances
6. Carry out appropriate health surveillance	• Monitor any adverse effects of exposure to hazardous substances
7. Prepare plans and procedures to deal with accidents, incidents and emergencies	• Set up warning systems • Set up lines of communication in the case of an incident
8. Ensure that employees are properly informed, trained and supervised	Provide suitable and sufficient information, instruction and training, to include: • the names of the substances they work with or could be exposed to and the risks • the main findings of the risk assessment • the precautions that should be taken to protect themselves and others • how to use personal protective equipment and clothing • the results of any exposure monitoring and health surveillance (without giving individual employees' names) • any emergency procedures that need to be followed

COSSH is important in a leisure centre swimming pool, which contains different chemicals. Under COSHH, bacteriological testing should be carried out regularly. In public leisure centres such tests are checked by the HSE. In private leisure pools this responsibility often falls to the Environmental Health Officer, who will take random bacteriological tests.

Health and Safety (First Aid) Regulations (1981)

The Health and Safety (First Aid) Regulations (1981) require that, in order to provide first aid to their employees who are injured or become ill at work, employers must have adequate and appropriate equipment, facilities and personnel. The regulations also state that an organisation must provide:

▶ first aid equipment, including first aid boxes, a list of controls and their locations and supplementary equipment such as a spine board and resuscitation kit

▶ a first aid room (the regulations also specify the size, design and location)

▶ first aiders and any necessary training programmes (this includes a list of those people who have received a certificate from an authorised training body – certificates are normally valid for at least 1 year).

Manual Handling Operations Regulations (1992)

The Manual Handling Operations Regulations (1992) apply to any situation where employees are carrying, lifting or moving loads. Loads are not identified with a maximum weight, so each task requires a risk assessment that considers the weight to be lifted or carried and the working environment.

Employers are required to 'avoid hazardous manual handling operations' as far as is reasonably practicable.

Professional bodies in the sport sector

A professional body is normally an organisation that does not try to make a profit but promotes the integrity of a particular profession or trade. Professional bodies speak on behalf of their members, protecting their interests, and ensure high standards are maintained.

Link

Refer to page 149 for additional information about CPD.

Many of these professional bodies also offer training to their members to help their continuing professional development (CPD).

▸ **Chartered Institute for the Management of Sport and Physical Activity** – representing all practitioners of physical activity in the UK, it offers courses in operating and managing sport and physical activity and provides a framework to keep a record of CPD.

▸ **Register of Exercise Professionals** – the UK regulator for fitness professionals, which works to ensure they meet the national occupational standards and provides courses in CPD that help maintain registration.

▸ **UK Sport** – has a list of all national governing bodies that provide coaching qualifications, for example UK Athletics, Badminton England and the Professional Golfers' Association (PGA).

▸ **The British Association of Sport and Exercise Science (BASES)** – a professional body for sport and exercise sciences in the UK; offers the Certified Exercise Practitioner qualification.

▸ **The Register of Personal Development Practitioners in Sport (RPDPS)** – recognises the experience and qualifications of those working with athletes in a variety of sports and supports training needs and career progression.

▸ **Adventure Activities Licensing Authority (AALA)** – ensures the safety of those providers that offer outdoor and adventurous activities. It offers licences to those who conform to its strict regulations so users can feel safe in taking part.

Research

In small groups, research one of the professional bodies discussed in this unit, focusing on the cost of annual membership, the benefits of joining, the type of services they offer and the training they provide, if any. Present your findings as a short leaflet to share with the group so that you all have a resource for each of the professional bodies.

Industry codes of practice

Most professional bodies also operate a code of practice that their members have to follow, in order to help maintain standards. Two examples are listed below.

▸ **Fitness and exercise** – the Register of Exercise Professionals (REPs) is an independent register which recognises the qualifications and expertise of exercise instructors in the UK. It ensures instructors and trainers meet the health and fitness industry's agreed **National Occupational Standards (NOS).** REPs was set up to prevent rogue traders with no training and experience, to protect the public and to recognise the qualifications of exercise professionals.

▸ **Sports coaches** – Sports Coach UK administers the minimum standards for active coaches. This is a set of agreed core standards for sports coaches in the UK. These standards are important for the following reasons:

- to ensure coaches have the right level of qualification, knowledge and skills for their coaching role
- to safeguard coaches and the participants they coach
- to ensure coaches have the right level of insurance.

Key term

National Occupational Standards (NOS) – these specify UK standards of performance that people are expected to achieve in their work, and the knowledge and skills they need to perform their role effectively. NOS, which are approved by UK government regulators, are available for almost every role in every sector in the UK.

▶ Sports Coach UK is a national and charitable agency

National governing bodies (NGBs) also have codes of practice for coaches. It is important that NGBs assume this role because they can develop specific codes for specific sports.

Ⅱ PAUSE POINT   Can you explain what a professional body is?

> **Hint**   Using paper, a whiteboard or a tablet, write down the purpose of a professional body and say why you would want to join one.

> **Extend**   Set up your own imaginary professional body for skateboard coaches. Consider what you would offer members and what other services you could offer.

Sources of continuing professional development (CPD)

Continuing professional development (CPD) is the process of gaining new skills, knowledge and experience, both formal and informal, as you work after any initial training. You should keep a record of your experience and learning and file it in a folder or online.

CPD is often undertaken as a requirement of your profession (not necessarily your employer). If you ensure your training and development log is updated regularly it can become a valuable record of reflections and actions in your role as a professional.

Theory into practice

Consider the advantages of training and development in the sports industry. Using the list of sectors in the sports industry – exercise and fitness, physical education, outdoor learning and sports therapies – explore at least three ways in which professionals in different roles take care of their respective training and development needs.

Training and development are similar but not the same.

▶ Training could involve a sports coach attending a course in safeguarding or a sports therapist learning a deep muscle manipulation technique. It is related to a skill or specific **competence**. Sometimes the training is compulsory, such as updating your knowledge of first aid or safeguarding.

Key term

Competence – the ability to perform a technical task that will have required training and practice.

▶ Development is usually less formal and is more related to a competence than a qualification. For example, a sports teacher may be asked to deliver a range of sports at a basic level: it is impractical to be an expert in more than a few sports, but the right development will allow them to follow a basic set of principles so they can competently introduce a range of sports. Development is likely to focus on transferable skills such as leadership, project management and event organisation.

CPD can be as simple as taking on a new challenge or experience, such as working with a cross-sector organisation or helping with an elite performance programme for the first time.

Professional development in sports therapies

CPD for this sector is offered by a range of organisations. In health professions, perhaps more than any other, membership of professional bodies such as the Society for Sports Therapists depends on the compulsory completion of a set number of hours of CPD. This might be specific training such as:

- electrotherapy
- new stretching or taping techniques
- sports first aid.

It might also require you to host or attend meetings covering day-to-day issues and demonstrate competence in an organisation.

Professional development in exercise and fitness

- The Register of Exercise Professionals (REPs) requires you to maintain your membership so that you can log your CPD against a points system.
- You need to gain 24 points in a 2-year period. Points are gained by taking part in a range of CPD events such as ones on water fitness instruction or training to deliver exercise for special populations.

Professional development in physical education

Key term

Advocacy – acting in a manner that advises while supporting.

- The Association for Physical Education is an association, not a professional body – this means membership is not compulsory – which offer members a number of ways to enhance their career as a PE teacher. This includes CPD sessions on professional leadership and **advocacy** as well as updates on curriculum changes and workshops on subjects such as the use of ICT in PE and dance activities.
- Teachers who join this organisation enjoy access to a range of local and national conferences.

Professional development in physical activity

- The Chartered Institute for the Management of Sport and Physical Activity (CIMSPA) supports CPD by providing free and paid-for activities, workshops and seminars. It also helps professionals to log and record their CPD and to design personal CPD plans.
- It has several categories of CPD which include training events, reading and research, and network events on subjects such as presentation skills, leadership, and health and safety.
- CIMSPA has a system where its members can gain points over a set time frame.

Professional development in sports coaching

- Sports Coach UK aims to have all its members register for coaching licences.
- Part of the licence requires that the coach participates in targeted training events that cover a range of subjects such as **equity** in coaching, safeguarding children and analysing sports performance. The courses can be as short as a few minutes and can often be delivered at evenings or weekends.
- They aim for sports coaches to be considered as professionals who participate in and log CPD as a vital part of their profession.

> **Key term**
>
> **Equity** – being impartial and fair.

Types of CPD in the sports industry

▸ **Qualifications** – any academic or professional qualifications that support and develop members in their role or future career.

▸ **Training** – can include workshops, short training courses, masterclasses, online learning and, increasingly, seminars and webinars.

▸ **Networking events/conferences** – professional body CPD events and other events that increase knowledge.

▸ **In-house/in-company training** – undertaken as part of an organisation's planned development scheme, which may be linked with performance development and appraisal.

▸ **Sharing of knowledge** – writing published books, papers, journals or articles that focus on principles relating to the sports industry.

▸ **Mentoring and coaching** – sharing knowledge and experience with colleagues and associates, usually in support of new people, such as a trainee lifeguard.

▸ **Reading and research** – time spent improving knowledge and skills by studying by yourself. Such activities include online research, learning new job-related skills, reading sector publications and research.

When thinking about the CPD that you want to do, it will help if you have an outline career plan. For instance, you might want to study a part-time university or college course to broaden your knowledge of sport. Universities and colleges offer a range of different qualifications, including courses focusing on exercise, fitness, nutrition, psychology and coaching.

For many careers in sport, a university degree is not essential. Instead, Foundation degrees can allow you to work while you study, and on completion many providers will have a partnership agreement that allows you to gain a degree.

> **Research**
>
> In a small group, carry out research to determine in which of the following roles a university education is 'essential', 'desirable' or 'not necessary'. If university is essential, then describe the entry criteria for each of the degree courses that you discover. If university is not necessary, what are the requirements of the role? What kind of experience and training are employers looking for in an applicant? Present your findings to the group.
> - Sports coach
> - PE teacher
> - Sport psychologist
> - Duty manager – Leisure.

PAUSE POINT

What is professional development? Can you explain why it is important for your career plans?

Hint   Find out what kind of training events there are in a profession that interests you, and feed back to the rest of your group.

Extend   What kind of training would help you develop if you were a PE teacher? Research available courses and training and sketch out a year plan. Remember to keep room in the plan for your professional responsibilities.

Assessment practice 3.1

A.P1 A.P2 A.M1 AB.D1

Your school is hosting its annual open day and you have been asked to give visiting parents and potential students a written report titled 'Careers in Sport'. Your report should demonstrate how it is possible to seek a career in two contrasting sports roles – as a personal trainer and a PE teacher. You need to carry out some research into the two careers, showing that you understand the requirements of each position and how, as a sport student, you could go about seeking employment in these jobs.

You will need to outline the short and long-term prospects of each job role and build them into a career development action plan, supported by a personal skills audit that reflects the skills needed for each position.

Plan
- What is the task? What am I being asked to do?
- How confident do I feel in my own abilities to complete this task? Are there any areas I think I may struggle with?
- I will gather my thoughts on the information the report should contain and how it should be structured.
- I will research both roles using a mixture of sources, adverts for vacant positions and websites such as the National Careers Service.

Do
- I know what it is I am doing and what I want to achieve.
- I will write the report starting with an introduction that states the aims and provides some background.
- I will describe each job role, outlining the requirements of the roles and including the CPD requirements of each role, with details of professional bodies etc.

Review
- I will explain what the task was and how I approached it.
- I will explain how I would approach the more difficult elements of the task differently next time.
- I will use my conclusion to reflect on the entire process, how I carried out my research and what I might have done to improve. I will also reflect upon issues that my research has raised, such as finding fitness training courses or learning more about the National Curriculum.

B   Explore own skills using a skills audit to inform a career development action plan

Personal skills audit for potential careers

Getting a clear idea about what you want to do as a career can be confusing. Everyone will have different ideas about what they want to do based on what their friends and families think, what their experience of those professions is and perhaps even their perception of the job and what it entails. Sometimes people lack an understanding of a particular job role and have not considered their own qualities and skills.

A skills audit is a way of assessing the skills needed for a particular job and comparing them with your own current skills to see how closely they match. This can be used to help you plan your career development so that you can learn, train for and develop the skills you need in order to secure the job that you want.

This section will help you to construct a skills audit that will be personal to you. It will help you to assess if what you want to do is right for you and help you to make an informed choice.

Building a skills audit

Interests and accomplishments

The first step is to consider your personal interests and accomplishments.

Your interests are an important factor. It would be silly to pursue a career in hockey if you do not like hockey, or to pursue a career that involves working in a leisure centre if you prefer working outside. Listing your personal interests can help you focus on the job roles that are most suited to you.

There are a number of ways in which you can design a skills audit. If you have ever been involved in any work or work-based experience you will appreciate that it is good practice to be aware of your own strengths and attributes as well as any relevant experience. It is equally important to be aware of the gap that exists between your current experience and that of a professional working practitioner, e.g. PE teacher. It is only by recognising these factors that you will be able to analyse your current skills.

When considering your accomplishments, think of your sporting achievements that might be of interest to a future employer (e.g. selection for county or regional squads, captaincies) and performance-based achievements (e.g. completing endurance events). Have you assumed roles that require additional qualities, looked after newer or younger players, officiated or helped organise events like club competitions? This is a good opportunity to demonstrate your passion for sport or exercise to an employer.

Personal accomplishments could also include volunteering in your spare time to raise money for good causes or helping with the organisation of a sports event.

Perhaps the most important process that completing a skills audit will teach you is the ability to be **self-reflective**. This means the ability to look at your own achievements and accomplishments and identify your strengths and weaknesses. When reviewing your skills audit, look at a range of job descriptions to identify skills that you may not have considered you have, and those that you hope to gain.

Personal qualities

Another key feature in a skills audit is your assessment of your personal qualities. These make you the person you are and are valuable attributes employers consider in all of their workforce. Key qualities include:

▶ **reliability** – can an employer trust you to turn up, be on time and do what is expected of you?
▶ **organisational skills** – when given complex tasks, are you able to prioritise, sort and then approach tasks in a methodical fashion?
▶ **commitment** – are you willing to go 'above and beyond expectations', stay late, start early and persevere with tasks?
▶ **resilience** – how do you cope with difficult situations? Faced with a problem, what is your approach, and how do you deal it?
▶ **empathy** – how do you relate to others? Can you anticipate how someone might feel about something? Do you recognise the reasons for people's behaviour, and if you do, do you know the best way to respond?

Basic skills

Most employers expect a level of basic skills and it is important you develop these skills wherever possible, as they are common to all aspects of professional life. Generally these will include competence in literacy, numeracy and IT.

> **Reflect**
>
> Think of examples from your studies and/or your sporting experiences that might illustrate your personal qualities. For example, getting up early three times a week to go for a run before school or college shows commitment. Planning your personal study so that you hand in your coursework on time shows organisational skills.

Experience

It is important to detail any experiences that might be relevant for your career. If you have volunteered as a sports coach with a group of children, this can relate to the role of lifeguard in a busy swimming pool. It will demonstrate your experience with young people, managing behaviour issues and communicating with children and parents.

This is also the best place to highlight any leadership experience, perhaps with the Scouts or Guides, or helping new players in a tennis club. Sometimes even travelling abroad can be relevant, as experiencing other cultures and customs can help you to appreciate the needs of a diverse population.

Qualifications

Qualifications are important in any industry, and in the sports industry, academic qualifications such as GCSEs, particularly in Maths, English and PE, will help you to progress through further and higher education. You should also consider other specialist qualifications.

Research

The following qualifications might be considered essential to carry out the role of an archery instructor properly:

- Archery Instructor Award
- First Aid Certificate
- Safeguarding Children (Sports Coach UK workshop).

Assuming that you have none of these qualifications, conduct research with a partner to find out where you can study the courses. How much would each course cost, and how long would it take? Present your findings to your class, individually or in a small group.

▶ Archery coaches need more than just coaching qualifications

Employability skills

A skills audit should also consider and include the common skills that are likely to be required by all employers. Table 3.4 shows some of the most common ones. Try completing the table, giving yourself a rating for each skill. Once you have done that, consider what you think could be added, removed or changed.

▶ **Table 3.4:** Generic skills for employment

Generic Skills for Employment					
Read the statements below and circle the number that applies to you using the following guide: 1 = wide experience 3 = a little experience 5 = do not know 2 = some experience 4 = no experience					
Written communication I can write clearly and concisely in a range of different formats to communicate messages effectively to varied audiences.	1	2	3	4	5
Oral communication/presentation skills I can summarise and communicate information effectively when speaking with people or delivering presentations.	1	2	3	4	5
Time management I can manage my time and prioritise my workload to ensure that I produce high-quality work within set deadlines.	1	2	3	4	5
Problem-solving I know how to find logical, constructive, and realistic solutions when I am presented with complex problems.	1	2	3	4	5
Teamwork I am able to work effectively as a member of a team in order to help my team achieve its goals.	1	2	3	4	5
Leadership I am able to use a range of approaches and techniques to lead a team towards its goals.	1	2	3	4	5
Information skills I am able to find sources of information (including online sources) quickly and easily. I am able to evaluate different sources of information to determine their reliability.	1	2	3	4	5
Independent learning I am able to manage my own workload and complete tasks on my own with minimal input or supervision from my tutor.	1	2	3	4	5

Specific technical skills

Each career also has a range of specific skills. Coaching and teaching can be specific. A cycling coach will have a basic proficiency in all disciplines, but most cycling coaches have a preferred discipline such as BMX or Cyclocross.

▶ Some football coaches work exclusively with goalkeepers, while some rugby coaches work only with forwards.

▶ Some sports have training methods that require extra competence: for instance, cricket coaches need extra training to use a bowling machine, while trampoline coaches need to train to use overhead rigs.

▶ If your role requires you to administer fitness tests, you need to understand the importance of delivering each test correctly so that the results are reliable and valid.

Each career you look at will have a range of specific and required skills. Part of putting together a good skills audit is identifying what those skills are and making sure that your audit reflects these skills, with solid examples from your life and career to date.

▶ Most sports coach roles need specific technical skills, such as knowing how to conduct a fitness test or use equipment

SWOT analysis

Once you have considered your skills and characteristics, you should carry out a SWOT analysis. 'SWOT' stands for **strengths**, **weaknesses**, **opportunities** and **threats**. It will allow you to identify areas where you are already strong and evaluate areas where you can plan for future improvement, in this case to assist in career and employment planning.

SWOT analysis is a useful way of creating a personal and professional profile, and if done well it can be edited and added to throughout your career. In most professions there are opportunities to progress and improve, but even if you are applying for your first job you can benefit from this type of planning.

Reflect

Take a look at the example of a SWOT analysis shown in Table 3.5. This is the profile of a 17-year-old who wants to work as a personal trainer.

Complete a SWOT analysis like this for yourself in a career of your choice. Where possible ask your friends and family to offer their input – it is easy to forget obvious characteristics or perhaps miss an opportunity that others have more knowledge about.

Table 3.5: Example SWOT analysis

Strengths	Weaknesses
• Good IT skills • Experience in using fitness equipment and exercise classes • Committed to working in the fitness industry	• No experience of working in fitness industry • Sometimes struggle balancing study and personal life, missing important deadlines • No fitness qualifications
Opportunities	**Threats**
• Potential work placement as part of BTEC Sports course • A chance to study exercise and fitness at university • Local courses in nutrition, exercise for special populations and first aid	• Not achieving at school/college due to distractions and missing deadlines • Not good at working with older and unfit people

Planning personal development

Career action planning

Having completed a detailed skills audit, the next stage is to produce an action plan. This is a plan that shows how to achieve the career and job you want. In most cases this will be a long-term plan and so it is helpful to have a staged approach, over months and years.

As part of the action planning you need to identify key timescales that you can relate to achieving particular tasks to help you accomplish your career goal. These timescales could be immediate or could take place over a number of years. For each of these timescales, identify any training or educational needs and experience you will need to achieve. You should also have a clear plan for how you will complete each step.

An example of a career action plan for someone starting a BTEC National in Sport is shown in Table 3.6.

Case study

Alia is a sports therapist who has her own practice, a shop-front facility in a busy town that offers a range of health services with other colleagues. She has been practising for five years. Most of her work is with sportspeople, helping them to recover from injury or prevent further damage, using different massage and manipulation techniques.

A few years ago, at the start of her BTEC National in Sport course, Alia's career action plan might have looked like the one shown in Table 3.6.

- Consider what the key features of a 5-year plan are. (Think SMARTER!)
- Draw up a list of rules for a realistic 5-year plan.
- Individually design a 5-year plan for a career of your choice.

Theory into practice

Remember that SMARTER objectives are:

- **Specific** – Be precise about what you want and need to do.
- **Measurable** – How will you know you have achieved your goal?
- **Achievable** – Do not expect to walk into a job at Arsenal FC as a physiotherapist. Aim for something more achievable given your experience.
- **Realistic** – Do you have the skills you will need: for instance, are you really patient and a good communicator? If you are unsure, ask someone who knows you well.
- **Time-framed** – Without an end date there will be no sense of urgency. Always add a date to your target.
- **Exciting** – Developing enthusiasm will increase motivation and is shown to benefit participants' performance.
- **Recordable** – Reviewing previous achievements or failures will allow you to assess progress and develop further targets.

Table 3.6: An example career action plan

Timescale	Goal/target	Actions to achieve goals	Support needed	Deadline	How will you know that this has been achieved?
Immediate actions	Complete my first Sports Injury Assignment.	Research at home and in the library, produce poster.	Access to the internet, books and journals.	End of October	My tutor will assess my work and return it for my portfolio.
1 year	Complete the first year of my BTEC course with at least a Merit grade overall.	Complete all assessments on time and manage my spare time properly.	Guidance from my tutors and the help and support of my parents.	July next year	I will have a certificate that confirms my achievement.
2 years	Start a university course in Sports Therapy in Birmingham.	Apply through UCAS, visit the university and achieve the grades that I need.	Support from my parents in looking at universities, help in applying through UCAS.	October next year	I will have started my course.
5 years	Complete my undergraduate degree and be set up as a registered Sports Massage Therapist.	Work hard at university, completing all work and exams satisfactorily and registering with Society of Sports Therapists.	The help of my tutors and friends, access to research materials and sufficient funds.	June in 5 years	I will have a degree from the university and be practising as a therapist.
10 years	To have developed a reputation in sports therapy in my local area.	Work hard to establish a reputation and have a substantial client list.	Colleagues and friends and particularly the services of a good accountant.	Ongoing	I will make a comfortable living with a good client base.

Getting careers guidance

You can get careers guidance from a number of sources depending on the sector of the sports industry in which you are seeking advice and information.

▶ A good starting place is professional bodies such as ScUK, CIMSPA or REPs who have a variety of support tools and advice for those in and around their respective professions.

▶ Careers officers and support staff in your school/college will be able to offer advice. Your tutors, many of whom will still be connected to the industry in some way, are also a great source of guidance.

▶ The National Careers Service provides careers advice and guidance on hundreds of jobs and offers profiles of real people in the industry.

▶ You can also speak to a practitioner. There is nothing better than speaking to someone who is already in the job you want. They will have lots of relevant information and will also be able to offer tips on what to avoid and how to get the most out of your studies.

Career development action plan (CDAP)

Putting everything together into a specific career development action plan (CDAP) is key to providing a framework for your career development and producing a roadmap for future progression.

What should be in a CDAP?

As well as all of the detail in your earlier skills audit, a CDAP should also contain:

▶ your short, medium and long-term goals – what is important in your career and life?

▶ your current list of competencies, skills and abilities from your skills audit – what can you offer an organisation?

- your development needs, including broad aims and SMARTER goals
- how to specialise in certain areas
- achieved milestones
- milestones yet to be achieved. Who can help you achieve these goals? What blocks do you need to overcome?

Be flexible, review your CDAP regularly and be willing to adapt and change it.

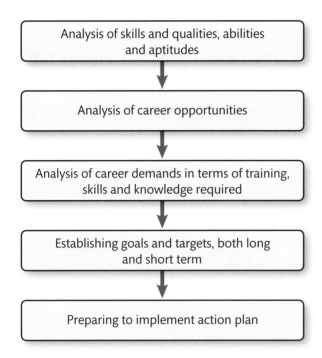

▶ **Figure 3.2:** Flow diagram of CDAP construction

Professional development activities

It is never too early to start taking your potential career seriously. Earlier, this unit covered the role of professional bodies in the development of practitioners (page 148). Many of these bodies offer workshops or classes for people with a similar interest or need: for example, a group of new teachers who need help in using technology to improve their lessons. Quite often these workshops are not restricted to those in the profession. To find a suitable workshop, identify your training need and then run a simple web search. Alternatively go straight to one of the regulated professional bodies, e.g. Sports Coach UK.

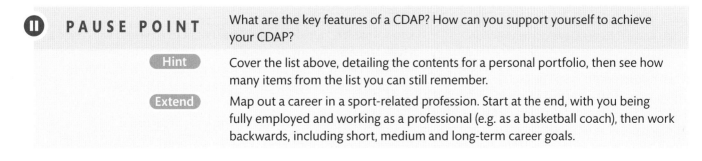

⏸ PAUSE POINT	What are the key features of a CDAP? How can you support yourself to achieve your CDAP?
Hint	Cover the list above, detailing the contents for a personal portfolio, then see how many items from the list you can still remember.
Extend	Map out a career in a sport-related profession. Start at the end, with you being fully employed and working as a professional (e.g. as a basketball coach), then work backwards, including short, medium and long-term career goals.

Maintaining a personal portfolio/record of achievement and experience

While many organisations invite applicants to apply online, a well composed personal **portfolio** or record of achievement demonstrates your commitment to gaining employment. A good personal portfolio should contain:

▸ educational certificates, e.g. GCSEs, BTECs and others

▸ sport-specific awards and achievements based on competence and proficiency, as well as possibly officiating and/or coaching

▸ testimonials – positive statements about you from respected people: sports coaches, head teachers, respected members of the community. These people may also act as referees if you apply for a job

▸ press cuttings or screen grabs from appropriate websites – if your sporting achievements have been featured by the local media

▸ details of work experience – a summary with details and, where possible, positive comments from placement supervisors

▸ details of volunteering – any times you worked for worthy causes or relevant organisations.

You should also have at least one specific *curriculum vitae* (CV) that has been adapted to target your desired sports industry jobs. You can read more about CVs later in this unit (page 164).

Assessment practice 3.2   B.P3 B.P4 B.M2 B.M3 ABD1

Following the successful sports careers event, it is time to consider your own career in sport.

For this assessment you will need to build a portfolio of evidence. This could be presented in a variety of ways but must include both a personal skills audit (PSA) and a Careers Development Action Plan (CDAP).

The finished portfolio will be useful when planning your actual career in sport, so take time and care and include as much detail as possible.

Plan
- What is the task? What am I being asked to do?
- I will start by making a list of contents for my portfolio, using this chapter for guidance. I will remember to include all potentially useful evidence such as certificates, references and my CV, as well as my PSA and CDAP.

Do
- I know what it is I am doing and what I want to achieve. I will create a detailed timeline for my progress.
- I will think clearly about who might ask for access to this portfolio, perhaps at a university interview or a potential employer.

Review
- I will explain what the task was and how I approached it.
- I will explain how I would approach the difficult elements differently next time.

C Undertake a recruitment activity to demonstrate the processes that can lead to a successful job offer in a selected career pathway

Applying for a job

Applying for jobs can be a challenging process. First you have to know where to look. Research suggests that most people now look for jobs online.

General job search websites can be run by large organisations that are not industry-specific. Typically they require you to register and enter details about the type of job you are looking for. They provide you with a job alert service that will send regular emails or text alerts when they have a job that matches your criteria. Examples of this kind of website include www.indeed.co.uk, www.gov.uk/jobsearch and www.fish4.co.uk.

An alternative is to use the websites of professional bodies in the industries you are interested in, or job search providers that target the sports industry, such as:

▶ www.careers-in-sport.co.uk
▶ www.sportcareers.co.uk
▶ www.globalsportsjobs.com

If you want to narrow your job search to a specific part of the sports industry, there are specialist online search facilities including:

▶ Sports Sciences – www.bases.org.uk
▶ Physical Education – www.tes.com/jobs
▶ Leisure, Health and Fitness – www.leisurejobs.com
▶ Public Sector Sports – www.uksport.gov.uk/jobs-in-sport

You can also find jobs in other ways – through newspapers and trade magazines, or through possible employers, such as at leisure centres.

Job advertisements

In order to attract the right kind of applicant it is necessary to place an advertisement in a location where likely and qualified applicants might look. This will include company websites, trade websites, sport governing body websites and specialist websites such as www.leisureopportunities.co.uk.

Designing a job description needs careful planning and consideration. It is the initial opportunity for an employer to attract suitable applicants. There are many approaches to job advertisement design; think about the different style of advertisement that might be needed for a Groundskeeper compared to a Sports Therapist.

Guidelines on writing a job advertisement

Write an appealing job title that is descriptive and credible.

Set out a structure – perhaps like this:

1 Short introduction
2 Roles and responsibilities
3 Person specification
4 Rewards
5 Your company
6 What to do next / how to apply

Appeal to the audience by considering their needs when designing the advertisement.

Job analysis

A job analysis identifies detailed job duties and requirements and the relative importance of these for a particular job. The prospective employer collects data about the specific duties in the job and uses it to create a job description. As someone applying for the job, you will not usually get to see the job analysis.

Job description

A job description contains details of exactly what the job entails. Generally the features of the job are listed in order of importance, so for a PE teacher you would expect to see the following:

▶ lesson preparation

▶ teaching and making sure that everyone learns

▶ behaviour management

▶ administering and arranging sport fixtures in and out of school

▶ ensuring health and safety regulations are followed

▶ setting and marking homework and assignments

▶ preparing learners for examinations and coursework

▶ attending meetings and training

▶ speaking with parents and carers about each learner's progress.

Many job descriptions also include a statement that covers tasks or responsibilities that may not have been anticipated when the job description was originally created. In most cases this is why you see a criterion in job descriptions that says something similar to, '...all other reasonable duties as determined by the Senior Management Team.' This means that reasonable changes to a job can be added to the duties that were originally advertised.

When applying for a position that requires you to send a CV, it is worth changing the key features of your CV to suit the application. You can easily place an emphasis and re-prioritise skills and qualities so that they match each job description.

Case study

A dry-ski slope employs over 20 staff including instructors, catering staff, reception and administration staff, and a manager. The business has grown and the equipment now needs regular repair and servicing. Until now the manager has paid external contractors for large jobs and carried out the rest of the work herself with the help of the instructors. Now that business has picked up, there is no time to perform these tasks. Because income has grown the manager has decided to recruit a technician.

Since the role has never existed before, the manager needs to carefully consider what the role requires, what kind of person would be suitable and how to develop a person specification.

Draw up a possible job analysis and job description for this role.

- Make a simple list of all the duties that the technician might perform such as the maintenance and repair of the ski surface, the ski lift and the safety run offs.

- Draw up a list of daily, weekly, monthly and annual duties.

- Think about the most appropriate hours of work. Do you need someone to be available all the time, part time, at particular hours, or with set hours and a call out?

- Design a suitable job description. Where would you advertise this position?

Person specification

A person specification is less centred on the tasks of the job and more on the kind of person who would suit the job: their skills, qualities, experience and competencies. Figure 3.3 shows an example person specification for the role of Tennis Coach. Note that the E at the end of a criterion means 'essential' (the applicant <u>must have</u> this), while D means 'desirable' (the applicant <u>should have</u> this).

Person specification for a tennis coach

Experience
- Proven experience in a similar role **E**
- Experience of working within a tennis club environment **E**
- Strong experience/awareness of offering exceptional service **D**
- Prior experience of working with children **E**
- Disclosure and barring service (DBS) certification **E**
- Minimum of 3 years' experience in a tennis instructor role **D**

Skills
- LTA Level 2 Tennis Coach **E** or other equivalent qualification **E**
- Minimum 2-day first aid certificate **E**

Qualities
- Team player able to manage, supervise and motivate the team **E**
- Strong administrative and organisational skills **E**
- Excellent verbal and written communication skills **E**
- Commitment to customer care **E**
- Influencing skills **D**
- Problem solver **E**

Personal attributes/behaviours
- Enjoy working as part of a team and with a wide variety of people **E**
- Good communication and interpersonal skills **E**
- A love of tennis **D**
- An outgoing nature and enthusiasm **D**
- Good teaching skills **E**
- Motivational skills and a positive approach to learning **D**
- Desire to keep improving own skills and techniques **E**
- Patience **E**
- Organisational skills **E**
- A good sense of humour **D**
- The ability to use own initiative while following established drills and teaching techniques **E**
- Ability to complete paperwork to deadline **E**
- Ability to provide honest feedback to individuals in a tactful manner **D**
- Stamina and desire to work long hours in tough conditions **E**

▶ **Figure 3.3:** Example person specification for a tennis coach

Application form

Applying for a job is usually straightforward. Once you have registered an interest – over the phone, by email, text or social media, as appropriate – the employer will either send you a paper application or link you to an online form.

There are several rules to consider when applying for any job.

▶ For written applications always write neatly and in black pen (black ink shows up better if they photocopy it). It is worth photocopying the blank form and filling out a draft copy first so you can correct any mistakes or add information.

▶ Be honest. Do not lie about what you have achieved; you will nearly always be found out and will lose out on the job and possible future opportunities.

▶ Do not guess. If the form asks a question you do not understand, ask someone you trust for guidance.

▶ List previous jobs (if you have had any) chronologically with the most recent first. If you have not had a job, do not be embarrassed: say so, but be prepared to list your other experiences, especially volunteering.

▶ Do not leave filling out the form and submitting it until the last minute. Always set your deadline well before the actual one – this demonstrates organisational skills and the ability to prioritise.

▶ When writing your **supporting statement** make sure you respond to the question and keep to the point. If the form says to write 500 words, then keep within this guide. Read the job description and person specification and sell yourself; be direct without being over-confident.

▶ When asked for references, always use someone who has credibility to an employer, for example a previous employer, a head teacher, a tutor or a person in a position of authority. Do not use family members. Always ask the referee if they are prepared to offer a reference before you write down their name – you would not want a potential employer to be told your referee has declined a reference or not sent one.

▶ Make sure you follow the instructions on the form. Return all completed forms and any additional information requested, such as copies of certificates or disclosures.

> **Key term**
>
> **Supporting statement**
> – a personal statement that supports a job application and represents an opportunity for an applicant to demonstrate their ability to communicate effectively in writing while making their case for employment.

Personal CV

A CV is essentially a list of your work experiences and is a document you can add to and develop throughout the course of your life as you gain new skills and experiences. Most employers will ask for a CV from job applicants, so it is always a good idea to have one ready to send.

Key features and suggested structure of a CV

▶ Name, address and contact details – make sure any email address you give looks professional.

▶ Profile – this is a statement of about 30–40 words describing your work skills (for example 'highly organised', 'able to work in a team or alone' and 'motivated by a challenge'). Do not just list your personal ambitions here: employers want to hire people who will add value to their organisations, so tell them what you are going to be able to do for them.

▶ Qualifications – start with the most recent first.

▶ Work history – again start with the most recent first. If you lack work experience, include any relevant volunteering you have done.

▶ Interests and hobbies – if you have an interest where your talent has been recognised or awarded, or a hobby that demonstrates your personal qualities, then describe it in detail – up to 40 words. Remember it's not just what you did, but how you did it that will impress a prospective employer.

▶ References – these should be credible and willing to act as your referee.

Organising a CV

In its final form your CV should:

▶ be word processed and printed on good quality paper using a clear font

▶ be concise – aim for no more than two sides of A4 paper

▶ list education and work experience in reverse date order (most recent first)

▶ emphasise relevant skills, achievements and experience

▶ be truthful – do not be tempted to lie – you are likely to be found out at interview

▶ be thorough and accurate – show your CV to a tutor, colleague or careers counsellor, and have it checked for spelling, grammar and typing errors.

Research

There are many opinions about the most appropriate style of CV. Only a few details remain constant, such as personal details. In pairs, see if you can find four different styles of CV. Choose your favourite and suggest why you think it is more effective than the others. Pay particular attention to CVs that demonstrate the best of your experience, particularly if you have little employment experience.

In the United States they use the word *resumé* instead of CV.

Letter of application

Some employers may ask you to send them a letter of application, also known as a covering letter. The letter must follow some rules to make sure it makes a good impression on a potential employer. The following statements, used in this order, will help you compose a good letter of application:

▶ Say why you are writing, e.g. for which job and where you saw the vacancy advertised.

▶ Explain what you are currently doing, e.g. in employment or education.

▶ Discuss briefly why you are applying for the job and what appeals to you about it.

▶ Justify briefly why you are suitable for the position, e.g. discuss your relevant experiences or skills.

▶ End by saying you can attend an interview and hope to hear from them soon.

❚❚ PAUSE POINT   Can you explain the difference between a person specification and a job description?

Hint   Look at examples of person specifications and job descriptions and identify the main information in each type of document.

Extend   Design a person specification for a sports job of your choice. Try to imagine what the role involves and what kind of person you would need. Look at other person specifications and compare them with yours.

Interviews and selected career pathway-specific skills

Interviews can be a daunting prospect, but for the well-prepared they are an opportunity to show off skills and achievements, to get the job or at least to do your best in trying. It is important that you consider what it is you need to do to prepare for an interview.

Communication skills for interviews

The two-way process of communicating is at the heart of the employment decision. In an interview you will be expected to demonstrate your personality. You should always speak in a professional manner and not talk at length about yourself out of context of the role you are applying for. Try to focus all of what you say and do on the job at hand, and relate everything to the job. You must never forget the messages that your body is sending: see Table 3.7.

Applying for some roles might require a suit; for other roles, such as casual lifeguards or sports coaches, it may be better to dress for interview in sports clothing that still presents a professional appearance. You may also be asked to demonstrate technical skills, perhaps in a **microteach** or a mini coaching session. If this is the case, then you must practise and prepare fully for these scenarios.

Reflect

Look at Table 3.7 and read the advice for effective communication in interviews. In pairs, find a job you would each like to apply for (either now or in the future). Imagine you have been invited for interview. Draw up a set of guidelines that will help you to prepare for the interview. Some advice will be about how to behave, while some will be about what to expect and be ready for. Prepare a set of questions and answers and practise the interview with your partner.

▶ **Table 3.7:** Communication skills for interviews

Body language and dress	Formal language	Skills and attitudes of interviewee
• Sit or stand upright and with confidence. • Maintain eye contact regularly but do not stare. Smile and nod your head. • Wear smart/appropriate clothing that will demonstrate your respect for the position and the interview panel. Requirements may vary but always be smart and clean.	• Refer to other professionals as Mr, Mrs or Ms. • Avoid informal, casual or over familiar language (e.g. 'mate') or the kind of language you would use with a friend in a text message or email. • Be aware of your posture; speak clearly and a little more loudly and slower than normal, as being anxious or nervous may make you speak softly or quickly.	• Research the company, look at their website, and know their products and services. • Practise answers to common question types.
Role play	**Listening skills**	**Interview questions**
You may be asked to come up with a solution to a problem or imagined incident. • If you are part of a group, make sure that you take part and allow others to take part. • If you have the opportunity, explain your role in the process. • Ask questions and stay calm.	• Face the person with an open, attentive posture. • Active listening reflects back what the speaker is saying in other words to clarify your understanding: paraphrase and repeat back key points.	Expect questions like: • Tell me about yourself. • What are your strengths? • What are your weaknesses? • What would you offer us? • Where do you see yourself in 5 years' time?

Presentation skills: microteaching and microcoaching

Many interview candidates will be asked to deliver a short microteach session to their peers. These short sessions are an opportunity to demonstrate skills, knowledge and understanding. Time will go quickly so it's best to rehearse the session in advance. A microcoach session is very similar to a microteach but focuses more on coaching skills and less on the learning that takes place – it looks more at how you deliver the session and demonstrate your skills and knowledge.

Planning your session

Think carefully about the topic you will deliver and have a realistic aim which can be achieved within the time allocated. Prepare a session plan which shows the teaching, learning and assessment activities to be used (along with timings for each) and shows the resources you will need.

There are lots of things you will need to consider in advance, such as:

▶ How long will the session be? When and where will it take place?

▶ Who will observe you? Will they need a copy of your plan? Will they make a visual recording for you to view later?

▶ What equipment and resources are available for you to use?

▶ How many people will there be in the group? How can you find out their learning preferences, any individual needs, and any prior knowledge?

▶ Can you show a video clip? If so, how long can it be?

Your session should have a beginning (the introduction), a middle section (the development) and an ending (the summary/conclusion), which should show a logical progression of learning. Use a variety of teaching and learning approaches to cover all learning preferences and keep your learners engaged and motivated. You should not be speaking for the majority of the session, and your learners should be active (doing the talking or participating positively), not passive (listening and not fully engaged).

> **Key terms**
>
> **Body language** – your movements and posture and the way they show your attitudes or feelings.
>
> **Role play** – many organisations now use role play as part of their selection and recruitment process. This gives interviewees the chance to demonstrate negotiating, listening and teamwork skills.

If you are only delivering a 15-minute session you may not have time for group activities. If you do set activities, think about what you will be doing while your learners are working (moving around them and observing or asking questions shows you are in control). Longer sessions can benefit from a mixture of teaching and learning approaches and different assessment activities.

Delivering your session

You may feel nervous, which is quite normal. Try to imagine you are acting a role and this should help boost your confidence and calm your nerves. Stay focused, be in control, and do not let any personal issues affect you.

Keep your plan nearby to serve as a prompt if you need it. If you feel you might forget something, use a highlighter beforehand to mark key words which you can quickly glance at. If your mind suddenly goes blank, take a couple of deep breaths and look at your plan to help you refocus.

You will need to establish a rapport with your learners and engage and interact with them from the start. Asking the question 'What experience, if any, do you have of this topic?' is a good way of involving your learners in your subject from the start and helps you check any prior learning.

▶ Some interviews may include observing you delivering a session

Interview feedback form

The interviewers may use an interview feedback form to transparently record and justify their decision regarding who they appoint to the job. The form is used to record the information collected during your interview and helps them evaluate and compare different applicants once the interviews are completed.

Panel members must provide brief details in the comments section of the form to justify the rating they awarded the applicant. All panel members need to ensure that no irrelevant characteristics or 'protected attributes' are taken into account or considered during the interview process. For example, age, disability, marriage or civil partnership, pregnancy and maternity, race, religion or belief, gender or sexual orientation must all be disregarded when deciding who to give the job to.

Observation form

Sometimes when interviews are carried out, the interviewer, or one of the panellists, completes an observation record against a set of criteria that is established by the organisation. The observation form can include details about the way you perform, answer questions, work in a team, etc. The scoring on this form can be used to make an appointment or help decide between two candidates.

Involving a peer group in the interview process

Involving a peer group in the interview process involves job candidates meeting one-on-one with the company's employees. The candidate is able to ask the employees questions about the company and job, while the employees can evaluate the applicant and then tell the employer their thoughts.

In this process, which is becoming more popular, the interviewee is interviewed by the existing workers, often those in the same position they will be working in. The employees then complete a review form and return it to the management team for a final decision. This approach has some advantages and disadvantages compared to traditional panel interviewing – see Table 3.8.

Submitting applications to peer group

When using a peer interview panel there are some considerations. Before the process can start the manager should recruit the most appropriate peers, brief them on the interview matrix (the criteria for selection) and ensure that each of the peers is competent. At this stage it is really important that management are available for questions from the peer interview panel. Finally, the applications can be given to the panel prior to the interviewing process.

▶ **Table 3.8:** Advantages and disadvantages of peer group interviews

Advantages	Disadvantages
• Transfer of knowledge. Applicants are able to learn more about the company from employees (who are likely to tell it a little more like it is). • Guard is down. Applicants are more likely to let their guard down with peers, so the organisation will get a better sense of who their candidates are and how they'll fit. • Employees help to select their future co-workers. Being involved in the selection process is good for morale and productivity. • As employees are invested in the new person's success they are more likely to help them. Similarly, new employees start work knowing their peers support them.	• When unhappy employees are involved, the new applicants can be put off. • Some employees could be threatened by an applicant and not recommend him/her because of their own insecurities. • They can be time-consuming, including preparing, conducting the interview itself, and following up with recommendations.

The type of feedback the manager receives from peers is usually quite different from panellists in traditional interviews. Typically, the feedback from the peer group includes about specific applicants, coupled with more general feelings about the group of applicants.

In making decisions it is important to assess all of the comments and conclusions and decide which are the most valid and impartial. If the peer group is experienced and has had an input into the process they will give valuable comments and feedback related to how the applicant might fit into the role; this is particularly important for small teams who must work closely together.

Employer evaluation

Once the interview is complete and the applicant or applicants are appointed, organisations will often evaluate the interview process with questions such as:

1 How effective was the activity/activities, e.g. microcoach or role play exercise?

2 Were the correct questions asked?

3 Did the advertisement, job description and person specification appeal to the right candidates? Did they attract the best applicants?

4 Did the organisation follow all relevant legislation including equal opportunities?

PAUSE POINT   What are the main things to consider when preparing for an interview?

Hint   Consider all the questions you might be asked at an interview.

Extend   Imagine you have been asked to prepare at least ten questions for interviewing a sports coach to help a panel decide whether the applicant is suitable for the job. What would the questions be?

Assessment practice 3.3   C.P5 C.P6 C.M4 CD.D5 CD.D3

A large multinational leisure park is planned just outside your local town. With all of the planned rides, attractions, hotels and restaurants there will be a significant number of employment opportunities. You have noticed that the largest of the hotels will be recruiting fitness and leisure staff such as personal trainers, lifeguards and duty managers for their leisure complex.

Even though it is two years before the complex is due to open, there is a team of recruiters holding generic fitness and leisure interviews with a view to making appointments to these positions in two years' time.

1 Prepare a presentation that details the importance of communication skills in the fitness industry.

2 Prepare a 20-minute microcoach of a specific fitness session such as an exercise class or circuit class.

Plan
- How confident do I feel in my own abilities to complete this task? Are there any areas I think I may struggle with?
- Can I develop the scenario described and formulate an imaginary staffing structure, to identify potential roles that may become available?
- I will identify the key elements of effective communication to include in my presentation.
- I will decide on the content of my microcoach and practise my interview technique.

Do
- I know what it is I am doing and what I want to achieve.
- I will complete my slideshow so that it is ready for presentation and demonstrates my understanding of the selection and recruitment activities.
- I will deliver my microcoach, which will probably be fitness- or sports-focused.

Review
- I will explain what the task was and how I approached it.
- I will explain how I would approach the difficult elements differently next time.
- I will review both aspects, presentation and microcoach.

D Reflect on the recruitment and selection process and your individual performance

Review and evaluation

Whether you are successful with your interview or not, you should always evaluate how you performed during the process. This will help you improve your chances next time, or perfect your interview skills.

Self-analysis of interview performance

As part of the review of an interview there needs to be an element of self-reflection and a personal review of the process that includes a critique of all of the supporting paperwork, such as the skills audit, the CDAP and any prepared answers.

Look at the interview evaluation form shown in Table 3.9, designed to be used after a job interview. Using a template like this is an effective way to start the evaluation process and will help you to begin a new action plan for your next job interview.

To help with the process, here are some questions that you might consider after an interview.

▸ In general, how did the interview go? Did it proceed as you expected or were you surprised by the process in some way?
▸ How did your skills audit help in your interview?
▸ What was the most memorable part of the interview? (Maybe something the interviewer revealed or an event of some sort that occurred during the interview.)
▸ What do you think your best interview question was? Why?
▸ If you were to meet with the interviewer again, what new questions would you want to ask?
▸ Has your attitude toward the job changed in any way because of the interview?
▸ Did you find out what you had expected to by doing the interview?
▸ How will you adapt your CDAP following this reflection?

▸ **Table 3.9:** An interview evaluation form

Evaluation	Weak	Average	Strong
Role play activity: Did I read and understand the brief; stay on task and to the point; avoid conflict with others; demonstrate empathy?			
Organisational ability: Did I approach each part of the interview methodically; think and structure my responses; organise any other activities effectively?			
Communication: Did I express my thoughts clearly in writing and verbally; project a positive manner in all forms of communication; respond diplomatically?			
Problem solving/decision making: Did I demonstrate my ability to make decisions; involve others as appropriate; resolve issues?			
Building trust: Did I demonstrate my ability to keep commitments and meet deadlines; exhibit integrity and honesty with colleagues and customers; be open to views of others; take responsibility for my own actions in conflict resolution?			
Teamwork: Did I demonstrate my ability to work as part of a team; seek the perspective and expertise of others; look for opportunities to support others on the team?			
Learner/customer service oriented: Did I demonstrate strong customer service orientation with the ability to provide clear, consistent information and service?			

After an interview it is also good practice to consider what went well and what could be improved from a more analytical point of view. You will generally have a feeling about how the process went, but it is possible to have further reflections. If possible, ask for feedback or a rating from one of your interviewers to help with this.

Be objective about the situation. Were you prepared and had you practised, or did you 'throw it together and hope for the best'? Could you have been more effective with additional practice? What will you do to prepare for your next interview?

One of the most helpful things you can do after an interview is to let go of your self-recriminations by 'venting'. Go home or to a café and write about the interview. Let your thoughts pour out. When you have finished, put the writing away, and 'let it go'. Sleep on it and when you have had a chance to relax and digest the information, go back and revisit what you wrote. What can you learn from this experience? What will you do differently next time?

On a scale of 1–10 rate yourself on the following questions:

▶ Did you arrive on time?

▶ How was your introduction?

▶ Were you confident and professional?

▶ Did you speak calmly and clearly?

▶ How was your non-verbal communication?

▶ Did you have good engagement with the interviewer?

▶ Did you talk about your strengths?

▶ Did you talk about your weaknesses in a positive manner?

▶ Did you handle the difficult questions with ease?

▶ Did you ask good questions about the role?

▶ Were things left on a positive note?

If most of your rating numbers are in the 5–10 range, you are probably doing things right. Look carefully at the lower ratings and assess your shortcomings. You may want to consider practising with someone so that you can obtain more objective feedback on your answers and style.

You can then revisit your action plan and set about adding new actions or updating your existing actions as appropriate, thinking how you might improve in relevant areas. For example, if you scored 3 for 'How was your introduction', then you can further research and practise how to make a good impression at the start of the interview.

What to do if you are interviewing

To this point we have mostly considered the interview from the perspective of the interviewee. What about the skills of the interviewer? Here are some practical guidelines on how to carry out an effective interview. You could use these in preparing to play the role of interviewer.

▶ What do you want to ask? Prepare questions in advance.

▶ Choose the correct space to interview – it does not have to be overly quiet but should not be distractingly noisy.

▶ Act professionally and with respect – do not interrupt.

- Start with something that puts your applicant at ease – you want to get the best from them.

- Think about your questions. Closed questions (which could be given a 'yes' or 'no' response) get short answers. Try to start questions with what, why or how.

- Record your feelings about the quality of answers as they are answered. Many interviewers use a code that helps score the quality of the responses.

Updated SWOT and action plan

Once your initial appraisal is complete, you should update your SWOT analysis and action plan. As well as considering your interview performance to see if it was effective, you should also carry out a separate SWOT analysis of any role play activities you were asked to undertake.

The example in Table 3.10 shows a SWOT analysis based on an interview for the role of Recreation Assistant at a local swimming pool. As part of the interview there was a role play activity that simulated an emergency response scenario in the sports hall. It was a group role play and called for candidates to formulate a plan and act out the process of that plan as part of a team.

▶ **Table 3.10:** Example SWOT analysis after an interview's role play

Strengths	Weaknesses
• Good communication skills • Good rapport with interview panel • Experience of role play activities, having practised them • Good understanding of task presented • Good planning at early stage	• Lack of industry experience • Lack of job knowledge • Forgot to ask about the rules of the task • Could not remember all of the technical parts of the task
Opportunities	**Threats**
• To learn the role of Recreation Assistant • To build up more knowledge of sports hall activities and how to set up and take down equipment • To develop my role as a Recreation Assistant at the centre	• Nervous about working with an established team • Lack of time before I start to learn all procedures

Once you have completed your SWOT analysis of how you performed in the interview, including any role plays, you can go on to update your overall CDAP and identify some new actions for your action plan so you can conduct and participate in interviews more effectively.

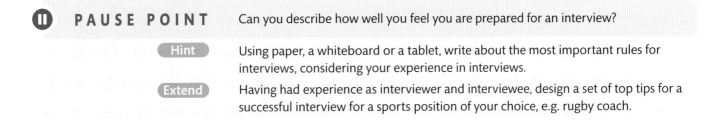

ⅠⅠ PAUSE POINT   Can you describe how well you feel you are prepared for an interview?

Hint   Using paper, a whiteboard or a tablet, write about the most important rules for interviews, considering your experience in interviews.

Extend   Having had experience as interviewer and interviewee, design a set of top tips for a successful interview for a sports position of your choice, e.g. rugby coach.

Assessment practice 3.4

C.P5 | C.P6 | D.P7 | CM.4 | D.M5 | CD.D2 | CD.D3

Following on from your recruitment experience at the leisure park, you need to review your own performance. This is going to take the form of an extension to your portfolio and is likely to include the following evidence:

1 A role play activity

2 A carefully considered appraisal of the recruitment activity with evidence of self-reflection, peer feedback and tutor/assessor feedback

3 A review document that allows you to reflect on your communication and organisational ability in the recruitment process

4 A SWOT analysis of your performance, informed by all parties

5 A review of the whole mock recruitment process, including your feelings on its value in relation to seeking future employment

6 An updated CDAP

Plan

- How confident do I feel in my own abilities to complete this task? Are there any areas I think I may struggle with?

- I will develop the scenario described and focus on the purpose of the role play activity.

- I will extend my existing portfolio to include the main areas for review.

Do

- I know what it is I am doing and what I want to achieve.

- I will complete the reflection and review process, taking on board the comments of all involved, and making an equal contribution to their reviews.

Review

- I will explain what the task was and how I approached it.

- I will explain how I would approach the difficult elements differently next time.

- I will update my CDAP.

Further reading and resources

Books

Hong, C.S. and Harrison, D. (2011) *Tools for Continuing Professional Development*, London: Quay Books.

Masters, J. (2011) *Working in Sport*, 3rd edition, London: How to Books.

Wells et al. (2010) *A Career in Sports: Advice from Sports Business Leaders*, Ohio, USA: Wells Books.

Websites

www.careers-in-sport.co.uk – Careers in Sport: information about career options in the sports industry.

www.nationalcareersservice.direct.gov.uk – National Careers Service: information about different careers and advice and guidance about the process of finding a job.

www.uksport.gov.uk/jobs-in-sport – UK Sport: Information about sports-related jobs in the UK.

THINK ▶FUTURE

Metin Terlemez

Sport and Public
Services Tutor

I was once a BTEC Sports learner at the college where I now teach. I knew that when I was finished I wanted to be a Further Education Tutor. I love the way that the learners are allowed to relax a little and work in an environment that is a little more work realistic. The job is very rewarding but also very challenging. As tutors, we are often required to assume roles that are outside what you might expect, for example helping learners to gain a work placement as part of their course.

It is difficult sometimes to try and include everyone in the learning process. In a typical lecture there are learners with vastly different learning styles, family backgrounds and expectations. In a college, learners have always come from at least four different schools, so even their school experiences can have been quite different. Add to the mix a few older learners, some in their twenties, and the group takes on a very different dynamic.

Focusing your skills

Managing behaviour

Most tutors will tell you that they have had to manage inappropriate behaviour at some point. For many it is a daily reality. There are any number of training courses, web resources and books on the best strategies.

- Try to understand the root cause of the behaviour because this will be a great place to start managing the behaviour.
- One of the most effective approaches is to consider interventions or strategies that might involve body language, voice control or attention focus. Other strategies include altering the layout of the teaching room and using cooperative learning.
- Recognising and respecting everyone's different approach is important. Ask your own tutor about their approach – you might be surprised!

Planning your delivery

You cannot just turn up and teach all of your lessons. Planning will help your lessons take shape, let those in your class feel as though they have been part of the process and help you to improve as a teacher.

- Start by focusing on who the lesson is for rather than the subject. You need to consider the different ways in which you can teach the lesson and whether these options are practical. You may use small group activities or maybe even a visit.
- Along with your lesson plan and scheme of work you will need to review each session and reflect on what went well. The ability to reflect and be self-critical is something we all have to learn in teaching.

Getting ready for assessment

Ellie is working towards completing the second year of her BTEC National in Sport. She has been given an assignment that covers learning aims A and B. She has already produced a report to complete the part of the assignment that covers learning aim A. Now she needs to complete the second half of her assignment, which asks her to explore her own skills using a skills audit. This will inform a career development action plan (CDAP) to help cover learning aim B. The CDAP needs to contain:

▸ information on relevant skills, qualities, experience and ambitions
▸ the kind of qualifications she would need to study to be successful in the industry.

Ellie shares her experience below.

How I got started

First I listed my experiences, qualifications, accomplishments and what I want to achieve in my sports career. Then I found a skills audit template online and set about completing it. When I showed it to my mum she reminded me of some things I had forgotten, like the voluntary work that I do for the Scouts and the 75-mile trek that we completed last year.

I am not really sure what I want to do yet for a job but I like PE and I think that it could be an interesting and rewarding career. I arranged a short placement at my old school and shadowed my old PE teacher – that was useful and has definitely steered me more strongly towards teaching.

How I brought it all together

Having completed the placement I designed my own CDAP, which was essentially a table in a word processed document. Once I'd finished it, it helped me focus on:
▸ analysing career opportunities in PE by searching current vacancies and focusing on person specifications and job descriptions
▸ analysing career opportunities by evaluating available jobs and making realistic personal targets
▸ analysing the skills and technical skills that I would need for the job – I did that by looking at the job descriptions
▸ planning for how to become a teacher within the next 5 years.

The completed template became my CDAP.

What I learned from the experience

Being back at school was weird at first, but the staff were helpful in guiding me and helping me think about university choices.

On reflection it would have been good to research the realities of the job first and to have thought about how I would tackle the tasks that I knew I would be involved in, like lesson warm-ups and supervising Year 7 gymnastics club.

It took a long time to find a good skills audit template, and with hindsight I think that I might have been better to design my own, as I knew what to put in the table anyway. I am still unsure about whether a career as a PE teacher is definitely for me, but I do at least know how I would get there if I wanted to.

Think about it

▸ If I were to start again, I would spend more time researching the professional development requirements of my chosen profession.
▸ Completing the skills audit is difficult. I could have asked my parents or friends what my strengths and weaknesses are – it is hard to be objective about yourself.
▸ Watching videos on good interview techniques would have helped my own techniques and ironed out my flaws quicker.
▸ Reviewing and redesigning my CDAP would have been easier with a good SWOT analysis.

Sports Leadership 4

Getting to know your unit

There are countless roles within the sports industry where strong leadership skills are essential. Leadership is vital to ensure that groups and individuals are able to achieve their goals. Principles of leadership must be applied to maintain safety, and to motivate and develop personal relationships. There are many styles of leadership and an exceptional leader will be able to adapt their style to meet the requirements of their team and situation.

How you will be assessed

This unit will be assessed internally by a series of tasks set by your tutor. These tasks might take the form of presentations or written documents. There will also be a strong emphasis on practical delivery during which you will be observed.

The assignments set by your tutor may take the following forms:
▶ creating a PowerPoint® presentation that analyses the qualities and characteristics of effective leaders and presenting it to the rest of the class
▶ producing a written document that evaluates psychological factors which may affect leaders
▶ leading a sports coaching session of your choice, making appropriate decisions as a leader and reviewing your performance.

The assessment activities within this unit are designed to help you practise and gain skills that will help you to complete your assignments. Leadership is something that is best developed through practice. The theories within this unit will give you the background information to enable you to complete the unit but will not guarantee you a particular grade.

To pass this unit you must ensure that you have covered all the Pass grading criteria. If you are seeking a Merit or Distinction grade then you must be able to show both an understanding of basic leadership concepts and also how to choose appropriate styles and tools to be effective.

Assessment criteria

This table shows what you must do in order to achieve a **Pass**, **Merit** or **Distinction** grade, and where you can find activities to help you.

Pass	**Merit**	**Distinction**
Learning aim **A** Understand the roles, qualities and characteristics of an effective sports leader		
A.P1 Discuss the skills, qualities and characteristics of three different leadership roles within different sport and exercise activities or environments. **Assessment practice 4.1**	**A.M1** Analyse the importance of skills, qualities and characteristics in the leadership role within different sport and exercise activities or environments. **Assessment practice 4.1**	**A.D1** Evaluate the impact of skills, qualities, characteristics on sports leadership within different sport and exercise activities or environments. **Assessment practice 4.1**
A.P2 Explain the importance of skills, qualities and characteristics in the leadership role within different sport and exercise activities or environments. **Assessment practice 4.1**		**B.D2** Evaluate the impact of key psychological factors on sports leadership within different sport and exercise activities or environments. **Assessment practice 4.2**
Learning aim B Examine the importance of psychological factors and their link with effective leadership		
B.P3 Discuss how key psychological factors may affect sports leadership within different sport and exercise activities or environments. **Assessment practice 4.2**	**B.M2** Analyse key psychological factors that may affect sports leadership within different sport and exercise activities or environments. **Assessment practice 4.2**	
Learning aim C Explore an effective leadership style when leading a team during sport and exercise activities		
C.P4 Demonstrate a chosen leadership style, using appropriate skills when leading a team during a sport and exercise activity. **Assessment practice 4.3**	**C.M3** Demonstrate a chosen leadership style, using effective skills when leading a team during a sport and exercise activity. **Assessment practice 4.3**	**C.D3** Justify your leadership style and its impact on team performance, suggesting alternative leadership styles that could be used to improve team performance. **Assessment practice 4.3**
C.P5 Review the impact of own leadership style on the performance of the team during the sport and exercise activity. **Assessment practice 4.3**	**C.M4** Analyse your chosen leadership style and the impact of it on team performance, considering own strengths and areas of weakness. **Assessment practice 4.3**	

Getting started

Effective sports leadership inspires and motivates. Give three examples of sports leaders you have experienced who you felt were effective and say why. Now give three examples of sports leaders that you have experienced who you feel need to improve their delivery and explain why.

A Understand the roles, qualities and characteristics of an effective sports leader

Before we are able to develop ourselves as sports leaders it is important that we reflect upon the sports industry as a whole and are able to identify leaders and the demands of their role.

> **Link**
>
> This unit can help when you are studying *Unit 6: Sports Psychology, Unit 8: Coaching for Performance, Unit 10: Sports Event Organisation, Unit 23: Coaching and Leading for Participation* and *Unit 31: Team Building.*

Different leadership roles

The sports industry is vast and the roles within it are very diverse. Table 4.1 gives an overview of some roles that call on leadership skills and qualities.

▶ **Table 4.1:** Different leadership roles in sport

Role	Description
Activity leader	A person who ensures that rules and regulations are kept to during games and competitions to maintain fair and safe activity.
Teacher / trainer	A practitioner who gives new knowledge to participants through a variety of methods and techniques.
Coach	A practitioner who works with participants to develop skills which normally already exist in order to improve performance.
Team manager / manager	Someone who oversees a group's or individual's performance as a whole and is responsible for both motivation and discipline. This person often has unseen duties such as logistical organisation (e.g. organising travel) and budget control.
Score keeper	A person who is responsible for monitoring and recording scores during competition.
First aider	Someone who is on hand to deal with incidents and injuries, and will keep potential casualties safe until further assistance arrives when needed.
Instructor	A practitioner who introduces new skills and techniques, normally in a practical environment.
Official	Someone who controls discipline and ensures fair play during a contest from within, or close to, the area of play.
Table official	Someone who ensures fair play, often records scores and attends to management of discipline from outside the area of play.
Health and safety officer / Risk assessor	Someone who ensures that the sporting environment is safe for participants and spectators.

Leadership skills, qualities and characteristics

Skills, qualities and characteristics can be developed and acquired. It is important to remember that leaders will always have strengths and weaknesses. Although the best leaders develop the ability to switch between styles, their own personality will mean they develop in different ways.

Many attributes of a leader are transferable and are generic to a variety of leadership roles. Some of the general skills, qualities and characteristics found within leaders are shown in Figure 4.1.

▶ **Figure 4.1:** Skills, qualities and characteristics of sports leaders

Skills

Building rapport

All leaders should be focused on getting the most out of those they are responsible for. This is generally easier if a positive relationship is built on trust, respect and honest communication. A relationship such as this is described as a good 'rapport'. Developing a good rapport will ensure that communication is easier and that objectives are met successfully.

Rapport is dependent on successful development of other leadership qualities and characteristics such as knowledge, patience, confidence and approachability.

Theory into practice

Imagine that you are tasked with looking after a new group. There are a number of simple techniques that you can use to help build rapport.

1　Maintain an open posture. Avoid crossing your arms and try to look approachable.

2　Show an interest in your group. Consider them as individuals and try to greet them each personally.

3　Emphasise your passion for the subject and try to project energy.

What else could you do to build rapport with your group? Find a group that you can practise building rapport with. This might be by volunteering at a local club or centre.

Confidence

A leader who lacks confidence is one who will struggle. Confidence is projected onto those that you are responsible for. If you are confident in your own ability and judgement, then those around you are more likely to share your confidence. Confidence is often considered one of the most important elements of a good leader. Having confidence, however, only comes from ensuring that other elements are all in place, allowing the leader to perform at their best. These elements include:

▶ being organised
▶ being appropriately resourced
▶ understanding the demands of the role
▶ having clear objectives
▶ being experienced.

Communication

The art of communication is complex and can be difficult to learn. Communication is successfully sharing information with one or more people. Different people take in information in different ways, and so a good communicator must develop a variety of tools to pass on this information effectively.

It is important to remember that there are two sides to communication. Listening is just as important as giving information. A good listener will enhance their image as being approachable and valuing other team members' thoughts, gaining a reputation for being a good collaborator.

Communication can be **verbal** or **non-verbal**. Many inexperienced leaders will be tempted to over-complicate verbal communication, giving people too much information at once and using technical terms where they are not necessary. Strong verbal communication will be clear and concise. The sports environment is often noisy and fast-paced. In order for a leader to ensure that their requirements are met, they must be able to project their thoughts and wishes to individuals and groups no matter what is happening around them.

Non-verbal communication can be split into the following forms:

▶ **Body language and facial expressions** – Even when verbal communication is the primary form, body language and gestures must be used to support it. If you look uninterested and lack passion or energy, you are unlikely to encourage others to work harder.

▶ **Gestures and hand signals** – These can be used from a distance, and many sports and activities have gestures and hand signals that are specific to them. Having a clear understanding of these will enable success as a leader.

▶ **Demonstrations** – Physically showing someone what you want is a clear way to communicate. A demonstration should be concise and delivered so that your audience can best observe.

▶ **Non-verbal sounds** – Whistles are common in sport. They are primarily used to attract attention so another form of communication can then be used.

> **Key terms**
>
> **Verbal communication** – communication that takes place using the spoken word.
>
> **Non-verbal communication** – communication that comes through gestures, facial expressions, eye contact, posture or tone of voice.

> **Discussion**
>
> As a class, split into two groups. One group must discuss all the benefits of verbal communication while the other group discusses the benefits of non-verbal communication. As a class, debate whether you feel verbal or non-verbal communication is more important in a sporting environment.

Being organised

Even the most exceptional leader cannot expect to deliver their best without planning and preparation. A leader who is not punctual, is poorly resourced or has not done any background research is set for failure. Being organised will not only give the leader confidence, but will also inspire others to have confidence in them.

Giving feedback

One of the key areas where a sports leader has to act in an ethical manner and with integrity is when they are giving feedback to their participants. Honesty is important, but the sports leader must be sure that they are also objective and do not allow any of their preconceptions to cloud their judgement or appraisal of the participant. This means that they must be attentive to the participants' performance at all times.

Qualities

Knowledgeable

A strong leader will be knowledgeable about both the activity and their team. Not only will they have a full understanding of the technical aspects of what they are trying to achieve, but they will also understand the individuals they are responsible for, what motivates them, and their strengths and weaknesses.

▶ **Knowledge of rules and laws** – Every activity has a set of rules and laws which are designed to keep participants safe and ensure fair play. These rules and laws vary between activities, and some activities have more complex systems than others. It is a leader's responsibility to maintain discipline and uphold rules so that participants have confidence in fairness and can perform without any safety concerns.

▶ **Knowledge of techniques, strategies and tactics** – Activities all have specific techniques, skills, strategies and tactics associated with them. These elements can be trained for, but in order for them to work they must be used at the right time in the right scenario. Sports leaders should consider conditions, environment and opposition when developing strategies. Techniques may be complex and need breaking down into small sections in order for a participant to learn them. For example, the start of a sprint race will involve an athlete positioning themselves in a set of starting blocks, exiting the blocks and taking the first few strides in the race.

▶ **Knowledge of team or participants** – In order to develop the best from an individual, a leader must understand what drives them. They must be aware of the participant's personality traits, motivations and aspirations. Only when a leader has **empathy** with, and understands, an individual can they understand how they fit within a team. They must also understand the participant's physical needs, such as any specific dietary requirements or old or existing injuries.

> **Key term**
>
> **Empathy** – when you understand and can share the feelings that someone else is experiencing. Having empathy for a team member will help you build a relationship with them and look for solutions to problems.

 **PAUSE POINT**   A good leader will be highly knowledgeable. What types of knowledge are important for a leader to possess?

Hint   Close the book and list as many types of knowledge as possible in two minutes.

Extend   Are there any sports that you have aspirations to lead? What specific knowledge would you need to be successful in these sports?

Empathetic

Both within a sporting environment and in everyday life there are stresses placed upon individuals. Being able to listen and empathise with team members will allow them to express any concerns or anxieties and feel valued and understood. Sometimes just having someone to talk to can boost an individual's morale.

Characteristics

Goal orientated

A leader who understands what those they are responsible for must aim for or achieve is able to set goals. An ultimate goal may then be broken down into attainable targets. Goals and targets provide focus, and in order to work most effectively a leader must learn and adapt to make these goals challenging and feasible.

Patient

Being a leader can be challenging. Your decisions will not always be popular, you may have individuals or groups who struggle to grasp skills or concepts, and there may be disruptive learners or participants. No matter what the situation, a leader must remain impartial and level-headed. It is vital that leaders develop strategies for coping with challenges.

Approachable

Leadership is crucially about relationships. In order to get the best out of an individual, you need to understand their motivations and anxieties. Being approachable will allow people to discuss their problems with you so that you may be able to help.

Consistent

Consistency is vital in order to promote fair play and ensure every member of a team feels equally valued. A leader cannot appear to have favourites or be biased – they must be objective. Additionally, when delivering instruction in techniques a leader must ensure they are consistent.

Role model

A quality leader will often lead from the front. Their behaviour and motivation will set the benchmark for every other member of the team to aspire to. This is particularly relevant when working with children, as they will often imitate the conduct of their coach or leader.

Role models set an example:

▶ **socially** in the way they integrate with both the team and outsiders in a spirit of cooperation and fair play

▶ **personally** by demonstrating life skills such as manners and punctuality

▶ **psychologically** by controlling emotions and projecting confidence and motivation

▶ **physically** by maintaining a healthy lifestyle through exercise, diet and good habits.

Committed

Most successful sports leaders are extremely driven. If a leader is to expect total commitment from those they are responsible for, then they must demonstrate that they are also willing to give 100 per cent commitment to support them. This can be through simple acts such as early starts for training or fetching a thirsty athlete water.

Ethical and having integrity

Being ethical and acting with integrity is understanding the accepted norms of right and wrong and acting in a manner that promotes right from wrong. Within a competitive context, right and wrong are often clearly defined by rules and regulations. However, acting ethically and with integrity should also be expected within training, and good, appropriate behaviour encouraged at all times.

Leads by example

A good leader shows what they want from their team by consistent demonstration of their expectations. Here are a few ways to clearly lead by example:

▶ Chelsea's John Terry earned a reputation for leading from the front and setting his team a benchmark

- share blame when things go badly as well as accept praise when they go well
- emphasise positive qualities and characteristics such as passion, knowledge and integrity
- be persistent and do not give up even when things are tough.

PAUSE POINT There are many skills and qualities of a leader. Can you describe them and explain their importance?

Hint Close the book and draw a spider diagram of skills and qualities important to leadership.

Extend Which three of the skills do you consider to be the most important and why?

Examples of leaders

Regardless of their specific role, almost all sports leaders are responsible for helping the participants in their charge develop their full potential. This involves creating the right conditions to allow improvements to take place, and educating the participants to develop their knowledge and understanding of sport. However, some skills, qualities and characteristics are more important in some roles than in others.

Worked example

Carefully examine the examples of leaders below. Are there any additional characteristics or qualities that you feel would be essential for success within these roles? Justify your thoughts in writing.

Is there a leadership role that you aspire to? Consider the characteristics and qualities you would need within this role. Choose the three you feel are most important and evaluate why.

Rock climbing instructor

- Organisation is essential, as any kit which is left behind will be out of reach when out at the climbing site.
- Communication must be clear so that climbers understand exactly what is required of them.
- The instructor must be firm and have excellent knowledge to ensure their group remains safe at all times.
- Patience is often needed to ensure individuals are encouraged to overcome psychological barriers as well as physical ones. This means that the instructor has to maintain their energy levels and commitment at all times.
- Motivational skills are also necessary to help nervous or inexperienced participants.
- Being friendly, outgoing and approachable, with good listening skills, will ensure that anxious participants feel comfortable and teaching can be adapted accordingly.

Cricket captain

- Motivation is vital. Captains must often lead by example and are responsible for inspiring the rest of the team. A skilful captain must be motivational.
- Having confidence in their own ability as a captain will influence the team and help them gain confidence. This confidence can come from experience and knowledge of the sport.
- Fairness will encourage inclusivity and ensure that every team member feels equally valued. The captain needs to be a good vocal communicator, praising others and conveying their passion for the sport.
- Experience is essential for a captain as they must understand the game thoroughly, know and enforce the rules, read the game, and use strategies and tactics well.

Swimming coach

- Keeping schedules and resources organised will allow a coach to use time effectively and ensure every session runs smoothly.
- Good observation skills will allow the coach to spot areas for improvement, while being able to break down a technique and analyse the component parts to help pinpoint specific goals.
- Having strong delivery will encourage confidence in the coach's ability and could lead to further clients and work.
- Being capable of clear demonstrations will help show participants exactly what is required of them.
- Questioning participants effectively will help the coach to assess understanding of a technique, and giving clear feedback will ensure that both strengths and areas for improvement are understood. This will also help to build rapport.
- Swimming pools can be hazardous areas, so strong safety awareness is essential.

Ski race official

- An authoritative manner will help keep discipline and ensure races are safe. Ski courses can be large and officials may need to make decisions without support, and so common sense is essential.
- Clear communication between officials will ensure the entire event runs smoothly.
- To ensure all participants feel the event has been run fairly, consistency is very important. Understanding of the rules of racing is essential to achieve this, and good communication with other officials and competitors will help ensure decisions are clear.
- In the case that bad weather halts racing, decisions to abandon or postpone a race may be very unpopular. The person making that judgement will need to be confident in their decision and communicate the reasons for a decision that keeps participants safe.
- Accurate timekeeping must be used, not just to record individual descents but also to make sure the whole event runs to schedule.

Gymnastics teacher

- Teachers are accountable for the safety of the participants and students in their care. Organisation and the planning of each lesson will support this.
- A lesson must be adaptable to enable teachers to focus on new skills which are proving difficult to learn.
- For any teacher, being engaging and inspirational will keep students focused and positive about their learning.
- Being confident in yourself and what you are teaching will ensure discipline.
- Being passionate about a subject and enthusiastic in delivery will help to keep participants motivated. It is also important to offer praise when appropriate.
- When participants are struggling to learn a skill, additional practice may be required. Teachers may need to be resourceful and creative to deliver a topic or concept. They also have to be dedicated and determined to help the student succeed.

Assessment practice 4.1   A.P1   A.P2   A.M1   A.D1

You are the manager of a busy sports centre that delivers a wide variety of activities. You are updating your staff training procedures. As part of this process, you are designing observation feedback forms for your deputy managers to use when observing staff.

You have chosen to trial the new procedures with three roles: pool lifeguards, youth squad football coaches, and over-50s circuit training instructors. You are preparing a presentation to deliver to your deputy managers, to make sure they understand exactly what to do.

Within this presentation:

1 discuss the skills, qualities and characteristics that you expect in each role

2 explain the importance of these elements and analyse why they are important to the strong delivery of each activity and to the success of the centre as a whole

3 evaluate the impact that these skills, qualities and characteristics will have on other roles in the sports centre.

Plan
- What is the task? What am I being asked to do?
- How confident do I feel in my own abilities to complete this task? Are there any areas I think I may struggle with?

Do
- I know what it is I am doing and what I want to achieve.
- I will identify when I have gone wrong and adjust my thinking/approach to get myself back on course.

Review
- I will explain what the task was and how I approached it.
- I will explain what I would do differently next time in order to improve my work.

B   Examine the importance of psychological factors and their link with effective leadership

The **psychological factors** that affect our performance are numerous and varied. Sporting environments can be challenging and pressure on leaders high. Not only do sports leaders have to cope with internal psychological factors, but external psychological factors outside the leader's control will also have a large impact on performance. Psychological factors can have a profound effect on any sporting activity, affecting:

- how safely the activity is conducted
- the management of resources and environment
- the way that participants interact together
- the way that spectators interact with participants
- the final outcome and, ultimately, the success or failure of the final goal.

Key term

Psychological factors – factors that are in the mind or related to mental attitude.

Theory into practice

Within your class, split into groups of 4–6 people. Each group should have a small ball of sticky tack and 30 cocktail sticks. You have five minutes to build the highest tower possible using just the sticky tack and cocktail sticks.

After five minutes which group has built the tallest tower? What contributed to the success of this team? Evaluate how your own team performed and suggest how this performance might be improved in future tasks.

External psychological factors

Team cohesion

Success or failure is always dependent upon how the team works as a cohesive unit. Team cohesion can be split into two forms:

▶ **task cohesion** is the degree to which a group works together to reach a common goal, such as a hockey team applying tactics to win a hockey match

▶ **social cohesion** is when a group works together through mutual respect for one another and often very simply because members enjoy each other's company.

The degree to which a group successfully bonds is affected by a variety of factors. Table 4.2 shows these factors and gives some examples.

▶ **Table 4.2:** Factors affecting team cohesion

Factor	Examples	Example scenario
Personal factors	• Historic relationships • Individual fatigue • Injury or illness • Gender • Age	If individual members of the team are tired, injured or unwell, they may struggle to participate fully in the game.
Team factors	• Aligned goals • Supportive relationships • Experience • Abilities	A hockey team with some experienced competition players may find that they are able to maintain a more controlled game due to the positive effect that their experience brings to the team.
Leadership factors	• Leader's ability to lead by example • Leader's decisiveness • Leader's approachableness	When running a gruelling expedition, a tired and haggard-looking leader will have a very negative effect on the morale of the group.
Environmental factors	• Access to appropriate resources • Weather • Venue	A football team that has access to indoor training, astro turf pitches and quality equipment will have greater options when it comes to training.

The factors shown in Table 4.2 can vary, but they can also be affected by strong leadership. A leader can encourage cohesion within their team by:

▶ encouraging a team identity, perhaps by introducing a uniform or kit

▶ avoiding turnover of team members by retaining individuals through positive leadership

▶ maintaining strong communication through team meetings, briefs and debriefs

▶ having empathy with individuals' frustrations and emotions

▶ setting clear, challenging, yet achievable goals

▶ making every team member feel valued and appreciated

▶ promoting a 'one team' atmosphere rather than allowing smaller social **cliques**.

Group formation

It is possible that you could bring together a line-up of the world's greatest athletes yet still have a weak team. Teams evolve: they do not form immediately and high levels of skill within their membership do not mean the team will develop faster.

> **Key term**
>
> **Clique** – a smaller group of people that keeps itself apart from others, often based on common interests, views, etc.

Figure 4.2 shows the stages that are used to describe the evolution of a team. An effective leader will be able to identify what stage their team is at and what challenges they must overcome to keep progression on track.

Link

This content links to *Unit 6: Sport Psychology*.

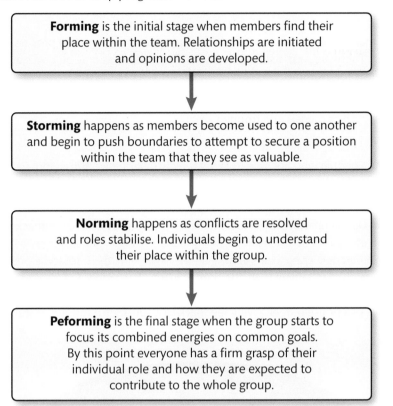

▸ **Figure 4.2:** Stages in the evolution of a team

Discussion

Think of a group you spend a large amount of time with, such as your class or a team you are part of. At what stage of formation do you feel it is?

Social loafing

In 1913, a Frenchman called Maximilien Ringelmann observed that in groups individuals pulling on ropes did not perform as well as their personal ability might suggest. A loss of motivation can be seen in individuals within a team which is now defined as 'social loafing'. It is known that people will often value individual success over group success and thus levels of motivation will be higher when people have personal goals.

Personality

Our personality is how we are projected to others and affects how we interact with those around us. Everyone is different and no two personalities are ever the same, but it is possible to generalise individuals into two categories: introvert and extrovert.

▸ **Introverts** tend to be quieter, less verbally communicative and unlikely to promote their own success. Often they are drawn towards individual sports and activities such as long distance running, rock climbing and other activities where training can be done individually or in very small groups.

▸ **Extroverts** tend to be very outgoing, communicative and enjoy social situations. They are likely to be drawn towards team sports such as football or netball.

Motivation

For some people simply taking part in an activity or sport is reward enough. They are motivated by the pleasure of participating. This is referred to as being **intrinsically motivated**.

However, many activities and sports offer rewards beyond the actual process of taking part. These are **extrinsic motivations**. These rewards may be physical or psychological, for example:

▶ financial compensation for time or success

▶ rewards such as medals and trophies

▶ perceived admiration from peers and onlookers.

Those sports people who are able to avoid the distraction of extrinsic motivations will often find that they are able to perform in a less inhibited manner, under less pressure and ultimately often succeed over others.

Motivation can be provided by leaders who use praise and positive feedback as the foundation of their feedback sessions. Many leaders use the 'praise burger' to deliver feedback. When delivering a 'praise burger', we begin with 'the bun' and a positive comment, we then follow up with 'the burger' in which we identify an area for improvement and we then finish with the second 'bun' and another positive comment. An example of a praise burger, giving feedback to a 100-metre sprinter, is shown in Figure 4.3.

Once you were up to speed, your posture was excellent.

Next session, we should look at your reaction from the block as this is hindering your overall performance.

Your stamina is strong at present, and your finish is fast.

▶ **Figure 4.3:** 'Praise burger' of feedback to a sprinter

Arousal and anxiety

Human nature suggests that we have a need to succeed: when we are put into a situation where failure is a possibility, then we feel the effects of stress on our **psyche**.

Arousal can help us focus and motivate ourselves. However, when we become 'over aroused' or anxious this will have negative effects, reducing both focus and control. This is clearly displayed in the inverted-U theory, shown in Figure 4.4.

Key terms

Psyche – the centre of a person's thought – their mind, soul and spirit.

Arousal – a physiological state that is alert and ready for action.

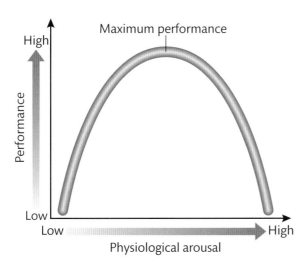

Figure 4.4: The inverted-U theory

The difficulty comes when trying to predict where the point of maximum performance found at the very top of the graph might come. This point varies depending on the activity. For example, sports such as snooker or archery take tremendous amounts of concentration and high levels of arousal can be negative. However, within power lifting and sprinting much higher levels of arousal can be beneficial to promote increased motivation.

An individual's personality will also affect the amount of arousal they can tolerate before negative signs are observed.

Leaders must be aware of how arousal and anxiety contribute to success or failure within specific activities. They should also aim to work with individuals to understand how they are personally affected by various levels of stress. Where necessary, leaders must be able to help with the management of stress. This might be through the use of:
▸ breathing techniques and meditation
▸ repetitive training of the task linked to increased stress levels to condition the athlete's body
▸ tasks designed to build confidence and self-esteem.

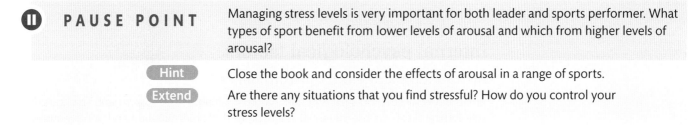

Ⅱ PAUSE POINT   Managing stress levels is very important for both leader and sports performer. What types of sport benefit from lower levels of arousal and which from higher levels of arousal?

    Hint   Close the book and consider the effects of arousal in a range of sports.

    Extend   Are there any situations that you find stressful? How do you control your stress levels?

Link

This content links to *Unit 6: Sport Psychology*.

Confidence

The belief that you can be successful at performing an activity is about having confidence. This could be any activity from lifting a heavy weight, scoring a goal in football, climbing a rock face or swimming the English Channel. A lack of confidence will affect motivation, increase anxiety and reduce the level at which an individual can expect to perform. This is sometimes known as a **self-fulfilling prophecy**.

Key term

Self-fulfilling prophecy – when someone believes a scenario will happen so strongly that they increase the likelihood of it happening.

During the 2014–15 Premier League season Chelsea FC were dominant and ultimately Premiership champions. However, the following season they started with poor results. It appeared that the team entered a run of bad form or a self-fulfilling prophecy. Lack of belief in their own ability to win could have been linked to team dynamics, team management, or fans' confidence.

1 What do you think was responsible for the sudden change in Chelsea's level of performance?

2 As a leader of that team, what could you have done to help build their confidence and break the cycle of a self-fulfilling prophecy?

Confidence can be increased in a variety of ways.

▶ Experience and previous success will generate an expectation of equal or better performance.

▶ 'Vicarious experiences' are those gained by watching other people. Observing success in others who are perceived as having equal or lesser ability will generate a belief that an individual can succeed.

Verbal enforcement by a leader – or by peers – that a task can be achieved will only work if there is trust: if you tell someone that they can achieve, they must believe you.

Case study

During the 2015 Rugby World Cup, Japan was responsible for one of the biggest shocks in Rugby Union history when they beat South Africa 34–32 in one of the opening matches.

Many sports commentators compared the two teams' approach to the game and levels of confidence. The Japanese players were described as having belief in themselves and a hunger for victory. South Africa was described as looking complacent and overconfident. Clearly, South Africa underestimated their rivals.

1 Evaluate how overconfidence might have affected South Africa's performance.

2 How do you think that Japan's victory might have affected the confidence levels of other teams that were scheduled to meet South Africa later in the competition?

Internal psychological factors

Attribution theory and self-confidence

Whether we succeed or fail, it is human nature to attribute this to a reason. This could be an internal reason, such as personal ability or level of determination and perseverance, or an external reason outside our own control, such as the ability of an opponent, the weather, sickness or injury.

What we attribute success and failure to is directly linked with our own personal levels of self-confidence. A world-class diver such as Tom Daley would attribute his own success to excellent preparation and his own ability. A new diver who manages to make a good dive is more likely to attribute this to luck.

A 'winning streak' is a common term often used lightly. However, there is some reality in this theory. A winning sports person will gain confidence but may still attribute success to luck. If they win again they will generate further confidence in themselves and begin to attribute success to their own ability. As it becomes easier to attribute success to ability, confidence grows, and as confidence grows so will a sportsperson's ability to succeed.

Tennis ace Serena Williams has been dominant in her sport since winning her first major tournament in 1999 and yet her own confidence is linked to a number of personal superstitions. She wears the same socks for an entire tournament, she has to tie her shoes in the same way before each match, and Serena makes sure to bounce the ball exactly five times on her first serve and twice on her second serve. On losing matches she has gone as far as to blame her defeat on not keeping to these strict routines.

Investigate examples of three more sports stars whose self-confidence is affected by routine and/or superstition.

Self-esteem

Our own opinion of our self-worth is known as our **self-esteem**. Often confused with self-confidence, self-esteem in a sporting context is whether we feel we deserve to win or lose. An athlete who believes that their success is based on luck or chance probably has quite low self-esteem.

When leading a team, you should be aware that self-esteem can be directly linked to a member's integration within that team and whether they believe they belong or deserve to be there. A person with low levels of self-esteem may find that being surrounded by people with high self-esteem has a negative effect on their belief in their own self-worth. This is why team cohesion is so important: so that everyone feels equally valued and in return values their own contribution.

Past experiences

Whether we have a history of success or failure will dictate our own self-belief. When we are winning it can sometimes seem easy to keep winning. However, when we are losing, the challenge of overcoming failure can seem too much. Self-belief is most essential at this point to enable maintenance of motivation and determination.

Leaders can use video footage of past successful experiences to illustrate a team member's ability to win. Spoken commentary is also good, and in the absence of either of these, newspaper articles can be used. Some leaders have been known to encourage meditation techniques to enable athletes to relive positive experiences and attempt to harness the positive feelings these past experiences generate.

Self-serving bias

Our own need to maintain belief in ourselves and protect our confidence can lead to us displaying self-serving bias. This is when we attribute success to our own ability and effort, but attribute failure to an external factor, such as a 'cheating' opposition or poor conditions. Although confidence is usually a good thing and high levels of self-esteem are required for success, we must also be able to reflect on defeat honestly in order to develop strategies for improvement.

Reflect

Has there been a time when you mistakenly blamed your own failure on an external reason? Be honest! Discuss and compare your experience of this with others in your class.

Behaviour

The behaviour of an individual can be attributed either to their own personality or to external factors. Our normal behaviour is how our personality is perceived, i.e. whether we are naturally grumpy, happy, or excitable. As part of a team, our team mates and leader will begin to understand our standard patterns of behaviour. This behaviour is known as **intentional behaviour**.

When placed within an environment that we find stressful, such as a sporting situation in which we feel pressure to succeed, we are more likely to demonstrate **accidental behaviour** characteristics. It is crucial that sportspeople are able to manage many accidental behavioural traits. For example, when playing rugby and other contact sports where adrenaline is flowing and arousal is high, it is relatively common for athletes to make mistakes or let their emotions get the better of them. However, the difference between a disciplined game and one governed by emotion can be the difference between winning and losing. There are plenty of examples of athletes who have allowed emotion to govern their behaviour in a way that has then hindered their success. Consider the Australian tennis player Nick Kyrgios's behaviour during the 2015 Rogers Cup, when he was subsequently fined $10,000 by the ATP for making an offensive remark aimed at French Open champion Stan Wawrinka during a match.

Case study

Cassie is a talented up-and-coming boxer. She has just started to fight at a national level and is so far undefeated. She is renowned for projecting high levels of confidence before, during and after matches. Her demeanour in and out of the ring projects her belief that she is the best in the world. During interviews with the media, she never hesitates to project pure confidence.

When she walks into the ring she looks relaxed and ready for action.

After every fight she ensures she acknowledges her opponent; however, she always spends time celebrating her victory and posing for cameras.

1 How do you think that Cassie's attitude affects her opponents?

2 How do you think that her self-belief affects her own performance?

3 Could Cassie's attitude ever have a negative effect upon her fights?

 **PAUSE POINT** Which of the features described in this section seems most relevant to your own experience of leadership?

 List as many external and internal psychological features as you can remember.

 In what activities can high levels of arousal quickly have negative effects on performance?

Forms of leadership

Different leadership styles will work to varying degrees with different individuals and teams. The success of a style is very much dependent on the psychological profile of those being led. However, no matter what form or style of leadership a person adopts, an effective leader is likely to possess a number of key psychological elements, such as:

▸ an ability to build positive relationships

▸ a clear and focused vision, an ability to avoid distractions, and an ability to plan, organise and set clear objectives

▸ self-belief that will allow decision making and solution finding

▸ an image that projects positivity and assertiveness

▸ perseverance and the robustness to learn from failure and move forward after failure.

Situational leadership

Situational leadership is a theory developed in 1969 by Paul Hersey and Ken Blanchard. Their theory suggests that a leader is only as effective as their ability to adapt in a situation.

> **Discussion**
>
> Use the internet to find out more about the situational leadership model. Find out the difference between directive behaviour and supportive behaviour and suggest situations in which each type of behaviour might be used.

Transformational leadership

Transformational leadership requires large amounts of self-belief and the ability to project passion, energy and inspiration to a team. A transformational leader is as concerned about the process of reaching a target as achieving the actual goal.

There are four components to transformational leadership.

1 **Intellectual stimulation** – this type of leader will encourage creativity and search for opportunities for innovation and change.

2 **Individualised consideration** – individuals within a transformational leader's team are recognised and their ideas appreciated. Supportive relationships are developed to encourage free flowing communication.

3 **Inspirational motivation** – these leaders have a clear vision and are able to project this to their team.

4 **Idealised influence** – leading by example and as a role model are fundamental to this type of leadership. Trust and respect are encouraged by positive examples.

Transactional leadership

A transactional leader will manage a team and expect every member to understand their own role while also recognising their position as leader. Clear structure is used so that team members understand the chain of command.

Transactional leadership revolves around the theory that success or failure should be met with reward or punishment and this is what motivates individuals to succeed. These leaders use rewards such as praise, events or financial compensation. In contrast, failure might result in reprimands or punishment such as physical exertion.

> **Research**
>
> For each of the forms of leadership – situational, transformational and transactional – think of an example of a leader that you feel fits that style. Evaluate how leading in this way has affected the performance of the team that they are responsible for and ultimately whether that team was successful.

Assessment practice 4.2

B.P3   B.M2   B.D2

Managing a netball team, coaching a downhill skier and refereeing a rugby game are three very different leadership roles. Each has its own challenges and each will present psychological barriers for the leader to overcome.

Create a written document discussing which psychological considerations a leader might have which are common to all of these activities and which may be different.

Analyse and evaluate how each of these considerations might affect the performance of a leader. What might a leader do to ensure that they are successful and to overcome these psychological challenges?

Plan
- What am I being asked to do?
- Do I understand the three sports leader roles given to me?

Do
- I will give clear evidence of my thinking and justify my comments.
- I will present this information in a clear and concise manner.

Review
- I will identify areas for improvement in my work.
- I will make suggestions on how I might tackle and present this task differently next time.

C Explore an effective leadership style when leading a team during sport and exercise activities

Teams will have very clear expectations of their leader. However, a team also has a duty to its leader and the leader should have expectations of them.

> **Discussion**
>
> As a leader, which of the following attributes do you possess?
> - Knowledge that will enable you to develop skills, techniques and tactical understanding
> - Ability to control and educate an individual or a team
> - Passion to inspire and motivate other people
> - Dedication to lead by example
> - Motivation to share an individual's or team's goals
> - Confidence to lead and strive for success
>
> Discuss your thoughts with the rest of the class.

A team's expectations of their leader will vary depending on the leader's ultimate role. However, the same core features are likely to be required in some degree no matter what the role. In general, a team is likely to expect their leader to:
▶ have the ability to lead and help the team to achieve their goals
▶ have the ability to teach/coach them towards success and control the team when needed
▶ have knowledge of the activities and skills associated with the sport and also techniques and tactical understanding to develop the team's performance
▶ share the team's goals, share their drive for success and have passion to motivate them towards their shared goals, including creating an atmosphere where everyone helps each other
▶ have the ability to inspire, lead by example and project energy.

Where appropriate, the team will also expect their leader to employ their sport's rules and regulations successfully and to keep scores accurately.

❚❚ PAUSE POINT   Can you remember what expectations a team might have of their leader?

Hint   Consider your expectations of your own sports coach or tutor.

Extend   Which expectations do you feel are the most important?

Discussion

Within your group, discuss what other expectations a team might have of their leader.

The things that a sports leader should expect from their team in return are shown in Figure 4.5.

▶ **Figure 4.5:** What a sports leader should expect from their team

Skills and delivery for different leadership styles

The skills and delivery of different leadership styles will depend on the situation: different skills will be needed for different situations. A leader's strengths and weaknesses will dictate how they perform and integrate with a team or individual.

Link

This section links to *Unit 6: Sports Psychology*, Learning aim B3: Leadership in creating effective groups.

Delivery

▸ **Transactional** – a transactional leader focuses upon supervision, organisation and group performance.

▸ **Transformational** – a transformational leader will identify and then empower change by providing vision and inspiration.

▸ **Situational** – a situational leader will use both of the previous styles, depending on which is most appropriate for the task and scenario.

Styles

▶ **Autocratic** – an autocratic leader likes to be the sole decision maker, dictates tasks and does not like to consider opposing opinions; they are very goal orientated.

▶ **Democratic** – a democratic leader wants to share responsibility and collaborate when making decisions and is a concerned coach.

▶ *Laissez-faire* – a *laissez-faire* leader steps back and has a 'hands off' approach, placing the emphasis on the rest of the team to make decisions. This style can lead to the lowest productivity and improvement compared with others.

▶ **Transformational** – a transformational leader uses inspiration to encourage others to push themselves further than they thought possible.

▶ **Paternalistic** – a paternalistic leader adopts a position of complete authority but understands the people they are in charge of and cares for them completely. They act with high levels of self-discipline, kindness and moral integrity when controlling the group members.

The following case studies give examples in which leaders chose a style for a new team and in which they made a mistake.

Case study 1

A new boxing coach takes on a class at a gym. The group is relatively new and no one really knows each other. The leader chooses an autocratic style because he wants to stamp his authority on the class to maintain discipline. Only 50 per cent of the class come back the following week. The leader had clear goals but did not consider the needs of the group or of the individuals within that group.

1　How would you have approached this scenario differently?

2　What other leadership style could the boxing coach have adopted?

Case study 2

A women's football coach takes on a new team. There are some strong characters who have played for the team for a long time. The coach adopts a *laissez-faire* style because she wants to prove that she has faith in the team and wants the experienced players to feel valued. The first session breaks down because there is no focused leadership. Arguments break out between players with different ideas and the session is wasted.

1　What dynamics within the team might have indicated that a *laissez-faire* style could be unsuccessful?

2　When do you feel a *laissez-faire* style might be used to best effect?

 **PAUSE POINT**　Close the book and see if you can list the five styles of leadership. Do you understand what makes them different?

Hint　To help you remember the different leadership styles, think of leaders you have encountered.

Extend　Everyone has a natural style. Which style do you think you exhibit as a leader?

Planning and preparing an activity

The role of a leader starts well before and finishes well after they ever interact with anyone. Successful leaders will use a process similar to the flow diagram shown in Figure 4.6 to ensure that they fulfil the goal of every session.

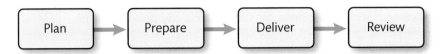

▶ **Figure 4.6:** Four stages of an activity

A leader who does not plan and prepares inadequately is unlikely to succeed. When considering the delivery of a session a leader should start by asking themselves three questions:

▶ What is the desired outcome of this session?

▶ How can I ensure that the session is delivered to the best of my ability and meets the desired outcome?

▶ How will I keep my team safe?

Theory into practice

Imagine that you are planning to run a game of dodgeball for a group of 11-year-olds. None of them have played the game before but all are very excited to play a new sport.

- Consider the most likely desired outcome of this session.
- How would you prepare so that the session is effective and meets the desired outcome?
- What safety considerations would you have to be aware of and prepare for?

Session outcomes

Identifying the outcome of a session is key to the session's overall success. A good leader may have to adapt their delivery during the session in order to ensure it is a success, but they will always go into the session with a well-prepared plan.

The outcome of a session may be pre-determined or might be decided by the leader. When considering or setting a session outcome, a sports leader should look at the individual or group, where they have come from and what their objectives are. A quality leader is unlikely to deliver exactly the same session in exactly the same way more than once.

You should consider your group in terms of:

▶ **ability** – experienced participants are likely to need less supervision and direct instruction than beginners. It may be that a group has a variety of abilities within it. If that is the case, you might consider splitting the participants into smaller groups or finding another way in which participants can be grouped in order to ensure that everyone is challenged.

▶ **age** – the age of the participants will have both physical and psychological effects on their participation. Younger participants will have less strength and speed. Often they will also have less focus and a shorter attention span than more mature participants. Older participants are more likely to have a history of injury and less stamina.

- **gender** – as males and females mature, their different physical strengths become more noticeable. Younger groups can easily be taught in mixed gender classes. However, as participants get older it may be appropriate to split the genders into separate groups.
- **cultural issues** – cultures are diverse and different customs must be respected. Without compromising safety, adjustments to delivery must be made to accommodate cultural differences such as dress and personal beliefs.

> **Discussion**

When planning an activity, differentiation within a group must be made to ensure that individuals are best placed to succeed. However, you must ensure that you do not discriminate on grounds of gender, culture or disability. With a partner, discuss how you could ensure that this is done.

- **medical issues** – some medical conditions such as asthma and diabetes are relatively common, others less so. Medical forms should be completed by all participants before a session so you are aware of any relevant medical details. This will allow you to adapt your session and to protect participants from harm, such as ensuring they carry their inhaler.
- **disabilities** – for many people with a disability, integration into mainstream activity is possible and welcomed. For example, someone with a visual impairment can very often play in a local football team. However, it may be that dedicated sessions are more appropriate, for example an activity for people who are **paraplegic** such as wheelchair basketball.
- **size of group** – the number of participants may mean that additional staff and resources are required. Larger groups are challenging, and maintaining supervision and a safe environment can be difficult for even the best of leaders.

> **Key term**
>
> **Paraplegic** – paralysed (unable to move) from the waist down.

① PAUSE POINT   On individual sticky notes, write the various considerations you need to make when looking at a group that you have been tasked with leading.

Hint   Order the notes from the most important to the least important (in your opinion).

Extend   Are there any activities in which one or more of these considerations might become more or less important? Adjust the ranking of the notes to match.

Learning outcomes

Once you know the nature of the group then you can consider the session's outcomes. It is vital that a leader understands their role in relation to a desired outcome. Table 4.3 shows a few examples of leadership scenarios and the associated outcomes.

▶ **Table 4.3:** Example leadership scenarios and desired outcomes

Leadership scenario	Desired outcomes
Referee at an adult football match	• Deliver an unbiased result • Ensure safe participation that is free from conflict • Generate a spectacle that is exciting for spectators
Kayaking taster session for a group of 8-year-olds	• Ensure that the group has fun and enjoys the experience • Ensure that safety is maintained at all times • Ensure that the group wants to come back and have further sessions
Personal training session with a national-level cyclist	• Assess fitness levels • Generate a plan for subsequent sessions that will lead to increased levels of performance
Pre-season warm-up with a local female rugby team	• Encourage cohesion and a team ethos • Inspire confidence and motivation

Setting SMARTER targets

An effective leader will set targets both for themselves and for the person or people they are leading. Target setting will ensure focused sessions in which everyone understands the task in hand. They will also allow later performance reviews and assessment of how the session went.

One of the most used target setting techniques is 'SMARTER'. SMARTER stands for specific, measurable, achievable, realistic, timed, exciting, recordable.

▶ **Specific** – precise targets will encourage focused performance.

▶ **Measurable** – a target will not work unless there is a clear way of measuring success.

▶ **Achievable** – is everything in place to encourage success? Targets will normally require resources such as support, equipment or time.

▶ **Realistic** – targets should be challenging and improvements are not made without pushing yourself, but at the opposite end of the scale a target that is set too high can be damaging to motivation.

▶ **Timed** – having a starting point and finishing point will focus efforts.

▶ **Exciting** – when approaching a goal that has clear benefits to an individual or team's performance, participants' motivation is likely to be far higher. Having enthusiasm about a goal is a crucial element for target setting.

▶ **Recordable** – having the ability to review previous achievements or failures will allow participants and leaders to assess progress and more accurately develop further SMARTER targets.

Case study

A personal trainer at a gym has a regular client who plays for a local rugby team. The team has had a tough year, and the client wants to improve his form to help and improve the team's performance next season. Specifically, he wants to improve his pushing power in the scrum. The personal trainer comes up with the following targets:

- **Specific:** Improve my client's squat 1 rep max.
- **Measurable:** Increase weight lifted from 90 kg to 115 kg.

- **Achievable:** I have access to a gym and excellent resources.
- **Realistic:** He has already made good progress in the last 6 months.
- **Timed:** It is 4 months to the start of the new season.
- **Exciting:** This will help his performance within the rugby scrum, motivate him and ultimately may help his team win.
- **Recordable:** I have collated his 1 rep max monthly for the last 6 months and can chart his progress.

Using resources

It may be that you are incredibly lucky as a leader and have unlimited resources. More often than not you will find resources are limited and you must work with what you have available. Resources can be categorised as follows.

Staff

Levels of staffing required will depend on the activity and the nature of the group. Those activities which have a higher perceived risk will normally require a higher staff-to-participant ratio. For example, basketball requires a lower level of staffing than windsurfing. Within the confines of the activity, levels of staffing may also need to be adapted depending on the group. For example, younger groups will require more supervision than older ones.

Environment

The environment in which an activity takes place may be fixed or may change depending on the session. A cricket coach may spend their entire time at one ground and a personal trainer may work from a specific gym. But a cycling instructor is likely to adapt the route that is taken depending on the group of riders.

No matter what environment a leader is working in and how often they have delivered from that venue, complacency should be avoided. Leaders should be continually aware of the risks associated with their environment.

Equipment

Lack of equipment or poorly maintained equipment will affect morale within a group and the confidence they have in their leader. The equipment selected for a session must be fit for purpose and any specific training associated with its use should be delivered at the start to maintain safe practice.

Time

Within sport leadership, the length of a session is often pre-determined, for example when refereeing a football match. Wherever possible, though, the length of a session should be adapted to meet the requirements of the group and session. Factors such as the individual's stamina and concentration must be considered. A leader should ask themselves whether participants might need a mid-session rest or whether they need to set aside time for set up or changing.

PAUSE POINT   Can you remember the four categories of resources?

> Hint   Consider a sport you have experience in. Use your experience to help you list the categories.

> Extend   Are there any sports in which one or more categories might be less relevant?

Safety

Safety should be at the forefront of every leader's mind and is vital to avoid injuries and ensure participants can take part with confidence.

There are numerous ways in which participants might come to harm during an activity and every activity has different risks and hazards associated with it. When looking at the levels of safety associated with an activity, the easiest way to break it down is by environment, resources and people.

Environment

Whether the activity is taking place inside or outside, there will be environmental risks. Outside these can include weather elements, such as the temperature being too hot or cold, rain or reduced visibility from the session taking part at night or in fog. Inside, poorly ventilated venues can mean difficult and dangerous environments in which to perform.

The playing surface is a common cause of injuries. Inside, wet floors are hazardous, while outside on grass poorly maintained pitches can cause trip hazards.

Resources

Resources and session-appropriate equipment should be kept in working order and checked regularly. Some resources, such as gym machines, may require specialist training so that participants can use them safely.

Research

Activities are normally regulated by a governing body. The governing body will set standards that may include recognised leadership awards, participant/leader ratios and pre-set schemes for delivery. What governing body is responsible for the following activities, and do they have any guidelines for delivery?
- cycling
- volleyball
- kayaking

People

Many activities involve physical contact with other participants, but you must take care to ensure that this is done as safely as possibly.

Where environments are shared with other teams, or onlookers and passers-by might be present, care must be taken to ensure that the space is managed and contact avoided.

A leader planning an activity will benefit from as much information as possible about who they are working with. The factors discussed earlier in this section – such as age, gender, experience, ability, disabilities and medical history – will all dictate how a session can be run safely. A questionnaire should be used with new participants or team members, allowing the leader to plan adequately.

Theory into practice

Imagine that you are involved in organising a sports event based on a beach. There will be opportunities for primary school children to try touch rugby, beach volleyball, softball and various other team games. There are going to be marquees, an area to get refreshments and a PA system to make announcements. Organisers expect about 150 participants over a four-hour period. The event will take place at the end of July in the height of summer.

- What potential hazards might you expect to come across and in the event area?
- What precautions could you take to protect participants?

Risk assessments

A risk assessment is a vital part of planning for an activity. Although dynamic risk assessments should be being done constantly during the session as the activity evolves, a physical risk assessment should be conducted before the session. Risk assessments consider **hazards**, the risks associated with those hazards and the severity of any potential injury.

Risk is calculated by considering:
▶ the likelihood or probability that a hazard will cause an injury
  - **low** likelihood – unlikely to happen as long as sensible steps are taken
  - **medium** likelihood – reasonable chance that it might happen
  - **high** likelihood – very likely to happen
▶ the severity of the injury should the hazard cause injury
  - **low** severity – short-term injury such as cuts, scrapes and bruises that will have little effect on performance
  - **medium** severity – significant injury such as breaks, strains and sprains, or concussion that would halt an activity and need serious medical attention
  - **high** severity – severe or potentially fatal injury.

Once the likelihood and severity have been assessed, the overall risk can be calculated using a grid such as the one shown in Table 4.4. Figure 4.7 shows an example of a risk assessment and the precautions taken.

Key term

Hazard – something that has potential to cause harm to an individual or group.

▶ **Table 4.4:** Using likelihood and severity to calculate risk

		Likelihood		
		Low	**Medium**	**High**
Severity	**Low**	Very low risk	Low risk	Medium risk
	Medium	Low risk	Medium risk	High risk
	High	Medium risk	High risk	Very high risk

Hazard	Immediate risk	Precautions to be taken	Ultimate risk
Slippery pool side	Medium risk	• Maintain non slip matting. • Ensure participants are briefed to not run and to watch their footing.	Low risk
Shallow water	High risk	• Brief all participants not to jump or dive into shallow end. • Ensure warning signs are clearly visible.	Low risk
Collisions with other pool users	Low risk	• Use swim lanes to regulate flow of swimmers.	Low risk

▶ **Figure 4.7:** Example risk assessment for a swimming session

Case study

Max has got a new job at a busy sports centre. One of his duties is to teach aqua aerobics. This class has been established for many years and has been very popular within the centre. Max is fairly nervous as the previous instructor was very popular and had a fantastic reputation.

The session is delivered at the shallow end of the pool. There is access to a variety of resources suitable for use in the water. The session starts at 11:30 a.m. and finishes at 12:15 p.m. every Tuesday. There is always an additional lifeguard present, as well as the aerobics instructor.

The group is 90 per cent female and many of them are over the age of 60. After each session they use the centre's café to enjoy a cup of tea and a chat.

1 What considerations should Max make when choosing resources?

2 What safety elements may affect delivery of this session?

3 What do you feel are the two key desired outcomes from this session?

You can use a template like the one shown in Table 4.5 to help you plan an activity.

▶ **Table 4.5:** Session planning template

Session planner	
Date	Venue
Start time	Finish time
Group name	Number of participants
Special requirements of participants	
Desired outcomes from session 1 2 3	
Resources required	Additional staff required
Safety considerations	
Introduction / warm-up	
Content phase 1	Content phase 2
Content phase 3	Content phase 4
Wrap up / cool-down	

Leadership into practice

When you have assessed all of the requirements of a session, the variables between groups and the resources that you have available, only then can you really assess what sort of leader you need to be. It is likely that you have a preferred leadership style. You need to ask yourself three questions about your own ability to be successful as a leader:

1   Is my natural leadership style going to work for this scenario?
2   Do I need to adapt it to meet the needs of my team?
3   If my leadership style is not working, how am I going to make changes to my own leadership to ensure I am able to perform as I need?

Reflect

Leadership comes naturally to some and is harder for others. The best way of developing as a leader is through practice. Can you identify ways in which you can practise as a leader and develop styles which may not come naturally to you?

⏸ PAUSE POINT   Do you feel that you could successfully plan a session?

> **Hint**   What are the three questions that you should ask yourself before starting planning?
>
> **Extend**   What considerations should you make about the group?

Structuring and delivering the activity

Briefing

Learning outcomes, safety considerations and the session's requirements should all be communicated from the leader to the participants. All good sessions will start with a brief from the leader. This might include:

▶ a recap of previous sessions

▶ the desired outcomes of the session they are about to deliver

▶ a breakdown of how these outcomes will be achieved

▶ any safety considerations

▶ timings

▶ use of resources and the environment.

Breaking a session down

Whether it is best to run a continuous session, or one with just one break, or a session that is split into smaller sections, will depend on the group, time and desired outcome. The leader must decide on an appropriate structure to enhance delivery of the subject matter.

Usually, when you have to deliver a complicated subject, this subject matter and therefore the session will be broken down. This will allow you to deliver the subject in manageable sections and means you can effectively monitor progression and give feedback where appropriate.

Sessions can be broken down in a pre-planned format into two main types of delivery.

▶ **Leader-led delivery** – Most of the delivery will be leader-led. This is when the sports and activity leader makes the decisions, dictates the activities and directs the focus of the session. This delivery style is relevant to sessions involving beginner and low-level participants.

▶ **Participant-led delivery** – Allowing individuals in a group to have a say in the development of a session. Contributing to decision making can empower participants and increase levels of motivation. This is particularly effective when a group is highly skilled or already has high levels of motivation.

Types of learners

A strong leader will understand that individuals within a group learn in different ways.

▶ **Auditory learners** prefer to discuss a new skill or subject and listen to explanations.

▶ **Visual learners** prefer to observe delivery of a new skill through demonstrations.

▶ **Kinaesthetic learners** prefer to practise a new skill and learn by doing.

Effective leadership will ensure that all these learning styles are catered for during delivery of a session. By ensuring that delivery of a subject matter is diverse, all individuals should be attentive and motivated.

Demonstration

An essential leadership tool is the art of demonstration. Demonstration does not have to be a physical act, nor does it need to be done by the leader themselves. Use of video showing an expert or example is a valuable way of demonstrating a skill or technique. Asking a member of the team to demonstrate something they have learned will empower them and potentially make the subject matter more accessible for the rest of the learners.

When making an effective demonstration a leader should consider the following points:

▸ A demonstration is visual and therefore commentary should be kept to a minimum to allow focus.
▸ Avoid distractions by positioning the demonstration appropriately.
▸ Consider the environment. When outside, make sure the group is not positioned facing into the sun.
▸ Where possible, demonstrate slowly. If the subject matter is something that can be broken down into small sections, then clearly identify each section so the group understands its significance.

Theory into practice

Choose an activity that requires ball control skills and is one that you feel confident with. Practise a technique until you feel you can demonstrate it as effectively as possible.

Choose a learner that you know will have little experience of this technique. Explain to them that you are going to teach them something and you will do this without speaking.

Demonstrate the technique to the best of your ability. Break it down into sections and watch as the learner practises.

Analyse how successful you were at this task. Ask the learner for feedback. How might you improve your delivery in the future?

Delegating responsibility

A strong leader will not be afraid to recognise others' ability. Delegating responsibility to other team members will make them feel valued and can allow a subject to be delivered more effectively. This is especially relevant when faced with a large group. Some skills may require the group to be split into smaller groups – using higher-level participants to lead each smaller group. This will ensure that focus is maintained and will allow the overall leader to float effectively between groups, contributing where needed.

Differentiation

Differentiation involves recognising that, although a team may ultimately be united, each individual's strengths and weaknesses are different. This is an important factor for a leader to acknowledge. Additionally, individuals' roles within a team may vary. For example, many sports have dedicated defenders and attackers, and there would be little point spending time coaching scrum delivery to a winger in a rugby team.

Session debrief

Every session should end with a debrief. This review of the session should examine both its strengths and weaknesses and identify areas for improvement. It should also refer back to the session's intended outcomes to see how these have been met. This form of debrief, where the leader compares final performance with actual targets or goals, is called **summative assessment**.

In contrast, **formative assessment** is an ongoing process that takes place at regular intervals within most sessions. This involves the leader monitoring progress and performance. Formative assessment will allow a strong leader to adapt their session if necessary to ensure success.

Reviewing effectiveness of leadership

An effective leader is a reflective leader. Leadership is something that we can all develop and improve. On completion of an activity session, all leaders should consider their own strengths and weaknesses. A leader's role is often what defines the success of a team. In order for a team, or those a leader is responsible for, to improve, the leader must be prepared to improve, too.

Personal performance

On completion of a sports leadership exercise you will have some idea of the success of the task and how your own performance directly contributed to it. You should ask yourself three fundamental questions:

1 Do I feel the aim of the task was achieved?
2 Was it done in a safe manner?
3 Is my team happy and motivated?

If the answer to any of these questions is 'no', then further evaluation must be done to understand why not. Being honest with yourself about your performance as a leader can only make you a better and stronger leader in the future. Consider these questions to develop your performance:

1 Was your leadership style appropriate?
2 Were you successful in adapting your leadership style to meet the session's aims?
3 How can you improve your performance in the future and develop further leadership styles?

Feedback

Feedback is essential to help you analyse your performance as a leader. Feedback can be given by anyone who has taken part in, or observed, your session. Good sports centres will integrate observations from senior staff into every leader's ongoing development, and these observations will be linked to ongoing performance targets. Table 4.6 shows some common methods of gathering feedback.

Participant feedback

Whether a participant feels that they have succeeded or failed will be a strong indication of the effectiveness of the leader. A leader's main function is to encourage success in those that they are responsible for; positive and negative feedback should be taken seriously.

Observer feedback

Observations of the sports leader in action could be made by senior staff, colleagues, parents or officials. Observations might be pre-arranged (taking place on an agreed date) or they might be dynamic (carried out without any prior notice).

▶ **Table 4.6:** Methods of gathering feedback

Feedback methods	Description
Witness statements	A written statement from someone who observed the event discussing positive feedback and noting areas for improvement.
Interviews	Interviews may be conducted by telephone or face-to-face. To give them focus it is useful to have bullet points listing the information you are interested in discussing.
Questionnaires and surveys	A series of focused questions presented in written paper format or online. Some questionnaires may ask for short written statements. However, in order to encourage people to actually complete them, most use tick-boxes so people can complete them quickly. They are sometimes completed during, or straight after, the session or event if time allows. Many are sent out by post or email when the event is completed.

▶ **Table 4.6:** Methods of gathering feedback – *continued*

Feedback methods	Description
Observation forms	Anyone can complete an observation form; however, they are most useful from an industry expert. Observation forms are completed during the session to ensure they are accurate. As they are often completed by experts, they tend to pick up on subtle areas for improvement or positive features that might otherwise be overlooked.
Comment cards	Comment cards are a good way of collecting anonymous feedback. They are usually completed at the end of the session and then posted into a comment box. Often comment cards do not ask for personnel details, which means feedback may be more honest.
Satisfaction buttons	Although still relatively rare due to the expense of setting them up, computerised satisfaction buttons allow people to quickly and anonymously rate their satisfaction with an event as excellent, good, average or poor. This is a great way of getting quick feedback from large numbers of people.

Reflect

A good leader should have the confidence to ask for feedback and act on it as necessary. Can you think of any times following your delivery of a session or presentation when you should have asked for feedback?

SWOT analysis

A SWOT analysis is a clear way of considering your performance as a leader by looking at your own strengths, weaknesses, opportunities and threats.

▶ **Strengths** – A session's positive elements should be recognised so that they can be used again in the future.

▶ **Weaknesses** – No matter how minor, areas for improvement should be highlighted so that they can be eliminated for subsequent delivery.

▶ **Opportunities** – Change is an important part of the leadership process. Learning new techniques, developing or improving resources, or gaining access to new venues are all opportunities that a good leader will look for and try to integrate into their delivery.

▶ **Threats** – Elements that might prevent success are varied. They might be time constraints, lack of access to appropriate resources, or potential injury. Threats should be identified early so preventative measures can be put in place to eliminate or reduce their impact.

Action planning

When a clear understanding of a leader's performance has been developed, then an action plan can be designed to enable improvement. There are many ways to set out an action plan. Whichever you choose, there are three basic questions that you must ask yourself.

▶ **Where am I now?** An overview of experiences. What have been highlighted as your strengths and weaknesses?

▶ **Where do I want to get to?** Discuss your ambitions. Set a long-term goal but make sure that it is achievable.

▶ **How am I going to enable this?** Use short-term goals and use SMARTER targets to develop a strategy for success. Breaking a goal down into several targets will enable success and encourage motivation and confidence.

 PAUSE POINT Why is reviewing your own performance so important upon completion of a leadership session?

> Hint Consider how you evaluate others' success in a leadership role.

> Extend How might you go about gathering feedback from other people so that you can better evaluate your own performance?

Assessment practice 4.3

Choose a leadership role in which you must lead a team that you feel comfortable with and can use to practise and develop new skills. This could be anything from coaching a primary school group dodge ball to running a canoeing session for disabled adults.

Demonstrate the skills associated with good leadership during planning, preparation and delivery to the best of your ability. Produce a brief written report to review your successes and areas for improvement.

Why do you think that your chosen leadership style and attributes were relevant and successful? If you do not feel you were successful at any point, why not? Justify any decisions that you made as a leader and suggest ways in which you might improve your performance in the future.

Plan
- What role is going to suit me best and provide the best opportunities for practice?
- What resources and support do I need to achieve this task?

Do
- I have a clear plan and feel confident in what I want to achieve.
- I am able to justify my decisions as a leader and understand how they might affect the performance of my team.

Review
- I will listen to feedback from my team and any observers and understand both strengths and areas for improvement.
- I can make suggestions on how I might improve my own performance in the future and understand how to put these suggestions into practice.

Further reading and resources

Martin, B., Cashel, C., Wagstaff, M. and Breunig, M. (2006) *Outdoor Leadership Theory and Practices*, Champaign, IL: Human Kinetics.

Prentice, E. and Bliszczyk, R. (2012) *Sport Leadership: Winning with your Mind*, Prahran, Australia: Tilde University Press.

Roe, K. (2014) *Leadership: Practice and Perspectives*, Oxford: Oxford University Press.

THINK ▶FUTURE

Katy Parker

Strength and conditioning coach for an America's Cup sailing team

My role is to develop the athletes' athletic capabilities in line with the demands of their roles on the water. These athletes are world-class and as such have a great deal of experience. Sometimes they can be difficult to direct. Racing an America's Cup boat is exceptionally physical and highly dangerous and there are some big characters attracted to the sport.

I have to be incredibly patient with many of the athletes as well as being firm when I need to be: after all, I am the professional and I understand what is best for their strength and conditioning development.

As the racing takes place around the world, I have to spend long periods of time away from home with the rest of my team. As part of an America's Cup team everyone is expected to muck in where needed. When a job needs doing we will work all hours until it is done. There is no place for shirking, as success will ensure we maintain our sponsorship and financial backing.

Focusing your skills

Handling pressure

The best leaders end up in the best roles at the top of their game. As the role increases in prestige, so do the responsibilities and demands. A leader should expect to have significant pressure to perform as an individual and to enhance the effectiveness of the team.

- Take part in activities that will push you out of your comfort zone. Do not avoid pressure, and look for opportunities to practise leadership skills in an environment that you will find challenging. Are there any clubs that you could volunteer for to help gain experience?
- Do not be afraid of failure. Often it is the best way to learn.

Developing skills

Effective leaders will be self-reflective and constantly looking for ways to improve their performance. No one knows everything, and looking to improve as a leader will inspire the rest of the team to follow and push to better themselves.

- Constantly ask for feedback on your performance and ensure that you act on it to improve your own performance.
- Do you have an opportunity to shadow or observe a leader within an elite team? If so, assess what characteristics this leader has and if possible ask them to give you tips for success.

Getting ready for assessment

George is midway through a BTEC National in Sport. He was given an assignment titled 'Plan, prepare and deliver a practical coaching session'. He was able to choose the sport that he felt most comfortable with and had to deliver a practical session for a group of 9-year-olds from his local primary school. He had to:

▶ ensure that he considered his group and set an appropriate learning outcome
▶ maintain safety throughout the session
▶ demonstrate practical leadership skills after selecting a style of delivery.

George discusses his experience below.

How I got started

Initially I was nervous about delivering a session to a class of young children. I chose basketball as this is an activity I play regularly and I have seen my coach deliver many sessions for my team. I made sure that I had a clear understanding of the group by emailing their teacher. That way I knew what to prepare for and could spend time thinking about how to lead the session.

I decided that I should use a structured session plan. I listed resources I might need and the safety considerations, and I broke the one-hour session into 10-minute chunks to allow me to plan effectively.

I have already had a practice at running a session as part of my BTEC. I asked my classmates to give me some feedback on how they felt I performed and provide some suggestions on how I might improve my delivery.

How I brought it all together

I arrived early so that I could prepare my resources and go over my plan. I knew that my group was going to be excited and full of energy. I decided that I needed to focus on group control by using a transactional form where positive behaviour was rewarded with praise and negative behaviour managed by the child sitting out of the game for two minutes.

To ensure that I maintained a balance and kept the session fun and fast-paced, I wanted to focus on being an inspiration and projecting confidence and motivation. I believe my style was transformational as I really wanted to engage with my group and push them hard to keep involved in my session.

As a tool to keep my session exciting, I broke it into short, sharp chunks no longer than 10 minutes. Each chunk introduced a different skill. In the last 10 minutes we played a quick game to try and pull all the skills together.

What I learned from the experience

I really enjoyed the experience. I wish that I had had more practice at running sessions before my assessment. I could have gained this by volunteering at my local basketball club and helping to coach a younger team.

I think that I did well at motivating my group. There were a few problems with group control and although I aimed to use a transactional form of delivery I did not follow up my threat to make boisterous learners sit out. They quickly realised this and I think they took advantage of my priority to make things fun.

Think about it

▶ How can you gain some more leadership experience? Do you have access to a team you could volunteer with?
▶ Do you have a session plan that you can use to structure your session?
▶ Do you have a clear understanding of the various leadership forms and styles and which type most complements your natural personality?

Application of Fitness Testing 5

Getting to know your unit

Fitness is a fundamental aspect of all sporting performance, and sports performers need to maintain and improve their fitness levels to excel in their sports. It is important that they take part in regular fitness assessments so they can establish their baseline levels and use this information to plan specific training programmes.

This unit explains the principles of fitness testing including factors affecting the selection and administration of tests, such as ensuring the validity, reliability and suitability of tests. You will explore a range of laboratory- and field-based fitness tests and the administration process of each fitness test. You will then consider the selection of appropriate tests for specific sports performers, demonstrating your ability to conduct a range of fitness tests in accordance with safety and ethical requirements. Finally, you will evaluate and compare results to draw meaningful conclusions about a specific person's fitness.

How you will be assessed

This unit will be assessed through a series of assignments set by your tutor. Throughout this unit you will find useful assessment activities that will help you work towards your final assignments. Completing each of these assessment activities will not necessarily mean that you achieve a particular grade, but each will help you through relevant research or preparation that can be used towards your final assignments.

To ensure that you achieve all the tasks in your set assignments it is important that you cover all the Pass criteria. Make sure that you check each of these before you submit your work to your tutor.

If you are hoping to achieve a Merit or Distinction you must consider how you present the information in your assignment and make sure that you extend your responses or answers. For example, to achieve a Merit you must explain the use of specific fitness tests, outlining why these have been chosen, and further explain the results. To achieve the Distinction criteria you must further analyse the results and be able to justify the recommendations that you make for each component of fitness based on this information.

The assignments set by your tutor will consist of a number of tasks designed to meet the criteria in the table. They are likely to consist of written assignments but may also include:

▶ planning a series of fitness tests for multiple sports performers
▶ safely conducting a number of fitness tests for each component of fitness
▶ creating and assessing a fitness profile for a specific, selected sports performer.

Assessment criteria

This table shows what you must do in order to achieve a **Pass, Merit** or **Distinction** grade, and where you can find activities to help you.

Pass	Merit	Distinction

Learning aim **A** Understand the principles of fitness testing

A.P1 Explain the importance of validity, reliability, practicality and suitability in relation to fitness testing. **Assessment practice 5.1**	**A.M1** Recommend methods that can be used to ensure fitness testing is conducted in a valid, reliable, practical, suitable and ethical way. **Assessment practice 5.1**	**AB.D1** Analyse own administration of selected fitness tests against practicality, suitability and ethical guidelines justifying suggestions for improvement. **Assessment practice 5.2**
A.P2 Explain how ethical requirements should be met when planning and conducting fitness testing, giving examples. **Assessment practice 5.1**		

Learning aim B Explore fitness testing for different components of fitness

B.P3 Select six valid fitness tests for selected sports performers. **Assessment practice 5.2**	**B.M2** Assess practicality and suitability of each selected fitness test for selected sports performers. **Assessment practice 5.2**	
B.P4 Safely administer and accurately record the results of six fitness tests for a sports performer. **Assessment practice 5.2**	**B.M3** Administer six fitness tests, demonstrating skills to ensure the test results are accurate and reliable. **Assessment practice 5.2**	
B.P5 Interpret fitness test results against normative data. **Assessment practice 5.2**	**B.M4** Suggest areas for improvement in the administration process of fitness tests based on test results. **Assessment practice 5.2**	

Learning aim C Undertake evaluation and feedback of fitness tests results

C.P6 Create a fitness profile for a selected sports performer following fitness testing, providing feedback to the performer on their fitness test results and how they can impact on sporting performance. **Assessment practice 5.3**	**C.M5** Assess the strengths and areas for improvement from fitness test results providing feedback for a selected sports performer. **Assessment practice 5.3**	**C.D2** Justify the fitness profile for a selected sports performer including identified areas for improvement related to their selected sport. **Assessment practice 5.3**
		C.D3 Evaluate the effectiveness of methods used to test the components of fitness and provide feedback to sports performers. **Assessment practice 5.3**

Fitness is an essential ingredient in all sport and exercise performances. Write a list of the different components of fitness and how these can affect sporting performance. Now consider a sport of your choice and describe the main components of fitness that are needed in order to be successful.

A Understand the principles of fitness testing

Link

This unit can tie in with *Unit 2: Fitness Training and Programming for Health, Sport and Well-being*. It also links with *Unit 8: Coaching for Performance* and *Unit 28: Sports Performance Analysis*.

To safely and effectively administer laboratory-based and field-based fitness tests, you need good knowledge and understanding of tests for different components of fitness, and the procedures and protocols to follow. You need to be aware of the advantages and disadvantages of different fitness tests and their implications when selecting and administering tests.

Validity of fitness tests

Validity is essential in fitness testing because it relates to whether you are actually measuring what you planned to measure. Without validity you might use a test that does not actually measure the component of fitness you were aiming to measure. For example, if you used a sit and reach test to measure strength, your results would be invalid. Therefore it is essential that when you undertake fitness tests you understand the purpose of the test and that the results relate to the component of fitness that you set out to measure.

The test should also target an element of fitness that is relevant for the sports performer being tested. For example, it would be pointless to test a weight lifter to measure their reaction time, but appropriate to test them to measure their strength.

Reliability of fitness tests

What is reliability?

A reliable fitness test is one which, if repeated, would give the same or similar results. However, **reliability** can be claimed without results necessarily being correct. For example, if you always ask the wrong questions in research, you will always get the same wrong answers. This will mean the test is reliable because you have received the *same* wrong answers, even though they are not accurate ones.

In quantitative research (research that sets out to gather numbers and measurements), reliability can be one researcher conducting the same test on the same individual on a number of occasions and getting the same or similar results. Alternatively, it can be different researchers conducting the same test on the same individual and getting the same or similar results.

Key terms

Validity – the accuracy of the results. This means whether the results obtained are a true reflection of what you are actually trying to measure.

Reliability – the consistency and repeatability of the results obtained. That is, the ability to carry out the same test method and expect the same results.

There are certain factors you should take into account that can affect reliability. For example:

▶ errors can happen when you do not know how to use the equipment correctly

▶ the equipment may be poorly maintained

▶ the wrong type of equipment may be selected for the fitness test

▶ testing conditions may vary between tests (e.g. when conducting a sprint test outside, the wind speed may affect the results).

Benchmarking data

In order to compare the results of your fitness tests, benchmarking data is commonly used. This is data gathered from a number of studies that allows you to see a normal range of results, and allows you to make a judgement against the data that you have collected. Data will generally be put into a number of categories, including age and gender, which means that you will be able to compare your results with similar groups. Benchmarking data can also be used to compare your results with elite sports performers. By using benchmarking data you will be able to develop a fitness plan including target setting.

Ⅱ PAUSE POINT   Do you understand the differences between 'validity' and 'reliability'?

> **Hint**   Close the book, then write a definition of what is meant by validity and what is meant by reliability.

> **Extend**   Consider why validity and reliability are important in fitness testing and what your results would mean if these were not considered.

Methods of ensuring reliability

To ensure that the test results are reliable there are a number of different factors that you must remember and follow in your role as an administrator.

Pre-test

▶ **Calibration of equipment** – before you start any fitness test you must ensure the equipment you are using is fully functional and in good working order. To do this you must check that any device used for measuring is reset and that the equipment is fit for purpose. In some cases, you may need to seek specialist help to ensure that the equipment is serviced and in good working order.

▶ **Warm-up** – many of the fitness tests will require strenuous exercise, and therefore it is important that subjects are fully prepared to ensure that injury does not occur. This is especially important where flexibility is being measured as well as where sudden power tests are conducted. It is also important to make sure the time spent warming up or practising is the same before each test; for example, sit and reach scores will vary depending on how much warming up or stretching has been done before the test. Tests that measure resting heart rates should be carried out before a warm-up or after the heart rate has returned to normal resting levels.

▶ **Fitness test technique practice** – to ensure that your test results are reliable you must make sure that the subject uses the correct technique when conducting a fitness test. It is useful to demonstrate the technique that must be used during the test and then allow the subject to practise before starting the actual test. During the practice, highlight and correct any poor techniques. Sometimes incorrect technique will be used when the subject begins to tire, so it is important to watch for this and correct if necessary.

During the test

▶ **Skill level of the administrator** – the more experienced you are in administering a range of fitness tests, the more reliable the results will be. Therefore it is useful to practise each test so that you increase your skill levels as well as improve your confidence. Your own skill will also reassure your subjects during the tests.

▶ **Adherence to test protocol** – to ensure that the fitness test results are reliable and that these can be compared to normative data, you must always follow the standard set test protocol. If you deviate from the set methods, your results may become invalid as they are likely to be inaccurate. For example, if you undertake the multi-stage fitness test but only measure 15 metres instead of 20 metres, your test result will be inaccurate and unreliable. Protocols for specific fitness tests are described on pages 222–246.

▶ **Constant conditions** – the administration of fitness tests can generally be categorised into two broad areas:
  • field-based tests, which usually take place outside or where the sport or exercise usually takes place. As such, the test may be affected by factors such as the weather, the outside temperature or the condition of the testing surface (e.g. running track)
  • laboratory-based tests, which can be used to eliminate the factors that can affect field tests and to ensure that the exact same conditions are used every time you undertake the same test. However, testing indoors can be restrictive, especially where a large space is needed such as for the 60-metre sprint test.

▶ **Appropriate rest periods between tests** – to ensure that your subjects are able to perform in the selected fitness test, and for the results to be reliable, you must ensure that they are fully rested. This is particularly important where the subject may have practised a test or where a test involves working at a maximal level, for example, a VO$_2$ max test. Therefore you must ensure that your subject is fully rested before commencing any test. Further you must consider the order in which you undertake the fitness tests because some tests will require the subject to recover before starting the next test. Without recovery time built into the testing protocol, there is a risk that subsequent test results will be affected.

Practicality and suitability of fitness tests

At the centre of successful fitness testing is the ability to identify the component of fitness that is to be assessed, before selecting and administering a suitable test, and then being able to record and interpret the results. However, there are a number of additional factors that you must consider that will affect your ability to undertake a range of fitness tests.

Factors affecting the practicality of fitness tests

Cost

A significant factor when measuring fitness is the cost of the equipment. Many tests will require highly advanced laboratory equipment which is very expensive. However, a number of tests, including many of those outlined in this unit, only require basic and affordable equipment such as a stopwatch, tape measure and cones.

Time

Fitness testing can be very time consuming, especially when you are working with large groups of people such as a team. Some tests can be quick to administer while others can take much longer. Likewise, some tests, such as the sit and reach test, require you to work on a one-to-one basis while other tests, such as the multi-stage fitness test, can be administered to a large group of subjects at the same time.

It is important that you consider the test you are going to select and plan enough time to undertake it, including time to give feedback to the subject or subjects. Remember to consider the order of the tests to ensure you allow sufficient recovery time between them, especially for activities that require increases in heart rate.

Equipment

Having the correct equipment is important when measuring the components of fitness. Many tests can be conducted using basic equipment while some tests will require more advanced (and expensive) equipment. Whatever equipment you use, ensure that you are familiar with how it works, check that it is serviced or well maintained, and check that you can calibrate it if necessary. Do not undertake a fitness test using damaged equipment, as this might be dangerous and could also lead to inaccurate and unreliable results.

Some components of fitness can be measured using different tests, and in some cases the data that you obtain will be predicted results rather than actual results. An example of this is measuring aerobic capacity (VO_2 max) where the multi-stage fitness test will allow you to predict your aerobic capacity, whereas a maximal oxygen consumption test will give your actual aerobic capacity.

Facilities available

Using an appropriate facility will help to ensure that results are accurate and reliable. Always check facilities before use and identify any hazards. Likewise, having changing facilities and a rest area will help make your subjects comfortable.

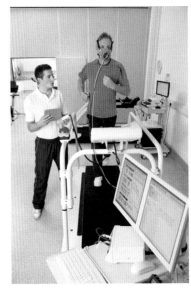
▶ Laboratory equipment used for fitness testing can be expensive

> **Reflect**
>
> Think about the different fitness tests you have observed or participated in, perhaps through your local sports club or through another programme of study. What were the advantages and disadvantages of the tests? Think about factors like cost, time and equipment required. Write a list and discuss in pairs or small groups.

Suitability

When planning fitness testing, ensure that the tests you select are suitable for the components of fitness used in the chosen sport. Each sport requires certain attributes and relies on some factors more than others for successful performance. For example, you would not necessarily want to test a marathon runner for sprint speed – your testing time could be better spent doing more relevant tests.

Likewise you should consider the fitness levels of the performer and only undertake tests that are relevant and suitable. For example, if a performer has low levels of aerobic fitness it would not be suitable to conduct a maximal aerobic test with them.

⏸ PAUSE POINT   What is meant by 'practicality' when considering fitness testing?

Hint   What are the factors that will affect the practicality of fitness testing?

Extend   How might you address each of these factors to ensure that your fitness tests are valid and reliable?

Ethical issues associated with fitness screening

Before you start any fitness testing session you must get **informed consent** from the participants (see pages 248–249). You must also **ensure the welfare of the participant** at all times when carrying out fitness tests. You can read more about the health and safety aspects of fitness testing, including reasons for terminating a test, later in this unit, starting on page 248.

Pre-test preparation

To ensure that the results you gain from a series of fitness tests are valid and reliable, you must make sure that the participant is fully prepared for the testing session.

Before the test, the participant should be fully rested and free from injury. Likewise they must be fully recovered from any previous exercise and should not have participated in exercise immediately prior to the test.

For tests such as body composition using bio impedance the participant must be fully hydrated. This is also important for tests where aerobic and muscular endurance are being measured so that the participant does not become dehydrated during the test.

For a number of tests, including flexibility and power and strength tests, a full warm-up should be conducted to reduce the possibility of injury.

Research

For more information about ethics and codes of conduct, visit the website of the Register of Exercise Professionals (REPs) at www.exerciseregister.org.

Ethical clearance for tests

Ethical practice involves setting rules to ensure appropriate behaviour is maintained at all times. Codes of ethics for fitness trainers exist to make sure that clients' welfare is always a primary concern. This means that fitness trainers are responsible for their clients' safety at all times and must maintain high professional standards.

In your role as a fitness tester you are expected to act in a professional and ethical way. You must respect the rights and dignity of the participants at all times. You are also responsible for setting and monitoring the boundaries between a working relationship and friendship with the participant, and this is particularly important when the participant is a young person.

If you are using the results of your fitness testing as part of a research project, you must gain ethical clearance from your tutor, college or school **ethics** committee. An ethics committee is a group that looks at your research proposal and decides whether it is safe and ethical and will confirm whether you can start work on your project.

Key term

Ethics – rules of conduct that should be respected at all times and which ensure that all people are treated fairly.

Data protection

As part of your pre-screening and collection of fitness test results, you will collect confidential data. Any data you collect is protected under the terms of the Data Protection Act (1998) and must be stored in a locked filing cabinet or on a password-protected computer, accessible only by you or your supervisor. It must not be disclosed to anyone else without the permission of the subject.

Case study

Protecting client privacy

George has recently started working as a fitness testing assistant in a sports club. He has met a number of athletes and worked on a one-to-one basis, recording their personal information and performing a number of fitness tests. He has recorded this information on the appropriate forms and stored these in a locked filing cabinet.

George has recently been approached by a coach from the sports club who he has never met before. The coach is keen on looking at the test results for all the athletes.

Check your knowledge

1 What should George do? Why?

2 How will you record client information?

3 How will you ensure that this information remains confidential?

4 Where will you store the clients' information when it is not being used?

Research

Visit the government website for more information on the Data Protection Act (1998) and why it is important. To access this website go to: www.gov.uk/data-protection/the-data-protection-act

 **PAUSE POINT**   What is meant by ethical issues in fitness testing?

Hint   What is ethical practice?

Extend   Why is it important for a fitness tester to behave in an ethical way?

Assessment practice 5.1   A.P1   A.P2   A.M1

Your college football team would like to prepare for the new season by undertaking a series of fitness tests in order to develop a specific training plan. The football coach has asked you to prepare a presentation and supporting leaflet that explains the importance of validity, reliability, practicality and suitability of fitness testing in relation to football.

You should also include information and examples on how ethical requirements should be met when conducting fitness tests.

The last part of the presentation should recommend methods which can be used to ensure fitness testing is conducted in a valid, reliable, practical, suitable and ethical way.

Plan

- I will make sure I consider ethics and why they are important in fitness testing.
- I will define reliability, validity, practicality and suitability.

Do

- I will complete the leaflet in as much detail as possible.
- I have practised my presentation skills and asked my peers to give me advice on how I can improve.

Review

- I can explain what the task was and how I approached it.
- I will reflect on my own work and the feedback from others, and make any necessary changes to my leaflet.

B Explore fitness tests for different components of fitness

To safely and effectively administer laboratory-based and field-based fitness tests, you need good knowledge and understanding of tests for different components of fitness, and the procedures and protocols to follow. You will need to be aware of the advantages and disadvantages of different fitness tests and how these affect which tests are chosen and how they are used.

The components of fitness can be divided into two broad categories, as seen in Table 5.1.

▶ **Table 5.1:** Elements of physical and skill-related fitness

Physical or health-related fitness	Skill-related fitness
Aerobic endurance	Balance
Muscular endurance	Power
Muscular strength	Agility
Flexibility	Coordination
Speed	Reaction time
Body composition	

Fitness testing is also carried out in health clubs where instructors screen clients for **contraindications** to exercise, administer fitness tests, and use the results to design exercise programmes that meet the clients' personal goals. Fitness tests can also be used to identify those clients requiring medical referral.

Regardless of the fitness element being assessed, all fitness tests must be administered safely and effectively, using the correct units of measurement. Relevant health and safety procedures and test protocol guidelines should be followed, and tests should be selected that are suitable for the sports performer and their fitness levels.

Fitness tests to assess components of physical fitness

Flexibility

Flexibility is defined as the range of movement around a specific joint. Most sports will require a good level of flexibility either to perform specific movements (e.g. gymnastics) or to prevent injury. Flexibility can be either:

▶ static flexibility – where a joint is held in a particular stationary position

▶ dynamic flexibility – where a full range of motion is used during an action (for example the arching of the back during a pole vault).

There are a number of different tests that you can perform to measure flexibility.

Sit and reach

This test is an indirect measure of static flexibility. It measures trunk forward flexion, hamstring, hip and lower back range of motion. A standard sit and reach box is used.

1　Perform a short warm-up prior to this test. Do not use fast, jerky movements as this may increase risk of injury. Remove your shoes.

2　Sit with your heels placed against the edge of the sit and reach box. Keep your legs flat on the floor, i.e. keep your knees down.

3　Place one hand on top of the other and reach forward slowly. Your fingertips should be in contact with the measuring portion of the sit and reach box. As you reach forward, drop your head between your arms and breathe out as you push forward.

4　The best of three trials should be recorded. Use Table 5.2 to interpret your results.

▶ **Table 5.2:** Interpreting the results of the sit and reach test

Rating	Males (cm)	Females (cm)
Excellent	25+	20+
Very good	17	17
Good	15	16
Average	14	15
Poor	13	14
Very poor	9	10

Shoulder flex test

This simple test is used to assess the flexibility of the shoulders, which is important in sports such as tennis, badminton and throwing sports. This is a comparative test that can be repeated over time to measure progress following flexibility or to compare against peers. The equipment required is a stick and a tape measure.

1 Start by holding a stick in front of the body with both hands wide apart and palms facing downwards.

2 Lift the stick over the head to behind the back, maintaining the hand grip on the object.

3 Repeat the test, moving hands closer together each time until the movement cannot be completed.

4 Your score is determined by the minimum distance between the hands.

Calf muscle flexibility test

This is a simple test that measures the indirect flexibility of the calf muscle. There are no norms for this test but it will give an athlete a starting point when undertaking a flexibility training programme. A tape measure is required to record the results.

1 Perform a warm-up, including stretching.

2 Stand flat-footed the maximum distance you can away from a wall while still being able to bend your knee to touch the wall.

3 Measure the distance from the toe to the wall.

4 Repeat for each leg.

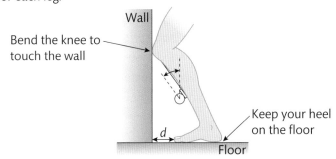

▶ **Figure 5.1:** Calf muscle flexibility test

Trunk rotation test

The purpose of this test is to measure the flexibility of your trunk as well as your shoulders. This is particularly useful for sports such as golf or bowling in cricket where trunk rotation is important. You will need a pencil or piece of chalk and a tape measure.

1 Draw a vertical line on a wall.

2 Stand directly in front of the line with your feet shoulder width apart and your back towards the wall. Make sure you keep enough room behind you to turn.

3 Extend your arms straight out in front of you.

4 Twist your trunk to your right and then touch the wall behind you with your fingertips, keeping your arms extended and parallel to the floor. You are allowed to turn your shoulders, hips and knees as long as your feet do not move.

5 Mark the position where your fingertips touched the wall, and measure the distance from the line in centimetres.

6 A point before the line is a negative score and a point after the line is a positive score.

7 Repeat for the left side with your feet in the same position.

8 Take the average of the scores. Use Table 5.3 to interpret your scores.

▶ **Table 5.3:** Interpreting the results of the trunk rotation test

Ratings	Score (cm)
Excellent	20
Very good	15
Good	10
Fair	5
Poor	0 (or less)

Strength

Strength can be defined as the ability to apply a force against resistance. It is important in most sports but particular sports, such as rugby, will require this as a primary component of fitness.

Bench press 1 repetition maximum ('1RM') test

The bench press 1 repetition maximum (1RM) is a test of the dynamic strength of the bench pressing pectoral muscles of the chest. It is a dynamic test used to assess upper body strength. The test can be safely carried out using a bench press resistance machine.

1 An informed consent form (see pages 248–249) must be completed before undertaking this maximal test.

2 Carry out a standard warm-up and stretching of the major muscle groups.

3 Determine a comfortable weight to start to press.

4 Breathe out on exertion, i.e. as the weight is lifted. Ensure you do not hold your breath as this will cause an increase in blood pressure.

5 Each bench press weight successfully lifted should be noted.

6 Allow a 2-minute rest between trials before increasing the weight by 2.5–5 kg.

7 Continue this protocol until a maximum weight is successfully lifted. This is recorded as your 1RM.

8 Perform a standard cool down.

9 Divide your 1RM result (kg) by your body weight in kg. Use Table 5.4 to interpret your results.

▶ **Table 5.4:** Interpreting the results of the bench press 1RM test

Rating	Males (1RM kg/kg body weight)	Females (1RM kg/kg body weight)
Excellent	>1.26	>0.78
Good	1.17–1.25	0.72–0.77
Average	0.97–1.16	0.59–0.71
Fair	0.88–0.96	0.53–0.58
Poor	<0.87	<0.52

Grip dynamometer

This measures the static strength of the grip-squeezing muscles, where the whole hand is used as a vice or clamp. A grip dynamometer is a spring device – as force is applied, the spring is compressed and this moves the dynamometer needle which indicates the result. Digital dynamometers are also available.

1 Adjust the handgrip size so that the dynamometer feels comfortable to hold/grip.

2 Stand with your arms by the side of your body.

3 Hold the dynamometer parallel to the side of your body with the dial/display facing away from you.

4 Squeeze as hard as possible for 5 seconds, without moving your arm.

5 Carry out three trials on each hand, with a 1-minute rest between trials, and record your best result. Use Table 5.5 to interpret your results.

▶ A grip dynamometer

▶ **Table 5.5:** Interpreting the results of the grip strength dynamometer test

Rating	Males aged 15–19 (kg)	Females aged 15–19 (kg)
Excellent	52+	32+
Good	47–51	28–31
Average	44–46	25–27
Below average	39–43	20–24
Poor	<39	<20

Seven stage abdominal strength test

This test measures your abdominal strength and can be performed in large groups together. Abdominal strength is important as it provides back support and core stability which will help maintain posture. The test requires a flat surface, a 2.5 kg and a 5 kg weight, as well as pen and paper to record your results. The test has eight levels ranging from very poor (0) to elite (7). The highest correctly performed sit-up level is recorded.

1 Lie on your back, with your knees at right angles and feet flat on the floor.

2 Starting with level 1, attempt to perform one complete sit-up for each level in the correct manner as outlined in Table 5.6.

3 Each level is achieved if a single sit-up is performed in the correct manner, *without the feet coming off the floor*.

4 You can make as many attempts as necessary but ensure that you are fully rested before starting the test again.

Theory into practice

Experiment with the grip dynamometer test by carrying the test out on your dominant hand and your non-dominant hand. Compare the results to find out how great the difference might be.

▶ **Table 5.6:** The different levels of the seven stage abdominal strength test

Level	Rating	Description
0	Very poor	Cannot perform level 1
1	Poor	With arms extended, the athlete curls up so that the wrists reach the knees
2	Fair	With arms extended, the athlete curls up so that the elbows reach the knees
3	Average	With the arms held together across abdominals, the athlete curls up so that the chest touches the thighs
4	Good	With the arms held across the chest, holding the opposite shoulders, the athlete curls up so that the forearms touch the thighs
5	Very good	With the hands held behind the head, the athlete curls up so that the chest touches the thighs
6	Excellent	As per level 5, with a 2.5 kg weight held behind head, chest touching the thighs
7	Elite	As per level 5, with a 5 kg weight held behind head, chest touching the thighs

Link

You can read more about aerobic energy in *Unit 1: Anatomy and Physiology*.

Aerobic endurance

Aerobic endurance is the ability of the cardiovascular and respiratory systems to supply the exercising muscles with oxygen to maintain the aerobic exercise for a long period of time, for example over two hours during a marathon. Also known as stamina or cardiorespiratory endurance, aerobic endurance is important for daily tasks such as walking to school or college, or doing tasks around the house. It is also important for a range of sport, leisure and recreational activities.

There are a number of events that rely almost exclusively on aerobic endurance, such as marathon running, long-distance swimming and cycling. But aerobic endurance forms the basis of fitness for most sports. If an athlete has a reduced aerobic endurance, possibly due to a long-term injury, this leads to a decrease in other fitness components such as muscular endurance. Poor aerobic endurance leads to poor sporting performance in many sports and can also lead to injury.

There are a number of different methods for measuring aerobic endurance.

Maximal oxygen consumption test (VO₂ max)

The maximal oxygen consumption test (or **VO₂ max** test) is a laboratory-based fitness test that directly measures aerobic capacity. This test involves expensive laboratory equipment including oxygen and carbon dioxide analysers, Douglas bags (used to collect exhaled air), a heart rate monitor and a treadmill or cycle **ergometer**.

The test involves exercising initially at a moderate level and then increasingly harder until a maximal level is achieved. Oxygen uptake is calculated from measures of ventilation and the oxygen and carbon dioxide in the expired air, and the maximal level is determined at or near test completion.

The subject is considered to have reached their VO_2 max when a plateau in oxygen uptake is recorded and while maximal heart rate is achieved. A basic method of determining your maximum heart rate is using the calculation of 220 minus your age.

Key terms

VO₂ max – the maximum amount of oxygen your body can consume while exercising at your maximum capacity.

Ergometer – a piece of equipment that measures the amount of work or energy used during exercise.

Multi-stage fitness test

This test is used to *predict* your maximum oxygen uptake (aerobic fitness) levels and is performed to a pre-recorded soundtrack that plays bleeps at decreasing intervals. It should be conducted indoors, usually in a sports hall using two lines (or cones) placed exactly 20 metres apart.

1 Perform a short warm-up.

2 Line up on the start line and on hearing the triple bleep run to the other line 20 metres away. You must reach the other line before or on the single bleep that determines each shuttle run.

3 Do not get ahead of the bleep – you need to make sure you turn to run to the other line on the bleep. You will find that the bleeps get closer and closer together, so you will need to continually increase your pace.

4 Continue to run to each line. A spotter is used to check you have reached each line in time with the bleep. If not, you will receive two verbal warnings before being asked to pull out of the test.

5 Continue running until you are physically exhausted, i.e. you have reached maximum exhaustion, at which point your level and shuttle reached is recorded.

6 Use Table 5.7 to predict your maximum oxygen consumption (ml/kg/min).

7 Use Table 5.8 to interpret the maximum oxygen uptake result.

▶ **Table 5.7:** Predicted maximum oxygen uptake values for the multi-stage fitness test (ml/kg/min)

Level	Shuttle	VO$_2$ max	Level	Shuttle	VO$_2$ max	Level	Shuttle	VO$_2$ max	Level	Shuttle	VO$_2$ max
4	2	26.8	10	2	47.4	15	2	64.6	19	2	78.3
4	4	27.6	10	4	48.0	15	4	65.1	19	4	78.8
4	6	28.3	10	6	48.7	15	6	65.6	19	6	79.2
4	9	29.5	10	8	49.3	15	8	66.2	19	8	79.7
5	2	30.2	10	11	50.2	15	10	66.7	19	10	80.2
5	4	31.0	11	2	50.8	15	13	67.5	19	12	80.6
5	6	31.8	11	4	51.4	16	2	68.0	19	15	81.3
5	9	32.9	11	6	51.9	16	4	68.5	20	2	81.8
6	2	33.6	11	8	52.5	16	6	69.0	20	4	82.2
6	4	34.3	11	10	53.1	16	8	69.5	20	6	82.6
6	6	35.0	11	12	53.7	16	10	69.9	20	8	83.0
6	8	35.7	12	2	54.3	16	12	70.5	20	10	83.5
6	10	36.4	12	4	54.8	16	14	70.9	20	12	83.9
7	2	37.1	12	6	55.4	17	2	71.4	20	14	84.3
7	4	37.8	12	8	56.0	17	4	71.9	20	16	84.8
7	6	38.5	12	10	56.5	17	6	72.4	21	2	85.2
7	8	39.2	12	12	57.1	17	8	72.9	21	4	85.6
7	10	39.9	13	2	57.6	17	10	73.4	21	6	86.1
8	2	40.5	13	4	58.2	17	12	73.9	21	8	86.5
8	4	41.1	13	6	58.7	17	14	74.4	21	10	86.9
8	6	41.8	13	8	59.3	18	2	74.8	21	12	87.4
8	8	42.4	13	10	59.8	18	4	75.3	21	14	87.8
8	11	43.3	13	13	60.6	18	6	75.8	21	16	88.2
9	2	43.9	14	2	61.1	18	8	76.2	–	–	–
9	4	44.5	14	4	61.7	18	10	76.7	–	–	–
9	6	45.2	14	6	62.2	18	12	77.2	–	–	–
9	8	45.8	14	8	62.7	18	15	77.9	–	–	–
9	11	46.8	14	10	63.2	–	–	–	–	–	–
–	–	–	14	13	64.0	–	–	–	–	–	–

▶ **Table 5.8:** Interpreting maximum oxygen uptake results (VO$_2$ max, ml/kg/min)

Rating	Males (aged 15–19) (ml/kg/min)	Females (aged 15–19) (ml/kg/min)
Excellent	60+	54+
Good	48–59	43–53
Average	39–47	35–42
Below average	30–38	28–34
Poor	<30	<28

▶ Performing a VO₂ max test

The 12-minute Cooper run test

The aim of the 12-minute Cooper run test is to cover as much distance as possible through running in 12 minutes so that you can determine your predicted VO_2 max. The test is designed to be maximal, which means that you should be working as hard as you can.

The equipment you will need is a flat, oval running track (400 metres), marker cones and a stopwatch.

1 Before you start, markers should be placed at 50-metre intervals around the track to help to measure the completed distance.

2 When instructed, start running. Walking is allowed, though you should push yourself as hard as possible so that you can maximise the distance covered.

3 After 12 minutes you must stop and the distance covered should be measured and recorded. Use Tables 5.9 and 5.10 to interpret the results.

▶ **Table 5.9:** Interpreting 12-minute Cooper run test (for men)

Age	Excellent	Above average	Average	Below average	Poor
20–29	>2800 m	2400–2800 m	2200–2399 m	1600–2199 m	<1600 m
30–39	>2700 m	2300–2700 m	1900–2299 m	1500–1899 m	<1500 m
40–49	>2500 m	2100–2500 m	1700–2099 m	1400–1699 m	<1400 m
50+	>2400 m	2000–2400 m	1600–1999 m	1300–1599 m	<1300 m

▶ **Table 5.10:** Interpreting 12-minute Cooper run test (for women)

Age	Excellent	Above average	Average	Below average	Poor
20–29	>2700 m	2200–2700 m	1800–2199 m	1500–1799 m	<1500 m
30–39	>2500 m	2000–2500 m	1700–1999 m	1400–1699 m	<1400 m
40–49	>2300 m	1900–2300 m	1500–1899 m	1200–1499 m	<1200 m
50+	>2200 m	1700–2200 m	1400–1699 m	1100–1399 m	<1100 m

Harvard step test

The Harvard step test is a measure of aerobic fitness and uses a person's ability to recover from strenuous exercise to predict their aerobic fitness. Recovery heart rate is measured and compared to normative data.

To conduct this test you will needs a step that is 50.8 cm (20 inches) high, a stopwatch and a metronome.

1 When instructed you must step up and down on the step or box at a rate of 30 steps per minute (every 2 seconds). The metronome should be set to keep you in time or rhythm.

2 Continue to exercise for 5 minutes or until exhaustion. Exhaustion is defined as when you cannot maintain the stepping rate for 15 seconds.

3 On completion of the test immediately sit down. The total number of heart beats are then counted between:

- 1 to 1½ minutes after finishing
- 2 to 2½ minutes after finishing
- 3 to 3½ minutes after finishing.

Note: you are using the total number of heart beats in the 30-second period, not the rate (beats per minute) during that time.

4 A score is used to determine your aerobic fitness by using the following equation: (100 × test duration in seconds) ÷ (2 × total (sum) of heart beats in the recovery periods).

5 Use Table 5.11 to interpret your results.

▶ **Table 5.11:** Interpreting Harvard step test results

Rating	Fitness Index
Excellent	>96
Good	83–96
Average	68–82
Low average	54–67
Poor	<54

Case study

Harvard step test results

Dan is a 17-year-old cricket player. He has recently completed the Harvard step test as part of a fitness testing session. His results are as follows.

The total test time was 300 seconds (because Dan completed the whole 5 minutes) and the number of heart beats recorded was:

- 90 between 1–1½ minutes
- 80 between 2–2½ minutes
- 70 between 3–3½ minutes.

Check your knowledge

1 Using the above results, work out Dan's aerobic fitness.

2 What does this result mean?

3 What advice would you give Dan to improve his aerobic fitness?

Rockport walk test

This low intensity test is used to predict maximum oxygen uptake. Because of the non-stressful nature of the test, it can be particularly useful in assessing those who are unfit. The test is best performed on an indoor athletics track, or an outdoor track on a day when weather conditions will not adversely affect test results.

1 Perform a warm-up.

2 On the starter's orders, walk a distance of 1 mile as fast as possible.

3 On crossing the finishing line:
  - record the time taken and convert it to decimal minutes where decimal minutes (t) = [min + (s/60)]
  - take your pulse rate for 15 seconds and convert it into heart rate (beats per minute) where:
    15-second pulse rate × 4 = beats per minute

4 Use the equation below to predict maximum oxygen uptake (VO_2 max l/min) and interpret this using Table 5.8 on page 227.

VO_2 max (l/min) = 6.9652 + (0.0091 × wt) − (0.0257 × age) + (0.5955 × gender) − (0.2240 × t) − (0.0115 × HR)

Where:
  - wt = body weight (kg)
  - age = years
  - gender = 0 = female; 1 = male
  - t = time in decimal minutes
  - HR = heart rate (beats/minute)

Case study

Rockport walk test

James is a 19-year-old male who completed the 1 mile walk test in a time of 13 minutes and 26 seconds. His body weight is 79 kg. On crossing the finishing line, James's 15-second pulse was 29.

- To convert 13.26 to decimal minutes (where decimal minutes (t) = [min + (s/60)]) = [13 + (26/60)] = 13.43 decimal minutes

- To convert the 15-second pulse into beats per minute = 29 × 4 = 116 beats/minute

Use the equation to predict maximum oxygen uptake (VO_2 max ml/kg/min):

- VO_2 max (l/min) = 6.9652 + (0.0091 × wt) − (0.0257 × age) + (0.5955 × gender) − (0.2240 × t) − (0.0115 × HR)

Therefore:

- VO_2 max (l/min) = 6.9652 + (0.0091 × 79) − (0.0257 × 19) + (0.5955 × 1) − (0.2240 × 13.43) − (0.0115 × 116)
- VO_2 max (l/min) = 3.45 l/min

Convert **absolute VO_2 max** (l/min) to **relative VO_2 max** (ml/kg/min):

- VO_2 max (ml/kg/min) = [(3.45 × 1000) ÷ body weight (kg)]

Therefore:

- VO_2 max (ml/kg/min) = [(3.45 × 1000) ÷ 79 kg] = 43.7 ml/kg/min

Using Table 5.8 on page 227, James's fitness rating is average.

Check your knowledge

1 How does your own predicted VO_2 max from the 1 mile walk test compare to normative data?

2 How do your results compare to those of your peers?

3 Calculate your results and discuss in small groups

> **⏸ PAUSE POINT**   What is aerobic endurance?
>
> **Hint**   List and describe three tests that measure aerobic endurance, explaining the strengths and weaknesses of each.
>
> **Extend**   Why should you measure aerobic endurance for sport or exercise?

Speed

Speed is defined as the ability to move over a distance in the quickest possible time. Athletic sports such as the 100-metre sprint and long jump require high levels of speed for an athlete to maximise performance.

Sprint tests

Sprint or speed tests can be performed over a variety of different distances, and the distance used (20 metres, 30 metres, 40 metres, 50 metres or 60 metres) will relate to the specific sport in which the athlete is training. For example, a winger in football would benefit from undertaking a 60-metre sprint test whereas a goalkeeper should undertake a shorter test. In all cases the equipment used is cheap and easily obtainable and will include a tape measure or trundle wheel to measure the distance, cones to mark the distance and a stopwatch. **Reliability is greatly improved if timing gates are used, but these can be expensive. Using a dedicated non-slip running surface will improve the accuracy** of the results.

To perform a sprint test you will need a tape measure or marked track, a stopwatch, cones to mark distance and a flat, straight area that is at least 60 metres in length, with enough space for a run-off. **The test involves running a single maximum sprint over varying distances depending on the test selected, with the best time recorded. For each test you should carry out the following.**

1 Perform a thorough warm-up including stretching.
2 Practise your starts so that you are fully prepared for the test.
3 Putting your front foot on or behind the starting line will ensure you start from a stationary 'standing start' position.
4 When signalled you must sprint in a straight line with maximal effort.
5 Your time will be recorded from the moment you start to the moment you cross the finish line. You can have three attempts and the best result is recorded to the nearest two decimal places.
6 The fastest recorded time is used to assess your performance.

This is a benchmark test that can be repeated over time to determine progress.

Muscular endurance

Muscular endurance is needed where a specific muscle or muscle group makes repeated contractions over a significant period of time (possibly over a number of minutes). Examples in sport include a boxer making repeated punches or a 400-metre sprint in athletics.

One-minute press-up test

This test is used to assess the endurance of the muscles of your upper body.

1 Position yourself on a mat facing down, with your hands on the floor shoulder-width apart and arms fully extended, and straight legs supported on your toes. Next, lower your body until the elbows are at 90° away from the torso.
2 Return to the starting position, with your arms fully extended.
3 Repeat, making sure your push-up action is continuous, with no rests in between.
4 The total number of press-ups is recorded for 1 minute. Use Table 5.12 to interpret your results.

People with reduced upper body strength and women may choose to use a modified press-up technique. The positioning is similar to the standard method, but in the starting position a bent knee position is assumed. Table 5.13 can be used to interpret results.

▶ **Table 5.12:** Interpretation of results from the full body press-up test

Rating	Males	Females
Excellent	45+	34+
Good	35–44	17–33
Average	20–34	6–16
Poor	<19	<5

▶ **Table 5.13:** Interpretation of results from the modified press-up test

Rating	Number of reps
Excellent	39+
Good	34–38
Average	17–33
Fair	6–16
Poor	<6

One-minute sit-up test

This test assesses the endurance and development of your abdominal muscles.
1 Lie on a mat on your back with your knees bent, and feet flat on the floor, with your arms folded across your body.
2 Raise yourself up to a 90° position and then return to the floor.
3 Your feet can be held by a partner if you wish.
4 The total number of sit-ups is recorded for 1 minute.
5 Use Table 5.14 to interpret the results.

▶ **Table 5.14:** Interpretation of results from the one-minute sit-up test

Rating	Males	Females
Excellent	49–59	42–54
Good	43–48	36–41
Above average	39–42	32–35
Average	35–38	28–31
Below average	31–34	24–27
Poor	25–30	18–23
Very poor	11–24	3–17

Wall sit test

This is a simple test that requires only a stopwatch, a flat dry surface and a wall. The purpose of the test is to measure the strength endurance of your lower body, particularly the quadriceps muscle group.
1 Stand comfortably with your feet approximately shoulder width apart, with your back against a smooth vertical wall.
2 Slowly slide your back down the wall to assume a position with both your knees and hips at a 90° angle.
3 The timing starts when one foot is lifted 5 cm off the ground and is stopped when you cannot maintain the position and the foot is returned to the ground.
4 After a period of rest, the other leg is tested. Use Table 5.15 to interpret results (note that it is used for the results from one leg at a time).

▶ Conducting a wall sit test

▶ **Table 5.15:** Interpretation of results from the wall sit test

Rating	Males (seconds)	Females (seconds)
Excellent	>100	>60
Good	75–100	45–60
Average	50–75	35–45
Below average	25–50	20–35
Very poor	<25	<20

Body composition

Body composition is the amount of body fat and lean body tissue the athlete has. It is important from both a health and a sports performance perspective. There are a number of different tests that can assess body composition including:

▶ skinfold calipers

▶ bioelectrical impedance analysis

▶ body mass index (BMI)

▶ girth measurements.

Key term

Body composition – what your body is made from, including bone, fat, muscle, organs and skin tissue. In sport, body composition refers to the proportion of fat and fat free mass.

Research

The average man has 15% to 17% body fat, while the average woman has between 18% and 22%. In small groups, research why there is a difference in the average body fat percentages between males and females.

Now consider elite athletes. Research their body fat percentages and discuss why these are different between average people and elite sports performers.

Skinfold caliper testing

Skinfold caliper testing can be used to predict percentage of body fat. A relationship exists between subcutaneous, internal fat and body density. Skinfold testing for the prediction of percentage of body fat is based on this relationship. This section covers Durnin and Womersley's (1974) generalised prediction equations to predict the percentage of body fat.

For males and females, skinfolds are taken on the following four sites (see Figure 5.2).

▶ **Biceps** – a vertical fold on the anterior surface of the biceps muscle midway between the anterior axillary fold and the antecubital fossa.

▶ **Triceps** – a vertical fold on the back midline of the upper arm, over the triceps muscle, halfway between the acromion process (bony process on the top of the shoulder) and olecranon process (bony process on the elbow). The arm should be held freely by the side of the body.

▶ **Subscapular** – a diagonal fold taken at a 45° angle 1–2 cm below the inferior angle of the scapulae (point of the shoulder blade).

▶ **Suprailiac** – a diagonal fold above the crest of the ilium, taken in the anterior axillary line above the iliac crest (just above the hip bone and 2–3 cm forward).

Research

There are many different protocols for measuring body fat composition using the skinfold technique, using three, four or even seven sites. At Level 2, you are likely to have studied the Jackson-Pollock method (which uses three sites). Here, however, we have used a four-site protocol.

Research the differences between the various skinfold protocols. Why might you choose to use one technique rather than another in certain situations?

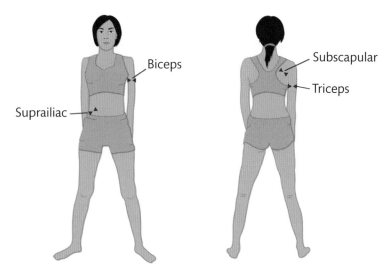

▶ **Figure 5.2:** The four sites where skinfold measurements are taken

Following a standard method will help ensure your results are valid. You will need skinfold calipers (such as Harpenden or Slimguide) to take the skinfolds as well as a tape measure and pen to mark each site.

1 Measurements should be taken on dry skin on the right side of the body. Exceptions to this would be if the participant has a tattoo or deformity on the site location, which means the left side of the body would need to be used. The participant should keep their muscles relaxed during the test.

2 Mark each skinfold site with a pen and use a tape measure to find the midpoints.

3 Grasp the skinfold firmly between your thumb and index finger and gently pull away from the body. The skinfold should be grasped about 1 cm away from the site marked.

4 Place the skinfold calipers at right angles to the fold, on the site marked, with the dial facing upwards.

5 Maintaining your grasp, place the calipers midway between the base and tip of the skinfold and allow the calipers to be fully released so that full tension is placed on the skinfold.

6 Read the dial of the skinfold calipers to the nearest 0.5 mm, 2 seconds after you have released the calipers. Make sure you continue to grasp the skinfold throughout testing.

7 Take a minimum of two measurements at each site. If repeated tests vary by more than 1 mm, repeat the measurement.

8 If consecutive measurements become smaller, this means that the fat is being compressed, and will result in inaccurate results. If this happens, go to another site and then come back to the site to be tested later.

9 Make sure you record each measurement as it is taken.

10 The final value is the average of the two readings (mm).

Once you have taken the readings, you can then calculate the percentage of body fat.

1 Add up the results for the four skinfolds (mm).

2 Use the calculations shown in Table 5.16 to determine body density.

3 Next, complete the following calculation, where d = density, for the prediction of percentage of body fat. Interpret the results using Table 5.17.

$$\left[\frac{4.57}{d} - 4.142 \right] \times 100\% \text{ body fat}$$

▶ **Table 5.16:** Calculating body density

Males (16–29 years)	Body density (d) = 1.162 – [(0.063) × (∑ log of four × skinfolds)] where ∑ is the sum or total
Females (16–29 years)	Body density (d) = 1.1549 – [(0.0678) × (∑ log of four × skinfolds)] where ∑ is the sum or total

▶ **Table 5.17:** Interpretation of percentage of body fat results

Rating	Males % body fat (16–29 years)	Females % body fat (16–29 years)
Very low fat	<7	<13
Slim	7–12	13–20
Acceptable	13–17	21–25
Overweight	18–28	26–32
Obese	28+	32+

Case study

Skinfold testing

Grace is an 18-year-old cyclist who has completed the skinfold testing with the following results recorded:

- Biceps = 10 mm
- Triceps = 14 mm
- Subscapular = 16 mm
- Suprailiac = 16 mm
- Sum of skinfolds = 56 mm
- Log of skinfolds = 1.748188

Using the calculation for females, Grace's calculation of body density is:

- = 1.1549 – [(0.0678) × (∑ log of four skinfolds)]
- = 1.1549 – [(0.0678) × (1.748188)]
- = 1.1549 – (0.1185271)
- Body density (d) = 1.0363729

Grace's calculation of percentage of body fat is:

- $\left[\dfrac{4.57}{d} - 4.142\right] \times 100\%$ body fat
- [(4.4096097) – 4.142] × 100 = % body fat
- [0.2676097] × 100 = % body fat
- = 26.8% = overweight

Check your knowledge

1 What validity and reliability issues should you consider when undertaking skinfold testing?

2 How do your percentage of body fat results compare to normative data and to data for elite performers?

3 What other factors could affect body fat results?

Bioelectrical impedance analysis (BIA)

Bioelectrical impedance analysis (BIA) is a method used to predict the percentage of body fat of an individual. A BIA machine is required to conduct the test (for example, Bodystat 1500) which is used to pass a small electrical current through the body. Modern bathroom scales often include this feature but these are considered less accurate and should not be used in fitness testing.

The method is based on the fact that fat-free mass in the body (muscle, bone, connective tissues) conducts electricity, whereas fat mass does not. Therefore, the higher the resistance to a weak electrical current (bioelectrical impedance), the higher the percentage of body fat of the individual.

1 Hydration levels can affect validity of test results. To ensure the test is valid, you should not: exercise for 12 hours prior to the test; eat or drink within 4 hours of the test; or drink caffeine prior to the test.

2 You should lie down and remove your right sock and shoe.

3 Place the BIA electrodes on the right wrist, right hand, right ankle and right foot.

4 Attach the cable leads (crocodile clips) to the exposed tabs on the electrodes.

5 Enter appropriate data into the BIA machine (for example age, gender, height, weight and activity level).

6 The test only takes a few seconds. You must lie still as the weak electrical current is passed through your body.

7 The percentage of body fat test result will be shown on the LCD display of the BIA machine.

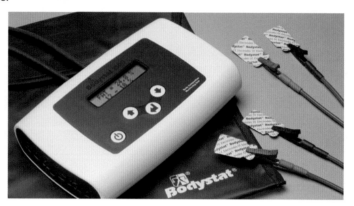

▶ A bioelectrical impedance analysis (BIA) machine

Body mass index (BMI)

BMI is a measure of body composition in kg/m^2 and is used to determine to what degree someone is overweight. It is only an **estimate**, as the test does not take into account the individual's frame size or muscle mass. Research shows a significant relationship between high BMI and incidence of cardiovascular disease, and high BMI and diabetes.

To obtain BMI, measure the individual's body weight in kg and height in metres, and calculate the BMI as weight divided by (height × height). This will give you a value for the BMI in kg/m^2.

▶ For women, a desirable BMI is 21–23 kg/m^2.

▶ For men, a desirable BMI is 22–24 kg/m^2.

The risk of cardiovascular disease increases sharply at a BMI of 27.8 kg/m^2 for men and 27.3 kg/m^2 for women.

Weight (kg)

Height (cm)	54	59	64	68	73	77	82	86	91	95	100	104	109	113
137	29	31	34	36	39	41	43	46	48	51	53	56	58	60
142	27	29	31	34	36	38	40	43	45	47	49	52	54	56
147	25	27	29	31	34	36	38	40	42	44	46	58	50	52
152	23	25	27	29	31	33	35	37	39	41	43	45	47	49
158	23	24	26	27	29	31	33	35	37	38	40	42	44	46
163	21	22	24	26	28	29	31	33	34	36	38	40	41	43
168	19	21	23	24	26	27	29	31	32	34	36	37	39	40
173	18	20	21	23	24	26	27	29	30	32	34	35	37	38
178	17	19	20	22	23	24	26	27	29	30	32	33	35	36
183	16	18	19	20	22	23	24	26	27	28	30	31	33	34
188	16	17	18	19	21	22	23	24	26	27	28	30	31	32
193	15	16	17	18	20	21	22	23	24	26	27	38	29	30
198	14	15	16	17	19	20	21	22	23	24	25	27	28	29
203	13	14	15	17	18	19	20	21	22	23	24	25	26	28

☐ underweight   ☐ healthy weight   ☐ overweight   ☐ obese

▶ **Figure 5.3:** BMI chart

Girth measurements

Beneath your skin is a layer of subcutaneous fat, and by taking the girth measurements at selected points on the body with a measuring tape it is possible to predict your percentage of the total body fat. However, more commonly girth measurements are used to see whether your body is in proportion.

Girth measurements are popular due to the fact that they do not require expensive equipment, only a tape measure. The most common girth measurements are taken around the waist and hip and used to determine fat gain/loss, as these girth measurements are based on fat that tends to accumulate around the midsection. If these measurements increase, then it is likely that the client has increased their body fat percentage.

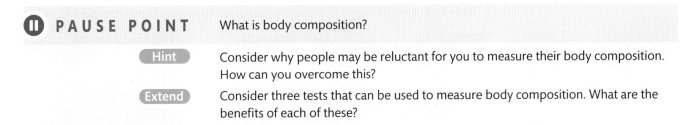

❚❚ PAUSE POINT   What is body composition?

Hint   Consider why people may be reluctant for you to measure their body composition. How can you overcome this?

Extend   Consider three tests that can be used to measure body composition. What are the benefits of each of these?

Fitness tests to assess components of skill-related fitness

In addition to physical fitness components there are a number of skill-related fitness components that are important in performing the technical aspects of sport. The skill-related fitness components are:

▶ agility

▶ balance

▶ coordination

▶ power

▶ reaction time.

Agility

Agility can be defined as your ability to accurately change direction at speed. It is an essential aspect of most sports. Specific examples of sports where agility is vital to success are football, basketball, rugby and tennis.

Illinois agility run test

The Illinois agility run is a common test that is used to measure agility. The test requires a tape measure, marking cones and a stopwatch, and requires the subject to run through a marked course as quickly as possible.

The course should be measured as 10 metres long by 5 metres wide and cones should be set out as illustrated in Figure 5.4.

To conduct the test, the subject must lie flat on their front with their head behind the start line. When instructed by the starter to go, they must get up and run as quickly as possible around the marked course without knocking over the cones. They should be timed completing the course, and then their performance can be compared with the norms shown in Table 5.18.

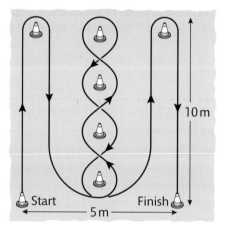

▶ **Figure 5.4:** Layout of the Illinois agility run test

▶ **Table 5.18:** Interpretation of Illinois agility run test results for men and women aged 16 to 19

Rating	Males (seconds)	Females (seconds)
Excellent	<15.2	<17.0
Good	15.2–16.1	17.0–17.9
Average	16.2–18.1	18.0–21.7
Fair	18.2–18.3	21.8–23.0
Poor	>18.3	>23.0

T-test

Similar to the Illinois agility test, the T-test requires a subject to run between cones in the fastest time possible. For this test you will need a tape measure, marking cones and a stopwatch. A course should be set out as shown in Figure 5.5.

The subject starts at cone A. On a command from the timer, the subject sprints to cone B and touches the base of the cone with their right hand. They then shuffle sideways to the left to cone C and touch its base, this time with their left hand. Then they shuffle sideways to the right to cone D and touch the base with their right hand. They then shuffle back to cone B touching it with their left hand, and run backwards to cone A. The stopwatch is stopped as they pass cone A. The subject must not cross one foot in front of the other when shuffling or fail to face forwards throughout the test.

The time taken can then be compared with the norms shown in Table 5.19.

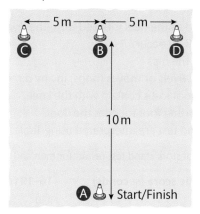

▶ **Figure 5.5:** Layout of the T-test

▶ **Table 5.19:** Interpretation of T-test results for men and women aged 16 to 19

	Male (seconds)	**Female (seconds)**
Excellent	<9.5	<10.5
Good	9.5–10.5	10.5–11.5
Average	10.5–11.5	11.5–12.5
Poor	>11.5	>12.5

Side-step test

There are a number of side-step tests. An easy one to set up and measure involves a subject jumping from side to side for 1 minute. This test requires a tape measure, stopwatch and tape or chalk to mark a distance of 30 cm.

Starting at a centre line you must jump 30 cm to the side (e.g. right) and touch the marked line with your closest foot. Jump back to the centre then jump 30 cm to the other side, then back to the centre. This is one complete cycle.

You must try to complete as many cycles as possible in 1 minute. The score is the number of repetitions in 1 minute. Use Table 5.20 to interpret your results.

▶ **Table 5.20:** Interpretation of side-step test results for men and women aged 16 to 19

	Poor	**Fair**	**Average**	**Good**	**High**
Female	<33	34–37	38–41	42–45	46+
Male	<37	38–41	42–45	46–49	50+

Balance

Balance is very important in many sports and can be defined as being able to maintain stability or equilibrium while performing. There are two forms of balance:

▶ **static balance** where the athlete is stationary (for example in a handstand in gymnastics)

▶ **dynamic balance** where the athlete is moving (for example a basketball player sprinting with the ball).

Stork stand test

The purpose of the stork stand test is to measure static balance on the ball of the foot.
1 To start you must remove your shoes and socks and place your hands on your hips.
2 Position the non-supporting foot against the inside knee of the supporting leg and practise balancing on one foot for 1 minute.

▸ **Figure 5.6:** Conducting the stork stand test

3 When you are ready to start the test, raise the heel of your supporting leg to balance on the ball of the foot.

4 The stopwatch is started as the heel is raised from the floor and the stopwatch is stopped if any of the follow occur:

- the hand(s) come off the hips
- the supporting foot swivels or moves (hops) in any direction
- the non-supporting foot loses contact with the knee
- the heel of the supporting foot touches the floor.

The results of the stork stand test are interpreted using Table 5.21.

▸ **Table 5.21:** Interpretation of stork stand test results for men and women aged 16 to 19

Rating	16–19 male score (seconds)	16–19 female score (seconds)
Excellent	>50	>30
Good	41–50	23–30
Average	31–40	16–22
Below average	20–30	10–15
Poor	<20	<10

Beam walk

The beam walk test is a 'pass or fail' test that measures dynamic balance. To complete this test you will need a beam or curb which is approximately 10 cm wide and 6 metres long and a stopwatch. The aim of the test is for you to walk the entire length of the beam and back in 30 seconds.

1 Starting at one end, step up onto the beam, walk the length to the other end, make a 180° turn and return back to the starting point.

2 If your feet touch the ground before they touch or cross the finish line, this counts as a fall.

3 You are allowed one fall off the beam.

Coordination

Most sports require a high level of coordination to perform specific skills. Consider the action of a tennis serve and how the various parts of your body interact to perform a complete movement. Coordination is the ability to move two or more body parts in a set sequence.

Wall-toss test

This test measures hand–eye coordination and requires a tennis ball, a stopwatch, a tape measure and a wall.

1 Following a warm-up you must stand facing a wall and throw the ball underarm with your right hand against the wall, catching the ball with your left hand.

2 You must then throw the ball using your left hand and catch it with the right hand.

3 Keep this rotation sequence occurring for 30 seconds and count how many successful catches you make in 30 seconds. The results can be compared with Table 5.22.

▸ **Table 5.22:** Interpretation of wall-toss test results for 15 to 16 year olds

Rating	Score (in 30 seconds)
Excellent	>35
Good	30–35
Average	20–29
Fair	15–19
Poor	<15

⏸ PAUSE POINT   Do you understand the importance of equipment in measuring fitness?

Hint   List three fitness tests and the equipment required for each test. Is this equipment affordable and readily available?

Extend   What must you consider when using equipment to conduct a fitness test?

Power

Power is the ability to generate and use muscular strength quickly over a short period of time and is determined by both strength and speed. Power is important for sprinters when pushing away from the blocks, footballers striking a long range drive and boxers delivering a punch, as well as in other sports.

Vertical jump test (Sargent jump test)

This is a test of the anaerobic power of the quadriceps muscle group. A standard vertical jump board is used for the test. The jump height may be digitally recorded or alternatively chalk on the fingertips may be used.
Perform a short warm-up prior to the test.

1   Stand with your dominant side against the board, feet together, and reach up as high as you can and record your standing reach height.

2   Only one dip of the arms and knees is permitted. Make the jump while simultaneously touching the vertical jump board at the peak of your jump.

3   Perform three trials. No rest is required between trials. Observe and record the height of the jump. Use Table 5.23 to interpret the results of the test.

▶ **Table 5.23:** Interpretation of vertical jump test results for men and women aged 16 to 19

Gender	Excellent	Above average	Average	Below average	Poor
Male	>65 cm	50–65 cm	40–49 cm	30–39 cm	<30 cm
Female	>58 cm	47–58 cm	36–46 cm	26–35 cm	<26 cm

A nomogram (see Figure 5.7) can also be used to obtain the results of the test. Use the Lewis nomogram to predict power of your quadriceps in kgm/s.

1   Plot the difference (D) between your standing reach height and your best jump height (cm) on the nomogram line (D).

2   Plot your weight in kilograms on the nomogram line (Wt).

3   Join up the two plots, which will cross over the power line (P) to give a prediction of the anaerobic power of the quadriceps (in kgm/s).

Standing long jump test

The standing long jump test (or broad jump test) is a measure of the explosive power of the legs and requires a tape measure and chalk to mark. The aim of the test is to jump as far as possible, landing on both feet without falling backwards.

1   You must start behind a line marked on the ground with feet slightly apart.

2   When you are ready you must take a two-foot take-off, swinging your arms and bending the knees to provide forward drive.

3   The measurement is taken from the take-off line to the nearest point of contact on the landing (back of the heels).

4   Three attempts are allowed and you record the longest distance jumped, i.e. the best of three attempts. Use Table 5.24 to interpret your test results.

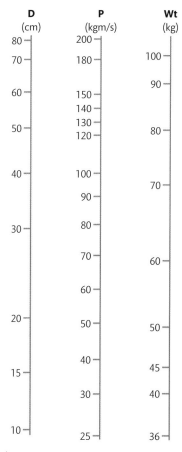

▶ **Figure 5.7:** The Lewis nomogram

Gender	Excellent	Above average	Average	Below average	Poor
Male	>2.44 m	2.29–2.44 m	2.16–2.28 m	1.98–2.15 m	<1.98 m
Female	>1.91 m	1.78–1.91 m	1.63–1.77 m	1.50–1.62 m	<1.50 m

Margaria Kalamen power test

The Margaria Kalamen power test is a measure of power of the lower extremities. The test requires the subject to sprint up a flight of stairs taking three steps at a time. Only basic equipment is required:

▶ stopwatch
▶ a flight of 12 steps about 17.5 cm high
▶ weighing scales
▶ cones for marking.

> **Safety tip**
>
> When doing the Margaria Kalamen power test, make sure that the area is clear and that a warning is displayed to prevent other people from coming up or going down the stairs.

1 Before the test starts, you must mark a starting line with cones 6 metres in front of the first step. You must then clearly mark the third, sixth and ninth steps by placing a cone on and to one side of the step.
2 Measure the vertical distance from the third to the ninth step (in metres).
3 Measure your weight (in kg).
4 Starting at the 6-metre line, you must run forward when given the command 'GO'.
5 Sprint to and up the flight of steps taking three steps at a time landing on the third, sixth and ninth steps. The stopwatch should be started when your foot lands on the third step.
6 The stopwatch should be stopped when your foot lands on the ninth step, with the time taken recorded in seconds.

Power (watts) is calculated from the formula: $P = (M \times D) \times 9.8 \div t$ where:

▶ P = power (watts)
▶ M = athlete's weight (kg)
▶ D = vertical distance (m) from third to ninth step
▶ t = time (s).

This is a benchmark test that should be done at the start of a fitness programme and then repeated in order to gauge progress.

Worked Example

The Margaria Kalamen power test

Joe is a basketball player who wishes to improve his lower body power. He has undertaken the Margaria Kalamen power test to measure his power.

- weight = 75 kg
- distance = 105 cm
- time = 1.7 seconds

Using the formula: $P = (M \times D) \times 9.8 \div t$:
$P = (75 \text{ kg} \times 1.05 \text{ m}) \times 9.8 \div 1.7$
= 454 watts

Seated medicine ball throw

The aim of the seated medicine ball throw is to measure upper body power. By keeping the back in contact with a wall, the power of the upper body (in particular the arms and chest) is tested. Basic equipment is required:

▶ 4 kg medicine ball

▶ tape measure.

1 Sit on the floor with your legs fully extended, your feet shoulder-width apart and your back against a wall.

2 Holding the ball with your hands either side of it, you must throw the medicine ball vigorously and as far straight forward as you can while keeping your back against the wall. Your forearms should be positioned parallel to the ground.

3 The distance thrown is recorded to the nearest centimetre with the best result of three throws used.

This is a benchmark test that should be done at the start of a fitness programme and then repeated in order to gauge progress.

Cricket ball throw test

The cricket ball throw test involves **throwing a cricket ball for a maximum distance and is a measure of power in the shoulder and arm muscles. The test is particularly useful for any athletes who perform throwing actions in their sport.**

1 Using a 10-metre run-up you must throw the ball as far as possible without crossing the start line. If the line is crossed the throw is deemed a foul.

2 The distance from the starting line to where the ball first lands is recorded to the nearest metre.

3 Three attempts are made and the best result of three throws is recorded.

This is another benchmark test that should be done at the start of a fitness programme and then repeated in order to gauge progress.

Wingate test

The Wingate cycle test predicts the anaerobic power of the quadriceps muscle groups using a 30-second all-out maximal sprint on a mechanically-braked cycle ergometer such as the Monark 824E. Informed consent is required before participating in this arduous test.

1 Measure your body weight in kg. To calculate the weight to add to the cycle ergometer basket, use this formula:
   • weight to add to basket = body weight × 0.075 minus 1 kg for the basket weight
     = weight to add to basket

2 You will need to wear a heart rate monitor for the warm-up. You need to cycle for between 2 and 4 minutes at an intensity sufficient to cause the heart to beat at 150–160 bpm. During the warm-up include two or three all-out bursts of cycling for 4–8 seconds each.

3 Following the warm-up you should rest for approximately 3 to 5 minutes during which you can carry out stretching of the major muscle groups.

4 On command from the timer, pedal as fast as possible to overcome the inertia of the flywheel. The weight will then be lowered onto the basket.

5 When the final load has been added to the basket, timing will commence. Continue to pedal as fast as possible for 30 seconds. You will require motivation from peers to help continue to sprint on the bike as fast as possible and keep the pedals turning for the full 30 seconds of the test.

6 An assistant will note the revolutions per minute (RPM) achieved for each 5-second period. This can be noted electronically from the cycle ergometer display.

▶ Performing a cricket ball throw

7 For cool down, and to minimise the risk of fainting, continue cycling with no load on the basket, for 2 to 3 minutes after the test.

8 You will need to be given help from assistants to get off the bike and should then, as a precaution, assume the recovery position.

9 The results can be interpreted using Table 5.25.

> **Research**
>
> The **recovery position** is used to prevent choking. You may have already done first-aid training as part of your BTEC National in Sport programme. If you have not, use a reliable internet site to find out what the recovery position is. Practise it with a partner and get a first-aid qualified person to check you have positioned each other correctly.

▶ **Table 5.25:** Interpretation of anaerobic power

Rank (%)	Male (watts)	Female (watts)
90	822	560
80	777	527
70	757	505
60	721	480
50	689	449
40	671	432
30	656	399
20	618	376
10	570	353

⏸ PAUSE POINT What is power?

Hint List five sports that require power as a key component of fitness. Describe why this is important to each of these sports.

Extend How can you measure power? Identify three tests that can be used to measure power.

Case study

Wingate cycle test

Gary is an 18-year-old student. His results for the anaerobic Wingate cycle test are shown in Tables 5.26–5.30.

Using the information in these tables:

- Calculation of anaerobic capacity (W):
  - = kgm-30s/3
  - = 2016/3
  - = 672 W (average mean power)

Check your knowledge

1 Undertake the maximal anaerobic Wingate cycle test. From your results, calculate:
  - peak anaerobic power (W)
  - anaerobic capacity (W) – your average mean power.

2 Plot a graph to show your data results. On the *Y*-axis plot anaerobic power (W) achieved for each 5-second period (plot time in seconds on the *X*-axis).

3 Show your average mean power (W) by drawing a straight line across your graph intersecting the *Y*-axis at your power result.
  - What is your average mean power result (W)?
  - How do your anaerobic power results compare to those of your peers?

> **Table 5.26:** Calculation of weight to add to Gary's ergometer basket

Gary's body weight	= 85 kg
Weight to add to basket	= Body weight × 0.075
	= 80 × 0.075
	= 6.0
Minus 1 kg for basket weight	**= 5.0**

> **Table 5.27:** Gary's revolutions per minute for each 5-second period

Time (s)	RPM
5	115
10	118
15	118
20	109
25	105
30	105

> **Table 5.28:** Calculation of Gary's anaerobic power

Time (s)	Anaerobic power (w)
Anaerobic power (W) = total weight on basket (kg) × revolutions × 11.765	
5	6.0 × (115 ÷ 60 × 5) × 11.765 = 676.5 W
10	6.0 × (118 ÷ 60 × 5) × 11.765 = 694.1 W
15	6.0 × (118 ÷ 60 × 5) × 11.765 = 694.1 W
20	6.0 × (109 ÷ 60 × 5) × 11.765 = 641.2 W
25	6.0 × (105 ÷ 60 × 5) × 11.765 = 617.7 W
30	6.0 × (105 ÷ 60 × 5) × 11.765 = 617.7 W

> **Table 5.29:** Calculation of Gary's total revolutions in 30 seconds

Time (s)		5s revs
5	115/60 × 5	9.58
10	118/60 × 5	9.83
15	118/60 × 5	9.83
20	109/60 × 5	9.08
25	105/60 × 5	8.75
30	105/60 × 5	8.75
Total revs		**55.82**
		= 56 (closest rev)

> **Table 5.30:** Calculation of Gary's anaerobic capacity

Anaerobic capacity (kgm-30s)	– total revs in 30s × 6m* (* one revolution of Monark flywheel is 6 metres) × force (kg)
	= 56 × 6 × 6.0
	= 2016 (kgm-30s)

Reaction time

Reaction time is the time between a stimulus to move and the start of a movement, such as a starting pistol (the stimulus) and the sprint start (the movement) in sprint events.

Ruler drop test

A simple reaction time test is the ruler drop test, which uses only a 1-metre ruler. This test uses the known properties of gravity to determine how long it takes a person to respond to the dropping of an object by measuring how far the object can fall before being caught.

1 The ruler is held by an assistant between the outstretched index finger and thumb of your dominant hand, so that the top of the thumb is level with the zero centimetre line on the ruler.
2 You must catch the ruler as soon as possible after it has been released.
3 The assistant releases the ruler and you must catch the ruler between your index finger and thumb as quickly as possible.
4 The distance between the bottom of the ruler and the top of your thumb where the ruler has been caught is recorded.
5 The test is repeated twice more and the average value used.

To calculate the reaction speed the following formula is used: $t = \sqrt{(2d \div a)}$ where:

▸ d = distance in metres
▸ a = acceleration due to gravity = 9.81 m/s^2
▸ t = time in seconds

Worked Example

Stuart drops a ruler and records a distance of 9 cm.
Using the equation: $t = \sqrt{(2d \div a)}$

• $t = \sqrt{(2 \times 0.09 \div 9.81)}$

• $t = \sqrt{(0.01835)}$

• $t = 0.135$ seconds

Stuart uses Table 5.31 to interpret his result.

▸ **Table 5.31:** Interpretation of ruler drop test results

Excellent	Above average	Average	Below average	Poor
<7.5 cm	7.5–15.9 cm	15.9–20.4 cm	20.4–28 cm	>28 cm

❚❚ PAUSE POINT

Do you understand the difference between skill-related components of fitness and physical components of fitness?

Hint

Close the book and under the different categories list the skill-related components and the physical components of fitness covered in this unit.

Extend

Now list a fitness test that will measure each of these components of fitness.

Planning tests

Subject requirements

Each of your subjects will be different, with different levels of fitness. Therefore you must be able to select a range of fitness tests that are appropriate to the needs of the individual subject. Factors that you must consider include understanding the physical demands of a particular sport or physical activity and being able to test the specific components of fitness that are relevant.

You should also consider the individual's age, gender and current physical activity levels when selecting tests. For example, if a subject has low levels of aerobic fitness then a maximal test such as the multi-stage fitness test would be inappropriate.

Selection of appropriate fitness tests

When selecting appropriate tests you must remember to consider the suitability, validity, reliability and practicality of each test and the resources required for it. One particular consideration is the sequence in which you perform a range of tests, as each test may affect the results of the next test. As a general guideline the sequence should be as follows.

1 **Health checks** – resting heart rate and blood pressure should be measured first when the subject is fully rested. These can be measured as part of the screening procedure.

2 **Body measurements** – can be measured after the health checks as they do not require physical exertion.

3 **Flexibility tests** – should be conducted after a warm-up to prevent injury.

4 **Skill-related tests** such as agility, balance, coordination and reaction time – should be conducted after a warm-up and after flexibility tests.

5 **Speed and power tests** – should be conducted before tests for power, muscular strength, muscular endurance and sprint tests. A full warm-up must be conducted before these tests. Muscular strength tests should always be conducted before a muscular endurance test.

6 **Muscular endurance tests** – always ensure that your subject is fully recovered from any preceding muscular strength test. A minimum of 10 minutes of recovery time will allow the subject to prepare for this test.

7 **Aerobic endurance tests** – most submaximal aerobic tests are based on a heart rate response to exercise and may be affected by the previous tests and by the mental state of the athlete. Therefore these should be scheduled accordingly. Remember that fatiguing maximal exercise tests, such as a VO_2 max or the multi stage fitness test (bleep test), require your subject to exercise to exhaustion so should always be scheduled at the end of a session and should not be repeated in the same session.

Case study

Choosing the right fitness tests

Victoria is an 18-year-old tennis player who has just been selected to represent her county. She wishes to prepare for an upcoming tournament and has approached a personal trainer, Kerrie, to help her with her fitness goals.

Step 1: Kerrie meets with Victoria and discusses what her training goals are. At this meeting they identify the key components of fitness required for tennis.

Step 2: Having identified the main components of fitness, Kerrie selects a fitness test that will measure each one and explains the purpose and protocol of each of these. She then completes a pre-testing health questionnaire with Victoria as well as an informed consent form which both parties sign (see pages 248–249).

Step 3: Victoria undertakes each of the selected fitness tests and Kerrie records the results after each of these.

Step 4: Once Victoria has cooled down, Kerrie meets with Victoria to discuss her results. She uses normative data to identify Victoria's specific fitness levels (linked to each component) and makes training recommendations based on each of these.

Step 5: Using the information, Victoria undertakes a specific training programme that addresses each component of fitness. After six weeks she returns to Kerrie who re-tests her to ascertain whether improvements have been made.

Check your knowledge

1 What would be the main components of fitness required for tennis?

2 Identify a fitness test that measures each of these components.

3 What factors would affect the selection of each of these tests?

4 Why is a signed informed consent form important when undertaking fitness testing?

5 What must Kerrie consider when using normative data?

Test procedure

Your subject may be nervous or uncertain about being part of a fitness testing session. Therefore it is important in your role as the tester to reassure the subject and fully explain the purpose and procedure of each test. To do this you can give a demonstration so that the subject can visualise the test and what to expect. Following this, allow the client to practise while you give clear instructions. For more complicated tests, it is useful to break down the test into smaller components and give clear instructions for each phase of the test.

Health and safety

When conducting fitness assessments, you must always adhere to strict health and safety procedures, and test protocol guidelines, and be able to identify those clients requiring medical referral. Therefore you must discuss the subject's current fitness and activity levels as well as lifestyle factors that may affect the tests. If you are uncertain as to whether the subject is able to undertake a selected test, do not conduct it. You must also monitor them throughout the tests to safeguard their welfare.

Subject screening

Health screening involves collecting information regarding an individual's current physical activity levels, dietary habits and lifestyle. Health screening questionnaires can be used to collect such information. Questionnaire results identify those who could have risk factors, such as for heart disease, and highlight where lifestyle changes are required.

Health screening questionnaires are likely to contain specific questions relating to the following areas:

▶ physical activity history and current physical activity levels
▶ injuries
▶ personal training goals
▶ smoking and alcohol consumption
▶ stress levels
▶ dietary habits.

During the screening you will need to ensure the individual feels at ease – develop a rapport, keep them fully informed and show discretion. Remember that it is just as important to listen to your client as it is to ask questions. Be aware of your body language and the non-verbal messages you are giving out. Finally, you must clearly communicate your findings and the implications of these.

Reasons for terminating a test

Individuals should be closely monitored while they are undertaking fitness tests. Reasons to terminate a test include your subject:

▶ requesting to stop the fitness test
▶ reporting chest pain
▶ experiencing severe breathlessness or wheezing
▶ showing signs of poor circulation, for example pale, cold, clammy skin
▶ showing signs of poor coordination, confusion and/or dizziness.

Informed consent

Before administering any health or fitness tests, the individual to be tested should complete an informed consent form. This is documented evidence that shows that you have provided the individual with all the necessary information to undertake the tests.

The informed consent form must include the following information:

▶ a description of the fitness test

▶ details of the procedure to be followed and confirmation that they are able to follow the test methods

▶ details of any risks and also potential benefits for the participant

▶ a section showing they know that they are able to ask you any questions relating to the tests and confirming that these have been answered

▶ a section indicating that they have fully consented to their participation in the fitness tests but understand that they can withdraw their consent at any time

▶ a section that explains that any information collected about them will remain confidential.

Theory into practice

Search online to find examples of informed consent forms. Design your own informed consent form that can be used for any fitness tests you choose to administer.

- Why is informed consent important in fitness testing?
- What health screening questions should be included?

What should you do if a subject refuses to complete a health questionnaire or informed consent form?

Link

See *Unit 2: Fitness Training and Programming for Health, Sport and Well-being* for more information about health screening questions.

The consent form should be signed and dated by:

▶ the individual to be tested (the participant)

▶ their parents/guardians (if under 18)

▶ you (the tester)

▶ a witness (usually your tutor/assessor during your BTEC course).

Pre-test warm-up

Before any exercise you must allow the subject to warm up. This will prepare them for the physical and psychological demands of the tests as well as reduce the risk of injury.

Theory into practice

If you are well rehearsed in test techniques, your results are more likely to be valid and reliable. Good planning will help you to feel more confident in administering fitness tests, particularly if it is someone you do not know.

1 Consider a range of fitness tests. Are you confident in being able to conduct each of these?

2 Do you know what the results mean?

3 In pairs, select a component of fitness and an appropriate fitness test. One of you should act as the subject while the other one will conduct the test.

4 After the test, give feedback to the subject. What were your strengths? What area do you need to further develop?

PAUSE POINT   Do you understand why health and safety is important in fitness testing?

     Describe three ways in which you can ensure that health and safety is maintained before and during fitness testing.

     Plan a health questionnaire that can be given to a subject before a fitness testing session. What questions will you ask? Why?

Administering tests

You will need to be well planned and organised throughout the administration of the fitness tests. It is important that you know and understand your role and responsibilities as a tester.

Role of tester

The role of the fitness tester is not only to conduct a range of fitness tests in a safe manner but to also ensure that the client is at ease and comfortable with the procedure. From the moment you meet the client and throughout the test you should remain positive and enthusiastic, building a good rapport with them.

The role of the tester includes:

▶ organising the equipment on the day and making sure that the facility is clean and safe before the client arrives – this may include conducting a risk assessment
▶ ensuring that the client has completed a consultation and other pre-test procedures, and that all the documentation has been recorded properly
▶ demonstrating the tests and taking the client through a full warm-up
▶ acting as a motivator to encourage the client to perform at their best and continue to motivate them when they are getting tired
▶ recording the results of each test in an organised and accurate manner
▶ being able to use this information to compare with normative data and make judgements and recommendations.

Responsibilities of tester

As the tester you are responsible for the welfare of your client throughout the session. As such you must make sure that the fitness tests that you select are suitable for the client and meet their needs, taking into account their age and fitness levels. You must also ensure the client uses the correct technique throughout the fitness test in order to prevent injury.

> **Safety tip**
>
> Remember, if you are unsure whether a client can safely complete a selected fitness test, do not conduct the test.

Remember that:

▶ you need to be very familiar with the test methods
▶ good planning will improve your confidence
▶ you will need to use published data tables to interpret results and give feedback to the individual
▶ practising test procedures and protocols will give you more experience in how to interpret results obtained. Results should be interpreted in a valid, effective and appropriate manner.

Pre-test checks

Pre-test checks are used to make sure that fitness tests are accurate and reliable, and that your client is safely able to complete the chosen tests. Before conducting any test, you must make sure all equipment is clean and ready to use, and that the testing area (including the floor or work surface where the tests will take place) is free of hazards. For example, the floor must be clear of obstructions and dry, so your client cannot trip or slip. If you are conducting tests outside, you must check the ground for litter or uneven surfaces and consider the weather and temperature, which could affect your client's ability to complete a given fitness test.

You must also make sure your client has completed all screening documentation accurately and filled in a PAR-Q form (see pages 77–79), so you know that they are physically fit to complete the chosen tests. Finally, you should ensure your client understands the purpose and procedures of the tests they are about to complete and ask them to sign an informed consent form (see pages 248–249).

Assessment practice 5.2   B.P3 B.P4 B.P5 B.M2 B.M3 B.M4 AB.D1

Now that the coaches of the football club have an understanding of fitness testing, they want you to identify and safely administer six valid tests that measure relevant components of fitness for football. For each test you must accurately record the results and interpret them against normative data.

Points to consider are outlined below.

- Ensure that the tests you select are valid for the chosen sport.
- Assess the practicality and suitability of each test.
- Suggest areas for improvement in the administration process of each test.

Once you have completed the tests, reflect on your own performance. Write a short summary analysing your own administration of the fitness tests and suggesting improvements, explaining why you have made these suggestions.

Plan

- Can I identify the specific components of fitness for a football player? What tests will be valid?
- What equipment do I need? Do I have the correct paperwork to record the results?
- How do I organise the fitness testing sessions? Where and when will these take place?

Do

- Am I confident in administering the fitness tests?
- Do I know how to record the results and can I interpret these against normative data?
- Have I taken into account any factors that may affect the results?

Review

- Can I explain what the task was and how I approached it?
- Have I reviewed how I administered the tests and what I could do to improve next time?

 C Undertake evaluation and feedback of fitness test results

Producing a fitness profile for a selected sports performer

After you have completed the fitness testing session, your client or subject will want to know their levels of fitness either compared to normative data or against previous results. Therefore you must prepare a summary report that highlights the results in a clear and simple fashion with a short explanation of the result meanings and your recommendations.

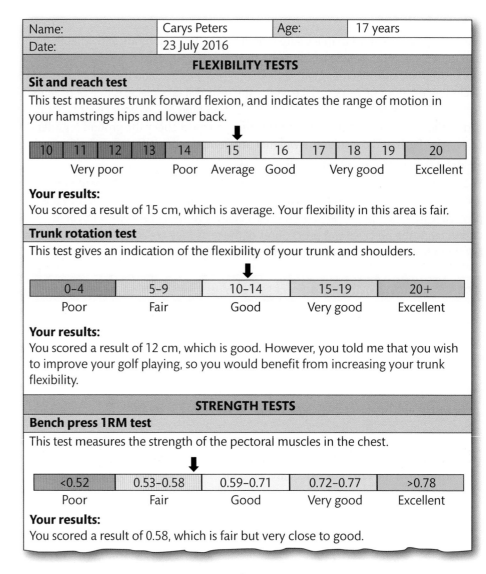

Name:	Carys Peters	Age:	17 years
Date:	23 July 2016		

FLEXIBILITY TESTS

Sit and reach test

This test measures trunk forward flexion, and indicates the range of motion in your hamstrings hips and lower back.

10	11	12	13	14	15	16	17	18	19	20
Very poor					Poor	Average	Good		Very good	Excellent

Your results:
You scored a result of 15 cm, which is average. Your flexibility in this area is fair.

Trunk rotation test

This test gives an indication of the flexibility of your trunk and shoulders.

0–4	5–9	10–14	15–19	20+
Poor	Fair	Good	Very good	Excellent

Your results:
You scored a result of 12 cm, which is good. However, you told me that you wish to improve your golf playing, so you would benefit from increasing your trunk flexibility.

STRENGTH TESTS

Bench press 1RM test

This test measures the strength of the pectoral muscles in the chest.

<0.52	0.53–0.58	0.59–0.71	0.72–0.77	>0.78
Poor	Fair	Good	Very good	Excellent

Your results:
You scored a result of 0.58, which is fair but very close to good.

▶ **Figure 5.8:** An example of a fitness profile

Interpret results against normative data

Once the fitness tests are over, you need to interpret the results against normative data. The data interpretation tables presented earlier in this unit can be used to help you do this. You can also use published data interpretation tables to compare your data against data for sports performers and elite athletes.

Your choice in selection of data tables for interpretation of fitness test results will depend on your selected individual, their needs and their personal goals. However, most individuals will be interested to know how they compare against normative data (population norms) including their peers. Using the recorded data will also allow you to compare against published data for acceptable health ranges.

Suitability of fitness test selection

Another key post-test task is to assess the suitability of the fitness tests chosen. You must make sure that the tests that you have selected are appropriate to the needs of the selected sports performer and that you have only measured the relevant components of fitness. For example, it would be important to measure the aerobic endurance of a rower but less important to measure their agility.

Providing feedback to a selected sports performer

Method of feedback

Having administered a number of different fitness tests for a subject, you need to provide feedback to the individual regarding their test results, discussing what they mean and giving your recommendations for future activities or training. Your feedback may be given verbally to the individual, supported by a written copy of their data results and interpretation of their levels of fitness against normative data.

Discussion

To help with feedback it is useful to practise with a friend. Adopt the role of a fitness instructor and conduct the fitness assessment that would be expected in a real-life vocational context. Once you have collected the results, prepare and give feedback.

1   Consider what your strengths are when giving feedback.

2   Now discuss with your friend any areas that you need to develop further when giving feedback.

Test results

The test results will be the key point of your feedback, as your subject will want to know how they have done. In your feedback, recap the tests carried out and why these particular tests were appropriate for the individual. Discuss in detail their data results and what these mean in terms of their fitness levels. Make sure the results are laid out in a way that is easy for the subject to read.

Levels of fitness

The key to fitness testing is being able to measure the components of fitness and being able to interpret the results, making a judgement on the subject's level of fitness. Therefore you should use the collected results and compare this to normative data and indicate how the subject's level of fitness compares. Remember that the subject may have different levels of fitness depending on the components measured.

Strengths and areas for improvement

Once you have outlined the test results and stated the subject's existing levels of fitness, your feedback can go on to discuss their strengths, areas for improvement and your recommendations for appropriate future activities or training. You should give the individual the opportunity to ask questions about your statements or views, and be prepared to justify your reasoning for each component of fitness that you tested.

⏸ PAUSE POINT   Do you understand how to give feedback following a fitness testing session?

> **Hint**   What information should you give the subject? How do you know whether the results are above or below average?

> **Extend**   How can you use normative data to help you interpret the results? How will you give your feedback? What sort of questions might you be asked?

Having successfully completed a range of valid fitness tests for the college football team, you are required to meet with each player to give feedback. As part of this one-to-one meeting you must prepare a short summary report for the player that will include a copy of their results and explain what the results mean and how they will impact on sporting performances.

Your summary report and verbal feedback should assess the strengths and areas for improvement from the results.

Finally you should explain and justify the fitness profile recommendations you have made and further evaluate the effectiveness of the methods used to test the components of fitness.

Plan

- How confident do I feel in my own abilities to give verbal and written feedback? Are there any areas I think I may struggle with?
- Have I prepared a well organised and professional looking summary report for the player and coach?
- Have I organised a time and suitable location where I will meet with the player to give feedback?

Do

- Do I know what it is I am doing and what I want to achieve?
- Am I confident in giving feedback?
- Do I know how to interpret these results against normative data and assess the strengths and areas for improvement?
- For the areas for improvement, can I make recommendations?
- Can I explain and justify why I have made these recommendations?

Review

- Can I explain what the task was and how I approached it?
- Can I explain how I would approach the hard elements differently next time?
- Have I reviewed how I selected, administered and gave feedback for the six fitness tests? What would I do to improve next time?

Further reading and resources

Books

Archer, D. and Coulson, M. (2015) *Practical Fitness Testing: Analysis in Exercise and Sport* (Fitness Professionals), London: Bloomsbury.

Morrow et al. (2010) *Measurement and Evaluation in Human Performance* (fourth edition), Champaign, IL: Human Kinetics.

Websites

www.brianmac.co.uk/ – Brian Mac Sports coach: a wide range of information related to fitness and training.

www.pponline.co.uk – Peak Performance: free advisory newsletter that discusses strength and fitness.

www.topendsports.com – Top End Sports: a range of fitness tests and normative data.

THINK ▶▶FUTURE

Freddie Vosper
Fitness Coach

Freddie works in a private health and fitness centre. He is responsible for instructing clients in the gym, undertaking health screening and client fitness assessments, and designing personal fitness programmes.

Consultations begin with a comprehensive screening process where the client completes questionnaires covering their medical and physical history. Freddie then carries out health monitoring tests like blood pressure and lung function and gives the client feedback on their results and the implications for future health.

'I then do a range of fitness tests depending on the goals of the client and the different components of fitness to be tested. After giving feedback on their test results and agreeing their training goals, I design a personal programme and closely monitor their progress throughout. Every six weeks or so, a client will book in with me for a reassessment of their health and fitness.

'For this job you need good communication skills and must be able to motivate people, develop a rapport and lead by example. I find the job very rewarding. Providing good education helps people to recognise where they may need lifestyle improvement and my role is to help clients to implement positive lifestyle changes.'

Focusing your skills

Preparing and conducting fitness tests

With fitness testing it is important that you understand what the main components of fitness are, the tests used to measure each of them, the equipment needed, how to undertake each of these tests and what the results mean. Here are some key tips to help you.

- Carefully consider the sport or exercise and the key components of fitness required to be successful in these.
- List the main components of fitness and select a test that can measure these.
- Consider what equipment you will need. Is this expensive or is it readily available?

- Is the equipment available and is it in good condition? Has it been checked, calibrated and serviced?
- Practise a wide range of tests on a friend so that you are confident in how to conduct a test.
- Prepare record sheets and normative data tables so that you can record results and interpret results easily.
- Practise giving feedback.
- Ensure that you are able to interpret results and give these in a clear and professional manner. Prepare a short written report for each subject and discuss the results and your recommendations in detail.

Getting ready for assessment

Joanna is working towards a BTEC National Extended Diploma in Sport and Physical Activity Development. She was given an assignment with the following title: 'Conducting a range of fitness tests on a Sports Performer' for Learning aim B. The assessment included:

▸ selecting and administering six valid fitness tests
▸ interpreting the fitness test results against normative data.

How I got started

First I collected all my notes on this topic and put them into a folder. I decided to divide my work into three parts: the principles of fitness testing, the components of fitness and the tests used to measure these, and the evaluation and feedback of fitness tests.

I researched the main components of fitness and used these to identify which ones are important in a variety of different sports. I then researched the fitness tests that measure each of these components, paying particular attention to the practicality of each test and equipment required to undertake the tests.

Having identified the components of fitness and the tests that I would be using, I set about practising how to conduct these tests. I used a range of people to help me practise the administration of the tests and asked for their feedback on how I had performed.

Once I had completed the tests I looked at the results and interpreted what they meant. I practised my calculations and then prepared a sheet of normative data which helped me with the analysis.

How I brought it all together

When I felt confident in how to administer fitness tests I identified a suitable athlete to conduct the test on. I used a prepared data collection form to record the results and once I had completed the tests I recorded the information in a summary report. I made sure the summary report explained the purpose of each test as well as what the results meant compared to normative data.

I then made my suggestions and recommendations. I paid particular attention to how the report looked and tried to ensure that it was easy to read and that it looked professional, checking for spelling errors.

What I learned from the experience

I really enjoyed the experience, although I realised that being able to administer fitness tests takes a lot of practice. The experience also made me realise that different sports require different components of fitness, and now I am confident in identifying these.

Think about it

▸ Have you written a plan that includes the key terms and allows enough time for you to meet the agreed submission date?

▸ Have you practised your fitness testing techniques and are you able to select the appropriate test for each component of fitness?

▸ Have you written your report in your own words and have you given clear recommendations? Are you able to justify any recommendations that you have made?

Sports Psychology 6

...ur unit

...rts psychology is increasingly prominent in today's sport. Often, the ...factor in successful sport performance and finding sport enjoyable ...individual's psychological qualities. Having an understanding of ...ifferent psychological factors that can affect sports participation ...erformance, as well as how to develop these qualities, is important ...ose working in the sports industry, such as athletes, teachers, and ...es.

How you will be assessed

This unit will be assessed internally by a series of tasks set by your tutor. There will also be opportunities for formative assessment where you will be able to receive feedback on your progress, strengths and areas for improvement.

The assignments set by your tutor may be a:
▶ written report on psychological skills training programmes
▶ presentation.

The activities within this unit are designed to help you gain knowledge, understanding and skills that will help you complete your assignments. Your understanding of sport psychology will be gained through understanding key theories and their application in different sporting contexts. You can develop your understanding by applying the model of asking:
▶ what?
▶ how?
▶ where is the evidence?
▶ what is the theory?
▶ how does it apply?
▶ where are the examples to support your ideas?

To pass this unit you must ensure that you have provided sufficient evidence to cover all of the Pass assessment criteria. You can see these listed in the table on the next page.

If you are seeking a Merit or Distinction grade then you must be able to show an understanding of different psychological skills and analyse the effects of personality, group dynamics and psychological skills training on sports performance.

Assessment criteria

This table shows what you must do in order to achieve a **Pass**, **Merit** or **Distinction** grade, and where you can find activities to help you.

Pass	Merit	Distinction

Learning aim **A** Understand how personality, motivation and competitive pressure can affect sport performance

A.P1

Describe how personality and motivational factors may impact on sports performance.
Assessment practice 6.1

A.P2

Describe how differing levels of arousal, anxiety and self-confidence can affect sports performance.
Assessment practice 6.1

A.M1

Explain how personality and motivational factors may impact on sports performance.
Assessment practice 6.1

A.M2

Explain how control of arousal, anxiety and stress and self-confidence can impact on sports performance.
Assessment practice 6.1

A.D1

Analyse the relationship between motivational factors, anxiety and stress and self-confidence and their impact on sports performance.
Assessment practice 6.1

Learning aim **B** Examine the impact of group dynamics in team sports and its effect on performance

B.P3

Describe how group cohesion and leadership contribute to the development of a successful sports team.
Assessment practice 6.2

B.P4

Produce sociograms showing relationships between members of a sports group.
Assessment practice 6.2

B.M3

Explain sociogram results and how they can be used to improve group cohesion and leadership potential in sport.
Assessment practice 6.2

B.D2

Analyse how group cohesion and leadership can contribute to success of a sports team.
Assessment practice 6.2

Learning aim **C** Explore psychological skills training programmes designed to improve performance

C.P5

Describe different psychological skills that could be used to improve performance.
Assessment practice 6.3

C.P6

Design a psychological skills training programme to improve performance.
Assessment practice 6.3

C.M4

Explain the design of your psychological skills training programme, making comparisons between your design and others.
Assessment practice 6.3

C.D3

Evaluate the design of your psychological skills training programme, suggesting and justifying alternative techniques that could be used to improve performance.
Assessment practice 6.3

Getting started

At Super Bowl 50 in 2016, the Denver Broncos beat the Carolina Panthers 24–10. American football is a sport that presents players with physical, psychological and emotional challenges constantly throughout a game and over the course of a season. Alongside this, the Super Bowl is one of the largest sporting spectator events in the world. Produce a mind map of all the different ways that you think sport psychology could help an American football player to prepare for a Super Bowl game.

A Understand how personality, motivation and competitive pressure can affect sport performance

Link

This content links to *Unit 4: Sports Leadership* and *Unit 8: Coaching for Performance*.

Key terms

Personality – the sum of characteristics that make a person unique.

Personality traits – the relatively stable or consistent characteristics that make up an individual's personality.

Arousal – a state of alertness and anticipation that prepares the body for action.

Gross motor movements – sporting movements that involve coordination of large body segments, such as the arms and legs.

Personality factors and assessment of personality

The role of personality in sport participation and performance is one of the oldest aspects of sport psychology. While people still debate the role of personality factors in sporting success, there are three schools of thought that consider the role of personality. These are the trait centred approach, the situational or social learning theory approach, and the interactional approach.

Personality traits

The earliest approach to understanding the role of **personality** in sport was to examine people's **personality traits**. Early trait theorists like Eysenck and Cattell argued that traits are mainly inherited and are relatively stable aspects of personality. There are two main dimensions to personality:

▶ an introversion–extroversion dimension

▶ a stable–neurotic dimension.

Introverts are individuals who do not actively seek excitement and would rather be in calm environments. This is because introverts can have higher than natural levels of **arousal** so do not need a great deal of additional excitement or stimulus to function well. They tend to prefer tasks that require concentration and dislike the unexpected. These factors partly explain why introverts tend to be drawn to sports where there is continuous, repetitive activity (e.g. marathon running) or activities that require quiet concentration (e.g. archery).

Extroverts tend to be more naturally under-aroused, so can become bored quickly, are poor at tasks that require a lot of concentration and constantly seek change and excitement. This constant change, particularly when they interact with others, gives extroverts higher levels of stimulation. This helps them to maintain optimal levels of brain functioning and, as a result, concentration and performance. Extroverts also tend to prefer sports that involve lots of **gross motor movements**. Collectively, these factors can explain why extroverts are often drawn to high-energy team sports, such as football and rugby.

Stable individuals can be more easy-going and even-tempered. **Neurotic** (unstable) people can be restless and excitable, with a tendency to become anxious and more highly aroused.

Often, people will conclude that trait views are too simplistic and that personality alone cannot predict success in a sporting environment. It can, however, be used to help explain why individuals choose certain sports.

Situational or social learning theory

The situational approach says that behaviour is largely dependent on your situation or environment, rather than character traits. There is some support for the situational approach in explaining sporting behaviour. Individuals displaying characteristics such as tolerance and shyness may participate in a sport that requires them to be extroverted.

Social learning theory suggests that personality is not a stable characteristic, but constantly changing as a result of experiences in different social situations. The theory states that individuals learn in sporting situations through two processes: modelling and social reinforcement. **Modelling** occurs when individuals try to emulate the behaviour of athletes that they can relate to. **Social reinforcement** is important because, if an individual's behaviour is reinforced or rewarded, it is likely that the same behaviour will be repeated.

Bandura, a leading psychologist, identified four main stages of observational learning that demonstrate how modelling influences personality and behaviour.

1 **Attention** – you are more likely to learn through observation if you have respect and admiration for the model you are observing. The amount of respect depends on the model's status. If the model is successful and dominant, they are more likely to hold your attention.

2 **Retention** – for modelling to be effective, you must retain the observed skill or behaviour in your memory, so you can recall it when needed.

3 **Motor reproduction** – you must be able to physically perform the task you are observing. You need time to practise the skill and learn how to perform it.

4 **Motivational response** – unless you are motivated, you will not experience the first three stages of modelling. Motivation is dependent on reinforcement (for example praise, feedback, sense of pride or achievement), the perceived status of the model, and task importance.

> **Discussion**
>
> Do you think that there are any differences in the personality types of athletes and non-athletes? Do the personality types of elite and non-elite athletes differ? Consider athletes who take part in individual sports or those who play in teams.

Interactional theory

The interactional theory says that you must consider how the situation and personality traits link and work together. Some people argue that situational factors and personality traits are equally important in determining behaviours. Others suggest that when situational factors are strong, such as during competitive sporting situations like penalty shoot-outs in football, they are more likely to predict behaviour than personality traits. The athlete who is quiet and shy in an everyday situation may run screaming towards an ecstatic crowd if they scored the winning penalty.

 **PAUSE POINT** Do you understand the different theories of personality? Can you explain the differences between them?

 Hint Produce a table that summarises the key features of the theories of personality.

Extend Which theory do you think best explains the role of personality in sports participation and performance, and why?

Assessment of personality

There are a number of personality tests that you can use with athletes. Generally, you should not use personality tests as part of team selection or to try to predict how athletes might behave in sporting situations.

Two methods of assessing personality are Eysenck's Personality Inventory and Cattell's 16 Personality Factors (16PF). While some argue that Cattell's 16PF offers a more comprehensive view of personality, the validity and reliability of personality testing is questionable as the results are affected by many different factors. These range from how the athlete thinks the test results may be used (to select or de-select them), to changes in mood, or other stresses the athlete is experiencing. Given the criticisms and the acceptance that there is no such thing as an athletic personality, there is little rationale for using these tests in sporting settings. Most sports psychologists prefer to use sport-specific measures of individual personality traits when working with athletes to provide more detailed and appropriate information.

Type A and Type B personalities

In the 1950s, two cardiologists, Friedman and Rosenham, suggested that there were two basic personality types among their patients, based on levels of anxiety and stress.

▸ **Type A personalities** lack patience, have a strong urge for competition, a high desire to achieve goals, rush to complete activities, will happily multi-task when under time constraints, lack tolerance towards others and experience higher levels of anxiety.

▸ **Type B personalities** are more tolerant towards others, more relaxed and reflective than their type A counterparts, experience lower levels of anxiety and display higher levels of imagination and creativity.

These categorisations can be used in sports psychology to predict how people might behave in particular situations.

Research

Research the 'big five' personality traits. What are they and how do you think they could affect sports participation and performance?

Motivational factors

Motivation is one of the most important qualities for any athlete. If your levels of motivation are too high, you may run the risk of injury; too low a level of motivation and you may not be able to rise to the sporting challenge.

Commonly, motivation is defined as the direction and intensity of your effort, so what you are motivated towards as well as how motivated you are. Other common definitions of motivation consider the effects of internal and external factors, which arouse and direct behaviour. There are two main types of motivation: **intrinsic motivation** and **extrinsic motivation**.

Intrinsic motivation

Intrinsic motivation refers to someone participating in an activity without an external reward and/or without the primary motivation being the achievement of an external reward. This is motivation that 'comes from within'. Fun is the most common form of intrinsic motivation, but intrinsic motivation can also be affected by:

▸ **accomplishment** – when athletes wish to increase their level of skill to get a sense of accomplishment

▸ **stimulation** – seeking an 'adrenaline rush' or some form of excitement

▸ **knowledge** – being curious about performance; wanting to know more about it and to develop new techniques or skills that benefit performance.

Extrinsic motivation

Extrinsic motivation is when someone's behaviour is influenced by an external factor. Common forms of extrinsic motivation are tangible and intangible rewards. **Tangible rewards** are physical rewards, like money and medals, whereas **intangible rewards** are non-physical rewards such as praise or encouragement.

For extrinsic motivation to be effective, rewards must be effective. If a reward is given too frequently, it will be of less value to the athlete, and may lose its impact on performance. Equally, if an athlete starts to place too much emphasis on the reward and it is then removed, their motivation levels could decrease. A coach needs to have an in-depth knowledge of their athletes to maximise the effectiveness of extrinsic rewards.

⏸ PAUSE POINT Can you understand how to contrast and link intrinsic and extrinsic motivation?

Hint Produce a table that provides examples of intrinsic and extrinsic motivation.

Extend How do you think that intrinsic and extrinsic motivation can interact to influence sport performance, both positively and negatively?

Achievement motivation

Athletes may be grouped into two categories: those who need to achieve (Nach) and those who need to avoid failure (Naf). Nach athletes strive for success, keep trying when things go wrong, and feel a sense of pride in their accomplishments. There is less focus on comparing skill, ability or performance against other athletes. They place greater emphasis on setting realistic and challenging personal goals.

Athletes who are high achievers typically set themselves challenging goals, prefer competition against worthy opponents and perform well when being evaluated. Naf athletes avoid these types of scenarios. For example, an athlete with low achievement motivation is likely to prefer playing against a poor opponent so they are virtually guaranteed success, or against an opponent who is so good that they are guaranteed to fail. Everyone has aspects of both Nach and Naf, but the balance of the two motives determines a person's achievement motivation.

⏸ PAUSE POINT Can you explain achievement motivation?

Hint Produce a table of key characteristics of high and low achievement motivation athletes.

Extend Why does playing against opponents where they are virtually guaranteed to lose present a low level of perceived risk for low achievement motivation athletes?

The effect of the environment on motivation

Think about when you arrive at a sports venue. Usually you will prefer it to be clean and tidy and to have working equipment. There is evidence to suggest that the quality of facilities and equipment in sporting environments can affect motivation. Having a clean, welcoming and well-equipped environment can enhance athlete motivation. This may be more important for younger, developing athletes than senior athletes, and the equipment that is provided is likely to be affected by the level at which you perform (i.e. elite athletes are more likely to be provided with state-of-the-art equipment). However, there is also **anecdotal evidence** that suggests some athletes prefer plain environments with minimal equipment (e.g. using ropes and tyres for strength and conditioning) in order to be motivated to train.

Key term

Anecdotal evidence – evidence drawn from people's experiences rather than formal research.

263

The influence of the coach, teacher or instructor on motivation

Coaches, teachers and instructors can have a significant effect on motivation as they play a key role in creating the motivational climate. Often, a mastery-orientated climate is preferred, particularly when working with young athletes in talent development environments.

Mastery climate

A mastery climate (sometimes called a **task-orientated climate**) is a motivational climate that focuses on the mastery of tasks (i.e. where athletes receive positive reinforcement and there is greater emphasis on teamwork, cooperation and mutual support). It helps to develop motivation through improving the athlete's attitudes, effort and learning techniques.

There are many benefits to mastery-orientated climates, including increased intrinsic motivation, increased information processing, decreased stress and anxiety, and an increase in overall psychological well-being. Collectively, these factors are likely to enhance performance.

To develop an effective motivational climate, use the TARGET technique.

- ▸ **Tasks** – having a range of tasks that require the athlete to participate in learning and decision-making.
- ▸ **Authority** – giving athletes control over monitoring and evaluating their own learning and decision-making.
- ▸ **Reward** – using rewards that focus on individual improvement rather than comparing levels to other athletes.
- ▸ **Grouping** – giving athletes the opportunity to work in groups so that they develop skills in a group-based environment.
- ▸ **Evaluation** – focusing on an individual's effort and improvement.
- ▸ **Timing** – timing activities effectively so that all of the above conditions can interact successfully.

Competitive climate

Often an athlete is in an environment where there is a lot of focus on the outcome. They might feel they will be punished if they make mistakes, competition may be strongly encouraged, or they may think that only those with the highest ability will receive attention. This is a competitive climate, or an **outcome-orientated climate**. In this environment, athletes with the highest ability will receive most attention, and competition between team members is encouraged. This often leads to less effort and persistence from athletes, and failure attributed to lack of ability.

Attribution theory

In sport, attribution theory looks at how people explain success or failure. Attributions provide explanations for successes or failures and fall into one of the following categories:

- ▸ **stability** – is the reason permanent or unstable?
- ▸ **causality** – is the reason something that comes from an external or internal factor?
- ▸ **control** – is the reason under your control or not?

Table 6.1 provides examples of different attributions. Knowing these is useful, as they can help you to understand key factors such as the motivation behind specific behaviour and the expectations of future success and failure. For example, a young boxer attributing their points victory to stable, internal and controllable factors is more likely to feel confident and motivated to carry on with the sport because they think they will win again.

> **Theory into practice**
>
> Mark is a competitive power lifter. He trains hard because he wants to improve his personal best and sees himself as his major competition. In training, he always sets challenging goals that relate to self-improvement. This is an example of a mastery or task-orientated climate. However, in competitions, Mark always focuses on beating his opponents. He needs everybody else to know he is the best. When he does not win, his training regime sometimes slows and he tells himself that he is not good enough. This is an example of a competitive or outcome-orientated climate.

▶ **Table 6.1** Types of attribution with examples from boxing

Type of attribution	Winning example	Losing example
Stability	• 'I was more able than my opponent' (stable) • 'I was lucky' (unstable)	• 'I was less able than my opponent' (stable) • 'We didn't have that bit of luck we needed today' (unstable)
Causality	• 'I tried really hard' (internal) • 'My opponent was easy to beat' (external)	• 'I didn't try hard enough' (internal) • 'My opponent was impossible to beat' (external)
Control	• 'I trained really hard for this fight' (under your control) • 'He wasn't as fit as I was' (not under your control)	• 'I didn't train hard enough for this fight' (under your control) • 'He was fitter than I was' (not under your control)

Reflect

Think about the last time you won and the last time you lost in sport. What reasons did you give to explain the events? How would you define the types of attribution?

Research

Research 'need achievement theory', 'achievement goal theory' and 'competence motivation theory'. How do they help us to understand more about achievement motivation?

Arousal–performance relationship theories

Arousal is a state of alertness and anticipation that prepares the body for action. It involves both physiological activation (increased heart rate, sweating rate or respiratory rate) and psychological activity (increased attention). Arousal is measured along a continuum, with deep sleep at one extreme and excitement at the other. Individuals who are optimally aroused are mentally and physically activated to perform. A number of theories have tried to explain the arousal–performance relationship; these theories are the drive theory, the inverted U hypothesis, the catastrophe theory, and individual zones of optimal functioning (IZOF).

Drive theory

The drive theory views the arousal-performance relationship as linear. This means that as arousal increases, so does performance. The more 'learned' a skill is, the more likely it is that a high level of arousal will result in a better performance (see Figure 6.1). However, there is little research to support this theory, as there is evidence to suggest that arousal benefits athletic performance only up to a certain point.

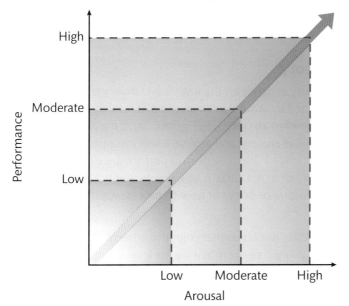

▶ **Figure 6.1:** According to the drive theory, what is the arousal–performance relationship?

Inverted-U hypothesis

The inverted-U hypothesis was born out of the limitations of the drive theory. It states that at optimal arousal levels (usually a moderate level of arousal), performance levels will be at their highest, but when arousal is too low or too high, performance levels decrease (see Figure 6.2). It argues that performance levels will be lower because the athlete is neither physiologically nor psychologically ready; heart rate and concentration levels may be too low or too high. The final key argument from this theory is that the performance decrease after the optimal level of arousal will be gradual.

The inverted-U hypothesis is more widely accepted than the drive theory because most athletes and coaches can report personal experiences of under-arousal (boredom), over-arousal (excitement to the point of lack of concentration) and optimum arousal (focusing on nothing but sport performance). However, there are questions surrounding the type of curve demonstrated. These questions include:

▶ Is optimal arousal always a single point or do some athletes experience optimal arousal for a longer period of time?

▶ Is the decrease in performance always a steady decline or can it be more dramatic?

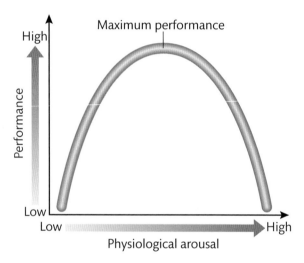

▶ **Figure 6.2:** According to the inverted-U theory, what is the arousal–performance relationship?

Catastrophe theory

The catastrophe theory expands on the inverted-U theory by suggesting that performance is affected by arousal in an inverted-U fashion only when the individual has low levels of **cognitive anxiety** (see Figure 6.3a). If the athlete is experiencing higher levels of cognitive anxiety, and arousal levels increase beyond the athlete's threshold, they experience a dramatic drop in performance levels (see Figure 6.3b). The key difference between the catastrophe theory and the inverted-U hypothesis is that the drop in performance does not have to be a steady decline when arousal levels become too high.

Catastrophe theory does not argue that cognitive anxiety is completely negative. The theory suggests you will perform at a higher level if you have a degree of cognitive anxiety because your attention and concentration levels increase. However, when levels of cognitive anxiety combine with hyper-elevated levels of arousal, performance levels decrease dramatically. This theory is questioned by some over claims that everybody's optimal arousal is at the same single, moderate point.

Key term

Cognitive anxiety – negative thoughts, nervousness or worry experienced in certain situations. Symptoms of cognitive anxiety include concentration problems, fear and bad decision-making.

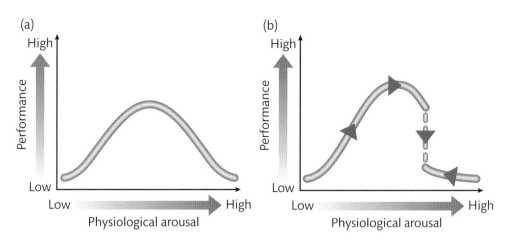

▶ **Figure 6.3:** According to the catastrophe theory, what is the arousal–performance relationship?

Individual zones of optimal functioning (IZOF)

This theory expands on the previous theories by arguing that each person (i.e. individuals with different personalities, participating in different sports) has a different optimal level of arousal and can remain in that zone of arousal for a period of time (see Figure 6.4). This means that athletes can perform at a higher level of performance for a longer period of time. The main differences between the inverted-U hypothesis and IZOF are:

▶ where the inverted-U hypothesis sees arousal at an optimal point, IZOF sees optimal arousal as a bandwidth

▶ where the inverted-U hypothesis sees every athlete's optimal point at a mid-point on the curve, IZOF says the optimal point varies from person to person.

IZOF and the inverted U hypothesis are similar in that they both propose that after the optimal point of arousal, performance decreases gradually.

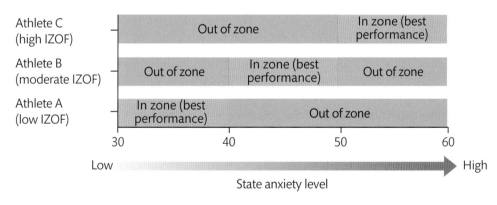

▶ **Figure 6.4:** According to the IZOF theory, what is the arousal–performance relationship?

Discussion

In a small group, discuss the different theories that try to explain the arousal–performance relationship, and suggest sporting examples that explain each theory.

Ⅱ PAUSE POINT   Can you explain the arousal–performance theories?

Hint   Using only the diagram of each theory, explain to a friend how each theory tries to explain the arousal–performance relationship.

Extend   Considering their strengths and limitations, which theory do you think best explains the arousal–performance relationship?

Attentional focus and sports performance under competitive pressure

The World Cup Final. The Olympic 100m final. Your first game for a new team. Your first game back after a lengthy injury. These are all examples of scenarios where you might feel a great deal of pressure. A key challenge for sport psychologists is to help athletes to maintain and enhance attentional focus under pressure.

Attentional cues

Athletes receive many attentional cues when performing. Some of these are relevant attentional cues whereas others are irrelevant attentional cues. Relevant attentional cues are factors that can directly affect performance (e.g. position of teammates, position of opposition and flight of a ball). Irrelevant attentional cues are factors that can distract you from your overall performance (e.g. crowd noise, insults from opposition).

Two important aspects of attention relate to attentional cues. Think about when you have played sport and there have been lots of things going on around you. Sometimes, you need to focus on one specific, relevant cue and block out the irrelevant cues. This is called **selective attention**. An example of this is a basketball player waiting to take a free throw: they have to focus on the relevant cue of the basket while blocking out irrelevant cues, such as crowd distractions and gamesmanship from opponents.

At other times, you will need to focus on lots of relevant cues and complete more than one task at a time. This is like mental multi-tasking and is known as **divided attention**. An example is Lionel Messi dribbling a football. He has to maintain control of the ball and will usually have lots of relevant cues to focus on (e.g. how many opponents are trying to tackle him, what their positions are in relation to his, where his teammates are, etc.), so he will need to keep his head up and look around to see what his options are.

Elite athletes are able to use selective attention and divided attention well, depending on each situation.

Types of attentional focus

You can view attentional focus in two dimensions: a width dimension (broad–narrow) and a direction dimension (external–internal).

- A **broad attentional focus** allows you to take in and interpret lots of information from lots of different sources to make your decisions in sport. This is important for athletes like a centre in netball, a centre midfielder in football or a point guard in basketball who have to take in information from lots of relevant cues in order to make a decision about which play to make next.

- A **narrow attentional focus** occurs when you only have one or two pieces of information to take in to be able to make your next play. For example, a golfer going to putt for the win at the Open will need to consider the distance from the pin and the ground patterns.

- An **external attentional focus** directs your attention to an external relevant cue, such as a cricket batsman judging the flight of a ball or a quarterback in American football noticing the run of their wide receiver.

- An **internal attentional focus** is directed inwards towards your own thoughts and feelings, for example a long jumper mentally rehearsing their performance in order to relax before an event.

Key terms

Selective attention – focusing on relevant cues that can aid performance.

Divided attention – performing two or more tasks concurrently while focusing attention on lots of relevant cues.

Shifting attentional focus

Being able to shift attentional focus is an important quality for elite athletes. In high-pressure situations, the ability to make decisions quickly and effectively is one of the differences between successful and unsuccessful athletes. For example, when rugby players get into fights or football players commit serious foul play, they will often report 'seeing red'. This is a form of anger and aggression that results from players placing too much focus on irrelevant attentional cues and not being able to shift attentional focus. When a football player commits a serious foul, they may have been paying more attention to something that happened previously in the match that they can no longer change. This, together with a narrow external focus (focusing all of their attention on one opponent that they want to foul), means that they cannot shift to a narrow internal focus (focusing their attention on their internal thoughts and feelings to calm themselves down).

> **Reflect**
>
> Think about a time when you played sport and things did not go well. Think about the critical incidents in the game that you were involved in (e.g. a missed tackle, a missed scoring opportunity). What type of attentional focus did you use? Was it the one you should have used?

Attentional strategies

Attentional strategies in sport fall under two broad headings: associative and dissociative. **Associative strategies** focus your attention on internal sensations in order to identify and control things that can affect performance, such as muscle tension and breathing. **Dissociative strategies** focus your attention externally in order to distract yourself from sensations of fatigue or pain: for example, admiring the view while running a marathon.

Causes of attentional problems

When you think about playing sport, consider the different things that distract your attentional focus. These distractors fall under two broad headings of **internal** and **external distractors**.

▸ **Internal distractors** are your thoughts (e.g. remembering mistakes that you made in previous sports events), feelings (e.g. worrying about previous performances) and psychophysiological sensations (e.g. fatigue) that can distract your attention from performance.

▸ **External distractors** come from the environment you are performing in. Environmental distractors vary from sport to sport, so something that might distract an athlete in one sport may not have such an effect in another. For example, a ringing phone when a golfer is about to attempt a difficult putt would be a big external distractor for them. However, a phone ringing during a football match with 50,000 fans in attendance would not significantly distract the football players. The most common external distractors in sport include gamesmanship, sudden changes in noise levels, spectator movements, bad weather conditions and fans creating a hostile environment.

> **Research**
>
> Research the typical home-crowd behaviour at Galatasaray Football Club in Turkey. What types of behaviour do fans display? What type of distractor is this? If you were the coach of a visiting team, how would you try to prepare your players?

Choking

In sporting terms, choking is an extreme form of nervousness that causes athletes to fail to perform or to make mistakes at a crucial time, such as when a golfer misses an easy putt that is required to win the Open. Choking can occur in high-pressure situations and is largely based on the subjective importance of the event (i.e. what the event means to the individual athlete). Choking can be more apparent in the presence of significant others (e.g. parents, peers) or large audiences and can occur as a result of changes in attentional focus.

Effect of different arousal levels on attentional focus

During heightened states of arousal the attentional field, which focuses attention and concentration, can narrow. This means that the more aroused you become, the lower the number of relevant cues you can concentrate on. For example, in a game of basketball, when at an optimal state of arousal, the point guard will be able to focus on the opposing player in possession of the ball as well as her position on the court and the position of other players. However, during heightened states of arousal, she may only be able to focus on the opposition player who has the ball and may disregard other cues.

Just as a heightened state of arousal can narrow the player's attention, it can also broaden it to the point where it decreases performance. In this scenario, the point guard player would concentrate on irrelevant information like crowd noise, as well as the relevant game cues.

Case study

Fara's World Cup penalty

In the 2015 FIFA Women's World Cup, Fara Williams scored a penalty in the third-place playoff against Germany to give England their first win over Germany in a competitive fixture in over 30 years (and after 20 fixtures). The penalty occurred in the 108th minute of the game (in the second half of extra-time) with the score at 0–0. This fixture came after the England women's team had lost the World Cup semi-final 2–1 to Japan. Fara was England's women's most capped player.

Using your knowledge of attentional focus and sports performance under competitive pressure, answer the following questions.

1   What will have been the different attentional cues?

2   What type(s) of attentional focus will Fara have used while preparing for and executing the penalty kick?

3   What do you think Fara's attentional strategies will have been?

▶ Fara Williams taking a penalty in the 2015 FIFA Women's World Cup

Stress, anxiety and sports performance under competitive pressure

Stress and types of stress

Stress is a mental or emotional response of the body to any demand made on it. Stress is often seen negatively, but there are two types of stress: **eustress** and **distress**.

▶ **Eustress** is a 'good' form of stress that gives you a feeling of fulfilment. Some athletes actively seek out stressful situations as they like the challenge of pushing themselves to the limit. This helps them increase their skill levels and focus their attention on aspects of their sport. The benefit is that increases in intrinsic motivation follow.

▶ **Distress** is a 'bad' form of stress and is normally what you mean when you discuss stress. It is an extreme form of anxiety, nervousness, apprehension or worry resulting from a perceived inability to meet demands. It can lead to an excessive increase in arousal and a potential decrease in performance levels.

Stress process

The stress process is a four-stage process that was developed to explain the effects of stress on performance (see Figure 6.5).

1 At stage one of the stress process, some form of environmental, physical or psychological demand is placed on the athlete in a particular situation. This could be taking the last penalty in a penalty shoot-out to win the UEFA Champions League.

2 At stage two, the athlete perceives this demand positively or negatively. If you perceive the demand positively, you are more likely to see it as a positive challenge, whereas if you perceive the demand negatively, you are likely to see it as a negative threat. The negative perception of the demand causes a negative mental state, lack of self-confidence and lack of concentration. If the demand is perceived as too great, you may find it difficult to concentrate on what you must do to meet the demand.

3 Stage three when is the perception increases the arousal levels of the performer and initiates a stress response. During this stage, you experience heightened arousal, higher levels of cognitive and **somatic anxiety** and changes in your attention and concentration levels. If at stage two you have perceived the demand more positively, you are more likely to experience eustress, which will result in an increase in motivation and energy towards the demand. If you have perceived the demand negatively, you are more likely to experience hyper-elevated worry and be distressed about the demand.

4 Ultimately, stage three determines the behavioural consequences that can affect the outcome of performance (stage four). If you have experienced eustress you are more likely to have an increase in performance, whereas if you have experienced distress you are more likely to experience a decrease in performance. The outcome of performance will likely affect the athlete's perception of similar demands the next time they experience a similar situation.

> **Key term**
>
> **Somatic anxiety** – the awareness and perception of physiological changes (such as increases in heart rate, sweating and increased body heat) when you start to play sport.

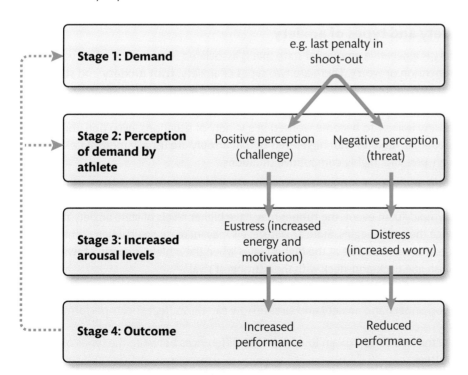

▶ **Figure 6.5:** How does the stress process explain the relationship between stress, arousal, anxiety and performance?

Signs and symptoms of stress

There are a number of signs and symptoms of stress. These can be grouped under biological, cognitive, somatic or **behavioural considerations**.

▶ The main biological consideration is the increase in cortisol and adrenalin levels that mobilises the body for the **fight or flight response**. While this is a natural response to stress, it can be quite detrimental in circumstances such as injury because cortisol reduces the rate of tissue repair, thus slowing down recovery.

▶ Cognitive considerations are increased feelings of worry and an inability to concentrate, both of which may decrease performance levels and reduce an athlete's state of well-being.

▶ Common somatic considerations are an increase in pulse rate and blood pressure, as well as an increase in muscle tension. If not controlled, this increase in muscle tension can increase the risk of injury as well as leading to a condition known as **freezing**.

▶ Behavioural signs and symptoms include rushing, talking quickly and fidgeting. These can decrease performance by reducing the quality of communication between athletes and may mean that certain technical components of performance (e.g. the timing of runs) reduce in quality.

There are many ways in which these signs and symptoms can be effectively managed, including the use of psychological skills training and through effective **social support**.

Anxiety and types of anxiety

Anxiety is a negative emotional state that is associated with feelings of nervousness, apprehension or worry. There are two types of anxiety: **trait anxiety** and **state anxiety**.

▶ **Trait anxiety** is part of an individual's personality. Someone with a high level of trait anxiety is likely to become worried in a variety of situations, even non-threatening situations. Athletes with high levels of trait anxiety are usually more state-anxious in high-pressure, highly competitive situations.

▶ **State anxiety** is a temporary, ever-changing mood state that is an emotional response to any situation considered threatening. For example, at the start of an Olympic 400m event, the runner may have higher levels of state anxiety that drop once the event begins. State anxiety levels may increase again when coming up to the final bend and be at the highest level when the athlete is coming towards the finish line neck-and-neck with their strongest rival.

PAUSE POINT   Do you understand anxiety and stress? How can they affect sports performance?

> Hint

Close the book and explain to a friend the differences between the types of anxiety and stress.

> Extend

Try to think of scenarios when anxiety could be both positive and negative, drawing on your own experiences.

Consequences of stress and anxiety

The definition of anxiety suggests that it is a negative mental state characterised by worry and apprehension. It is thought that if you worry too much, your performance will suffer.

Constantly worrying about an event can make you think that you are not good enough to succeed (decreased self-confidence). This can make you feel like you are less likely to win (decreased expectations of success).

Heightened cognitive anxiety means there is an increase in nervousness, apprehension or worry. One of the things athletes worry about is failing. The problem with this is that once you start to worry about something, you are focusing on it. This increases the likelihood of it happening. Heightened fear of failure could result in negative physiological responses like hyper-elevated muscle tension and lack of movement coordination, which will also negatively affect performance.

Multidimensional anxiety theory

The multidimensional anxiety theory (Martens et al. 1990) suggests that somatic and cognitive anxiety can affect performance in different ways and that they will change in the build-up to an event. Cognitive anxiety is thought to decrease performance, whereas somatic anxiety is thought to enhance performance up to a certain point.

However, there are exceptions. For example, where somatic anxiety is low in the build-up to an event, having slightly elevated levels of cognitive anxiety can enhance performance. This slight increase in worry can arouse and direct an athlete's attention towards the upcoming performance; however, if the cognitive anxiety becomes too great, then performance will be reduced.

Reversal theory

The reversal theory suggests that, rather than anxiety levels *per se*, it is the **perception** of anxiety that can have an effect on performance. For example, if an athlete perceives the symptoms of anxiety as positive and beneficial for performance, they are more likely to enhance performance. This explains why some sport psychologists will highlight the role of some of the signs and symptoms of somatic anxiety (e.g. increased heart rate, increased breathing rate and increased temperature) in successful sport performance. They aim to turn anxiety from an unpleasant worry into a pleasant excitement.

⏸ PAUSE POINT	What do the theories on this page tell us? Can you explain the impact these theories have on sports performance?	
	Hint	Close the book and write a summary of the multidimensional anxiety theory and the reversal theory.
	Extend	Discuss which theory you think best explains the relationship between anxiety and performance, justifying your answer.

Self-confidence and sports performance under competitive pressure

What does a confident athlete look like? It might be a player who wants the ball all of the time, even when under pressure, or a player who maintains positive body language throughout the game even when things are going wrong. Without high levels of self-confidence, athletes may not always involve themselves in their sport in this way.

Self-confidence is a psychological state empowered by the belief that you have in your ability to perform and achieve specific outcomes. An individual's level of self-confidence is influenced by their experiences in training and games, so it is important that you know how to help people build confidence in your sessions. Think of confidence as a solid brick wall – your job is to help athletes build their wall, brick by brick.

► Many sprinters display supreme self-confidence before a race

Reflect

Think about a time when a coach told you that you needed to be more confident. How did you behave during that performance? How would you change your behaviour in future to show your increased confidence?

Benefits of self-confidence

Self-confidence can benefit the athlete by encouraging positive emotions, aiding concentration, inspiring effort and controlling game play and tactics. For example, if an athlete has a high level of self-confidence then they may want to take responsibility for set pieces in football (controlling game play and tactics) because they feel that they have paid attention to various positions and behaviours of their teammates (aiding concentration), and that they can increase the chances of a successful performance.

Optimal self-confidence

Optimal levels of self-confidence can help to improve and maintain an enhanced level of performance. However, if an athlete has lower levels of confidence or is over-confident, then performance can decrease. It can affect their overall psychological well-being and can increase the risk of injury. Additionally, they may begin to miss relevant information about performance because they are less likely to be paying full attention to the sport.

Some people believe that this optimal point of arousal works in a similar fashion to the inverted-U hypothesis (see page 266). Others subscribe to the idea that athletes have an optimal zone of confidence that they can maintain for a period, similar to the IZOF approach (see page 267).

Research

Research the negative consequences of over-confidence. For each negative consequence that you find, provide an example of how it may affect sport performance or an athlete's well-being.

How expectations influence performance

The expectations that you have of yourself and the expectations that others have of you can affect the way that you behave in sport. If you have high expectations of yourself – or your coach has high expectations of you – it is likely that these are based on a perception of competence (i.e. a feeling that you are good at something). If you or somebody else has these expectations, they are more likely to enhance your levels of confidence. Enhancing confidence means that you are likely to demonstrate more intent and effort towards achieving your goals.

Link

This content links to *Unit 4: Sports Leadership* and *Unit 8: Coaching for Performance.*

Key term

Efficacy – the ability to produce a desired or intended result.

Bandura's self-efficacy theory and its applications in sport

Bandura, an eminent psychologist, produced the self-**efficacy** theory. This theory explains how self-efficacy and, as a result, self-confidence can be developed. As a coach, tutor or fitness instructor, it is important to understand the principles of building self-confidence into your everyday sessions. The self-efficacy theory tells us that performance accomplishments, vicarious experiences, verbal persuasion and emotional arousal will create efficacy expectations, which will increase the chances of heightened athletic performance (see Figure 6.6).

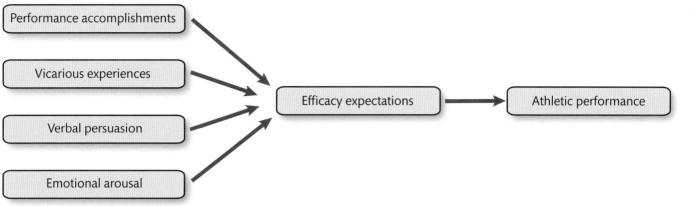

▶ **Figure 6.6:** How can you apply Bandura's self-efficacy theory to your favourite sport?

▶ **Performance accomplishments:** Think about a time when you played well in a sport; how did you feel afterwards? The likelihood is that you enjoyed it and could not wait to play again, because you believed you would be able to do well again. Recent performance accomplishments are the strongest source of self-confidence, so it is important that, particularly with children and young people or those returning to sport after a lengthy absence, you structure practices to allow for achievement of challenges and for athletes to receive feedback on these accomplishments.

Coaches and sports leaders need to give specific examples of accomplishments and praise/reinforce the effort that it has taken to reach the accomplishment. For example, if a basketball player successfully performs their first three-point jump shot, do not just praise the scoring of the three points. Make sure that you praise the effort they have put into achieving it, such as the time they have spent practising, the questions they have asked you about how to get the timing of the jump correct, etc.

▶ **Vicarious experiences:** The second strongest source of self-confidence is vicarious experiences. This occurs when an athlete sees somebody of a similar age or performance level perform a skill successfully. This is because seeing somebody similar successfully complete a task can enhance your self-belief in being able to perform the same task. Drawing on Bandura's Social Learning Theory (see page 261), seeing somebody else perform the task can have a modelling effect. This is enhanced if the athlete you are observing is somebody significant to you, such as a close friend or talented teammate.

To enhance the modelling effect, some coaches also use video footage of elite athletes performing a task. This can be aspirational without creating any negative social comparisons between teammates. This is important, as recent research in football has shown that negative social comparisons between team mates can reduce a player's chance of reaching an elite level in football, due to the effects it can have on their confidence (Gledhill and Harwood, 2015).

▶ **Verbal persuasion:** This is a useful way to enhance self-confidence and occurs when somebody who is important to you, such as a coach or team captain, tells you that they believe in you and that you are able to perform well. This is similar to positive motivational self-talk, but it comes from an external source who is persuading you that you are good enough and that you have what it takes – hence the term verbal persuasion. For coaches, it is important to role model this behaviour for two main reasons:
• As a coach, you are likely to be the most influential person in a young athlete's sporting life, closely followed by their teammates and parents, so the message that comes from you is likely to have the most impact.

- If, as a coach, you model the behaviour of verbal persuasion, you are more likely to have the athletes you work with model that behaviour. In doing so, you will help to create a climate of confidence-building in your athletes and create more social support networks within the team. Creating these networks becomes important during setbacks, such as slumps in performance or serious injury, as athletes then feel more empowered and able to cope with these situations, as well as feeling a greater sense of team cohesion (see page 278).
  ▶ **Emotional arousal:** This is the least impactful factor affecting self-efficacy. If you are sad or upset prior to a competition, this may make you think that your confidence is low.
  ▶ **Efficacy expectations:** These are an athlete's beliefs and expectations about their ability to perform tasks, and can play a role in how successful they are.

 PAUSE POINT How does self-efficacy theory explain performance?

> Hint Describe each of the sections of self-efficacy theory.

> Extend Provide a sport-based example of self-efficacy theory.

Assessment practice 6.1 | A.D1 | A.M1 | A.M2 | A.P1 | A.P2 |

You are on work experience with a netball coach at a local netball club. They have asked you to prepare a report on personality, motivation, self-confidence, arousal, stress and anxiety, and their respective influences on performance. Not only would the coach like to know how they affect performance individually, they would also like to know about any relationships between the different factors and any further impact that they may have on performance. The purpose of the report is to educate the coach about these topics.

Plan
- What aspects of the task do I think will take the most/least time?
- Do I need clarification on how different theories might apply in sporting situations?
- Are there any areas that I think I might struggle with?

Do
- Am I using all of the support available to me, such as the recommended sport psychology resources, people that I may have worked with in sport and my tutors?
- I understand why I have decided to approach this task in a particular way.

Review
- I can explain what elements I found easiest.
- I can explain which elements I found hardest.
- I can say whether I met the task's criteria – as well as where and how – by providing specific examples.

B Examine the impact of group dynamics in team sports and its effect on performance

Group processes

For a group of people to become a team, it is suggested (Tuckman, 1965) that they must go through four developmental stages: forming, storming, norming and performing.

This approach to understanding group development is an example of a linear perspective. All groups progress through all stages, but the time they spend at each stage and the order in which they go through the stages may vary. Once a team has progressed through the four stages, it does not mean that they will not revert to an earlier stage: if key members leave, the team may revert to the storming stage as others begin to vie for position within the team.

▶ **Forming** – during the forming stage, group members familiarise themselves with each other, trying to decide if they belong in that group. Group members assess the strengths and weaknesses of other members, and test their relationships with others in the group. Individuals get to know their roles within the group and make decisions about whether or not they feel they can fulfil (or want to fulfil) those roles. Formal leaders (e.g. managers) in the group tend to be directive during the forming stage.

▶ **Storming** – during the storming stage, conflict begins to develop between individuals in the group. Individuals or cliques start to question the position and authority of the leader, and start to resist the control of the group. Often, conflicts develop because demands are placed on the group members and some individuals try to acquire roles that are more important. During this stage, the formal leader in the group takes on more of a guidance role with decision-making and helps the team to meet expectations in terms of professional behaviour.

▶ **Norming** – during the norming stage, conflict that occurred in the storming stage is replaced by cooperation. Members of the group start to work towards common goals rather than focusing on individual agendas, and group cohesion begins to develop. As this happens, group satisfaction increases as tasks are achieved and levels of respect for others in the group increase. In this stage, the formal leader expects group members to become more involved in the decision-making process, and to take more responsibility for their professional behaviour.

▶ **Performing** – the performing stage involves the team progressing and functioning effectively. The group works without conflict towards the achievement of shared goals and objectives and there is little need for external supervision as the group is more motivated. The group is now able to make its own decisions and take responsibility for them.

> **Research**
>
> Research life cycle and pendular perspectives on group development. How do they differ from Tuckman's linear view and how might this extend our understanding of group development?

Steiner's model of group productivity

Steiner's (1972) model explains group effectiveness. It is:

  actual productivity = potential productivity – losses due to faulty group processes

▶ **Actual productivity** refers to how the team performs and what results they get.

▶ **Potential productivity** refers to the perfect performance the team could produce based on the skill and ability of each individual athlete and the resources available. Losses due to faulty group processes relate to the issues that can prevent the team from reaching its potential performance. Losses are normally due to two main areas: **motivational faults/losses** and **coordination faults/losses.**

The Ringelmann effect

The Ringelmann effect is a phenomenon where, as the group size increases, the individual productivity of the people in the group decreases. The Ringelmann effect is caused by motivation faults or losses rather than coordination losses. This occurs when people are not accountable for their own performance.

> **Link**
>
> This content links to *Unit 4: Sports Leadership, Unit 8: Coaching for Performance* and *Unit 31: Team Building.*

> **Key terms**
>
> **Motivational faults/losses** – occur when some members of the team do not give 100 per cent effort.
>
> **Coordination faults/losses** – occur when players do not connect with their play, the team interacts poorly or ineffective strategies are used. Generally, sports that require more interaction or cooperation between players are more susceptible to coordination faults or losses.

Social loafing

Social loafing (see page 189) is group members failing to put in 100 per cent effort in a team-based situation. The losses in motivation causing social loafing are evident when the individual contributions of group members are not identified or are dispensable. It occurs when some players appear to be working harder than others.

Individuals who display social loafing lack confidence, are afraid of failure and tend to be highly anxious. They may not feel they can make a useful contribution to overall team performance, which might be why they do not want to participate.

Case study

The faltering American football team

You are on a work placement with an American football team. You notice there are a few players who do not seem to be trying very hard. When feeding the ball to the quarterback on set plays, they seem to be very slow on the snap.

You also notice that the wide receiver seems to be misjudging the quarterback's passes on a regular basis and there does not seem to be a great deal of intent when players are supposed to be blocking. The other players on the team appear to be working harder to try to make up for this. However, despite their efforts, there is little interaction between spikers and setters.

1   What evidence of Steiner's model, the Ringelmann effect and social loafing can you find in this case study?

2   If you were the coach, how could/would you improve these faults?

Cohesion in effective group performance

A sports team is a unique type of group. They may spend a lot of time living, training and competing together and, because of this, the levels of cohesion can have a significant effect on performance. There are two key types of sports team: **interactive teams** and **coactive teams**.

▶   **Interactive teams** – team members directly interact and co-ordinate with each other in order to achieve a successful performance. Sports such as hockey are typical examples of this type of team.

▶   **Coactive teams** – there is no direct interaction between team members during the performance. Members are required to achieve success in their individual games, events or performances to achieve overall team success. An example is a gymnastics team, where each member takes their individual turn on the different apparatus but their individual success scores points for the team.

Task and social cohesion and how these create an effective team climate

Cohesion is a dynamic process reflected in the tendency for a group to stick together and remain united in the pursuit of its goals and objectives. There are two key types of cohesion: **task cohesion** and **social cohesion**.

▶   **Task cohesion** relates to how well group or team members work together to achieve common goals and objectives. High levels of task cohesion are usually associated with higher levels of team role acceptance and task interdependence, which can increase team performance.

▶   **Social cohesion** relates to how much team members like each other. Socially cohesive teams tend to provide greater levels of social support, subscribe to more positive social norms, have a stronger sense of team identity and are more comfortable with structured and clear communication. Collectively, these contribute to increased team performance and can increase athlete well-being.

Team climate is a term used to describe how well the different players in the team get along. It is affected by both task and social cohesion. Creating the team climate is the responsibility of both the coach and the team.

> **Research**
>
> Research the Chicago Bulls basketball teams of the 1990s and read newspaper stories about relationships within the team. Which type of cohesion do you think they most often displayed? How would you describe their team climate?

Factors affecting cohesion

Carron's conceptual model of cohesion (1982) explains the four factors affecting cohesion (see Figure 6.7): environmental, personal, leadership and team.

▶ **Environmental** – groups whose members are located closer together, and which are smaller, are more cohesive because members have greater opportunities to interact and form relationships.

▶ **Personal** – the individual characteristics of members are important in group cohesion. If players are motivated to achieve the group's aims and objectives, are from similar backgrounds, and have similar attitudes and opinions and similar levels of commitment, there will be more satisfaction among group members and the group is more likely to be cohesive.

▶ **Leadership factors** – leadership styles, behaviours, communication styles and the compatibility of the coach and athletes' personalities all that affect cohesion.

▶ **Team elements** – if the team stays together for a long time, experience success and failure together and can be involved in the decision-making process, the group is more likely to be productive and cohesive.

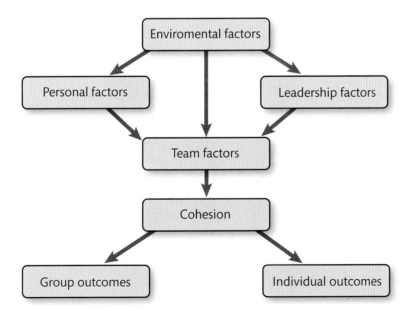

Figure 6.7: How does Carron's (1982) conceptual model of cohesion explain factors affecting cohesion?

Relationship between cohesion and performance

It is easy to say that the greater the level of cohesion, the higher the level of performance. Interactive sports like football and volleyball require direct interaction and coordination between players, so cohesion (especially task cohesion) is important. Coactive sports like golf and archery require little, if any, direct interaction or coordination. Cohesion affects the performance in interactive sports more than it does in coactive sports.

Consider the relationship between cohesion and performance: what is the direction of the relationship? It is plausible that cohesion affects performance and performance affects cohesion. It is understandable that the members of a team that wins on a regular basis may get along better, but equally understandable that a team whose members get on better is more likely to be successful. Because of this, many people now accept that the cohesion–performance relationship is circular: an increase in performance leads to an increase in cohesion, which leads to further increases in performance, and so on.

Strategies to develop an effective group and cohesion

It is best to develop a group and effective cohesion by starting the process early, for example during pre-season training. Doing so gives people more opportunity to get to know one another and establish important group norms. This can be particularly important if there has been a large turnover of team members or if there has been a change of coach or manager. Developing an effective group and levels of cohesion should be the collective responsibility of all staff and team members. Table 6.2 demonstrates some ways that different people can contribute.

▶ **Table 6.2:** Ways different people can help build team cohesion

Coach strategies	Team member strategies
• Communicate effectively	• Be responsible for their own activities
• Ensure everybody knows their role	• Resolve conflict quickly
• Keep changes to a minimum	• Try as hard as possible
• Encourage a group identity	• Get to know each other
• Set both group and individual goals	• Help each other
• Get to know the athletes	

Leadership in creating effective groups

Leadership is an important aspect of creating effective groups. Leaders need passion and they need to inspire people. However, being a leader is difficult, so the first stage of understanding leadership is understanding some of the theories behind leadership.

Theories of leadership

The four main theories of leadership are trait, behavioural, interactional and multi dimensional.

Trait approach

The trait approach says there are certain personality characteristics that predispose an individual to be a good leader and that leaders are born, not made. This theory says that leadership is innate and a good leader would be good in any situation. This approach has had little support and it is now accepted that there is no definitive set of traits that characterise a good leader.

Behavioural approach

The behavioural approach to leadership argues that a good leader is made, not born, and anyone can learn to be a good leader. They can do this by observing good leaders' behaviours in a variety of situations, reproducing those behaviours in similar situations and having behaviours reinforced. For example, if you have observed a football coach letting players make decisions and mistakes and seen the players learn from this (observation), you might use a similar coaching style (reproduction). If the players that you are coaching improve or enjoy their football more and you get positive feedback from their parents (reinforcement), you are more likely to act in this way again.

The focus of this approach is trying to discover leadership behaviours displayed by all great leaders. These include the ability to develop mutual trust, earn and show respect, communicate clearly, demonstrate good organisational skills, and provide clear examples of how things can be done.

> **Discussion**
>
> Discuss why each of the behaviours listed under 'Behavioural approach' demonstrates good leadership. Can you think of any other behaviours that might be important?

Interactional approach

While the trait and behavioural approaches to leadership place emphasis on the personal qualities of a coach, the interactional approach considers interaction between the individual and their situation. Two main types of leader are identified through the interactional approach:

- **Relationship-orientated** leaders focus on developing relationships with individuals in the group. They work hard to maintain communication with members and develop respect and trust with others. Relationship-orientated leaders are more effective with experienced, highly skilled athletes.
- **Task-orientated** leaders are concerned with meeting goals and objectives. They create plans, decide on priorities, assign members to tasks, and ensure members stay on task, with the focus on increasing group productivity. Task-orientated leaders are effective with less experienced, less skilled performers who need constant instruction and feedback.

Different athletes will prefer task-orientated or relationship-orientated leaders. In principle, a leader who gets the right balance between providing a supportive environment and focusing on getting the job done is the most effective leader. It is a leader's role to get to know their performers so they know where to concentrate their efforts. Most leaders will change from task-orientated to relationship-orientated (or vice-versa), depending on the situation.

Multidimensional model of sport leadership

The multidimensional model of sport leadership (Chelladurai, 1978) says the team's performance and satisfaction with the leader will be highest if the leader's required behaviours, preferred behaviours and actual behaviours all agree. Figure 6.8 shows Chelladurai's model.

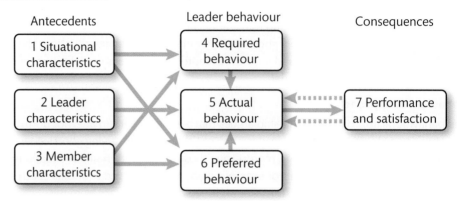

▶ **Figure 6.8:** How does this model help us to understand the factors that can create high performance and satisfaction?

The leader's **required behaviours** are generally determined by the situation the leader is in (e.g. the sporting organisation) and the expectation that the leader conforms to the expected norms. For example, how many times have you seen a football manager punished by the Football Association for criticising a referee after a game? The established norm is that leaders should not criticise match officials, so that is the behaviour expected of the leader.

The **preferred behaviour** is determined by the people within the group or team. Their preferences relate to factors including personality, experience and skill of the athletes; and non-sport related aspects such as age and gender. For example, a senior elite athlete might expect their coach to behave differently towards them than they would towards a youth-level athlete just starting their career.

The **actual behaviour** is directly determined by the characteristics of the leader, and indirectly by the situational factors and the preferences of the group. For example, a grass roots sports coach might adopt more relationship-orientated behaviours because their primary goal is to enhance enjoyment and maintain young people's sport participation, whereas a coach in a world championship final might display more task-orientated leadership to try to maintain the team's focus on winning.

Case study

An organisation has asked you to run sports sessions for a group of young people from an inner-city area in the North of England. When you are given information prior to the sessions, you find out that there are usually around 30 children attending, aged between 8 and 13 years old. Many of the children have behavioural difficulties; they are often in trouble at school and some of them have troubled family backgrounds. The organisation asking you to run these sessions is trying to use sport to develop personal and social responsibility skills in young people. You have a range of abilities in the sessions and the children play sports including football, cricket, rugby, and track and field athletics.

1 What are the key pieces of information in this case study that might determine how you work with the children and young people?

2 How can you use the information that you know about relationship-orientated and task-orientated leaders to decide how you might lead the group?

3 How can you use information from the multidimensional model of sport leadership to decide how you might lead the group?

Prescribed vs. emergent leaders and how this might affect a sports group

Leaders are either prescribed or emergent.

▶ **Prescribed leaders** are appointed by an authority. For example, Pep Guardiola was appointed Manchester City Football Club manager from the start of the 2016/17 season.

▶ **Emergent leaders** achieve leadership status by showing specific leadership skills or being skilful at their sport and gaining the respect and support of the group. For example, Wayne Rooney became an informal leader of Manchester United FC before eventually being appointed club captain. He emerged because of his impressive performances, gaining the respect of others. In some situations, emergent leaders can be more effective than prescribed leaders as they already have the respect of existing group members.

> **Discussion**
>
> Think about situations when one of a team's senior players is promoted to become their new manager. What effect might this have on the relationships they have with their former team mates whom they are now managing? How might this affect the team as a whole?

Autocratic and democratic leaders

Autocratic leaders have firm views about how and when things should be done. They are inflexible in their approach to the group. This type of leader dictates who does what tasks and when, and often how the task should be done as well. They use phrases like 'do this', or 'do it the way I told you to'. The leader does not seek the views of people within the group, and rarely gets involved on a personal level with group members.

Democratic leaders make decisions only after consulting with group members. They encourage group involvement, adopt an informal and relaxed approach to leadership and listen to ideas relating to the prioritisation and completion of goals. They use questions like 'How do you think we can do this?' Working in this way shows that they value the group's input, yet they still maintain their position as the leader by making the final decision.

> **Reflect**
>
> Think about situations in which you have led a group, as either a prescribed or an emergent leader. Do you think you were more autocratic or democratic? Why did you act in that way? How would you change it if you were in the same situation again?

Impact of processes, cohesion and leadership on a team and performance

The impact on performance is always a key concern when thinking about group effectiveness. There can be positive or negative impacts.

Positive impacts

The most obvious positive impact is an increase in performance. However, what is more important to understand is how this performance increase happens. Often, this is attributed to everybody in the group having clearly assigned roles that they understand and feel they are able to fulfil well. They set and work towards common goals, and maintain clear communication as a group.

Negative impacts

Where group processes are faulty, where there is a lack of cohesion or where there is a poor level of leadership, performance will usually decrease. This is because there will be misunderstandings over roles and responsibilities (often caused by poor communication or a lack of communication), there may be team members who become selfish or greedy, and there is an increased chance of social loafing.

Measuring the impact of processes, cohesion and leadership on a team and performance using sociograms

A sociogram is a way of measuring group cohesion by showing ways in which different team members relate to each other. You can use sociograms to monitor group interactions, athletes' choices, or the preferences of individuals within the group. Sociograms can be used to identify different relationships within a team and to identify the effectiveness of group processes, as well as identifying leadership potential.

The over-arching purpose of sociograms is to identify instances of attraction and rejection within the group, with a view to enhancing the group environment.

Constructing sociograms

You construct a sociogram by asking team members questions – anonymously – and then collating the responses into a diagram. For the process to be effective, you should encourage honesty and reinforce this by stating the confidential nature of results – nobody in the team will know who has given which responses. Questions and statements can include: 'Name the three people that you enjoy training with the most and three people that you enjoy training with the least', and 'Name three people that you would most like to share a room with on a trip and three people that you would least like to share a room with'. The most frequently selected individuals go towards the centre of the sociogram and least frequently selected towards the outside. Team members' names are linked by arrows, with the direction of the arrows depicting the nature of the relationships.

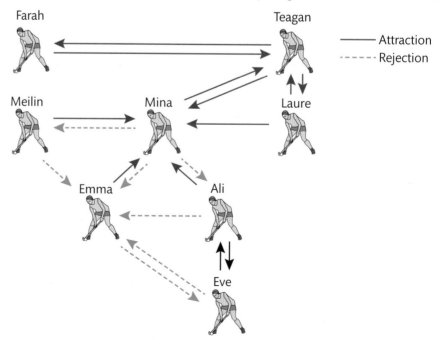

▶ **Figure 6.9:** How does a sociogram help you to determine the effectiveness of your team?

II PAUSE POINT Do you understand the uses of sociograms? How are they used to help sports performance?

> Hint   Close the book and explain to a friend what a sociogram is and how you can construct one.

> Extend   Explain the potential positive and negative impacts of using sociograms in team-based settings.

Assessment practice 6.2   B.D2 B.M3 B.P4 B.P3

A local rugby team has asked you to deliver a workshop on team cohesion. The team manager has approached you as there have been breakdowns in relationships between players lately, mainly because the team has been on a bad run of form and lost a lot of matches. The team manager would like you to deliver a presentation on group cohesion and leadership and how these affect successful performance in rugby.

They have also asked you to find out if there are cliques or if any members of the team are being left out. As well as completing your presentation, you decide to complete a sociogram and provide the results to the team manager.

Plan
- What is the task?
- What am I learning about team cohesion and why is this important?
- Are there any areas that I think I might struggle with?

Do
- I have spent some time planning my approach to the task.
- I can seek others' opinions.
- I am recording any problems I am experiencing and looking for ways/solutions to clarify queries.

Review
- I can accept that I am responsible for my actions.
- I can explain how I approached the task.
- I can say whether I met the task's criteria.

C Explore psychological skills training programmes designed to improve performance

Psychological skills

Think about the demands of competitive sport. You are required to concentrate for long periods under changeable circumstances, and often you have to be able to cope with setbacks and motivate yourself to continue. These are all things that psychological skills can help with. Key psychological skills that can benefit athletes include self-talk, goal setting, arousal control techniques and imagery.

Self-talk in sport and exercise

Have you ever been playing in a match and said something to yourself such as 'Come on!' or 'Focus, keep your eye on the ball!'? This is self-talk and is something that most athletes do, sometimes without even doing it for any specific purpose. Self-talk is a psychological skill that enhances learning, increases performance and motivates athletes. The two main categories of self-talk are **positive** and **negative self-talk**.

Positive self-talk

Positive self-talk is used for motivational purposes, to increase energy levels and produce a positive attitude in athletes. Positive self-talk involves statements such as 'Keep going!' or 'I can do this!' rather than having task-specific instructions. Sometimes athletes will use **cue words** instead of phrases, with some athletes going to the extent of writing cue words on their hand or wrist, or even sewing them into clothing or equipment.

Historically, sport psychologists have believed that positive self-talk is beneficial for all sporting activities. However, more recently, some sport psychologists (e.g. Hatzigeorgiadis *et al.* 2011) have suggested that positive, motivational self-talk may not be as effective if an athlete is performing in sports that require fine movements.

Negative self-talk

Generally, people have believed negative self-talk to be a negative aspect of performance. It is a self-critical process that some sport psychologists have argued gets in the way of an athlete achieving goals and can foster self-doubt. Common self-talk statements include 'that was a stupid mistake to make' and 'I can't believe how bad I was'. However, recently, some researchers (e.g. Tod *et al.* 2011) have argued that negative self-talk does not always impede performance.

> **Discussion**
>
> In a group discuss ways in which negative self-talk may impede or enhance performance.

Key terms

Cue words – single words that are a form of self-talk and used to trigger a desired response in an athlete. Common cue words include 'believe', 'relax', 'focus' and 'strong'.

Instructional self-talk – a task-specific form of self-talk that involves the athlete giving instructions to themselves about different aspects of performance (e.g. technical or tactical elements).

Uses of self-talk

There are many uses of self-talk. Three of the most popular uses are self-confidence, arousal control and as part of pre-performance routines.

▶ **Self-confidence** – Self-talk can help to enhance self-confidence, providing the athlete with a sense of belief in their actions. Positive self-talk can redirect the athlete's attention away from negative thoughts or things that have gone wrong, increasing the athlete's level of confidence.

▶ **Arousal control** – Self-talk can be useful to regulate arousal. Cue words or positive phrases are used to re-direct the athlete's attention away from negative aspects of performance that are the cause of higher levels of arousal.

▶ **Pre-performance routines** – Athletes can often use positive self-talk and another form of self-talk – **instructional self-talk** – as part of pre-performance routines. Positive self-talk helps to motivate athletes for the upcoming game as part of a pre-performance routine, whereas instructional self-talk can be used to provide sport-specific instructions for the athlete to concentrate on during the game.

> **Reflect**
>
> Virtually everybody uses some form of self-talk. When have you used it? Was it positive or negative self-talk? Why did you use it? How did it impact your activity and performance?

PAUSE POINT   Do you understand self-talk? What benefits and uses does it have?

> Hint   Consider how you might use self-talk and when.
>
> Extend   Can you think of times when positive self-talk may have a negative effect, and when negative self-talk might have a positive effect? Be specific with examples and reasons.

Influencing motivation through goal setting

Consider the different factors that can affect motivation. You may have experienced performance setbacks or injuries, you may have struggled to manage the demands of sport and education, or you might have a number of competitions coming up and feel overwhelmed. These situations can all be improved through effective goal setting.

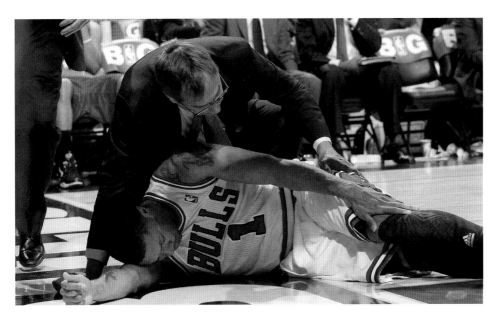

▶ How can goal setting be useful for enhancing motivation in injured athletes?

Timescale for goals

Goals should be set in a coherent, progressive and linked manner. You should use a combination of short-term, medium-term and long-term goals, as solely having a long-term goal has little effect on performance and motivation. Having a series of short-term and medium-term goals can make progress towards the long-term goals more realistic, and the constant sense of achievement through achieving the short-term and medium-term goals enhances the athlete's motivation to continue.

Avoid being too prescriptive with timescales for some goals and allow flexibility for them to be revised if the athlete is struggling to achieve them all. Table 6.3 shows an example of short-term, medium-term and long-term goals that might be used with an international rugby player who has ruptured their anterior cruciate ligament and had this surgically repaired.

▶ **Table 6.3**: Why do you think it is important to have a logical progression of goals?

Goal setting for an athlete who is recovering from anterior cruciate ligament reconstruction surgery	
Duration of goal	**Example**
Short-term	Progress to standing up, full weight bearing within 72 hours of surgery
Short-term	Have swelling eliminated and approximately up to 100° range of movement within two weeks post-surgery
Short-term to medium-term	Be able to perform a full squat, have unrestricted balance and control when walking and have c.130° of knee flexion within two weeks to three months post-surgery
Medium-term	Have full range of motion, full strength and straight line running ability by 3–5 months post-surgery
Medium-term to long-term	Be able to perform change of direction running and return to restricted sport-specific drills within 4–6 months post-surgery
Long-term	Have a full return to competitive sport within 6–12 months post-surgery

Types of goals

There are different types of goals that are each thought to have different effects on motivation. The key types of goal fall under headings of outcome and process goals, and mastery and competitive goals.

Outcome and process goals

Outcome goals focus on the result of the event. This type of goal is often the least effective when it comes to motivation, as goal achievement is dependent on the opposition as well as the athlete themselves. For example, an athlete could run a personal best in a 400-metre event but still finish last. If the outcome goal is always to win, this could negatively influence motivation, even if performance is improving.

Spending too much time thinking about this type of goal, before or during competition, can increase anxiety and decrease concentration, reducing motivation. However, this type of goal can improve short-term motivation. Think about when you have lost to somebody that you really wanted to beat. It probably spurred you on to train harder so you could beat them next time.

Process goals are based on what the athlete has to do to improve their performance. For example, a basketball player wanting to improve their jump shot accuracy might focus on releasing the ball at the height of the jump. This type of goal is useful for improving motivation as it gives a specific element of performance to focus on, which facilitates learning and development.

You should try to incorporate both types of goal when goal setting with athletes; they should complement each other and are more likely to enhance motivation.

Mastery and competitive goals

Mastery goals (sometimes referred to as task or learning goals) focus on self-challenge and improvement, or at least not doing any worse than a previous performance. You do not make any comparisons between your athlete and other competitors. Some sport psychologists argue that this type of goal is best for enhancing motivation as mastery goals help an athlete strive for greater competence and give the athlete more control over their achievements.

There are two types of mastery goal: **mastery-approach goals** (MAp) and **mastery-avoidance goals** (MAv).

▶ MAp goals focus on performing a task well and outperforming yourself (e.g. setting new personal best times). These goals tend to create the greatest levels of intrinsic motivation in athletes and can have positive effects on performance.

▶ MAv goals focus on not making mistakes or not letting your performance worsen from previous levels. These goals can have negative effects on an athlete's well-being but do not always decrease performance.

Competitive goals (sometimes referred to as performance goals or ego goals) focus on demonstrating your superiority over, or not being out-performed by, another athlete. Some people think that these goals are detrimental to motivation because their achievement is not fully in the athlete's control. However, they can be beneficial for motivation if the athlete setting the goals has a high perception of competence.

There are two types of competitive goal: **performance-approach goals** (PAp) and **performance-avoidance goals** (PAv).

▶ PAp goals focus on performing better than another athlete. They can have a beneficial effect on motivation, especially when an athlete feels more competent, and have been shown to enhance performance in competitive situations.

▶ PAv goals focus on not being out-performed by another athlete. They are widely recognised as the worst type of goal as they focus heavily on negative aspects of sport and can create higher levels of stress and anxiety, and lower levels of motivation as a result.

In the 2015 Rugby World Cup, England lost 28–25 to Wales despite England leading 22–12 at one stage in the second half. Some critics felt that England had played as though they were simply trying to avoid defeat, rather than as though they really wanted to win. This could be seen as a negative approach.

1 If a team sets out to avoid losing, what type of goal are they using?

2 In knockout tournament settings, why do you think a team might set up the aim of avoiding defeat after they have won their first match?

3 If you were a coach, how would you convince your players that setting up to avoid defeat was a good game plan?

Principles of goal setting

Setting effective goals is essential if you want them to benefit the athletes. Using the acronym SMART will help to set the right type of goals. SMART stands for:

▶ **S**pecific – goals should show exactly what needs to be done
▶ **M**easurable – goals should be quantifiable
▶ **A**chievable – the goals can be attained and are relevant
▶ **R**ealistic – goals should be within your reach
▶ **T**ime-constrained – there should be a reasonable timeframe by which the goal should be achieved.

Link

SMART targets are looked at in more detail in *Unit 4: Sports Leadership*.

Reflect

Think about the last time you set goals for yourself. Did they include timescales for the goals? Did they include the different types of goal? Did they include the principles of effective goal setting? How would you improve the goals that you set for yourself in future?

Arousal control techniques

Arousal control techniques can be used to either increase or decrease arousal. Techniques that increase arousal will energise the athlete, whereas arousal reduction techniques will help to relax the athlete.

Relaxation techniques

Common relaxation techniques include:

▶ **Progressive muscular relaxation** – An easy-to-use technique that helps to reduce muscle tension. It is a useful technique because it raises your awareness of your levels of muscle tension and, through the relaxation phase, helps you to distinguish between states of tension and relaxation. The technique involves tensing and relaxing groups of muscles in turn over the whole body. The process involves tensing a muscle group for five seconds, releasing the tension for five seconds, taking a deep breath and repeating. It is called progressive muscular relaxation because an athlete progresses from one muscle group to the next until all muscles have been tensed and relaxed.

▶ **Breathing control** – A slow and deliberate inhalation–exhalation process. It is best used during breaks in play and is useful when athletes are getting anxious. A simple method of breathing control is to work on a 1:2 ratio of breathing in to breathing out, with people most commonly taught to breathe in for four seconds and then breathe out for eight seconds.

Safety tip

You should find out if your athlete has any respiratory conditions – such as asthma – that could affect their ability to breathe in deeply, prior to starting any breath control techniques with them.

▶ **Autogenic training** – Autogenic training is a type of self-hypnosis and can take a number of months to learn. It helps to develop feelings of warmth and heaviness. This programme of self-hypnosis uses a series of sentences, statements or phrases to focus attention on the different feelings the athlete is trying to produce. A normal autogenic programme has six stages:

1 Heaviness in the arms and legs, e.g. my left leg feels heavy
2 Warmth in the arms and legs, e.g. my right leg feels warm
3 Regulation of cardiac activity, e.g. my heart rate is normal
4 Regulation of breathing, e.g. my breathing rate is normal
5 Abdominal warmth, e.g. my abdomen feels warm
6 Cooling of the forehead, e.g. my forehead is cool

Discussion

It can take a long time for athletes to learn to perform autogenic training. Some people suggest that it can take up to 40 minutes per day over a period of months for athletes to become proficient with this method. How do you think this might affect an athlete's engagement with the skill?

Energising techniques

Common energising techniques include both audio and visual tools.

▶ **Music** can narrow a performer's attention and divert attention from tiredness. Exciting music can increase body temperature, heart rate and breathing rate, all of which can improve sport performance. Music is also helpful for avoiding negative thoughts.
▶ **Pep talks** are short talks designed to instil enthusiasm in athletes and increase their determination to succeed. They are usually informal but will be passionate. In team situations, pep talks are usually delivered by the team leader (e.g. coach or captain), but can be delivered by anybody in different situations.
▶ **Energising imagery** can be achieved using high-energy images of competition (e.g. a hard tackle in rugby), playing well (e.g. crossing the finish line first in a race) and high levels of effort (e.g. being able to lift a new weight in the gym).
▶ **Positive statements** can be used alone or alongside other arousal-increasing techniques, such as energising imagery, to increase arousal levels. When using positive statements, consider the following factors so you create as much positive impact as you can.
  • Phrase statements using the first person singular, and be personal with your statements. Say 'I', 'me' or your first name, so they are personal to you.
  • Make statements as positive as possible. Avoid the use of 'no', 'don't', and 'not', because if you ask yourself **not** to think about something, you are more likely to think about it.

- Phrase statements in the present tense. Use statements like 'I am confident of achieving the best result'.
- Make statements short, clear and simple. Statements that are too long are difficult to internalise, so shorter and simpler is better.
- Make statements emotional: use phrases that make you feel happy, empowered and self-assured, such as 'It makes me happy when I know I've competed hard'.

❚❚ PAUSE POINT   What are the energising techniques?

> **Hint**   Close the book and create a list of all the energising techniques and their benefits.
>
> **Extend**   Identify situations when you think it would be inappropriate to use different energising techniques, and explain why.

Imagery

Imagery is creating or recreating images in your mind, rather than physically practising a sports skill or technique. It should involve as many senses as possible, as well as recreating emotions experienced through the activity you take part in. The most effective imagery uses **visual**, **auditory** and **kinaesthetic** senses, and can be used:

▸ **to increase self-confidence** – through imagery, the athlete will be able to experience the feelings of success and will be able to come up with strategies to help them be successful in performance. As the performer sees that they can complete the performance successfully (in their minds), their levels of self-confidence will increase.

▸ **to relax** – imagining emotions associated with relaxation, sometimes together with the use of other techniques such as breathing exercises, can more effectively control anxiety, arousal and stress levels.

▸ **as part of pre-performance routines** – imagery can be used as part of all types of pre-performance routine as it helps the athlete to mentally rehearse the action before physically performing the activity.

▸ **to imagine goals** – imagery can be used to create a mental experience of you achieving your set goals (e.g. the process of winning a medal or surpassing your personal best).

> **Key terms**
>
> **Visual** – you concentrate on the different things that you can see during the movement.
>
> **Auditory** – you concentrate on the different sounds that you associate with a sporting movement.
>
> **Kinaesthetic** – you concentrate on the feel of the movement.

> **Reflect**
>
> Think about a time when you played sport and things did not go as well as you wanted them to – maybe you made some mistakes or you lost a game that you really wanted to win. Which of the psychological skills would you use if you were in the same situation again? How do you think they would benefit you?

Designing a psychological skills training programme

Have you ever turned up to an important game and thought: 'I can't do this?' Have you started something new feeling like you wanted to give yourself the best chance of being a success? These are situations where psychological skills training (PST) is useful. PST is an approach to sport psychology that equips athletes with different skills that can increase performance and well-being. Sometimes you may see PST referred to as mental skills training. Like any other skill, athletes need time to be able to practise and develop their psychological skills so that they can get the greatest benefit from them.

Identification of an appropriate individual

Anybody can take part in PST programmes. Once athletes become familiar with them, PST programmes are useful for most. However, you will encounter some athletes who will not want to take part in PST for different reasons. They may feel a bit silly taking part, or may not see any benefit from the programme. For these athletes, you could try to educate them about the benefits of PST programmes but, if they decide not to **consent** to the programme, you should not force them to take part.

Identification of techniques to develop psychological skills

Earlier in this unit, you learned about common psychological skills that are used in PST: goal setting, arousal control techniques, self-talk and imagery. The techniques that you actually use with an athlete should be specific to the athlete and be based on a clear needs analysis.

Assessment of psychological skills

Before you can determine which psychological skills you should include in your PST programme, you should first conduct an initial assessment of psychological skills. Discovering an athlete's strengths and areas for improvement is the first stage of this.

Strengths and areas for improvement

Before deciding on the aims and objectives of the PST programme, you should perform an initial assessment of the psychological strengths and areas for improvement in your athlete. You can achieve this through:

▸ **interviews** – **semi-structured interviews** are often best.

▸ **questionnaires** – to assess levels of different psychological factors in sport and the athlete's current psychological skills. There are many questionnaires available that either give you a general overview or help you to assess specific qualities.

▸ **performance profiling** – to help you to understand the athlete's and the coach's perception of performance and skills and to get a clear, consistent understanding of the demands of the sport.

Use of questionnaires and interviews

Using a combination of questionnaires and interviews is a particularly good way of getting to know your athlete. It can often be easier to build a picture of your athlete's current situation if you have a greater depth of information. Using this combination of techniques provides a way of double-checking the information that the athlete has given you. Two things that you need to be aware of when using interviews and questionnaires with athletes are **social desirability** and **self-serving bias**.

Some common questionnaires used in sport include:

▸ the Athletic Coping Skills Inventory-28 (ACSI-28, Smith *et al.* 1995), which is a general measure of overall psychological skills and qualities

▸ the Injury-Psychological Readiness to Return to Sport (i-PRRS, Glazer, 2009), which measures an athlete's confidence in their return to sport after injury to see if they are ready to return

▸ the Competitive State Anxiety Invetory-2 (CSAI-2, Martens *et al.* 1990).

It is important that you do not use these types of questionnaire unless you know why you are using them, how to interpret the results and how it might affect the athlete when you explain the results to them.

> **Key terms**

Consent – permission given by an athlete to involve them with an activity. Permission is sought after the athlete has received all of the information they need to make an informed decision.

Performance profiling – a technique used to identify key strengths and areas for improvements in athletes, often used to form the basis of goal setting and to enhance coach–athlete communication regarding the demands of a sport.

Self-serving bias – athletes giving answers that purposefully make them appear better than they are.

Semi-structured interview – an interview where you have set questions, but you add additional questions during the interview when an interesting or important piece of information comes up that you want to explore further.

Social desirability – athletes giving you answers that they think you want to hear.

Case study

Activity: Athletic coping skills inventory

Below is a copy of the ACSI–28 (Smith *et al.*, 1995). Complete the questionnaire and analysis as follows:

- Read each statement and tick the response you most agree with (honestly!). Remember, there are no right or wrong answers and you shouldn't spend too much time on any statement.

- Work out your score for each subscale using the scoring system. Each scale has a range from 0 to 12, with 0 indicating a low level of skill in that area and 12 indicating a high level of skill in that area.
- Add up each subscale score to get a total score for psychological skills. Your total score will range from 0 to 84, with 0 indicating low levels of psychological skill and 84 signifying high levels of skill.

Statement	Almost never	Sometimes	Often	Almost always
1. On a daily or weekly basis, I set goals for myself that guide what I do.				
2. I get the most out of my talent and skill.				
3. When a coach or manager tells me how to correct a mistake I've made, I can take it personally and can get upset.*				
4. When I'm playing sports, I can focus my attention and block out my distractions.				
5. I remain positive and enthusiastic during competition.				
6. I tend to play better under pressure because I can think more clearly.				
7. I worry quite a bit about what others think of my performance.*				
8. I tend to do lots of planning about how I can reach my goals.				
9. I feel confident I will win when I play.				
10. When a coach or manager criticises me, I become more upset rather than feel helped.*				
11. It is easy for me to keep distracting thoughts from interfering with something that I am watching or listening to.				
12. I put a lot of pressure on myself by worrying about how I will perform.*				
13. I set my own performance goals for each practice or training session.				
14. I don't have to be pushed to practise or play hard; I give 100%.				
15. If a coach criticises me, I correct the mistake without getting upset about it.				
16. I handle unexpected situations in my sport very well.				
17. When things are going badly, I tell myself to keep calm and it works for me.				
18. The more pressure there is during a game, the more I enjoy it.				
19. While competing, I worry about making mistakes or failing to come through it.*				
20. I have my game plan worked out in my head long before the event begins.				
21. When I feel myself getting too tense, I can quickly relax my body and calm myself.				
22. To me, pressure situations are challenges that I welcome.				
23. I think about and imagine what will happen if I make a mistake.*				
24. I maintain emotional control regardless of how things are going for me.				
25. It is easy for me to direct my attention and focus on a single object or person.				
26. When I fail to reach my goals it makes me try even harder.				
27. I improve my skills by listening carefully to advice and instruction from coaches and managers.				
28. I make fewer mistakes when the pressure is on because I concentrate better.				

Use the following scale to calculate your skills:

For statements that do not have an asterisk (*) next to them:

- almost never = 0
- sometimes = 1
- often = 2
- almost always = 3.

For statements that have an asterisk (*) next to them:

- almost never = 3
- sometimes = 2
- often = 1
- almost always = 0.

Coping score (0–12)

Sum your scores for statements 5, 17, 21 and 24. The higher your score on this scale, the more likely you are to remain calm, positive and enthusiastic when things go badly. You are more likely to be able to overcome setbacks in a performance situation.

Coachability score (0–12)

Sum your scores for statements 3*, 10*, 15 and 27. The higher your score on this scale, the more likely you are to be receptive to guidance from your coaches or managers, and to concentrate on using their instructions to benefit your performance, rather than getting upset and taking the comments too personally.

Concentration score (0–12)

Sum your scores for statements 4, 11, 16 and 25. The higher your score on this scale, the less likely you are to become distracted by different things. You are also likely to focus on important aspects of your sport performance.

Confidence and achievement motivation (0–12)

Sum your scores for statements 2, 9, 14 and 26. The higher your score on this scale, the more likely you are to give 100 per cent in both competitive and training situations. You are also more likely to be confident in your skills and abilities, as well as being motivated by challenges.

Goal setting and mental preparation score (0–12)

Sum your scores for statements 1, 8, 13 and 20. The higher the score on this scale, the more likely you are to set yourself effective goals and produce appropriate plans to achieve your goals. You are more likely to plan out your sport performance effectively.

Peaking under pressure score (0–12)

Sum your scores for statements 6, 18, 22 and 28. The higher your score on this scale, the more likely you are to find high-pressure situations challenging. It is likely that you will use them to help performance, as opposed to viewing them as threatening and allowing them to hinder performance.

Freedom from worry score (0–12)

Sum your scores for statements 7*, 12*, 19* and 23*. The higher your score on this scale, the less likely you are to put pressure on yourself by worrying about performance, making mistakes and what others think about your performance (particularly if you perform badly).

Total psychological skills score (0–84)

Sum all of your subscale scores. The higher your score on this scale, the higher the level of psychological skills you have.

Psychological demands of the sport

Do you think that a rugby player and a snooker player will require the same psychological skills and qualities? Understanding the psychological demands of the sport that the athlete takes part in is an important aspect of designing an effective psychological skills training programme. Performance profiling is a common way to understand the psychological demands of the sport. Performance profiling has five main stages.

Step by step: Performance profiling

1 Identify and define key qualities for performance. Introduce the idea by asking the athlete what attributes they think are important for top performance. When using performance profiling in a sports setting, ask the athlete to think of an elite performer and to write down that athlete's qualities. Table 6.4 highlights some prompts to use with different athletes. It is useful for the athlete to record and define the qualities necessary for performance in a table format. This helps the athlete and practitioner to develop an understanding of what the terms mean. To avoid misunderstanding, the practitioner must make sure the athlete devises the definitions used. Some people suggest aiming for 20 qualities; however, this will vary from athlete to athlete and sport to sport. Explain that there are no right or wrong answers.

2 Profile the practitioner's perceptions of the athlete's levels and profile the athlete's perceptions of their levels. This is an assessment by you and the athlete of their current level of performance. You and the athlete write the key qualities in each of the blank spaces around the outside of the circular grid. Give each quality a rating from 0–10 (see Figure 6.10).

3 Discuss the practitioner's and the athlete's profiles. In this stage, use the results from the performance profiles to identify perceived areas of strength and areas for improvement. When looking at the two profiles (shown in Figure 6.10), if there are large differences between levels (two points or more), you should have a discussion with the athlete about why the different levels have been given.

4 Agree on goals and how they will be achieved, including setting benchmarks for each goal. Use the results to set the goals through the PST programme. Normally, each of these desired benchmarks will be at level 10 – any target level below this on the athlete's behalf would suggest that there is some form of resistance to achieving the ultimate level of performance.

5 Repeat the profiling to monitor the athlete's progress. The aim is that the athlete will gradually progress further towards the outside of the scale (closer to the rating of 10). If the athlete does not make the desired progress, you and the athlete need to discuss why. Usually this is because the training programme did not take into account a quality (errors in design of programme), you have different views on the importance of a quality (errors in communication and understanding) or the athlete has not put in the effort to achieve the improvements in performance.

Table 6.4: Examples of demands of sports. What are the five most technical demands of your sport?

Psychological	Physical	Attitudinal/character	Technical
Confidence	Strength	Weight control	
Concentration	Stamina	Discipline	
Reflection	Endurance	Determination	
Commitment	Flexibility	Will to win	
Resourcefulness	Power	Positive outlook	
Control	Speed		
Creativity	Balance		
Resilience	Reaction time		

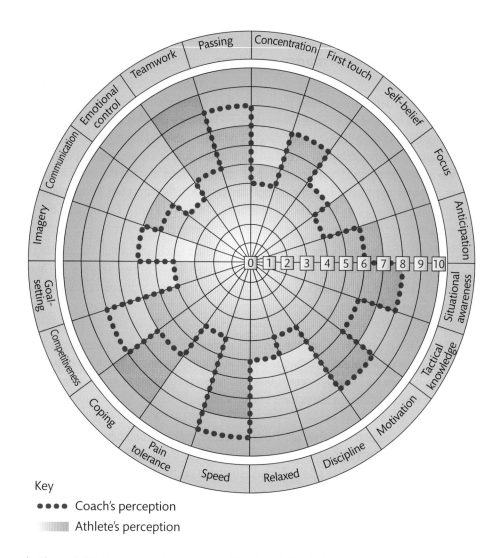

Key

●●●● Coach's perception

░░░░ Athlete's perception

▶ **Figure 6.10:** How can performance profiling benefit both the coach and the athlete?

Benefits of a psychological skills training programme

There are a number of myths about psychological skills training (PST) programmes in sport, such as that PST is only for elite or 'problem' athletes. Knowing the benefits of an activity is likely to increase engagement from the athlete and their coach. This will increase the effectiveness of the programme.

It is important that coaches and athletes are aware that PST programmes are not a 'quick-fix' solution for things like slumps in performance. Effective PST takes time for athletes to learn and develop their skills and it is important that they know this before embarking on their PST programme.

For many athletes and coaches, the most important question they will ask is 'How will this affect my performance?' A simple answer to this is that research shows that successful athletes have better developed psychological skills than less successful athletes. An effective psychological skills training programme will lead to:

▶ performance enhancement

▶ increased enjoyment

▶ enhanced self-satisfaction.

All of the techniques covered in this unit have evidence to suggest that they can improve performance. When athletes are performing well, they are more likely to enjoy their sport. This is because they feel more satisfied that they are able to compete at an appropriate level and offer something to their team. In addition, as an athlete's performance improves, they are more likely to feel that they have learned something new and developed as an athlete. Because of this, athletes are more likely to enjoy their sport and their satisfaction will increase.

It is important that you, the athlete and the coach continue to work together to increase the level of challenge for the athlete so that they can keep developing. If their development **plateaus**, they are likely to become more dissatisfied with their sport. Reviewing and revising your PST programme at timely intervals is one way that you can help to increase the level of challenge for an athlete.

> **Key term**
>
> **Plateau** – a 'levelling out' in performance that can lead to a lack of commitment, motivation, enjoyment or satisfaction if the athlete does not improve or find a way of improving soon after.

> **Research**
>
> Research the 'Challenge Point Hypothesis'. What does this theory tell you about the importance of increasing the level of challenge for athletes? How could PST programmes be used to appropriately increase the level of challenge for athletes?

Designing a training programme

Effective, well-planned PST programmes should reflect a thorough understanding of the reasons and benefits behind the techniques that you use. There is no such thing as a 'one size fits all' approach – the athlete's individual needs should always be taken into account.

Individual situation

You can assess an athlete's individual situation in a number of ways including questionnaires, performance profiling and interviews (see page 292). Once you have completed these, you should summarise your findings on a needs analysis form. See Figure 6.11 for an example of a completed needs analysis form.

Aims and objectives

The aims and objectives of the PST programme are what you and the athlete want to achieve through the programme. Without clear aims and objectives, you will find it difficult to effectively plan the programme or monitor progress. It may be necessary to agree goals with the coach. However, maintaining client confidentiality is an important aspect of the work that you complete.

When you have decided on the aims and objectives of the programme, you should work with the athlete to prioritise them. The biggest areas for improvement, or the skills that are most important to the athlete's performance, require the highest priority.

Action plan to address aims and objectives

After you have prioritised the aims and objectives, you need to produce an action plan with SMART targets. When producing a plan for any PST programme, think about how much time is required for different aspects of the programme. If you are introducing new skills to the PST programme, then 15–30 minute sessions, in addition to physical practice sessions, 3–5 times a week are beneficial. The aim is to move gradually away from needing distinct sessions and, instead, to integrate the psychological skills with normal practice. However, this only becomes possible when athletes are more proficient in their new skills.

Needs analysis

Client's name Adrienne Robertson

Sports psychologist's name Mark Johnson

The following initial assessments were undertaken (*name the assessment methods and state what they were used for*)

1 ACSI-28 – Measure overall psychological skills

2 One-to-one interview – develop rapport with client

3 Performance observations – monitor client in performance environment

Results from assessment 1

Moderate psychological skills use

Low levels of confidence, low peaking under pressure

Results from assessment 2

Client said they sometimes lose confidence when they start to lose, they don't think that they can get back into the game

Results from assessment 3

Always lots of effort from client

Sometimes body language changes when they start to lose

Your main strengths are

High concentration levels, lots of effort during matches

Your main areas for improvement are

Low levels of confidence

You could improve your performance by using the following techniques

Imagery – rehearse positive situations

Breathing – Refocus/calm self in competitive scenario where you start to lose

Self-talk – use of positive statements relating to your ability

▶ **Figure 6.11:** Why is it important to complete a detailed needs analysis?

Key term

Holistic – this approach means that you support the whole athlete's development, not just the technical aspect of their sport.

Timeframe

When planning your PST, you should take into account the short-term (ST), medium-term (MT) and long-term (LT) planning. This planning links to your ST, MT and LT goals. You should include PST activities that will help athletes **holistically**. Using a PST programme that supports the athlete's development in physical, psychological, technical, tactical and lifestyle areas will help to make them more successful in sport.

Figure 6.12 shows an example of how you might work with an injured athlete.

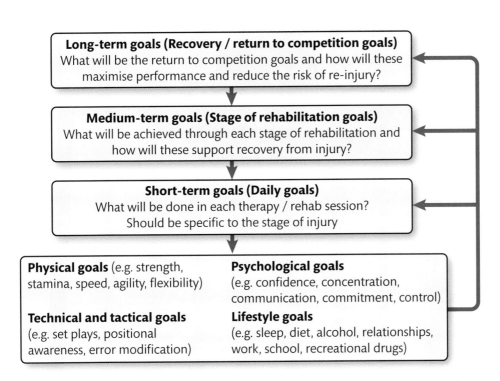

Figure 6.12: Why is having a short-, medium- and long-term plan essential for effective work with athletes?

Link

This content links to *Unit 17: Sports Injury Management.*

Weekly and daily content of the programme

The sport psychologist, coach and athlete should decide the daily and weekly content together. This means the daily and weekly content is decided objectively and considers different perspectives. Including the athlete in the design of the daily and weekly content increases their motivation to adhere to the programme. If an athlete invests time and effort in the programme's design, they will feel like they have more control over the process. Another important reason behind the inclusion of both the athlete and the coach is to ensure the daily and weekly content is manageable. You can also show how the PST programme fits with the normal training routine.

Methods of evaluating the effectiveness of the programme/measurements of key milestones

Evaluating your PST programme is important as it provides an opportunity for:

▶ feedback from both the athlete and the consultant
▶ highlighting the strengths and limitations of the programme
▶ subjective and objective assessment of the programme.

The main ways of reviewing a PST programme are interviews, questionnaires and monitoring physical performance (including collecting objective performance data). These are all ways of getting feedback that is key to reviewing your programme.

Using **questionnaires** can be useful at key milestones of the PST. Comparing scores to the initial questionnaires completed when producing your needs analysis will allow you to see if there has been any improvement. You could also re-visit the performance profiling that you conducted with the athlete to see if there have been any changes in the scores in the priority areas.

Interviews provide you with a good way of getting more in-depth information from your athletes regarding the effectiveness of the PST programme. Use semi-structured interviews as this allows you to probe different areas that might arise during the interview. Figure 6.13 shows a sample interview guide that you could use in either group or individual settings. It helps you to get qualitative feedback from athletes.

Research

Research the basic psychological needs of competence, autonomy and relatedness. How can they help you understand the importance of including the coach and athlete in programme design? How do you think satisfying these basic psychological needs can affect the athlete's motivation to take part in the PST?

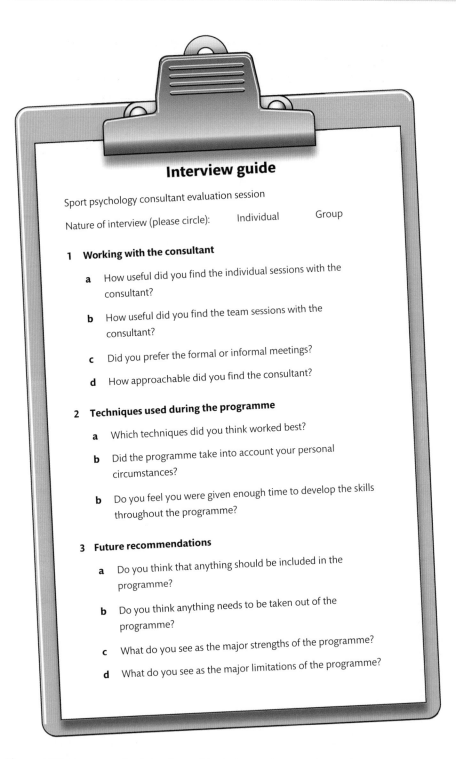

Interview guide

Sport psychology consultant evaluation session

Nature of interview (please circle):   Individual   Group

1   **Working with the consultant**

   a   How useful did you find the individual sessions with the consultant?

   b   How useful did you find the team sessions with the consultant?

   c   Did you prefer the formal or informal meetings?

   d   How approachable did you find the consultant?

2   **Techniques used during the programme**

   a   Which techniques did you think worked best?

   b   Did the programme take into account your personal circumstances?

   b   Do you feel you were given enough time to develop the skills throughout the programme?

3   **Future recommendations**

   a   Do you think that anything should be included in the programme?

   b   Do you think anything needs to be taken out of the programme?

   c   What do you see as the major strengths of the programme?

   d   What do you see as the major limitations of the programme?

▶ **Figure 6.13:** How can using interview guides help to gain an understanding of the athlete's opinion?

Observing your **athlete's performance** is useful in assessing the effectiveness of your PST work because it enables you to detect any changes in physical performance. It allows you to collect any objective data relating to performance. When you observe performance, you can look for:

▶ changes in psychological factors (such as arousal and somatic anxiety)

▶ changes in body language

▶ differences in the skill level of the athlete.

Anybody working in sport environments should always reflect on their own work so that they can improve in the future. As well as evaluating the athlete during and after the PST, it is also useful to evaluate your own performance as the sports psychologist. Evaluation forms can give qualitative and quantitative feedback on:

▶ your characteristics (e.g. liaising with your athlete)
▶ your effectiveness (e.g. how well did you communicate with your client?)
▶ suggestions for your future work (e.g. if you were to work with similar athletes in future, which areas could you improve on?).

The form in Figure 6.14 shows the type of questionnaire used to review the effectiveness of the PST programme. This form can be used for both athletes and coaches.

> **Research**
>
> Recently, the 5Cs (commitment, communication, confidence, control, concentration) have become prominent in the sports environment as important psychological qualities for sporting success. Research the 5Cs and decide which behaviours you would look for when observing athletes. How would this help you if you were coaching a group of young athletes?

Consultation evaluation form

Client's name _____

Consultant's name _____

1 Characteristics of the consultant

For each of the following statements, please provide a rating from 1–5, with 1 being the lowest rating and 5 being the highest.

Statement	Rating
a The consultant provided me with information on skills training that applied directly to my sport.	
b The consultant produced a programme that was geared to my individual needs.	
c The consultant was flexible and was happy to work around me.	
d The consultant was positive.	
e The consultant made me feel comfortable.	
f I understood exactly what the consultant expected of me.	

2 Effectiveness of the consultant

Please circle the number that you feel best describes how effective you feel the consultant was in helping overall sporting performance.

a Overall individual performance										
Limited performance									*Helped performance*	
−5	−4	−3	−2	−1	0	1	2	3	4	5

b Overall team performance										
Limited performance									*Helped performance*	
−5	−4	−3	−2	−1	0	1	2	3	4	5

3 Recommendations for improvement

Please use the space below to provide any recommendations you feel will increase the quality of service provided by the consultant. Please continue on the back of this form if necessary.

▶ **Figure 6.14:** Why is it useful to ask these types of question when working with athletes?

Assessment practice 6.3

C.D3 C.M4 C.P6 C.P5

A T53 classification wheelchair athlete from your local athletics club has come to see you as they have been struggling with their performance. They feel anxious in the build-up to big events and think that there are certain athletes that they will never be able to beat. They are keen to learn and develop as an athlete and just want to be happy in their sport, feeling as though they can perform well.

As the athlete is a T53 classification, they have little abdominal control so find certain types of breathing activities difficult. You have spoken to the athlete's coach who has a background in sport psychology and he is happy to supervise you through the production of an appropriate psychological skills training programme.

Produce a psychological skills training programme that will address the key considerations presented by the athlete. Ensure that you include only relevant techniques and that you clearly say what these techniques are and how they will benefit the athlete.

Plan
- What is the task?
- Do I need clarification on anything?
- What aspects of the task do I think will take the most/ least time?

Do
- I can make connections between what I am reading/ researching and the task, and identify the important information.
- I can set milestones and evaluate my progress and success at these intervals.

Review
- I can explain what the task was and how I approached it.
- I can explain how this learning experience relates to future experiences.
- I realise where I still have learning/knowledge gaps and I know how to resolve them.

Link

This content links to *Unit 1: Anatomy and Physiology*.

Further reading and resources

Burton, D. and Raedeke, T.D. (2008) *Sport Psychology for Coaches*, Champaign, IL: Human Kinetics.

Bush, A., Brierley, J., Carr, S., Gledhill, A., Mackay, N., Manley, A., Morgan, H., Roberts, W. and Willsmer, N. (2012) *Foundations in Sports Coaching*, Harlow, Essex: Pearson Education.

Forsdyke, D. and Gledhill, A. (2014) Reaching out for a helping hand: The role of social support in sports injury rehabilitation. *sportEx Medicine*, 61, 8–12.

Gledhill, A. and Forsdyke, D. (2015) The challenges of youth: Psychological responses to sports injury and rehabilitation in youth athletes. *sportEx Medicine*, 63, 12–17.

Hemmings, B. and Holder, T. (2009) *Applied Sport Psychology: A Case-based Approach*, Chichester, West Sussex: Wiley-Blackwell.

Karageorghis, C. and Terry, P. (2010) *Inside Sport Psychology*, Champaign, IL: Human Kinetics.

Kornspan, A.S. (2009) *Fundamentals of Sport and Exercise Psychology*, Champaign, IL: Human Kinetics.

Weinberg, R.S. and Gould, D. (2014) *Foundations of Sport and Exercise Psychology*, 6th edition, Champaign, IL: Human Kinetics.

Williams, A.M. (2012) *Science and Soccer: Developing Elite Performers*, Oxford: Routledge.

Journal

Athletic Insight: The Online Journal of Sport Psychology. Available at: www.athleticinsight.com

THINK ▶FUTURE

Umair Ali

Sport Psychologist

I have been working as a sport psychologist in professional football for four years. During this time, I have encountered many different athletes who have benefitted from sport psychology. After I completed my BTEC Level 3 in Sport, I went to university and completed a BPS-approved degree in Psychology, as I needed this to be able to use the title 'Psychologist'. This complemented my existing football coaching qualifications so I am happy that I have the subject-specific knowledge as well as an understanding of the sport.

Having an understanding of the sport you work in is essential for effective work as a sport psychologist. So is the ability to develop and maintain effective working relationships with different individuals. In doing so, you are more likely to be able to get to know your athlete, which is useful when it comes to designing psychological skills training programmes. This is important as there is no such thing as a universal psychological skills training programme and you should always tailor your work to the needs of your athlete.

Focusing on your skills

Designing effective PST programmes

It is important to be able to design effective PST programmes for athletes. Here are some tips to help you do this:
- Before completing any work with a client, make sure that you have their consent.
- Make sure that you conduct an appropriate needs analysis with the athlete and discuss your findings with them.
- Find out if the athlete has any previous experience of using PST programmes – they may already prefer certain psychological techniques.

- Ensure that you are able to provide a clear rationale for the psychological techniques that you adopt. You can usually do this by linking the needs of the athlete with the benefits of the techniques and then supporting your suggestions with appropriate evidence.
- Reviewing your athlete's progress at scheduled interviews is key for monitoring their progress. This can really help their motivation levels and can help you to alter your programme design as and when required.
- Make sure that you always work within your limitations of practice. If there is anything that you are unsure of, speak to professionals or refer your athlete to them.

Getting ready for assessment

Bruno is taking a BTEC National in Sport. He has been given an assignment to produce a psychological skills training programme for an athlete in a sport of his choice and write this up as a report. Bruno had to:

▶ discuss the different psychological skills that can be used with athletes in sport

▶ produce a psychological skills training programme for an athlete and discuss how the programme would benefit the athlete.

How I got started

First, I decided on which athlete I wanted to base my report. I chose a sport that I am interested in because I knew this would make me more motivated and committed to doing a good job on the work.

I collated all of my notes for learning aim C and separated them into different sections that looked at the different psychological skills and how to design a PST programme. After this, I created a summary table describing the different psychological skills and their benefits and looked at how they might link to my client.

I looked at the different ways that you can assess an athlete's strengths and areas for improvement and how I could identify the demands of different sports. Then, I looked at how I could organise the different skills that would benefit my athlete into a coherent PST programme.

How I brought it all together

To start, I wrote a short introduction outlining the purpose of the work that I was doing. After this, I discussed each of the psychological skills that can be used in sport, with:

▶ an introduction to each of the different psychological skills

▶ a discussion of the proposed benefits of the psychological skills for different athletes.

After doing this, I planned my PST programme for my athlete, ensuring that I covered all of the unit content. I made sure that I included the key benefits of the PST programme for my athlete, as well as suggesting any alternatives in case my athlete wanted different PST activities to do.

What I learned from the experience

There are many different psychological skills training activities that can be used with athletes so it is important to be able to link the proposed benefits of these activities to the needs of athletes. This made the assignment a little bit difficult at times because I was unsure which to select.

Next time, I would group my PST activities under headings (e.g. psychological skills that can enhance relaxation), look at the key benefits and any difficulties athletes might have when learning these and use all of that information to select the best ones for my athlete.

I think I spent a bit too much time focusing on the structure and layout of my PST programme and not enough time providing evidence to support the arguments that I was making, so I would look to improve this if I was to do the same assignment again.

Think about it

▶ Have you planned your assignment so that you know you will be able to complete it by the submission deadline?

▶ Do you have the recommended resources to help you to provide evidence and references to support and develop the arguments that you plan to make?

▶ Is your assignment written in your own words?

Practical Sports Performance 7

Getting to know your unit

Assessment

You will be assessed by a series of assignments set by your tutor.

People's desire to participate in and enjoy sport continues to increase. While some are content to enjoy the long-term benefits of a healthy lifestyle, others enjoy sport as an opportunity to push themselves to the limit, aiming for the perfect performance and to achieve the highest accolades. Sports performers can be at many different levels: from early beginners to elite level athletes. All of them, however, will need to build the same understanding of the skills, techniques and tactics of their sport. The better your understanding of these factors, the more effective your sports performance will be.

This unit will give you the opportunity to improve your own knowledge and practical ability in a selection of individual and team sports, introducing the skills, techniques and tactics as well as reflecting on your own performance. Effective reflection on your performance will allow you to identify how to improve and develop as a performer – a vital skill that will guide your development in the sport.

How you will be assessed

This unit will be assessed by a series of assignments set by your tutor. Throughout this unit you will find assessment activities that will help you work towards your assignments. Completing these assessment activities will not mean that you have achieved a particular grade, but you will have carried out useful research or preparation that will be relevant when it comes to your final assignments.

In order for you to achieve the tasks in your assignment, it is important to check that you have met all of the Pass grading criteria. You can do this as you work your way through the assignment.

If you are hoping to gain a Merit or Distinction, you should also make sure that you present the information in your assignment in the style that is required by the relevant assessment criterion. For example, Merit criteria require you to analyse and discuss, and Distinction criteria require you to assess and evaluate.

The assignments set by your tutor will consist of a number of tasks designed to meet the criteria in the table. This is likely to consist of both practical assessments and written assignments but may also include activities such as:

▶ summarising how participants comply with the rules/laws of team and individual sports

▶ reviewing the skills, techniques and tactics required to perform effectively in different sports

▶ completing a practical assessment of your ability to apply the skills, techniques and tactics in conditioned and competitive situations in both individual and team sports

▶ reviewing and reflecting on your own performance in individual and team sports.

Assessment criteria

This table shows you what you must do in order to achieve a **Pass**, **Merit** or **Distinction** grade, and where you can find activities to help you.

Pass	**Merit**	**Distinction**

Learning aim Examine National Governing Body rules, laws and regulations for selected sports competitions

Pass	**Merit**	**Distinction**
A.P1 Summarise how participants comply with the rules/laws and regulations in individual and team sports. **Assessment practice 7.1**	**A.M1** Assess how participants comply with the rules/laws and regulations and the impact on individual and team sport. **Assessment practice 7.1**	**AB.D1** Evaluate how participants use skills, techniques and tactics required in individual and team sports and their compliance with rules/laws and regulations impacts on individual/team performance. **Assessment practice 7.2**

Learning aim Examine the skills, techniques and tactics required to perform in selected sports

Pass	**Merit**	**Distinction**
B.P2 Discuss the skills, techniques and tactics required in two different sports. **Assessment practice 7.2**	**B.M2** Assess the skills, techniques and tactics required in two different sports. **Assessment practice 7.2**	

Learning aim Develop skills, techniques and tactics for sporting activity in order to meet sport aims

Pass	**Merit**	**Distinction**
C.P3 Demonstrate in a competitive situation the appropriate combination of skills, techniques and tactics from isolated and conditioned practices for an individual and a team sport. **Assessment practice 7.2**	**C.M3** Demonstrate in a competitive situation the effective combination of skills, techniques and tactics from isolated and conditioned practices for an individual and a team sport. **Assessment practice 7.2**	**C.D2** Demonstrate in a competitive situation the effective adaptation of the relevant skills, techniques and tactics from isolated and conditioned practices and full and accurate compliance of the rules and regulations for an individual and a team sport. **Assessment practice 7.2**

Learning aim Reflect on own practical performance using selected assessment methods

Pass	**Merit**	**Distinction**
D.P4 Discuss the selected assessment methods used to review a practical sports performance. **Assessment practice 7.3**	**D.M4** Analyse own performance to reflect strengths and areas for improvement in an individual and a team competitive sport using feedback from others and different assessment methods. **Assessment practice 7.3**	**D.D3** Justify recommendations for personal performance improvement using wider understanding of compliance of rules and regulations and use of skills and techniques in an individual and a team competitive sport. **Assessment practice 7.3**
D.P5 Discuss own performance using different assessment methods and feedback from others in an individual and a team competitive sport. **Assessment practice 7.3**		

Getting started

Participation in some sports is increasing, whereas in other sports participation levels are decreasing. Changes in levels of sports participation are often linked to media coverage of a sport. Write down a list of sports which you have seen covered in the media over the last six weeks. When you have completed this unit you will have a thorough understanding of a variety of different sports; see if some of the sports that you have listed are the sports you will be studying.

A Examine National Governing Body rules, laws and regulations for selected sports competitions

Sport could be defined as 'an organised competitive physical activity, governed by set rules and regulations'. This definition clearly includes sports such as tennis, badminton, athletics and gymnastics, but leaves others such as snooker, pool and darts open to debate. The debate will continue to grow as the popularity of these sports increases.

Often as a sport grows, an international governing body is established to govern its rules around the world, and this is often a determining factor in its classification as a 'sport'. All such sports must have governed rules and regulations. These are organised and regularly updated by the appropriate governing bodies at the highest level, and are then enforced by officials who represent the governing bodies, both at national and international levels.

An athlete needs to be aware of the rules and regulations of any sport in which they participate. Researching the rules and regulations of their sport can help to make players more competent and better role models for others. The better an athlete understands the rules and regulations of their sport, the more they will appreciate the work of the officials who implement them.

Rules and laws in sports

Before the development of organised governing bodies, **rules** for sporting activities were set at local level, meaning that similar games played had varying rules and formats in different villages and towns. It was in England during the nineteenth century where the **codification** of most sports occurred. This was because of the development of public schools and universities where, in the nineteenth century, young boys and men from different areas of the UK came together with their regional variations of traditional games. With a desire for competition, there was a need for common rules. These rules were devised in the public schools and this was where the governance of sports began. The rules, laws and regulations of a sport are set out to provide players with standards to adhere to and ensure that they all play fairly.

Research

Select a popular sport and research when the first sets of rules of the sport were devised. If you can get a copy of the first set of rules, have a look at these and compare them against the modern day rules that you are familiar with for this sport.

In modern day sport it is the international sport federations that decide on the rules for a sport. It is also these organisations that decide on the appropriate sanctions that should be applied following a breach of the rules. These rules obviously apply to the players but they can also apply to administrators of the sport as well.

Discussion

In the media there are often examples of how players in various sports have broken the rules. Examples include a player getting sent off from the field of play or an inappropriate reaction to an umpire or official's decision.

Using a recent example from both a team sport and an individual sport, discuss the rule which has been broken and the action which has been taken by the national governing body (NGB) or International Federation. Do you think the sanction was appropriate?

Sports can be classified into many different categories which are linked by their many different features. For your BTEC National in Sport qualification, Pearson has categorised sports as 'team' and 'individual'.

▶ A **team sport** includes a minimum of two individuals who compete to win against opposing teams. Examples of team sports include netball, hockey, football, rugby union, rugby league and basketball.

▶ An **individual sport** is a sport in which the individual performs on their own against other individuals. Examples of individual sports are tennis (singles), badminton (singles), golf, boxing and most cycling events.

In team sports, the number of participants per team is restricted, and it is usual for each team to have an equal number of players. For example, in a game of rugby union each team is allowed to start with a maximum of 15 players; a side starting with fewer players will be at an obvious disadvantage.

Some rules do not differ much compared with another sport. For example, in rugby league and rugby union the rules regarding losing control of the ball and knocking the ball forward are similar; likewise in table tennis and tennis the rules regarding the number of times a ball is allowed to bounce are similar. However, most sports' rules differ quite considerably.

This section will look at some components of sports which remain constant although varying from sport to sport. This includes the start of a competition, scoring or methods of victory, the competitive environment and time. These are examples of rules which are managed and maintained by national governing bodies (NGBs) and international sports federations (ISFs).

National and international governing bodies

NGBs are the organisations responsible for a sport within a specific country. In 2016 Sport England recognised 33 NGBs for sport. NGBs are responsible for organising and running their own sport in the UK. Mainly due to participation levels, some NGBs are much larger than others; because of this, some NGBs are financially self-sufficient whereas others rely heavily on subsidies from Sport England and the National Lottery.

ISFs are responsible for the formulation of rules that NGBs will ensure are followed by players and consistently applied by officials. ISFs organise international competitions and they also arrange sponsorship and television contracts for international competitions.

The rules and regulations of sports are normally established and governed by the NGB or, when one exists, the relevant ISF. NGBs work closely with the ISF to ensure that the rules, structure and development of the sport are managed appropriately.

Most NGBs and ISFs are recognised by UK Sport, the International Olympic Committee or both, depending on the nature of the sport.

Tables 7.1 and 7.2 each show selected sports (team sports in Table 7.1 and individual sports in Table 7.2) and list their relevant NGB and ISF.

▶ **Table 7.1:** The NGB and ISF for ten team sports

Team sports	NGB	ISF
Football	Football Association	Fédération Internationale de Football Association (FIFA)
Rugby union	Rugby Football Union	International Rugby Board (IRB)
Rugby league	Rugby Football League	Rugby League International Federation (RLIF)
Volleyball	English Volleyball Association	Fédération Internationale de Volleyball (FIVB)
Basketball	England Basketball	Fédération Internationale de Basketball (FIBA)
Hockey	England Hockey	International Hockey Federation (FIH)
Cricket	England and Wales Cricket Board	International Cricket Council (ICC)
Rounders	Rounders England	National Rounders Association (NRA)
Netball	England Netball Association	International Federation of Netball Associations (IFNA)
Lacrosse	English Lacrosse Association	Federation of International Lacrosse (FIL)
Rowing*	British Rowing (formerly Amateur Rowing Association)	Fédération Internationale des Sociétés d'Aviron (FISA)

*Rowing can sometimes be an individual sport (e.g. single scull)

▶ **Table 7.2:** The NGB and ISF for ten individual sports

Individual sports	NGB	ISF
Boxing	Amateur Boxing Association	International Boxing Association
Golf	Royal and Ancient (Golf Club of St Andrews)	International Golf Federation
Badminton	Badminton England	Badminton World Federation
Gymnastics	British Gymnastics	Fédération Internationale de Gymnastique
Athletics	UK Athletics	International Association of Athletics Federations
Cycling*	British Cycling	Union Cycliste Internationale (UCI)
Tennis	Lawn Tennis Association	International Tennis Federation
Sailing	Royal Yachting Association	International Sailing Federation
Table tennis	English Table Tennis Association	International Table Tennis Federation
Judo	British Judo Association	International Judo Federation

*Cycling can sometimes be a team sport (e.g. track team pursuit and road team time trial events)

NGB and ISF regulation of rules and laws

The rules and laws decided by NGBs and ISFs determine how a sport can be won or lost. In the past decade a number of sports have introduced changes to the rules and regulations to make them more entertaining for spectators. For example, in 2014 FIFA adapted the laws of football allowing goal line technology to be used at the World Cup in Brazil to inform match officials when the football had fully crossed the goal line, and in 2006 the Badminton World Federation adapted its method of scoring to ensure that for every successful shot a point was awarded to the player(s) who completed it.

The process of changing the rules requires a trial period; once the ISF agrees that the rule change is appropriate, the change is sanctioned, the rules and laws of the sport are amended, and the appropriate information is passed to the NGBs. This information should then be passed on to officials, clubs, coaches, performers, teachers and spectators, and applied in all future competitions and events.

In most sports, rules and regulations are updated regularly and it is the responsibility of everyone involved in a sport to have a thorough knowledge of these changes.

Competition rules/laws and regulations

All sports have space and time restraints, rules and a clear competitive structure. The focus of all sports is to determine who is the best. However, the process for deciding the ultimate result may differ between competitions.

In some sports, performers are matched or categorised to ensure that their opponents are given equal circumstances during competition. For example, in Paralympic sports, participants with different disabilities are categorised to compete with individuals with similar disabilities.

Link

Paralympic sports are categorised in accordance with an athlete's disability. You will cover this in more depth in *Unit 24: Provision of Sport for People with Physical and Learning Disabilities*, if that unit is part of your qualification.

Leagues and knockout competitions

Sport competition can have many different formats. The ultimate objective of a sports competition is for there to be a clear winner.

▸ A league format is often used for sports performers and sports teams to compete in. A league is a formation of a group of teams or individual sports performers that compete against each other in a specific sport. A league format involves every team or performer competing against each other at least once (this is also known as a round-robin). League competitions are provided for sports performers of all abilities, from beginners to elite performers.

▸ A knockout tournament is a competition in which an individual or team competes against other individuals or teams in a 'winner takes all' format. The format of this tournament means that when a team loses they can no longer compete in the tournament. The winner of the tournament is the individual or team that goes the entire length of the tournament undefeated.

The Olympic Games

The modern Olympic Games are seen by many sports performers and figures in the media as the biggest international sporting event in the world, with more than 200 nations participating. The modern Olympics feature both summer and winter games, in which thousands of sports performers from around the world participate in a wide range of sports with the aim of winning an Olympic medal.

The Paralympic Games is an international event for elite athletes with disabilities; the Paralympic Games is also part of the modern Olympic Games. The Paralympics always follow the Olympic Games every two years, with both summer and winter games.

During both Olympics and Paralympics, the numbers of entrants are limited within each event through ranking systems. Competition during the Olympics is heavily regulated to ensure that competition is completely fair.

> **Research**
>
> Not all sports are played at the Olympic Games. For a list of all the sports that are represented at the Olympic Games, see www.olympic.org/sports. For some sports with a limited profile (and funding), to be included in the games would be a huge benefit for the sport.
>
> Carry out an investigation into which sports are currently being considered to be 'demonstration sports' for the 2020 Summer Olympic Games in Tokyo.

World championships and other tournaments

In some sports a regular competition is held to enable sports performers and teams from all over the world to compete against one another, to determine who is the best in the world. These events are organised by the ISFs (see Tables 7.1 and 7.2). Table 7.3 shows examples of the world championship competitions organised for specific sports with an indication of the regularity of the competition.

The formats of these competitions vary enormously, including straight knockout competitions and ones that involve mini-league or 'group' stages before progression to a knockout stage.

▸ **Table 7.3:** Example world championship events

Sports	Name of event	Regularity
Netball	International Netball Federation (INF) Netball World Cup	Every 4 years
Athletics	International Association of Athletics Federations (IAAF) World Championships in Athletics	Every 2 years
Rugby union	International Rugby Board (IRB) Rugby World Cup	Every 4 years
Hockey	Hockey World Cup	Every 4 years
Snooker	World Snooker Championship	Every year
Rowing	World Rowing Championship	Every year
Football	Fédération Internationale de Football Association (FIFA) World Cup	Every 4 years
Gymnastics	World Artistic Gymnastics Championships	Every year (except the year of an Olympic Games)
Cricket	International Cricket Council (ICC) Cricket World Cup	Every 4 years
Swimming	FINA (Fédération Internationale de Natation / International Swimming Federation) World Aquatics Championships	Every 2 years

In pairs, research two World Championship tournaments in different sports. What laws, rules and format does each tournament have? What are the similarities and differences? What might be the reasons for this? Prepare a short report of your findings.

 PAUSE POINT

Do you understand the function and purpose of NGBs in organising and running sports and competitions?

Hint   Why do you think each sport needs a central body to provide its rules and laws?

Extend   Carry out further research into the governing body for your sport. What changes have there been in the past ten years?

Unwritten rules and etiquette

Unwritten rules and **etiquette** are the ethics and values which all athletes are expected to follow, both in training and in competitions. The concept of fair play revolves around equality, not just the desire to succeed. The founder of the modern Olympics, Baron de Coubertin, is believed to be one of the earliest exponents of the concept of 'sportsmanship'; his words express the importance of a moral intention in all sports:

> *'The most important thing in the Olympic Games is not to win but to take part, just as the most important thing in life is not the triumph but the struggle.'*

The rules, regulations and laws of sport are written down and provided for all participants and officials, as well as the spectators. They exist to define what constitutes a victory. But there are other rules which are not written down or governed but which all sports performers are nevertheless expected to observe.

Sportsmanship

Sportsmanship is the belief that all athletes should conform to both the written and unwritten rules of their sport. Fair play means treating an opponent as an equal, and adhering to the rules at the same time as striving to win.

The concept of fair play includes:

▶ respect towards coaches, officials, spectators and other players

▶ playing within the rules and spirit of the sport

▶ the ability to accept success and failure, victory and defeat well.

Sports performers should also consider the attitudes they should eliminate to ensure they are demonstrating sportsmanship at all times. Unacceptable behaviours include:

▶ highlighting weaknesses of team mates or opposition

▶ demonstrating aggression after losing

▶ hurting an opponent or team mate through words or actions

▶ boasting after success

▶ cheating or attempting to gain an unfair advantage

▶ questioning the ability of, or decisions made by, an official.

Link

This section links with *Unit 27: The Athlete's Lifestyle.*

Key term

Etiquette – the rules that govern how people behave with others. In sport, etiquette is also known as sportsmanship and fair play.

It is very important for all sports performers to demonstrate compassion and self-discipline with team mates, opponents, coaches, officials and spectators. Without these two factors, it is difficult to demonstrate a philosophy of sportsmanship.

It is important to share the concept of sportsmanship with young people and those who are starting their 'journey' in a particular sport. Giving consistent messages, enabling sports performers to feel safe and secure in the sporting environment, is a key building block to create an ethos of sportsmanship.

Case study

The unwritten rules in team sports

In a football match between West Ham and Everton in 2000, the Everton goalkeeper, Paul Gerrard, was injured. The West Ham player Paolo di Canio had an ideal opportunity to score: an open goal, during injury time. Instead, however, he caught the ball and indicated that Gerrard needed medical attention. Fortunately, Gerrard was not seriously injured, but di Canio's actions earned him a lot of respect from other players and from the supporters.

Check your knowledge

1 What unwritten rules do you think were applied in this situation?

2 Can you identify any other acts of sportsmanship that have been applied in team sports recently?

3 Do you think there is a place for sportsmanship and fair play in team sports today?

4 Discuss the phrase 'Winning isn't everything, it's the only thing'. Do you agree? If yes, why? If not, why not?

5 Can you identify five ways people can cheat in team sports?

Case study

The unwritten rules in individual sports

On 29 March 1981, Dick Beardsley and Inge Simonsen completed the first ever London Marathon hand in hand: they had been so evenly matched throughout the race that they agreed to share the victory. In 2015, to mark the 35th anniversary of the marathon, 'fun runners' were encouraged to repeat this gesture and cross the finish line hand in hand.

Check your knowledge

1 What unwritten rules do you think have been applied in this scenario? Can you identify any other acts of sportsmanship which have been applied in individual sports recently?

2 Is there a place for sportsmanship and fair play in individual sports today?

3 Discuss the phrase 'nice guys finish last'. Do you agree? If yes, why? If not, why not?

4 Can you identify five ways people can cheat in individual sports?

▶ Paula Radcliffe finishes the 2015 London Marathon holding hands with Rob Danson

Competitors' welfare

When considering the concept of sportsmanship, the main focus is to ensure that everyone applies the rules of the sports at all times, and ensures the reputation of the sport is not tarnished by an act of foul play or disrespect towards players, officials or spectators.

When considering sportsmanship, it is important that the well-being of team mates and opponents is considered at all times. When participating in sport it is important that the desire to win does not impact on the physical or mental well-being of an opponent or team mate (when appropriate).

In some instances, sports performers have not consistently applied this concept and, because of their desire to win, the physical and/or mental well-being of their opponents has been impacted. In addition to the obvious example of physical injury being caused deliberately, in modern sport the concept of 'barracking', 'banter' and 'sledging' can also have a negative impact on the psychological well-being of sports performers.

An example of performers supporting the welfare of their opponents is when an injury occurs during a competitive situation. Rival players (when appropriate) may demonstrate sporting behaviour by ensuring that the injured sports performer is able to continue, or seeing whether they require first aid. In some sports, efforts can be made by the other performer to stop the game, although in other sports play cannot stop until a point is lost or a race is won.

> **Research**
>
> Look back at some of the most recent 'big' sports events – Olympic Games, World Championships, European Championships, etc. Look to see if there were any examples of other sports performers demonstrating sportsmanship to other competitors. Were there any examples of sports performers cheating? Consider and discuss which of the examples created the most media coverage.

Regulations for sports under competition rules

Regulations are the rules or principles that are applied consistently in a sport. These differ from one sport to another, which is why each sport requires a governing body.

Regulations for players and participants

The regulations governing different sports are varied, but all will include regulations that relate to the players or participants.

Different sports have different numbers of players participating in competitive situations. Sports like badminton, tennis, judo, golf and cycling are considered to be individual sports (with some exceptions, e.g. doubles in tennis and badminton, and team pursuit in cycling). Others, such as rugby union, rugby league, hockey, netball and basketball, are considered to be team sports. Team sports restrict the number of players that are allowed to be involved in a competitive situation at any one time.

Any competition has to have a clear beginning and end. In all sports, the start will be administered by an official. Consider the examples of the starting of events below.

▶ In basketball a player from each of the two teams will compete to gain possession through participating in a tip-off conducted by the umpire.

- In cricket, the umpire must allow the captain from one of the two teams to decide who is going to start the batting or the bowling: this is decided by the toss of a coin. The winner of the toss then decides whether their team will bat or bowl first.
- In a 100-metre sprint race the start is controlled by the starter: the athletes will go when they hear the gun or starting signal.
- Before a tennis match, the umpire tosses a coin and the winner of the toss chooses whether to serve first, and on which side of the court to start the game.

Many sports have different rules with regard to the number of interchanges that can take place during a competitive situation.

An example of a player/participant regulation which is applied to the concept of interchanges is the law/rules around the process of substitutions in football.

Football substitution rules

- A maximum of three substitutes may be used in official competitions. In other competitions (e.g. friendly games) teams may agree on a maximum number but the referee must be informed before the match.
- Substitutes must be nominated (named) before the start of the game and the names of the substitutes must be given to the referee and other officials.
- In a competitive situation the player who has been replaced by the substitute cannot return to the field of play.
- When all three substitutions have been made (during a competitive situation) no other player can enter the field of play, even if a serious injury occurs to a player through no fault of his/her own.
- Only those nominated may participate. A substitute may replace a player sent off by an official before the start of a match.
- A substitute sent off before the start of a match by an official may not be replaced.
- A substitute is under the match referee's authority during the game and may be cautioned and sent off.
- A substitute who enters the field of play without the permission of the referee should be cautioned.

Equipment

It is important in sport that all players are safe at all times. Therefore, all equipment must be constantly regulated to ensure sports performers are protected at all times, and many sports will specify what type of equipment must always be worn or used in order to protect the participants.

When considering equipment for sports performers the NGBs and ISFs have to consider both the sports performers and their opponents. For example, in American football the player may be more protected by metal helmets, but the opponent may be more seriously injured by a clash with a metal helmet than by a hard plastic helmet.

When NGBs and ISFs consider what equipment is or is not acceptable in sport, consideration is also given to whether the equipment may provide more of an advantage to some competitors than others. For example, when metal woods were first introduced to golf, the Professional Golf Association banned them from all major competitions until testing had been carried out.

Playing surfaces

The surfaces which competitive sports can be played upon are also governed and regulated by the ISFs and NGBs. Some sports can be played at a competitive level on

Research

Hi-tech polyurethane suits were banned by FINA (International Swimming Federation) in 2010. Consider other sports which have banned particular equipment because it gave sports performers an unfair advantage. Discuss your findings with the rest of your group.

more than one surface, and the rules around the type of surface need to be constantly monitored because of advances in technology.

For example, association football can be played on either grass or third-generation grass surfaces, and tennis can be played on a variety of surfaces in a variety of facilities (indoor or outdoor). However certain surfaces, such as clay, are generally only suitable for outdoor use, whereas other surfaces are used both indoors and outdoors, e.g. hard court.

Up until 2012, rugby league was only allowed to be played competitively on grass pitches. However, due to the development of artificial turf technology, in 2012, Widnes Vikings became the first club to play and train on artificial grass.

For some sports competition can only take place outside in the open air, whereas in other sports competition can take place either inside or outside. An example of a sport which can be played both inside and outside at an elite level is tennis. In 2009 a retractable roof was installed at Centre Court at Wimbledon (seen by many as the most prestigious tennis venue), allowing tennis to be played either outside or inside, at any time of the day, and regardless of the weather.

Boundaries for participation

The area where sport is played may have many names, such as court, pitch, ring, course or track. These boundaries remain the same, although some sports can be played both inside and outside them.

In order for a sport to be governed, and the rules to be administered by officials, a set boundary is often required. In most sports this will be a closed environment such as a football pitch, basketball court or rugby pitch in team sports, and tennis court, badminton court or boxing ring in individual sports.

In some sports boundaries are more open, although there are still restrictions regarding the route or course an athlete has to take. For example, a sailing race will have limited boundaries and a specific route, but due to the nature of the event the boundaries are flexible.

Facilities

One of the key regulations in any sport is the provision which is used to facilitate a competitive situation. In some instances the facility will require more regulations than others. The facilities in sport vary depending upon the sport, and the different types of facilities include courts, pools, tracks, rings, pitches, courses, etc. The size of the facility will depend on the sport. In some instances the same type of facility will be required for every event but the size of the facility will vary. For example, a pool is required in both swimming and diving but the dimensions of the pool will vary because of the different needs of the sports.

When considering the dimensions for a diving pool, it is not just the size of the pool that matters: the distance and space between the diving boards and platforms, and the depth of the water under each, must also be considered to create a safe diving environment for the diver. In contrast, for swimming, FINA (International Swimming Federation) state that all international swimming competitions use a 50-metre Olympic-style pool.

Health and safety

Health and safety is partly affected by the size of the facility, the surface of the facility and the equipment used. The key role of the regulations that are applied to equipment, surface and facilities is to prevent the risk of injuries to sports performers, officials and, when appropriate, spectators.

An example of regulations which have been developed to consider the safety of all sports performers are the rules that were brought in by the Football Association in 2008 to ensure that all goalposts used at sports clubs, schools, playing fields and leisure centres are safe and meet strict regulations. The regulation was introduced to reduce the number of injuries that had been caused historically on 'old' unsafe goalposts. The responsibility of goalpost management belongs to the clubs, councils, schools or private providers that have overall responsibility for each of the facilities.

Scoring

In some sports, scores are given for achieving a goal, while in others success is assessed by a time or a distance. The points, games, time, or distance determine who wins and who loses.

▶ A cricket team will win a game if they score more runs than the opposing team. There can be restrictions on the number of overs a team may bowl in order to obtain a set number of runs (limited overs cricket), but some matches (test matches) can have unlimited overs but are restricted to a set number of days.

▶ In a sailing regatta, the winner will be the team which completes the race in the fastest time.

▶ A 100-metre sprinter will win the race by attaining a faster time than all the other athletes in the race.

▶ In tennis, on the other hand, a player has to win a certain number of points to win a game, a certain number of games to win a set and a certain number of sets to win the overall match.

Spectators

Most sports rely on spectators to engage in order to make them financially viable. Spectators are obviously an important part of any sporting event. However, as with any variable, spectators must maintain codes of behaviour in order for competition to take place fairly and smoothly. The three key ways in which spectators are generally expected to conduct themselves are:

▶ staying clear of the competitive area

▶ avoiding causing distractions during periods of focus for an athlete

▶ refraining from language or behaviours which might offend or intimidate competitors or other spectators.

The extent to which these elements are enforced varies between sports. However it is not uncommon for spectators to be removed from sporting arenas for breaking codes of conduct.

Time

Many team sports limit the length of time a game/match can last. Some include breaks, to give the players a rest and to allow coaches and managers the opportunity to discuss the application of tactics and strategies.

In basketball there are four quarters or two halves; the amount of time per quarter/half depends on the age of the players. If a match ends in a tie, extra time, called 'overtime', is added in order for one of the two teams to win the match.

The rules of some sports demand that there must be a winner at the end of a match, whereas in other sports, such as hockey, if a match ends with an equal score on both sides, a draw will be declared, and equal points will be awarded to each team and added to a tally of points. The formulations of these points are governed by the appropriate NGB.

Research

Pick one individual sport, such as tennis, and one team sport, such as cricket. Explore the different scoring rules of both of these sports and prepare a brief report, explaining the scoring systems and identifying differences.

Few individual sports have time constraints, although some combat sports such as boxing and judo do. In boxing, a set number of rounds are agreed (a maximum of 12 is allowed for championship matches, though amateur bouts usually have four). If a bout goes the full number of rounds, the winner will be the boxer who has landed the most punches and obtained the most points (awarded by the officials/adjudicators). Sometimes a winner may be declared before the end of the allocated time; this could be due to a knockout or a stopped fight by the ring or match official.

Situations where rules/laws have been broken

Every athlete needs to have a good knowledge of how the rules are applied in various situations within their sport. This will give them the necessary understanding of what actions are within the rules and which ones are illegal. It will also explain any sanctions that may be imposed when they or another player breaks the rules.

There are many sports where the effective use of rules can be used to gain a competitive advantage. Examples of this can often be seen in sailing races where, if an athlete has already gained enough points within a series to be winning, they might use tactics and rules to dominate their nearest opponent in a final race. This ensures the rival has no chance of gaining enough points to close the gap and threaten the competition for first place; they can legally ruin their opponent's race by aggressive sailing.

In some sports, development of equipment can lead to rules being updated to accommodate these developments. A prime example of this is the trend that occurred when swimmers used full body suits to gain a competitive advantage. As the use of these suits became better understood, the rules have been updated to make them illegal in most arenas.

A greater understanding of the rules and regulations will increase athletes' appreciation of the officials within the sport and the job they do. All sports demand a high level of respect for the officials who enforce the rules in competitive situations, and in many sports, any athlete who fails to respect these individuals can expect to have sanctions imposed on them.

Rules can be broken in many different circumstances in sport. Table 7.4 demonstrates some examples of when rules/laws can be broken in various sports.

▶ **Table 7.4:** Examples of rule breaking in sport

Breaches	Possible examples
Health and safety breaches	• In football a player cannot go into a challenge with an opponent with both feet (and studs raised). • In rugby union a player cannot tackle an opponent around the neck. • In boxing a contestant is not allowed to punch their opponent below the waistline.
Start/restart of competition	• In football when the game is being kicked off to restart play (either at the start of a half or after a goal has been scored) each player in a team must stay in their own half, until the ball has been kicked. • At the start of an athletics track event, the athletes must not start to run until the starter pistol has sounded.
Sports boundaries	• In both athletics and swimming when racing (on the track or in the pool) each competitor must stay within their lane. • When serving in tennis the player cannot step onto the court when the racket is making contact with the tennis ball.
When defending	• In football when a defender makes a back pass to the goalkeeper, the goalkeeper is not allowed to pick the ball up (unless the ball is headed back to the goalkeeper). • In rugby league when a player has tackled another player the defender is not allowed to slow play down by holding the attacker down after being tackled. • In netball no contact can be made with the attacker when they are shooting at goal.
When attacking and scoring	• In basketball a team must not take longer than 24 seconds to take a shot at the basket. • In field hockey the whole ball must be over the line in order for a goal to be scored.

Can you identify the key rules and regulations in a selected sport?

Hint

What information would you give a young sports performer who was playing this sport for the first time?

Extend

Think about the key elements of competition, the playing area, how to start, how to finish, how to win, and how to score.

Roles and responsibilities of officials

Sports involve many officials, each with clear roles and responsibilities regarding the application of the rules and regulations. See Table 7.5 for examples of key officials and their duties.

▶ **Table 7.5:** The role of key officials

Official	Example sports	Roles
Umpires	Tennis, cricket, netball, hockey, athletics, badminton	The umpire is responsible for all on-field activity during a game. The umpire will ensure that the rules/laws of the game are maintained. The umpire will be the official who will make the key and final decisions. The umpire is responsible for stopping play and communicating the decision which has been made, using the appropriate method of communication.
Referees	Football, rugby union, rugby league, basketball, cricket, judo, swimming	The role of the referee is to ensure that all rules/laws are followed and adhered to by the sports performers. Normally the referee will be part of the on-field competition, although in some sports the referee may not be part of play.
Tournament directors	Judo	The tournament director is responsible for the organisation of the event, and then the on-site running of the event. They coordinate the schedule and take overall responsibility for all the officials. They field questions from coaches, players and spectators regarding everything apart from refereeing queries.
Judges	Boxing, judo, athletics	The role of the judge is to ensure that the rules/laws have been correctly followed and to make a judgement on performance. It is often the judge's decision that will determine whether a rule/law has been broken and who has won or lost.
Timekeepers	Swimming, athletics, cycling, rugby union, rugby league, basketball	The timekeeper is responsible for ensuring that the clock starts and stops during play. Their use allows the on-field match official (if appropriate) to concentrate solely on making the correct decisions.
Starters	Swimming, athletics, cycling	The starter has the role of starting a competition in line with the rules/laws of the sport. The starter is often required to communicate the start of a race using a set procedure, ensuring that all participants are aware of the start time.
Third umpires	Cricket	The third umpire is an official who will use television coverage to adjudicate or make key decisions on a specific event. Third umpires can only be used when the equipment is available; they are limited to use in professional or elite sport.
Fourth umpires	Football, rugby union, rugby league	It is now common in elite football, rugby union and rugby league to see a fourth official. For rugby union and rugby league the fourth official is also known as the video referee – their role is similar to that of a third umpire. In football the role of the fourth official is to support the other officials. In the event of an injury to any of the on-field officials, the fourth official would be called upon to replace him or her.
Referee assistants	Football, rugby union, rugby league	Referee assistants (or linesmen) are there to support the decisions made by the referee. They communicate to the referee when they have spotted an infringement or a reason why the competition has to be stopped. In some sports the assistant referee will have specific rules which they have to apply during competition. For example, in football the assistant referee will indicate when a player is in an off-side position.

Responsibilities of officials

An official has many responsibilities in addition to their duties, and control of the competitors is just one of them. They must consistently apply, understand and implement these responsibilities in order to be a successful official in any sport.

Figure 7.1 shows the responsibilities which a key official may have to demonstrate when officiating in a selected sport. Obviously some officials have different responsibilities from other officials in the same sport.

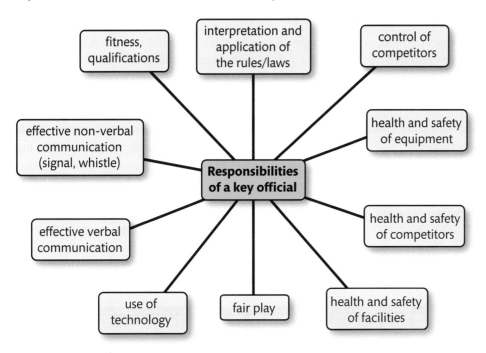

▶ **Figure 7.1:** Typical responsibilities of a key official

Interpretation and application of the laws

An effective official must have an up-to-date and thorough understanding of the rules/laws of the sport. In addition to having a clear understanding of the rules, the official must also have an understanding of how to apply the rules during a competitive situation. All officials in all sports have to ensure that the rules/laws of the sports are correctly applied during a game.

Health and safety

A key responsibility of an official is managing the safety of the **participants** involved in a competitive situation. When working with anyone under 18 this responsibility becomes a legal obligation of a duty of care. During competitive situations all officials have the responsibility to keep participants safe and free from harm. At all times the health and safety of all participants is at the forefront of their mind when applying the rules/laws of the sport.

At the start of their career, officials will work with younger performers, hence they need to be aware of child protection and the importance of safeguarding children at all times. As well as keeping them free from injury, an official should be aware of the signs and symptoms of child abuse and understand what to do if they notice anything suspicious. Anyone working with children must undergo the appropriate checks, which will be carried out by the organisers of the competition or the league.

Officials also have a major responsibility to ensure **facilities and equipment** used during a competitive situation are checked prior to participation. The playing area must also meet the required regulations. Prior to starting a competitive situation, the referee will check the pitch, equipment and players. If they notice any hazards or risks to the participants, they will ensure that appropriate adjustments are made.

Safety tip

If in doubt, ask to see the risk assessments for a venue and competitive situation. Risk assessments are written documents clearly listing all risks and hazards associated with an activity.

When sport is played outside, the official should also take into account the weather and consider whether the conditions could injure the participants. For example, when playing rugby if the grass surface is frozen players are more likely to be injured.

Fair play

It is important that officials are the advocates of fair play at all times; this can be demonstrated by the way in which an official approaches their roles and responsibilities and, more importantly, how these are applied when the official is applying the rules/laws of sport. The official should ensure that they always show respect to the sports performers, coaches and spectators; this may be through the way they communicate with them. All officials should also do their utmost to promote sportsmanship and fair play during a competitive situation, in addition to ensuring that the rules of the sport are effectively applied at all times.

Use of technology

As the development of technology in sports becomes more prevalent, so does the need for officials to be able to understand how to use technology. In some instances third umpires, video referees and match umpires will simply use the technology provided to support the application of rules. The majority of technology is highly accurate and the rules/laws of sport have written rules which apply to the software and its usage during a game.

▶ Technology is now in use in a number of sports to support decision-making

In some instances the referee or umpire also has to be aware of when the technology should be brought into the competitive situation to ensure that the rules are applied correctly in any given situation. The lead officials have to ensure that technology is only used when absolutely required.

Research

Consider the different technologies used in tennis, cricket, rugby union and football. For each of the sports identify when the technology was first introduced. As a group consider the impact the technology has had on the sport. Do you think it has benefited each sport or not? Do you think the introduction of technology has devalued the position of the officials in each sport?

Communication

Officials have to use **effective communication** when applying the rules of the sport in a competitive situation. Officials are required to display information about the rules/laws that they apply to players, coaches and spectators.

Officials mainly use verbal communication, often talking players through the decisions which they are making or have made. However, for the coaching staff and spectators, officials also have to consider using universal **non-verbal communication** methods. These methods are prescribed to the officials in the laws of the game but they indicate to a coach and knowledgeable spectator which rules/laws have been broken.

In sport the types of non-verbal communication differ, although, in the main, hand signals are used to highlight which rule the official is applying. In some sports, in addition to hand signals, officials also communicate using equipment such as a whistle. For example, in rugby union the touch judge uses a flag to attract the attention of the referee, although each signal used has a different meaning.

Fitness requirements

In some sports there is a requirement for the match official to be on the field of play and to keep up with the play to ensure rules are applied appropriately. In addition to being able to keep up with the play, the official must also be alert and capable of making appropriate decisions. This requires a high level of fitness, as play in some sports can be very fast at times, and the official may even do more running than some of the players on the pitch.

In some sports the fitness of the officials is regularly assessed. Failure to meet the guidelines (which will be set by the NGB or ISF) results in the removal of an official from the list that can officiate at a particular level. Obviously the higher the level of performance, the greater the fitness requirements in sports which require on-field officials.

Qualifications

In most sports (and certainly at an elite level in all sports), officials are required to hold appropriate and recognised officiating qualifications. Appropriately qualified officials ensure that the sport is played within the rules/laws of the game, and that the participants, coaches and spectators are safe at all times.

All NGBs provide training and qualifications to educate officials. The level of qualifications for officials often varies depending upon the age and experience of the applicant. For example, in football there are ten different levels for officiating. In order to achieve the highest level (level 1) a match official must have passed appropriate qualifications and gained significant experience.

The officiating qualification is often also recognised by the ISF. This enables the officials to officiate in international competitions if they are appropriately qualified.

Case study

Knowing the rules

Holly is a coach for a local netball team. She has had several issues finding officials for her matches; on a number of occasions during the season parents of players have had to stand in to officiate competitive matches.

Some of the parents and players have been challenging the decisions made by the stand-in officials during competitive situations. In order to overcome this Holly would like to educate both the parents and players in her team about the rules of netball and how they are applied in specific situations.

Check your knowledge

1. List the officials required to officiate a game of netball.

2. Can you provide the parents and players with a summary of the roles and responsibilities of each official?

3. Can you provide a summary for the parents and players of how to start a competitive game of netball?

4. Can you provide a summary for the parents and players of how to score a goal in a competitive game of netball?

PAUSE POINT　　Can you identify the role of key officials in a selected sport?

> **Hint**　　What information would you give someone who was officiating an event for the first time?

> **Extend**　　What do you consider to be an official's three most important duties? Write them in order of importance?

Assessment practice 7.1　　　　　A.P1　A.M1

A local coaching company is thinking about building a workshop into its summer coaching programme which further develops the participants' understanding of the rules/laws of sport. The director of the company would like some resources which will be shared with the coaches who will be delivering the session to the participants. The resources should be informative and provide both the coach and the participants with all the information they need regarding the rules and regulations of an individual and a team sport of your choice.

Produce some resources which summarise how the participants on each of the coaching programmes will comply with the rules/laws and regulations in both a team and an individual sport.

To further enhance understanding of how to apply the rules of the sport you should provide examples for each sport where rules/laws have been followed and also where they have been broken.

Within the resources, make sure you include a summary of the different officials and their roles and responsibilities when applying the rules in competitive situations in each of the sports.

Plan
- What is the task? What am I being asked to do?
- What resources will I need to support me in completing this task?

Do
- I know what I am doing and what I need to achieve.
- I can identify when I have gone wrong and adjust my thinking.

Review
- I can explain what the task was and how I approached the task.
- I can explain how I would approach the difficult elements of this task differently next time.

B & C　Examine and develop the skills, techniques and tactics required to perform in selected sports

As well as being either a team or an individual sport, sports can be classified as 'athletic', 'gymnastic' or 'games'. They can then be divided further, for example within the 'games' category there are net and wall games, invasion games, striking and fielding games, combat games, target games, track athletics and field athletics.

Every sport will have a range of applicable skills, techniques and tactics associated with it. Some may be common between sports and, although obviously much of this will be practical, there will be a range of 'soft skills' required as well, such as communication and team work.

> **Link**
>
> This section links with *Unit 2: Fitness Training and Programming for Health, Sport and Well-being* and *Unit 26: Technical and Tactical Demands of Sport.*

Technical demands required to perform in sport

Skills

A skill in sport is the ability to produce a combination of movements using a variety of muscles and joints to produce a coordinated action. Skills are acquired through learning, then mastered through practice and observation. Athletes develop skills through support and feedback from experienced and knowledgeable coaches and/or athletes. Mastering a skill means being able to continually produce it successfully with little effort.

Skills vary, however. Some can be transferred from sport to sport. For example, an athlete who masters the skill of catching when receiving a pass in rugby can transfer this skill to other sports that involve catching, such as basketball, cricket or netball.

To achieve success in sport, an athlete has to successfully master a range of skills. For example, a basketball player will have to perform the following skills successfully: dribbling, passing, free throws, jump shots, lay-ups, rebounds, blocking, stealing. A tennis player must successfully perform serves, volleys, forehands, backhands, slices and top spins.

> **Discussion**
>
> In a group or pairs, think of some other sports where skills can be transferred to enhance an athlete's performance. Why is this? Feed back to the rest of the group.

Different types of skills

Skills can be classified according to the environment in which they are performed. They may be **open skills** or **closed skills**. We also classify skills by the pace with which the athlete controls the timing of an action: skills are said to be **self-paced**, **externally paced** or somewhere between the two. See Table 7.6 for more information.

For some skills the athlete can control the start of the action, but thereafter the movement takes place at an externally set pace.

▸ An example from a team sport is a goalkeeper making a save during a football game: the goalkeeper will decide when to dive towards the ball, but once the decision is made, the goalkeeper no longer has any control over the speed at which she/he travels towards the ball.

▸ An example from an individual sport is a 10-metre board diver who decides when to start the dive, but having left the board is unable to control the rate at which she/he heads towards the water.

▸ **Table 7.6:** Different types of skill

Type of skill	Description	Individual sport example	Team sport example
Open skills	Skills the athlete is constantly adapting, according to what is happening around them	Badminton return: the receiver is unaware where the shuttlecock will be played, so reacts to their opponent's moves to select an appropriate return. The choice of return shot will also be affected by the opponent's position.	Footballer dribbling a ball, unaware of the location of all the members of the opposing team. Defenders challenge to try to get possession of the ball. The decisions the player dribbling will make depend on the actions of the opponents.
Closed skills	Pre-learned patterns of movements the athlete follows with very little reference to the surrounding environment	An archer takes aim, pulls back the bowstring and releases the arrow towards the target.	Rugby player taking a conversion during a match. The movement pattern remains the same every time the player performs the skill.
Self-paced skills	When an athlete controls the timing of the execution of the skill	A golf shot: the golfer determines when to start the swing and may choose to wait until a gust of wind has dropped.	A volleyball server decides when to start the action; the timing may depend on the location of opponents and readiness of the server.
Externally-paced skills	When the timing of the skill is determined by what is happening elsewhere	A windsurfer will have to alter the angle of his/her sail, depending on the direction of the wind.	With a hockey pass, the skill is determined by the location of players on the same team and the opposing team.

Fine and gross body involvement

Skills can also be classified as fine or gross, depending on the muscles involved.

▸ **Fine skills** involve small movements of specific parts of the body. For example, taking a close-range shot at goal in netball will only require the goal shooter and goal attack to move their fingers and wrist to produce the required skill. An individual shooting a rifle on a shooting range will only have to move their trigger finger.

▸ **Gross skills** involve large muscle groups and movement from the whole body. An example of this form of skill in a team sport is the bowling action in cricket, while an individual example is the javelin throw.

Continuous, discrete and serial skills

▸ **Continuous skills** are those which have no obvious beginning or end – they can be continued for as long as the performer wishes, with the end of the skill becoming the beginning of the next, for example in running, where one stride becomes the start of the next running stride.

▸ A **discrete skill** has a clear beginning and end – it can be repeated, but the athlete will start the full action again in a controlled and timely manner. A team sport example is a rugby conversion, while an individual example is a golf putt.

▸ A **serial skill** is a series of discrete skills put together to produce an organised movement – the order of the movement is often important, but each part of the skill requires specific development. A team sport example is when a footballer dribbles with the ball, steps over it to beat a defender and then shoots at goal at the end of the movement. An example from an individual sport is a pole vault.

> **Theory into practice**
>
> In groups, identify whether throwing a javelin is:
>
> - an open or closed skill
> - a fine or gross skill
> - a self-paced or externally paced skill
> - a continuous, discrete or serial skill.
>
> List the skills in your own sport and identify which categories they fall into.

Within some sports, skills can be broken down further into attacking or defensive categories. They will still also be classified in the previous manner, but it will be clear whether they are relevant to attack or defence. For instance, in rugby a drop goal is clearly an attacking skill whereas a tackle is clearly defensive.

Techniques

A **technique** is the way an athlete performs a skill. In some sports, players use different techniques to produce the same outcome. For example, Lionel Messi and Cristiano Ronaldo have different techniques when taking direct free kicks, and Andy Murray and Novak Djokovic have different serving techniques

The most effective way to consider a technique is to consider how the skill can be broken down. For example, a long lofted pass in football can be broken down into its component actions as follows: run-up (preparation stage), alignment to the ball, feet position, body position, contact with the ball and follow-through. An example from an individual sport might be a tennis serve broken down into its component actions: feet position and movement, body position, action of the racket-holding arm, action of the other arm, ball toss, racket swing and follow-through.

Breaking down skills like this develops athletes' understanding of how to improve their application of each skill. The technical elements for each component will be different for each individual, but the components of the skill will remain the same.

> **Key term**
>
> **Technique** – a way of carrying out a particular skill.

Effective use of skills during participation

When using any skill it is important that it is technically correct – if a sports performer does not apply the correct technique to the application of the skill it may affect the outcome, but it may also consume additional energy which could have been better used to secure victory in a competitive situation. In order to consider the correct application of a skill, a sports performer must think about the position that each part of the body is in during each stage of the skill.

Modern technological advances have affected sport just as much as other aspects of our lives. In elite sport detailed subjective analysis of performance provides sports performers with the required detail to amend a technique so it can be used effectively. Technological advances used in this way are covered later in this unit.

> **Research**
>
> Carry out some research into the success of the British Cycling Team since 2008, when performance director Dave Brailsford claimed that a lot of the success was down to a 'marginal gains' mentality.
>
> Think about your own sports performance and the marginal gains you could introduce to improve your sports performance.

 **PAUSE POINT**   For a selected sport, can you break down the components of the technique for a particular skill?

> **Hint**   Think about each of the stages of the skill and the final outcome.
>
> **Extend**   How does the role of each body part relate to each stage of a skill?

Tactical demands applied in sports performance

> **Link**
>
> This section links with *Unit 26: Technical and Tactical Demands of Sport.*

Tactics are the skills a player uses in any type of sport in order to win; for example during a hockey or tennis match, each team or player will apply specific tactics and strategies to try to beat and outwit their opponent(s). While techniques are the way we apply skills in a selected sport, tactics are how we apply skills successfully in competitive situations. The most skilful and talented performer can lose if they do not apply the skills tactically in specific situations.

> **Key term**
>
> **Tactics** – the skills and strategies a player uses in any type of sport in order to win.

Factors that affect tactics include the opposition, the playing conditions and possibly the timing of the game, match or tournament in a season. Some tactics are determined before the event starts – these often target a player's or a team's weaknesses. Pre-event tactics can involve carrying out research on an opposing player or team.

The main factors affecting the application of tactics in team and individual sports are:

▶ attacking and defending
▶ the situation in the game – are you winning or losing?
▶ your own/team's strengths – what parts of the race/game are you stronger in and which parts of your game are weaker?
▶ your opponents' strengths and weaknesses.

You will need to demonstrate effective use of skills, techniques and tactics in a range of different situations, including:

▶ **isolated practices** – practices which are devised to develop a skill or technique; often a drill or exercise which develops each component of the skill

▶ **conditioned practices** – practices with special rules or restrictions that support the development of a skill, technique or tactic in a natural, game-like scenario, for example 3 v 3 in basketball

▶ **competitive situations** – events or contests where more than one sports performer competes to achieve a set goal, following all of the rules/laws and regulations applied by a recognised official.

Attacking and defending

Tactics in sport are mostly concerned with attacking and defending, so they are often categorised into **attacking strategies**, used to attack opponents, and **defensive strategies**, used to prevent opponents scoring points or gaining ground. Each sport has strategies for attacking and defending; a couple of examples are outlined below.

▶ In netball, one team may spot a weakness in one of the opposition and as a team try to exploit this to gain an advantage. On the other hand, if a netball team is suffering because of a particular player in the opposing team, changes may be made to mark that player very closely.

▶ In tennis a serve could be seen as an attacking shot, but the application of the skill alone cannot guarantee this. The player performing the serve may adjust their serve to disadvantage their opponent, in which case the serve becomes defensive.

It can be difficult to coach athletes in applying tactics in a competitive environment, as this knowledge is developed through experience. Coaches can try to develop the knowledge and ability to apply appropriate strategies through simulating specific practices. After athletes have experienced specific scenarios, they will be able to react appropriately.

Decision making

When skills have been mastered in isolation, sports performers then need to demonstrate that they can apply these skills effectively, appropriately and strategically in a competitive situation.

The process of making the correct decision in a competitive situation is often the difference between a good sports performer and a very good sports performer. The decisions made by sports performers in these highly pressured situations can mean the difference between winning and losing.

> **Research**
>
> Carry out some research into England's performance in the 2015 Rugby Union World Cup. Examine the team's exit from the World Cup. Can any of the reasons for their exit be linked to a weak tactical performance from any individual players?

Communication

The ability to communicate with other people during competitive situations can also impact upon the use of tactics during performance. When used effectively, communication (both verbal and non-verbal) can have a positive impact on the outcome of a situation.

Sports performers in a team game may communicate with each other about how to apply a tactic in a specific situation. In order to do this effectively the other team members need to have an excellent knowledge of the sport, opponents and their own team mates.

In some sports, sports performers need to communicate tactics during play to each other. In some instances teams may also apply code words or non-verbal signs to indicate a tactic in a particular situation. For example, in rugby union when a team is preparing to take a line out, the player who is nominated to throw the ball will communicate to his team mates to whom and where he will target the throw. In baseball the catcher will use hand signals to suggest different types of pitches to the pitcher.

For sports performers who have close contact with their coach during competitive situations, it may be communication from the coach to the player which may influence the tactics used in a particular scenario during competition. When doing this the coach will often assess the situation and use his/her experience to consider what a sports performer needs to do. In order to apply this effectively, the coach's communication to the sports performer needs to be very clear, and the sports performer's listening skills need to be very good to ensure that the message is well received and understood.

Environmental conditions

It may be appropriate in certain conditions for a sports performer to apply different tactics. In some instances the weather may impact upon the decisions that a sports performer makes. For example, if it is particularly windy some sports performers may have to change tactics; if it is very hot they may need to reconsider their tactics.

The gradient of the surface may also impact upon the decisions that a sports performer makes. For example, if a marathon runner is running on a hilly marathon course, they would need to apply different tactics to those that may apply if they were running on a flat marathon course.

It may be relevant to apply different strategies within different situations in an attempt to gain an advantage over sports performers' opponents.

Case study

Developing tactical awareness

Darren is head coach for an under-18s basketball team which competes in the regional league. The team had a very good start to the season, winning their first three games. However, since these victories the team has lost the last five consecutive games.

Darren's assistant coach, Malcolm, believes that the reason for recent losses is because of the team's poor tactical awareness.

Check your knowledge

1　Can you provide Darren with a summary of what tactics are?

2　Can you provide Darren with some examples of attacking plays in basketball?

3　Can you provide Darren with some examples of defending tactics in basketball?

While on work experience at a local secondary school, you have been asked by one of the PE teachers to provide some materials which will promote table tennis and rounders to Year 7 learners. The aim of the materials is to further develop the learners' knowledge of these sports. At present, the learners have very little knowledge about either sport.

You have been asked to provide some materials which will go on one of the notice boards in the sports hall which summarise the skills, techniques and tactics in each sport. Within your materials you should ensure you assess and evaluate how participants use skills, techniques and tactics effectively.

In addition to the materials for the notice board, the PE teacher would also like you to provide a video which demonstrates the appropriate combination of skills, techniques and tactics in both table tennis and rounders. The video will be used to show the learners the correct application of the skills, techniques and tactics in both table tennis and rounders.

Plan

- Do I know the skills, techniques and tactics in each of these sports?
- Do I have the ability to perform the skills, techniques and tactics in each of these sports?

Do

- I know what I am doing and what I need to achieve.
- I can identify when I have gone wrong and adjust my thinking.

Review

- I can explain what the task was and how I approached the task.
- I can explain how I would approach the difficult elements of this task differently next time.

D Reflect on own practical performance using selected assessment methods

Athletes are constantly seeking to develop and improve their performance. Although a pivotal person in this process is the coach, an athlete should also take responsibility for their own development. Being able to reflect on their own practical performance is an important skill.

As an athlete becomes more reflective about their performance, they should follow the performance cycle shown in Figure 7.2.

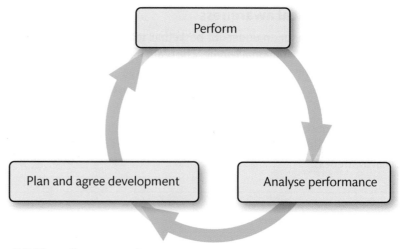

▶ **Figure 7.2:** The performance cycle

This section looks at a variety of methods that you can use to assess the performance of other athletes. More importantly, you will learn how to assess your own performance and draw conclusions from your findings regarding self-development in individual sports.

Assessment methods

There are four areas of performance to assess: the physical, psychological, technical and tactical demands placed on a performer in a competitive situation. The methods used to assess sports performance are important if weaknesses are to be identified and worked on. To ensure that the best results are obtained from the analysis, the most appropriate assessment method must be selected. The method may depend on the sport, the area of performance being analysed, existing knowledge of the sport and, if observing others, knowledge of the player(s) that are being observed.

SWOT analysis

A SWOT analysis is used to evaluate the strengths, weaknesses, opportunities and threats involved in the performance of a player or team. You need to understand the performance demands of the sport you are analysing. Normally, only experienced coaches carry this out, although as athletes develop it is beneficial for them also to carry out SWOT analyses so that they can compare and contrast their findings with those of their coach and agree on targets for future performance.

▶ Strengths – first identify the player's or team's strengths in a SWOT grid like those shown in Table 7.7 (for a team) and Table 7.8 (for an individual). This information could come from objective data or subjective observations. Compare the performance against an ideal model for each performance demand. It is important that you have clear criteria against which to assess the performer(s) when carrying out the performance and SWOT analysis.

▶ Weaknesses – with the support of the data, identify any weaknesses such as technical inefficiencies in the performance of specific skills, or the incorrect application of tactics and strategies in a game or a simulated practice.

▶ Opportunities – note any opportunities that the player or team have to develop their performance, such as access to training sessions or specific coaches to support technical development. It may also include information about any opponent(s), such as objective data on previous performances (times, results, etc.) or subjective assessments of their effectiveness, possibly in the form of a scouting report.

▶ Threats – identify any short- or long-term threats to the performance of the player or team.

When assessing the performance demands of a sport, it is important that all four key elements of the performance are assessed: physical, psychological, technical and tactical.

▶ **Table 7.7:** SWOT analysis of West Side netball team

Strengths	Weaknesses
• Good defensive organisation • Excellent centre (country standard) • High fitness levels for all sports performers	• Inconsistent results • Poor space awareness • Poor shooting
Opportunities	**Threats**
• Developed attacking tactics • Opponents are weak in attack • Recently appointed new head coach (very experienced with lots of ideas)	• Opponents have two county netball players: wing attack and goal attack • Mental strength – easily frustrated after a poor performance • Relegation from the league

▶ **Table 7.8:** SWOT analysis of Darren Milner, badminton player

Strengths	Weaknesses
• Good overhead clear • Good agility on the court • Excellent court coverage • High fitness levels	• Inconsistent short and long serve • Poor backhand technique, clear, smash and drop shot • Late to react to opponent's position on the court • Poor shot selection
Opportunities	**Threats**
• Developed short serve through intensive coaching sessions • Opponent also has a poor drop shot • Ability to move around the court gives performer an advantage when returning shots and generating rallies	• Opponent is a better player • Mental strength – easily frustrated after a poor shot • Wrong shot selection in long rallies

Link

This section links with *Unit 28: Sports Performance Analysis.*

Key term

Notational analysis – the recording of movement patterns and other performance data by an observer.

Performance profiling

In order to complete a full assessment of their performance, an athlete may choose to carry out a performance profile: a full assessment of the technical, tactical, physical and psychological requirements of their sport.

A performance profile uses a variety of assessment methods including **notational analysis** and performance observation. The assessment involves awarding a grade or mark which should be set against an achievable target performance or goal relating to the athlete's development.

It is important that athletes and coaches have realistic expectations regarding developmental goals. Consider the two examples below.

▶ A 10-year-old footballer could compare their performance against another player in the same league who is the top goal scorer in the league. So on a scale of 1 to 10, 1 may be a player who has scored no goals in the season, while 10 may be a player who has scored 30 goals. It would be unrealistic to compare their performance to that of Lionel Messi because of the difference in age, ability and skill levels.

▶ A golfer with a handicap of 16 could compare their performance against a golfer with an 8 handicap. So on a scale of 1 to 10, 1 may be a 16 handicap while a 10 may be compared to a 4-handicap golfer. It would be unrealistic to compare their performance to Rory McIlroy, because of the difference in ability and skill levels.

▶ Performance profiling allows golfers to compare their performance against each other

When coaching beginners, a sports coach will need to complete an initial performance profile to determine which elements of their performance require development. As an athlete develops in age and ability, performance profiles should be completed by both the coach and the athlete. After the completion of the performance profile, both athlete and coach should discuss the findings and agree a plan that can be followed to address any technical, tactical, psychological or physical weaknesses in their performance.

Use of technology

Over the past decade a range of technology has been introduced to support the process of assessment.

▶ Prozone is a computer program that analyses performance and generates data. It can provide post-match performance information for both home and away games, allowing the assessor to analyse every aspect of team and player performance. Prozone provides post-match analysis that enables coaches to supplement their own subjective observations with objective performance data.

▶ Dartfish technology is a program that can slow down a movement and freeze-frame each component of a skill to enable an assessor to assess the effective application of a technique at each stage.

▶ Kandle technology is another form of video analysis software which is used to support coaches' observations of performance.

The more complex the skill, the greater the requirement for software to enable sports coaches to analyse it in greater detail. However, more basic technology can also be used. Many club running coaches, for example, will use a smartphone or tablet to record videos of their athletes running. With the right app, they can then play it back slowly, freeze frames and even draw diagrams over the image to illustrate points about running form.

> **Link**
>
> You can read more about using technology to assess sports performance in *Unit 28: Sports Performance Analysis*.

Testing

Tests can give an objective picture of an athlete within a team's current performance levels. For example, psychometric tests may be used to assess an athlete's mental state, and fitness tests may be used to assess the physical and skill components of fitness required.

> **Link**
>
> Fitness testing is covered in detail in *Unit 5: Application of Fitness Testing* and also in *Unit 28: Sports Performance Analysis*.

An example of a psychometric test is the 'profile of mood states' test (POMS). This measures an athlete's mood during training and can indicate whether they are overtraining. It is mostly used for athletes who are looking jaded in performance or showing a lacklustre attitude when training, and is designed to examine the reasons behind the problem.

Interviews

One of the easiest methods of analysing performance is to interview an athlete after a training session or a competition. This gives valuable feedback on how they felt their performance went, and what areas of their performance they feel require further development and improvement. Using the athlete's own views on their personal strengths and areas for improvement allows them and their coach to develop training strategies to help future performances.

Objective performance data

It is possible to assess a team's or individual's performance 'live' at a training session or competition, or on video after the event, by collecting objective performance data. This involves gathering statistical data on a performance in a competitive or training situation. This data can take many different forms and allows an objective assessment based on the use of numerical data or statistics. For example, if during a football match a team has 15 shots at goal, only three of which are on target, it is possible to conclude that the team needs to work on its shooting.

This data can be collated for teams, but can also be used to assess the effectiveness of individual players within a team and athletes in individual sports. For example, if a boxer landed 37 left jabs out of 43 attempts and only 23 right jabs out of 53 attempts in a bout, it is possible to conclude that the boxer's strength is their left jab and their weakness is their right.

This objective performance data can be collected using notational analysis, where an observer/assessor records data by completing tallies. See Figure 7.3, which shows how notational analysis could be used to assess the effectiveness of a tennis player's first and second service during a game.

number of first serves in	number of first serves out
JHT JHT JHT JHT II	JHT JHT JHT JHT JHT JHT IIII
number of second serves in	number of second serves out
JHT JHT JHT JHT JHT JHT II	II

▶ **Figure 7.3:** How notational analysis could be used to assess the effectiveness of a tennis player's first and second service during a game

From this data, you might conclude that this tennis player needs to develop their first service. However, this example also highlights a flaw that may be encountered when using objective performance data: the player may have hit 22 aces from each of the first serves they landed, and therefore the first serve may not be as much of a weakness as the data suggests.

Completed passes in the final third	Failed passes in the final third
JHT JHT JHT JHT II	JHT JHT JHT JHT JHT JHT IIII

▶ **Figure 7.4:** How notational analysis could be used to assess the effectiveness of a footballer's passing ability

Figure 7.4 shows how notational analysis could be used to assess the effectiveness of a footballer's passing ability. From this data, you might conclude that this footballer needs to develop their passing in the final third of the pitch in order to improve their own performance and that of the team. Again, this information can be used to highlight a flaw that may be encountered with objective performance data: the player might have completed 22 passes and set up three goals from three of the passes they completed. The 34 incomplete passes may have been the result of excessive marking from the opponents after the impact of the earlier passes on the game, so the player's passing ability may not be as much of a weakness as the data suggests.

The collation of data does not always assess technical efficiencies as it does not include observation, so observations remain important.

> ### Theory into practice
>
> In groups of two or three, watch a game of football and record simple information such as:
> - successful passes
> - shots on target
> - shots off target
> - number of corners
> - successful tackles
> - goals scored
> - goals conceded.
>
> Analyse the data you have collected. What does it show? Discuss the findings with the rest of your group, then answer these questions.
>
> 1 Discuss what was good about the method of objective data analysis that you used.
> 2 What problems did you encounter?
> 3 How could the information you collate in the future be more accurate and effective for the analysis you have to complete?

> ### Theory into practice
>
> In groups of two or three, watch a game of singles badminton and record simple information such as:
> - successful forehand returns
> - successful backhand returns
> - number of serves
> - number of successful serves
> - points won on service
> - points won on return of serve.
>
> Analyse the data you have collected. What does it show? Discuss the findings with the rest of your group, then answer these questions.
>
> 1 Discuss what was good about the method of objective data analysis that you used.
> 2 What problems did you encounter?
> 3 How could the information you collate in the future be more accurate and effective for the analysis you have to complete?

Subjective observations

Subjective observations and assessments of a team or an individual are based on your judgements, interpretations, opinions and comparison against an ideal performance.

Observation analysis is a popular technique for assessing performance and effective application of skills, techniques and tactics. All coaches need to be effective observers, to enable them to identify strengths and weaknesses during performance.

Observation analysis should be used to identify the needs of a team or individual, and should inform a coach's plans to develop performance. The full analysis of overall performance should form the basis for a training programme with the aim of addressing the most significant weaknesses.

Many performance observations and assessments combine objective performance data and subjective observations. For example, an observation of a basketball player may include notational analysis of their application of each skill during a match, then the coach may observe their performance and compile feedback based on both these things.

⏸ PAUSE POINT   Can you explain the difference between objective and subjective analysis?

> **Hint**   Think about the different methods of assessing sports performance.
> **Extend**   When would you use each type of analysis and why?

Review performance in selected sports

To support their own development, an athlete must demonstrate effective analysis skills, including self-analysis. Analysis of performance is the ability to observe and make appropriate judgements, including of the technical and tactical elements of a specific performance. An athlete should be able to identify strengths and prioritise performance targets for both their own and other athletes' development.

In order to complete an effective analysis of performance, the athlete needs to have a clear understanding of what to expect at each stage of their development. Analysis requires the athlete to assess any faults they observe in the whole performance, a skill which takes time and experience to develop. Once done, it will allow them to identify their own strengths and areas for improvement.

> **Reflect**
>
> Think about the last time you watched sport on television. Did you make a judgement about an athlete's performance? If you made a negative judgement, who or what were you measuring the performance against?

Even the greatest athletes have weaknesses which may not be spotted by everyone; even their own coaches may not spot their faults. That is why elite athletes may change coaches or seek support from others, or build a team of coaches to work on specific areas of their performance.

Specific to sport

When analysing the performance of an individual athlete, the assessor should be aware of the demands of the sport they are assessing. For example, the skills and physical requirements of basketball and football, or of snooker and boxing, are very different and the assessor will have to take this into account in order to make an appropriate judgement on the performance.

Application of skills

When carrying out an assessment the assessor must understand the correct application of each skill ('the perfect model'). Without this understanding, the quality of feedback will be limited. For example, when assessing netball an assessor should be able to compare the application of the players' skills, techniques and tactics to an ideal application of the technique/skill being observed. This comparison against an ideal will enable the assessor to examine the performance for strengths and areas for improvement. If the assessor is unable to spot any weaknesses in the performance, then the athlete should consider consulting a more knowledgeable and experienced coach/assessor.

Technique analysis and assessment

The skills in many sports are built up of complex contractions and actions, such as the volleyball serve or the tennis serve. To gain a greater understanding of these skills, they are broken down into smaller stages to allow a clear assessment of each stage of the technique.

This method of analysing an athlete's skills may require the assessor to slow the action down (video analysis would be helpful here) and assess each part of the technique. For example, at full speed the service of a volleyball or tennis player may look fine; however, slowing it down may show that the ball toss is too far away from the body of the server, which may weaken the player's overall performance.

Tactical analysis and assessment

It is important when analysing an athlete's performance that the assessor understands the tactics and strategies. They should compare the performance they are watching against an ideal. The athlete must understand what is required and be able to execute the strategy effectively.

This tactical assessment should also consider the athlete's application of any relevant rules and the effectiveness of their decision making.

▶ Technology can help analysis of techniques such as a volleyball serve

Achievements

When analysing the performance of an athlete or a team, it may be useful to look at their previous achievements, which are likely to help form a useful impression before the observation is started. An assessor may find it helpful to look back at recent matches to see if there is a pattern in the wins/losses, and whether this is related to the performers' physical attributes.

Such information may not always be helpful, but it may help to paint a picture prior to any assessment of performance.

Strengths

The feedback collated during the observational analysis should be drawn from the observer's subjective and objective views. The subjective views are their opinions of the performance and the objective views may come from data compiled during the observation. With this information, the observer should be able to identify the strengths of the performer observed.

Areas for improvement

As with the strengths identified, areas for improvement should be identified from the observations made regarding the performance and, if appropriate, the data produced from the observation.

For example, who would have thought that Usain Bolt could have run the 100-metres any faster than he did in the Beijing Olympic final in 2008? However, by developing elements of his performance throughout a four-year period, he managed to beat his own Olympic record in the Olympic Games in London in 2012.

Developments to improve performance

Following a performance analysis, the player or team and the observer/assessor should agree a development plan which takes into account the findings from the analysis and introduces activities to improve performance. This is essential, as without a development plan and agreed goals and targets for future performance, an athlete's or team's performance could **plateau**.

Aims and objectives

Before formulating a development plan, a team/player and coach should agree clear aims. These should consist of things they would like to achieve, e.g. promotion to the higher league, or improving sprint starts, by the start of next season.

In order to achieve their aims, a team or athlete will also need to have objectives that express how they will meet each of their aims. Each aim should have an objective, e.g. 'In order to improve our league position we will have to work on defending', or 'To improve my sprint start I am going to have to work on my reaction time and leg power'.

Goals

After the completion of performance assessments and player or team analysis, the observer and the team should agree specific goals for future development. Goal-setting should be used by individuals and teams to increase their motivation and confidence for future sports events. Goal-setting should be the first stage of the planning process for any team and coach, because by setting goals they can set clear targets for personal development. Goals should provide both direction and motivation. Goals are often set over various periods of time: teams can set short-, medium-, and long-term goals.

▶ **Short-term goals** are set over a short period, between one day and one month. A short-term goal could be a target that a team or performer wishes to achieve after the next training session, or a specific technique they would like to develop by the end of the next month.

▶ **Medium-term goals** should progressively support the team or individual achieving the long-term goals. These goals can be measured at specific points within a season.

▶ **Long-term goals** are set for and with a team or individual to help them determine where they want to go, what they want to achieve and the best way of getting there. A coach should use these goals to shape their coaching schedule for a season or longer if appropriate.

SMART targets

Wherever objectives and goals are set for teams or individuals, they should be SMART.

▶ **S**pecific – the goals set should be as precise and detailed as possible for the team or individual.

▶ **M**easurable – the goals set should define a method of measuring the success of the team or individual. They should set achievement targets: what and by when?

▶ **A**chievable – the goals set should be attainable within a set period of time and should be relevant for the team or individual.

▶ **R**ealistic – the goals set should be appropriate for the team or individual.

▶ **T**ime-bound – ensure you agree a timescale, even if it includes mini-targets for athlete development (short-, medium- and long-term goals).

Opportunities

Formulating a plan for future development may open new doors for teams' and individuals' personal development as well as sporting achievement.

It may be a requirement or an agreed target that an athlete will attend courses and obtain qualifications that involve them learning new skills and techniques, or developing knowledge about a specific area of their sport. They might learn about the treatment and prevention of sports injuries, technical requirements of a sport, sports nutrition or tactical development.

Research

In your own sport, find out about appropriate courses and/or qualifications an athlete could take to improve their knowledge about the areas listed below. Give the name of the course, provider, location and cost.

- Treatment and prevention of sports injuries
- Technical requirements of a sport
- Sports nutrition
- Tactical development.

For example, if an athlete has suffered a number of injuries, their coach may think it would be beneficial for them to attend a sports injury and rehabilitation course. Here they will learn about different methods of treating sports injuries and may also learn how to avoid or prevent injuries. By completing these courses an athlete can increase their portfolio of qualifications.

The development plan agreed between the coach and the team may also introduce a team or individual to new methods of training and possibly new coaches. This may freshen up the current methods and develop further motivation. It may also provide an opportunity to improve overall performance.

Possible obstacles

Although the development plan produced for a team or individual may cover every possible eventuality and provide some excellent opportunities, unforeseen circumstances may arise and hinder progress towards attaining the set goals. These could include:

▶ injury and illness

▶ bad weather

▶ lack of funding

▶ failure to qualify for competitions/events

▶ family and/or peer pressure.

When participating in a training programme, athletes should be given every opportunity to meet their goals and targets. Athletes can seek support from within their club, or from their sport's NGB if appropriate. This support may deflect any obstacles that threaten to prevent them attaining their targets.

 PAUSE POINT   Do you understand how to analyse your own performance?

 Hint   Think about your performance in a sport. What could you do to improve it?

Extend   Try drawing up a series of short-, medium- and long-term SMART goals to improve your sporting performance.

The managing director of a local sports coaching company has contacted your college and invited some learners to meet with her staff to discuss ways of reflecting on sports performance.

She has asked you to provide a summary of different assessment methods used to review practical sports performance. She would like this to be in the form of a presentation to the sports coaches at the company.

To support the presentation, the managing director has also asked you to provide some video footage that puts the theory into a real-life context. She wants you to:

- take part in a competitive situation in both a team and individual sport, and have a video made
- use the footage to assess your own performance and provide a justification of what you will need to do to improve your performance in each sport
- produce a development plan which states what you will do to improve in each of the sports.

The managing director would like you to use the development plan to show how sports coaches can reflect on the performances of their sports performers.

Plan

- I will compile a list of each of the assessment methods used to review performance of sports performers.
- I will ensure that I have a video recording of myself competing in both a team and an individual sport.

Do

- I can reflect upon and review my performance in each sport.
- I can use appropriate assessment methods to review my performance and consider developments for further performance in each sport.

Review

- I can identify how this learning experience relates to future experiences.
- I can make informed choices based on reflection.

Further reading and resources

Cassidy, T., Jones, R. and Potrac, P. (2008) *Understanding Sports Coaching: The Social, Cultural and Pedagogical Foundations of Coaching Practice*, Abingdon: Taylor and Francis Ltd.

Crisfield, P. (2001) *Analysing Your Coaching*, Leeds: Coachwise.

Miles, A. (2004) *Coaching Practice*, Leeds: Coachwise.

Robinson, P. (2014) *Foundations of Sports Coaching*, Abingdon: Taylor and Francis Ltd.

THINK ▶▶FUTURE

Rose Wallace
Professional
Surfer and Writer

When I was growing up I always dreamt of travelling the globe and surfing for a living. I never thought that I would be good enough to make enough money from surfing to be comfortable. I accept that I am not the greatest surfer in the world but from years of consistent practice I have reached a good standard and have developed my skills so that I can tackle some fairly tough surf breaks.

During my travels I write a regular blog, have articles commissioned by magazines and manage a surf travel forum. My husband takes photos of our trips and so between us we are able to provide some great images and content. As my exposure has become greater I have attracted sponsors who provide equipment for me and help towards the cost of our trips. In return I ensure their brands receive coverage in our blog and the magazines I write for.

I don't have to compete at all, which is fantastic for me as I don't really enjoy competitive surfing. I am able to use my skills to live the life I want and I love every minute of my work.

Focusing your skills

Consistent practice

To make a living from taking part in sport you need to be at the top of your game. Once you have reached a high standard it is too easy to relax and let standards slide. In order to maintain sponsors and keep yourself in the media you must be performing at an excellent standard.

Practice is key to success, even when you may not want to practise because conditions are poor or you do not feel like it. Sports professionals are highly motivated and will push themselves at all times. That way when a camera is pointed in their direction or they have an expectation to perform they can do so with the confidence that they have done everything they can to prepare.

Developing other skills

There are many sports in which it is quite possible to make a career from being a professional athlete without ever having to compete. For those who pursue one of these careers it is essential that they develop a range of other skills to complement their sporting prowess and allow them to make a living from it. These skills might include:

- writing – to contribute to books, magazines and online platforms
- public speaking – so that they can promote their exploits through paid presentations
- general communication – to negotiate with sponsors and potential supporters
- organisation – in order to keep to busy schedules and meet targets and deadlines
- budgeting – to ensure that expenses are balanced against possible income streams.

Getting ready for assessment

Luke is working towards a BTEC National in Sport. He was given an assignment with the title 'Complete a reflection of your own performance in a Team and Individual Sport' for Learning aim D. He had to complete an analysis of his own performance in two sports in the form of a presentation; he was then going to present his findings to a group of sports coaches. The presentation had to:

▶ include information on the different assessment methods that could be used to review his performance when participating in different sports
▶ review his own performance using selected assessment methods in each sport
▶ discuss activities he will use to improve his performance in each of the selected sports.

Luke shares his experience below.

How I got started

First I collated video evidence of my badminton (individual sport) and rugby union (team sport) performance. I completed a summary of the methods I could use to assess my performance of skills, techniques and tactics in sports. I used this to decide which method of assessment I would use.

I then started to assess my performance while competing in each sport. I listed my strengths and areas where I required further development in each of the sports. I also needed to improve my knowledge of high level performance in each sport. I decided to observe sports performers performing at the highest level. I arranged to watch a live performance of an international badminton competition and my local professional rugby union club play.

How I brought it all together

I completed a SWOT analysis for each sport. To start, I wrote a short introduction describing the different methods that can be used to assess sports performance and which methods I felt were most appropriate to assess my own performance. For each sport I:

▶ created a table saying which methods of assessment I would use to assess my performance, with a short summary of each
▶ explained why I selected these methods to assess my performance
▶ completed a SWOT analysis table with a rationale for each part of the assessment
▶ summarised my ability to apply the skills, techniques and tactics, and the rules of each sport, ensuring I make the correct decisions at all times
▶ completed a development plan for my performance in each sport, which highlighted how I could improve.

I compared my own ability against the elite performers that I had observed. Finally, I wrote a short summary as a conclusion to the presentation.

What I learned from the experience

I wish I had developed a greater understanding of elite performance before completing my self-analysis. With a better understanding of the sport it would have been easier to think about the methods required to improve my performance. Next time I would compile the criteria for a performance profile in each sport, before completing a self-assessment.

I focused too much on the methods of assessing sports performance. I could have focused more on my own performance and provided a more detailed summary of how I could have improved my performance in each sport. I struggled to assess my own performance, although I did find it much easier to assess the performance of elite performers.

Think about it

▶ Have you written a plan with timings so you can complete your assignment by the submission date?
▶ Do you have video recordings of yourself performing in each sport that you are going to review? Remember one must be a team sport, and one must an individual sport.
▶ Is your information written in your own words and referenced clearly where you have used quotations or information from a book, journal or website?

Coaching for Performance 8

Getting to know your unit

There is more to being a good coach than producing good athletes or excellent teams. The best coaches are those who give athletes a positive experience and motivate them to continue. The role of a sports coach can go beyond that of a skilled and knowledgeable coach who is dedicated to developing athletes. A coach might be called on to act as a fitness trainer, social worker, motivator, disciplinarian, friend, mentor, manager or secretary, as well as many other roles.

With sport participation increasing throughout the UK, there is a strong demand for coaches who can develop athletes' performances. In this unit you will investigate the work of successful coaches and examine the skills and techniques required to develop sports performance. You will plan and deliver a coaching session; after its completion, you will assess your performance and produce a development plan to support the improvement of your planning and delivery skills.

How you will be assessed

Coaching is fundamentally a practical skill and as such there will be a strong emphasis in this unit on practical learning. Throughout this unit you will find a range of assessment activities designed to consolidate your learning, give you valuable experience and assess your learning. Completion of these activities will give you the opportunity to demonstrate your knowledge but will not guarantee you any particular grade.

It is important that you follow a structured approach to these activities to ensure that you cover all the learning aims. This will be good practice for when you tackle your actual assignments, helping you provide the required evidence to achieve a pass grade.

For a merit or distinction grade, additional information will be required and presented in the appropriate format. For example, for a merit grade, you may be asked to compare or analyse whereas for a distinction you may be asked to evaluate.

Your tutor will design tasks that will challenge you and provide opportunities to evidence your understanding at all levels. This may take the form of:

▶ providing a written document to explain and analyse the skills and knowledge required to be a strong coach

▶ presenting a plan for an individual session and showing how it links to an extended series plan

▶ delivering an individual practical performance session

▶ conducting a thorough review upon completion.

Assessment criteria

This table shows what you must do in order to achieve a Pass, Merit or Distinction grade, and where you can find activities to help you.

Pass

Learning aim A Investigate the skills, knowledge, qualities and best practice of performance coaches

A.P1

Explain the skills, knowledge, qualities and best practice of a performance coach, reflecting on personal coaching ability.

Assessment practice 8.1

Learning aim B Explore practices used to develop skills, techniques and tactics for performance

B.P2

Explain practices to develop skills, techniques and tactics for sports performance.

Assessment practice 8.2

Learning aim C Demonstrate effective planning of coaching for performance

C.P3

Produce a detailed plan for an individual performance coaching session that reflects planning considerations and an overall series plan.

Assessment practice 8.3

Learning aim D Explore the impact of coaching for performance

D.P4

Deliver your individual performance coaching session showing consideration of health and safety factors.

Assessment practice 8.4

D.P5

Review your delivered coaching session, reflecting on your planning and coaching performance.

Assessment practice 8.4

Merit

A.M1

Analyse the skills, knowledge, qualities and best practice of a performance coach and your personal coaching ability.

Assessment practice 8.1

B.M2

Analyse practices and their practicality, suitability and effectiveness to develop skills, techniques and tactics for sports performance.

Assessment practice 8.2

C.M3

Discuss the inter-relationship between your individual plan, planning considerations and an overall series plan.

Assessment practice 8.3

D.M4

Analyse your delivered individual performance coaching session and the impact of your planning and coaching performance.

Assessment practice 8.4

Distinction

A.D1

Evaluate personal coaching ability, suggesting and justifying recommendations for future personal development.

Assessment practice 8.1

B.D2

Evaluate practices and their practicality, suitability and effectiveness to develop skills, techniques and tactics for sports performance, making recommendations for adaptations.

Assessment practice 8.2

CD.D3

Evaluate the impact of your planning and coaching performance on an athlete and/or team performance, justifying future coaching developments.

Assessment practice 8.4

Getting started

Positive coaching takes practice and skill. You will probably have worked with a coach in real life and should be able to give an account of how they performed. Consider a coach you have observed. What strengths did they exhibit? What do you feel they could have done better? What skills and qualities do you think you possess that would help you as a coach?

A Investigate the skills, knowledge, qualities and best practice of performance coaches

> **Link**
>
> This unit has strong links with *Unit 4: Sports Leadership*.

In this section you will examine the skills, knowledge, qualities and best practice of a sports coach. You will reflect on how coaches should and do meet the requirements of each of their roles, responsibilities and skills. Remember that in order to be an excellent coach you do not have to fulfil every role, responsibility or skill covered in this unit: even the greatest coaches may not demonstrate excellence in all the areas covered. But as a sports coach you can always improve and should always seek to develop in order to support the athletes you work with.

Skills and knowledge for coaching for performance

Organisation of session

Planning training programmes and sessions requires a coach to demonstrate high levels of organisation. An organised session will motivate athletes and maintain interest. In order to be fully prepared and organised for a session a coach should ensure that:

- they know how many participants are taking part
- the activities are appropriate for all the participants (to do this the coach will need to know the ability levels of each participant)
- they have decided what equipment they will need prior to the event and checked that it is available and ready for use on the day of the session
- the facility where the session is taking place is booked well in advance and that they are aware of its safety procedures
- at the end of the session the facility and equipment are left as they were when the session started
- they have clear methods of stopping and starting the session. This could be discussed with participants at the start of the session; for example, when the coach blows the whistle, all participants must stop.

When they first start coaching, many sports coaches keep a written record of each session they deliver and collate their records to make a logbook. They can then refer to it when creating future session plans. Although these session plans and logbooks are an important part of organising the planning and delivery of coaching sessions, coaches also need to know how to adapt sessions if activities are not working. It is in these situations that a coach's knowledge, experience and organisational skills will be pushed to the limit.

Consider the sport you feel most confident in and imagine you have been tasked with providing a coaching session for a group of Year 9 students. How many students would you coach at any one time? What would you cover in your coaching session? What resources and facilities would you need for successful delivery?

Rapport building

It is very important that a sports coach has an excellent relationship with their performer(s) or team. A coach must ensure that the sport performer(s) or team trust the coach to ensure that they get the best out of their performance in training and during competitive situations. If a coach can develop a good relationship with the performer(s) or team, then communication between the two becomes much easier.

To develop a good rapport a coach will need to find common ground between themselves and the sports participant. This will help develop a close and harmonious relationship with each sports performer that they work with.

Communication

Communication is possibly the most important skill required to coach athletes effectively. Coaches have to exchange information, not only with athletes, but also with parents, other coaches, officials, other staff at a sports club, tutors, spectators and many other people.

The three main forms of communication used by sports coaches are verbal communication, non-verbal communication and listening skills.

In **verbal communication** it is important to keep language simple and free from technical and complex jargon, unless the athlete understands what it means. A coach should ensure that what they are saying is correct and appropriate, and that they have the attention of the person/people they are speaking to. After providing the information, they should check for understanding by questioning the audience or observing the performance of the athlete.

Non-verbal communication can take many forms, for example body language. Most body language is unconscious (done without thinking). An athlete will be able to read positive and negative body language and this information will indicate the coach's mood.

Other forms of non-verbal communication used by coaches are hand signals and demonstrations. Hand signals can direct athletes or provide instructions during training and competitions. Demonstrations are used to show the correct technique and to outline each component of a skill, technique or tactic.

As well as communicating information, it is important that a coach can receive information. In order to improve their **listening skills** a coach should:
▶ concentrate when someone is talking to them
▶ make eye contact with the speaker
▶ avoid interrupting the speaker
▶ ask questions or summarise what has been said to confirm their understanding.

Consider your classmates. As a group, decide who you think is the best communicator in the class. Discuss your decision and justify your thoughts. What is it about them that makes them strong at communication?

Diplomacy

It is important that a sports coach can communicate to sports performer(s) and or teams using **diplomacy** when appropriate. At times sports performers can be very difficult to communicate with, possibly due to a dip in form, a recent injury, or possibly even just because the sports performer is losing during a competitive situation.

During these difficult times the sports coach has to use diplomacy skills to communicate key messages to the sports performers in a way that does not upset them. This can be especially tricky during difficult periods in form, when the coach will need to convey appropriate messages to help the sports performer improve their condition or their performance, sometimes by giving constructive criticism. In such circumstances the coach must ensure that the messages they give the athlete are concise and clear.

Case study

Dave Brailsford, Cycling Coach and Manager

Sir Dave Brailsford is widely credited with turning UK cycling around over the last decade. Brailsford is famous for his 'marginal gains' philosophy that if you break a sport down into its component parts and improve your performance in each of those parts by just 1% the total gains will be significant. He is also known for his 'no compromise' attitude in which he sees only the best as close to good enough.

Brailsford's hunger for success is apparent: he leads by example, never asks anyone to do something he is not prepared to do himself and places himself firmly in the driving seat of the team. But without the 'buy in' from his team and athletes, it is of little value.

Check your knowledge

1 Considering Dave Brailsford's approach to coaching, what skills do you think he needs in order to ensure that his team follows him and accepts his vision?

2 Can you name any other famous coaches with a no nonsense approach who inspire their team and are fundamental to the success of their athletes?

Motivator

Success and enjoyment are critical when trying to motivate sports performers of all ages and abilities. A sports coach needs to adequately plan for progressive and challenging practices to ensure they maintain their participants' **motivation** and drive to take part and persist during a competitive situation. It is very important that the sports coach uses a variety of techniques to maintain this high level of motivation for their sports performers.

There are two different types of motivation which a sports coach could use to motivate the sports performers: **intrinsic** and **extrinsic**.

▶ **Intrinsic motivation** – prompted by internal factors such as enjoyment. A coach may use intrinsic motivation to support a sports performer by ensuring that the activity sessions which the sports performers participate in are varied and enjoyable. The coach must ensure that performers can achieve success and develop their skills, ensure that the session is appropriately stimulating, and set the session at an appropriate level.

▸ **Extrinsic motivation** – prompted by external factors such as rewards. A coach may use tangible or intangible rewards to motivate the performers. Tangible rewards are things that can be physically given to a sports performer like money, medals or trophies. Intangible rewards are non-physical things such as praise or encouragement.

Setting goals for athletes

Goal-setting should be used by coaches to increase athletes' motivation and confidence. It should be the first stage of the planning process for any coach, as goals should provide both direction and motivation for athletes. Goals may be short-term, medium-term or long-term.

▸ **Short-term goals** could extend from one day to one month, for example a target that an athlete wishes to achieve after the next training session, or a specific technique they would like to develop by the end of the next month.

▸ **Medium-term goals** should progressively support the progress of the athlete and their coach towards achieving the long-term goals. These goals can be measured at specific points in an athlete's season.

▸ **Long-term goals** are set for and with athletes to help determine what their ultimate aims are and the best way of achieving them. A coach should use these to shape their coaching schedule for a season or longer if appropriate. Long-term goals can also run over a number of years, for example for an elite athlete who sets themselves a target of competing in the next Olympic Games, which may not take place for another three years.

Reflect

Motivation is a transferable skill and is important in all aspects of life. Has there ever been a time when you have lacked motivation? What do you believe caused your lack of motivation? How did you manage to combat this and get the task done?

 **PAUSE POINT**   The skills required for success will vary between scenarios. However, there are many core skills which are fundamental to success as a coach.

Hint   There are many skills associated with success as a coach. Can you remember the ones discussed previously in this unit?

Extend   Which of these skills do you feel are the three most important? Justify your answer.

Knowledge of correct technical performance models

Link

This section links with *Unit 7: Practical Sports Performance* and *Unit 26: Technical and Tactical Demands of Sport*.

It is important that a sports coach has a thorough understanding of the sport they are coaching so that they can teach their athletes the correct technical performance models. This will help them to decide on appropriate activities to develop the performance of each sports performer. The coach may have gained this knowledge through their own history of participation, but they may also have to consult other resources in order to refresh their memory as to the correct technical performance model. You can read more about establishing technical ideal models and benchmarks in Unit 26 (starting on page 416).

The coach should have a detailed understanding of what practices to apply when coaching sports performers' various skills and tactics.

When learning skills and techniques, sports performers require progressive challenges. The challenges which are presented to a sports performer should focus on a complete or whole experience of the skill or technique, or they can be broken down into smaller parts. For most skills it is more supportive for the sports performers if the coach uses a combination of the two methods.

Techniques are the basic building blocks of skilled performance and are simply the most efficient way for any sports performer to overcome a physical task or problem within the rules of the sport. A skill is mastered when a sports performer has the ability to perform the skill with very little effort and thought. When coaching skills it is important that the sports coach understands how competent a sports performer is at delivering that skill.

A sports coach would generally introduce a skill to a sports performer by a demonstration and/or an explanation of the skill and then let the sports performer have a go. After observation the sports coach should then consider the most appropriate method to coach the correct technical application of the skill. Below are some methods that can be used by a sports coach to develop skills and techniques in different sports.

Whole and part learning

If a sports performer is struggling with the basics of a skill, the coach may break the skill down into its component parts and practise each part separately. For example, when coaching the triple jump in athletics, if a sports performer is unable to apply all of the components as one whole movement, a sports coach – after observing the sports performer trying to complete the triple jump as one fluent movement – would break it down into the run up phase, hop phase, step phase, and the jump and landing phase.

This 'whole–part–whole' method works well as each part of the skill requires complex technique. When it has been broken into parts it can be put back together again easily by linking the movements back together stage by stage (sequentially) until the performer can undertake the whole movement.

> **Discussion**
>
> Rowing is a popular water sport that requires great skill and coordination. The paddle stroke can be broken down into distinct phases and this is how performance is coached. As a group, can you list the various phases of a paddle stroke in rowing?

Chaining

Breaking a skill into parts is also used in the 'chaining' method of coaching. It is called this as it links the skill together in the same way that a chain links together. Again this method is suitable for complex skills with parts that can be broken down easily into different sub-parts.

When applying this method to coach a skill the sports coach should:

▶ demonstrate the whole skill
▶ demonstrate the first part of the skill (the first part of the chain)
▶ let the sports performer practise the first part
▶ demonstrate the first and second part of the skill (the first two parts of the chain)
▶ let the sports performer practise the first and second part
▶ demonstrate the first, second and third part of the skill
▶ let the sports performer practise the first, second and third part of the skill
▶ and so on until the whole technique is covered.

Chaining a tennis serve

The serve in tennis can be broken down into the following links:

1 correct positioning of feet at the start of a serve
2 correct ball toss
3 correct back swing of racket
4 correct connection with racket and ball
5 correct follow through
6 correct body position after serve.

Shaping

Breaking things into parts does not work as well when the parts of the skill need to be carried out simultaneously and/or quickly, such as a somersault or a backflip in gymnastics. There is very little time between each part of the skill, so it is very difficult for the coach to break down each part of the skill for a sports performer.

A sport coach can instead simplify the action, by modifying the skill or leaving some parts of the skill out, then adding them back in as the sports performer masters the other parts. This is known as 'shaping' a skill, and involves the sports coach:

▶ demonstrating the whole skill

▶ demonstrating a simplified technique that includes the most important parts of the skill

▶ letting the sports performer practise the modified version of the skill

▶ gradually working on the areas for development and adding back in the components of the skill that have been removed until the skill is shaped into its full form, and is executed appropriately by the sports performer.

Research

Tom Daley is a world class diver who performs complex moves in a very short space of time. How are divers coached to develop difficult dives? Does all their coaching take place in the pool?

▶ Divers such as Tom Daley have to perform complex moves in a very short space of time

Knowledge of correct tactical performance models

It is also important that a sports coach has an appropriate level of understanding of tactics in order to pass this knowledge on to the sports performer. Tactics vary from

---

Link

This section links with *Unit 7: Practical Sports Performance* and *Unit 26: Technical and Tactical Demands of Sport.*

sport to sport, although in general tactics are when a sports performer has to make a decision which will impact either offensively or defensively on their performance. As with techniques, the coach may have picked up this knowledge during their own competitive career, but they may need to refresh their memory. You can read more about how to establish tactical ideal models and benchmarks in Unit 26 (starting on page 416).

Before coaching tactical knowledge, a coach will need to analyse the existing performance of the sports performer(s) that they are coaching and the performances of opponents, and possibly compare these to the best performers in the sport. The coach will then develop strategies (or tactics) that the sports performer(s) they are coaching can use to overcome the strengths or weaknesses of the opponent.

A coach may also set up a performance strategy for their athlete. This will allow them to compete in a manner that plays to their strengths while ensuring, where possible, that their weaknesses are not exposed.

Once a sports coach has devised and considered these strategies they need to go through how the sports performer(s) will implement these strategies in a competitive situation. For most sports coaches this will be done in either **conditioned practices**, which mimic a competitive situation, or in a **competitive situation** during training. You can read more about conditioned practices and competitive situations later in this unit (starting on page 375).

> ### Key terms
>
> **Conditioned practices** – practices with special rules or restrictions that support the development of a tactic in a natural game-like scenario.
>
> **Competitive situations** – full-scale 'mock' competitive events used during training to mimic a real-life competitive event, such as an 11 v 11 training match in football.

> ### Theory into practice
>
> Rugby is a complicated sport with many rules and tactics that can be used to improve a team's chances of winning. Keeping the ball moving forward is crucial for building momentum and keeping pressure upon the opposing team.
>
> Can you design a brief practical coaching session in a competitive situation that will help teams focus on moving the ball forward and keeping pressure high?

Sports activities to challenge and develop performance

It is important that a sports coach has a bank of activities they can use when coaching. Using a range of activities is important to maintain interest and motivation. It also enables a coach to develop a programme to ensure sports performers develop as required and to ensure that they remain appropriately challenged as they progress.

A sports coach may also have specific activities which focus on particular techniques. For example, a football coach may use isolated practices to further develop the technique of a long lofted pass. The coach may then make the drill more complicated by adding barriers for the performers to avoid with the ball to further enhance their application of the skill.

> ### Discussion
>
> When working with sports that use frequent and accurate passing of a ball, coaches spend a lot of time looking at moving the ball between players quickly and accurately.
>
> Consider a ball sport. As a group, discuss some ways in which you might adapt the usual rules of play to encourage passing during a training session.

Planning for progression

It is important when planning sessions that the coach considers what challenges each performer needs and how the session is going to challenge each performer to progress. To manage this the coach must have a good knowledge of the performers and the ability to effectively analyse their performance.

When planning for progression it is important that a coach sets appropriate goals. Progression may be mapped out over a longer period of time and a coach may plan a series of sessions rather than hoping to achieve progression of all performers in a single session. The concept of planning multiple sessions is known as 'programme planning'.

Sport adaptations to challenge and develop performance

It is important that a sports coach has the ability to adapt their sessions as appropriate to ensure that the sports performers are challenged and entertained for the duration of the session. The adaptations that a coach can make can relate to:

▶ the **space** that the session takes place in – the coach could expand or reduce the amount of space available to challenge participants in different ways

▶ the **time** available – time restrictions can further challenge the participants

▶ the **equipment** used – different pieces of equipment can be introduced to further challenge participants or shift the focus onto specific areas that need addressing

▶ the **pace** – the speed with which a drill is performed can also be adapted to present new challenges

▶ the **people** involved – for instance in a team sport the coach might set up a 'defence vs. attack' drill in which one side has a numerical advantage.

You can read more about these adaptations later in this unit (in the section *Adaptation of practices to promote development of performance'*, starting on page 368.)

starting on page 368.

> **Discussion**
>
> Have you ever been involved in training where progression was mapped over an extended period? What goals were you set during this journey?

Planning for changing conditions

A good coach should be prepared for every eventuality; this is known as contingency planning. When undertaking a contingency plan it is important to:

▶ consider everything that could possibly go wrong or not quite work as originally planned – for instance with the athletes, the equipment, the weather, the location or the facilities

▶ do everything you can to ensure that none of these things happens – so check all equipment, the availability of the facility, the number of participants and the specific needs of the participants at least the night before the event

▶ have an alternative plan and be prepared in case something does go wrong.

For example, a sports coach has to have different activities in the back of their mind to take account of changing conditions. A golf coach may have different activities to use in different weather conditions: shot selection for golfers changes with the weather conditions, and a sports coach would need to develop the shot range for sports performers for a variety of conditions.

▶ Coaches must be able to adapt sessions to changing weather conditions

Maintaining safety in changing conditions

As conditions change, a sports coach must make sure that the health and safety of the participants is maintained. An environment that was safe at the start of a session might not be safe by the end of it. A coach should be prepared to end a session early if safety becomes affected. Alternatively, they may be able to adapt the session as the conditions change, for instance by moving from an outside environment to indoors.

You can read more about carrying out risk assessments of environments and activities later in this unit, starting on page 359.

PAUSE POINT   To be an effective coach you need a wide range of skills and knowledge. How many specific skills and examples of knowledge can you write down?

> Hint   Close the book and list as many examples as you can in 2 minutes.

> Extend   Of all these examples which do you think are most important? Justify your thoughts.

Qualities for coaching for performance

This section covers some of the qualities that are desirable for performance sports coaches. A coach displaying these qualities is more likely to earn the respect of participants, colleagues and others, and is therefore more likely to achieve success. These qualities are shown in Table 8.1.

▶ **Table 8.1:** Qualities for coaching for performance

Quality	Description
Professionalism	Always behave appropriately. The coach's conduct and behaviour will determine the experience and future behaviour of the athletes. A good coach will: • dress appropriately for the coaching session • speak clearly, using appropriate language at all times • respect all athletes of all abilities and treat them all equally • respect and support all officials and their decisions • promote **fair play and honesty** • reward effort • follow any national governing body (NGB) codes of conduct.
Good time keeping	It is important that a coach always arrives at the session with enough time to set up and prepare the session for the sports performers. The coach should also make sure that the session ends on time. It is also important to make sure that: • all the athletes attending the session are aware of its location and start time • the facility is booked in advance • the equipment required is prepared and ready for use • the session is planned and all appropriate arrangements are made.
Positive attitude	An enthusiastic, positive coach will encourage sports performers to succeed. Coaches should treat the performers with the same level of respect and fairness that they would expect to receive themselves, ensuring the needs of the performers are placed first and that any feedback is positive and constructive. Being positive does not mean a coach cannot highlight areas of development for a performer, but relates to the method they use to do this.
Positive role modelling	A coach should set a good example to the participants, demonstrating appropriate behaviour and using appropriate language. Coaches should accept responsibility for the conduct of the athletes they coach and encourage positive and non-discriminatory behaviour. A coach should 'set the tone' by wearing appropriate clothing and footwear, and using appropriate equipment to coach the session.

▶ **Table 8.1:** – *continued*

Awareness of environment and social setting	The coach should be aware of any issues which may impact the performance of a sports performer. This will include where the player lives, their family background and any social considerations which may impact their physical or mental well-being.
	Understanding these issues supports the coach's understanding of the sports performers they are working with. For example, if a coach is aware a performer has to travel a long distance from their home to the training venue, the coach might adapt the session start time to accommodate the needs of the performer.
	However, a coach should not become too intrusive in a sports performer's personal life. A coach must ensure they maintain a professional relationship with each sports performer they coach.
Adaptability and proactivity in problem solving	Coaches must be able to find solutions to any number of issues. It is important that a sports coach looks to find a solution to a problem quickly; the quicker a coach can resolve an issue and provide an alternative solution the more efficient the coach will be become.
	When possible always look for a solution to a problem, even in the most adverse situations, using their experience and quick thinking to adapt to the situation. A sports coach who gives up at the first hurdle is one who lacks the drive and motivation to succeed.
Empathy	It is important that a coach shows **empathy** for the circumstances, ability and pressures of the performers they coach. The coach should do everything they can to support performers to enable them to develop. At times a coach may need to be patient due to factors beyond their control, such as a family bereavement. In this example, performers may not have the same level of motivation as they had prior to the bereavement.
Approachability	Performers should have the confidence to approach their coach to discuss anything – they should feel able to ask questions and seek advice and guidance when appropriate. A coach should demonstrate their approachability by maintaining a friendly demeanour, although they should always be careful not to become too friendly and get too close to the performers, but must maintain a professional relationship.
Appropriate personal appearance	It is very important that coaches consider their appearance prior to coaching a session, as this can have a major impact on people's perception of them. Personal appearance is one of the most important ways people judge an individual's personality, and how the sports coach looks is a major factor that will influence the sports performers' first impressions.
	A coach should arrive wearing appropriate kit for the sport and the conditions, and with appropriate personal equipment. Sports performers will start the session with a higher level of respect.
Enthusiasm	An enthusiastic coach can leave a lasting impression on a sports performer, and the more enthusiastic a coach is, the more enthusiastic the athletes are likely to become.
	A coach can demonstrate their enthusiasm by showing that they enjoy the sessions and activities they are delivering. This behaviour is likely to rub off on the performers participating in the session.
Appropriate levels of confidence	A coach should have the confidence to stand in front of a group of performers with a range of abilities and direct them towards achieving an agreed objective. They need to have confidence in their own ability to identify areas for development of performers, and apply tactics using their own judgement in specific situations.
	At times coaches may also have to deliver messages to the performers which are not going to be well received. When delivering such messages, the coach must demonstrate faith in their own opinions and deliver this to the sports performer(s) in a way which inspires confidence.
Reflective practice	A coach has to learn from their experiences if they are to develop. The coach must evaluate each and every session they deliver, considering its strengths and weaknesses.
	The coach should then consider what they would do in the future should a similar circumstance arise to ensure the session is a complete success.
	Figure 8.1 shows the reflective practice model. It is important that a sports coach encompasses this process throughout their coaching career.

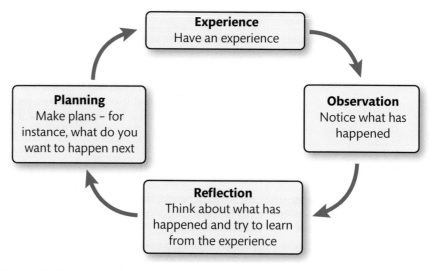

```
        Experience
      Have an experience
```

```
Planning                    Observation
Make plans – for            Notice what has
instance, what do you       happened
want to happen next
```

```
        Reflection
      Think about what has
      happened and try to learn
      from the experience
```

▶ **Figure 8.1:** The reflective practice model

Theory into practice

Imagine you have been tasked with teaching a group of adults basic hockey skills. Create a checklist you might use to ensure you complete all the tasks needed when preparing for this session. On your checklist indicate when you are going to complete each task, i.e. 10 minutes before the session or two days before the session. Justify your plans and timings.

Case study

Argentina in the 2015 Rugby World Cup

No one expected Argentina to do as well as they did in the 2015 Rugby World Cup. Compared to countries like England and France, Argentina has far fewer grass roots players and a much smaller pool of talent to pick from.

In the years leading up to 2015, Argentina's rugby performance came a long way. They also benefitted from being refused permission to join the Northern Hemisphere Six Nations Cup, instead joining the Southern Nations Tri Nations Cup: Southern Nations Rugby is currently dominant as a world force and Argentina's performance has been strengthened by consistent competition against the world's best teams.

However, their coaches have had much to do with Argentina's fantastic performance.

Check your knowledge

1 Carry out research to identify the type of atmosphere that Argentina's coaches try to promote in their team, from preparing in the changing rooms to getting on the field.

2 What would you say is the main difference between Southern and Northern Hemisphere Rugby and what is the difference in the focus of coaching?

3 Do you believe that Argentina can continue to improve or has their coaching peaked?

II	**PAUSE POINT**	A good coach will have many qualities. Which qualities do you consider most valuable?
	Hint	Are there any qualities that you might have already which will help you as a coach?
	Extend	Are there any qualities that you may need to develop? How might you go about developing these qualities?

Best practice for a coach for performance

Away from the training pitch or practice court, there are other requirements to being a successful sports coach. A sports coach can fail if they do not follow certain practices, no matter how good their grasp of the principles of delivering a session.

Safeguarding

All coaches who work with children have a responsibility for safeguarding them while they are under their care and supervision. The definition of safeguarding is to protect children and young people from harm or damage with an appropriate measure. Safeguarding involves following a process to protect children from abuse and neglect, but also includes preventing the impairment of a child's development.

▶ Coaches need to be aware of safeguarding issues

Any professional working with children has a duty to place the child's welfare as their paramount concern at all times. All organisations must have clear safeguarding policies and procedures in place that should be followed. It is common for NGBs to have standardised procedures that should be followed for specific activities.

Coaches must be able to recognise the main forms of child abuse, which include:

▶ **physical abuse** – physical hurt or injury caused by an adult to a child (could be displayed when a child displays unexplained bruising, cuts or burns)

▶ **sexual abuse** – adults, both male and female, using children to meet their own sexual needs (could be displayed when a child demonstrates over-sexualised behaviour)

▶ **emotional abuse** – could be a persistent lack of love and affection (this could be displayed when a child becomes reserved and withdrawn from social contact with others)

▶ **neglect** – failure to meet the child's basic needs such as food and warm clothing (this could be evident from a child's appearance and clothing).

If a child says or indicates that he or she is being abused, or information is obtained which raises concerns that a child is being abused, the coach or anyone receiving the information should:

▸ react calmly in order not to frighten the child
▸ tell the child they are not to blame and they are right to tell someone
▸ take what the child says seriously
▸ keep questions to an absolute minimum
▸ reassure the child
▸ make a full record of what the child has said
▸ not promise the child that no one else will be informed
▸ report the findings to a designated child protection officer at the school or sports centre, or report the information directly to the police as soon as the conversation has ended.

As a sports coach you should also be aware that coaches have caused harm to children through over-training, bullying and other forms of mistreatment, and that it is vital that a coach always treats children fairly and with respect.

Disclosure and Barring Service (DBS) checks

Prior to working with children in any capacity a coach must be the subject of a Disclosure and Barring Service (DBS) check to find out if they have a criminal record. Any previous convictions will be listed and a decision will be made by the organisation after they have viewed the DBS's feedback. This will determine whether or not the candidate is appropriate for the work. In some instances those with criminal records will not be able to work with children – this includes people on the sex offenders' register and those with violent criminal records.

The DBS was created through a merger between the Criminal Records Bureau (CRB) and the Independent Safeguarding Authority. You may still hear some people who have worked in the industry for some time refer to them as 'CRB checks'.

 **PAUSE POINT**   Many coaches work with children and young people. As professional sports coaches we have a duty of care to ensure these young people are well looked after and not put at risk.

 Hint   Close the book for a moment. What are the four main types of abuse to children?

Extend   What steps should we take as professionals within the sports industry to ensure that children are kept safe?

Key terms

Equality – treating everyone equally.

Inequality – social disparity, e.g. inequality between the pay of men and women in sport.

Prejudice – intolerance or a dislike for people based on race, religion, sexual orientation, gender, age or disability.

Equal opportunities

A sports coach will need to deliver their coaching sessions to a range of sports performers with a variety of abilities and from a range of ethnic and social backgrounds. Some sports coaches will also deliver sessions to sports performers with physical disabilities, both male and female.

It is important that, when working with any sports performer, the coach gives everyone the same opportunity to develop and improve their performance – this is what equal opportunities is about. A sports coach should ensure that they demonstrate **equality** at all times. Sports coaches should coach sports sessions without any **inequality** or **prejudice** and must ensure that all participants are treated equally and included in all of their sessions.

Qualifications and CPD

It is important that sports coaches develop themselves to the best of their ability. Sports science is always progressing, and it is important that coaches keep up to date with the latest theories and practices in their field.

Coaches must also look to continue their professional development (CPD). CPD can take place while a coach is coaching a team, and may be part of the coach's own development. CPD can be set by the coach themselves, but a coach can also be directed towards CPD through a supervisor or mentor.

This takes place in most sports through the attainment of recognised qualifications. It is important that coaches take the career qualification pathway best suited in order to fulfil their own ambitions: qualifications that tend to be more 'hands on' are provided by NGBs, while academic qualifications are also available.

Link

You can read more about this topic in *Unit 3: Professional Development in the Sports Industry*.

National Governing Body qualifications

Sport NGBs have developed coaching and leadership awards which will support a developing coach. Almost all NGBs now have a coach education structure which produces qualifications from the level of an assistant coach (often level 1 on the ladder), up to elite sports coach level (this may be level 4, 5 or higher).

It is important that a coach aims to gain the appropriate qualification required to coach the performers that they are working with. In some sports it is necessary to have a specific qualification to work with performers of a certain ability. In some sports now there is also a move to ensure that all sports coaches at all levels obtaining or working towards a recognised coaching qualification.

Academic qualifications

Academic qualifications are qualifications that are obtained in educational institutions; these include GCSEs, A levels, BTECs (various levels) and degree courses (BSc and BA). Some of these courses will further enhance the coaching ability of a sports coach. For some of the more advanced coaching awards a high standard of academic education may be needed to support the theoretical element of the course.

Risk assessment of environment and activity

Sports coaches have a **duty of care** at all times to provide a safe environment for the athletes who participate in their sessions, in order to comply with all relevant health and safety legislation, e.g. the Health and Safety at Work Act (1974). They must also make sure that the activities they deliver do not put the participants at risk.

Link

You can see an example of a risk assessment form in *Unit 4: Sports Leadership* (Figure 4.8, page 204).

Key term

Duty of care – a legal obligation imposed on an individual, requiring that they adhere to a standard of reasonable care while performing any acts that could possibly harm others.

A key part of this is risk assessment in order to reduce or remove the risk of harm or injury to players, spectators and coaches. Risk assessment requires the coach to examine all equipment and the facility/playing surface where the activity is taking place. Once a hazard has been identified, the coach must eliminate the hazard and/or risk. If the hazard can be eliminated then the session can proceed; if not, the coach must classify the degree of risk. Risks are usually classified as:

▶ low – no or minimal risk of injury

▶ medium – some risk of injury

▶ high – high risk of injury.

If the risk is anything higher than low, the coach must take action to eliminate the hazard, where possible, or reduce it to an acceptable level by reviewing and adding precautions. If a coach encounters such hazards, they must consult a more senior coach or member of staff and discuss whether the session should proceed.

There are two major types of risk that can cause injuries:

▶ **extrinsic risks** – something outside the body that may cause an injury, such as a slippery floor or bad weather

▶ **intrinsic risks** – a physical aspect of the body that may cause an injury, such as not eating enough before training or taking part with an existing injury.

Discussion

As a group, plan a circuit session for a group of 17 year olds. Once you have planned the session complete a risk assessment (like the one in Figure 8.2). Then go into the sports hall and carry out the session. Individually, and as the session takes place, look for any other health and safety considerations that you have missed and add these to your risk assessment. Discuss your findings with the rest of the group.

Location ....

Date ....

Sports coach/Assessor ....

Possible hazard	Risk	Likelihood of risk occurring (low/medium/high)	How to eliminate or minimise the risk

▶ **Figure 8.2:** A risk assessment form

Emergency procedures

Although a coach may assess every risk and hazard, and use methods of reducing injury and keeping harm to a minimum, injuries can and will occur during sport and physical activity sessions.

Sports coaches may benefit from obtaining a first-aid qualification to ensure they know what action to take if an athlete is injured. If you are not a qualified first-aider, you should make provision for first-aid during coaching sessions, for example by ensuring that a qualified first-aider is present. A coach should ensure that athletes seek professional advice as soon as possible if:

▶ a major injury is sustained during a session – fracture, severe bleeding, head injury, severe swelling or bruising with pain

▶ a minor injury is sustained during a session – muscle strain, muscle contusion (bruising), minor cuts or bleeding

▶ they become ill – vomiting, headache, sore throat, dizziness.

A coach also needs to be aware of all the emergency procedures for the facility. They should follow these procedures and should also share their knowledge of them with athletes at the start of every session. A coach will therefore need to familiarise themselves with:

▶ the fire drill at a facility/organisation

▶ the evacuation procedures at a facility/organisation

▶ the first-aid procedure at a facility/organisation

▶ the location of qualified first-aid staff at a facility/organisation

▶ the location of telephones at a facility/organisation in the event of the emergency services being needed

▶ the risk-assessment procedure at a facility/organisation.

Prior to a coaching session a coach should carry out last minute health and safety checks to ensure the facility is prepared and safe for physical activity to commence.

Administration for coaching

Administration refers to the paperwork that becomes part of the role of coaching sports performers. The days of a sports coach simply turning up at a venue and coaching a session have almost disappeared. Owing to a number of factors – most importantly the safety and protection of children and young people – sports coaches now have several different administrative tasks to carry out before, during and after delivering a session.

Planning and preparation

All coaching sessions should be planned in advance and the session plans should be kept by the coach as a record of the activities that have been delivered. This also allows the coach to reflect after a session on what went well and what parts of the session would need to be amended in the future.

In order to aid development of sports performers a coach may also plan a series of coaching sessions. When planning more than one session a sports coach would not plan all the detail of each session; instead they would plan a schedule which outlines the topics which each session will focus on, before drawing up a detailed plan for each session.

Registration

In order to ensure that a sports coach has a record of who is present at a coaching session, he or she should take a register. Players should be signed in to the session, and for children and young people the coach should also sign the players out when they leave with their parents.

A register is used both for health and safety purposes and for performance development measures: a sports coach can use a register to track which sessions a sports performer has attended and therefore what knowledge they have already been taught.

Record keeping

A coach might also need to keep track of payment of subscription fees, fines, entry fees for competitions, etc. depending on the role allocated to sports coaches within different clubs. If this is the case, it is very important that a sports coach keeps a record of all money that has been received and from who.

Insurance

Sports coaches must have appropriate insurance cover to participate in physical activity as well as to lead a sport or physical activity session. A coach is responsible for the safety of the athletes while they are under his or her supervision. If an athlete is injured during a coaching session, the coach is considered liable (legally responsible) and could be considered negligent (at fault).

If an incident does happen, insurance companies may want to see copies of the session plans and the risk assessments that the coach completed before they were delivered.

Self-reflection on personal coaching ability

A sports coach should quickly develop an understanding of how to reflect on their performance as a sports coach. It is very important that a coach does this effectively to ensure that they can develop their own performance and the performance of the sports performers who they coach.

In order to do this a coach must reflect on their current level of understanding of:

▶ skills and knowledge for coaching activities for performance
▶ qualities for coaching activities for performance
▶ best practice for a coach performance.

A coach should review their performance in each of these areas and be able to identify strengths and areas for improvement in their own performance, using each of these qualities and attributes to plan for further development as a sports coach.

You can read more about self-reflection later in this unit (see pages 379–381).

 **PAUSE POINT**   Accidents will always happen when playing sport. However, it is our duty as coaches to minimise the risk. As coaches, what can we do to ensure that sessions are run smoothly and safely?

 Hint   Close the book and list as many methods as you can within 2 minutes.

Extend   Are there any risks that you feel are common between many sports? How can we lessen the risk of injury associated with these risks?

Assessment practice 8.1

Imagine that you are the head coach for a sports team. You have six junior coaches working under you who are all new to their roles and lacking experience.

Create a presentation for your junior coaches that carefully explains the skills and qualities associated with being a strong coach, analysing why you feel they are relevant. To enforce the importance of self-reflection, use yourself as an example, highlighting your own strengths but also areas for improvement, justifying your thoughts as you go.

Plan
- What resources do I need to do to complete this task?
- Do I have enough experience as a coach to complete this task or do I need to gain some practice?

Do
- Do I clearly understand what makes a good coach?
- Do I have a clear structure that I can use to communicate this through a presentation?

Review
- Am I able to justify why I tackled this task as I did?
- Can I make suggest improvements I would make if I had to redo this task?

B Explore practices used to develop skills, techniques and tactics for performance

It is important to understand that coaches use different practices in different sports to develop the specific skills, techniques and tactics for that sport, with a focus on developing them in competitive situations. A coach must have a thorough understanding of these skills, techniques and tactics for their sport.

A coach needs to develop an understanding of a variety of practices that can be used to work with a variety of performers. In some sports, activities used for a beginner may also be used for an elite performer; the difference lies in the method with which the performers apply the skill. In other sports some practices are not appropriate for beginners for a number of reasons. A coach must always make a judgement about when to introduce a particular practice to a performer, or group of performers.

Skills, techniques and tactics

The definitions of skills, techniques and tactics are outlined below.

- A **skill** in sport is the ability to produce a combination of movements using a variety of muscles and joints to produce a coordinated action. Skills are acquired through learning, and mastered through practice and observation. Athletes develop skills with the help of support and feedback from experienced and knowledgeable coaches and/or other athletes. Mastering a skill means being able to continually produce it successfully with little effort.
- A **technique** is the way an athlete performs a skill. In some sports, players use different techniques to produce the same outcome.
- **Tactics** are the skills a player uses in any type of sport to be able to win: for example, during a hockey or tennis match each team or player will apply specific tactics and strategies to try to beat and outwit their opponent(s).

While techniques are the way we apply skills in a selected sport, tactics are how we apply skills successfully in competitive situations. The most skilful and talented performer can lose if they do not apply the skills strategically in specific situations.

> **Key terms**
>
> **Skill** – something we learn how to do.
>
> **Technique** – a way of undertaking a particular skill.
>
> **Tactics** – the strategies a player or team uses in any type of sport to be able to win: for example, during a hockey or tennis match, each team or player will apply specific tactics and strategies to try to beat and outwit their opponent(s).

The main factors affecting the application of tactics in team and individual sports are:

▶ attacking and defending
▶ the situation in the game – are you winning or losing?
▶ your own/team's strengths – what parts of the race/game are you stronger in and which parts of your game are weaker?
▶ your opponent's strengths and weaknesses.

Discussion

There are many sports which involve individuals performing on their own, one-by-one, for example, gymnastics. Although there might not initially appear to be many tactics in these sports, in reality there are. Working in a small group, list a few examples of such sports and discuss ways athletes might use tactics to gain an advantage over competitors.

Link

You can read more about skills, techniques and tactics in *Unit 7: Practical Sports Performance* and *Unit 26: Technical and Tactical Demands of Sport*.

Practices to develop skills, techniques and tactics for performance

A sports coach should have an excellent knowledge of all the skills, techniques and tactics of their particular sport. A coach's main responsibility is to ensure that the practices which they use develop the ability of the sports performers to:

▶ effectively apply the skills, techniques or tactics in a practice environment
▶ later and more importantly, apply the skills, techniques or tactics in a competitive situation effectively.

The coach must consider the choice of practice for the sports performer(s) participating in a session. The session must be enjoyable but appropriately challenging for the sports performer(s).

The following sections look at the different types of practices that a sports coach may use to develop the skills, techniques and tactics of sports performers.

Isolated practices

Isolated practices are devised and used by coaches to develop skills, techniques and tactics during a coaching session. An isolated practice for skills, techniques and tactics is often a drill or exercise which breaks the skills, techniques or tactics which are being coached into parts.

An example might be in volleyball when a coach is trying to improve a long serve. They might ask an athlete to repetitively serve to a specific area over the net while giving feedback. The serve is never returned, so the practice is therefore 'isolated'.

A coach usually uses isolated practices to introduce skills and techniques the performer has not fully mastered, and in some instances never used. They are used mainly for beginners and intermediates, but as sports performers develop their ability, isolated practices are used to rehearse and refine the technique and skill.

Isolated practices can be adapted to help a sports performer when they are struggling to master a technique or skill. They can also be adapted to increase in difficulty when performers have mastered a skill and require further challenges.

> **Research**
>
> Get into a small group. Individually within your group, try and find three activities which you feel would benefit from isolated practices. Compare your notes with those of the rest of your group. Are there any activities that more than one of you chose? Between you, choose the three which you feel are most suitable for isolated practice.

Isolated practices can also be used to further develop a performer's ability to apply tactics. In a similar way to how a coach uses isolated practices to develop skills and techniques, coaches use isolated practices to introduce tactics to performers. In team sports, like rugby union, a coach will replicate a particular component of the game, like a line-out. In order to develop tactics, a coach will continually work with a group of players to ensure they understand the tactics to use in that particular situation. When a team has mastered a tactic, the isolated practice may be used to further refine the tactic's application. The coach may then progress the coaching session by asking the performers to apply the tactic in a conditioned practice.

▶ Isolated practices can be used to develop specific skills or techniques

Conditioned practices

Conditioned practices are used by coaches to recreate elements of specific competitive situations during coaching sessions. The focus of these practices is for the performer to master the correct application of skills, techniques and tactics in these situations; after rehearsing them, the performer can apply them in specific competitive situations.

An example of this is practising a line-out in rugby and the subsequent moving of the ball back into aggressive play. The coach might split the team into attack and defence and play the game on for just 1 minute after each line-out, each time practising a different scenario.

During conditioned practices, a coach will often stop the practice to coach the performer(s), providing specific guidance, feedback and reinforcement to shape their behaviour should the situation arise in a competitive situation.

A coach would normally only use conditioned practices for performers who already have a very good understanding of a sport and who have mastered all, or the majority, of that sport's skills and techniques. Often these practices are used to shape tactics and refine a performer's knowledge of when to use a particular skill to support a particular tactic.

Conditioned practices often have special rules or restrictions to support development in a natural, game-like scenario. For example, in basketball a coach may only use half a basketball court and play three attackers against two defenders. This practice is used when coaching an attacking play to demonstrate to the attackers how to apply appropriate skills, techniques and tactics in this particular situation.

Usain Bolt

It has been remarked that you cannot make a world class athlete: the athlete must already be there. The coach's job is to facilitate the use of the athlete's assets to enable success.

When coaching an activity such as the 100-metre sprint you might think that the options for coaching are limited due to the brief nature of the actual competition. However, this is not so. When working with world class athletes where success is dictated by tiny margins, small adjustments to technique can lead to big results.

A great deal of science is utilised in Usain Bolt's training, as with many top level performers. It took two years of focused training before the 2008 Olympic Games, a milestone in Usain's career, to redevelop his technique to bring his performance to the next level.

Allowing small errors in technique can result in an athlete wasting time when developing their performance later in their career. Coaches must make a judgement about when to enforce changes to technique and when to allow them to be overlooked, focusing on improvements that might result in greater, short-term rewards.

Check your knowledge

1 In what scenario is it advisable to ignore small mistakes in technique and focus on fast-paced development?

2 What other sports could be compared to the 100-metre sprint, where coaching very small adjustments to technique can give big rewards?

3 To be able to work with a world class athlete such as Usain Bolt, what additional skills and knowledge might a coach need to develop?

Competitive situations

Competitive situations are created by coaches in coaching sessions to rehearse the tactics the coach has taught the sports performers throughout their coaching sessions. They mimic a real-life competitive event, following the usual rules/laws and regulations of the sport. They are used by coaches to provide performers with the opportunity to apply skills and techniques developed and previously mastered, in a competitive situation, and further challenge performers in coaching sessions.

A sports coach will also often use a competitive situation to observe particular components of a performer's or team's performance and observe their offensive and defensive ability.

Offensive

When a sports performer is attacking, they are classed as using skills and techniques and applying tactics offensively. The offensive team or performer is attempting to attack their opponents to gain an advantage in a competitive situation. In team sports, designated players are given positions to focus on attacking their opponents, whereas in individual sports performers may look to focus on the weaknesses of their opponent's play in an offensive attack. The offensive performers or teams will use a variety of tactics to attack their opponents.

Defensive

Defensive play is the act of resisting an attack from an opponent. A sports performer or team will have a number of skills, techniques and tactics which focus on defending in these situations in an attempt to overcome the attack. For example, in hockey, when defending an attack, defenders use appropriate skills like tackling and blocking, and tactics like man-to-man marking and zonal marking, to prevent opponents from scoring a goal and gaining an advantage. The defensive sports performer or team uses a variety of tactics to defend against attack from their opponents.

> **Theory into practice**
>
> Many sports involve scoring goals. Think about a sport you have played where points are awarded through scoring goals. Draft three brief plans for practice sessions which focus upon accuracy in shooting for goal. Ensure one is an example of isolated practice, one is of conditioned practice and one is of a competitive situation. Which session do you feel might be most effective?

Evaluation of practices

It is important that a coach evaluates each practice they use in each of their sessions. A coach should constantly assess the practices they have used and consider whether they can be used again to support the development of sports performers.

The coach should consider the practice's practicality, suitability and effectiveness in terms of developing the sports performers (see Table 8.2). After the coach has considered each of these areas, they can then choose whether to use the practice again in future sessions.

▶ **Table 8.2:** Evaluating practices

Practicality	The coach should consider: • the time it took to set up the activity • the amount of and use of equipment during the activity • the outcome of the activity. After the coach has considered each of these points they can make an effective judgement on whether each practice is appropriate for future use.
Suitability	When considering what is and is not a suitable practice a coach should consider: • whether the activity adequately challenged the performers within the session • whether or not the activity supported the coach to achieve their own outcomes (aims and objectives) for the session they had planned.
Effectiveness	• After each session a coach should consider which practices were effective in developing performers and which practices were not as effective. • A coach may also use an assessment of the effectiveness of each practice to adapt practices to ensure the practice will be more effective in the future for sports performers.

 **PAUSE POINT**   Can you list the examples of types of practice commonly used by coaches?

> Hint   Briefly describe each one in no more than a paragraph.
>
> Extend   When reviewing the success of a coaching session, what should the coach consider?

Adaptation of practices to promote development of performance

A coach can consider many different ways of adapting practices in order to further challenge performers and develop their performance. It is important that a coach is aware that performers learn at different speeds, and that ability levels within groups will differ. A coach must ensure each performer is adequately challenged in a session. At times this may mean practices are changed for some performers, but not all.

A coach may adapt a coaching session by altering the participants, the environment and/or the equipment.

The participants

A coach will need to consider what to do with participants during a coaching session to ensure each sports performer is adequately challenged and enjoys the session.

Size of the group

With younger sports performers the size of the group may be large to ensure the coach can include lots of competitive games to develop skills and techniques through competition. As performers become more advanced, the size of the group may reduce.

A coach may also decide to reduce the numbers of performers in a practice to make the practice easier, and increase the number to make the practice harder. In individual sports when coaching elite performers, the coach may work one-on-one. For example, a boxing coach works with one boxer in the lead-up to a big fight.

> **Research**
>
> Can you find any examples of sports which involve competitors competing individually but in which it is common practice to develop skills or techniques in large groups?

Role of individuals

A coach may also give different performers different roles within a session.

Where some performers are more advanced than others, the coach may give the advanced performers roles which support other members of the group. A coach may also give advanced performers roles which require more advanced application of skills and techniques.

Less advanced performers may be given roles which involve them in the session while allowing those with a higher level of skills the opportunity to develop and be challenged.

A coach has to be very careful when allocating sports performers' roles as, in some instances, it can be seen as favouritism or isolating performers from the session and development.

Technique restrictions

A coach may adapt a practice to increase its difficulty for more advanced sports performers, to challenge them, while supporting the sports performers who are not as advanced in the session. For example, during a conditioned practice in football, a coach may allow some performers to play with their favoured kicking foot while the rest of the performers will have to play with their weaker foot. In order to include everyone in a session like this the coach can ask all the performers to switch but ensure that the stronger players in the groups do this for longer than the weaker players.

Theory into practice

Peer coaching is widely used in grass roots coaching. This is when a sports performer who has mastered a skill or technique is in turn encouraged to coach team members who may be struggling. This technique should only be used when appropriate as it has both strengths and potential weaknesses.

Strengths

- It can boost a performer's confidence by giving them further responsibility.
- As they have only recently learned the technique they are more likely to show real empathy for the other learner(s).
- The experience will reinforce the technique by forcing the original learner to break it down for themselves.

Weaknesses

- Unless the original learner has fully mastered the skill or technique, bad habits can be passed on.
- The less able learner might be made to feel less able as you are highlighting the fact that someone else is better.
- This exercise can make it appear as if there are favourites in a team unless managed correctly.

Do you belong to a team or sports club? Is there a specific element involved in training that you feel very confident about? Ask your coach if you can practise some peer coaching if appropriate. Do you feel this is a positive exercise?

When coaching a group of beginners the coach may adapt a practice to enable weaker players to work on particular components of their technique. For example, in football when delivering a dribbling drill a coach may ask the group to only dribble with certain parts of their feet, and then progress the activity to work with other parts when the coach is satisfied that all performers have mastered that component.

The environment

The environment that we coach in can be altered to enhance training sessions and focus upon specific skills. When working outside, the prevailing conditions can be very fickle. To allow the best use of time, many outside sports are coached inside to enable positive learning.

Some sports coaches use space to adapt practices to increase or decrease the difficulty level of a practice. For example, a basketball coach may use a full court when coaching beginners how to dribble but as the ability levels of performers progress, the amount of space may be reduced to demonstrate control of the dribble.

Equipment

Some coaches use equipment to adapt practices to challenge performers. In some sports, when working with performers for the first time, using the least equipment possible will help performers to settle into the sport. For example, a rugby coach will look to develop ball handling skills by only using rugby balls and no other equipment. However, as players progress, the amount of equipment a coach uses to develop skills will increase.

Research

Can you find any examples where a coach might work with an athlete by fine-tuning their equipment to try and find a mechanical advantage over competitors?

In other sports, because of the amount of safety implications involved for performers that are new to the sport, more equipment is needed from the start. For example, when a gymnastic coach coaches a somersault on a trampoline, a sports performer will perform the activity with a number of coaches supporting a safety harness. As the performer develops their confidence and skill level, the amount of equipment supporting the performer will be reduced until eventually no coach or equipment is needed to support the performer.

Some coaches will use equipment for different purposes: with beginners some equipment will have a very different purpose to that used for more advanced sports performers. For instance, a swimming coach might use a pull buoy with beginners to help them 'feel' the right body position by lifting the legs, whereas a more experienced swimmer will use a pull buoy to remove the kicking action and focus on building upper body strength and technique.

 PAUSE POINT   Give yourself 1 minute to jot down a spider diagram showing examples of ways a coach might adapt a session.

Hint   Which of these considerations do you feel you would be most likely to use? Justify your thoughts.

Extend   Are there any considerations that might prove challenging for a coach? How might they adapt a session in these scenarios?

Assessment practice 8.2   B.P2   B.M2   B.D2

Think back to Assessment practice 8.1. For the next stage in your junior coaches' development, you must now produce a written document that explains a variety of practices to develop skills, techniques and tactics for sports performance. Evaluate these practices within this document, discussing their suitability and practicality within your chosen sports club. Suggest ways that you might adapt these practices for your chosen sport.

Plan
- Do I understand how to plan a document so that it is clear and easy to read?
- Have I done appropriate research into a variety of practices and do I have a strong understanding of the topic?

Do
- Am I able to motivate myself to generate a document that is thorough?
- Do I have the IT skills to ensure that it is presented in a professional manner?

Review
- Am I able to identify ways in which I could improve this document in the future?
- Do I have access to classmates and tutors who can give me feedback on my work?

C   Demonstrate effective planning of coaching for performance

Planning considerations

Several areas must be considered prior to planning a coaching session. It is important for a coach to gather as much information about the performers as possible. Gathering this information will allow the coach to develop a greater understanding of the athletes and the group that will be participating in the session.

When planning coaching sessions, the activities must be suitable for the performers. It is they who should determine the types of activities and the method of delivery and instruction for a particular session. The information the coach gathers should include:

▶ group size
▶ age
▶ ability level of sports performers
▶ gender mix
▶ individual needs of participants.

All information about the participants should be highlighted on the session plan.

Research

Can you find an example of a sport that is coached at an elite level with males and females training together?

When a sports coach has collected all this information, they can start to plan the content and detail of the session. When planning a session, a coach should initially consider what the overall **aim** is for the group. In addition to the aim a coach may also have specific targets for individuals to achieve within the session. The targets set for a sports performer may be very different to the session's aim as outlined by the coach. A coach should also document the targets for individuals on a session plan.

Key term

Aim – something you want to achieve – a goal.

Environment and equipment

A coach's session planning should understand the environment in which they are going to deliver the session and the equipment that will be available.

They should be aware of the space in the environment and its possibilities for a coaching session. A coaching session can take place in a number of different spaces, as shown in Figure 8.3.

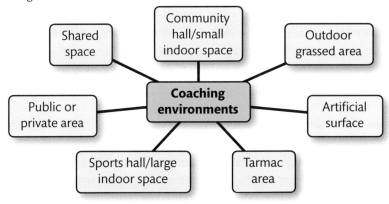

▶ **Figure 8.3:** Coaching environments

The equipment available must also be considered when planning. A coach should ensure they know the equipment requirements for each part of the session and what is available on the site. A rationale should be provided on the session plan, detailing the purpose of the equipment for each activity. This rationale would also include diagrams to show how to set up each activity.

The environment being used might offer minimal or even no equipment, but this is not necessarily a problem if the sessions can be planned around these restrictions.

If equipment is available, the coach should select which pieces to use for different purposes to challenge performance.

Planning the activities

After considering the make-up of the group and the environment/equipment available, the coach can set about designing the activities to be delivered.

▸ **Selection of skills and techniques** – the coach must choose which skills and techniques are used to ensure the session aims are met and that performers are challenged and developed appropriately. The coach should ensure they have appropriate knowledge of the correct technical model to coach the sports performers correctly, and identify the correct coaching model for each skill coached within a session.

Key term

Objective – how a sports coach is going to meet their aim.

▸ **Set clear learning aims and outcomes** – each aim should be an expected outcome, which will be achieved by all or some of the sports performers within that session. For example, 'by the end of the session everyone will be able to correctly complete a long lofted pass, and some performers will be able to correctly complete a long swerve pass.' To achieve the aim, a sports coach will need to set out some **objectives**. These should also be written clearly on the session plan and should express how you will meet each of the aims listed on the session plan.

▸ **Selecting activities/adaptations to develop skills and techniques** – a variety of activities should be used within every session, each included to support the coach to achieve the aims they have set for each performer, challenging them and supporting the development of every performer. Within a session plan a coach should include appropriate detail about how they will deliver and set up each activity.

▸ **Differentiation through adaptation of activity** – there will be parts of some sessions in which performers of all abilities participate. During these activities, a good coach should look to challenge performers of different abilities by adapting activities. The coach should have adequate control and understanding of how to do this. Each adaptation should be clearly stated in the session plan.

▸ **Contingency** – finally, within each session plan the coach should consider plans for every eventuality, indicating a number of alternative options if something goes wrong, or even if the session has to be stopped.

Health and safety considerations

The key priority of the coach should be to manage the health and safety of the participants before, during and after the session. To effectively manage the safety of performers a coach must assess all the potential risks which could occur during a coaching session. This involves considering:

▶ risks posed to and by the athletes and the group

▶ risks posed by the environment

▶ risks posed by any equipment used, or ways that equipment could be used to minimise risk.

Refer back to the section earlier in this unit on risk assessment of the environment and the activity (starting on page 359).

Planning for an individual session for performance

Individual session plans normally cover all of the elements outlined below.

Introduction aim/target setting

At the start of every session there should be an opportunity for a coach to outline to the performers the aims of the session and, if required, to set individual targets for sports performers. The session should start with all the performers together, where the coach clearly communicates the aims and objectives of the session.

Individual targets should not be shared in front of the group; this is to save possible embarrassment. The coach should look to give individual sports performers their targets by pulling them out one-by-one and discussing the targets with them.

▶ Coaches should start every session with an introduction and target setting

Warm-up

Every coaching session should start with a warm-up to prepare the athletes both physically and mentally. This should last for at least 10 minutes and should take a methodical approach which:

▶ initially increases body heat and respiratory and metabolic rates

▶ stretches the muscles and mobilises the joints that will be used in the session

▶ includes rehearsal and practice of some of the skills/techniques that will be covered within the main part of the session.

Imagine that you are preparing a warm-up for a group of young gymnasts. Consider the three elements that should be included in every warm-up. Write a brief plan, keeping in mind the age of your learners and how you might engage them in the start of a session as well as fulfil your other objectives.

Technique/tactic introduction

It is important that a coach introduces each activity within a session appropriately to the performers. This is particularly important when introducing a technique or tactic: the content the performers are required to take on board is key. This is why both communication and the method used are carefully considered.

Verbal communication should be clear and concise. A coach will often give technical instructions using both verbal and non-verbal means. Non-verbal communication usually consists of some form of demonstration, while verbal communication involves giving instructions and guidance during and after demonstrations.

An effective coach should have a good knowledge of the technical requirements of the sport they are coaching, including knowing how to break down the components of each skill or technique to share it with the session participants. When instructing athletes, it is important to explain the significance and relevance of the instruction in relation to their overall development.

When providing technical instructions, a coach should:

▶ plan what they are going to say and how they are going to deliver the information (this may depend on the audience)

▶ gain the attention of all the athletes before they speak

▶ keep the instructions simple but ensure the information is accurate

▶ when possible, use demonstrations/visual examples to reinforce the instructions

▶ check at the end of the instructions that all members of the group have understood.

As with any learning process, an athlete's ability to take in information will depend on what stage of learning they are at. For each stage, a coach should provide different levels of instructions and support (see Table 8.3).

▶ **Table 8.3:** Matching instructions to the appropriate stage of learning

The stages of learning		
Cognitive	**Associative**	**Autonomous**
Athletes are trying to grasp the basics of the skills/tasks set; they often have few experiences to relate to in the sport being coached. They will demonstrate a lot of errors and technical inefficiencies.	Athletes try to develop skills and techniques. They do this through practice. As they develop, they make fewer errors, although there will still be errors in the application of skills.	Athletes can produce skills with little effort and with almost 100% accuracy and success. At this stage they should be able to apply skills successfully in competitive situations.
Coach should: • use simple technical explanations and demonstrations • use simple basic drills and practices to develop skills • create fun and enjoyable sessions • encourage performers to practise unopposed • use lots of positive feedback.	Coach should: • use instructions and demonstrations to give athletes more information on the correct application of the skills • simulate training sessions and activities to develop specific skills • provide constructive feedback and promote peer- and self-analysis to assess performance.	Coach should: • use video demonstrations to demonstrate perfect application of skills • use complex technical instructions to fine-tune skills • discuss tactical application of the skills mastered.

 **PAUSE POINT**   The three stages of learning are important points for a coach to be able to identify and respond to. Can you describe them?

> Hint   Close the book and list the three stages of learning, briefly describing each stage.
>
> Extend   How should an effective coach respond to each stage and change their delivery?

Technique/tactic development and advancement

Once the technique/tactic has been introduced, it can be developed. When a performer has mastered the application of a technique or tactic, the coach must develop the practice to increase the difficulty level of the application of the technique or tactic under increased pressure.

For example, if a sports performer has learned a technique by taking part in an isolated practice, the sports coach may add in conditions which require the sports performer to apply the technique in a more competitive, game-like environment. The timing of this progression is crucial. If a performer is left on the same practice for too long without progression, they will quickly become bored and lose interest. On the other hand, a coach may need to adapt a particular practice to further support a performer who is struggling with it. It is just as important that a coach knows how to adapt a practice to make it easier as it is to be able to increase its difficulty.

A coach should understand which techniques and tactics are more complex and consider how and when to introduce these into a session, based on the ability of the performers and the support they will need.

In some situations, sports performers will need to combine a number of techniques and tactics in order to compete or perform successfully. Coaching sessions should allow sports performers to practise applying techniques or tactics in combination, both in conditioned practices and in simulated competitive situations.

Conditioned and competitive situations

It is important that conditioned and competitive situations are used by coaches to develop sessions and ensure performers enjoy taking part. In some practices a coach may adapt a practice to allow an element of competition.

In some sports, like athletics and swimming, conditioned practices are not as easy to apply as they are in team sports, like hockey and netball. In these sports a coach may use more competitive situations.

Adaptations for performance

A coach needs to consider, both within the session plan and during the session, how to adapt practices to promote and develop sports performance. When doing this, coaches need to ensure the practices used within a session become more difficult for some (but not all) performers. Adaptations may include applying more speed, accuracy, force or pressured situations for the performers to carry out the practice.

Cool down

At the end of the session a coach should ensure all participants spend an appropriate amount of time cooling down. This brings the body back to the pre-exercise condition gradually. It should prevent muscle stiffness and injury and improve flexibility, provided that stretches are performed correctly and controlled effectively by the coach.

Plenary coach/athlete feedback

At the end of each activity and throughout a session, time should be allocated for the coach and athletes to feed back about the performance of each skill or technique covered. Coaches always give athletes feedback. This is usually verbal, although with the development of technology and sports-analysis software, more coaches are using video and objective data.

It is essential a coach discusses with athletes how well they have done in a session and in what areas they can develop. Inexperienced performers and children are less able to make sense of what happened during the session, so need more feedback. As athletes gain experience, they are more able to compare their own experiences with previous attempts and thus more able to contribute to a coach-led discussion.

The plenary should also be an opportunity for the coach to reflect on the session and consider whether or not performers met the aims set by the sports and also whether individual performers met the targets the coach set at the start of the session.

Planning for a series of sessions for performance

Coaches who work with clubs, teams and more established performers will set aims, targets and goals for the season. Because of this, coaches need to plan programmes which cover a full season or periods of time within a season. The aim and target of the coach will determine the structure of the training programme.

When planning a programme for a group of performers, a coach should consider how many sessions it will take to fulfil the aim and target. A series of sessions normally covers a minimum of four sessions, or covers a build-up towards a major competition or a season. When planning a series of sports coaching sessions a coach will often consider using a macrocycle, mesocycle or microcycle.

- A **macrocycle** is an extended period of time defining the available preparation time up to a major competition, e.g. school club, district, regional or national championship, Olympics, world championships, etc. When planning a macrocycle, the programme will be built up of several developmental periods called mesocycles.

- A **mesocycle** usually extends from 2–6 weeks and has a specific target, e.g. introduce and develop the concept of man-to-man full court press defence in basketball.

- A **microcycle** is a shorter training period, usually of about 7 days; again the focus of the microcycle will be to target a particular component of a sports performer's focus for development.

When planning a series of coaching sessions, the coach has to consider how they are going to link the sessions to help the performer progress and develop in order to meet the aim/target in full by the end of the sessions. The focus of the coach and the performer(s) has to be the end result after the series of sessions. The sports coach may do this by:

- **developing different skills and techniques combined to create an end product performance** – during a number of different sessions, a coach would work on different skills and techniques through specific practices, which in turn will be linked together to create the desired outcome

- **developing a selected technique** – a coach may consider developing a series of sessions to develop a particular technique. A coach would need to ensure each of the sessions progresses the development of the performers and appropriately challenges them. The final outcome of the session is easily measured through the ability of the performers to undertake the technique

- **developing a tactical application –** a coach may use a series of sessions to implement a particular tactic. It may take a series of sessions to coach performers in the skills and correct timing used when applying a tactic. The outcome is easily

Discussion

Why might it be important that a coach includes strengths as well as areas for improvement during all plenary sessions?

managed through observing the ability of the performer(s) to demonstrate the tactic successfully, both during training and in a competitive situation.

The focus culmination/end product of a series of sessions

A series of coached sessions will always work towards a particular end product. The end product will either be a competitive element, or a non-competitive aim or target.

▶ A **competitive element** can be demonstrated through the performer(s) completing a series of sessions prior to a race or tournament. This can include an element of 'tapering' where the physical demands of training are eased off in order to leave the participant fresh for the competitive event.

▶ A **non-competitive aim** or target could be the performer acquiring additional skills or competency in a particular component of a sport by a certain date.

 **PAUSE POINT**   Do you understand the differences between macrocycles, mesocycles and microcycles?

            Hint   Roughly how long is each cycle? Can you give examples of when they might be used?

            Extend   How might a coach ensure that they reach their desired objective at the appropriate time?

Assessment practice 8.3   C.P3   C.M3

Choose a sport that you are most confident in delivering. Choose an individual or group that you feel you can work with to practise your coaching skills. Generate a session plan that meets a pre-defined purpose for the session, ensuring that it links into an overall series plan.

Write a document that discusses the relationship between your individual plan, planning considerations and a series plan.

Plan
- Have I chosen a sport that I am confident in delivering?
- Do I understand who my sports performer or performers are and what the objective of the session is?

Do
- Is my plan detailed and clear?
- Have I considered my objectives and do I believe my plan to be both realistic and practical?

Review
- Am I able to highlight strengths within the plan and areas where it might need improvements?
- For future plans, am I able to implement my suggestions for improvement?

D   Explore the impact of coaching for performance

Delivering for coaching performance

When leading sports coaching sessions, coaches need to demonstrate a variety of attributes to show their ability to coach and to develop performers effectively. These attributes include:

▶ appropriate knowledge of coaching theory and best practice

▶ skills and techniques to support the development of participants

▶ personal qualities as outlined in Table 8.1

▶ the ability to adapt plans for coaching sessions if something goes wrong to ensure targets and aims are met.

Performance analysis

Link

This section can link to *Unit 5: Application of Fitness Testing, Unit 26: Technical and Tactical Demands of Sport* and *Unit 28: Sports Performance Analysis.*

A coach should be able to effectively analyse the performers within each session. The most effective way to assess the performance and application of the skills, techniques and tactics during a session is by using observation analysis. Coaches need to be effective observers so they can identify strengths and weaknesses during performance. This analysis is then used to develop future coaching plans.

Observation analysis should be used to identify an athlete's needs, with the coach completing a full analysis of their overall performance and developing a training programme around it, aiming to improve significant weaknesses. There are two basic ways of formulating judgements:

1 **subjective analysis** which is based on observational judgements, personal interpretations and opinions

2 **objective analysis** which involves measuring and comparing performance data, for example the ability to perform a basketball free throw could be assessed objectively by counting how many free throws a player scores out of ten. The same assessment could be carried out subjectively if a coach compares the player's technique and skill against a mental image of an ideal technique.

The most commonly used method of observation analysis is notational analysis where the coach records the number of skills completed effectively in a competitive situation. Once this objective analysis is complete, the coach can make subjective observations on the outcome of the athlete's overall performance.

When carrying out observation analysis, a coach must be careful to remain unbiased. They will have built up a relationship with the athlete they work with, but must view their performance in as unbiased a light as possible.

Feedback to athletes

Feedback is essential to learning and a coach must remember to give feedback to performers during and after each session. There are two main sources of feedback:

▶ **intrinsic feedback** – feedback from the performer themselves, after they have carried out a movement or skill, or applied a tactic; this type of feedback is always available to the performer

▶ **extrinsic feedback** – feedback from an external source, such as a coach, a spectator, another sports performer or even from video replay of a performance.

When providing extrinsic feedback, the coach must ensure they understand the performer and their ability level. The coach should ask the performer questions about their performance to encourage self-analysis. Feedback should build on the strengths of the performance, not just highlight areas for development, and should be limited to only one or two points at a time.

Feedback should be simple and easily understood, avoiding technical jargon where possible. The coach should ask questions to ensure the points raised have been understood.

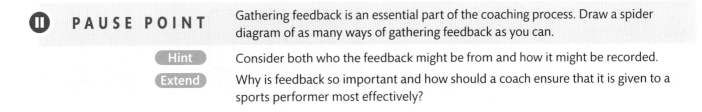

PAUSE POINT   Gathering feedback is an essential part of the coaching process. Draw a spider diagram of as many ways of gathering feedback as you can.

Hint   Consider both who the feedback might be from and how it might be recorded.

Extend   Why is feedback so important and how should a coach ensure that it is given to a sports performer most effectively?

Reflection on session

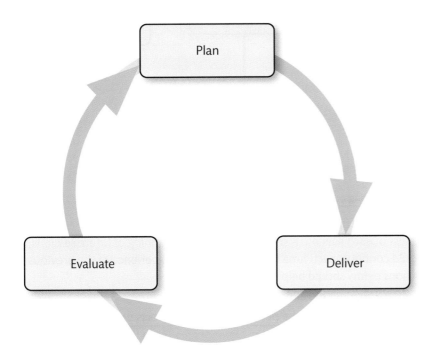

▶ **Figure 8.4:** The process of reflection

Coaches often spend a lot of their time and effort concentrating on developing the athletes and sports performers who participate in their sessions, but rarely spend the same amount of time and effort improving their own performance as a coach. In order to improve, a coach must undertake regular self-assessment and reflection.

Self-assessment and self-reflection are something we all undertake. For example, the last time you played sport at a competitive level you probably considered how well you played, and the last time you delivered a presentation in class you will have assessed your presentation skills. When you reflect on yourself in this way you also consider what you would do differently if you were put in that situation again. Reflection enables you to learn from your experiences and consider what to do if the same situation arises again.

For a coach, reflection is just like any other attribute. Some coaches are far more effective at this skill than others. A good coach should ensure they reflect after each session they deliver. Coaches work on the principle that performers learn as much from their mistakes as their successes. However, a coach can learn from every session they deliver, if self-assessment and reflection take place after it.

When reflecting on each session a sports coach should consider each of the areas shown in Figure 8.5.

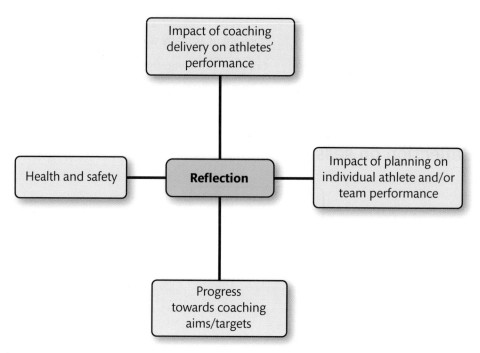

▶ **Figure 8.5:** Carrying out post-session reflection

The reflection stage of the coaching process is when the coach should reflect upon the effectiveness of each session. It should influence the planning of future sessions. The cycle should continue, each time benefiting from the experience of the previous stage. The questions below should help in assessing a session.

1 Did the session meet the aims and targets set at the start?
2 Did the session impact on the performance of the sports performers who participated in the session?
3 What went well in the session and why?
4 What did not go well in the session and why?
5 Did the session impact on the overall plan for the sports performers?
6 Were the performers and spectators safe at all times?
7 What would you do to improve the session if you had to deliver it again?

Theory into practice

It is possible to practise the reflective process without actually coaching a session yourself. Ask to observe an experienced coach's session. Use the seven questions above to give structure to your observation. Make sure that you have some notes for every question. If they are comfortable with it, discuss your thoughts with the coach.

Coaching development based on reflection

Link

This section links with *Unit 3: Professional Development in the Sports Industry.*

After reflecting on their coaching performance, the coach should consider how to address the feedback obtained and the opinions they have developed. Their conclusions should form the basis of a development plan, consisting of targets they have set themselves.

Personal development recommendations

After reflecting, a coach can consider how they can improve their own performance in future sessions. When reflecting on their personal performance, a coach should consider whether and how to improve:

▶ skills and knowledge needed for coaching activities for performance

▶ personal qualities for coaching activities for performance

▶ best practice for a coach for performance.

When considering how to develop, a coach should have a clear set of standards to work towards. As with the athletes they coach, who should have a perfect and ideal model in mind that they are trying to replicate, a coach should use role models and consider how they effectively apply each of these areas. They can then aim to mirror the behaviours and practices of their role models.

Session development recommendations

A coach should also consider the methods they used during each session, judging:

▶ their effectiveness

▶ how appropriate they were

▶ how manageable they were in reality.

The coach should consider each of these areas and the actions they would take in the future to develop the session if they delivered it again.

Opportunities

In their development plan the coach should identify specific goals, for example:

▶ completing specific coaching qualifications

▶ working with specific sports coaches

▶ observing sports coaches working with specific groups.

The plan should clearly identify the methods the coach wishes to use to improve their performance, with a justification of how and why.

Assessment practice 8.4
D.P4   D.P5   D.M4   CD.D3

Look back to Assessment practice 8.3. Deliver your pre-prepared plan to your group or individual. Ensure that during the delivery you use appropriate skills and techniques and demonstrate the qualities of a strong coach. Consider health and safety factors during your session and take steps as necessary to keep your group or individual safe.

Analyse your performance as a coach and the impact of both your planning and delivery on the individual or group. Evaluate your performance, suggesting and justifying ways to develop your own performance in the future.

Plan
- Am I confident in my plan and do I believe it will engage and benefit my group or individual?
- Have I prepared my environment and resources and do I have everything I need in order to succeed?

Do
- Have I identified my own areas for improvement and do I know how to work on them during delivery of my session?
- Have I identified any risks and hazards and am I confident that my group is going to remain safe?

Review
- Are my strengths and areas for improvement clear to me and do I have the means to practise further?
- Am I confident enough to ask my group or individual for feedback and act upon what they tell me?

Further reading and resources

Books

Cassidy, P. (2005) *Effective Coaching: Teaching Young People Sports and Sportsmanship*, Yardley, PA: Westholme Publishing.

Cassidy, T., Jones, R. and Potrac, P. (2009) *Understanding Sports Coaching: The Social, Cultural and Pedagogical Foundations of Coaching Practice*, Abingdon: Taylor and Francis Ltd.

Earle, C., Craine, N. and Andrews, W. (2004) *How to Coach Children in Sport – Coaching Essentials No. 6*, Leeds: Coachwise Ltd.

Websites

www.1st4sport.com – 1st4Sport: an online shop for a range of resources to help you work as a sports coach.

www.coachwise.ltd.uk – Coachwise: advice and support for people involved in sports coaching and increasing participation in sport.

www.sportscoachuk.org – Sports Coach UK: information, advice and learning resources for anyone interested in sports coaching.

www.sportsleaders.org – Sports Leaders UK: information and advice about awards and qualifications for sports leaders.

www.topendsports.com – Top End Sports: a range of fitness tests and normative data.

THINK ▶FUTURE

Natalie Ward

Sports Coach

Sports coaching is a great job. I get to work with lots of really keen young people, which is great. Helping them to develop is really fulfilling. It isn't all easy, though, and there are some difficult parts. One of the biggest problems that I face is when I am working with different age groups. I currently coach girls' hockey teams at the following ages: under-10s, under-12s and under-14s, so there are lots of different things that I need to take into account when I am planning and running sessions.

At times it can get a little confusing, especially when I'm working with some of the 'older' 14-year-olds who are more mature or more advanced than some of the 'younger' 12-year-olds! I often think that working with people based on their age group is not the best way to work, especially between the ages of 10 and 14. This is where there are some of the biggest differences in growth and maturity and I'm always trying to find better ways of working with my players to meet their individual needs rather than just the needs of their age group.

Focusing your skills

Managing people

Coaching is not just about teaching people how to play a sport. You need to be a leader and manager as well as an expert in your sport.

- Developing your team working and leadership skills is important. Try and identify any opportunities to do this. For example, if you take part in a group discussion in class, volunteer to lead the discussion.

- Coaching is a professional environment. Make sure you are familiar with the attitudes and responsibilities you will need to follow in a professional environment.

- Part of leading sessions is understanding that everyone is different – both in personality and how people are best motivated. Talk to friends and family: how do they motivate themselves? What do they look for in a leader? The different answers you receive will show you the range of options for leadership styles that coaches have.

Organising your time

One of the major things Natalie needs to deal with professionally is organising other people's time as well as her own. Understanding how to plan and organise your time is a crucial skill. The more organised you are, the more authoritative and professional you will become – and the more respected you will be as a coach.

- Try to plan your time – get used to organising yourself and work out the best ways you can structure your time. It may help to organise your tasks into achievable chunks.

- When working in a group in class, review and organise the tasks you have been given. Work out a plan that will allow you to achieve everything you need to do within the time you have been given.

Getting ready for assessment

Mark is working towards his BTEC National in Sport and Activity Development. He particularly enjoys the practical units and in the future hopes to find a job in coaching or sports leadership. He has ensured that he has gained plenty of experience by volunteering as an assistant coach at his local swimming pool. It has helped him to practise his own skills and also be in an environment where he can learn from more experienced coaches.

His tutor has encouraged each learner to organise their own coaching assessment for Learning aim D. This way, she explains, they will be able to perform in an environment that they feel comfortable in and will enable them to do their best.

Mark discusses his experiences below.

How I got started

I have managed to gain quite a lot of experience by volunteering as an assistant coach. However, having my tutor attend a session and observe me was quite nerve-racking. To make sure that I could deliver my session confidently I ensured that my planning was thorough and that I understood the needs of my group and the desired outcome.

The session was 45 minutes long and in my plan I broke it down into bite-sized chunks, each with a clear objective. I arrived early for my session which gave me ample time to prepare my resources and go over my plan one last time. To ensure that I was able to keep to my plan accurately I brought a stopwatch.

How I brought it all together

The group I was working with were already familiar to me as I had helped coach them before. I ensured that when I welcomed them my brief was very clear so that everyone knew what we were going to do, what was expected of them and what the objective was. I knew that my group had a slight mixture of abilities so I tried to differentiate between individuals using floats to help develop their strokes.

It soon became clear that individuals develop at different speeds. I had to adapt my plan slightly, splitting the group in two and giving the more able group a slightly more challenging task to ensure that they were pushed.

What I learned from the experience

It was clear that my practice helped me with my session. As I already had some experience and was familiar with my group it helped me perform confidently. The planning and preparation I spent a long time on gave me a good basis to work from. However I soon discovered that it isn't always possible to keep to a plan and that you might need to adapt a session so everyone gains as much as they can from it.

I tried to gather plenty of feedback after the session from my group to help with me evaluation. Although I felt uncomfortable initiating this exercise, there were plenty of positive comments as well as some areas for improvement. One of my group reminded me that, 'I was still inexperienced and so there were obviously going to be areas for improvement. The only way I was going to get better was by taking advice and practising.'

Think about it

▶ Are you confident in your plan and is your preparation sufficient?

▶ Are you able to communicate this plan effectively and make adaptations if needed?

▶ Do you have the tools to collect feedback and are you confident that you can make improvements to your own personal performance as a coach?

Technical and Tactical Demands of Sport

26

Getting to know your unit

All sports contain an element of technical execution and the application of appropriate tactics. Some basic skills, such as catching, running and throwing, are the foundation skills of specific sports. Tactics, however, are plans for different scenarios and will help performers be better prepared for certain situations and the skills they will need to use.

This unit will allow you to consider the nature and type of skills required in a range of sports, the tactics that can be employed and the way in which key stakeholders such as coaches and analysts can help to improve performance.

How you will be assessed

This unit will be assessed by a series of internally assessed assignments set by your tutor. Throughout this unit you will find assessment activities that will help you work towards your assignment. Completing these activities will not mean that you have achieved a particular grade, but you will have carried out useful research or preparation that will be relevant when it comes to your final assignment.

In order for you to achieve the tasks in your assignment, it is important to check that you have met all of the Pass grading criteria. You can do this as you work your way through the assignment.

If you are hoping to gain a Merit or Distinction, you should also make sure that you present the information in your assignment in the style that is required by the relevant assessment criterion. For example, Merit criteria require you to analyse and discuss, and Distinction criteria require you to assess and evaluate.

The assignment set by your tutor will consist of a number of tasks designed to meet the criteria in the table. This is likely to consist of a written assignment but may also include activities such as:

▶ a presentation that focuses on technical and tactical skills, using specific examples from sports, as well as a comparison of the application of techniques and tactics
▶ a written report that investigates the ways in which you can measure technical and tactical performance – this might involve the production of your own assessment tool
▶ a written report in which you take a look at technical and tactical analysis at different levels of performance, from beginners all the way through to international athletes.

Assessment criteria

This table shows what you must do in order to achieve a **Pass**, **Merit** or **Distinction** grade, and where you can find activities to help you.

Pass	**Merit**	**Distinction**
Learning aim  Examine the technical skills and tactical components of sport that contribute to effective performance		
A.P1 Explain the technical skills required for successful sport performance in contrasting sports. **Assessment practice 26.1**	**A.M1** Analyse the professional development requirements and opportunities for specialism or promotion in different career pathways and the associated job opportunities in the sports industry. **Assessment practice 26.1**	**A.D1** Evaluate technical and tactical components and the importance of their combination in different situations of different sports. **Assessment practice 26.1**
A.P2 Explain the tactical components required for successful sport performance in contrasting sports. **Assessment practice 26.1**		
Learning aim **B** Investigate methods to measure technical and tactical performance in sport		
B.P3 Explain methods of measuring technical and tactical performance. **Assessment practice 26.2**	**B.M2** Analyse methods of measuring technical and tactical performance, comparing against produced measurement tools and protocols. **Assessment practice 26.2**	**B.D2** Evaluate methods of measuring technical and tactical performance, ideal models and benchmarks, justifying against selection of produced measurement tools and protocols. **Assessment practice 26.2**
B.P4 Explain ideal models and benchmarks for performance in a selected sport. **Assessment practice 26.2**	**B.M3** Analyse ideal models and benchmarks, comparing against produced measurement tools and protocols. **Assessment practice 26.2**	
B.P5 Produce a measurement tool and protocol to gather observational data on technical and tactical performance for both elite and non-elite developing athletes. **Assessment practice 26.2**		
Learning aim **C** Explore the technical and tactical performance at different stages of the performance continuum		
C.P6 Collect observational data through assessment of a performance of an elite and a non-elite developing athlete, using own produced measurement tools and protocols. **Assessment practice 26.2**	**C.M5** Analyse the collected observational data of an elite and non-elite developing athlete, making recommendations for development of each athlete. **Assessment practice 26.2**	**C.D3** Evaluate the collected observational data, justifying the recommendations made for the development of each athlete. **Assessment practice 26.2**
C.P7 Explain the collated observational data of an elite and non-elite developing athlete. **Assessment practice 26.2**		

Getting started

Sports have many different skills and techniques. Choose two sports: one team sport and one individual sport. List as many skills for these sports as you can. Then pick three important skills and compare the execution of these by an elite performer and the same skills performed by a beginner. Make a note of the key differences, and you will have started to analyse performance – this is the skill which lies at the heart of this unit.

A Examine the technical skills and tactical components of sport that contribute to effective performance

Technical skills in sport

As a starting point, it is important to understand what we mean by the term **skill**, what the different types of skill are and how they form the component parts of sporting activity. Skills can be classified according to the environment in which they are performed or by what determines the pace with which the athlete controls the timing of an action (self-paced, externally paced, or somewhere between the two). Refer to Learning aims B and C in Unit 7 for more information about the classification of skills in sport.

> **Key term**
>
> **Skill** – in sport this refers to the ability to select the appropriate techniques at the right time. It is characterised by the movements and actions needed to perform, for example, shots, strokes, jumps or throws.

Types of skill

At its most basic level, sport must still contain elements of skill. Before considering the sport-specific skills such as an off spin delivery in cricket or a top spin lob in tennis, it is worth considering the core skills that make up so many sports:

▶ throwing and catching
▶ striking with the hand
▶ striking with an implement
▶ striking with the feet.

In addition to this there are other key skill competencies such as stability, balance, rotation, jumping, walking and running.

Classification of skill

Different sports use different ranges of skills. Figure 26.1 shows different classifications of skills, but it is not always possible to define a skill in terms of extremes: sometimes a skill falls somewhere in between. For example, for skills on the open–closed continuum a penalty kick in football or rugby is essentially a closed skill, but when you factor in the potential actions of the opponent/s and in the case of the rugby penalty kick the environment, especially the wind, then the skill cannot be classified as either open or closed but rather it fits somewhere between the two.

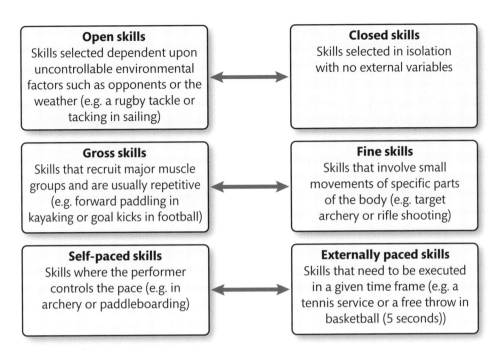

Open skills		Closed skills
Skills selected dependent upon uncontrollable environmental factors such as opponents or the weather (e.g. a rugby tackle or tacking in sailing)	←→	Skills selected in isolation with no external variables

Gross skills		Fine skills
Skills that recruit major muscle groups and are usually repetitive (e.g. forward paddling in kayaking or goal kicks in football)	←→	Skills that involve small movements of specific parts of the body (e.g. target archery or rifle shooting)

Self-paced skills		Externally paced skills
Skills where the performer controls the pace (e.g. in archery or paddleboarding)	←→	Skills that need to be executed in a given time frame (e.g. a tennis service or a free throw in basketball (5 seconds))

▶ **Figure 26.1:** Types of skill used in sport

Any of the skills shown in Figure 26.1 can also be classified as either continuous or discrete skills.

Continuous skills

Continuous skills have no obvious beginning or end and have a regular rhythm. An example is on display in rowing – see Figure 26.2.

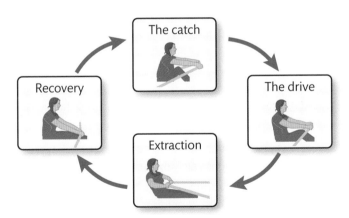

▶ **Figure 26.2:** A continuous skill exhibited during rowing

Discrete skills

Discrete skills are the opposite of a continuous skill and have a clear beginning and end. They are performed in one clear movement. The breakdown of the components of a snooker shot is an example of a discrete skill.

A snooker player should keep their body as still as possible when playing a stroke and should concentrate on the cue brushing their chin as they push the cue through to strike the cue ball. The player should have their eyes fixed on the spot where they have aimed the centre of the cue ball to be when it strikes the object ball, so they can see if they have hit it where they intended.

Serial skills

Serial skills are made up of discrete and/or continuous skills. They are a series of skills which follow each other in quick succession in an orderly sequence to become one movement. For example, high jump technique is made up of a sequence of events that need to be in the right order and which are outlined below.

▶ Approach: the run is J-shaped, straight for the first 3–6 strides and then curved for 4–5 strides. For the initial stride, the foot plants on the ball of the foot, the body leans slightly forwards, speed increases throughout the approach, the body leans naturally into the curve, and the body is lowered in the penultimate stride.

▶ Take off: the foot plant is quick and flat with a 'down and back' action. The take-off leg is bent slightly and the knee of the free leg is driven up to horizontal and stopped. The body is vertical at the end of the take-off.

▶ Flight: as the body gains height, the take-off position is held. The leading arm reaches up, across and over the bar. By arching the back and lowering the head and legs, the hips are raised over the bar. The head is brought up towards the chest to bring the legs clear of the bar.

▶ Landing: the head is drawn up towards the chest. The athlete lands on their shoulders and back, with knees apart.

Interaction continuum

Some skills can be performed by one person alone (individual skills), while others rely on more than one participant in order for them to be successfully achieved (interactive skills). Others fall somewhere between the two extremes. This creates what is called an **interaction continuum** (Figure 26.3), which defines the extent to which others are involved in the skill's success, either partly, wholly or not at all.

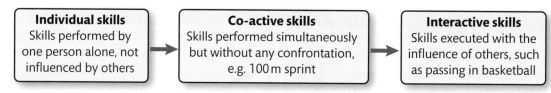

▶ **Figure 26.3:** The interaction continuum

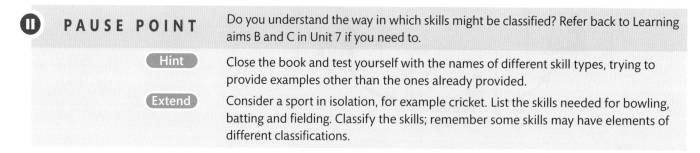

PAUSE POINT

Do you understand the way in which skills might be classified? Refer back to Learning aims B and C in Unit 7 if you need to.

Hint Close the book and test yourself with the names of different skill types, trying to provide examples other than the ones already provided.

Extend Consider a sport in isolation, for example cricket. List the skills needed for bowling, batting and fielding. Classify the skills; remember some skills may have elements of different classifications.

Fundamental motor skills

Fundamental motor skills are skills we generally learn as children. Simple skills like hopping, jumping, throwing, catching, kicking and striking form the basic components of the majority of sports. More complex and refined skills are learned later once the basic ones are mastered.

Learning the fundamental motor skills when young is a critical stage for performance development in later sporting life. This is because, if skills are learned with technical errors, they will affect the refined skills developed later, restricting development and success. In many cases the way in which young people learn and develop skills can be the key determiner in their ability to perform refined skills in later life.

Discussion

Think about the issues in terms of technical skill development for a 6 year old who learns to play table tennis with no instruction. It is not inconceivable that athletes can develop quite technical skills by watching or modelling other players. Compare that to an example of the same child being coached, learning tried and trusted techniques. Think about how their different experiences will impact on their later performance and coaching experiences.

Developing fundamental skills such as walking, running, throwing and catching in a challenging yet safe environment is very important, and at the core of this development are three categories of basic movement skills:

▶ **locomotor skills**, involving the body moving in any direction from one point to another, such as walking, running, dodging, jumping, hopping or skipping

▶ **stability skills**, involving the body balancing either in one place (static) or while in motion (dynamic), such as landing, balancing (either static or dynamic) or rotating

▶ **manipulative skills**, involving handling and controlling objects with the hand, the foot or an implement (a piece of equipment such as a stick, a bat or a racket). Manipulative skills include catching, throwing or striking with the hands, feet (kicking, dribbling) or a piece of equipment (e.g. batting).

Catching and throwing

Catching and throwing are important to learn together but are quite different from a skill-learning point of view.

▶ When catching or receiving, the body controls a ball or object, relying on the ability of the eyes to track the ball and prompt adjustments of the receiving part of the body.

▶ Throwing involves the propulsion of a ball away from the body towards a target and is therefore known as a target skill.

These skills are difficult to practise in isolation from each other, and both require specific attention in practice. Many coaches practise throwing but fail to introduce the principles of catching. Young children often say that they are scared of catching the ball because it hurts.

Principles of throwing

1 Bring your throwing arm as far back as possible and transfer your weight to your back foot. This means more force is transferred to the ball when throwing.

2 Under control, bring the arm forward and transfer your weight to your front foot in a swinging action. The straighter your arm in the forward swinging motion, the greater the force and therefore the faster the ball.

3 Try to extend your arm to its fullest and in doing so the swing will be faster and the ball will potentially go further.

Principles of catching

1 To absorb the force of an incoming object, spread the force over a large surface area for as long as possible.

2 When catching a ball, reach for the ball with your hands, spread your fingers or cup your hands together and 'give' with the ball (i.e. bring the ball into your body).

3 Your body should ideally be balanced and facing the ball so that it is coming directly towards you, with your legs or body providing a wide, firm base of support.

4 To establish a more secure base of support, lower your centre of gravity. For example, to field a ground ball in cricket, you kneel to one side, which provides a firm, low and wide base of support.

Running

Running is essentially like walking except there is a short amount of time when both feet are off the ground simultaneously. Most sports involve running in some form, such as sprinting, dodging, jogging or running backwards. Most runners know you apply force in a forward direction from the back leg, and the body, via a system of levers, propels itself forwards. Leaning slightly forwards assists the momentum in that direction.

Coaching points to improve running are outlined below.

▶ Hold your head up and look ahead.

▶ Lean the body slightly forward.

▶ Lift the knees.

▶ Bend the arms at the elbows and swing them backwards and forwards from the shoulders.

▶ Move the arms in opposition to the legs.

▶ Land on the forefoot or midfoot to limit the amount of **coupling**.

As running speed increases, push off with the balls of the feet, increase the body lean and arm action, and land on the balls of the feet.

Striking with and without an implement

Striking and controlling a ball with an implement (racket, stick or bat) happens in many ways, depending on the sport. For example, a **horizontal striking pattern** is used in rounders, while a more vertical pattern is found in golf and hockey. Many sports (e.g. tennis, badminton and cricket) include striking in several planes, and share the same movement concepts as striking with the hand.

Some of the key considerations in ball striking are outlined below.

▶ Grip is a key factor in ball striking, as is keeping your eye on the ball and extending the arm or following through after contact.

▶ When trapping/blocking with an implement, move your body directly in the path of the ball, as in a shot stop by a hockey goalkeeper.

▶ Keep your eye on the ball until contact is made – this is as true for hitting a moving ball, for example a tennis ball, as it is for a static one such as in golf.

Key term

Horizontal striking pattern – this describes the way that an object such as a ball is hit: contact made with a bat, stick or racquet that is parallel to the floor and has a force in the same direction. Examples of this include a forehand or backhand shot in tennis or badminton, a pull shot in cricket or a baseball hit.

Research

'Eccentric force' sounds like a strange concept but it is quite simple really. It separates the good from the great in all ball sports and it is important to understand it. In small groups research the terms 'eccentric force' and 'Magnus effect' and apply them to one of these scenarios:

• a tennis player hitting the ball for a topspin lob
• a golfer hitting a fade drive
• a football player bending a free kick.

Aim to demonstrate your findings with the help of a series of diagrams as part of a presentation to the rest of the group.

Science of a golf swing

Golf is easy: all you have to do is hit the ball, long and straight. However, if it was that simple everyone would be a professional golfer.

There are actually many ways to hit a golf ball and there are also many different clubs and a range of ground surfaces (usually called lies). However, there is some science that explains the process of hitting a golf ball. It might not make you a top ten player but it will help you understand the physical mechanics involved. The key principles are shown in Table 26.1.

▶ There is science behind the swing of golfers like Michelle Wie

Tips for a successful swing

- **Centrifugal force** – keep your forward arm straight through the swing and feel the clubhead as the heaviest part of the club with a force extending out away from your shoulder through your arm. The clubhead will return smoothly at the same level where it started. This is exactly the position you want to be in at impact. This is similar to swinging a bucketful of water: keep your elbows straight and the

action smooth and the water stays in, but shorten any aspect and everyone around gets wet!
- **Acceleration** – at its fastest point the clubhead should still be accelerating through the ball. This will put a positive spin on the ball so it is far more likely to travel in the intended direction. Slowing through impact will change the angle of the clubhead, making the ball more likely to be affected by wind and any other off-centre forces.
- **Launch angle** – because so many people now use very large clubheads it is recognised that shots will contact on the upward phase of the swing. This means higher launch angles generally have greater success because the speed of the clubhead (usually around 100 mph) responds to being hit through (still accelerating).

Check your knowledge

1   Assuming that there is little wind or any other distraction, could you offer some general advice for someone who is very new to golf? You do not need to be a golf expert to help someone new to the sport by following the mechanical principles above. Use all of the information available and be as simple as you can in your explanation.

2   Jot down a short list of these tips and be ready to discuss them with your peers/ tutor.

Sport-specific skills

Once fundamental motor skills have been gained, athletes need to take on more complex and specific skills for their sport. Different sports have different skills. Many are unique to that sport, such as kayak paddling or bowling in cricket, but others have a degree of transferability. Think about the action of a tennis serve and throwing a ball – not too different, are they? You tend to find that people who can throw overarm well do not take too long to learn a tennis serve. This is called the transfer of skills, in which a series of basic movements can be replicated for skills in other sports.

▶ **Table 26.1:** The science behind a golf stroke

Balance/stability	Production of force	Accuracy
This happens when your feet and/or legs are comfortably spread to provide a wide, stable base of support.	More force is gained by increasing the distance of your backswing and cocking your wrist at the top of the backswing.	If you strike a ball in line with the ball's centre of gravity (middle) and at a right angle to the direction you want it to go in, the ball will travel in a straight line.
Bending your knees will lower the centre of gravity to further increase stability. Balance is important to provide a secure base of support for the swing and strike.	Straightening your arms as the club is moved towards the ball also adds force.	If you hit the ball above or below the centre of gravity, it will spin away, losing distance and speed. Many golfers make the ball spin off-centre to change the direction of the flight. This is called draw or fade.

Here are a set of skills for paddleboarding with some guidance on their execution.

Forward stroke

- Keep your bottom arm straight and relatively still.
- Pull your top arm toward your body to extend the paddle forward.
- Rotate your top shoulder forward and extend your reach.
- Insert the paddle into the water as far forward as possible and bury the paddle into the water.
- Rather than pulling your paddle through the water, think about pulling past your paddle.
- To stay in a straight line, take a few strokes on one side then switch to a few strokes on the other. Always remember to switch the position of your hands when your paddle changes sides.

Turning with the forward sweep stroke

- To turn left, place the paddle in the water on the right side. At the same time, turn your torso to the left side.
- Keep a low stance and pull to the right, towards the tail with the paddle, while twisting and leaning to the left with your torso. You will feel the board shift to the left quickly.

Turning with the reverse sweep stroke

- To turn right, place the paddle near the tail and pull toward the nose while shifting your torso to the right. This will spin your board's nose to the right hand side. The more you bend your knees, the easier it will be to turn the board.

> **Discussion**
>
> Choose a sport that you play on a regular basis with a peer. Identify as full a list of skills and techniques as you can. Remember to consider the differing skills needed for different positions. When your list is complete, compare your lists in small groups. What similarities and differences are there? You could then research in technical manuals or online to come up with a more complete picture for the skills of your chosen sport.

Sports skills can be further categorised in the following ways.

▶ **Cognitive skills** – e.g. problem solving. A typical example would be the split-second decision that a tennis player needs to make that will get them out of trouble after having had to chase a ball down, whether to play a defensive or attacking shot.

▶ **Perceptual skills** – e.g. interpreting incoming information from the senses – for example, a running rugby player with the ball must consider whether to pass, dummy, side step or go to ground according to his perception of the location of his team mates and of the opposition, the environmental conditions, and the tactical significance at that point in the game.

Different technical skills in different positions/roles

Phase-specific demands

Most sports are comprised of different phases or parts of play that form components of the whole game, usually classified by a name. Table 26.2 shows similarities and differences between sports in these stages.

▶ **Table 26.2:** Phases of play for a selection of team sports

Sport	Offence	Defence	Transition (offence to defence, defence to offence)	Set pieces	Other phases
Football	✓	✓	✓	✓ Free kicks, penalties, throw ins	✗
Triathlon	✗	✗	✓ From one discipline to another – triathletes call transition 'the fourth discipline'	✗	✓ Swimming, cycling, running
Basketball	✓	✓	✓	✓ Free throws, out of bounds	✗
Cricket	✓ Batting	✓ Bowling and fielding	✗	✗	✗
Rugby	✓	✓	✓	✓ Place kicking	✗

The skills selected by the participants will be influenced by the phase and the tactics employed during that phase. For instance, basketball can be divided into offensive, defensive and special situations (other sports may call these set pieces).

▶ During the offensive phase, the skills chosen may include passing, shooting, dribbling, lay ups and dunks, as well as a significant amount of movement without the ball, such as screening or cutting.

▶ The defensive phase requires a different set of skills, such as matching up, lateral and backward movement, offensive and defensive rebounding and boxing out.

▶ Special situations require skills specifically related to out of bounds possessions, jump balls and potentially even the movement from offence to defence or defence to offence known as 'transition'.

The tactics employed during each phase might change depending on timing issues related to the event. For instance, a football team that is losing with little time remaining to play may opt to switch to a more pressing defensive strategy and to attack more vigorously. This can also have an impact on the skills selected: for instance, a team in this situation may need to deliver more long passes rather than shorter ones.

Individual roles

In addition to this there are specific skill requirements for certain positions in sports. Examples include point guard in basketball, fly half in rugby or centre in netball: each position has a unique and specific set of skills as well as the skills required of all performers in that sport.

Performers with specific roles can be measured in terms of their execution and success in these specific skills, and their overall effectiveness can also be measured. To do this, you must first define the position's **key performance indicators (KPIs)**.

> **Key term**
>
> **Key performance indicator (KPI)** – a measurement of factors that are crucial to successful performance.

KPIs for a football striker – Adam Furze

In order to make an assessment of the quality of a sporting performance you must establish what important skills, techniques and tactics make up its KPIs. Adam is an aspiring non-league football player who wants to be a professional player. In order to help him improve, his coach has established a set of key performance indicators that are used to assess his skills and tactical choices. These are his KPIs:

- minutes per goal – how many minutes it takes Adam to score a goal, on average
- shots on and off target
- minutes per shot/shot on target
- shot accuracy – on target and went where it was aimed (this is hard to know unless you are an expert observer)
- chance conversion – judged by the coach, who determines whether the player had a genuine or only slight opportunity
- clear cut chance (CCC) conversion – represents genuine opportunities for a player to score or hit the target
- set pieces – from free kicks and penalties
- goals via CCC – shows whether a player is reliant on good passes and through balls from team mates or whether they create opportunities for themselves.

The data the coach gets from these KPIs is compared to other strikers at different levels to help determine whether Adam has what it takes.

Statistics only ever tell part of the story of performance. Important variables such as effort, leadership and experience are difficult to measure and are just as important.

Check your knowledge

If you had to choose your top three KPIs from the list above, which would they be and why?

1 The KPI that focuses on 'miss-per-shot on goal' would be reliant on service. What does that mean? Explain your answer with examples from elite football.

2 Should penalties count as shots on target? Does this skew the data in terms of goal opportunities in favour of the penalty taker? Is there a danger that to the casual observer the penalty taker is a better striker?

PAUSE POINT   Do you understand the range of different skills needed in sports?

> Hint   How might the skills you need change depending on the position and role you play in the sport?

> Extend   Take a look at the sport of Ultimate Frisbee.

Relationship between skilled and ability performance

It is important to understand the difference between a skill and an ability.

▶ Skills are specific sports techniques that are learned and goal-directed responses, accurately and consistently performed. They are efficiently executed, often with the minimum amount of energy being expended.

▶ Abilities are enduring, stable and genetically pre-determined characteristics that underlie skills. Motor abilities are those concerned with actual movement of the body so include the fitness components (e.g. strength or flexibility). Perceptual abilities are those concerned with judging and interpreting information from the environment (e.g. rate control and aiming).

So whereas kicking a ball is a skill that all of us have and which we can practise to improve, we rely on specific abilities in order to do it.

Skills

Skills may be simple or complex:

▶ **simple skills** require little conscious thought or decision making, and are an almost instinctive reaction (e.g. throwing from a fielding position in cricket)

▶ **complex skills** require decision making and may be influenced by external factors, such as opponents, and generally result from a thought process (e.g. a combination of counter punches for a boxer).

Skilled performance is a learned behaviour. The ultimate aim is a skill that is consistent, coordinated, precise, aesthetically pleasing, fluent and efficient. **Practice** is a key component to all skill production.

Skilled actions are **deliberate,** meaning they are under conscious control: skill selection or **application** is a process whereby a performer can react quickly to incoming 'scenes' and make an appropriate skill selection from a set of learned, practised and deliberate skills.

Ability

Skills in sport also rely on the ability of the performer.

Ability is said to be innate (naturally-occurring as opposed to learned) and limited (in the sense that ability alone is not enough, and that naturally occurring talent of this nature needs nurturing and so learning must also take place).

Another characteristic of ability is that it is non-specific – this means that while sports will require particular skill learning and execution, performers with natural ability might not perform those skills without having to learn them. However, they are far more likely to learn complex motor patterns more quickly and with fewer barriers to learning. The following are abilities as opposed to skills – manual dexterity, stamina, control precision and reaction time.

Abilities can be used and combined in different ways in order to perform specific tasks. Proficiency in one task does not guarantee proficiency in a similar task, for example being able to strike a ball in hockey does not guarantee success in striking a ball in tennis.

To perform sporting actions, we learn how to use our abilities in an organised way, including limb coordination, reaction time, manual dexterity, aiming, static strength, explosive strength, flexibility, stamina and balance.

Differences between abilities and skills

To illustrate the difference between ability and skill, consider how a dive at the start of a swimming race is performed.

Initially the swimmers balance on the blocks. They then need to display good reaction time, limb coordination, power and flexibility to explode off the blocks and into the water when the starting signal sounds.

These abilities need to be put together to perform an effective movement pattern. This is done through practice in training, which will then be performed again easily in the pressure of a race. If a swimmer did not have fast reactions (ability) or lacked power (skill influenced by natural ability) then their start would be ineffective and this would put them at a disadvantage in the race. Similarly, if someone had high levels of these abilities, then they would only have an effective start if they learned the movement pattern. This means practice is needed to develop the resultant skill of diving.

Do you understand the differences between skills and abilities? Can you describe these?

Hint Can you list four fundamental skills? Close the book and see if you can name some.

Extend Produce a Skill and Abilities Profile for a sport or sporting position. Consider exactly which components of a sport are innate and which have been learned.

Tactical components in sport

Key terms

Tactic – a plan that aims to improve the chance of an individual or team winning or improving their performance.

Strategy – a particular approach to a competitive scenario that may or may not include specific techniques and tactics but is characterised by a general approach.

Gameplan – a specific and detailed tactical approach that has considered not only the strengths and weaknesses of the opponent but also the appropriate course of action for a range of competitive scenarios.

Tactics and **strategies** and **gameplans** are just as important as skills and their technical execution. Tactics depend on a number of factors including:

▶ the opposition
▶ players available for selection
▶ importance of the game/match
▶ conditions (pitch/court, weather).

Even the greatest players in the world must have tactical awareness and consider the factors which affect them. Tactics can ultimately mean the difference between successful and unsuccessful performances.

Tactics are game plans set up for a specific purpose during a performance or match, and are involved in all sports. They are discussed before a competitive situation (even in an individual sport, where the athlete will usually discuss them with their coach) and are part of the winning formula, so a performer must be able to carry them out successfully.

Tactics vary depending on your chosen sport and whether it is a team or individual sport. However, common tactics include:

▶ positioning – to outwit or mark the opposition
▶ choice and use of correct/appropriate skills – to outplay the opposition
▶ variation – to outsmart the opposition
▶ use of space – to give more time to make decisions or receive the ball and attack.

An example of a tactic in tennis would be to move your opponent around the court. A tactic in football might be the formation and style of passing you are to play. But within that overall tactic, the athlete also has to make constant tactical decisions about what sort of skill to use at any moment during the competition. For instance, a tennis player looking to move an opponent around the court will be deciding on whether to play a baseline drive or a drop shot. A footballer will be deciding whether to control the ball before passing or pass it with their first touch.

A player or team will go into a match with a strategy and the tactics will have been planned and employed to meet the objectives of the strategy. But the opponent will also be trying to apply their own tactics, so a competitive encounter becomes a battle of wits as the participants adapt their tactics to try and ensure success.

Theory into practice

Using your own sport as an example, come up with at least two tactics you have seen or been asked to play. These could include guidance on where to position yourself, what to do in certain situations or what you did to confuse the opposition.

- Present your tactic to your peers and try to give it a name (unless it already has one).
- Consider what you would do about the tactic you employed if you were the opposition coach. In other words, what tactics would you use to counter your own tactics?

Tactical strategies

Tactics often vary depending on whether you are attacking or defending. For example, in football some tactical demands are:

▶ when defending:
  - restricting time and space
  - challenging and recovering
  - defending set plays (corners, throw-ins)
▶ when attacking:
  - creating space
  - passing and movement
  - attacking set plays.

Some of the tactics are influenced by whether the team is in possession of the ball (attacking) or without the ball (defending). There are always tactics relevant to attacking or defending in any sport where there is direct opposition. For example, in rugby the back line will be formed at a steep angle when attacking or in a flat line when defending.

Discussion

Tactics are evident in most sports. Using the principles of tactical application – e.g. limiting possession, formations, creating space, creating shooting opportunities, preventing scoring opportunities or any other examples – in small groups select a sport and research the tactics available to performers.

Individual sports will focus on both the strengths of that individual and the perceived weaknesses of their opponents. In team sports, tactics are generally more elaborate and specific to certain scenarios. When presenting your findings:

- for specific teams outline the tactics they have adopted, formations, rules of play, etc., for example for Barcelona versus Real Madrid, or for the England rugby team compared to the New Zealand rugby team
- for individual sports, show how recognised individuals have prepared to compete against others, for example in tennis Andy Murray versus Novak Djokovic.

Offensive/attacking

These tactics are restricted to when a team or individual is attacking. They are based on the ability and understanding of that team/individual, the amount of practice and potentially a perceived weakness in the opposition. The dribble drive in basketball is an example.

Dribble drive – basketball

The offence focuses on spreading the offensive players in the half court, so that helping on dribble penetration or skips becomes difficult for the opposition defence, because the help will leave an offensive player open without any defenders near him. As an example a guard can drive through the defensive gaps for a layup or dunk, or pass out to the perimeter if the defence collapses onto him.

Defensive

These tactics establish a plan or a set of principles for defending. In the example below there is a combination of man-to-man and zone tactics that is effective against teams that do not all shoot well from the perimeter.

'Triangle and 2' – basketball

Two defenders play man-to-man against the two best scorers. The other three defenders play zone. Two play on the low blocks and have corner responsibilities too. Your very best, fastest, hardest-working defender plays the middle position starting at the free-throw line. He must cover the free-throw line area and above. He must also cover the ball-side low block when the ball goes into the corner.

Containing/limiting

Containing tactics are usually applied when a team or player is defending a lead, perhaps with very little time left in the game, for example in football when a team keeps the ball in the corner and runs the clock down. In basketball a team with a lead and very little time left might retain possession of the ball for a full 24 seconds without shooting, denying the opposition possession of the ball and any opportunity to score. In rugby, a team with a lead might be more tempted to keep the ball and ruck or maul instead of clear from their own half, retaining possession and denying the opposition an opportunity to score.

Formation and team selection

Formations and the way teams set up to play others will depend on the qualities and skills of their own players and squad, plus the perceived strengths and weaknesses of the opposition.

Case study

FC Barcelona – a unique approach to tactics

Founded in 1899, FC Barcelona has 110,000 members and teams across a range of professional and amateur sports, including handball and roller hockey. But football is the club's main activity and the one it is most famous for. FC Barcelona's football philosophy is based on three fundamental principles, including:

- winning the largest number possible of titles (League, domestic cups, Champions League, the UEFA Europa League, UEFA Super Cup and Mundialito of clubs)
- playing attractive football
- having as many similarly trained players as possible.

FC Barcelona speak in terms of numbers of positions rather than specific players, implying that tactics come first, not the skills of the player. In this way players must suit the position and not the other way around. Look at Figure 26.4 which details tactics related **just to passing**. In theory every player is aware of these pass lines not just for their own position but for the others, too.

Check your knowledge

1 Would the approach that FC Barcelona use be as successful for other teams? Explain why or why not.

2 Could this kind of approach be adopted by other sports and, if so, how exactly?

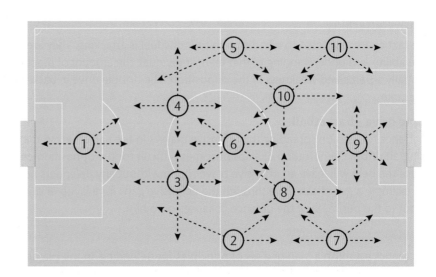

▶ **Figure 26.4:** FC Barcelona pass lines – their ideal direction and location of intended passes

In English football, traditionally the most common formation is 4-4-2. It is made up of four defenders, four midfielders and two strikers and is an adaptable system with strength in midfield and plenty of width. Two strikers means the front line has extra support rather than waiting for the midfield to reach them. This formation, like others, frees up the fullbacks giving them more time on the ball than midfielders, particularly if the opposition is playing 4-4-2 as well.

But some coaches see the two central midfielders in this formation as defenders and the fullbacks as attackers. This formation offers the chance for one of two central midfielders to get forward and support the strikers. Sometimes the two midfielders will take turns pushing forward to keep defenders guessing. In the past some teams, such as England, favoured a more solid approach, assigning a midfielder to a deeper, defensive role to cover the defence. This gives the more attacking midfielder greater freedom to push forward and support the strikers. This type of formation has been called the 'diamond formation' as the four midfielders form a diamond-like shape: it favours a team which does not have strong wingers.

Tactical considerations

Choosing the right tactic for the right situation is critical and depends upon some key variables. Figure 26.5 shows some of the key considerations when making tactical decisions.

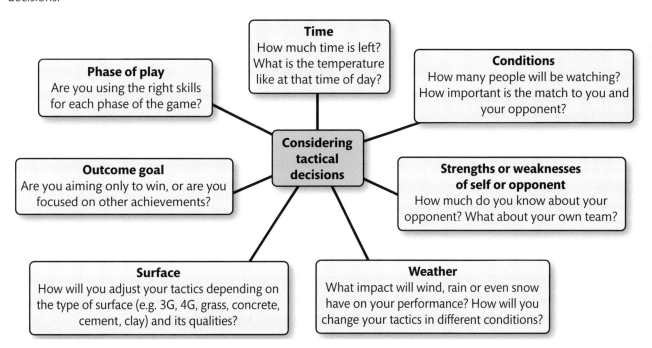

▸ **Figure 26.5:** Key considerations when making tactical decisions

It is worth looking in more detail at 'conditions', mentioned in Figure 26.5. Conditions can be internal or external. **Internal conditions** may depend on the importance of a match in relation to your team's position in a league or cup. Psychological factors like confidence, motivation, anxiety, focus and concentration are also conditions under which a match is played. Alternatively, you may be coming back from injury or key members of your team may be injured. **External conditions** are those that are not necessarily under any influence from the performer, for example the location of sport and recreation facilities would come under this heading, as would issues such as the attitudes and behaviour of team mates and opponents, the performance of officials and, to a significant extent for outdoor sports in the UK, the weather.

> **Link**
>
> You can read more about psychological factors in *Unit 6: Sport Psychology.*

Tactics and technical skill selection

When choosing a particular strategy or tactic, it is important to recognise the skill set and ability of the performer/s. For example, the long ball tactic in football has only been successful for teams who have key target players who have the particular skill of being able to create space while holding off defenders and control defenders with their backs to the goal, ready to play quick passes or flicks into the path of oncoming players to create quick shooting opportunities.

The case studies below, for a team and an individual sport, demonstrate the impact of tactics on technical skills in relation to player positioning and timing and refer to the specific demands of phases.

Case study

Team sport: volleyball

Choice of strokes and shots – tactics

A volley is a two-handed pass above the forehead. The flight is high and slow and, therefore, a beginner has a chance of assessing the ball's flight and can move to make efficient and correct contact. The volley is an accurate pass.

The volley – technical skills

The pass is used to set up an attack. A consistent contact point with the ball will come from:

- being ready
- being able to correctly judge the flight of the ball – where and when it will be at its highest point
- positioning the body behind and under the ball
- good flexibility of the knees upon ball contact
- knee extension and using the whole body to complete the action.

The serve – technical skills

The serve is used to start a game. This is the only skill in volleyball over which the player has complete control. An accomplished player will put pressure on the opponents through their serve by using more power or tactics. There are several different serves:

- the underarm serve
- the overarm serve
- the overarm float serve
- the overarm topspin serve
- the jump serve.

Variation – tactics

The smash is the principal attack shot in volleyball. The player runs in and jumps above and close to the net to hit the ball with one hand down into the opposite court.

Variations include:

- smashing a high set cross-court, or down the line
- smashing a quick set
- hitting the ball off the block and out of court
- tipping the ball just over the block (similar to a drop shot in tennis).

Use of space – tactics

Developing tactics should accompany technical skills in any sport. In volleyball, you should think about where and how best to attack and where you should stand in order to have the best opportunity to defend. The main aim of defence is to prevent the ball being smashed down the centre of the court. The defence can stop this attack option when the block is used to defend the middle of the court against a powerful smash. Powerful attacks are made from above the height of the net and close to it. By being in this position, the attacker opens up the options for attacks and gives defenders the minimum amount of time to play the ball.

Check your knowledge

1. Aside from the service, there are really only three basic skills required to begin playing volleyball. What are they?

2. What would be the advantage of an overarm serve in volleyball?

3. Volleyball is characterised by high levels of team cohesion and player rotation. What impact does this have on player development?

Case study

Individual sport: tennis

It is important you have a range of skills in your shot selection. The more range you have, the greater your tactical options. You should also always aim to hit the ball deep to force your opponent back. The following are guidelines to help you develop tennis tactics.

- Attack the net as many times as possible.
- Always hit the safest shot to reduce the risk of unforced errors.
- Under pressure, hit the ball up – it will give you more time.
- Try to upset your opponent's rhythm – mix up your shots.
- Do not always play to a weakness; sometimes attack a strength.

Tennis players must have good balance. When a player moves from being balanced to unbalanced, a sprinting action begins because they are forced to move their feet rather than fall. When a tennis player swings a racket, another part of the body, usually the arm, comes across to counter the movement of the racket arm. The player then retains control over the body, keeping their centre of gravity over their base of support. When a tennis player serves, the centre of gravity moves in the direction of the arm that is swinging upwards to toss the ball.

Positioning – tactics

In tennis, players have to follow the ball's movement in order to position themselves properly in relation to the ball. This is difficult if the ball is moving quickly or is very high or low. Throwing and catching the ball following a gentle arc pathway is the best way to initially practise following the ball.

When a player is developing their strokes and techniques, they often run too far from the ball or too close. Many players looking to approach the net will hit their shot into the corner of the court to give themselves more time to position themselves at the net. However, an opponent who moves and can read the game well will be able to position themselves in order to return the shot or even drive the ball past you. Hitting the ball deep but down the middle of the court stops your opponent from hitting their return by using angles created by the approach. Hitting deep into the middle of the court will cut off the options available to your opponent.

Choice of strokes and shots – tactics

The technique used by less skilled players is the straight backswing. Few professionals use this, as it is difficult to hit a ball with high velocity because the racket stops before it starts to move forward. The most common swing used by professionals is the small loop backswing. The body prepares for the backswing by moving into the correct position. The foot on the racket side turns outwards and the hips and shoulders rotate. The back foot then pushes forwards. The upper limbs control the stroke but the power comes from timing and the lower limbs. The arm and the racket must generate speed before impact occurs in order to successfully hit through the tennis ball.

If a player stops their swing at impact, they will lose control of the shot and probably hurt themselves. Therefore, a good follow-through is necessary to make an effective shot and to avoid injury.

Check your knowledge

1 Why is balance important to a tennis player?

2 Being in the ready position (research this) is critical in shot preparation. Why?

3 What would be a good strategy when playing a tall, powerful opponent?

 PAUSE POINT   What are the key considerations when deciding on a tactic?

Hint   See if you can redraw the key considerations diagram. You might also be able to provide a sporting example.

Extend   Exactly what tactics are available for elite performers? Some American sports have 'playbooks' – these are plans and strategies for given situations that might occur in game situations, a sort of 'What to do if...' set of rules relating to tactics. Could you design a playbook for your sport? See if you can come up with a set of typical scenarios in a competitive contest and a series of 'what to do if' responses.

Technical skill selection

In a team or partner sport, such as that featured in the next case study, the range of possible tactics and skill selections is further challenged by the recognition of a team member/s. Knowledge of the relative strengths and weaknesses of your team mate/s and yourself will enable you to devise strategies and effective tactics.

Case study

Badminton (doubles)

Doubles badminton is an exciting, fast paced, high adrenaline sport that requires extraordinary power, strength and agility. In doubles, two players are tactically referred to as the front and back players, named for the position relative to the net.

What choices does the back player have?

- Smashes – high percentage point winners. It is nearly always a good shot as it puts the opponent on the defensive and forces them into error situations.
- Drop shots – shots that barely clear the net are great for changing the pace of a rally and forcing opponents nearer the net. At an elite level many drop shots are recovered, but the shuttle comes over high and slow and is easier to smash as a result. This tactic helps break the rhythm of the opponent, taking it from fast to slow.
- Fast drop shots are ones near to the opponent's service line as opposed to slow drops that fall near the net, which allow the opponent more time. Slow drops are great against slower opponents.
- Clear shots are those that are hit defensively, with the aim to hit the shuttle high and to the back of the opponents' court. These are common in singles but often seen as negative in doubles, unless you find yourself in difficulty in a rally!

What choices does the front player have?

- Net kills – like a smash but flatter; this forces the opponent to lift their reply which should be easier to smash.
- Pushes – exploiting the open space. A great shot when you notice an opponent charge the net after an overhead and the shuttle is close to the service line at chest height. Simply push the shuttle to one of the tram lines (wide) and force your opponent to stretch.
- Drives – a shot that aims to force the shuttle over at pace and is hit 'through' the shuttle and so has more force as a result; great for when the shuttle is too low to smash but not low enough to lift (underarm).
- Lift – when nothing else will do, and to buy yourself some recovery time, hit underneath with as much **disguise** as possible.

Check your knowledge

1 Is it better to play front and back or sides when playing doubles badminton? Justify your answer.

2 Why is disguise such an important technique in badminton?

Key term

Disguise – making one shot appear like another. For example, playing a lift in badminton might be preceded by the kind of approach used for a drop shot, forcing your opponent into preparing for the wrong shot.

Tactics in different types of sport

In individual sports, tactics take on a very personal edge. There is often no one else from whom you can gain support, so the correct decision can be critical. Here are some tactics from open water swimming, one of the UK's fast growing sporting activities:

▶ drifting in an opponent's wake

▶ zigzagging

▶ applying different breathing techniques, such as bilateral breathing

▶ pacing and sighting.

Team sports with a significant number of team mates, such as rugby, extend the amount and type of tactical options even further. For example, a player with the ball can consider running or going to ground or passing or dummying or kicking (not to mention different kicks). Add to that the position of the player's team mates and the opposition and the potential resultant scenarios, and choosing tactics actually becomes critical to the overall success of the team.

To simplify often complex scenarios in team strategies or tactics, many teams develop philosophies that seek to provide very simple rules that apply to all players at most times. This means that, even if precise execution is not observed, then at least a general ethos or pattern can be followed. In the following case studies there are fewer specific strategies and more philosophical approaches to the game.

Case study

Rugby

The blind side

Every break down or scrum has a blind side and an open side. The blind side is the smaller side, 'blind' to the majority of the defenders who are on the open side, where there is more space to cover.

The blind side is usually attacked when the space is big enough to send two players down but the open side is still big enough to only have one defender spare, thus creating a two-on-one situation and a potential try scoring situation.

The open side

The opposite of the blind side, the open side is the side with the most space. This gives the attacking team more space to play the ball, but more defenders cover the open side and so often cancel the space out.

Down the middle

Often to tie in defenders and to free up a quick ball, a team will put the ball 'down the middle'. This involves giving the ball to a big runner to run into contact in the middle of the pitch. This will hopefully prompt some of the wide defenders to move in to help with the tackle and so leave more space on the wings to attack.

Quick ball

The speed with which the ball comes back from the ruck (or maul) limits what moves you can play. For example, teams playing champagne or 15 man rugby will aim to move the ball quickly to expose an unprepared defence and so want a quick ball. Teams playing ten man rugby want a slow ball so they have time to organise themselves and slow play down to catch their breath.

Ten man rugby

The main play consists of three stages, outlined below.

- The fly half kicks the ball downfield – if within the 22 aiming to put it straight into touch – if outside aiming to bounce it into touch.
- The forwards pressure the opposition line-out in an attempt to win the ball.
- When they have the ball they will maul it forward until they cannot maul forward anymore before passing to the fly half, repeating the steps again.

Champagne rugby

Champagne rugby is the exact opposite of ten man rugby. The ball is moved as quickly as possible and as far around the pitch in an effort to make use of faster players and to tire a less fit team. The Welsh are famous for this style of game, although the phrase originates from New Zealand. It involves offloading out of the tackle, keeping the ball in play more and avoiding contact.

15 man rugby

The ultimate in rugby, a team who can master this will beat the world. A combination of champagne rugby and a rugged pack of forwards, the team will aim to play the ball down the middle first, using a big forward and head straight into contact, before throwing the ball wide and using the fast men to avoid contact and score.

Check your knowledge

1   What are the main advantages of playing the blind side in rugby?

2   Why would the forwards pressure the opposition line-out in the ten man game?

Twenty20 cricket

Twenty20 cricket is the newest and, some would say, most exciting form of the game. This version of the game is shorter, generally played in the afternoon or evening to attract more spectators, and is infused with music, colourful kit and fireworks. As a result greater pressure is put on batsmen, bowlers and fielders, and tactics can and do change ball by ball – see Table 26.3.

▶ **Table 26.3:** Common tactics in Twenty20 cricket

Technical component	Tactic	Effect on skill selection (opposition)
Captaincy	Plan before the game	None – though each team should predict their opponent's approach by asking 'What would you do against us?'
	Force opposition players to do things they would not normally do – batting particularly	More pressure generally means more mistakes
	Create pressure with field placings	Adds pressure and makes opponents uncomfortable
	Change the bowlers or even alter the pace of the game	Direct effect on concentration
	Protect your boundaries	Prevents easy boundary scores
Bowling	Bowl at the stumps a lot more (compared to other forms of the game)	Batsmen playing across the line can miss, and bowler can get a leg before wicket decision if they are hitting the stumps
	Vary your run-up to disturb batter's rhythm	Added strain on concentration and pressure
	Variables like flight, length and line	Potentially more wickets
Batting	Opening batsmen look to score quickly and attack all of the bowling	Pressure on the bowlers
	One boundary an over with four or five singles	Destroys the confidence of fielding team
	Target a certain bowler	Upsets the confidence of the bowler and scores more runs

Check your knowledge

1 Compare the Twenty20 cricket format with that of the traditional five-day test match. In the early days of the newer format, many of the five day specialists failed to succeed. Why do you think this is? Answer in terms of specific skills and tactics.

2 Research a list of cricket techniques for batting, bowling and fielding. Then create two profiles, one for an ideal Twenty20 batsman, the other for a five day test player.

Application and importance of technical and tactical skills in effective performance

How strategies and tactics affect selection of technical skills

Tactical awareness is the ability to make the correct choice of strategies and tactics relative to the strengths and weaknesses of the opposing player or team. By having a game plan and good tactical awareness, an athlete can:

▶ control the structure of the game

▶ exploit the opposition's defensive weaknesses

▶ reduce the likelihood of conceding goals, points or runs

- ▶ avoid wasting energy
- ▶ increase the attempts on goals/opportunities to score points
- ▶ create more attacking moves
- ▶ make effective use of set plays
- ▶ vary the game.

Elite performers need to be able to 'read' a game. This is a perceptual ability rather than a visual one. Elite performers will be able to:

- ▶ anticipate the opponent's movement direction or the pass or stroke to be made
- ▶ predict the outcome of a range of different situations, based on previous experience – for example, by recognising the potential passing/stroke/shot option open to the player in possession
- ▶ recall patterns of play.

An athlete who has good tactical knowledge and can read the game will be able to choose and adapt strategies and tactics as the game progresses, choosing technical skills and techniques that are appropriate for their specific strategy at any particular moment of the game.

Selecting tactics in response to strengths and weaknesses

To make the right choice in terms of tactics, athletes need to know their own strengths and weaknesses, and those of their opponents. One of the best ways to do this is to use a performance profile that focuses on the athlete's use of technical skills and tactical knowledge.

A performance profile allows the performer and coach to focus on targets to improve performance. A performance profile:

- ▶ highlights perceived strengths and areas for improvement
- ▶ monitors change
- ▶ identifies any mismatch between the perceptions of the coach and the player
- ▶ analyses performance following a competition.

> **Discussion**
>
> The purpose of analysing a sporting performance is to provide detailed feedback to the athlete or team in order for them to improve their game. When analysing the performance of an individual or team, you should consider a variety of questions, which might include:
>
> - How well are specific skills executed?
> - How focused and motivated are the athletes?
> - Are the athletes using the correct techniques?
> - Are the correct tactics adopted at the right time?
>
> Choose a sport and, as a group, watch a performance and start a discussion using the playback, pause and even slow motion features to answer the questions above.

> **Link**
>
> You can read more about performance profiling in *Unit 28: Sports Performance Analysis*.

Scouting opponents

In many sports it has become normal to scout opponents before a competition. When carried out effectively it can provide very useful information that prepares you for the contest more thoroughly. In football many clubs employ the services of respected experts and analysts to provide data on perceived strengths and weaknesses of opponents, by position.

Scouts will focus on many aspects of performance (again using football as an example).

- ▶ For the opposition team as a whole:
  - their general philosophy or approach to the game
  - key threats and weaknesses
  - set piece routines including penalty takers and their preferences.

▶ For the opposition players:
- **goalkeepers:** reflexes, one-on-one ability, command of the penalty area and aerial intelligence
- **centre backs:** heading and tackling ability, height, bravery in attempting challenges, concentration
- **fullbacks:** pace, stamina, decision making, tackling and marking abilities, work rate
- **central midfielders:** stamina, passing ability, team responsibility, positioning, marking abilities
- **wingers:** pace, technical ability like dribbling and close control, off-the-ball intelligence, creativity
- **forwards:** finishing ability, composure, technical ability, heading ability, pace, off-the-ball intelligence.

Once you have a complete profile of yourself/team and your opponent you can consider the most appropriate tactics to use. Remember your choice of tactics depends largely upon your sport and these other factors:

▶ the strengths and weaknesses of your own team and the opposition

▶ the particular strengths of individual players within the structure, strategy or composition of your team

▶ the experience of players in your team or opposition and previous results

▶ how long you can apply the structure, strategy or composition

▶ the score in the game, time left in the game and weather/ground conditions

▶ the amount of space to perform in and type of apparatus selected.

❚❚ PAUSE POINT   How can tactics and skill selection affect the result of a game or match?

Hint   What is a tactic? See if you can name five tactics from a sport of your choice.

Extend   Why do some teams get it wrong? Research or watch a video of an unsuccessful performance and make a list of what went wrong and more importantly what you suggest to put it right.

Assessment practice 26.1   A.P1   A.P2   A.M1   A.D1

A local cricket and tennis club wants to improve the way they approach the technical and tactical demands of both sports. There are several new coaches working with club members of all ages and the club would like the coaches to be able to analyse sporting performance. To do this, the coaches must understand the technical and tactical demands of those sports.

In order to achieve this you have been asked to:
- research and produce a profile for either cricket or tennis that details the techniques and tactics that impact on performance
- produce a detailed leaflet that describes each of the techniques and tactics.

The last part of the leaflet should be an appropriate schematic that includes all of the factors identified, like a performance profile.

Plan
- I will use a variety of sources for both sports when researching techniques and tactics.
- I will build the leaflet with brief descriptions of each of the techniques and tactics, and consider when to use diagrams to improve the visual quality of my work.

Do
- I will complete the leaflet in as much detail as possible.
- I will be ready to present the leaflet to my peers for some additional ideas on improvement.

Review
- I can explain how I would approach the difficult elements differently next time.
- Once I have reflected on my own work and any feedback from others, I will make any necessary changes to my leaflet.

B ## Investigate methods to measure technical and tactical performance in sport

Having identified skills, techniques and tactics, and looked at how they might be used to your advantage, it would seem logical to find a way to observe and record them. Generally it is not enough to just offer an opinion like a football pundit, so what are our choices?

> **Link**
>
> This section links with *Unit 28: Sports Performance Analysis*.

Measuring technical and tactical skills

As sport has grown to be a multi-million pound industry, many sports have tried to professionalise their outlook, and this includes the way they measure technical and tactical skills. Many sports performers are now valuable commodities who are traded on transfer markets, which means that their skill and ability must be measured. These days:

▶ premier league football teams have player databases that cover more than 100,000 players, and their performance data is updated regularly by scouts and analysts

▶ tactical databases are also stored and recorded

▶ there is a move by some sports to professionalise the skills of performance analysis and scouting in recognition of their importance.

Methods

Video analysis

Video analysis is usually carried out on performers in live or recorded scenarios, and should be completed against an established set of performance criteria, like KPIs. Video analysis lets you analyse performance with the huge advantage of playback, slow motion and freeze frame features. This means incredible detail can be observed in a way that cannot be achieved through observing in real time.

Software applications allow the analyst to extract data, draw and notate and even calculate joint angles, such as in the case of trampolinist performing their ten bounce routine or a snowboarder analysing their latest skill.

You can read more about video analysis in Unit 28 – see page 490.

Notational analysis

Notational analysis assesses sport performance by counting different observations, for example, how many shots were successful versus unsuccessful.

It is used by sport scientists to collect objective data on the athlete's performance. It can be used to observe tactics, techniques, individual athlete movements and work rate. This then helps coaches and athletes to learn more about performance and gain an advantage over opponents.

You can read more about notational analysis in Unit 28 – see page 491.

Movement

Television coverage of sport shows lots of statistics and diagrams, such as the distance a player has covered in a game or the directions in which they have made most of their runs. These are different examples of the term 'movement' used in sports. Other factors to look at when examining a player's movement include:

▶ work rate (for example, measuring heart rate using heart rate monitors)

▶ positional play and movement patterns (for example, how well a player fulfils the positional roles in a team or the movements a player performs during a game)

▶ distance covered (for example, how far a player has travelled during a game, sometimes broken down into walking, jogging and sprinting)

▶ movement patterns.

Increasingly advanced systems are now being developed so that elite and non-elite teams can have access to notated data. In the early of days of notation, paper charts and concept keyboards were used to gather data. However, advanced movement and target tracking software has become so sophisticated that individual players can be recorded and tracked with ever more impressive functionality.

One of the most well-known examples of analysis software is Prozone, which is used by nearly all professional football clubs in the UK, and also by television companies to analyse performances, for example in tennis and cricket.

You can read more about global positioning system (GPS) and movement analysis in Unit 28 – see page 489.

Tally charts and rating scales

Tally charts are a useful tool for observing sporting performance. The tally chart may simply be used to count performance factors such as:

▶ shots on target in football

▶ number of fouls committed in basketball

▶ wide balls bowled in cricket

▶ number of double serves in badminton

▶ number of shots played to the forehand and backhand in tennis.

Tally charts can be used without any in-depth analysis, merely counting the number of occurrences.

Research

In small groups watch a recording of a volleyball match and conduct a basic tally analysis. Each member of the group should count occurrences of one of the following:
- successful serves
- unsuccessful serves
- shots to the front of the court
- shots to the back of the court
- smashes completed
- unforced errors.

Using the information you have collected, discuss your findings with your group and identify any areas for improvement.

Ratings scales are slightly more involved as they generally ask the observer to make a series of value judgements on aspects of performance, for example on scales of 1 to 5 where 1 = poor skill execution and 5 = excellent.

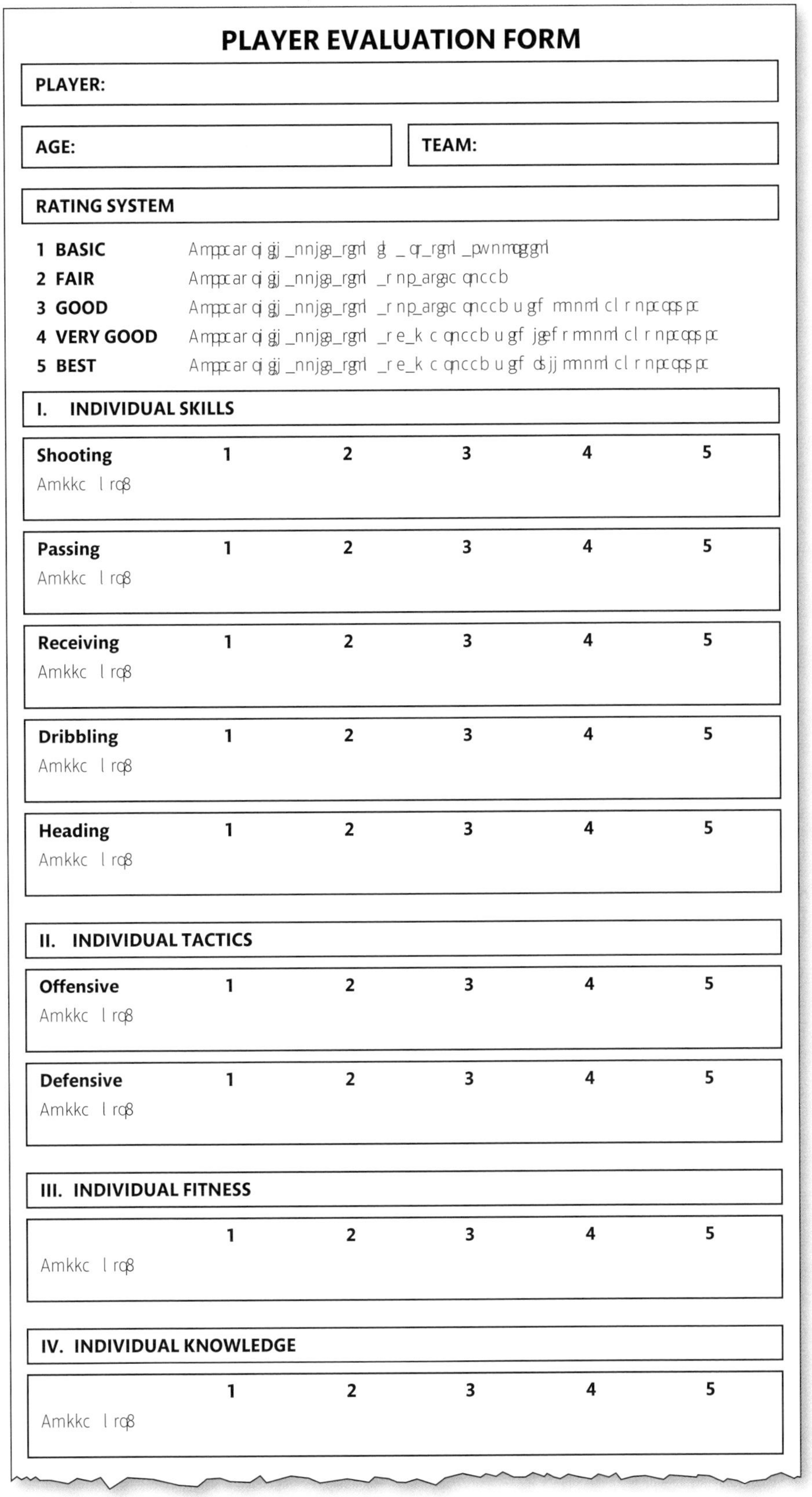

PLAYER EVALUATION FORM

PLAYER:

AGE: **TEAM:**

RATING SYSTEM

1 BASIC	Ampcar oi gij _nnjga_rgnl gl _ar_rgnl _pwnmggnl
2 FAIR	Ampcar oi gij _nnjga_rgnl _r np_argac qnccb
3 GOOD	Ampcar oi gij _nnjga_rgnl _r np_argac qnccb u gf mnnml cl r npcqps pc
4 VERY GOOD	Ampcar oi gij _nnjga_rgnl _re_k c qnccb u gf jgef r mnnml cl r npcqpspc
5 BEST	Ampcar oi gij _nnjga_rgnl _re_k c qnccb u gf dsjj mnnml cl r npcqpspc

I. INDIVIDUAL SKILLS

Shooting   1   2   3   4   5
Amkkc l ra߀

Passing   1   2   3   4   5
Amkkc l ra߀

Receiving   1   2   3   4   5
Amkkc l ra߀

Dribbling   1   2   3   4   5
Amkkc l ra߀

Heading   1   2   3   4   5
Amkkc l ra߀

II. INDIVIDUAL TACTICS

Offensive   1   2   3   4   5
Amkkc l ra߀

Defensive   1   2   3   4   5
Amkkc l ra߀

III. INDIVIDUAL FITNESS

            1   2   3   4   5
Amkkc l ra߀

IV. INDIVIDUAL KNOWLEDGE

            1   2   3   4   5
Amkkc l ra߀

▶ **Figure 26.6:** A typical rating scale approach to performance analysis

Checklists

An easy way to carry out an assessment is to use a checklist, as these are inexpensive and information can be processed quickly. This can assess an athlete's technical and tactical ability, covering:

▶ technical skills

▶ selection and application of skills

▶ tactical awareness and its application

▶ sport-specific skills, such as the ability to defend and attack, and shot selection.

Producing a checklist can be divided into stages.

1 Use the checklist to identify the player's strengths and areas for improvement in their sport.

2 Explain these strengths and areas for improvement.

3 Justify the development suggestions for your chosen player.

Many of the sections are transferable from one sport to another.

Avoiding bias

When using checklists and rating scales to assess athletes, it is important that you record information without bias. This means not pre-judging an athlete – if you go into an assessment expecting an athlete to be weak in a certain area, there is a risk you will 'see what you expect to see'. It also means ensuring you make a fair assessment of the overall picture.

If you are analysing live matches, it is difficult to observe every movement because of the speed of the game/sequence and you may miss important movements. Poor weather conditions may also pose problems.

You may have a smaller checklist associated with a specific area you want to assess, for example key skills and tactics. Observation could be focused on a particular period of time during a competition.

Having completed the checklists, you can then identify the strengths and areas for improvement.

> **Theory into practice**
>
> Using the ideas presented to you, design an observation checklist to assess the performance of a team or individual. Form groups if several of you are designing a checklist for the same sport. Ensure your checklist covers:
>
> - technical skills
> - selection and application of skills
> - tactical awareness
> - application of tactics
> - ability to defend and attack
> - shot selection.
>
> Observe a colleague and test your checklist by analysing their skills. Does it give you all the information you need to assess your chosen performer?

Environments for analysis

The best conditions under which analysis takes place will depend on the kind of data required, whether it is **qualitative** or **quantitative**, or if it is generated in a 'real' competitive scenario or an artificially created practice scenario. Table 26.4 shows the main features of the three different types.

> **Key terms**
>
> **Qualitative** – information or data that is based on qualities that are descriptive, subjective or difficult to measure.
>
> **Quantitative** – information or data that is based on quantities or numbers.

▶ **Table 26.4:** Environments for analysis

Open competition	Closed specific trials	Conditioned situations
During an actual live competitive event	Training sessions that have been designed with the main purpose of performer selection	Training or competitive situations that have been loaded to focus on specific tactics or skills
• The most common and perhaps most valid of all analysis environments • Analysis occurs in a natural environment and in the presence of true competition	• Trials can be designed to make direct technical and tactical comparisons and can be altered and managed, i.e. tests altered or conditioned to provide comparative data • The structure of the trials can focus on very specific detail and be used to identify strengths and areas for development in a way that competition will not allow	• Games and practices can be altered to provide data for comparison on specific focus. For example, a basketball coach tracking offensive movement without the ball might condition a practice to encourage this movement, perhaps by adding a no dribble rule

Timing

Analysis can also provide valuable information at different points of the competitive calendar. Table 26.5 shows a sequence of times when analysis might be conducted. Naturally, data is only reliable for a short time and does not take into account technical or tactical improvement over a period of time, say a season. Data that compares patterns of skill or tactical improvement (or regression) over a period of time is likely to be more beneficial to coaching staff, not to mention more valid.

▶ **Table 26.5:** Times to conduct analysis

Pre-season	This is critical for coaching staff to calculate and plan for the entire season. Analysis might be focused on fitness or on testing tactical formations and playing positions.
Pre-practice	Analysis can also take place before practice, particularly for strategic planning, like learning plays from a playbook in ice hockey or fitness assessments.
Post-practice	The end of a practice is a good time to make qualitative reflections. Successful football teams like FC Barcelona review video footage of their own games and their opponents in preparation for the next game.
Pre-competition	Generally pre-game analysis is low key and serves as a basic reminder. Tennis players often have tactical reminder cards summarising tactics for the next opponent, e.g. serve out wide to deuce court or serve volley in third set.
During competition	This is the best data for comparative purposes in real competitive situations.
After competition	Win or lose, it is important for players and coaches to reflect after a performance. Most coaches prefer not to analyse immediately after a game, but allow time for arousal to reduce and reflect on the most useful post-match data.
Pre-training	This is analysis that occurs prior to training, for example survey data or fitness testing data.
During training	This is the analysis that occurs in game and is generally recorded for further analysis, although increasingly sophisticated applications can capture data and analyse in-game.
Post-training	This is traditionally the time used to synthesise the data, such as video, statistical or basic observation. Post training also potentially allows for reflection and more access to performers to create a more rounded picture.

Protocols

Protocols are rules that aim to give clear guidelines about how an assessment should be carried out to ensure ethical and valid analysis or assessment. They aim to ensure that any analysis is done in a fair and balanced way. Many existing protocols are available for well-established methods, but you might have to create your own if you are adapting an existing test or creating it from scratch. It is worth considering these rules for analysis.

▶ **How** – what is the best of all the available methods for your needs? What can you afford? What will yield the most useful data?

- ▶ **Where** – this can cover training, competition and, more precisely, what perspective any observation or filming is done from.
- ▶ **When** – timings must suit the kind of data that you want to be able to compare or consider.

Evaluation

Evaluation of sporting performance can be considered in simple reflective terms, as in Figure 26.7.

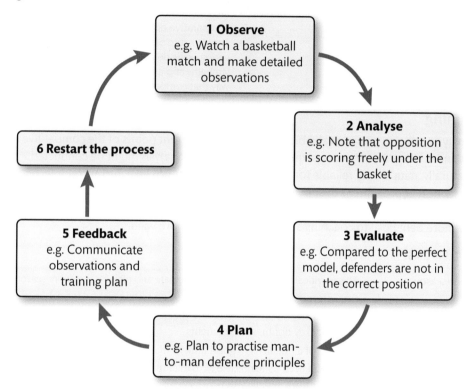

▶ **Figure 26.7:** The sports analysis evaluative process

But there are also more intricate, detailed approaches to evaluation, as outlined in Table 26.6.

▶ **Table 26.6:** Choosing the correct evaluation type

Evaluation type	Determinant	Example
Evaluation of process/performance	• How the techniques/tactics are performed • Accuracy, efficiency, timing, pace, power, correct selection, defining factor technique, ability or chance	• Floor routine in gymnastics • Lob and volley tactic in tennis or number of created chances to score in rugby
Evaluation of outcome	• Result of performance • Success • Time • Accuracy • Placing • Win/loss	• Consequence of winning or losing • Personal best (PB)/season's best/even distance from own PB or national/international records, e.g. for elite swimmers
Evaluation of performance	• Effects on outcome • Probability of successful repetition • Validity • Relevance • Accuracy	• Did it result in a win or a performance improvement? • How likely is it that you could perform the same way again? • Was the performance what was required?

Any evaluation should also end with consideration of the evaluation itself. This should consider whether the chosen evaluation method or methods produced information that is valid, relevant and accurate. It should be reflective at this stage so that any repeated analysis gains from the findings of the previous analysis.

❚❚ PAUSE POINT   How well do you think you could apply what you know about measuring sporting performance?

> **Hint**   What are the main tools that you can use for measuring performance? Describe each of them in your own words.

> **Extend**   Imagine you have been asked to analyse the performance of an athlete in a sport with which you are not very familiar. How would you go about deciding which assessment to use and what equipment would you need?

Technical and tactical ideal models and benchmarks

Any sporting analysis needs a frame of reference, or an 'ideal model' or benchmark against which you can judge current performance. Most performers are usually only too happy to say who they model their performances on, usually someone they respect in their sport, for example an international player or potentially a world champion. When you know what you want to aim at, you can then break down the key attributes of this ideal performance and start trying to reproduce them.

> **Reflect**
>
> Who do you model your own performance on and why?

Sources of information and references for technical and tactical analysis

In order for analysis to be valid and useful, we need to consider how we decide what to measure and how to best apply those sources to each individual analysis.

One of the more usual forms of performance analysis is comparative analysis against elite performance, typically using television, internet videos and other video or still image sources to make comparisons and allow adjustments to performance.

You can also speak to coaches/tutors, consult coaching manuals and refer to information published by National Governing Bodies (NGBs) in order to find 'benchmark' performances against which you can compare your subject.

The perfect model

The **perfect model** occurs when a performance is at its very best and can be described as skilled and technically correct. Judging an individual's performance against the perfect model can help you to describe strengths and weaknesses in their performance.

First of all, however, you must know how to describe the perfect model. Understanding the perfect model can come from:

▶ playing experience

▶ watching others

▶ reading about a sport in depth

▶ listening to and watching top performers.

A perfect model is shown in Figure 26.8.

> **Key term**
>
> **Perfect model** – a faultless performance and one which can be used as a model by performers at the highest level.

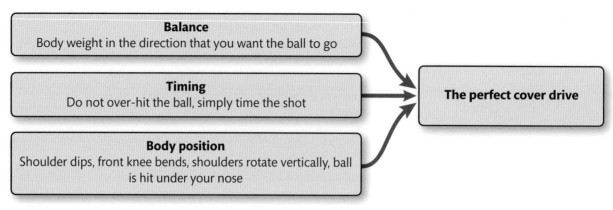

┌─────────────────────────────────────┐
│ **Balance** │
│ Body weight in the direction that you want the ball to go │
└─────────────────────────────────────┘

┌─────────────────────────────────────┐
│ **Timing** │
│ Do not over-hit the ball, simply time the shot │
└─────────────────────────────────────┘

┌─────────────────────────────────────┐
│ **Body position** │
│ Shoulder dips, front knee bends, shoulders rotate vertically, ball │
│ is hit under your nose │
└─────────────────────────────────────┘

┌─────────────────────┐
│ **The perfect cover drive** │
└─────────────────────┘

▶ **Figure 26.8:** Perfect model for a cover drive in cricket

Identifying evaluation constructs

Before you can decide what makes up your list of contents or menu for analysis, you need to consider exactly what features you should include.

When performers develop a high level of technical and tactical ability they may have the ability to compete at the highest levels. In order to undertake observations of elite performances it is important to understand what constitutes an elite performance in your sport.

Ideal models

Ideal models can be created from 'pinnacle performances', or performances that demonstrate the absolute best that anyone could achieve, or at the very least better than all other rivals, for example a Gold-medal winning performance in the Olympics. However, we must recognise that if we design a set of **constructs** based on the absolute best performance, we could limit those people who are not capable of achieving this performance. We could even limit them simply by identifying the constructs. It is important to recognise what is perfect and then what is ideal – and that these may not be the same.

National representatives are sports performers who are the best in their particular sport in their country and are selected to represent the country; for example, Andy Murray being selected to represent Great Britain in the Davis Cup or Eniola Aluko representing England at football.

National record holders are athletes who hold a record for performance in their particular sport. These records could take the form of points scored, wickets taken, time taken to complete a course, etc. These performances can be benchmarks for evaluative comparison, as can world record holders (those who have achieved a performance in a particular sport/event which has not been improved by anyone in the world). Examples of these include Jack Nicklaus's record number of wins in golf majors or Michael Johnson's world record in the 200-metres. These elite performers can help provide performance benchmarks.

Benchmarks

Benchmarks are essentially established, reliable and reviewed statistics. Their function is to provide a basis for comparison.

▶ Data and benchmarks exist for most sports at every age group, for both genders and for national and international comparison. Athletics, swimming and other sports speak in terms of personal bests or PBs. If you know the best times for national athletes, then you have a good baseline for comparison.

Key terms

Ideal model – not necessarily a perfect model as it takes into account the ability of the person who is modelling. For example, there is no point modelling a perfect performance if it is not physically achievable by the sports performer (for example, at an early development stage).

Constructs – any item that should be considered a critical part of something. In this context, a construct is a technique or tactic that should be included for analysis or evaluation.

▶ In team sports it is possible to obtain data from organisations like Prozone on possession of the ball, distance travelled, player pass completion rate and other KPIs (see page 395).

▶ Statistics can be found for national, world, Olympic, Commonwealth and a range of other parameters, as well as local competitions, county events – and potentially even your school or college.

Link

There is more about finding and using ideal models and benchmarks in *Unit 28: Sports Performance Analysis*, starting on page 499.

Producing measurement tools and protocols

The next stage of analysis is to construct your measurement tool, or the tool you will use to gather and analyse data. An example for junior basketball is outlined below.

Designing an assessment tool for junior basketball performance

1 **Establish ideal model** – this could be an elite performer from the NBA or from the wider world of basketball, e.g. FIBA (world governing body). Remember that FIBA along with many other NGBs has well-established national and international age group competitions, and that technical and tactical comparisons are perhaps more valid if they are age-related.

2 **Establish benchmarks and technical model** – technical models focus on descriptive analyses such as phases of play, or specific performance techniques rather than numerical data. In England all National League fixtures are required to use LiveStats, an application that will allow individual data to be gathered for each player on a range of constructs such as field goal percentage, baskets made, three pointers made and attempted, fouls and rebounds, etc. Benchmarks could include offensive and defensive rebounding, points made compared to shots taken, overall assists (passes that lead to points) etc.

3 **Summarise information** – after collecting data, consider the following questions related to the quality of the information.

   ▶ Validity – does it measure what it is supposed to? Is it useful?

   ▶ Reliability – if you were to use the same measurement tool, would it repeatedly reveal consistent information?

   ▶ Accuracy – can you check to see if what the data reveals is actually true?

   ▶ Bias – has the observer altered the outcome of an assessment due to subtle changes in the way he or she has interacted with the performer?

4 **Produce the measurement tool** – decide how you would like to collect your information, for example notation, questionnaire, video, stats application, IT application, tally chart, etc.

5 **Test it** – use it in a scrimmage or school game and see if it works. If necessary you can make changes before you use it in a 'live' situation.

6 **Go live** – use your measurement tool. Record on video anything you are analysing, even if you are not using video analysis. Often in fast moving sports like basketball, many things can happen very quickly in a very short amount of time. Video playback allows you to concentrate on particular sequences of play and is therefore more likely to be accurate, reliable and valid.

7 **Produce a protocol** – when you are satisfied that your tool works, draw up a set of guidelines about how it can be used so anyone can practise and use it themselves. You might want to clarify anything that is not clear, for example does a player who tips the ball away from their own basket get credited with a defensive rebound? Remember, there are always available definitions for these interpretations.

8 **Measure** – now use the data and benchmarks that you researched and make comparisons.

Hint   Name three ways in which you can measure technical or tactical performance.

Extend   What technical information would you want from your sport? Draw up a list of the technical considerations of your sport, then rank them in order of relevance.

Explore the technical and tactical performance at different stages of the performance continuum

Key terms

Technical measurement tools – tools which analyse specific skills, techniques or even fitness components and which could include use of video analysis or fitness testing equipment.

Tactical measurement tools – tools which focus purely on tactical approaches in given situations, such as observational analysis, statistical analysis and sport-specific attacking or defending analysis.

Assessing and developing elite sports performers

It is important to remember that, while all sports people take their sports seriously, the potential for greatness exists at the elite level. It could even be that some of the aspects of performance identified in analysis could mean the move from good to world class. Very few elite athletes, if any, will not have been the subject of careful analysis related to their technical and tactical skills. **Technical** and **tactical measurement tools** will have been used to assess their performance.

Observation of elite performers

When observing an elite sports performer there are several considerations and key variables, outlined in Table 26.7.

▶ **Table 26.7:** Considerations when analysing an elite sports performer

Consideration	Description
Talent identification	This is commonly referred to as scouting, and involves an experienced coach observing a performance and evaluating findings. This can help identify new players, or prepare for a match where information about the opposition will allow you to devise a specific tactic.
Monitoring current fitness levels	Using a variety of fitness tests, we can measure various components of fitness. This information can be a starting point for any training programme. Throughout training programmes, regular fitness tests can be conducted to ensure benefits are being gained. If results indicate that targets are not being met, training can be adjusted to take into account any changes.
Identifying strengths and areas for improvement	This is of particular importance when investigating technique. Once you have identified areas of improvement, it is possible to develop a training programme to address them. For example, analysis may show a goalkeeper is poor at gathering crosses. A training programme will incorporate specific training to improve this key area.
Performance assessment	By carrying out assessment during a competition situation, you can see whether players are affected by external factors, such as the crowd or opposition. This will allow you to develop specific tactics that can be used under game conditions. Using defined conditions during training allows a team to develop both their techniques and tactics. For example, if a basketball team struggles to defend using man-marking, a practice may include using specific drills to highlight marking, with the coach able to stop the practice and demonstrate if it has been effective or not.

▶ **Table 26.7:** – continued

| Recovery after injury | With injured athletes it is useful to perform a number of assessments before they restart training or performance. This ensures the athlete has recovered sufficiently so that injury does not recur. Simple fitness tests can be conducted both on the injured area, and also generally to identify a base level from which to start training again. It is important the athlete does not over-train, as this can result in continued injury and will prevent them from performing.

The analyst may also wish to talk to the athlete about their injury in case there are problems or concerns about a recurrence. A player may have been hurt by a tackle, and may have developed a fear of tackling. Using this information, the coach will be able to support and encourage the athlete to overcome any psychological factors. |
| Squad selection | Analysis can be used to monitor player performance both in training and competition. Sports such as rugby and football now use large squads of players and, through performance analysis, a coach will be able to select the players most likely to achieve success. If a player has been underperforming, this can be addressed and additional support given.

A coach can analyse the opposition team in preparation for a match, so that tactics involving certain players can be developed and used. |

Link

For more on training programmes, see *Unit 2: Fitness Training and Programming for Health, Sport and Well-being*. For more on fitness testing, see *Unit 5: Application of Fitness Testing*. For more on performance assessment, see *Unit 28: Sports Performance Analysis*.

The process of elite sports analysis can be summarised in Figure 26.9. Essentially the process has four stages.

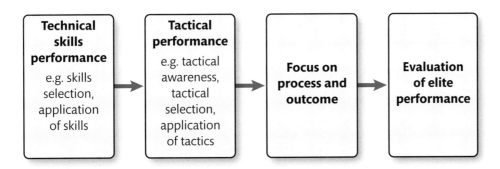

▶ **Figure 26.9:** Sports analysis of an elite sports performer

By way of an example consider the performance of an elite tennis player.

▶ Immediately following the performance, the process begins by analysing whether the shot selection at critical points was effective, for example lob or cross-court drive. This will be applied through the whole contest and may highlight differences in certain parts of the contest, for example the first set or at the end of the third set.

▶ Tactical analysis will focus on how the player exploited or failed to exploit identified weaknesses or even focused on key strengths. An amount of time will also be set aside to focus on the efficacy of the pre-contest tactical plan.

▶ The final stages of the analysis depend on the context of the analysis. If the tennis player is focused more on how they felt about their approach to the performance, for example in spite of losing they achieved near-to-ideal performance evidenced by numerical data, then the feedback can be about the process of the contest, and may even ignore the outcome or at the very least simply take it into account. This kind of approach is normal for a much lower-ranked player who faces a top ten tennis player. The outcome becomes less about winning and more about ensuring that the player plays their best game technically and tactically.

Research

Put the model shown in Figure 26.9 into practice. Choose an elite performer, team or position in sport. Build a set of relevant technical skills and locate a suitable video source that will allow you to analyse both techniques and tactics. Make a set of specific observations and, if you feel confident, make a list of recommendations for improvement. Use the internet and recognised coaching resources.

Development planning

The process of development planning for elite sports performers is essentially carried out in four steps.

1. Interpret the data

Collate the information and find the best presentation medium for your data, for example either numerically or via graphs, radar diagrams or collated statements. Figure 26.10 shows a radar diagram that allows you to differentiate between an athlete's personal perception of their performance compared to that of an established world class performance.

Link

There is more about collating and presenting analysis data in Unit 28: Sports Performance Analysis.

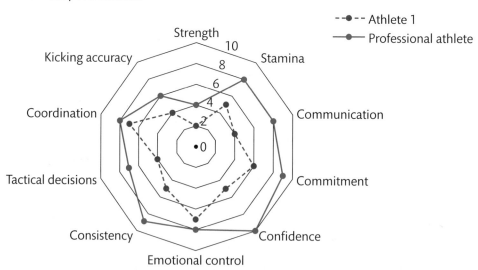

▶ **Figure 26.10:** Typical radar diagram used in sports analysis

2. Summarise the information

Summarising the information should include:

Link

Refer back to Unit 3: Professional Development in the Sports Industry to refresh your memory about SWOT analysis.

▶ mentioning the measurement tool used, alongside concise, accurate and valid conclusions

▶ comparing the results to the ideal model you have already identified

▶ identifying strengths, weaknesses and areas for improvement – this could be done by using a SWOT analysis as shown for football in Figure 26.11

▶ providing reasons why the athlete is at a particular stage of the performance continuum: this could be due to skill, ability, environment and/or external circumstances. This continuum seeks to place a performer at a particular point in their development in a sport, from the start point as a beginner through to world class performer. It takes into account the skills that have been learned, makes an allowance for natural ability, and factors in external influences such as peer pressure, injuries and social development.

Strengths	**Weaknesses**
• Movement to space after passing – give and go • Movement to support team mate with the ball • Movement to space away from ball anticipating play • On the ball – going to goal for shot • Accuracy to open space with left foot shot • Power of right foot shot • Tactical – positional responsibilities, principles of defence, team shape	• Tactical: alignment of formations • Tactical: principles of attack • Power of left foot shot • Volley shot with right foot • Volley shot with left foot • Tactical: transition from offence to defence and back • Tactical: restarts • Tactical: overall reading of the game
Opportunities	**Threats**
• Skill specific training • Access to ideal models for comparison • Working with quality coaches and analysts	• Lack of confidence and understanding • Injuries • Lack of access to pressure training environments

▶ **Figure 26.11:** Example of a SWOT analysis for a footballer

3. Plan for the development of an athlete

▶ Goal setting – when using detailed analysis and evaluation of performance, it is important that clear and well defined targets or goals are set by the coach and athlete. These goals can be seen as a target the performer wishes to achieve, and may be either short- or long-term goals. Goals should be set using the SMART principle (see page 338) and should be discussed openly by both coach and athlete. By including the athlete, it is likely they will remain motivated to train because they will feel in control of their training.

▶ Relating development goals to age – while you would not want to discriminate, in any sports there are athletes with long careers ahead, those in their prime and those nearer the end of their careers. Failure to recognise this when providing performance and analytical feedback ignores what an athlete could, should and ought to be targeting. For example, setting out a five year performance plan for an athlete near retirement would be pointless.

▶ Appropriate to ability – as part of SMART, ensure goals are achievable for the athlete's ability level.

▶ Appropriate to environment – a performer looking to make adjustments to their performance based on analysis will need to do so in the correct environment. This will vary from performer to performer. Certain skills and tactics can be practised in isolation (such as a trampolinist working on a single skill), under pressure (such as a basketball player shooting while being closely guarded) or even during certain weather conditions (for example for a sailing performance).

▶ Accessibility of resources – this is not usually an issue for elite performers, but you should not assume performers have unlimited access to all facilities or resources.

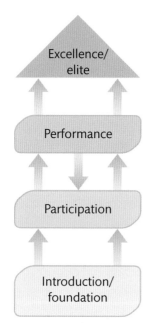

▶ **Figure 26.12:** The sports development continuum

4. Compare the performance and development plan

For development to occur it is necessary to **compare the athlete's performance** over a designated period of time. It is important to consider each of the technical and tactical components identified for improvement in the measurement tool, for example notation, and record their use accurately.

For example, a basketball player needs to improve their individual defence (technique and tactic) and the analysis has been focused on rebounding, boxing out and reducing their personal foul count, at the same time as improving power-based fitness. All of these performance measures can be easily measured and/or tested to produce data, but there can be no comparison from just one game or training session. The more data is gathered from different games, the easier it is to demonstrate trends in performance and hopefully show improvement. The focus of analysis also depends upon the level of performance. The next section highlights these differences.

There are many different levels of performance, depending on ability. This is best illustrated by the sports development continuum, also known as the 'sports development pyramid' (see Figure 26.12). Each level of the 'pyramid' represents the stage you are at in your chosen sport. Performance and development plans should look at the opportunities the athlete has at each stage, and be tracked against their progress through the continuum.

You can read more about the sports development continuum or pyramid in *Unit 27: The Athlete's Lifestyle*, starting from page 441.

Opportunities at different levels of the continuum

Opportunities for analysis exist at all stages of the continuum and while it is not entirely inconceivable that a beginner has access to elite resources, it is not normal. The following takes a look at a generalised example for the analysis of cricket in England and Wales.

▶ **Foundation** – at the very earliest form of introduction to cricket there is very little or no analysis of performance. The key focus at this stage is engagement and enjoyment.

▶ **Participation** – cricket at this level is beginning to focus on technical improvement. Analysis is provided mostly by objective observation and team, or one to one, coaching and advice. Some players, especially those who play at a club, may access better practice resources such as cricket nets and fielding equipment. Feedback on performance improvement is limited, but low level competition such as Kwik Cricket Festivals will provide those interested with outcome-focused analysis, i.e. festival winners. This is the earliest opportunity for talent identification and can help regional and NGBs decide where best to place their development resources.

▶ **Performance** – typically these will be those people who play a lot of cricket, for school, club and possibly beyond. Most clubs will have access to cricket nets, and some have bowling machines, fielding equipment and more exposure to higher level coaching. Video analysis is also quite common here; the use of portable high quality video is used to help improve technical ability at this point.

▶ **Elite** – the highest level, national players who can take advantage of the very best in technology and advanced analysis. The National Cricket Performance Centre in Loughborough contains a purpose-built practice facility with built-in video analysis software, fitness testing equipment, and access to advanced sports medicine and injury treatment advice.

Comparison of the development plans

The comparison of development plans can take into account improvement or regression in terms of technical or tactical components. Depending on the number of comparisons, it is possible to identify trends that could demonstrate even more useful data for coaching staff, such as the 'trainability' of the performer – this indicates how well the performer responds to training.

This is critical and raises the question of how much to involve the performer in the process of analysis. There is evidence that those performers who understand what is being analysed are more likely to improve. Care must be taken to avoid the 'Hawthorne Effect' – the idea that the subjects of any study behave differently because they know they are being studied.

Assessing and developing non-elite sports performers

For non-elite sports performers (those who are at foundation, participation or performance level on the sports development continuum), the process is essentially the same but with some key differences. Applying the same principles, take a look at the comparisons in approach shown in Table 26.8.

▸ **Table 26.8:** Differences when analysing non-elite sports performers

	Analysis stage and process	**Key differences for non-elite level analysis**
Interpret observational data	Collate and present information in a suitable format: numerically, graphs, radar diagrams, collated statements	This will depend upon the parameters measured but is likely to be presented in the same way.
Summarise information	• Make conclusions • Compare to the ideal model • Identify strengths, weaknesses and areas for improvement • Reason athlete is in particular stage of performance continuum: skill, ability, environment, external circumstances	The comparisons made here will be wide ranging. Elite performances will be far closer to the ideal model and will need a sharp, expert focus to narrow on specific performance differences. Ability could but might not always be higher in the elite analysis.
Plan athlete development	• SMART goal setting • Relation to age • Appropriate to ability and environment • Accessibility of resources	The key difference here will be the availability of resources – see the section *Accessibility of resources* below.
Compare performance and development plan	• Similarities and differences in the athlete's technical and tactical performance against different stages of the sports continuum: foundation, participation, performance • Opportunities at different stages of the performance continuum • Comparison of the development plans	The development plans will work on the same template but clearly the focus will be at either end.

Accessibility of resources

The non-elite performer may need more consideration when it comes to accessibility of resources. Non-elite performers are unlikely to have access to the same funding sources as elite performers, and this will affect their ability to access resources.

❙❙ PAUSE POINT   What are the key factors in analysing the performance of elite and non-elite athletes?

     Hint   List the stages of development planning for a non-elite performer and provide an example from a sport of your choice.

     Extend   Demonstrate the use of resources for analysis of a sport other than cricket at each of the levels in the sports development continuum.

Assessment practice 26.2

B.P3　B.P4　B.P5　C.P6　C.P7　B.M2　B.M3　C.M5　B.D2　C.D3

Following on from the success of the techniques and tactics leaflet that you prepared earlier, the same cricket and tennis club wants to go a step further and has asked you to complete some analysis.

Part 1: Measurement methods

In order to get this right there will be three steps to the process.

1　A comparison of your choices, e.g. hand notations, performance profiles, etc. – this should be presented as a poster which carefully describes the different methods, finishing with the measurement technique you intend to use for the cricket and tennis analysis. The poster will be displayed at the club for the coaches to see.

2　Choose an ideal model for comparison, either video-based or from technical manuals. Taking your source, adapt it into a short presentation. This can be presented as either a selection of short videos or animations that demonstrate near perfect technique.

3　Produce an information sheet explaining the measurement tool you have chosen and stating the rules for the collection of the data (the protocol). You must show you can use this tool to collect data for elite and non-elite athletes. Include examples of the range and parameters that you intend to measure.

Part 2: Observational analysis

The next part of the process is observing the performance of the elite and non-elite cricket and tennis players. This will involve examining video footage of performers and applying the measurement method to the entire process.

Lastly you will interpret the collated data for the elite and non-elite players and prepare a report for the tennis and cricket coaches.

Plan

- How confident do I feel in my ability to complete this task? Are there any areas I may struggle with?
- I will plan carefully, including deciding which measurement technique to use and which players to analyse.

Do

- I know what I am doing and what I want to achieve.
- I will follow each stage in sequence to help ensure it makes sense.

Review

- I can explain how I would approach the difficult elements differently next time (i.e. what I would do differently).
- I will reflect on the way I analysed and more importantly on the quality of the data that I interpreted.

Further reading and resources

Books

Charles, D. (2014) *Archery: Skills. Tactics. Techniques* (Crowood Sports Guides), London: Crowood Press.

Edwards, J. (2014) *Badminton: Technique, Tactics Training*, London: Crowood Press.

Hughes, M. (2015) *Essentials of Performance Analysis in Sport*, 2nd edition, London: Routledge.

Marcus, B. (2012) *The Art of Stand up Paddling*, Toronto: Globe Pequot Press.

O'Donoghue, P. (2014) *An Introduction to Performance Analysis of Sport* (Routledge Studies in Sports Performance Analysis), London: Routledge.

Prehn, T. and Pelkey, C. (2004) *Racing Tactics For Cyclists*, Manchester: Velopress.

Williams, T. and Mckittrick, J. (2008) *Rugby Skills Tactics and Rules*, London: Bloomsbury.

Also available are Crowood Sports Guides, a range of sport-specific guides covering sports including climbing, fencing, archery, boxing, tennis, football, canoeing and kayaking, badminton, cycling and hockey.

Websites

www.canoe-england.org.uk/ – Young paddler's resource.

www.cricketweb.net/tactics/ – Comprehensive cricket tactics and techniques.

www.fiba.com/pages/eng/cl/index.asp – World governing body coaching resource.

www.pponline.co.uk – Peak Performance: how performance analysis can improve your coaching methods.

www.teachpe.com – Teach PE: specifics about a range of sports and general skill and ability information.

www.topendsports.com – Topend Sports: information on all aspects of analysis and observation of sporting performance.

THINK ▶FUTURE

Jamie Coyle

Football Coach and Performance Analyst

I've been working with my local non-league football club for a few years now and in this time we have been promoted in three successive seasons and have aspirations of full-time professional football. Understanding the technical abilities and tactics of ourselves and our opponents has been a critical factor in our success.

Until recently, analysis of football performance was only practised by the elite. It is no longer necessary to pay for ultra-expensive software applications, and it is incredible just how much detail can be provided with very simple, inexpensive equipment. I only really need a couple of well-placed cameras, a laptop and some basic software.

The significance of this kind of analysis cannot be overstated. In an incredibly competitive league, where coaching and playing careers are decided by single points, this analysis can make all the difference. If just one tactical or technical improvement affects the outcome of the game, then we must invest and train analysts in all key areas.

People new to sport at this level are often surprised at the level of information and data that we process in order to prepare for each match. We look at all aspects from tactical formations against specific opponents to individual profiles based on technique such as tackling, heading, pass completion, pass accuracy and many more.

Focusing your skills

Assessing technical and tactical strengths and weaknesses

It is important to determine these strengths and weaknesses as they will be critical in any game plan. Here are some simple tips to help you do this.

- What are the skills you most want to know about? For example, typical formations, how do they set up for set pieces, strengths and weaknesses of key players, etc.?
- You will need to be able to live code first team matches home and away and identify team statistics and trends over the course of the season.
- To develop the culture at your club you should supervise the coding and analysis for the youth team and support analysts in their training.

Performance analysis guidelines

The role of the performance analyst is highly specialised and takes an amount of training and practice. Some of the tasks involved are outlined below.

- Film training and analyse the film.
- Produce pre-/post-match presentations.
- Prepare a breakdown of opposition analysis for meetings.
- Identify team statistics and trends over the course of the season.
- Carry out individual player analysis and breakdown of opposition analysis for meetings.
- Assist with recruitment structure within the club.
- Supervise assistants for filming/coding of U18–U9 matches.

Getting ready for assessment

Mariyan is working towards a BTEC National in Sport Development, Coaching and Fitness. She was given the assignment task along with some material that was specifically related to the value of notation. As a keen sportswoman with an analytical approach to her studies, Mariyan set to work on the task.

▶ Include information on how you have chosen the skills, tactics and techniques as well as the measurement tools in the latter part of the assessment.

▶ Discuss the way in which you intend to analyse, what you will analyse and how you will feed back.

Mariyan shares her experience below.

How I got started

First I collected all my notes on this topic and put them into a folder. I decided to divide my work into three parts: the techniques and tactics, the measurement tools and the analysis.

I began by researching cricket and tennis techniques and tactics, using a variety of online resources. Then I looked into the different ways of measuring and assessing technical and tactical skills. It was difficult to decide which method would be best but I decided on a hand notation for both sports and was able to adapt existing methods to meet my needs.

I arranged to go to the club to find two willing tennis players and two cricket players, and in each sport a talented elite player and a beginner with little experience. I was able to apply my notation coding to both elite and non-elite players.

How I brought it all together

When I had completed the analysis I put everything in a project folder.

▶ I took care to divide the folder logically, with a title page, an introduction that explained the context and methodology, the analyses and development plans, the results, the conclusion and some references.

▶ When reflecting I was careful to meet the criteria and to plan at each stage the exact evidence I would need to provide. It was important to me to have a very detailed plan, which my tutor helped me with. The plan helped me to focus on the important parts of each stage and allowed me to produce good work that looks useful for the performers.

What I learned from the experience

▶ I now feel that I am a competent analyst, and that I could apply a measurement tool in any scenario, particularly a hand notation.

▶ Until I had a plan I found this work quite daunting, and I didn't really know where to start.

▶ I really wanted to use video analysis using three different angles, but I realised that this was not practical, so I switched to a different approach using only one video camera and applying the footage to a hand notation that I designed for myself based on an existing one.

▶ I learned a lot about the expectations of each of the players. I was surprised by how interested the performers, particularly the non-elite ones, were in the results of my observations. Since then I have been asked by others at the club if I can analyse them. One of the cricket coaches has also asked for my hand notation template so that he can use it with his junior players.

Think about it

▶ Plan your work carefully. Think about the tasks you need to complete, then add completion dates for them so you can be sure you will finish everything by the deadline.

▶ Make sure that your analytical measurement tool actually does what you want it to do – consider practising on a peer before you apply the procedure to your subject/s.

▶ Your final report must summarise everything that you have done, as well as your understanding of the subject, so it is important to check your spelling and grammar, especially for sport-specific terms. You might want to consider showing your report to someone involved in the sport and asking for their objective opinion.

The Athlete's Lifestyle 27

Getting to know your unit

Assessment
You will be assessed by a series of assignments set by your tutor.

The world of sport presents athletes with an ever increasing range of challenges as they aspire to reach the elite level in their chosen sport. Physical and mental preparation are hugely important to the success of an elite athlete, but nowadays athletes need to be just as prepared to deal with the lifestyles they have chosen and are exposed to – these can have a big impact on performance. In this unit you will examine the different lifestyle choices facing elite athletes and learn about the support they can access to help them follow a career as a successful performer.

How you will be assessed

This unit will be assessed by a series of internally assessed tasks set by your tutor. Throughout this unit you will find assessment activities that will help you work towards your assessment. Completing these activities will provide useful research or preparation that will be relevant when it comes to completing your final assignment.

The assignment set by your tutor will consist of a number of tasks designed to meet the assessment criteria in the table below. It is likely to consist of a written assignment but may also include activities such as:

▸ a report on lifestyle factors that can affect the performance of elite athletes, including sources of funding and an athlete's financial responsibilities
▸ a report on positive role models and the importance of appropriate communication and behaviours
▸ a developed career plan with a written report justifying the decisions made.

In order for you to achieve the tasks in your assignment, it is important to check that you have met all of the Pass grading criteria. Plan to do this as you work your way through the assignment.

If you are hoping to gain a Merit or Distinction, you should also make sure that you present the information in your assignment in the style that is required by the relevant assessment criterion. For example, Merit criteria require you to analyse, compare, assess and justify, and the Distinction criteria requires you to evaluate.

Assessment criteria

This table shows what you must do in order to achieve a **Pass**, **Merit** or **Distinction** grade, and where you can find activities to help you.

Pass	**Merit**	**Distinction**

Learning aim **A** Understand lifestyle factors that can affect an athlete's sports performance

		AB.D1
A.P1 Explain how an athlete could reduce the impact of different lifestyle factors on sports performance. **Assessment practice 27.1**	**A.M1** Analyse how an athlete could reduce the impact of different lifestyle factors on sports performance with support available for young athletes. **Assessment practice 27.1**	Evaluate different lifestyle factors, the support available and financial factors that can influence sports performance and development towards becoming an elite athlete in a chosen sport. **Assessment practice 27.2**
A.P2 Explain the support available for the development of young athletes. **Assessment practice 27.1**		

Learning aim B Investigate different earnings, funding opportunities and financials of sports performers at different stages in their careers

B.P3 Explain the funding opportunities and financial factors of sports performers at the beginning of their careers to that of an elite athlete in a chosen sport. **Assessment practice 27.2**	**B.M2** Compare the funding opportunities and financial factors of sports performers at the beginning of their careers to that of an elite athlete in a chosen sport. **Assessment practice 27.2**	

Learning aim C Investigate the importance of effective communication skills in sports performance and coaching

		C.D2
C.P4 Explain how different types of media are used to demonstrate the behaviours of positive role models. **Assessment practice 27.3**	**C.M3** Assess the use of effective communication in different types of media showing consideration of the behaviours and attitudes of a positive role model. **Assessment practice 27.3**	Evaluate the use of effective communication with different types of media demonstrating the importance of appropriate behaviours. **Assessment practice 27.3**

Learning aim D Examine career planning directed to becoming an elite athlete

		D.D3
D.P5 Explain the content of a designed career plan for an athlete in a sport of your choice. **Assessment practice 27.4**	**D.M4** Justify the choices made in a career plan for an athlete in a sport of your choice. **Assessment practice 27.4**	Evaluate the choices made in a career plan for an athlete in a selected sport, demonstrating consideration to contingency planning. **Assessment practice 27.4**

Getting started

For a sport of your choice, draw up a list of lifestyle factors that can affect an athlete's performance. Hold a class discussion on the factors you have identified. Are there any common themes you have identified or distinct differences across the sports you have chosen to consider? Are there any factors that you think are more important in terms of their potential to positively or negatively impact on an athlete's performance?

A   Understand lifestyle factors that can affect an athlete's sports performance

Lifestyle factors that affect performance

Being a successful athlete is about more than just training and competing. It is a lifestyle that involves a huge commitment and many personal sacrifices. Lifestyle factors and choices can play both positive and negative roles in achieving sporting success and the maintenance of physical and mental well-being. The lifestyle choices that an athlete makes, such as how they spend their time and with whom, can help or hinder their performance.

Leisure time and social distance

Leisure time can be described as time available for rest and relaxation, when we are free from duties or responsibilities and can pursue pastimes and hobbies. To support high-level performance, elite athletes are advised to spend their leisure time resting and relaxing. However, some may engage in inappropriate activities that are not beneficial to performance such as gambling, drinking, smoking and recreational drug use. Being professional in all aspects of sporting life can help athletes to train more effectively, have good relationships with those they are working with, and to make the most of the opportunities that come their way.

'Social distance' relates to closeness of the athlete's relationships, or what some theorists call **relatedness**. Relatedness is considered by self-determination theorists to be one of the three fundamental psychological needs, along with autonomy (freedom or independence) and competence (being able to do something properly). By satisfying these needs, people are considered to optimise their potential and be in a better position to achieve set goals.

There is a risk that an elite athlete who is focused firmly on their performance goals might neglect to build or maintain good social networks. But when the demands of training are high, they may find that they also need the understanding of these networks for moral support.

Key term

Relatedness – a sense of connection or belonging to another person or group.

Research

Using the Internet, investigate the pastimes and hobbies of four elite-level sports people. After undertaking your research, hold a class discussion about your findings. Are there common pastimes and hobbies pursued by the sports stars you have chosen to investigate?

Overseas/long distance travel

Although long distance and international travel is now routine for many elite-level sports, it is not without problems. Many athletes will have their regular routines of training and competition disrupted when travelling. They might be excited or worried about planning for an unfamiliar environment. Vaccinations and visas may be required. At elite level, administrative and medical staff would usually manage these requirements.

After arrival, the athlete may suffer from travel weariness, disturbed sleep or jet lag. Jet lag can persist for several days and be accompanied by loss of appetite, difficulty sleeping, constipation and gastro-intestinal upset. The severity of jet lag symptoms is affected by a number of factors, in particular the number of time zones travelled. This will affect the plans put in place by the athlete and their support team to minimise symptoms and optimise performance.

Regular international travel, with frequent changes of time zones and therefore sleep patterns, can have a negative impact on any traveller, including athletes. As a result of this, elite-level athletes and their coaches give careful consideration to the competition schedule to ensure that they minimise the cumulative effect of travel on performance, particularly for major events and tournaments.

Case study

Sport and travel

Imagine you have been appointed as the team administrator for the Great Britain Hockey squad that is to travel to India for a 4-week tournament. It is your first visit to India and the first overseas trip for four of the younger members of the squad.

After undertaking appropriate research, outline the strategy you would adopt to ensure the squad succeed and survive this international trip.

Check your knowledge

1 What do you think will be the key challenges for this overseas trip?

2 How can you ensure that the players remain in peak condition for competition?

3 Develop a player fact sheet for coping with the trip.

Living away from family and friends

Many young athletes have to move away from home in order to train and compete at the highest level. Being away from friends and family can be daunting for a young athlete, but all athletes, no matter how old they are, must develop strategies to cope with these pressures. Strong personal leadership skills to minimise the issues of living away from home that might affect performance are at the core of being a successful elite athlete.

General healthcare, nutrition and fitness

Health and well-being are a necessary and important part of performance in sport: without them, world-class sport performance is less likely to be achieved. An athlete's health status reflects the body's homeostasis, or its attempts to maintain a relatively stable environment when confronted with changes in its external environment or **pathogens**. To reduce the risk of general infections, athletes should practise good hygiene at all times and wash hands regularly, especially before eating.

Eating well is one of the most important factors affecting health and performance and good nutritional practices are essential for an athlete's lifestyle. The most important nutritional goals of athletes are to maintain adequate energy and fluid balance – both can be subject to relatively rapid changes and are directly related to performance and health, particularly if competing in challenging environmental conditions.

Athletes of all ages and abilities benefit from a healthy, well-balanced and varied diet that is specific to the demands of their sport. Inappropriate food choices could lead to lack of energy to support training, competition and optimal recovery, or unwanted weight loss or gain. Poor nutritional practices can exacerbate (make worse) the negative influences that heavy training loads can have on an athlete's immune system.

Overtraining is the process of excessive exercise training that may lead to **overtraining syndrome**. Overtraining syndrome can lead to poor competition performance, difficulty in maintaining training loads, continual fatigue, recurrent illness, troubled sleep and alterations in mood state. There is evidence that several immune factors are suppressed during prolonged periods of intense training. Key considerations are the combination of poor nutritional practices and the built-up stress from protracted intensive training on the body's immune system. The stress associated with high-level training is influenced by training intensity and duration, the athlete's level of fitness, and the balance between training loads and recovery.

In addition, getting the right amount of sleep is important to maintaining health and achieving sporting success. Too much or too little sleep can cause problems with concentration and focus.

Being physically fit is about having enough energy, strength and skill to cope with the everyday demands of your environment. Individual fitness levels vary greatly, from the low levels required to cope with everyday activities to optimal levels required by some performers who are at the top of their sport. The preparation and construction of an effective training programme must be based on the way the body adapts to different training regimes. Training programmes, dependent on the phase of the competition calendar, can be constructed to emphasise one or many aspects of fitness, for example strength and power or aerobic endurance, giving careful consideration to relevant training principles.

Rest and recovery

Training and competing, particularly at the elite level in sport, places stress on many of the body's systems. Following high intensity or high frequency training, athletes go through the process of recovery so that they can return to a state of performance readiness. Adequate and well-planned rest is an essential element of the training process as it allows athletes to adapt to training, supporting them to train and perform while preventing overtraining and **burnout**. The recovery process allows the body to restore its energy stores and return to normal physiological and psychological function.

Ideal recovery plans are likely to include both total rest and active recovery. Active recovery can be used alongside total rest to achieve adaptations to training. Rest days will not involve any exercise training and elite athletes would plan to completely relax on rest days, perhaps to sleep in and spend the extra time with family and friends. Active recovery days will include activity but at an easy to moderate intensity, and may involve alternative activities for the athlete such as walking, swimming or cycling to get blood flowing to the muscles to facilitate recovery.

> **Key term**
>
> **Burnout** – physical and emotional exhaustion resulting in reduced performance.

> **Research**
>
> Burnout can happen if excessively high expectations are placed on young athletes by parents and coaches. Investigate burnout and the likely signs and symptoms to look out for. What strategies could an athlete develop to avoid and manage it?
>
> You might want to consider the role of goal setting, assertiveness training, problem solving and decision-making skills, coping mechanisms, and adequate rest and relaxation.

Time management

Athletes make many sacrifices to reach their potential. Commitment to sport often leads to pressure or sacrifices in other aspects of their lives, such as family, friends, work or education. Feeling that they have a lack of time or control over their lives can lead to stress, which will affect performance.

Athletes must consider how they are going to cope with time pressures in their lives. They are responsible for prioritising how to spend their time effectively. Time management is a critical element of effective stress management. It is about achieving tasks in good time by using techniques such as goal setting, task planning and minimising time spent on unproductive activities.

Pressure of training and competition

Pressure is put on athletes to perform, both in training and in competition. Pressure might come from coaches, tutors, parents, spectators, team mates, training partners or the athlete themselves. One reason why athletes drop out of sport is stress. This is

> **Discussion**
>
> As a small group, discuss the following questions.
> - How do you manage your time to maximise training and performance?
> - What things are important to you in your life?
> - How do you ensure you prioritise these over other things?
>
> Share the results of your discussion with the rest of the group and then, as a whole class, draw up a list of recommendations for how athletes could start to deal with some of these issues in their own lives.

often the result of well-intentioned parents or coaches who might set unrealistic goals. Young athletes in particular need to understand that mistakes or failing to achieve targets are part of the learning process and should not be feared.

Being able to deal with pressure is important if an athlete is to perform to the best of their ability. Training or performing when unwell or injured is likely to have a long-term damaging effect and should be avoided. Overtraining will be unproductive and significantly increase the risk of injury. A successful athlete will develop coping strategies through experience and discussion with their coach, tutor or parents.

Athletes are likely to experience higher levels of pressure during competition. The desire to win – combined with factors such as spectators, the venue and other athletes (or the opposition) – all play a part in putting stress on the athlete. Being able to deal with this is important if the athlete is to compete to the best of their ability. Remember that not all pressure is bad: a certain amount of pressure can help to improve motivation and concentration, having a positive effect on performance.

> **Link**
>
> You can read more about handling the mental side of sport in *Unit 6: Sports Psychology*.

> **Discussion**
>
> Discuss where pressure might come from. You might want to draw on examples from elite sport where top performers have appeared to crumble under pressure. Following your discussion, draw up a top tips list for controlling responses to pressure.

Education

Education is important for all athletes, no matter what their age. A young athlete might need to combine their training with studying for GCSEs, A levels, BTEC qualifications or the Advanced Level Apprenticeship in Sporting Excellence (AASE). An athlete in the middle of their career might be studying to become a coach. And older athletes might be thinking about what to do once they retire from sport and studying to help them change career.

> **Link**
>
> You can read more about education and continual professional development for sports people in *Unit 3: Professional Development in the Sports Industry*.

For younger athletes aged 16–19, the AASE programmes that run across many sports are a good way to prepare for life in professional sport or on the elite stage. Athletes on these programmes have the opportunity to improve their skills and learn how to manage their lifestyle in professional and elite sport while continuing with their education. These programmes are supported by expert coaching staff, high-quality training environments and access to conditioning experts, medical staff, sports scientists and athlete mentors.

An athlete who has achieved sporting success is an excellent source of advice and information for emerging athletes. They will be able to share their experiences and to give training and competition advice. The elite athlete can act as a motivator and further enhance the opportunities given to young performers. A positive role model in sport will have a positive effect on sports participation.

Other influences on athletes

How an athlete manages relationships can aid their success. Understanding other people around them and how best to work with them can have a positive impact on personal and professional development, and ultimately on performance. The pressures of elite-level competition can place increasing demands not only on the athlete, but also on their close family and friends, and the entourage (coaches, sports scientists, medical team, agents and representatives) that support them.

As part of competition and training, athletes also often have to deal with members of the public, including fans who might be aggressive or hostile towards them or their team. On the other hand, fans can be supportive, which often leads to improved performance. It is important that the athlete deals with these situations in a professional and effective way.

❚❚ PAUSE POINT   Think of your own lifestyle. What pressures have you had to face that have affected your ability to train and compete?

Hint   Consider factors that take up your time outside your sport – what impact might these have?

Extend   How might you overcome these pressures in order to keep your performance optimal? What strategies could you develop to support this?

Physiological and sociological lifestyle distractions

As well as the lifestyle factors we have already explored in this unit, athletes are also likely to face **physiological** and **sociological** lifestyle distractions that could affect their athletic performance.

Alcohol

Alcohol is sometimes used as a social tool in sport, for example in team sports to help team bonding, and is sometimes used to celebrate victory. But in elite sport athletes are expected to have a responsible attitude towards alcohol consumption, with some contracts requiring abstention (no alcohol) during the competitive season. Many alcohol companies use sport sponsorship as a marketing tool. However, alcohol is a drug that affects every organ in your body. Alcohol affects the body's ability to use energy efficiently, slows down reaction times, increases body heat loss and reduces endurance capacity.

Drinking to excess can lead to both short- and long-term problems. In the short term this can involve unruly and inappropriate behaviour, which can make the participant take unnecessary risks or attract negative media attention. In the long term, excessive alcohol use can have a detrimental impact on social and psychological health with the associated risks of developing stroke, cirrhosis, hypertension and depression.

Smoking

The dangers of smoking are widely publicised. Tobacco contains nicotine and tar which are both damaging to health. In recent years the government has spent millions on campaigns aimed at preventing smoking among young people. Many young people are attracted to smoking as they see it as 'cool'. Peer pressure is often an influencing factor when someone starts smoking.

Smoking can make exercise feel harder. When you exercise, your heart rate increases to meet the oxygen demands of your muscles. Cigarettes contain carbon monoxide that binds to the haemoglobin in blood more effectively than oxygen, which means that muscles are less able to get the oxygen they require during exercise. This results in the heart having to work harder.

Key terms

Physiological – related to the normal functioning of the body or its parts.

Sociological – related to the study of human behaviour dealing with social questions and problems such as cultural and environmental factors.

Research

Arsenal and England midfielder Jack Wilshere's activity around smoking has been highly publicised in the popular print media. Review some of the articles published and consider why being caught smoking was a controversial issue worthy of the media attention it drew. What are the likely implications of the reporting of such activity for an elite sports performer?

Drugs

As sport becomes ever more competitive, some athletes turn to drugs to try to give themselves an advantage. Drugs can be divided into two main categories:

▸ **recreational drugs**
▸ **performance-enhancing drugs**.

Common recreational drugs such as cannabis, cocaine or heroin are extremely dangerous and can have serious consequences for athletes. In the short term, their use will affect performance, making success unlikely. In the long term, the damage to health is considerable. All athletes should avoid such drugs as there is no benefit to their use.

'Doping' refers to using performance-enhancing drugs to gain an unfair advantage over opponents. Their abuse has been well publicised, with many high-profile cases of athletes found using them.

▸ **Table 27.1:** Examples of performance-enhancing drugs banned in sport

Drug	Effects	Examples of abuse in sport	Side effects
Anabolic steroids	• Increases power by increasing muscle strength and size • Increases training time so athlete able to train harder and longer • Helps to repair the body after training • Increases competitiveness and aggression	• Power events such as shot put, javelin or weightlifting • Sprint events	• Liver disease • Certain forms of cancer • Fluid retention • Infertility • Hardening arteries increase risk of coronary heart disease • Skin disorders
Beta blockers	• Steadies nerves and hand tremors	• Snooker • Darts • Archery • Shooting events	• Tiredness • Lethargy • Low blood pressure • Fainting • Breathing problems
Diuretics	• Reduces body weight	• Horse racing • Boxing	• Dehydration • Muscle cramps • Kidney failure
Stimulants	• Improves performance through increased awareness • Reduces fatigue	• Endurance-based sports	• Increased blood pressure • Increased heart rate • Paranoid delusions • Anxiety • Shaking and sweatiness • Sleeplessness and restlessness

Discussion

In a group, discuss why you think athletes might be attracted to the use of recreational drugs. What reasons and lifestyle factors might make this a temptation for elite athletes?

In many sports, athletes are tested regularly for all forms of drug use. If they test positive, athletes are likely to be banned from their sport for a long time, possibly for life, as well as facing the risk of police prosecution.

UK Anti-Doping has developed the '100% me' campaign. The ethos of 100% me is about being successful and confident and upholding the values of clean and fair competition. The campaign embodies five key values: hard work, determination, passion, integrity and respect. Over 50 sports receive direct educational support through this programme, which aims to support and educate athletes by providing practical anti-doping advice and guidance to ensure they are aware of the risks and responsibilities they face. All British athletes competing at the Rio 2016 Olympic games will be supported.

▶ Information about 100% me can be found at www.ukad.org.uk/athletes

Link

You can find out more about drug testing requirements in *Unit 13: Nutrition for Sport and Exercise*.

Research

Investigate the use of performance-enhancing drugs in your sport, then hold a group discussion about your findings. Are athletes in some categories of sport more or less likely to engage in the use of performance-enhancing drugs?

If you do not personally participate in structured sport you might want to look at some of the high profile cases reported in cycling, athletics or rugby.

Sanctions (the use of discipline, match bans and fines)

In the ever changing world of sport, particularly at the elite level, many associations provide guidance documents to ensure safe and enjoyable participation and a fair and transparent disciplinary process for those who breach the ethos of the sport. Any participant found to be breaching the ethos or rules of the sport may be subjected to match bans or fines to help ensure that appropriate standards of behaviour are upheld.

Case study

Sanctions

One of the most high profile examples of sanctions being imposed at the highest level of sport related to Luis Suárez of Uruguay following a biting incident in a game against Italy in the 2014 FIFA World Cup. Suárez was suspended for nine international matches, was banned from any football-related activity for four months and was issued a fine.

Check your knowledge

1   Hold a class discussion on the severity of these sanctions. Were they warranted for the offence, and if so why?

2   Broaden your discussion by considering examples from other sports. Do sanctions applied across different sports appear to have similar levels of severity and implications for athletes?

Use of social media

As an athlete, being active on social media offers a great opportunity to share the challenges and excitement of the sporting lifestyle. But athletes who engage with it should do so sensibly to make sure they always project a professional image. Athletes need to keep in mind that we live in a society that promotes free speech and freedom of expression, but this does not mean that they should not think carefully before posting comments to social media such as Twitter and Facebook. An athlete will also need to be resilient to the comments and opinions that other people may express; such comments can often be negative after a poor performance.

Many sporting organisations and teams now issue guidelines on the use of social media. For instance, both the International Olympic Committee (IOC) and International Paralympic Committee (IPC) have embraced social media and actively encourage its use, but have set guidelines on social media, blogging and internet use.

> **Research**
>
> Investigate the use of social media in sport. You may choose to do this by looking at a high profile athlete or team. Try to establish if there are any guidelines on the use of social media by their sport's governing body.
>
> You might want to look at the IOC and IPC guidelines produced for athletes and other accredited persons for the most recent summer and winter games and consider the impact these had.

Travel

As we have already seen earlier in this unit, travel – especially long distance travel – often puts athletes at greater risk of failing to meet their nutritional needs or succumbing to illness at a time when the demands on performance are at their greatest. Yet fixtures or competitions can often involve travel, and it is common to stay overnight in hotels beforehand or during an event. Athletes need to have a strategic approach when travelling to training events and competition and plan ahead for unexpected delays. They especially need to consider their nutritional needs when travelling to make sure that they have nutritionally balanced meals or snacks available that suit their training and competition requirements.

Family and friends

An athlete's ability to spend time with their family and friends will be affected by many pressures, such as strict routines and training plans that affect the amount of time available. But these support networks are important: an athlete might experience an injury that prevents them from training and competing, causing frustration and worry, and support from family, friends and employers can help the athlete to cope in such situations.

▶ Mo Farah celebrates with his family after winning an event

Family members will want to support the athlete to succeed, but this will not always prevent difficulties and tensions. A training programme should include time and space to relax with family members: it is important that time is spent enjoying their company, away from the pressures of training and competition.

Work or education alongside training and competitions means athletes may have little time to socialise. This can be stressful when combined with the pressure to achieve success through training and competition. Understanding and supportive friends are important if the athlete is to feel confident in their commitment.

❚❚ PAUSE POINT Consider a stressful situation you have encountered as a result of your sports participation. How did it make you feel and how did you deal with it? Could you have prevented this situation from occurring?

Hint This could be a situation related to travelling, tensions with friends and family, sanctions that have been imposed on you, or worrying about something you might have posted on Facebook or Twitter.

Extend Identify ways in which to manage stressful situations.

Case study

Lifestyle choices and priorities

Lifestyle choices are the things we prioritise in our lives that have a big effect on our enjoyment and satisfaction. By understanding our priorities and living by them we accept the consequences. For example, if study and achieving top grades is your number one priority, then you have to accept the consequences – good or bad – that come with it, such as better chance of employment or gaining a university place, or less time to spend with your friends.

Check your knowledge

1 How do you work out what your priorities are? Use a mind map to capture all of the things you choose to do and that are important to you. Then order them in terms of priority and reflect on them.

2 Can you see any conflicts in your priorities? If so, how might you overcome these?

The personal behaviour of an athlete

The way athletes conduct themselves during training and competition will have an effect not just on their own sporting success but also on the way that other people perceive them – and their sport, too. Appropriate behaviour both on and off the field of play is essential, especially with the rise in media coverage (of both sporting events and the private lives of elite competitors) and sponsorship opportunities.

It is essential for the athlete to develop a positive **self-image**. This is an important first step towards developing professional behaviour that will help achieve personal goals and satisfaction and will affect the image that they project to others.

It is also important that the athlete is seen to follow their sport's rules, regulations and codes of conduct. This can include the concept of sportsmanship, the often unwritten **ethics** and **values** that underpin the sport and ensure 'fair play'. Their behaviour reflects not just on themselves but on their team, the image of their sport, their coach – and even their family members. Behaving professionally and respectfully not only demonstrates the personal values of the athlete, but also that they value others.

Key terms

Self-image – the idea, conception or mental image you have of yourself – the way you think about and view yourself.

Ethics – moral principles or codes of conduct.

Values – ideals that form beliefs and actions.

Theory into practice

You should acknowledge when you have accidentally broken a rule without anyone noticing; for example when a goalkeeper knows that the ball has crossed the line but the referee has not awarded a goal, or when there was a bad line call in tennis.

Can you think of any high profile situations in sport where it has been clear that an athlete or team has not displayed sportsmanship or broken a code of conduct? What were the circumstances surrounding these situations? How might they have influenced the athletes concerned to behave in the way they did?

Athletes need to respect not just others within their sport but also those outside it. An athlete's behaviour can come under scrutiny from a wide range of people, including spectators and the media. Behaving professionally and respectfully not only demonstrates your own personal values, but also that you value others. Sport can be frustrating, especially when an athlete is performing below their best or when results are not favourable. Frustration can cause athletes to react badly to comments from spectators, and this can have a bad impact on the athlete's image and the sport as a whole. They must always follow the rules and respect their peers and others.

Elite athletes as role models

Elite athletes need to remember that they are often role models for younger people, fans and other non-athletes. Sports stars have the opportunity to be positive ambassadors for their sport. They can play an important role in introducing children to sport and encouraging increased participation. Children imitate their sporting heroes, both in the way they play and how they behave on and off the sports field. Athletes' actions can have both positive and negative consequences for which they should take responsibility. But athletes do not have to be famous to be a role model: younger athletes might look at older athletes and copy their performance or behaviour.

High-profile athletes often work within their local communities to provide encouragement to children and to act as sporting ambassadors. This provides positive experiences for children and can reflect well on the athlete. The media often report on these initiatives, raising the profile of both the athlete and their sport. These activities might be local, with local athletes working in schools and helping out with coaching, or on a national basis, with athletes endorsing specific nationwide campaigns.

Research

Investigate the sports initiatives undertaken in your local area by high-profile sportspeople. How do these initiatives benefit the local community and the athletes concerned?

 **PAUSE POINT**   Why is public image important for elite athletes?

 Hint   What does it feel like when people have a poor opinion of you?

Extend   If a sports performer has a negative image in the media, how might this affect their lifestyle and earnings?

Supporting athlete development

There are many different bodies that have been put in place to help support athletes to develop. Most sports have national governing bodies (NGBs) and there are many professional associations, clubs and sporting charities that exist to help support athletes in their career development. More information on these can be found in *Unit 3: Professional Development in the Sports Industry*, on page 135.

Sports development continuum

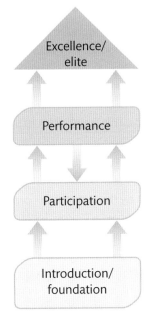

▶ **Figure 27.1:** The sports development continuum

Figure 27.1 shows the sports development continuum, which demonstrates how an athlete's participation develops over time in their sport. As an athlete moves up the continuum, their performance ability reaches a higher level. At each level of the continuum there are fewer and fewer athletes: only a few will reach elite level.

▶ Introduction/foundation – at this stage the participants are classed as novices, learning the basic skills and techniques of their sports. Participants will develop their 'physical literacy' (the physical competence of an individual). Even at this level, motivation, confidence, knowledge and understanding are crucial. It is important at this stage that equality and diversity are considered and all young athletes are offered the same opportunities. While performers at this stage are usually young, it is important they develop their social skills at this stage, including the ability to deal with losing and with conflict and anger.

▶ Participation – this stage involves regular participation in the sport and the further development of skills. Participation can be to socialise, for enjoyment, and to improve fitness and health.

▶ Performance – this stage consists of focusing on a specific sport and technique to develop. The athlete will show commitment to perfect their skills and will be at a club or regional standard. This level is reached through quality coaching and regular competition.

▶ Excellence/elite – this level consists of skilled performers at the peak of their performance. Very few people reach this stage. Those who do are usually professional athletes, competing for both **extrinsic** and **intrinsic** reward. They will often be representing their county and/or country.

Link

More on intrinsic and extrinsic rewards can be found in *Unit 8: Coaching for Performance*.

Young athlete development programmes

Young athlete development programmes are created to produce sequential progressive stages through the sport, to support the development of young athletes. These programmes will often recruit talented young athletes who have been scouted in one of many ways for different sports. For example, young athletes who are excelling in school teams and competitions might be encouraged to join local clubs. This can then lead to them being put forward to county or regional trials and, if selected, they can receive even more specialist coaching and better facilities. If successful at this stage the performers can then be put forward to national trials.

Once recruited to a young athlete development programme, the first stage is usually about developing the fundamental movement skills for a sport. This is usually followed by learning to train, training to train and finally training to compete. Each sport has its own development programme, for example:

▶ English Athletics runs Athletics 365, a multi-event young athlete development programme for 8–15 year olds. This event helps to initiate the fundamental movement skills.

▶ British Cycling offers a clear rider route development programme assisting potential athletes to become elite performers and the stars of world and Olympic cycling.

▶ Millfield School is recognised by the World Class programme and has its own Institute of Sport and Well-being which provides fantastic support for the potential athletes at the school.

▶ Girls4Gold is a talented athlete scheme for females which searches for highly driven and powerful athletes from the UK. UK Sport work together with the English Institute of Sport, targeting females aged 15–17 who have the potential to adapt to a new sport for the 2020 Olympics. Lizzy Yarnold won a gold medal in the Skeleton event at the 2014 Sochi Winter Olympics – she had never even attempted the sport before 2008.

Assessment practice 27.1

A.P1 A.P2 A.M1 C.M4 AB.D1

Your club has appointed a new coach. The key focus of their role will be to improve the performance of all young athletes within the club with the aim of supporting them to reach their full potential. The coach has spoken to each athlete individually and fully explained the importance of training and competition preparation.

The coach has asked you to prepare a short report on your own performance development needs and has asked that you pay particular attention to how lifestyle factors and choices can help or hinder your performance. Your report should:

- explain the main lifestyle factors that can affect athletes
- analyse ways of reducing the impact of lifestyle factors on your sports performance
- explain what support might be available to help your development.

Plan

- I understand that I am being asked to evaluate how lifestyle factors and choices I make might affect my performance.
- I will start by spending some time considering my performance goals for the next year and what is likely to impact on them.

Do

- I know I need to produce a report.
- This should be presented in a clear and logical format for ease of reference by the coach.

Review

- I will evaluate how I have approached the task and what I have presented.
- Have I identified lifestyle factors that impact on my performance?
- Have I considered how I could reduce the impact of these lifestyle factors on my sports performance?
- Have I produced a clear and logical report on my development needs and how these might be supported?

B Examine financial factors that influence an athlete's lifestyle

For an athlete to be successful it is essential that they have funding to support their training. In this section we will look at the different ways in which athletes are funded and their financial responsibilities.

Funding for athletes

Funding varies for different sports

The potential income for elite athletes can vary significantly based on their chosen sport. Football clubs in the Premier League will receive up to £150 million in prize money alone. This does not include the extra income they earn from playing live televised games. This money is distributed to players through a wages system which, in the Premier League, pays players an average of £30,000 a week – some players earn in excess of £250,000 a week.

At the other end of the pay scale a full-time international hockey player is unlikely to earn in excess of £40,000 a year. Even a potential medallist in athletics will only receive £23–40,000 a year in **funding**.

> **Key term**
>
> **Funding** – money provided to an athlete to support their training and competition.

> **Discussion**
>
> What do you think about the difference in potential earnings of different athletes? As a group discuss what this might mean for different sports, particularly team sports. How do you think this might create challenges for sports people?

How the level of the sport can affect funding

The sport an athlete participates in is not the only factor affecting their income. The level that the performer participates at will also affect their income, as outlined below.

▶ A **professional** is likely to train full-time, have a challenging schedule and tremendous discipline. They will probably have access to a range of sport scientists to support their training and development. They will need to train every day and their lifestyle is built around competitions and training schedules.

▶ An **amateur** participates in the sport for the love of the game, with the participation being more important than the result. They choose when they play and train. Amateurs will not receive any money for participating in events and will have to fund their own training, fees and any other costs incurred.

▶ **Local athletes** will usually compete against other athletes who study or work full-time and will only travel relatively short distances for their competitive fixtures. Many athletes will never progress beyond this stage.

▶ **National athletes** are increasingly likely to receive some financial support for taking part – but the amount can vary enormously from sport to sport. A national athlete is chosen to represent their country in international fixtures or competitions.

▶ **International athletes** participate in headline sports and are the athletes you are likely to read about in the newspapers or see on television. These athletes are highly likely to receive lucrative salaries, sponsorship and elite support.

Attracting funding

High-profile sports, such as football and Formula One, receive the majority of media attention, sponsorship and the income these bring. Niche sports, for example fencing, often receive very little funding and media attention.

In January 2011 the British Fencing association announced a five-year sponsorship deal worth £1 million with an insurance company. They have 21 fencers in a World Class Performance Programme which helps British Fencing fund those likely to achieve podium success at future games.

While this deal sounds like a lot of money, fencing is still considered a niche sport, especially compared to more mainstream (and high-profile) sports such as athletics. For instance, in 2015 Nike and UK Athletics signed a £15 million sponsorship deal.

Companies are prepared to invest substantial sums of money in sports that have realistic chances of international success and the media attention that comes with it. UK Athletics supports around 140 athletes on its World Class Programme at 'podium' or 'podium potential' level.

Check your knowledge

1 Do you think it is fair that different sports receive different levels of funding?

2 Do you think athletes should receive more funding when they are at the 'potential' stage to help them develop, or alternatively when they are at their prime but possibly receiving extra funding from elsewhere?

How career stage affects funding

For an aspiring athlete who has yet to become a household name it can be extremely challenging to raise enough money to pay for coaches, gym memberships, physiotherapy, travelling expenses, competition entries and other essential costs. These pressures can force some to give up due to the high financial cost. Income is lowest during the early stages of a career (often aged 17–19). Between the ages 20–24 income can increase steadily.

The chief earning time for athletes is usually between the ages of 25–29 as they are at their physical peak. Often well established in the media by this stage, they will have sponsors and some degree of success in their sport. They can often receive lucrative fees such as:

▶ **appearance fees**, which are paid for attending an event without necessarily competing

▶ **participation fees**, which are paid to an athlete for specifically taking part in an event

▶ **performance fees**, which are awarded to athletes for reaching predetermined goals. These could be based on achieving a specified position in a race, winning a medal, breaking a world record, or achieving a time or distance goal.

Some individuals continue to participate until they are in their mid-30s, but this is relatively rare. When they are no longer physically able to compete, lucrative earnings from participating in sport can stop. This can be difficult as retiring athletes are still healthy individuals with another 35–40 years of their working life ahead of them, for which they will need an income.

 **PAUSE POINT** Can you describe how funding varies for different sports? How does the level of performance affect funding? How can the stage of the career affect potential income?

 Hint — What are the common reasons for a sports performer to receive a high level of funding?

Extend — Research the funding sources available to elite athletes in a sport of your choice.

Types of funding

Athletes can receive funding from several different sources. Some of these sources get their money from the government, while others rely on money from corporate sponsors.

National Lottery funding (UK Sport World Class Programme)

UK Sport is one of 12 independent organisations that receive National Lottery funding, which they use for their World Class Programme. It supports every British athlete who has a realistic chance of winning a medal over the next two Olympic and Paralympic games. They focus on recognising and evaluating the athletes with ability and future medal chances. UK Sport's mission remains about getting the right support to the right athletes for the right reasons.

The programme has two levels:

▸ **podium** – supports individuals with genuine medal winning ability at the next Olympic/Paralympic Games (a maximum of four years away)

▸ **podium potential** – where the individual's performances suggest they have a realistic medal winning potential within the next eight years (the Olympics after next).

Currently there are approximately 1300 athletes receiving support from UK Sport's annual outlay of approximately £100 million a year. For athletes on the World Class Podium Programme, the funding is usually worth £36–£60,000 individually each year. Podium Potential level is £23–£40,000 per year for each athlete, although it can be less in certain sports.

The UK World Class Programme works in conjunction with various sporting NGBs.

National Governing Body (NGB) funding

Between 2013 and 2017 Sport England will provide more than £80 million of funding to support talented young sports people. They specifically support young athletes to give them access to high-class coaching, the best facilities and the chance to take part in challenging top-level competition. Although not every young athlete will achieve international success, it is still important that every young talented athlete fulfils their potential. UK Sport gives its individual governing bodies challenging performance-related targets. They are at risk of losing their funding if they are not successful at achieving podium places. The GB Basketball team had its £7 million funding withdrawn in 2014 after its poor performance at the 2012 games.

Various NGBs invest in youth sport to help the development of potential athletes, sometimes in partnership with sponsors. For example, the Football Association and Vauxhall work together to support and develop potential talent. NGBs also provide funding for specialist facilities and coaching, and encourage clubs to join their standard charter schemes to guarantee the quality of the coaching they provide.

Grants

There are many organisations that provide **grants** for sporting stars or teams to help them develop and fulfil their potential. Organisations do this for several reasons: to give back to the community/society; to support their nation's sports teams; or for the publicity that comes from association with a successful sports performer or team. Table 27.2 lists some sources of grants.

> **Key term**
>
> **Grant** – money provided for a specific purpose (in this case, to support an athlete) that does not have to be repaid.

Organisation	
Asda Athletes	Since 2008 Asda has worked with SportsAid to deliver finance and support to around 1,300 British athletes. The scheme has provided in excess of £1 million to many aspiring athletes and provides financial, practical and career support. In return, the athlete works with their local Asda store to help raise additional funds. This serves to develop their profile in the local community and builds support for the athlete.
GLL Sport Foundation	Since 2007 the GLL Sport Foundation has supported young gifted athletes. Their research indicated the annual cost of achieving top level national representation was roughly £6,000. £4.9 million of financial provision has been provided to 8,400 athletes at the beginning of their careers. The foundation particularly focuses on: • individuals from deprived areas • increasing wider participation • creating long-term legacies and managing national talent development pathways.
SportsAid	Established in the 1970s, SportsAid is a leading sports charity, raising money to assist gifted sports performers at the beginning of their career. It has provided over £30 million and approximately 2,000 awards are made every year.

Bursaries

A bursary is money that an athlete, or their school/college or university, can use to pay for specialist coaching and equipment for the sport. The availability of bursaries varies according to the area in which an athlete lives. Local or county councils offer bursaries to promising athletes, as do some businesses or charities. The process of application for each is often different, as is the support provided.

Scholarships

A scholarship is an award of financial assistance for an individual to further their education and help them fulfil their sporting potential. They are often awarded once specific criteria have been achieved. One significant advantage of scholarships is that they do not need to be repaid. In the US full scholarships can be worth over $50,000 a year to an athlete.

Sponsorship

Sponsorship is money or equipment given to an athlete or team by a company or individual. This allows the athlete to concentrate on training and competing rather than having to work to support themselves. The influence of sponsorship on the modern development of sport has been massive. Sport is now big business, with large companies spending millions of pounds to sponsor events or individuals.

Many companies want a high-profile athlete to endorse their product or company so that they gain media attention and, ultimately, sell more products. Companies such as Nike and Adidas invest millions of pounds in teams and individuals so that they wear their clothes. Such companies have been partly responsible for creating sporting icons such as Roger Federer and David Beckham.

Commercial companies recognise that elite sports stars can be fashion icons and role models so are keen to use them in their advertising campaigns. This is particularly true of sportswear, which is now a fashion product as well as a sporting one.

On a smaller scale, a Sunday League football team might gain sponsorship from a local business in order to pay for their kit or match fees.

Case study

Sport England's Talented Athlete Scholarship Scheme (TASS)

Sport England's Talented Athlete Scholarship Scheme (TASS) is financially supported by the government. It represents a unique partnership between gifted young athletes, NGBs, colleges and universities.

The scheme was created in 2004 and since then, over £25 million has been provided for athletes, with in excess of 6,000 individual awards. The scheme made an impact at the Beijing Olympic/Paralympic Games in 2008, when 19 TASS athletes won medals. At the London 2012 games, 200 TASS athletes competed, with 44 of them winning a medal.

Helen Glover, a rower, is one of the many successful athletes who have benefited from TASS at the early stage of their career, when the support was needed the most. The grant was used for coaching, physiotherapy, sport science support, equipment and clothing. TASS athletes are also given guidance on how to manage training with academic pressures.

Glover recently said: 'It was the extra things I never would have considered before, like having physio, looking after myself and having the right kit. Those things made a huge difference and tipped the balance. Having that support there means you've got a lot more in your favour and it massively brings those odds to the advantage of the athlete. It was the feeling there was a support system there, for me, specifically in my situation, that was really important.'

Tom Daley, Rebecca Adlington, Laura Trott, Zac Purchase and Greg Rutherford are other very successful athletes who have benefitted from TASS.

Check your knowledge

1 List the benefits of the TASS scheme to both the athlete and the governing body.

2 Explain how this support could help these athletes to develop.

3 In a small group, create a presentation that compares the success of the various grant schemes for athletes. You might wish to focus on one grant each in your groups.

⏸ PAUSE POINT   Can you explain the types of funding available to athletes?

> **Hint**   What are the positives and negatives of each type of funding? For example, when a sponsorship deal finishes, how could this affect the athlete?

> **Extend**   Look at NGB websites and find out what financial support they offer at a grass roots level and for potential medallists.

Other income sources

Part-time employment

For every professional multimillionaire superstar there are many athletes who compete on the global stage who are unable to train full-time and receive very little income. Some athletes have to work part-time in order to fund their chosen career.

It is easy to assume that athletes in events such as the 2014 Commonwealth Games and cyclists in the Tour de France train full-time. However, many athletes who devote their lives to their sporting careers receive very little reward. They could be the best in their sport but, with insufficient funding, it is not uncommon for them to supplement their income with coaching or other jobs. This lifestyle can be very demanding on the athlete as they seek to balance work, family, financial and sport commitments, possibly alongside education, too.

Image rights

For elite-level superstars, their image and name can be as valuable as a trademarked name like Adidas or Nike. 'Image rights' means an individual athlete has control over how their name and image is used and exploited commercially. Their image can be used to help sell products all over the world, creating significant financial income for the sports performer.

Many sports performers take image rights into careful consideration when negotiating contracts. For instance, a sports performer with a contract to a club might agree to divide their image rights income, sharing a percentage figure between the club (which may have invested a large transfer fee and be looking to maximise income to pay for the deal) and the individual. You might be aware of players and clubs who trademark their image and name to exploit its value.

Prize money

Prize money is a reward for achieving success in a sporting competition. Many athletes rely on prize money to maintain their sporting careers. The amount of prize money can vary depending on the size of the sport. In football, the winners of the 2015 UEFA Champions League received approximately €64 million, while in 2014 the Mercedes F1 team received close to $100 million. By comparison, the winner of the Tour de France receives £360,000 for achieving cycling's biggest prize.

> **Discussion**
>
> Nearly a third of sports reward males more than females, with the greatest differences found in football, cricket, golf, darts, snooker and squash. Why do you suppose this is? What changes could be made to introduce equality between male and female sports?

Advertising

Elite sports stars can be fashion icons and role models so commercial companies are keen to use them in their advertising campaigns. For the individual this can be an extremely useful source of income. On a smaller scale, a junior rugby team might be sponsored by a local business, helping them to pay for their kit.

Media work

Athletes sometimes work in the media as pundits, offering their opinion or commentary on a particular sport, usually the sport they participate in, or have participated in before retirement. However, the number of jobs available working in the media is limited and this is not an option for all sports performers.

Coaching

Athletes often undertake part-time coaching work to supplement their income. You may be aware of performers who use their expertise to help others develop. For example, overseas cricket players often come to the UK to play for a local club and undertake part-time coaching work, hoping to be spotted by a county team and turn professional.

PAUSE POINT   What are the most likely sources of funding for promising athletes? Can you think of any additional sources of funding?

Hint   Research individual elite athletes and identify how they gain additional income.

Extend   What are the potential positives and negatives of each form of additional funding?

Financial responsibilities

Elite athletes have many financial responsibilities and commitments which they need to manage carefully as careers in sport can often be relatively short lived. You may have seen media reports about sports stars who did not manage their finances with enough care and ended up in financial difficulties. Athletes need to make sure that their income is surpassing their outgoings (i.e. that they are bringing in more money than they are spending) and take into consideration their future cost of living. If an athlete marries, has a child or takes on a mortgage, then their cost of living will rise, and therefore they need to be prepared for that.

Athletes need to balance their moneymaking commitments with their training and competition commitments. If they do not spend enough time or focus on their commercial interests they will not generate enough revenue to maintain the required lifestyle to train and compete. Alternatively, spending too much time on developing commercial commitments might lead to a lack of time for training, and lead to fatigue. Athletes need to balance their training, rest and commercial commitments very carefully.

Budgeting

Athletes are likely to combine their sport with a job in order to reach their targets. Many sports are expensive, with the costs of equipment, travel and accommodation being met by the athlete. As we have seen, funding might be available to cover the essential support services, such as coaching, training camps, competition and sport science. UK Sport also offers money to help with the essential personal living and sporting costs incurred while training and competing as an elite athlete; this is called an Athlete Personal Award (APA).

Because their income often comes in 'lump sums' at irregular intervals (for example when they have won prize money or once a sponsorship award has been made), athletes have to be extremely careful with their budgets to make sure that they do not run out of money before the next payment is likely to arrive.

Agents and management companies

Athletes may feel that they need to have an agent as part of their support team. An agent would help them with:

▶ seeking out commercial and sponsorship opportunities

▶ giving contract advice

▶ managing external commitments such as public appearances

▶ negotiating contracts for fees and wages.

Athletes who feel that they do not have the time or expertise to maximise their commercial potential often use agents.

Athletes can also pay a proportion of their salary to sports management companies. Sports management and marketing companies often work with some of the biggest names in the world of sport. Their objective is to support gifted sports performers to achieve their athletic potential and to maximise their financial capability during their career. Services they provide include:

- competition scheduling and administration
- contract discussions and servicing
- marketing and promotion
- merchandising and brand building
- social media optimisation
- coaching
- financial and legal support
- medical services
- travel, visa and accommodation management.

Management companies and sport agents' services can generate substantial income for athletes, but this does come at a cost. The athlete will have to sacrifice some of their earnings to the company in return for the services they provide. For instance, agents often take a percentage of transfer fees, signing on fees and/or the performer's earnings. Sports agents usually collect between 4 and 10 per cent of the athlete's contract. For arranging endorsements, which can take up a greater proportion of their time, agents receive approximately 10–20 per cent of the contract. These amounts can vary significantly from sport to sport.

Accountants

Accountants can be paid to keep track of an individual athlete's financial situation and to maintain their financial records. This includes end-of-year reporting, paying tax and helping them to maimise their financial potential. It is part of their job to ensure income and expenditure are balanced. Often athletes nearing the end of their career, or who have retired, are unable to maintain their current cost of living, but some continue to spend and run into major financial difficulties.

Tax

Paying tax on income can be stressful, but it is important that athletes know what is required and how to do it. If the athlete gets part of their income from a fixed salary, tax should be deducted automatically before they receive their money. Any additional private work or self-employment involves declaring their income to HM Revenue and Customs.

An athlete in receipt of an Athlete Personal Award (APA) does not have to pay tax on it, but may have to pay tax on other earnings, such as sponsorship. If the government feels you are a professional athlete making a profit from sport, you will be taxed on your earnings from sport.

Insurance

Insurance can cover a number of things such as life, injury or property. For example, athletes may wish to protect expensive equipment against theft or damage. This means they will pay a small, regular monthly fee or premium to a company, which in return promises to pay to repair or replace the equipment if it is broken or stolen.

Savings and investments

The career of an athlete can be relatively short, with second careers often begun at the end of a competitive career. It is essential that an athlete saves some of their income so that they have a source of money in the future. Savings accounts vary greatly, with some allowing tax-free investment while others offer immediate access to money.

Either way, it is vital for an athlete to have savings they can fall back on. Savings accounts can be set up and managed online, so that the athlete can access them wherever they need to.

Investments are forms of saving designed for longer periods of time. Investments can come in many forms, such as buying shares in a company or buying property, with the hope that the value of the investment will increase over time. An athlete making money during their career may choose to invest some of their money in this way so that once they retire they can, if necessary, sell the shares or property, to generate income.

Economic failure can often be the end result of poor guidance and support at an earlier stage during the athlete's career. The combination of being young and earning thousands of pounds every week is attractive to those people trying to sell investments that claim to offer fantastic returns. When footballers go bankrupt, it is common that they do not know what has been going on with their own money. Frequently it affects players who have failed to adjust their expenditure and lifestyles when their income falls towards the end of (and after) their sporting careers.

❚❚ PAUSE POINT

List the financial responsibilities that an athlete might have.

Hint   Compare the funding responsibilities that an athlete might have.

Extend   Consider and analyse the financial responsibilities that an athlete might have.

Case study

Why footballers are increasingly being declared bankrupt

A charity for ex-football players, XPRO, suggests that 60 per cent of Premier League players, who earn an average of £30,000 per week, declare themselves bankrupt within five years of finishing the game.

In 2014 David James, the former goalkeeper for England, Liverpool, Manchester City, Aston Villa, West Ham and Portsmouth, declared himself bankrupt. As well as enjoying his playing career, he had also worked as a model, had personal sponsorship deals and image rights, and worked as a media pundit. It is estimated he earned £20 million during his career. However, despite his status he found it hard to find coaching work after his retirement and earn enough money to cover his outgoings.

James had been generous with his money, creating his own foundation and sponsoring many schemes in Malawi using his own income and donating his payment for a regular newspaper column to charity. The details of his bankruptcy are private, but a divorce from his first wife appears to have cost him considerably, along with other failed investments. He was declared bankrupt due to outstanding tax payments.

It is not just footballers who run into financial issues. In the NBA it is suggested that 80 per cent of players are bankrupt within five years. The explanations on both sides of the Atlantic are diverse but often seem to be linked to receiving bad advice – it is common for sports performers to make bad investments without really understanding what they are investing in.

Check your knowledge

1   What do you think can be done to help athletes to understand their finances?

2   Evaluate the different financial factors that have affected David James. Complete a short report looking at the different reasons for his bankruptcy.

Athletes receive different incomes based on the type of sport in which they participate, and the level at which they compete.

Choose a sport and consider an athlete at the start of their career in this sport and an elite athlete in the same sport. Produce a PowerPoint® presentation that compares:

- their funding opportunities
- the financial factors that are likely to affect them.

Evaluate the way that different lifestyle factors, the support available and financial factors may influence the young athlete's development towards becoming an elite athlete.

Plan

- I understand what I am being asked to produce.
- What do I already know about funding in different sports?
- In what areas do I need to develop my knowledge about funding in sport? Do I need to find out about the funding opportunities or the financial factors?

Do

- Do I know what I am doing and what I have to achieve in my presentation?
- Are there any potential problems when creating my presentation and how can I overcome them?

Review

- Have I met the objective of the presentation task?
- Can I describe the way I completed the presentation task?
- Can I evaluate what went well in researching, creating and completing the presentation?
- What did not go as well as I would have liked, when researching, creating and completing the presentation?

C Investigate the importance of effective communication skills in sports performance and coaching

The use of communication skills

Communication skills are increasingly essential to an elite athlete to help them promote their image. Styles of communication vary greatly, depending on who you are communicating with, your message and the situation you are in. There are three main styles of communication:

▶ **passive** – where others' needs are put before your own and you minimise your own self-worth

▶ **assertive** – where you stand up for your rights while maintaining respect for the rights of others

▶ **aggressive** – where you stand up for your rights but in doing so violate the rights of others.

There are several groups of people in sport with whom athletes need to be able to communicate effectively and appropriately. We touched on many of them at the start of this unit, but they include the following.

▶ **Team mates** – being part of a team is a vital ingredient in many sports. Athletes need to be able to communicate and talk with each other in a professional manner to help develop or maintain a team bond. Athletes should not blame – or give the impression of blaming – team mates or individuals for bad results or mistakes.

▶ **Coaches and support staff** – successful athletes work with a number of coaches and support staff at a variety of levels as their career develops. Athletes need to communicate well in order to understand what each of these coaches demands and expects in order to reach their sporting goals. Interacting in a professional manner will help in their pursuit of excellence.

▶ **Employers** – communicating with an employer in a professional and open manner allows the athlete to gain their support in developing their career. Establishing a good working relationship could mean more time can be spent on training, travel and competition. A flexible and open relationship is vital and beneficial to both parties: the employer gains a dedicated worker while the athlete feels valued in their work. For example, a part-time semi-professional rugby player who also has a part-time job will need to communicate with their employer about taking time off, or working at different times, due to their playing commitments.

▶ **Officials** – match officials are an essential part of sport. They are in charge of all decisions within a competition, and communicating with them in an inappropriate way could bring negative consequences! Their decisions are final and should never be questioned by athletes.

▶ **Fans** – when communicating with fans it is important that athletes maintain a positive image and a professional manner. Using multimedia can be a dynamic way of developing an athlete's image.

▶ **Sponsors** – a successful sponsorship deal can be long-lasting and beneficial, but requires the athlete to build strong, positive relationships with the sponsor. The longer the relationship lasts, the greater the value that can be gained from it.

Elements of communication

Speaking

Sport often uses technical terms and specialist language to describe performance and techniques. Non-athletes may be confused by this technical jargon, so you should avoid it when speaking to them. Coaches should also avoid using too many technical terms as athletes may be unsure about what is required, leading to confusion and poor performance.

What you are saying might be affected by the **intonation** and **clarity** of your verbal communication. People who speak very slowly in a non-expressive voice can be difficult to understand and uninspiring. Alternatively, someone with a lively, fast-paced voice may be speaking too quickly to be understood. You should learn to use your voice in a way that creates interest and is easy to listen to.

When being interviewed, verbal communication can often be relatively unplanned. This can take the pressure off but can also lead to athletes' views being taken out of context or them being misquoted.

Listening

When being interviewed by the media it is important that athletes focus on and listen carefully to the questions they are asked. A misguided response can instantly travel around the world and damage careers.

Good listening skills will also help improve performance as they will help athletes know what is expected of them by their coach in a task or situation.

Clear lines of communication should be open between people who rely on one another to get good results. Remember: what someone says and what we hear can be amazingly different!

Key terms
Intonation – the pattern and pitch of your voice.
Clarity – how clearly you speak.

Writing

Everyone involved in sport now has the potential, through social media sites, to write about their daily life for their followers, who can be anywhere in the world. But athletes have to use this platform with caution: there have been high-profile instances of athletes 'tweeting' inappropriate content which has directly cost them millions after their sponsors have withdrawn financial support.

Research

Use the Internet to find examples of responsible and effective use of social media – and bad examples too.

Athletes may also have to write to sponsors, managers, media or coaches regarding contractual issues or appearances. Many people are intimidated by having to write, but there are times when it is the best (or only) way to communicate.

Remember that written language is permanent and leaves a lasting record. Even for athletes it is important to pay special attention to spelling, grammar, punctuation, writing style and choice of words. Today's technology makes letter-writing and other written forms of electronic communication easier by providing reliable tools that check and correct misspelled words and grammar use. Letters and emails should always be checked thoroughly before sending to ensure they say exactly what is intended and that nothing could be misinterpreted.

Good writing skills can also sometimes be used after retirement from active sport as the basis of a new career – many sports correspondents for newspapers are former professional sports people.

Understanding

As an athlete, it is important to have good understanding skills. For example, if an athlete understands the physiological and psychological demands placed on them, they can cope better with the pressures that come with these. Being in a good state of mind is closely connected to producing a good performance.

Discussion

In groups of four or five, discuss why it is important for athletes and supporting individuals to have empathy with other people.

Athletes will also need a good understanding of tactics and their role in a particular sport (especially if they are part of a team) so they must be able to understand spoken or written instructions or directions, for instance, from their coach.

Body awareness

Body movements or gestures such as hand gestures, smiling or nodding are known as body language. This can help communication as it shows whether someone understands or is acknowledging what you are saying. It is important to understand body language and how it affects the way an athlete might be perceived. For example, yawning can show a lack of interest, while keeping your arms crossed might indicate a lack of openness. At elite level, an athlete must learn to control their body language as they are under scrutiny from a global audience, which can often be millions of television viewers. The athlete needs to learn to disguise their emotions, for example if they are tiring or losing their temper, as this can give their opponent an advantage.

Negotiating

All of the above elements of communication often come together when negotiating a new contract or other agreement. The key to a successful negotiation is to be prepared: the athlete should know what they want to say in a clear way but also be able to listen to others. It is also important to respect the other people involved in the negotiation, giving everybody the chance to put across their point of view.

Mentoring

The most successful elite sports performers from the UK often mentor young people to help inspire them, increase participation in sport and improve health and fitness. This is often done through visits to schools and youth groups where sharing inspiring stories of the athlete's personal journey, and how they have overcome challenges, can have a positive outcome on young people. The mentoring journey is sometimes tracked through the media where it can reach millions via television, Twitter, Facebook, Instagram and various other multimedia facilities.

⏸ PAUSE POINT   What do you consider to be the most important communication skills?

   List the communication skills that you believe are your strengths.

    Identify the communication skills that you need to develop and explain how you would plan to improve these.

Communicating with the media

Athletes will communicate with a wide range of media outlets, from local and national **written media**, to both local and national **broadcast media** and social media.

Elite athletes need to be able to communicate effectively with the media to develop a positive image and brand, which can lead to financial rewards by attracting sponsorship and appearance fees. With the development of global instant multimedia communications, it is essential that athletes are aware of the positive and negative aspects of any media involvement.

The media can have a massive influence on how athletes are perceived. It has the power to shatter myths and stereotypes, create overnight role models and celebrities, generate high profiles and large incomes, and build public appeal for athletes. It can also, just as quickly, condemn an athlete's lifestyle and career behaviour.

Having a positive relationship with the media is very important to athletes because positive coverage will help them develop and retain a positive public image.

Written media

The main types of written media are shown in Table 27.3. Roles in the written media can be broken down into four main areas, outlined below.

▸ **News reporters** look for an eye-catching story. They often report on scandalous or negative aspects of sport, such as alleged corruption in Fifa and doping scandals, but they may also look at positive achievements too.

▸ **Sports reporters** are generally supportive of athletes and their sport. They will report on failures, but usually have a balanced approach with the interest of sport at heart. Athletes should try to build a good relationship with these writers, as their articles can influence the public's perceptions of the athlete.

> **Key terms**
>
> **Written media** – term used to describe publications such as newspapers and magazines that were traditionally printed on paper, although many these days also have digital editions.
>
> **Broadcast media** – term used to describe media that is broadcast as sound and/or vision, traditionally transmitted by radio waves but now also by cables and the Internet.

- **Columnists** are looking for an overview and an 'angle'. They write regular features about sport. Their role is to give their opinion and to provoke thought and debate around an issue or personality in sport – positive or negative.
- **Feature writers** cover the sport or the athlete in greater depth than sports reporters. If an athlete is a known winner or has a good story, feature writers may look to have an extended interview with them before a competition. They may also write a long piece afterwards if the athlete has emerged as a champion.

▶ **Table 27.3:** Types of written media

Type of written media	Description
Local newspapers	Local newspapers operate in one area, such as a town, city or county. They will focus on reporting on local sports teams and events, playing both locally and nationally. They will talk to those involved and get their pre- and post-event opinions. Local newspapers can be vital in raising the image and profile of local athletes and teams.
National newspapers	National newspapers are published all over the country. They will report on athletes and teams from across the country, and they have a wide distribution. It is common for the national press to include a journalist's opinion on a team or individual athlete, and ex- or current players are also asked to give their professional opinion.
Specialist magazines	In recent years there has been a massive increase in specialist sports magazines, ranging from athletics through to activities such as climbing and mountain biking. Magazines regularly feature exclusive interviews with specific athletes, informing the public of their achievements and hopes for the future.
Club magazines	Club magazines are produced to inform athletes and sport club members of recent events, results and sport-specific news. They interview successful athletes on topics such as training, competition success and lifestyle away from sport.

Broadcast media

The broadcast media primarily consist of television and radio, but these days the Internet can also be used to broadcast video clips and live events. Television and radio usually broadcast at a national level, but may also include regional coverage. For instance, the BBC has slots throughout the day where it hands over television coverage to local news teams, and it has regional radio stations too.

Many large sporting clubs or organisations now offer their own broadcast channels, too, either over the Internet or via digital television, offering coverage of their own club's or organisation's events.

Television

Television offers athletes the most powerful opportunity to get their message across. Television can be an immediate outlet, with live broadcasting and regular news and sports programmes, including dedicated channels. Satellite links can bring fast transmission and communication of events, and studio editing can be used to create exciting and dynamic coverage of a range of sports. Television interviews can take place in a studio or at a venue as part of the outside broadcast unit. They may be broadcast live or pre-recorded.

▶ Television coverage offers athletes a chance to get their message across

Television's sport coverage operates in the following formats:

▶ live coverage

▶ pre-recorded coverage ('as live' or highlights)

▶ studio-based items

▶ outside broadcast items

▶ news bulletins

▶ documentary programmes

▶ linked websites, offering sports news and the chance to catch up with earlier programmes.

Radio

Radio is a flexible medium that operates 24 hours a day. It is also immediate because of its ability to turn around interviews and features quickly. It uses many of the same techniques as television. Radio covers sport in three basic forms:

▶ live coverage of events

▶ news bulletins

▶ magazines and documentary programmes that look behind the scenes.

Radio gives minor sports a great opportunity to gain coverage, especially through local and regional radio. Many sport radio stations also have their own linked websites.

Social media

Social media allows elite athletes to communicate with their followers instantly at any time of day, and to anywhere in the world that has network coverage. Messages can be directed straight to followers but the athletes need to be careful as negative comments can leave a bad impression and a lasting, negative digital footprint.

Working with the media

The media gives athletes a valuable opportunity to promote themselves and their sport. Making sure that communication is clear and open is a skill that develops with practice and experience. Athletes may have to give interviews to journalists from local and national television, or attend press conferences to give their views on individual or team performances. For example, all Premier League football managers have to give a pre-match and post-match press conference to their media partners.

It is important to understand how to communicate verbally and non-verbally in a professional way. The British Olympic Association (BOA) produces an information sheet for athletes that gives advice on dealing with the media. Here is a summary of the main points.

▶ Be yourself.

▶ Show how you feel.

▶ Think before you speak.

▶ Be natural.

▶ Speak clearly and not too fast.

▶ Look the interviewer in the eyes.

▶ Be open.

▶ Enjoy it: people want to know about you.

▶ Be proud of your achievements.

Many interviews are conducted immediately after a performance. Interviewers expect athletes to give a clear evaluation and opinion on sporting performance and it is important that this is conveyed in a clear and professional manner. Many broadcast media interviews will be broadcast live, so it is essential that communication is precise and accurate, even though you may be tired or disappointed after an energy-sapping match or event.

Interview practice

The old saying 'fail to prepare; prepare to fail' is true when being interviewed, and many athletes undergo public relations training in order to help them learn and practise interview skills.

An athlete must know what they want to say before speaking to a journalist, particularly after a match or event when they may be tired, disappointed or frustrated. They must remember to take their time in listening to the question that has been asked and respond confidently and with consideration.

When interviews are scheduled in advance, preparation can include research, preparing scripts or prompt sheets, and rehearsals. All these will help to prevent a poor or unexpected performance. This is essential when preparing to deal with the media, especially a press conference or live broadcast interview. Athletes need to be able to convey information in a clear and concise manner to aid understanding and avoid any embarrassing or controversial moments.

Being prepared might include asking yourself:

▶ What questions will I be asked?
▶ How should I respond to these questions?
▶ How should I present myself at the interview?
▶ What should my appearance be at the interview?
▶ Who can I seek help and advice from?

Theory into practice

Knowing the purpose of an interview beforehand will allow you to prepare. You will need to research what questions are likely to come up and what the answers should be. You should also prepare for the unexpected so that you are fully aware of the content of the interview or presentation.

Working in pairs, prepare to interview each other about your sports performance. Once you know what you are going to ask, begin to prepare the answers you might give to questions. Then interview each other.

People will not just be listening to what you say, they will be paying attention to how you say it. Be positive, open and clear, and remember not to let your body language become a distraction.

Audience

Speaking to an audience can be exciting; however, lack of preparation can make even the best-intended presentation a poor experience. To ensure that you are effective, ask yourself:

▶ Why am I giving this presentation or interview?
▶ What do I want the audience to take away from the presentation?

Sometimes an interview will be filmed in front of a live audience in a studio, but even when it is not you need to be aware of the audience that will be watching or listening to the interview. Knowing the level of knowledge within the audience means you can talk at the correct level and aid their understanding – is this a programme that will be watched/listened to by people who are fans of your sport? Or is it one that will be watched/listened to by the general public? Knowing the typical age of the audience members will also help you pitch the interview at the right level.

Rehearsals

A good way of improving your presentation skills is to rehearse in advance. Read through your notes so that when you have to do it for real you are familiar and confident with its content. Or you could conduct a 'mock' interview where someone plays the part of the interviewer.

Scripts and prompt sheets

Scripts and prompt sheets can be used to refer to during a presentation. They will give you confidence if you feel that you might forget something. However, do not rely solely on these as you may end up simply reading a script rather than presenting the information, which is not good viewing for the audience and does not convey a good impression of the athlete.

Language

It is essential when presenting information that you use the correct language: you should avoid slang and swearing. Your voice should be clear and words should be pronounced properly. Any difficult or unfamiliar words should be practised beforehand.

PAUSE POINT   List the reasons why athletes need to have a positive media profile.

    Hint   Can you explain why a positive media image will have a positive impact on the athlete and their sport?

    Extend   What could the consequences be of having a negative media profile?

Positive and negative impacts of the media

The media can have a considerable influence on the way that sports people are perceived. These impacts can be positive or negative. Table 27.4 gives some examples.

▶ **Table 27.4:** Positive and negative impacts of media coverage

	Positive impacts	**Negative impacts**
For the athlete	Increased income – corporations pay to invite athletes to events, or provide increased money for media broadcasting rights. Also increased interest from sponsors.	Intrusion on private lives – everyday lives of athletes are often followed and played out in the media; they often receive very little privacy.
	Increased exposure – for the athlete this can lead to them developing their own brand or image.	Media demands on athletes – can distract attention away from competition and training, as well as losing time for potential recovery and training.
For the sport	Positive role models – athletes provide models for young people to look up to and aspire to be like.	Reduced attendance – often for games shown live on television the actual number of spectators in the stadiums can be reduced.
	Education – people can acquire knowledge about sports.	Overkill – with many dedicated sport television channels some people would consider that there is too much sport on television.
	Inspiration – the media takes sport to audiences who do not usually get to see it and this can directly encourage participation.	Pressure from media organisers – on organisers of competitions to improve the broadcasting experience for viewers. Prestigious events can be run at a time suited to television companies, rather than the athletes. For example, scheduling an event at the warmest time of day.
		Bias – the most popular sports receive a great deal of airtime whereas the niche sports receive very little coverage.

Being a role model

As we have seen earlier in this unit, elite athletes can often be perceived as a role model by other people. It is important that they remember this whenever they are communicating with the media.

▶ They should uphold the highest principles of sportsmanship, spurn gamesmanship, and strive to maintain the ethics of their sport.

▸ Their personal behaviour should be exemplary when working with others, being involved in teamwork, negotiating or taking part in other cooperative enterprises.

▸ They should be careful when communicating to demonstrate a good attitude, taking extra care when expressing positive or negative views.

▸ They should always be aware of the influence that they have on team mates, sponsors, coaches and fans.

Case study

Attitude, expressing positive or negative views

The photo is one of the most well-known 'political' events in sports history. At the 1968 Mexico Olympics, Tommie Smith won the 200-metre race and fellow American international, John Carlos, took bronze. As the American national anthem played, and the pair stood on top of the medal rostrum to receive their medals, they dropped their heads and raised a clenched fist, echoing the 'Black Power salute'. Smith and Carlos both wore black socks and no shoes. They were booed when they left the rostrum.

The pair were opposing the treatment of black Americans and other minorities in the US. Together the athletes were barred from the games and condemned for their actions.

However, when returning to their home country both men were greeted as heroes by the African-American community. Some, however, considered them to be a negative influence and both received death threats. Three decades later they were both honoured for their role in promoting the civil rights movement. They were given awards by the US government and they also received the prestigious Arthur Ashe Courage Award.

Athletes' conduct and decisions can clearly get people thinking.

Check your knowledge

1 Why do you think these athletes acted as they did?

2 What reaction do you think their sponsors might have?

3 How do you think the governing bodies might react?

⏸ **P A U S E P O I N T**   Research ways in which athletes have tried to politically influence the public.

　　　Hint   Think about being a public figure. What impact could this have on how people respond to your views?

　　　Extend   How do you think sponsors would react when their athletes make political gestures?

The academy manager of your local League Two football club has approached you. One of their young players recently made some comments on Twitter that upset some of the club's supporters, and the academy manager is keen to make sure that this does not happen again.

The academy manager has asked you to produce a short report explaining the behaviours of positive role models in the media. Choose an athlete that you are familiar with – it does not have to be a footballer, but should be someone that young footballers can relate to. You might wish to do some online research to see this athlete's most recent interactions with various media organisations.

Your report should:

- explain the interactions between athletes and different types of media
- provide examples, which show the use of appropriate behaviours
- explain the possible negative effects of inappropriate behaviours.

Plan

- I understand what I am being asked to do to achieve this activity.
- What do I already know?
- Are there any areas I need to develop my knowledge in for the report?
- What content will I include in my report and where will I find it?

Do

- I can identify any potential problems I may face and develop a strategy to overcome this when writing the report.
- I am able to create the report with a logical structure.

Review

- I can explain what the objective of the report writing task was.
- I can identify my strengths and also areas for improvement in my report.

D Examine career planning directed to becoming an elite athlete

Being a successful athlete does not happen by chance. Sporting careers are well considered and well planned, with short-, medium- and long-term goals identified by the athlete and their coaching team. Progress may be made from local clubs to regional and national teams or competitions. But the athlete also needs to consider their post-athletic career – even before a planned retirement, factors such as injury or loss of form might result in secondary careers being required.

Career planning for a competitive athlete

Self- and needs analysis

Being able to carry out an honest self-appraisal is an essential skill for future success and achievement. It is important for long-term success that athletes have a clear vision of what they want to achieve before they start identifying how to accomplish this. Athletes must analyse all areas that could affect their performance, including physiological, psychological and specific sport-related skills. The analysis needs to cover all aspects of training, competition and their own personal needs, for example buying a house or starting a family. From this they need to identify what needs to improve and what they need to maintain for optimal performance.

It may be useful for athletes to perform a SWOT analysis. Originally this was a business concept used to plan and evaluate the strengths, weaknesses, opportunities and threats involved in any project or in a situation requiring a decision. Being clear and focusing on each of these key areas will allow the athlete to set long- and short-term goals, both in terms of performance and also long-term athletic career planning. If they find there is a gap between their performance and their goals, the next step is to identify how they will bridge this gap.

> **Link**
>
> You can read more about fitness programming and periodisation in *Unit 2: Fitness Training and Programming for Health, Sport and Well-being* (see page 119).
>
> You can read more about SWOT analysis in *Unit 3: Professional Development in the Sports Industry* (see page 156).

Goal setting

Short-term

To successfully achieve a long-term goal, athletes set smaller, short- and medium-term goals that build towards the long-term goal. They can then focus their efforts and energy into achieving these smaller goals, although they always have to remember the larger, long-term goal: an athlete getting up early on a wet, cold morning to complete a training session may have to motivate themselves by thinking of the long-term target of success.

Many athletes when setting short-term goals seek advice from experts and coaches. Talking to experienced athletes enables them to gain an invaluable insight into how they have achieved success. Coaches should help their athletes set career and performance goals, as well as encouraging them to achieve short-term goals.

Medium-term goals

Medium-term goals usually last between one month and six months and are a progression of short-term goals. It is important that athletes use periodisation when planning their goals, especially their medium-term ones – see Unit 2 (page 119) for more information.

Long-term goals

Athletes need long-term goals to aim towards. These are objective statements about specific, measurable achievements. These can be answers to questions such as, 'What is it that I want to achieve?' to which the answer might be: 'To finish tenth or above at the end of season' or 'To have a batting average of at least 50 at the end of the season'. Replies such as 'I want to win' or 'I want to be the best' say little about how to achieve these things, and they do not direct the athlete's behaviour.

Goal setting should follow the SMART principle, meaning goals should be:

▶ **S**pecific
▶ **M**easurable
▶ **A**chievable
▶ **R**ealistic
▶ **T**ime-bound.

Ⅱ **PAUSE POINT**   What are your short-, medium- and long-term goals?

   What do you need to do to achieve your goals?

Extend   How will you know that you have achieved them? What will be your measure of success?

Planning careers to manage personal expectations

It is important that athletes remain grounded when they first achieve success or, alternatively, maintain belief and a positive outlook if they struggle to make the progress that they wish.

Athletes need to make sure that they manage their own personal expectations carefully – they will often, for example, plan phases in their careers such as breaking into regional and national age group teams, with the ultimate goal of finally having full international representation and a successful career.

Athletes must be prepared for transitions in their career. For example, the jump can be significant when moving from national youth representation to full national representation, particularly in relation to the level of performance and expectation as well as exposure in the media.

Athletes must also be prepared for their careers not progressing as they would like or for a change in circumstances, which could include long-term injury, being dropped by a sponsor or failing to meet required targets. Having contingency plans and alternative sources of income can be extremely beneficial for athletes.

Education and qualifications

Nearly all occupations need specific qualifications and relevant work experience. Athletes might need to make difficult decisions about the future, after their sports playing career has finished. A lack of qualifications could make it difficult to find worthwhile employment at the end of their career. Athletes must also consider what they will need to do to find employment.

As part of their career planning, athletes should identify the alternative careers that interest them and the qualifications they require. Many careers will require further study at college or university and there are now hundreds of sports-related courses. Valuable insights can be gained by undertaking work experience, where the athlete takes on a job for a short period to see whether it is an area in which they enjoy working. Finally, some athletes will work full-time and operate as part-time professionals; in fact some athletes will actually earn a greater income by doing this.

> **Link**
>
> There is more about education and qualifications in *Unit 3: Professional Development in the Sports Industry*

Contingency planning

Athletes will experience many changes throughout their careers. These might include a change in coach, club or location, or a change in national or international status. There will also be the significant transition from participating in sport to their secondary, post-performance career. Athletes need to be flexible to manage changing circumstances.

▸ Changing teams can be difficult for players as the performance and dynamics may be different. It can be difficult to deal with, and integrate with, new players. On the other side of the coin, it can be challenging for remaining players to maintain motivation and performance levels if a star player leaves.

▸ Changing clubs can also be a difficult time for an athlete. They may be leaving friends or family and feel like they are 'the newbie' in the club. There are likely to be many unfamiliar faces and the prospect can seem daunting at first.

- An athlete may have to change coach and support staff. This may be due to career progression or when representing different teams. It is important that athletes accept this transition and are able to continue to perform at their best levels.

- Equipment changes for athletes can be challenging to deal with and disrupt their previous flow and focus. Any equipment changes need to be carefully planned for and tested before major competitions.

- As an athlete's career progresses, their status may change. They may be selected to represent their region, county or country. They need to consider carefully how their life will change, especially when moving from amateur to professional. Additionally, being made captain or a change in rankings can be prestigious for a sports person but can bring increased pressure and expectations. Similarly, losing status in a team or sport can be difficult to deal with.

- An unexpected illness or accident will prevent an athlete from performing or training. It may also be a setback in terms of competition preparation. As the nature of sport is often uncertain, injuries will occasionally happen, so it is important that there is a contingency plan in place. Injuries must be dealt with promptly and you should evaluate their impact on future training, practices and performances.

Many sports careers are cut short due to permanent injury. If this happens, the athlete may feel uncertain of their future as most of their life may have been dedicated to training and competition in their sport. It is important that athletes have a contingency plan and a future career plan in place for their life after retirement.

Career planning for a retired athlete

Sport can have many uncertainties. Clear and definitive planning does not prevent the unexpected happening, such as long-term or permanent injury, accidents or illness. Athletes should consider what options are available after their performance career has ended and what skills and qualifications these might require. They must learn to adapt to life outside competitive sport: a life that many may view as being slower and less structured than their sporting career. Sudden retirements brought on by injury can be particularly stressful.

Planning a career away from sport can be a daunting and stressful experience for athletes. For most of their adult lives, they will have been training and competing, and an uncertain future can lead to anxiety and stress. The better it is planned in advance, the less anxious and stressful it will be.

Reflect

Following retirement, only a small number of athletes are able to maintain the lifestyle they enjoyed when they were at their peak of earnings for competitive events. Nearly all athletes need to find a job simply to cover their outgoings. Think about your own interests and skills away from sport. Is there a broad category of work that might interest you once you stop taking part in regular sporting events?

Potential career opportunities

Careers after playing sport can be found both inside and outside the professional sports sector. Many of the skills within sport can be transferred easily to other employment areas. Athletes tend to be highly motivated and committed: these are valuable traits in any industry, as are teamwork and leadership skills. Identifying which careers are available, and the qualifications and experience required, will give athletes the direction needed to plan for the future.

There are also many careers that are related to sport, including physiotherapy, sports nutrition, coaching and teaching, working in the media or sports development. Each of these key areas still involves close contact with sport and competition. An example of a former athlete who continues to work in sport is television presenter Gary Lineker. After a successful career in football where he captained the England football team, Lineker went on to pursue a successful career in the media.

Most jobs or careers require qualifications and experience. As part of their post-competitive career planning, athletes need to identify the careers that interest them and the qualifications they require. Many careers will require further study at university and there are now hundreds of sports-related courses. But it may also be appropriate to consider retraining in a completely different industry by studying qualifications such as an NVQ in plumbing or another area that takes the athlete's interest.

Sometimes an athlete will start a second career while they are winding down their competitive sporting life, slowly transitioning to the new role over a period of time.

Table 27.5 shows some sports-related careers that athletes might consider.

▶ **Table 27.5:** Possible sports-related careers for retired athletes

Possible future career path	Description
Coach	Many athletes see this as a natural progression to continue in their sport as a coach. There are opportunities to coach at all levels, from grass roots through to elite. A number of specific and progressive coaching courses are now available.
Teacher	Teaching can be done at schools, colleges or universities. It is natural for sports teachers to have an active interest in sport and they often compete outside work. To be a teacher you must study to degree level in sports science or physical education and also hold a certificate in education. Study normally lasts for a period of three years in higher education.
Media roles	There are many jobs in the media such as a journalist or reporter. To undertake a career in this field, you should have a good command of written and spoken English and it is normal to study up to degree level.
Sports science roles	Sports science is expanding as we try to improve athletic performance. Areas include biomechanics, psychology, fitness testing and physiology. Each of these areas is designed to offer athletes support and to improve their performance. Sports scientists normally study at university and often continue their studies afterwards with research.
Sports development	Sports development is concerned with getting various groups involved in sport, such as elderly or disabled people, or children. Local authorities normally target groups that are under-represented in sport and offer schemes or sessions to get them actively involved. Sports development officers normally have a sports-related qualification as well as a range of coaching awards.
Physiotherapist	Athletes are often keen to become physiotherapists as they may have experienced injury during their careers. There are a number of courses available in the UK, but competition for places is stiff. A physiotherapist has to study to degree level and the course will involve working in general physiotherapy at a hospital. Sports injuries and rehabilitation are not studied in a physiotherapy undergraduate degree course.
Officiating	Officiating is becoming an increasingly popular choice for some athletes to turn to after retirement, or in some cases athletes combine part-time officiating with active competition. It can be used as a source of income for the part-time athlete. For the athlete in retirement it can be a way of staying in the sport and making a positive contribution.

Case study

Ben Burgess – a change of direction

At the age of 30, footballer Ben Burgess only managed to complete a couple of training sessions in the first three weeks of pre-season for his club Tranmere Rovers before he decided to retire due to long-standing knee injuries. When he knew he was going to have to retire he felt confusion, fear, anger, desperation and apprehension. He also knew that he would need to work for at least another 30 years.

To be a professional requires not just technical skill and high levels of fitness; players also need willpower, leadership and teamwork skills, the ability to perform under pressure, drive and flexibility. All of these skills are transferable to many other different jobs and appreciated by employers.

Ben took advantage of the Professional Footballers' Association's vocational and academic courses, taking a degree at Staffordshire University in Broadcasting and Writing. To gain experience he did some radio commentary and wrote some magazine articles. After ending his football career he started training for a Post Graduate Certificate in Education (PGCE), which enabled him to qualify as a teacher. He has created a whole new career and takes great joy in watching children learn and develop. While playing football he was ambitious and determined to be the best player he could be. In teaching he has the same ambitions and would like to progress to be a head teacher.

Check your knowledge

1 What did Ben do effectively to plan for the end of his career?

2 Explain the choices made in a career plan for a sports performer in a sport of your choice.

3 Evaluate the possible career choices that could be available to an athlete at the end of their sporting careers.

 PAUSE POINT   Why do sports people need to prepare for a second career?

       Hint   Why is it important for athletes to plan for the future?

       Extend   Analyse the potential career options available to athletes.

Assessment practice 27.4   D.P5   D.M4   D.D3

You are working as coach in your favourite sport's young athlete development programme. The scheme's lead coach has asked you to create a leaflet for podium potential athletes, advising them about how to build a career plan. As part of this, she has asked you to produce a sample career plan relevant to that sport. She has asked you to make sure that it also includes contingency planning.

Plan
- Do I need any clarification about the task?
- Are there any areas in which I need to develop my knowledge?
- What are the success criteria of this task?

Do
- I know what I am doing and what I have to achieve.
- I can identify any potential problems I may face when creating the leaflet and develop a strategy to overcome them.

Review
- I can explain the reason for creating the leaflet.
- I can explain what a successful career plan will look like.

Further reading and resources

Books

Balyi, I., Way, R. and Higgs, C. (2013) *Long-term Athlete Development*, Leeds: Human Kinetics.

Clark, N. (2014) *Nancy Clark's Sports Nutrition Guidebook: 5th edition*, Leeds: Human Kinetics.

Dixon, B. (2007) *Careers Uncovered: Sport and Fitness: 2nd edition*, Bath: Trotman.

Kennedy, E. and Hills, L. (2009) *Sport, Media and Society*, Oxford: Berg.

Lyle, J. and Cushion, C. (eds.) (2010) *Sports Coaching: Professionalisation and Practice*, London: Churchill Livingstone.

Mottram, D.R. and Chester, N. (eds.) (2015) *Drugs in Sport: 6th edition*, Abingdon: Routledge.

Websites

www.sportengland.org – Sport England: the English Sports Council, which aims to encourage the development of sport and improve opportunities, particularly for young people.

www.teamgb.com – The British Olympic Association (BOA): prepares and supports Olympic competitors and develops and promotes the Olympic Movement within the UK.

www.uksport.gov.uk – UK Sport: supports Britain's Olympic and Paralympic sports and athletes to achieve their full potential.

THINK ▶FUTURE

Stuart Smith

PE Teacher

PE teaching is a wonderful career. I get to work with fantastic young learners and be involved in my passion of sport every day. I get to see learners start as complete beginners, develop skills and tactics and become proficient in the sport, often choosing to continue with the sport outside school.

My job can be very busy with fixtures and training regularly after school and sometimes before school. I have to plan every lesson to specifically cater for every learner and make sure that everyone is achieving their learning goals and making progress every lesson. Being physically fit myself is really important because I often need to complete demonstrations and lead by example.

As an ex-professional cricket player, I'm aware of the importance of training and practice, especially as I continue to play semi-professionally and receive a small wage for playing and coaching the club juniors. I'm able to combine these two roles and find a suitable balance that allows me to commit to both. Being able to plan and prepare is an essential skill.

I'm highly committed to my job and my cricket. I have had to consider my family commitments outside work and cricket and each of these puts a tremendous amount of pressure on my time. I also understand the importance of positive behaviour both on and off the field, as I'm a role model to young people both as a PE teacher and as a cricketer.

Focusing your skills

Planning for two careers

- While playing full-time as a professional it is important to plan for when you can no longer compete and train as a full-time athlete. You need to get experience and qualifications for your chosen career. This could be through work experience.
- You may need to identify clubs/teams that would allow you to play on a part-time basis and would be happy for you to have another career and income source.

Managing two careers

- Discuss with your various coaches your expectations and key dates for when you are going to very busy. Rigorous planning can then be undertaken and any problems solved.

- Try to pursue work that will build your career and help you develop new skills.
- You need to accept that, at times, you will be very busy, but make sure you allow enough time to relax, recover and socialise.

Organisation

- Try to plan your time – get used to organising yourself and work out the best ways you can structure your time. It may help to organise your tasks into achievable chunks.
- Trying keeping a diary outlining your plans for the future that you can also review every day.

Getting ready for assessment

Sangita is working towards a BTEC National Extended Diploma in Sport and Physical Activity. She has recently completed an assignment that asked her to 'Investigate different earnings, funding opportunities and financials of sports performers at different stages in their careers' for Learning aim B. Sangita had to write a feature for a magazine that gives advice to aspiring young athletes. The magazine feature had to:

▸ include information on the various funding opportunities and the factors that affect their funding

▸ explain these funding opportunities and financial factors that affect athletes at the different stages of their elite careers.

How I got started

To start I chose which athlete and sport I was going to focus on: an Olympic Gold medal winning track athlete. I spent some time researching their career and sources of income. I saved all the information on the computer at college and also wrote some notes which I kept in a file.

I then created three clear sub-headings for my work:

1 Different earning opportunities
2 Different funding opportunities
3 Different stages of their career

After creating my sub-headings I carried out further research using websites and textbooks. To compare the funding opportunities and financial factors I created a mind map and lists of the similarities and differences. I also emailed an athletes' sports management company for information to support my work.

How I brought it all together

To write the magazine article I spent some time planning what was relevant and what should not be included. I also found several images to improve the appearance of the article. I decided to use an online blogging site to complete my work.

I created a table with further information about each source of funding for my chosen athlete. For the various sponsors I added links, which can take readers directly to the associated websites.

For the main body of the article I used my three headings. Under each heading I explained the various funding opportunities and financial factors. I created a timeline outlining the different stages of an athlete's career, with explanations in text boxes.

What I learned from the experience

I have developed my IT skills and have learned how to hyperlink and how to write a blog/magazine article. I feel these skills could be vital when I leave education. In fact I enjoyed writing the article so much I have decided to continue to write the blog about my own life.

I also learned how important it is to have a good plan in place before you start the write-up phase. I think the task would have been completed much quicker if I had done that, as I occasionally lost direction. Next time I will plan what I'm trying to do and list the content that I need to cover.

After proofreading my work for the first time I felt that I had not included enough detail in my explanations, so I spent some time rewriting my initial draft. I feel this significantly improved the overall quality of my work. I have learned that reviewing and adjusting my work is really important.

Think about it

▸ Have you completed a plan of what you are doing and when you are doing it?

▸ Have you undertaken enough research on the content that you are going to write about?

▸ Have you included all your sources of information in your references?

Sports Performance Analysis 28

Getting to know your unit

Sports performance analysis involves giving objective feedback to athletes to help them change or adapt their performance for the better. The analysis aims to inform the athlete what actually happened as opposed to what they perceived to have happened – sometimes, these two things can be very different.

In this unit, you will explore the components of successful performance in sport and the different methods of analysis applied to different areas of performance. You will look at performance profiling to identify different areas of performance, including measures of fitness and measures employed to assess technical and tactical components for success. Once factors affecting successful performance are established, suitable measures for performance will be produced and practical observation of athletes' performance made. Based on this structured observation, areas of improvement can be identified and feedback given to athletes.

How you will be assessed

This unit will be assessed by a series of internally assessed tasks set by your tutor. These tasks might take the form of written documents, presentations or short projects. There will also be a strong emphasis upon your practical analysis skills, which may be observed as part of your assessment.

The assignments set by your tutor may take the following forms.

▶ Produce a report on the different methods of analysing sports performance, evaluating their relevance and usability for a coach.

▶ Create a presentation explaining the performance demands, ideal models and performance benchmarks of an individual or team sport. Then, using this information, produce your own analysis method for this sport.

▶ Carry out an analysis of the performance of an individual athlete or team and provide a summary report with feedback on performance, incorporating feedback and setting goals for future development.

The exercises within this unit are designed to help you practise and gain the skills that will help you complete your assignments. The theories you will learn will give you the background information to enable you to complete the unit but not necessarily guarantee you a particular grade. The following table shows what you must do in order to achieve a Pass, Merit or Distinction grade, and where you can find activities to help you.

Assessment criteria

This table shows what you must do in order to achieve a **Pass**, **Merit** or **Distinction** grade, and where you can find activities to help you.

Pass	Merit	Distinction

Learning aim A Examine methods for analysing sports performance

A.P1 Explain methods and techniques for analysing sports performance. **Assessment practice 28.1**	**A.M1** Analyse methods and techniques for analysing sports performance, assessing validity, relevance and usability. **Assessment practice 28.1**	**A.D1** Evaluate methods and techniques for measuring performance analysis, recommending and justifying methods and techniques for individual or team performance analysis. **Assessment practice 28.1**

Learning aim B Explore ideal models, benchmarks and protocols for performance analysis

B.P2 Identify established ideal modes, benchmarks and protocols for performance analysis of an individual athlete or team. **Assessment practice 28.2**	**B.M2** Assess and establish ideal models, benchmarks and protocols for performance analysis of an individual athlete or team. **Assessment practice 28.2**	**B.D2** Evaluate established ideal models, benchmarks and protocols for performance analysis of an individual or team. **Assessment practice 28.2**
B.P3 Produce protocols and materials to use for performance analysis of an individual athlete or team. **Assessment practice 28.2**	**B.M3** Produce detailed protocols and materials to use for performance analysis of an individual athlete or team. **Assessment practice 28.2**	

Learning aim C Carry out an analysis of sports performance of an individual athlete or team

C.P4 Collate data and present in a suitable format, from an observation of an individual athlete or team performance. **Assessment practice 28.3**	**C.M4** Collate detailed data and present in different formats, from an observation of an individual athlete or team performance, comparing against own ideal performance model and benchmarks. **Assessment practice 28.3**	**CD.D3** Evaluate collated data, comparing against own ideal performance model and benchmarks, providing feedback that sets justified goals for future development. **Assessment practice 28.3**

Learning aim D Review the collected analysis data and provide feedback to individual athlete or team

D.P5 Review collated data providing feedback to an individual athlete or team on their sporting performance. **Assessment practice 28.3**	**D.M5** Analyse collated data providing detailed feedback to an individual athlete or team on their sporting performance that sets goals for future development. **Assessment practice 28.3**	

Coaches and athletes need to know how movement and physiology affect performance. Technical and tactical aspects of any sport are also important, as is a coach's ability to make changes or adaptations when necessary to gain success. There is also an increasing awareness of sport psychology, and how the mind can affect performance. These factors tell you about the importance of sports performance analysis. How can knowledge of these factors help you analyse sports performance and improve the athletes of tomorrow?

A Examine methods for analysing sports performance

> **Link**
>
> This unit has particularly strong links with *Unit 5: Application of Fitness Testing, Unit 6: Sport Psychology* and *Unit 7: Practical Sports Performance.*

Performance profiling

> **Key term**
>
> **Performance profiling** – giving objective feedback to performers who are trying to achieve a positive change in performance.

Performance profiling is a method used to identify and organise the training, development and preparation of athletes to help them achieve their goals. The method has no set format and depends on how the coach and athlete like to work, although a common approach is a visual display of important areas in a particular sport. The aim of performance profiling is, if applied correctly, to help focus the athlete on key aspects of their performance and help direct their training to the areas that require adaptation.

It is a way of giving the athlete information about what actually happened in their sport – rather than what they think happened. It involves analysing the athlete's performance through observation, and also understanding the athlete's state of mind. There may be occasions when the athlete has underperformed due to nerves or lack of concentration. Therefore the purpose of performance profiling is to:

▶ help the athlete with their physical and psychological needs

▶ assess scope for technical and tactical improvements

▶ improve the athlete's motivation and performance.

The coach should assess the athlete before and after the event, discussing physical, technical and tactical issues, and the following important psychological factors:

▶ confidence

▶ concentration

▶ commitment

▶ control

▶ refocusing of effort.

Understanding each of these will allow the coach to prepare a strategy to address any issues highlighted by the profiling.

Performance analysis follows a clear process of observation, analysis, evaluation, planning and feedback (see Figure 28.1). This model can be used repeatedly and for all aspects of training.

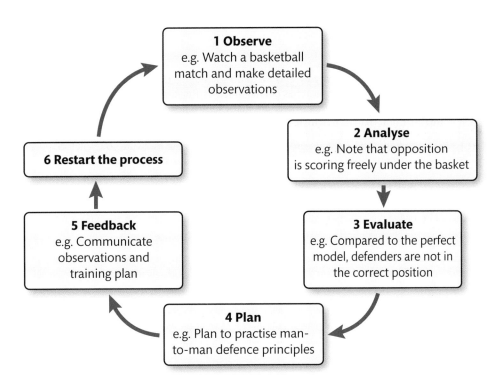

▶ **Figure 28.1:** The performance analysis model

Successful sports performance analysis aims to do the following.

▶ Improve overall performance – different sports have very different requirements, and the athlete and coach should be aware of the specific physical and psychological demands that must be met in order to achieve success. For example, a midfield player in football will need different physical and mental skills from those of a goalkeeper.

▶ Allow accurate assessment of current performance – a performance profile must be timely, accurate and objective. The methods of analysis must be carried out by a competent and qualified person, and then presented to the coach and athlete in a suitable format.

▶ Result in agreed development plan/strategies – once an analysis has been carried out and the relevant technical, tactical, physiological and psychological factors have been addressed, a development plan or strategy should be agreed by both the coach and the athlete which aims to adapt and improve performance.

▶ Prompt improved performance training and development – if a development plan or strategy is agreed, the coach will change the athlete's training schedule to accommodate the adaptations required to improve future performance. The athlete's progress will continue to be analysed (using the same system of performance profiling) to track improvements.

To do this, the performance profile will analyse psychological, physical, technical and tactical factors.

Psychological factors

It is impossible to observe mental factors directly: we only see the physical responses that arise from them. A performance is always conditioned by the mental processes that shape our behaviour through such aspects as motivation or arousal. This is why it is important to consider psychological factors when compiling a performance profile.

You can read more about sport psychology in Unit 6, but Table 28.1 gives an overview of the main factors.

Mental factor	Explanation
Motivation	Motivation is the desire to perform a certain task; it is why we choose to do something. Understanding what motivates athletes helps coaches to devise effective training sessions. It has been defined as 'the direction and intensity of effort' – what we choose to do, and the amount of effort we put in. There are many motivation theories but, in general, motivation can be regarded as **intrinsic** (internal) or **extrinsic** (external).
Stress	A certain level of stress is needed for optimum performance: too little and it is difficult to motivate yourself; too much and it can seriously affect your ability to focus. Both coach and athlete should recognise the symptoms to ensure performance is not affected. Stress occurs when: • you think what is being asked of you is beyond your perceived abilities • too much is asked of you in too short a time • unnecessary obstacles are put in the way of achieving goals. An optimum level of stress will give the alertness and activation that improves performance.
Anxiety	Anxiety is different from stress and comes from concern about a lack of control over circumstances, often resulting in negative thinking with a detrimental effect on performance: for example, an athlete worrying about what spectators think and fearing making a mistake.
Arousal	Arousal is a state of general preparedness when performing a specific sport/action. Every sport triggers a sense of excitement or anticipation, but if this becomes too great, the athlete may feel anxious, with a negative effect on performance. It is important that levels of arousal are suitable to the skills being performed.
Attention	Athletes are presented with a large amount of information; some will be important and relevant (e.g. a coach's instructions), while other information is of no use (e.g. spectators' negative comments). Athletes must focus on relevant information, ignoring negative factors. Concentration demands vary according to sport: • sustained concentration – distance running, cycling, tennis, squash • short burst of concentration – cricket, golf, athletic field events • intense concentration – sprinting events, skiing. Common distractions include anxiety, mistakes, fatigue, weather, public announcements, coach, manager, opponent, negative thoughts, etc.
Confidence	Confidence is the feeling that you are going to succeed in a given situation: self-confidence is the belief you can achieve your goal. The more confident you are, the more likely you are to achieve your goals, resulting in sporting success. A confident athlete will persevere even when things are not going to plan, showing enthusiasm and positivity, and taking their share of responsibility for success and failure.
Aggression	Some sports, such as rugby, require players to show levels of acceptable aggression, e.g. a player making a hard tackle to win possession. But in most sports excessive aggression is viewed as bad, e.g. a frustrated player throwing a punch. It is important athletes control their emotions and only use aggression in a controlled, appropriate way. Frustration at their own or others' performance may lead to anger, resulting in loss of concentration, deteriorating performance and loss of confidence. This in turn fuels more anger – a slippery slope to failure. A coach must teach players that, while aggression can be positive in trying to win, winning should only be achieved by playing within the rules of the game.
Relaxation	Relaxation is used to reduce unwanted anxiety. Key relaxation techniques are outlined below. • Mental imagery: athletes imagine themselves in a variety of situations – perhaps performing a certain skill at a specific place, or in a relaxing situation such as lying on a beach. Research shows the more detailed the imagery, the more likely the athlete is to feel prepared for a specific situation. Imagery is useful in developing: · self-confidence · strategies to teach athletes to cope with new situations before they encounter them · focused attention on a particular skill an athlete is trying to develop. • Progressive muscular relaxation: the purposeful contracting and relaxing of specific muscles. Each muscle is contracted for 4–6 seconds and then consciously relaxed, with the athlete making a mental note of how they feel. This process allows the muscles to return to a more relaxed state. • Meditation: used to reduce stress before an event. With experience, athletes can learn to relax different muscle groups and appreciate subtle differences in muscle tension. By making a note of their breathing and muscle tension, the athlete is able to relax and focus on the competition ahead.
Concentration	Concentration is the ability to focus and it will aid performance. It can be described as the ability to focus on a specific task. In sport, many factors can cause an athlete to become distracted – the crowd, the weather, negative thoughts, etc. An athlete needs to know how to concentrate, especially when under pressure.

Key terms

Intrinsic motivation – motivation derived from engaging in a sport for the sheer satisfaction and enjoyment of taking part.

Extrinsic motivation – motivation derived from an external source, such as a desire for money or trophies.

⏸ PAUSE POINT What psychological reactions may arise if an athlete is told their performance is sub-standard?

> **Hint** Think about how you might react if your coach said your performance was flawed and required improvement. How would that make you feel and what mental factors might come into play at this point?

> **Extend** Can you find any recent examples of an athlete who has underperformed during competition? Can you give any reasons why this may have happened?

Discussion

Imagine one of the greatest fears for any athlete in a big event or game: the fear of failure. What does this mean and how can it affect performance? Discuss this complex issue as a class debate.

Physical factors

Physical factors are crucial to any performance and form the platform from which the performer is able to participate in an activity. It is therefore crucial that physical factors are included in a performance profile. There are five main components of fitness:

- **strength** – the ability of a muscle or group of muscles to exert a maximal force, or overcome a maximal resistance, in a single contraction
- **aerobic endurance** – the ability of the heart, lungs, blood vessels and skeletal muscle to take in, transport and utilise oxygen efficiently and over a prolonged period
- **muscular endurance** – the ability of a muscle or group of muscles to make repeated contractions against a light to moderate resistance and over a prolonged period
- **flexibility** – a measure of ability to move a joint, for example the knee, through a complete and natural range of motion without discomfort or pain
- **body composition** – the body's physical make-up in terms of fat, muscle, bone and water measured as a percentage.

Being able to measure these will help the coach and athlete develop a training plan that will meet the specific requirements of the sport and the chosen area of fitness. Fitness tests can be conducted to measure each area, and the results analysed in order to develop a training programme.

Theory into practice

Rugby union players are split into two positional areas: forwards and backs. Each of these requires specific physical factors vital for optimal performance. The body composition of forwards is typically heavier and taller with high levels of strength in scrums and line-out situations. The body composition of backs is typically leaner than that of forwards as they spend more time free running, and wingers in particular require considerable speed and agility to out-manoeuvre opponents.

How would you go about profiling your class or group into forwards and backs? What criteria would you employ?

Link

You can read more about these physical factors and fitness training programmes in *Unit 2: Fitness Training and Programming for Health, Sport and Well-being*, and more about testing physical factors in *Unit 5: Application of Fitness Testing*.

Heart rate

This can be measured during exercise with a heart rate monitor. Athletes can train within target zones of their maximum heart rate, at a controlled intensity. Heart rate monitors can provide an indication of an athlete's training intensity: whether they are training too hard, not hard enough or just right for a particular session.

Warm-up

To perform at an increased level of performance, physical preparation before training and competition is paramount. A warm-up must always be performed correctly and the monitoring of how you warm up your muscles and increase your heart rate is a factor which can be analysed (via heart rate monitors and physical indicators such as reddened face) to prevent injury and ensure the body is prepared for exercise.

⏸ PAUSE POINT

What factors affect a resting heart test? What anomalies might occur during the test and why?

Hint

How might you feel if you were having your resting heart rate tested – relaxed or nervous?

Extend

How might you prepare a client to undergo fitness tests? What strategies might you adopt to ensure accuracy in your testing procedure and make sure that your client is relaxed?

Cool down

A cool down involves the gradual reduction in physical activity after training or competition. It is designed to return a body back to its pre-exercise state, by returning the heart rate back to normal, removing any waste products in the blood and returning the muscles to their original state. All these factors help maintain the body and reduce the risk of injury.

A cool down can be analysed (via heart rate monitors and physical indicators such as relaxed breathing) by a coach to ensure it is being carried out properly.

Lung function

Analysing lung function allows athletes to determine:

▶ the size of their lungs, and therefore how much air they can inhale

▶ the strength and efficiency of their lungs.

Being able to inspire oxygen and deliver it to working muscles is essential to athletes. Likewise, being able to expire waste products, such as carbon dioxide, is also vital to sporting performance. Research shows that the larger and stronger the lungs, the more they are able to deliver oxygen to working muscles, especially during intense exercise. For example, an elite rower can deliver up to 240 litres of air per minute in and out of their lungs; a typical value for an untrained male would be between 100 and 150 litres per minute during maximal exercise.

A spirometer is used to measure lung function. The athlete takes the deepest breath they can, then exhales into the spirometer as hard, and for as long, as possible. The following measurements are then taken:

▶ **forced vital capacity (FVC)** – the total amount of air forcibly blown out after full inspiration (in litres)

▶ **forced expired volume 1 (FEV1)** – the amount of air forcibly blown out in 1 second, in litres per second (along with forced vital capacity, this is considered one of the primary indicators of lung function)

▶ **peak expiratory flow (PEF)** – the speed of the air moving out of your lungs at the beginning of the expiration, also measured in litres per second.

▶ Spirometers can be used to measure lung function

Technical and tactical factors

> **Link**
>
> Technical and tactical factors are also explored in *Unit 7: Practical Sports Performance* and *Unit 26: Technical and Tactical Demands of Sport*.

> **Key term**
>
> **Technique** – a way of undertaking a particular skill.

Sport involves many complex skills and **techniques** which should also be assessed as part of a performance profile. **Technical skills** involve the execution of sport-specific movements or processes to achieve a task. As we learn and practise these skills, they become more 'natural' and we are able to refine and perfect them. For example, a cricketer will practise specific shots in training, to the standard needed to execute them as part of a competitive match. By analysing technique you will see how body movements are executed and whether these conform to an accepted or prescribed movement pattern.

Tactically performers need to understand where and when to deploy strategies and perform movements and skills. Athletes and coaches must focus on how skills are performed. This may involve observational analysis and feedback, and examining complex skills broken down into simpler parts. Skills can be divided into three categories:

▶ **discrete skills** which have a very clear beginning and end, for example a tennis serve

▶ **continuous skills** which have no obvious beginning or end but tend to merge and flow into one another as the skill or sport progresses, for example cycling or swimming

▶ **serial skills** which are composed of both discrete and continuous skills, for example a tennis player playing a shot on the run.

Tactical skills involve making decisions or reading a situation to enable the successful application of a technical skill(s) to gain an advantage. All sports require tactics or strategies to achieve success and these can also be analysed. Sport contains many examples of tactics that a coach, athlete or team may adopt to win, for example playing an offside trap in football, batting defensively in cricket or using zonal marking in basketball. When devising and using tactics, all players need to understand the tactic and when to employ it. Failing to do this may lead to confusion and disrupt performance.

Process of profile construction

The purpose of analysing sports performance is to provide detailed feedback to the athlete or team in order for them to improve their game. When analysing the performance of an individual or team, you should consider their performance by asking:

▶ How well are specific skills executed?

▶ How focused and motivated are the athletes?

▶ Are the athletes using the correct techniques?

▶ Are the correct tactics adopted at the right time?

This kind of analysis can be adapted to suit any sport. It compares where the athlete views their level of performance for each category against the perfect model of performance. Any differences can be identified and discussed.

Selection of characteristics

The first step when constructing a profile is to decide which factor(s) you wish to analyse. This will vary depending on the sport being assessed, the requirements of the athlete and whether there are any areas that have been flagged up for investigation.

A football coach may wish to determine the level of passing accuracy throughout a football team or shots on target. Equally, a long jumper may want to know how close their take-off foot is to the foul line when they hit the take-off board. In both cases, a set of characteristics must be selected before the start of the performance that will be analysed; deciding this beforehand will allow it to be given proper focus during the event.

In the two examples given, the football coach might decide to analyse two characteristics: the number of passes each player makes and which of those found their target successfully. The long jumper might analyse one characteristic: the distance from the tip of the toe to the foul line (measured with the aid of video analysis). In each case, the characteristic(s) selected for analysis is specific to the sport or technique being undertaken.

Discussion between coach, athlete and team

A coach will not simply try to improve an athlete or team by instructing them to 'try harder'. To be an effective coach, you should be able to analyse and correct specific techniques as part of a training programme. Coaches will often maintain a dialogue with an athlete before, during and after a training session to aid the development of specific techniques or tactical skills. Being able to break down complex movements into simple tasks allows the athlete to identify and correct specific aspects of his or her technique.

Grading of components

Once the coach and athlete have agreed which characteristics to concentrate on in their analysis, the athlete is then asked to complete a self-evaluation assessment of their current level on a scale of 1 to 10 (1 = poor, 10 = outstanding). Finally, the athlete should decide a performance rating on the same scale (1 to 10) for their perfect model or real athlete. This process enables the athlete and coach to construct a suitable comparison and then, construct realistic training goals to meet those aims.

Qualitative and quantitative analysis

Quantitative analysis involves a detailed, scientific approach to observation analysis. It uses direct measurement of a technique or performance, and is often very time-consuming due to the need for detailed data collection. It uses assessments based on numerical analysis, such as match statistics and performance checklists.

One method of collecting information is to watch a game and write down the action as it occurs – this is known as real-time analysis. However, sport is fast-moving and it is often necessary to video record a performance. This is known as lapsed-time analysis. For example, in a basketball match it would be very difficult to collect statistical data such as successful shots as the action occurred.

As technology has advanced, items of equipment such as video cameras and laptop computers have become more affordable. This has enabled coaches to collect data during training and competition and analyse it afterwards. Examples of quantitative analysis may include:

▶ recording patterns of play
▶ recording successful passes in basketball
▶ examining the techniques used by a bowler in cricket
▶ the number of successful tackles in football
▶ the number of turnovers in a basketball match.

Quantitative data can be presented using graphical representations (see Figure 28.2). Science has proved an important asset in improving and enhancing performance. Scientific principles are often applied to help record sporting performance, and the data can be analysed by the athlete, the coach or a sports scientist, with the aim of improving future performances. There are many different ways of displaying data including graphs, histograms, bar charts and cumulative frequency graphs.

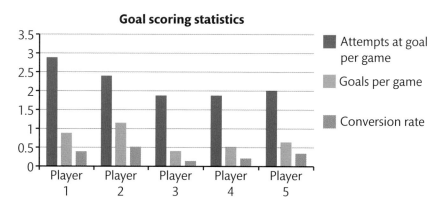

▶ **Figure 28.2:** Example of quantitative data presented in graphical form (a bar chart)

Key term

Key performance cues – performance-related technical or tactical factors which are important for focus during competition or training.

Qualitative analysis is less complicated than quantitative analysis, as it simply requires general observations of a performance to be carried out. The observer will look for **key performance cues** and use them to give judgements. This can be done by a coach, spectators or even other players. Because this method is largely subjective (or open to interpretation), the information gathered may be biased. Therefore, the more experience and knowledge an observer has, the more accurate the analysis is likely to be.

Horn or halo effect

The horn or halo effect is a psychological tendency which allows your judgement of another person or athlete to be unduly influenced by favourable (halo) or unfavourable (horns) first impressions based on appearances or a single **trait** of theirs, minimising the relevance of other evidence or data. This subjective and often inaccurate viewpoint may result in a negative bias and compromise any qualitative analysis.

Performance profiling cycle

An athlete should always evaluate their performance both during and after training or competition. Profiling will not be a one-off event. A coach will continue with the performance analysis and employ the various applications over short-, medium- and long-term goals. This creates a performance profiling cycle that is continuously used to try to improve the athlete's performance and iron out any remaining weaknesses.

▶ **Table 28.2:** The performance profiling cycle

Stage in the cycle	Description
1 Communication between coach and athlete/team	It is important when analysing performance that an honest, clear approach is adopted.
2 Establishing priorities	This will enable athletes to make decisions affecting future performance.
3 Identifying strengths and weaknesses	A coach may identify movements that are ineffective or unnecessary, and these can be altered or removed from a performance. Alternatively a coach can identify a physiological weakness which may be remedied with specific training methods and tested on a regular basis to detect any improvement.
4 Displaying data	There are many different ways of displaying data including graphs, histograms, bar charts, cumulative frequency graphs, radar diagrams and circles.
5 Agreed goals	An analysis of the data in relation to the chosen performance factors will indicate where improvements can be made, helping to create or clarify future goals.

ⅠⅠ PAUSE POINT Do you understand why communication between coach, athlete and team is important in performance profiling?

> **Hint** What other skills does a coach require to successfully improve aspects of an athlete's performance?

> **Extend** Research the career of a high profile coach or manager. What characteristics played an important part in their success?

Methods for analysing

Having access to analysis equipment and qualified support will enable athletes to focus on specific parts of their performance and training and develop strategies to improve. Such scientific support is usually only accessible to elite athletes because of the costs involved. However, 'low budget' alternatives using relatively inexpensive kit are available.

Cardiorespiratory tests

Unit 5 outlined how to carry out the following cardiorespiratory tests:

▸ Wingate anaerobic test

▸ 12-minute Cooper test

▸ Harvard step test.

However, there are also other tests that can be used to test cardiorespiratory function.

Astrand treadmill protocol

The Astrand treadmill test is designed to estimate an athlete's VO_2 max.

1 The athlete begins the test by walking on the treadmill and progressively builds their speed up to 8 km/h (5 mph) with an incline of 0 per cent. Once this speed is achieved, the athlete runs at this constant speed for 3 minutes.

2 After 3 minutes the gradient is increased to 2.5 per cent and the athlete runs for a further 2 minutes.

3 The gradient is then increased by 2.5 per cent every 2 minutes until the athlete fatigues and is unable to continue.

The athlete's VO_2 max is calculated using the following formula:

$$VO_2 \text{ max} = (\text{time} \times 1.444) + 14.99$$

'Time' is the athlete's total time on the treadmill in minutes and fractions of a minute.

Once the results are calculated they can be compared to the normative data for females and males found in Tables 28.3 and 28.4.

> **Key term**
>
> **VO_2 max** – the maximum amount of oxygen that can be taken in and utilised by the body. Also a measure of the endurance capacity of the cardiovascular and respiratory systems and exercising skeletal muscles.

▸ **Table 28.3:** VO_2 max normative data for females

Age	Poor	Below average	Average	Above average	Good	Excellent
13–19	<25.0	25.0–30.9	31.0–34.9	35.0–38.9	39.0–41.9	>41.9
20–29	<23.6	23.6–28.9	29.0–32.9	33.0–36.9	37.0–41.0	>41.0
30–39	<22.8	22.8–26.9	27.0–31.4	31.5–35.6	35.7–40.0	>40.0
40–49	<21.0	21.0–24.4	24.5–28.9	29.0–32.8	32.9–36.9	>36.9
50–59	<20.2	20.2–22.7	22.8–26.9	27.0–31.4	31.5–35.7	>35.7
60+	<17.5	17.5–20.1	20.2–24.4	24.5–30.2	30.3–31.4	>31.4

▶ **Table 28.4:** VO$_2$ max normative data for males

Age	Poor	Below average	Average	Above average	Good	Excellent
13–19	<35.0	35.0–38.3	38.4–45.1	45.2–50.9	51.0–55.9	>55.9
20–29	<33.0	33.0–36.4	36.5–42.4	42.5–46.4	46.5–52.4	>52.4
30–39	<31.5	31.5–35.4	35.5–40.9	41.0–44.9	45.0–49.4	>49.4
40–49	<30.2	30.2–33.5	33.6–38.9	39.0–43.7	43.8–48.0	>48.0
50–59	<26.1	26.1–30.9	31.0–35.7	35.8–40.9	41.0–45.3	>45.3
60+	<20.5	20.5–26.0	26.1–32.2	32.3–36.4	36.5–44.2	>44.2

YMCA cycle ergometer test

A cycle ergometer test involves the athlete cycling at 50 revolutions per minute for 6 minutes at a workload set at a level according to their gender and physical condition, as outlined in Table 28.5.

▶ **Table 28.5:** Workloads for YMCA cycle ergometer test

Unconditioned male	Conditioned male	Unconditioned female	Conditioned female
50–100 watts	100–150 watts	50–75 watts	75–110 watts

Their heart rate is taken in the last 10 seconds of each of the final 2 minutes of exercise (from 4:50–5:00 and from 5:50–6:00). The average of these two figures, corrected for your age (220 bpm – age), is used to estimate the VO$_2$ max.

Astrand cycle ergometer maximal test

The Astrand cycle ergometer maximal test is designed to estimate an athlete's VO$_2$ max. The athlete pedals on a cycle ergometer at a constant workload for 7 minutes. Heart rate is measured every minute and the **steady state** heart rate is determined.

1.5 mile running test

This test is best performed on an indoor athletics track, or on an outdoor track on a day when weather conditions will not adversely affect test results.

4   Perform a warm-up and stretching of major muscle groups.

5   On the starter's orders, run a distance of 1.5 miles as fast as you can.

6   Record the time taken.

7   Perform a standard cool down and stretching of major muscle groups.

Use Table 28.6 to interpret and analyse the results.

▶ **Table 28.6:** 1.5 mile running test VO$_2$ max normative data

Time (mins) for 1.5 mile run	VO$_2$ max (ml/kg/min)	Time (mins) for 1.5 mile run	VO$_2$ max (ml/kg/min)
<7.31	75	12.31–13.00	39
7.31–8.00	72	13.01–13.30	37
8.01–8.30	67	13.31–14.00	36
8.31–9.00	62	14.01–14.30	34
9.01–9.30	58	14.31–15.00	33
9.31–10.00	55	15.01–15.30	31
10.01–10.30	52	15.31–16.00	30
10.31–11.00	49	16.01–16.30	28
11.01–11.30	46	16.31–17.00	27
11.31–12.00	44	17.01–17.30	26
12.01–12.30	41	17.31–18.00	25

Queen's College step test

This test is similar to the Harvard step test, which was outlined in Unit 5.

A metronome is set up to the required number of steps per minute (males = 22 steps per minute, females = 24).

The athlete steps up and down on a step with a height of 41.3 cm in time with the metronome.

The test is stopped after 3 minutes and the athlete's heart rate is recorded. Once the results are calculated they can be compared to the normative data for males and females aged 16 to 19 shown in Table 28.7.

▶ **Table 28.7:** Queen's College step test data for men and women aged 16 to 19

Gender	Excellent	Above average	Average	Below average	Poor
Male	<121	121–148	149–156	157–162	>162
Female	<129	129–158	159–166	167–170	>170

Intensity testing (maximal and sub-maximal)

The PWC170 and PWC75% tests are examples of maximal and sub-maximal tests respectively. PWC stands for 'physical work capacity' – PWC170 approximates your working capacity at a heart rate of 170 beats per minute (bpm) and PWC75% estimates your working capacity at 75 per cent of maximum heart rate.

The tests are similar and require an athlete to perform three consecutive workloads on a cycle ergometer. Begin each test and measure the heart rate each minute and continue for 3–4 minutes until a steady heart rate is achieved. Continue the test for second and third workloads to achieve a heart rate of 115–130 and 130–145 bpm respectively.

Each of the three rates are graphed, with a line of best fit for the three points to estimate a workload that would achieve a heart rate of 170 bpm or 75 per cent of max heart rate.

Muscular assessment

Endurance

Endurance in the **upper body** can be assessed using the one-minute press-up test – see Unit 5, page 231 for details of how to administer this test.

The sit-up test assesses the endurance and development of your **abdominal** muscles.
1   Lie on a mat with your knees bent, and feet flat on the floor, with your arms folded across your body.
2   Raise yourself up to a 90° position and then return to the floor.
3   Your feet can be held by a partner if you wish.
4   The total number of sit-ups is recorded for 1 minute.

▶ **Table 28.8:** Sit-up test normative test data for men and women

Rating	Males	Females
Excellent	49–59	42–54
Good	43–48	36–41
Above average	39–42	32–35
Average	35–38	28–31
Below average	31–34	24–27
Poor	25–30	18–23
Very poor	11–24	3–17

Key term

Power – the ability to generate and use muscular strength quickly over a short period of time.

Power

The standard vertical jump test is used to assess the **power** of the quadriceps muscle group. You can digitally record the height of the jump, or alternatively gymnast's chalk may be used.

1   Stand with your dominant side against the board, feet together, and reach up as high as you can to record your standing reach height.
2   Only one dip of the arms and knees is permitted; make the jump while simultaneously touching the vertical jump board at the peak of your jump.
3   Perform three trials. No rest is required between trials. The time taken to observe and record the height of the jump is all that is needed for recovery between consecutive trials.

A nomogram can also be used to obtain rest results for this test – see Unit 5, page 241 for more information.

▶ **Table 28.9:** Vertical jump test normative test data for men and women

Rating	Males	Females
Above average	105+	90+
Average	95	80
Below average	<85	<70

Strength

The grip strength or dynamometer test measures the static strength of the power grip-squeezing muscles and can be tested using a grip dynamometer – see Unit 5, page 225, for more information.

Skill-related assessments

Flexibility

A good test of flexibility is the sit and reach test, which was covered in Unit 5 (see page 222).

A further test of flexibility is a goniometer test. This is used to measure the range of motion around a joint. The goniometer is placed at the axis of rotation (the joint), the arms are aligned with the bones of the attached segments and the measurement (in degrees) is taken.

Balance and stability

A simple method of testing balance and stability is the Romberg test. During this test the athlete stands with their feet together, arms at their sides and eyes closed. If the athlete begins to sway, cannot keep their eyes closed or moves from the standing support bases, there is likely to be a balance issue which may have ramifications on performance. The test can be made more challenging for the athlete by performing a single leg heel-to-toe movement with arms at the side and eyes closed.

A more dynamic method of testing balance and stability is the star excursion test. This is a low cost method in which a 'star' is constructed on the floor using tape. Cut four strips (2 to 3 metres in length), place two strips on the floor in the shape of a '+' and two in the shape of an 'x' at 45° to the '+'.

The athlete stands on one leg at the centre of the 'star' and reaches with the opposite leg in a direction on the star as far as possible. Mark the point on the tape and record the length from the centre for future reference and profiling. The test should be performed in all eight directions of the 'star' as shown in the photo.

▶ The star excursion test

Field tests

Field tests include the following, which were covered in Unit 5:

▶ Illinois agility test (page 238)

▶ 40-metre, 60-metre, 100-metre sprints (page 231)

▶ multi-stage fitness tests (page 226).

There are also two other field tests that can be used.

Pro-agility shuttle

To perform this test an athlete should run a 5-, 10- and 5-metre sprint. An athlete is required to sprint 5 metres in one direction, 10 metres in the opposite direction, then 5 metres in the opposition direction again to a finish. The test gives an indication of an athlete's speed and agility. Record the results and use them as a functional baseline to mark progress. This provides an effective method to measure an athlete's performance.

Arrowhead agility drill

The arrowhead agility test requires frequent changes of direction and speed. Research indicates athletes with increased agility are able to make the most of their physical attributes and coordinate more technical skills effectively.

Cones are laid out as shown in Figure 28.3. The athlete then runs as fast as possible to the middle cone, turns to run around the cone to the right of the arrow head, around the far cone at the tip of the arrow and back to the finish line. The athlete completes four attempts, two to the right of the arrow and two to the left. The final time is a combination of the best times for both left and right halves of the arrow. Record the results and use them as a functional baseline to mark progress, providing an effective method to measure an athlete's performance.

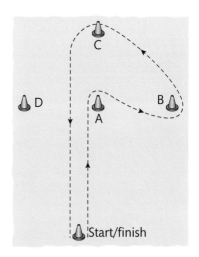

▶ **Figure 28.3:** The arrowhead agility drill

Health-related tests

The following can all be used to help assess the subject's health status:

▶ body mass index (BMI)

▶ skinfold test

▶ bioelectrical impedance analysis

For details about conducting and carrying out these tests, refer back to Unit 5 (pages 233–236).

Functional movement screening

Functional movement screening (FMS) is a system that analyses and grades movement patterns. The system of functional positioning measures any possible limitations or asymmetries within an athlete's range of movement. This process generates a score which is used to target potential problems and track the athlete's training or rehabilitation progress.

The movement tests include the overhead squat, hurdle step, in-line lunge, shoulder mobility, active straight leg raise, trunk stability push-up and rotary stability. Each movement pattern has specific criteria and is scored 3 (optimal), 2 (acceptable) or 1 (dysfunctional). If the athlete feels pain associated with any of the movements, they receive a score of zero and are considered susceptible to injuries related to that pattern. At this stage physiotherapy is sought as part of the training programme.

FMS can be performed anywhere, requires simple measuring equipment, creates a functional baseline to mark progress and provides an effective method to measure an athlete's performance.

Remember that, when you carry out any tests, it is important to assess the validity, accuracy, reliability, ease of use, cost, health and safety and accessibility of the methods you are using. More about these can be found in Table 28.11 on page 503.

▶ Athlete undergoing the three stages of FMS for shoulder mobility

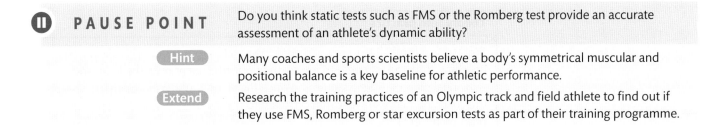

Discussion

In small groups discuss whether or not you think physiological laboratory tests replicate the pressures of sports performance sufficiently. If an athlete is used to performing in front of a crowd or outdoors, does the more 'clinical' environment of the laboratory have an effect and, thus, should the results be treated with caution? Discuss your findings with the rest of the class.

⏸ PAUSE POINT   Do you think static tests such as FMS or the Romberg test provide an accurate assessment of an athlete's dynamic ability?

Hint   Many coaches and sports scientists believe a body's symmetrical muscular and positional balance is a key baseline for athletic performance.

Extend   Research the training practices of an Olympic track and field athlete to find out if they use FMS, Romberg or star excursion tests as part of their training programme.

Techniques for sports analysis

When analysing sports performance, good technical skills are required for success.

In play and isolated skill situations

When studying sport it is possible to analyse performance through observation. This may be done either 'live', actually at a sports event, or by video after the event. In play, isolated skills can often be recorded using a range of technology. Coaches and athletes are increasingly using the medium of video to analyse performance in play, especially as video analysis software and GPS are available to help fine-tune any analysis and feedback.

The difference between quantitative and qualitative measures of performance were covered earlier on pages 481–482.

> **Key term**
>
> **Tactics** – the skills and strategies a player uses in any type of sport to be able to win.

Global positioning system (GPS) analysis

Global positioning system (GPS) is used in a wide range of sports from cycling to football. It is a precise tool that provides both athlete and coach with the ability to locate the position, and track the movement, of an athlete. GPS has the added advantage of being portable and can be worn by an athlete (or team of athletes) without discomfort, providing real-time data that is accurate, including a breakdown of distances covered and speeds achieved. For instance, professional football clubs often use GPS tracking vests to monitor player movement.

Both movement tracking via GPS, or motion analysis via more complex equipment and computer software, enable movement analysis using computerised data. Coaches use movement analysis as a method of enhancing and improving technique, correcting errors and aiding rehabilitation after injury.

Movement tracking can be inexpensive or costly.

- Inexpensive equipment provides basic data such as stride length, distance covered or jumped, average speed, etc.
- Costly equipment provides data such as angular motion, joint or total body kinematics.

Video analysis

Video offers both coaches and athletes an inexpensive means of analysing sports performance. Video footage offers considerable flexibility to examine and correct technique, and review individual and team performances. The aim is to record actual footage of an athlete or performer executing a skill, or a team playing a competitive game, for later analysis by a coach. Video can be used for analysis in two ways:

1 re-watching a game or performance during which the coach and performer can highlight numerous aspects of the performance
2 using the video footage as a data source for use with video analysis software.

Theory into practice

Professional football teams now record their matches on video. This allows the coaching staff and manager to review the performance of both the team and individual players. After a game, and once the video footage has been processed, the coaching staff will meet with the team to review team play (e.g. set pieces, positioning, etc.).

Video packages allow graphics to be drawn on top of the video footage to highlight and reinforce specific areas or phases of play, which can then be discussed as required. In addition, the footage allows statisticians or sports scientists to record functional data about the position of the ball, players involved, the time and outcome of passing, shooting, etc.

How do you think the coaching staff and manager will use this information to improve their team's performance?

Resources and process

Performance profiling requires coaches and athletes to create a reliable record of performance by employing a series of observations that can be analysed and used to make changes to an athlete's training. This process relies on two distinct approaches:

▶ **notational analysis** that uses different means to record elements of individual or team performance
▶ movement analysis that uses video to record the sporting impact of body movements.

Key term

Notational analysis – analysis which involves counting different aspects of sport performance. For example, a netball coach might use notational analysis to measure how many successful or unsuccessful passes are made by an individual player or team, or how many shots on or off target the goal shooter or goal attack have attempted.

To accommodate both these distinct approaches, video footage is essential. The aim of both approaches is to provide an accurate record of performance that can be reviewed at a later date. The equipment used for video analysis ranges in expense. An effective evaluation can be performed by a coach simply watching a performance and feeding back their findings or thoughts to the athlete. This can be done by recording a performance or drill using equipment as basic as the camera on a smartphone or a digital camcorder. Alternatively, technologically advanced equipment can be used to video techniques and evaluation software can be used to analyse specific movements. In both cases, coach and athlete must consider how the footage is to be recorded.

To extract the maximum amount of information, the following characteristics of the footage should be considered carefully to aid analysis:

▶ **position** – ensure the camera is positioned so it can capture the performance regardless of the angle or view

▶ **quantity** – consider how many attempts or games you wish to capture

▶ **duration** – ensure you have enough memory and battery life to capture a performance

▶ **quality** – make sure all aspects of the performance are clear to view (i.e. not a grainy image)

▶ **review** – check the footage meets the requirements for analysis.

Guidelines for video analysis

Here are some tips to ensure you get the most from video analysis.

▶ **Location** – camera positioning is important. Find a good vantage point with an uninterrupted view and the best position to capture critical performance areas. Be aware of environmental factors like sun, wind, rain and crowds!

▶ **Perspective** – most sports performances are best viewed from a position of height: sidelines simply will not do. This is often difficult but not impossible.

▶ **Storage** – footage could be presented in DVD/CD/memory stick format, mini discs and cassettes from video cameras, or a range of cards are also available.

▶ **Sharing** – as technology advances it has become possible to file share on a range of different applications.

▶ **Data protection/confidentiality** – never forget you will probably need consent to share any images captured.

▶ **Identity** – do not forget that, while you know which performer you are filming, the next person might not – be clear who you are observing in each scenario by using either audio or text confirmation.

Evaluation software

There are a number of evaluation software packages available, such as Dartfish, Kandle and Coach's Eye, which use a series of analysis tools that allow the coach to measure distance and angles directly over the video footage to aid interpretation of a performance. This software can slow down replay so that tiny movements can be studied and measured. Evaluation software also allows coaches to create a detailed report of the analysis of the performance, which can be referred to later. But this can be both expensive and time-consuming.

Notational analysis

Notational analysis studies movement patterns in team sports, and is primarily concerned with strategy and tactics. Notational analysis provides a factual record about the position of a ball, players involved, action concerned, and the time and outcome of a particular aspect (e.g. passing or shooting). The data is then presented in a statistical or graphical form, for example via a graph or bar chart, to help the coach and athlete to analyse a performance. This is different from the other aspect of performance profiling, or motion analysis, which focuses on an individual's biomechanical movement. In both cases the data collected tells you what happens, not how or why it happens.

The end product of notational analysis quantifies an athlete's or team's performance in a statistical or graphical format which highlights categories of strength or weakness for future consideration as part of a training programme. This information can then be used in planning tactics or strategy in subsequent matches to outperform opponents.

Theory into practice

Being able to analyse past performances and the performances of upcoming opponents is an essential tool used by modern football managers, and it is common to see a laptop or tablet on the training ground, or a television in the changing room.

Managers or head coaches will review video footage of matches to highlight the strengths and weaknesses of players as well as patterns of play. This enables the manager to give players feedback as part of the coaching process, highlighting specific areas to address.

List at least six specific areas of a football match (e.g. shots on target) you think a football manager would be interested in.

Notational analysis can be used to quantify the performance and movement patterns of an individual or a team. Think about when you have watched sport on television. Lots of statistics and diagrams are used, showing a player's distance covered in a game or the directions in which they have made their runs. These are different examples of 'movement' in sports. Other factors to look at when examining a player's movement include:

▸ work rate (for example, measuring heart rate using heart rate monitors)
▸ positional play and movement pattern (for example, how well a player fulfils the positional roles in a team or the movements a player performs during a game)
▸ distance covered (for example, how far a player has travelled during a game – sometimes broken down into walking, jogging and sprinting)
▸ movement patterns.

Positional play

Figure 28.4 shows an example of how the movement patterns and positional play of a footballer can be analysed.

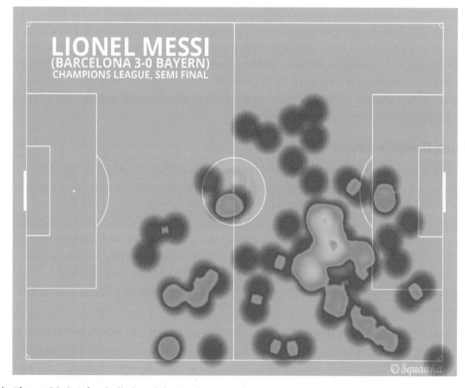

▸ **Figure 28.4:** A football player's 'action heat map'

Technical selections

The technical components you will look at in your technical model are dependent on the sport or activity you have chosen. You may produce your technical model around 'coaching points' of the different sports or activities based on the key **performance criteria** for that sport. For example, a technical component could be a successful pass to a team mate. Notational analysis can provide a factual record of the number of times each player makes a successful pass and use this data to aid future coaching requirements.

Key term

Performance criteria – aspects of sports performance which, if performed well, should lead to success.

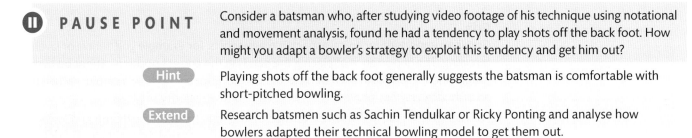

⏸ **P A U S E   P O I N T**   Consider a batsman who, after studying video footage of his technique using notational and movement analysis, found he had a tendency to play shots off the back foot. How might you adapt a bowler's strategy to exploit this tendency and get him out?

       Hint   Playing shots off the back foot generally suggests the batsman is comfortable with short-pitched bowling.

       Extend   Research batsmen such as Sachin Tendulkar or Ricky Ponting and analyse how bowlers adapted their technical bowling model to get them out.

Technique selection

Notational analysis often provides detailed information during a game or contest about which technical component is successful and which is not. For example, in basketball, one approach to a team's performance could be the ratio of shots taken to baskets scored. In golf, it may focus on the number of greens a player hits in regulation. Tennis is a good example of a sport that can benefit from detailed notational analysis both during and after a game. Graphical or statistical representations often tell whether the service to an opponent's forehand or backhand, or a wide service or a service down the centre of the court, is more successful. A combination of the notational analyses for an opponent may highlight a weakness to a service side (i.e. to their forehand or backhand). Consequently, the coach and athlete may choose a particular technique that targets this technical weakness and enhances their chance of victory over their opponent during a match.

To extract the fullest information from notational analysis, it is important to remember that technical components should not always be considered in isolation as they are often dependent on one another for successful athletic performance.

Body position

One of the most important aspects from a technical perspective is the body position of the athlete. If you consider the golf swing, every stage must be coordinated and executed correctly.

Shooting

Shooting is a technical component required in many sports. It is among the most used technical component in net games. Indicators of shooting behaviour in tennis, for example, such as the distribution of shot type (e.g. forehand or backhand) and of shot outcomes (e.g. where the ball landed on the court), allow both coach and athlete to determine which type of shot proved more successful against an opponent. An analysis of shot selection in tennis is easily transferred to numerical or graphical formats for evaluation.

Footwork

A tennis player's movement on the court is vital. Tennis performance depends on quick bursts of speed interspersed with variations of fast, side-to-side movements. In racket sports, footwork is often a key indicator of the potential success of other technical components. For example, correct footwork allows the athlete to be in a position for an effective shot or ball strike. Statistics show that 70 per cent of missed or poorly hit shots are due to poor footwork.

Balance

Static and dynamic balance are basic skills needed in practically every sport and exercise activity. From football to cricket, changing your centre of gravity to match your moves is key to skill execution. Identifying whether or not an athlete is 'balanced' during execution of a skill will contribute to the overall outcome's success or failure and can be recorded as such for analysis.

Grip

Grip is an important technical aspect in many sports, for example golf, tennis or javelin throwing. The importance of placing the hands in the correct position cannot be over-exaggerated. There is no such thing as the perfect grip, but holding a club or racket in an orthodox way has proved to be successful for the majority of players.

For example, in golf, a 'V' must be formed on the right hand by the thumb and lower section of the forefinger, pointing between the chin and the right shoulder, and only two knuckles are visible on the left hand to the player.

Stance

In combat sports such as boxing, the stance (the position of the body, particularly the feet) of the athlete is paramount. These sports require good balance and coordination, combined with the optimal stance. Within boxing, the most important factor when considering stance is perfect balance, enabling the boxer to move quickly and smoothly, shifting weight constantly from one leg to another and punching effectively. The collection of stance data (southpaw or orthodox) can be combined with other data (e.g. successful punch or defence) to determine the relative success of the stance adopted.

Kicking

A variety of kicking styles has evolved to suit different sports, ball types, game rules and the part that kicking plays in the game. Notational analysis is important in sports such as football to help determine the ratio of shots on target to goals or the shot accuracy with each foot (i.e. left or right).

Throwing

This is central to many sports (e.g. cricket, American football and rugby). Due to the differences in the type of ball (and the reasons for throwing), there are different techniques for different sports. However, all techniques can be noted in terms of success or failure or the ratio of throws attempted to throws finding their target.

Catching

One of the most difficult balls to catch in sport is the high kick in rugby. It is an important skill that every rugby player should learn. As it is likely the opposition will be surrounding you, you will need to catch the ball in the air. Notational analysis can help rugby players and coaches to track the number of catches made during a game, and whether these catches were made from a high kick or line-out.

Fielding

In cricket, when fielding, you should 'attack' the ball (move towards the ball if it is hit towards you, rather than standing still and waiting for it). During the course of a game, fielders will attempt to take catches, throw the ball at the stumps in the hope of a run out, or react quickly to prevent a run. In all cases, notational analysis can record the action concerned.

Batting

In cricket, there are many batting shots that require a high level of technical ability. For example, in a forward defensive shot the aim is to put the bat in front of the wicket to stop the ball from hitting the wicket. Alternatively, a batsman may adopt a more aggressive shot and hook a bowler for six runs. There are numerous shots in a batsman's repertoire and notational analysis can record which shots were used and how many runs were taken as a result. This can be displayed graphically (as a wagon wheel) or statistically by the ratio of balls faced to runs scored.

Dribbling

Dribbling must have an end product, such as a shot at goal/basket, etc. or a key pass. If it does not, the dribble is deemed unsuccessful. In either case, notational analysis can record the different outcomes.

Sprinting

Sprinting is a key aspect of many team sports (for example, a football winger sprinting after the ball to make a cross).

Two key elements in sprinting are stride length and frequency. Stride length is the distance an athlete covers with each stride (measured in metres). Stride frequency is the number of strides made in a specific time (usually one second). It is possible for notational analysis to record both elements or, indeed, the number of short sprints a footballer executes throughout a match.

Jumping

In track and field sports, there are a number of jumping events such as long jump, triple jump, high jump and pole vault.

These events are highly technical, since if the athlete has a poor technique it is likely to result in poor performance. Notational analysis can help in a number of areas: for example, recording the distance from the perfect take-off point, the number of foul jumps or the angle of take-off.

Success rates

Notational analysis provides a factual record of the technical components of a sport or event. The results, whether graphical or statistical, allow a deeper analysis of the relative success or failure of each component. Graphical representations allow for an easy-to-follow illustration for the athlete or team to digest and, together with a coach, identify areas or technical components that require further attention as part of the wider coaching cycle.

Remember that, when you are evaluating any performance data, it is important to assess the validity, accuracy, reliability, ease of use, cost, health and safety and accessibility of the methods you are using. More about these can be found in Table 28.11 on page 503.

 PAUSE POINT   Can you think of any disadvantages of analysing a technical component in isolation?

Hint   A great many sports movements are compound movements (i.e. a combination of
Extend   more than one technical component in succession).

Think of a complex sports movement and try to break it down into its technical components for further performance analysis.

Sports analyst Amy Hall and the performance analysis proposal

Amy is a postgraduate student studying for her MSc in Performance Analysis. She answered an advertisement for a part-time sports analyst to work with a county cricket league club that recently received a large development grant to invest in training resources for the team.

Amy played cricket while at university and excelled at both batting and bowling. This, combined with her sports analysis background, is why the cricket club offered her the role of part-time analyst.

Amy's first task is a tough one. The club's head coach has asked her to draft a report on the possible methods of analysing performance for batting and bowling, and to provide a summary of the relevance and usability of these methods. This report will then be discussed at the next committee meeting to decide on what equipment to purchase with the grant money.

Amy has to draw up a report for the cricketers that addresses the following key content of the methods of sports performance analysis:

- aims of performance profiling – how this can improve the overall performance of players and the team
- methods of analysis – what field or laboratory test she would recommend using.

Check your knowledge

1 Write down your own definition of performance profiling and explain why you think it is important in a modern coaching setting.

2 List as many techniques available to coaches for sports analysis as you can.

Assessment practice 28.1   A.P1 A.M1 A.D1

You have secured a position as a coach at a university rowing club. In addition to general fitness coaching, the club coach has asked you to design a presentation on the methods for analysing sports performance. The club has high expectations for success when competing against other universities this year and has decided to pay closer attention to the performance and training of all the club's rowers.

The club is expecting between 30 to 40 rowers to attend a pre-season meeting and you are on first. You have a 30-minute slot (20 minutes for a presentation and 10 minutes for questions and answers) to give your presentation. The club president has asked you to prepare a presentation for all those in the audience, in a format of your choice (PowerPoint®, posters, slideshow, etc.). The presentation must address the following key points:

- performance profiling
- methods for analysing
- techniques for sports analysis.

You will need to carry out some research on these points and demonstrate you understand what each of the them mean and how they may be applicable to rowers and their training. Make sure your presentation is relevant and informative. You will need to outline the importance of performance analysis and how this might benefit performance.

Plan

- What is the task? What is my presentation being asked to address?
- How confident do I feel in my own abilities to complete this task? Are there any areas I think I may struggle with?

Do

- I know how to examine methods for analysing sports performance.
- I can identify when my presentation may have gone wrong and adjust my thinking/approach to get myself back on course.

Review

- I can explain what the task was and how I approached construction my presentation.
- I can explain how I would approach the more difficult elements differently next time (i.e. what I would do differently).

B Explore ideal models, benchmarks and protocols for performance analysis

Coaches will often recognise potential from observing performance; good coaches realise that even the most gifted of performers can improve. To achieve this they often employ an ideal model or benchmark to perfect a technique. An outstanding coach will be aware of where such ideal models or benchmarks may be obtained and how best to use them to correct or improve technical skills or tactical performances.

Information sources

Observation/recordings

Observation and video analysis are an easy way to understand and analyse the performance of an athlete. This is best done by watching an elite or experienced athlete and noting their techniques, strengths and possible weaknesses. Having your performance filmed will provide you with an objective record of what happened with the advantage of being able to analyse it in slow motion or real time and compare it against the benchmark or perfect model.

Regardless of the type of benchmark or perfect model being viewed, it is important that both coach and athlete consider and evaluate the validity, relevance and accuracy of the source material being used. It is important the footage, images or commentary being used are genuine (i.e. not doctored), relevant and beneficial to the athlete. If not, they may give a false impression of what is achievable or, in some circumstances, may prove dangerous to replicate. Make sure the sources are reputable (i.e. sports governing bodies, reputable accounts on YouTube, television channels or recognised sports magazines/periodicals) and integrate these benchmarks into the wider coaching cycle.

Videos

Video analysis through observations and recordings is useful for identifying and correcting faults with an athlete's technique. There are a number of performance benchmarks that might be analysed using video footage, including:

▶ head and body positions during a performance (e.g. golf swing)
▶ angle of release for throwing events (e.g. javelin)
▶ joint angles and velocities (e.g. throwing an upper-cut punch in boxing)
▶ ball release velocity and trajectory of ball path (e.g. cricket bowling).

 **PAUSE POINT**   What factors might you need to keep in mind when viewing video footage of a golf swing?

        Hint   What biomechanical properties, issues surrounding perspective or camera specification would you need to consider in order to try and replicate the skill or technical selections on show?

        Extend   What filming strategies might you employ to ensure that, if you were filming a benchmark or perfect model, your footage is not blurred and able to demonstrate the key movements for others to analyse?

Pictures

Pictures can serve as a useful reference or benchmark for technical and tactical models. For example, football formations are often reinforced with images or pictures that illustrate where players should operate during attacking and defending phases of play.

Commentary

A commentary is generally an audio recording made by a coach or observer, usually in a match or competitive situation, that provides an indication or description of how an athlete or team are performing. This is a cheap source of information but any analysis is subjective because it provides only the viewpoint of the observer, and they can only record what they think or believe they see is happening.

National Governing Body sources

Every sport's **National Governing Body (NGB)** will publish a series of coaching manuals from Level 1 to Level 4. Within these manuals will be technical and tactical guidance relevant to their sport. They are excellent sources of information and often contain guidance on perfect models and physical and psychological requirements for that sport.

Comparative level of performance

NGBs are the custodians of specific performance data that demonstrates the various levels of performance (novice to elite athlete) that can be used as indicators in performance profiling and the coaching process, or enable athletes of a specific level to obtain additional funding towards their training costs.

Coaching courses

Most coaches will have gained a recognised qualification at some point in their career. It is generally accepted that to improve you should become qualified. Most NGBs will offer up-to-date qualifications that will not only train you but also keep you informed of relevant changes in coaching protocol and provide source material for performance benchmarks and perfect models.

▶ **Governing body coaching pyramids** – NGBs of sport have developed coaching awards which are designed to support a developing coach. Almost all NGBs now have a coach education structure which produces qualifications from the assistant coach (Level 1) up to an elite sports coach (Level 4 and 5). It is important that a coach aims to gain the appropriate qualifications required to analyse the performance of the athlete with whom they are working. This ensures that the athlete receives the support and experience recommended by the NGB.

▶ **Specialist qualifications** – higher education institutions offer specialist qualifications in sports analysis. These qualifications take the form of BSs (Hons) or MSc, and aim to develop a specialist knowledge that equips practitioners to carry out detailed or high levels of performance analysis.

> **Research**
>
> In small groups, research one of the NGBs; specifically research the coaching material or services available – can you find examples of ideal models or benchmarks for performance? Present your findings as a short leaflet to share with the whole group. This will mean that you will have a resource for each of the professional bodies.

Academic papers, journals and documents

Many academic papers are published each year, alongside journals and other relevant documents, that provide information about performance models and benchmarks. The best ones to consult will depend on the sport you are assessing.

> **Key term**
>
> **National governing bodies (NGBs)** – responsible for the rules and organisation of competitions for their sports. They also select representative teams and deal with funding and disciplinary issues.

They are available to help provide information about:

▶ **coaching** – The *International Sport Coaching Journal* (ISCJ) is published by Human Kinetics. Through its peer-reviewed research articles, essays, and project applications, the ISCJ aims to progress the education, development and best practice of coaches. The journal also presents relevant information about performance models and benchmarking

▶ **psychology** – The *Journal of Applied Sport Psychology* aims to advance thought, theory and research on applied aspects of sport and exercise psychology that promotes further research and intervention strategies that may be used in the analysis of sports performance

▶ **biomechanics** – The *Journal of Biomechanics* publishes research that examines the use of the principles of mechanics to address biological problems. The articles help to show how coaches and sports scientists can further analyse movement in a sporting capacity as part of the wider coaching process

▶ **nutrition** – The *Journal of the International Society of Sport Nutrition* examines the effects of sports nutrition and supplementation strategies that might complement or enhance training programmes and strategies

▶ **fitness training** – The *American College of Sports Medicine Health and Fitness Journal* examines the latest research in fitness training techniques that will aid performance profiling and fitness training as part of the wider coaching process

▶ **coaching manuals** – most NGBs produce their own coaching manuals, all of which contain sections on performance profiling and notational analysis guidance.

Coaches, tutors and sports scientists

As well as published sources of information about ideal performance models and benchmarks, the most obvious source is to consult with other coaches, tutors and sports scientists who are engaged in performance analysis.

Coach's ideal model

As part of the coaching process, athletes and coaches will evaluate the data from the notational and movement analysis. The planning component of the coaching process requires the coach to apply an ideal model to the training programme that helps the athlete adapt or change their performance for the better. Further analysis can take place requiring additional adaptation, and so the cyclical coaching process continues, until the ideal model is replicated by the athlete.

Benchmark data

Benchmark data is generally used to measure the progress of an individual or team over time, as and when a new training programme is implemented. However, it can also be used as a valuable coaching aid if an individual's test results are compared to competitors or to foster competition and motivation within a team setting. Athletes displaying a similar ability in the different tests undertaken, or similar results in a wider performance analysis, can be put to work together, generating a better training environment. In this way athletes will not be asked to work in a group that is too advanced or not advanced enough, in terms of potential ability and achievement.

Internet and social media

The Internet and social media are fast becoming platforms to establish ideal performance models and benchmarks. The speed and simplicity at which information can be uploaded and disseminated allows coaches and athletes to share ideas, technical models, tactical ideas and the latest research and results. It is important that footage, images or commentary being used are genuine (i.e. not doctored), and relevant and beneficial to the athlete. If not, they may give a false impression of what is achievable or, in some circumstances, may prove dangerous if they are imitated.

Match statistics

In sports such as athletics or swimming, the benchmark could be an athlete's personal best time or distance. However, in many other sports match statistics are important and are a relevant source of information regarding the performance of an individual or a team. Football, rugby union, rugby league and ice hockey are increasingly accompanied by statistical information concerning factors such as passing or time in the opposition's half. Sports such as cricket are naturally biased towards statistical information, yet even in cricket new innovations such as 'wagon wheel' run displays or 'Manhattan' run/wicket graphs are an increasingly common sight on television screens.

Match statistics provide a ready-made analysis of both individual and team performances. They come with the added advantage of being born out of a competitive environment.

> **Discussion**
>
> Match statistics are a key feature in football and many other team sports. We are told about a team's possession percentage or how many metres a player has covered during the game. What if the team with the least amount of possession ends up winning or the player who has covered the least amount of ground ends up 'man of the match'? Do match statistics tell the whole story or do we put too much emphasis on them?
>
> In small groups consider whether match statistics play an important role in understanding the game or are they unimportant and often unrelated to the results? Feed back your thoughts to the rest of the class.

Records and finish times

▶ **National records** – relevant for events such as athletics or swimming, national records are available from NGBs and provide an indication of elite benchmarks and performance. For example, see www.britishathletics.org.uk/world-class/gb-records/.

▶ **Age group records** – age group records for individual sports are available from NGBs and provide an indication of elite benchmarks and performance.

▶ **Finish time data** – provides comparative data, for example from track and field athletes or swimmers. This information is generally available from NGBs.

Protocols and material for performance analysis

Summary of sources of information

It is important that the source material used for performance analysis is relevant and accurate. Regardless of whether you are looking at ideal models or benchmarks, ensure your information comes from a reputable source such as an NGB, academic institution or reputable sports analysis organisation. Moreover, ensure your material is valid by being sports-specific – there is little point in coaching a footballer how to perfect a throw-on by using footage of a two-handed basketball pass.

Timing

Performance analysis can be a very time-consuming process. If an analysis is conducted, the coach will have to review the performance, interpret the data that has been collected, fully evaluate it and develop the results into training programmes or tactics. For an analysis to be effective, it is important that the coach and players allocate sufficient time to evaluate findings as part of the process. If evaluation is hurried, errors are likely to occur and the findings may be inaccurate.

During or after performance

Most analysis is done during performance as that is when the athlete is executing technical and tactical skills, and placing their body under physical and psychological pressure. Benchmark tests should not normally be carried out immediately after a performance as the athlete is likely to be suffering the effects of fatigue. However, in certain circumstances, it is possible to subject an athlete to post-performance analysis: this is usually done as a physical fitness indicator to determine the athlete's rate of recovery immediately after an event.

Timing of benchmark tests

Benchmark tests, for example VO_2 max tests, are not designed to be undertaken every day or week: they should be scheduled to take account of the athlete's season and performance events. In the case of a footballer training from July to May, benchmark tests are best taken pre-season (in July), twice during mid-season (November and January) and towards the end of the season (in May).

By spacing out the timings, an athlete can get a clearer picture of how they are performing throughout a season, which may give an indication of any additional training requirements.

Duration of benchmark tests

The duration of a benchmark test depends on which test is being undertaken. However, few last more than 10 minutes.

 **PAUSE POINT**

As a coach, why would you generally discourage the undertaking of a benchmark test after a training session?

Hint   Fatigue will have a negative impact on an athlete's ability to execute technical and tactical skills correctly.

Extend   Can you think of any circumstances when you might undertake a benchmark test after a training session?

Preparation of materials for gathering information

When you have decided which performance criteria you are interested in assessing and analysing, you must gather together any necessary equipment or other materials that may be needed. The equipment should also be checked to make sure that it is working, and its use assessed for any possible health and safety implications during the assessment. For instance, you would not want a star athlete to be injured by tripping over a video camera's tripod!

Selecting and reviewing equipment needed

The equipment a coach can use to perform an analysis varies greatly. A clipboard can be used to record observations during a match, and a simple stopwatch to record times. But more elite performers require highly detailed analysis with more advanced equipment, such as movement analysis software, force platforms and respiratory analysers.

The equipment needed will depend on the analysis to be conducted, but can include:
▶ video and/or audio recording equipment
▶ a computer, tablet or phone
▶ movement sensors
▶ modified equipment
▶ dynamometers
▶ power meters
▶ a stopwatch.

It can also be useful to have existing performance documentation to hand to act as a reference point during the analysis.

Creation of materials for analysis

As well as gathering together equipment, it can be useful to create documentation that will help you conduct the analysis (see Figure 28.5). Examples of the materials that might be useful are shown in Table 28.10.

▶ **Table 28.10:** Materials that might be useful during a performance analysis

Piece of equipment	Useful for:
Observation checklist	All sports – general overview of types of skills exhibited
Tally chart	All sports – notational analysis or snapshot of frequency with which an athlete demonstrates a skill, with added success rates
Tick list	All sports – general overview detailing if an athlete attempts or performs a skill from a pre-determined list
Formatted recording sheets	Sports-specific – recording the type and frequency of exhibited technical skills
Data sheets	Sports-specific (e.g. basketball, volleyball, etc.) detailing areas of play, other specifications and player requirements
Statistics sheets	Sports-specific (e.g. basketball, cricket) detailing player information, scoring systems and other statistical information
Adapted existing performance documentation	All sports – general written record compiled by a coach detailing athlete's continued progress in technical, tactical, physical and psychological fields

Fitness test results

Name:

Age (yrs/mths):

Height (m):

Weight (kg):

Body mass index (BMI kg/m^2):

Informed consent form completed *(insert date)*:

Fitness component	Fitness test	T1	T2	Av. result	Units	Interpretation of test results (rating)
Flexibility	Sit and reach				cm	
Strength	Handgrip dynamometer				kg	
		Result				
Aerobic endurance	1.5 mile run test				ml/kg/min	
Speed	35-metre sprint				s	
Muscular endurance	1-minute sit-up				Number of reps	
Body composition	Bioelectrical impedance analysis (BIA)				% body fat	

▶ **Figure 28.5:** A fitness testing data collection sheet

Considerations for the evaluation of performance measures

Be careful where you find your information about records, ideal models or even coaching techniques. Ensure your information comes from a reputable source such as an NGB, academic institutions or reputable sports analysis organisation. If you are unclear as to the **validity** of your source material, it may nullify your performance analysis process.

There are several key issues that will influence the quality of your analysis, and which you need to consider with your methods and resources. These are shown in Table 28.11.

> **Key term**
>
> **Validity** – whether a measurement actually measures what it is intended to measure.

▶ **Table 28.11:** Considerations for the evaluation of performance data

Influence	Description
Validity	Validity is essential in analysis as it relates to whether you are actually measuring what you planned to measure. There are different types of validity, but two key types are internal validity and external validity. • **Internal validity** relates to whether the results of the analysis can be attributed to the different treatments in the study. This means you need to ensure you have controlled everything that could affect the results of the analysis. • **External validity** relates to whether or not the results of the analysis can be applied to the real world.
Reliability	This relates to whether, if the analysis was repeated, you would get the same or similar results. In qualitative analysis, reliability relates to the same or different coaches or analysts placing results into the same or similar categories on different occasions. There are certain factors you should take into account that can affect reliability. For example: • errors can happen when coaches do not know how to use the equipment correctly • the equipment may be poorly maintained • the wrong type of equipment may be selected. Test–retest reliability relates to doing the same test on different occasions and getting the same (or similar) results. An example of a test–retest reliability issue in sport is the measurement of heart rate. Heart rate can be affected by different factors, such as temperature, time of day, diet, sleep patterns, physical activity levels and alcohol. If you measured the heart rate on the same person at the same time of day, but on different days, you could get different measurements.
Relevance	Always ask yourself: are you doing the right thing? It is important to make sure what you are doing or analysing is connected or appropriate to the performance being considered or carried out. For example, there would be little point in analysing the front crawl swimming technique of a marathon runner.
Usability	Ensure the equipment employed in an analysis is fit for use. For example, a video camera that is not waterproof should not be used to film a football match in the rain. Make sure any data you collect is usable; coaches or athletes do not want to be baffled by statistics.
Cost	Make sure the cost of analysis (equipment, time or personnel) is affordable. There is little point in planning a complex 3D analysis of a golf swing if your budget stretches to only a few hundred pounds.
Accuracy	Any analysis undertaken by a coach and athlete should be free from measurement errors. The coach should be aware how all equipment operates. For example, make sure the cuff of a blood pressure monitor is fitted correctly or timings are all recorded to the same decimal place.
Health and safety	Always ensure that any analysis an athlete undertakes is safe and will not cause injury or harm. This applies to the equipment used and the area in which the analysis is taking place.
Accessibility	The analysis process and the results should be available to the athlete when required and the results available for viewing or discussion with the coach when convenient to both parties.

 **PAUSE POINT**   What considerations should the evaluation of a Queen's College step test performance measure for your class or group include?

Hint   List any potential reliability, usability, accuracy, and health and safety considerations.

Extend   How do you think coaches might address similar considerations for their elite athletes who train in different locations around the world throughout the training year?

Sports analyst Amy Hall and the performance analysis models – part 1

Amy is progressing well as the cricket club's new sports analyst. Following a successful committee meeting at which the members approved the purchase of video equipment, evaluation software and various inexpensive field testing equipment (body fat callipers, cones, heart rate monitors, stopwatches, etc.), the club coach has asked Amy to help with the next step in the club's performance analysis programme.

Amy has been asked to work with the club coach to explore ideal models, benchmarks and protocols for performance analysis of the players. To make sure all components of the performance analysis are apparent, Amy has been tasked to produce a presentation in two halves: one for batting and one for bowling.

Amy has to make sure that her presentation:

- identifies, assesses and evaluates established ideal benchmarks for batting and bowling.
- includes detailed protocols and materials (e.g. what field or laboratory tests to use and what to video for analysis) for performance analysis for batting and bowling.

Check your knowledge

1 List the potential sources of information you would trust to provide a valid and reliable ideal model or benchmarks for the performance analysis of a footballer.

Assessment practice 28.2   B.P2 B.P3 B.M2 B.M3 B.D2

In Assessment practice 28.1 you prepared a presentation on methods of analysing sports performance for a university rowing club. Your presentation proved a success.

To take the season's aim of high expectations forward, the club president has asked you to prepare a report on the ideal models, benchmarks and protocols for performance analysis of the club's rowers. This will then be studied by the club's coaches and play an integral role in the season's training schedule.

To make sure all components of the performance analysis are addressed, the club president has secured the use of the university's sports science laboratories and analysis equipment. This is a rare opportunity, so your report should:

- identify, assess and evaluate established ideal models for performance analysis in rowing
- include detailed protocols and materials (e.g. what field or laboratory tests to use and what to video for analysis) for performance analysis for rowing.

You will need to carry out some research on these points and demonstrate that you understand how they may be applicable to rowers and their training. Make sure your report is relevant and informative. Remember, you have access to all the university's laboratory testing equipment and their indoor rowing machines, which may be very useful.

Plan

- What is the task? What is my report being asked to address?
- How confident do I feel in my own abilities to complete this task? Are there any areas I think I may struggle with?

Do

- I know how to explore ideal models, benchmarks and protocols for performance analysis in rowing.
- I can identify when my presentation may have gone wrong and adjust my thinking/approach to get myself back on course.

Review

- I can explain what the task was and how I constructed my report.
- I can explain how I would approach the more difficult elements differently next time (i.e. what I would do differently).

C Carry out an analysis of the sports performance of an individual athlete or team

Carrying out a sport analysis

Once the analysis protocols have been established, athletes can be filmed using video equipment during a live performance or tested using specific equipment under laboratory conditions. In both cases, a quantity of data will be produced which then needs to be presented in a format so that the coach can properly analyse the performance.

Throughout the analysis you should keep your focus on the performance and processes, not on the outcome. This involves both not getting 'caught up in events' and not being 'blindsided' by a successful outcome: an athlete may achieve success by employing a certain technique or tactic, but could they have employed it even more successfully?

Observation environments

Athlete in live competitive performance

Live competitive performances are ideal scenarios for analysing athletes under pressure. A competitive scenario will add factors such as pressure and anxiety to a performance, alongside external pressures such as crowd noise, all of which may further exacerbate technical or tactical flaws. This is often in contrast to training sessions where such pressures are often absent.

A live competitive performance is often filmed and reviewed the following day, when the coach or analyst will highlight key points or statistics which did not come to light during the game or event. This happens regularly in games such as football. With 22 players on the pitch at any one time, it is difficult for coaches to concentrate on everyone and individual performances. Once the recorded performance has been viewed and the statistical information analysed (e.g. percentage of passes completed, shots on target, etc.), the coach can discuss the team and individual performances with each of the players in greater depth.

Video of performance

When filming an athlete there is a chance that recording may have **perspective error** because you are filming a dynamic action. This is easily explained using a 100-metre sprinter. You may be interested in recording the time at 10-metre intervals, with the camera positioned at the 50-metre point. Figure 28.6 shows that you would need to film the athlete going through all the points at 10-metre intervals. The perspective error can be seen at the 80-metre point as the camera's line of sight is not perpendicular to the athlete's direction of travel, so you cannot say exactly when the athlete reaches the 80-metre point.

> **Key term**
>
> **Perspective error** – an error where objects seem to get bigger or smaller as they move towards and away from the camera and you cannot effectively judge their position.

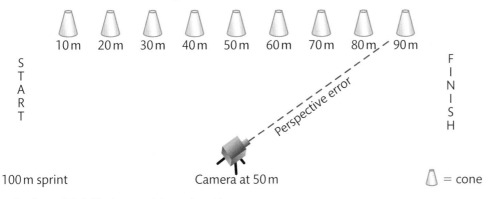

▶ **Figure 28.6:** Filming an athlete using video

Conditioned benchmark test

It can be difficult to decide which of the numerous tests to use when testing an athlete. Where possible, use benchmark tests as these can be repeated to judge an athlete's progress. However, you should ensure that, when the tests are repeated, they are performed in a similar environment or conditions to ensure the reliability, accuracy and validity of the results. For example, a coach will ask an athlete to perform the Illinois agility test every three months in a sports hall, rather than outdoors in different weather conditions.

Gym- or lab-based fitness test

By their very nature, gyms and labs tend to be reliable environments in which to carry out fitness tests as they are generally stable in terms of temperature and humidity, and they are relatively unaffected by weather and time of year.

To administer laboratory-based fitness tests safely and effectively, you need good knowledge and understanding of the test and how it is relevant to the performance analysis of the athlete(s) concerned. You will need to be well-planned and organised throughout the administration of the test(s). Use an appropriate data collection sheet to record the athlete's results as you go along (see Figure 28.5 on page 502). Ideally, for reliability of results, all fitness tests selected should be repeated. However, there may not be enough time to do this, and you may need to take this into account when giving feedback to the athlete or coach.

Use the correct units of measurement for the fitness tests you have chosen to administer. For some tests you may need to use tables to process raw data before you can interpret what the test results mean and provide feedback to the athlete. For example, the Astrand treadmill test result is recorded as a time. Use the formula (see page 483) to calculate the predicted VO_2 max of the athlete. You can provide feedback verbally to the athlete or coach, but ensure that your findings are published as a data table or spreadsheet in your report.

> **Theory into practice**
>
> If you want to search for performance analysis information concerning specific sports, look at one of these websites:
> - sports sciences – www.bases.org.uk
> - tennis – www.itftennis.com
> - football and rugby – www.prozonesports.com
> - general sport – www.eis2win.co.uk/pages/performance_analysis.aspx
> - cricket – www.lords.org/lords/mcc-cricket-academy/performance-analysis/
> - swimming – www.swimming.org/britishswimming/swimming/world-class/

Collating and presenting analysis results

As we have seen, information gathered during or after performance analysis will generate either quantitative or qualitative information, or a combination of both. The way that you collate and present these different types of information is important: the easier something is to understand, the better. Coaches and athletes do not want to be blinded with statistics: they want the information to be presented in a usable and informative format.

Collation methods

Once all the visual or statistical data has been collected from observing a performance, it has to be gathered together or collated into a usable format for use by the coach and performer.

Statistical analysis

Statistical analysis requires the coach to describe the data analysed and identify any trends that can be fed back to the athlete to help improve performance. For example, during a football match a striker had more shots on target using his left foot (7 out of 8 attempts) than his right foot (3 out of 6 attempts). The coach will then go on to present these findings in a graphical or numerical format for further study.

Totalling tallies

Tally charts are a useful tool when observing sporting performance. A tally chart may include simply counting performance factors such as:

▶ shots on target in football
▶ number of fouls committed in basketball
▶ wide balls bowled in cricket
▶ number of double serves in badminton
▶ number of shots played to the forehand in tennis.

Averages

Averages are simple numerical indicators that provide an indication of overall performance. They can provide an overview of factors such as:

▶ average speed in mph of a bowler during an over
▶ average drive distance for a golfer off the tee.

Averages can also be displayed in graphical format such as, for example, a bar chart.

Percentages

Much like averages, percentages are simple numerical indicators that provide an indication of overall performance. They can provide an overview of factors such as:

▶ possession time for both teams during a game of football
▶ number of successful first serves during a tennis match
▶ successful double out-shots in darts.

Percentages can also be displayed in graphical format such as, for example, a pie chart.

Summary statements

Summary statements should emphasise the key points or findings of the analysis for the benefit of the coach and athlete. The statements should be brief and to the point.

Presentation formats to allow conclusions to be made

Once your information has been collated, it needs to be presented in a way that is accessible for the coach and athlete. There are many different ways of displaying your data including graphs, histograms, bar charts and cumulative frequency graphs.

Statistical evidence

As a written format, summary statements are probably best presented in bullet point format, complemented by additional graphical or tabulated data such as bar charts, pie charts or tally charts.

Graphs

Graphs are an excellent method of turning raw data into an easy-to-understand picture for rapid examination. Graphs are a useful tool for comparing data over a period of time and therefore highlighting any trends, whether they are improvements or deteriorations in the factors of performance being tested. Bar charts and histograms are suitable examples of graphs for visualising comparative data (for example, passes with left foot versus passes with right foot, etc.). Line graphs are useful for showing trends (for example, an athlete's heart rate during a game).

Distribution diagrams

A normal distribution of data means that most of the test or analysis results within that data set are close to the 'average', while a few results are at one extreme or the other. Normal distribution curves have the following characteristics.

▶ The curve has a single peak.

▶ It is bell-shaped.

▶ The mean (average) lies at the centre of the distribution.

▶ The shape of the distribution is determined by the mean and the standard deviation.

From the point of view of performance analysis, distribution diagrams are useful tools to highlight the average performance of a group of athletes, to see who is underperforming and who is exceeding expectations.

PAUSE POINT

For the benefit of coaches and athletes, do you think numerical data is best displayed graphically (graphs or charts), in the form of a numerical spreadsheet, or as a combination of both?

Hint   A key aspect of sports performance analysis is to keep feedback clear and concise: brief but to the point.

Extend   Could you devise a checklist or input form to use with a chosen sport? What categories and information do you think you would need to include?

Edited video commentary

Edited video commentary on a performance provides auditory cues or explanations from an observer or coach. This can be in digital or MP3 format and can accompany video footage. As the commentary comes directly from a coach or observer, it can be subjective in its view.

Annotated video

Annotated video can be a powerful tool in performance analysis. Using appropriate software, a coach can simply highlight aspects of play by using a combination of drawing tools or playback facilities over the actual video footage. In this way, a coach can reinforce aspects of play that are positive or ones that need improvement. These annotated clips or screenshots can be repeated over time and compared to see if improvements have been made.

Research

Use the Internet to find some examples of annotated sports videos. You might be able to find examples on the websites of specific providers, such as Dartfish.

D Review the collected analysis data and provide feedback to individual athlete or team

Comparing data to benchmarks and ideal model

Once you have collated your data, you can compare your athlete's performance against the desired or ideal model that you chose earlier. This can be done easily using a table where you list the technical component being assessed, provide a description of the ideal model broken down into component parts, and then add a space where you can write notes on the observed performance.

This process can be aided with video footage, if budget permits, allowing you to highlight aspects of play by employing a combination of drawing tools or playback facilities over the actual video footage.

Using relevant evidence and data

In sport and exercise science, the term 'evidence-based practice' means you should base your recommendations on appropriate sources of information. Once you have undertaken a performance analysis and gathered a quantity of raw data, it is unlikely that all the data collected will be used to feed back to the athlete. It is the coach's role to sift through this data and determine what is relevant and usable for presentation to the athlete as an appropriate report. Ensure that any recommendations in your report are linked directly to your athlete's performance and your conclusions are considered alongside the data collected.

Process and outcome mismatches

Occasionally, mismatches or anomalies will occur during performance analysis that will require careful handling and feedback on the part of the coach. An instance would be when poor technical performance leads to a successful outcome. For example, a footballer may score from a corner attempting to head the ball when, in fact, it bounced off his shoulder. Although the athlete achieved a successful outcome, the likelihood of this outcome being repeated in a competitive scenario is small. Likewise, a 100-metre sprinter may have executed excellent technique and improved on his/her personal best, but ultimately failed to achieve the required time to compete in national competition. In scenarios like this, a good coach will concentrate on the positive feedback and use the present failure as a source of motivation for future attempts.

Developing outcomes

As you view the performance (either live or via video footage), poor technical execution will become apparent when compared to an ideal model. However, more discreet errors will require more in-depth analysis (for example slowing down the video footage to a speed where these tiny errors, which may be leading to poor technical performance, can be observed). The small movement of a golfer's head while driving the ball may not be obvious during the live performance, but once any video footage is slowed down, the technical error may be identified and a suitable recommendation for improvement incorporated into the feedback.

> **Theory into practice**
>
> In a team situation, a centre back in football may possess good technical skills, but their tactical or positional awareness may be poor. In this case, the performance analysis may identify that an opposition striker is getting goal-side of the defender too easily. This situation may be remedied with recommendations that the defender undergo specific drills or coaching on positional play without the ball.

Patterns and anomalies in performance

Using a perfect model can highlight certain detrimental patterns or habits in performance. Batsmen often tend towards patterns of play when faced with a type of bowling; for example, the batsman who attempts to hook the ball when faced with a short-pitched delivery. This type of shot carries a high risk of being caught, so a more considered approach based on a proven ideal model (i.e. Steve Waugh) would be to take avoiding action and let the ball continue through to the wicket keeper.

Anomalies are flaws in technique that can be identified and addressed. A recent example of this is Tiger Woods, who, due to a back injury that caused a lack of rotational mobility in his torso, was unable to drive the ball off the tee correctly. Through stages of analysis, Woods and his coaches realised this and opted for surgery to help address this flaw.

Providing feedback to an athlete on performance

Make sure the information you give an athlete or coach is simple and easy to follow and provides them with sufficient detail to help them develop. Too much scientific jargon could baffle them whereas very little detail is useless. There are several different factors to consider when feeding back to an athlete including:

▸ appropriate use of language – make it athlete/coach friendly

▸ strengths and areas for improvement

▸ positive and negative feedback

▸ clarity of information

▸ type of feedback (for example, written or verbal)

▸ having evidence to support the feedback you are providing

▸ any other factors that have influenced performance.

PAUSE POINT   What factors might you need to keep in mind when giving an athlete feedback on performance?

Hint   Do you think it is possible to impart too much information at once?

Extend   How might you break down your feedback into categories? What questioning strategies might you adopt to ensure your feedback is taken on board by the athlete?

Research

It can be argued that notational analysis is now big business. For example, Prozone is considered one of the world leaders in sports analysis. Visit www.prozonesports.stats.com and look at the software tools and services available.

Research Prozone's products. Compare this to what you might achieve with the equipment available at your school or college. Are both offering the same outcome in terms of performance analysis? You should be prepared to present your findings as a small group to the rest of your class.

When you are presenting your feedback, always focus on the performance and the process, not the outcome during the event analysed. In the event being analysed, the athlete may have enjoyed a successful outcome but that does not mean that there are not areas where the performance or process can be improved.

Always look for both strengths and areas for improvement when working with your athlete. When looking at strengths and areas for improvement consider:

▶ past performances (look for a pattern or profile)

▶ the influences on performance (such as motivation)

▶ separating the individual's strengths from the team's strengths, if applicable

▶ what the athlete needs to develop first (these will be the things that affect performance most significantly).

Using suitable formats

The most important outcome of performance analysis is that your findings make a positive difference to the athlete. How your analysis is presented to your athlete or coach is very much a personal choice based on what is likely to work best for them. It is important to ensure your information, data or recommendations are clear and concise. Remember that the ultimate goal is the promotion of technically and tactically correct performance to increase likelihood of future success.

The feedback should be presented in a way that reinforces the conclusions drawn. For example, shots attempted, shots on target and points scored can be presented in statistical or graphical form.

Sometimes, simple verbal or visual feedback is all that is necessary, for instance a quick discussion or playback of video footage. Often, however, more detailed analyses are required, particularly if improvement is not going to be obvious immediately. In this instance, a written report incorporating tally charts, graphs, annotated video footage, comparison with ideal models or statistical analysis may be required.

 **PAUSE POINT** What are the advantages of providing your athlete with a brief written report on his or her performance?

Hint Do you think it is a good idea that he or she can take something away and think about their performance?

Extend Should a written report have a section that allows the athlete to add their own comments or right of reply to the analysis?

Goal setting

Whichever method of feedback you select, remember that your input should make a positive difference to the athlete's future performance. Part of your role is to provide recommendations for the athlete or coach. There are different factors that you should consider, including:

▶ priority of future coaching and training

▶ team skills or drills

▶ individual skills training

▶ fitness training for specific components of fitness

▶ technique coaching specific to a movement.

Goal setting is a vital aspect of sporting performance; clear, well-defined targets are a valuable tool when giving feedback to an athlete. Goals should be SMART (specific, measureable, achievable, realistic and timed). Goals should develop from, and be backed up by, evidence from the observations.

Types of goals

When it comes to sports performance analysis, the goals you set should relate to two aspects: process goals and outcome goals. They should be aligned with the ideal model and benchmarks that you identified before the observation was carried out.

▶ **Process goals** address the technique or strategy required to perform. Examples include keeping the football close to your foot when dribbling or maintaining 30 strokes per minute throughout a 2000-metre rowing race.

▶ **Outcome goals** refer to a desired end result involving outperforming rivals or winning but are not always within an individual athlete's control. An example is if an athlete is selected to represent their country.

Agreed goals

When setting goals, it is important to understand that to achieve the 'dream' goal there should be a number of short- or medium-term targets to achieve on the way. An athlete dreaming of winning an Olympic 1500-metre gold medal will need to set short-term, 'day-to-day' goals to focus their effort.

▶ **Short-term or daily goals** provide a focus for training in each session. Past research on Olympic athletes found that setting clear daily training goals was one factor that distinguished successful performers from the less successful. The 1500-metre runner might set out to execute his routines with a tighter, more efficient running style which his coach films every session, reviewing the outcome afterwards with the athlete.

▶ **Medium-term or intermediate goals** are markers of where you want to be at a specific time in your training programme. For example, if the 1500-metre runner's long-term goal was to lower his 1500-metres personal best time by one second over ten months, a medium-term goal could be a half-second improvement after five months.

▶ **Long-term goals** seem a long way off and difficult to achieve. In time terms, they may be anything from six months to several years away. These goals should be made up of short- and medium-term goals. The 1500-metre runner might aim to set a personal best every 12 months. His goal after two years would be to win Olympic gold.

PAUSE POINT	What goals might you set for an elite athlete recently dropped from a national squad?
Hint	How would you break these overall goals into a plan including short-, medium- and long-term goals?
Extend	How would you incorporate performance profiling into this plan and how might this analysis impact on your proposed goals?

Sports analyst Amy Hall and the performance analysis models – part 2

Amy's presentation and report have helped the cricket club coach understand what sports performance analysis involves. As her work has been well received, the committee have asked if they can witness how the analysis process works in practice and what end products the club's players can expect. Therefore, Amy has been asked to undertake an analysis of both a batsman and a bowler and to submit her findings to the committee. If they are happy with her work, she can start the process with all players.

Amy has been given access to all the equipment mentioned in the previous case study. The committee and club coach are expecting her to produce a detailed performance analysis report as an end product. To achieve this Amy will do the following.

1 Collate detailed data and present this in different formats (e.g. graphs, checklists, annotated video footage, statistical analysis) from an observation of an individual batsman and bowler and compare the performance to ideal model and benchmarks.

2 Provide detailed feedback to the batsman and bowler within the report that sets goals for future development.

Check your knowledge

1 What feedback methods are available to a coach when following the analysis of an athlete's performance?

2 What are the different types of goals a coach can set an athlete, and how do they differ?

Assessment practice 28.3

`C.P4` `C.M4` `D.P5` `D.M5` `CD.D3`

The rowing club president is delighted with your efforts so far in explaining and establishing the methods, models, benchmarks and protocols associated with performance analysis. He tells you that the first regatta is in three months' time in Germany, so the performance analysis needs to begin soon.

The club president has discussed all requirements with the coaches, and they would like to see if your proposals work in practice prior to the start of training. They agree to allow one rower to undergo a full performance analysis within a gym environment to witness first-hand how you carry out an analysis, review the data collected and present your findings.

You have been given access to all the laboratory equipment, recording equipment and an indoor rowing machine. The coaches are expecting you to produce a detailed performance analysis report as an end product. To achieve this you must carry out the following tasks.

- Collate detailed data and present it in different formats (e.g. graphs, checklists, annotated video footage, statistical analysis) from an observation of an individual rower. Compare the performance to an ideal model and benchmarks.
- Provide detailed feedback to the rower within the report that sets goals for future development.
- Remember it is a detailed report, so make sure the data is evaluated, brief and to the point.

Plan

- What is the task? What is the analysis report being asked to address?
- Are there any areas of data collection I am not comfortable with? Is my report of a high enough standard, design and impact to be shared with coaches and athletes?

Do

- I know how to carry out and review an analysis of sports performance, including all the necessary information and referring to ideal models and performance benchmarks.
- I can identify where my report may have gone wrong and adjust my thinking/approach to get myself back on course.

Review

- I can explain what the task was and how I approached construction of my report.
- I can explain how I would approach the more difficult elements differently next time (i.e. what I would do differently).

Further reading and resources

Books

Franks, I. and Hughes, M. (2004) *Notational Analysis of Sport: Systems for Better Coaching and Performance in Sport*, Abingdon: Routledge.

O'Donoghue, P. (2014) *An Introduction to Performance Analysis of Sport*, Abingdon: Routledge.

Websites

www.dartfish.com

www.prozonesports.stats.com

THINK ▶FUTURE

Madeline Farrell, Sports Science student

After I completed the Level 3 BTEC Sports course, I went to university and studied for a BSc in Sport and Exercise Science. The BTEC course got me interested in sports performance analysis and I knew that I wanted to take my interests to degree level.

While at college, I was allowed to film the college basketball team during training sessions and matches. I then analysed the footage and used the results as my course project. I really enjoyed looking at the players' technique when they were shooting, playing the footage back to them and looking for ways to improve their technique. It must have made a difference because later that year the team won the annual county further education tournament. During my application to university I was asked to give a short presentation on an aspect of sports coaching or training I had undertaken at college. I talked about my work with the basketball team.

Now I'm in my final year and working on a dissertation. I'm working with a professional football club conducting performance analyses on their academy players. I can use the footage within my dissertation and make recommendations regarding the players' physical, psychological, technical and tactical development.

I don't mind which sport I end up working in – it is the day to day variety and complexity and the positive impact upon performers that make the role so interesting and worthwhile.

Focusing your skills

Using IT equipment

You need to understand how to set up and use various pieces of IT kit. If one piece is missing or not working, it could have a knock-on effect for the entire performance analysis process.

- Sports scientists should be familiar with the use of cameras and camcorders: how to track a moving athlete and download the data to a laptop or hard drive.
- You should be proficient with spreadsheets and data input software that produces graphs and other graphical interpretations of raw numerical data.
- Ensure all equipment is operational and ready to use, e.g. all batteries are charged and cables attached.
- Be able to use motion capture software and carry out screen annotations for performance profiling.

Coaching and fitness knowledge

While the majority of your role is the gathering of crucial data for the performance profiling of an athlete, you must have key fitness and coaching knowledge so you can better understand what it is you are analysing.

- A sports scientist needs to know how the body moves and functions, especially in sporting scenarios.
- It is often necessary to understand the techniques and skills involved in the sport you are analysing.
- Following a successful performance profiling, you must understand how to blend goals and motivational techniques into any training programme.
- Excellent communication skills are needed as it is important to discuss with both coach and athlete how you will record, analyse and present your findings.

Getting ready for assessment

Dean is working towards completing the second year of his BTEC National in Sport. He has been given an assignment that asks him to create a presentation that examines the methods for analysing sports performance. The presentation may be in a format of Dean's choice (PowerPoint®, posters, slideshow, etc.), but must address the following key points:

▸ performance profiling
▸ methods for analysing
▸ techniques for sports analysis.

Dean shares his experience below.

How I got started

First I wrote down a list of everything I learned during my lectures at college. I started by dividing my presentation using three key headings:

▸ performance profiling
▸ methods of analysis
▸ techniques for sports analysis.

I decided upon a PowerPoint® presentation so I could include photos. The first part was quite easy – I looked through my notes and compiled a framework of what makes up a workable performance profile. The second and third headings were more difficult because, apart from the few bits and pieces we'd done at college with a camera, checklist and clipboard, I wasn't too sure what else I could include. So I decided to ask my local non-league football club if they could help. They were excellent and invited me to a couple of their training sessions. The coaches there used fitness testing equipment and video analysis and fitted the players with heart rate monitors and GPS tracking devices so they could tell how far they had run during training. Fortunately, the club allowed me to take notes and photographs which I later included in my presentation.

How I brought it all together

Although my college course taught me a great deal about performance analysis, I'm so glad I picked up the phone and spoke to the football club. What I saw there put everything into perspective. A combination of the two approaches allowed me to:

▸ evaluate the different methods and techniques for measuring performance analysis
▸ justify the methods and techniques used to analyse individuals and team performances.

What I learned from the experience

I'm glad I gave myself plenty of time to plan my presentation. If I had left everything to the last minute, I wouldn't have had the opportunity to visit the football club and gain first-hand experience of what goes on in an elite sporting environment. Studying this unit made me realise a camera can be useful – not just for analysis but to record events that you can use in your assignments. If you go to watch a game, take a camera as you never know when the images may come in useful.

After I had spent time with the football club, my friends at college were keen to find out what I'd done. It was encouraging to explain to them that everything we'd been taught about performance analysis at college suddenly made sense. Moreover, the football coaching staff were very helpful in guiding me and helping me think about my presentation and future career choices. With hindsight I wonder if it might have been better to have gone to the football club for help with all my assignments, but I'm sure they'd have got fed up with me quite quickly!

Think about it

▸ Make sure you give yourself enough time to plan and write your assignments.
▸ Do not be afraid to look beyond your school or college for ideas and inspiration, but always consult your tutor.
▸ Remember you are a sports student. Go to sports events and observe, not only the athletes performing, but also the support staff and coaches who make it all possible.

Index